World Armaments and Disarmament

SIPRI Yearbook 1974

D0310072

# SIPRI

## Stockholm International
## Peace Research Institute

SIPRI is an independent institute for research into problems of peace and conflict, with particular attention to the problems of disarmament and arms regulation. It was established in 1966 to commemorate Sweden's 150 years of unbroken peace.

The financing is provided by the Swedish Parliament. The staff, the Governing Board and the Scientific Council are international. As a consultative body, the Scientific Council is not responsible for the views expressed in the publications of the Institute.

## Governing board

## SIPRI

### Stockholm International Peace Research Institute
Sveavägen 166, S-113 46 Stockholm, Sweden
Cable: Peaceresearch, Stockholm Telephone: 08-15 09 40

# World Armaments and Disarmament

# SIPRI Yearbook 1974

SIPRI

Stockholm International Peace Research Institute

The MIT Press
Cambridge, Massachusetts and
London, England

Almqvist & Wiksell
Stockholm

Copyright © 1974 by SIPRI
Sveavägen 166
S-113 46 Stockholm, Sweden

First published by Almqvist & Wiksell
26 Gamla Brogatan, S-111 20 Stockholm

in collaboration with

The MIT Press
28 Carleton Street
Cambridge, Mass 02142

and

126 Buckingham Palace Road
London SMlW 9SD

ISBN 0 262 19129 6

*Library of Congress Catalog Card
Number:* 74-8306

Previous volumes in this series:

SIPRI Yearbook of World Armaments and Disarmament 1968/69
SIPRI Yearbook of World Armaments and Disarmament 1969/70
World Armaments and Disarmament, SIPRI Yearbook 1972
World Armaments and Disarmament, SIPRI Yearbook 1973

Printed in Sweden by
Almqvist & Wiksell, Uppsala 1974

# PREFACE

This, the fifth issue of the *SIPRI Yearbook,* continues our analysis of the world's arms races, and the attempts to stop them, up to 31 December 1973. Unfortunately, the events of the past year have not provided any grounds for altering our previous assessment of the lack of progress in disarmament. SALT and certain other arms control measures have, of course, had very important, far-reaching political consequences. In particular, they have significantly contributed to the improvement of relations between some states. But, in general, they have not produced any actual disarmament, nor have they even stopped the arms race. In our view, disarmament—with the abolition of nuclear weapons having the highest priority and leading to general and complete disarmament—is essential if nuclear holocaust is to be avoided. *It is our basic commitment to effective disarmament that makes inevitable the "harshness" of our judgement of the value of existing arms control measures.*

It is sometimes argued that in the world as it exists today, disarmament can only be achieved as the end-product of a lengthy process. The first stage in this process involves banning weapons of little or no military value and weapons from environments of little or no military significance. This process, so it is claimed, will build such a degree of mutual confidence among the negotiating parties and so improve the climate of international relations that, in due course, far-reaching disarmament will be possible. History shows that this first stage will indeed be a lengthy one. In the meantime, it is said that we must learn to live with nuclear weapons.

At first sight, this argument appears convincing but it completely misses a crucial point. Military technology is advancing extremely rapidly. Weapons are being developed and deployed which produce periods of considerable instability. As time goes on, the intensity of instability increases. Sooner or later, a period of instability may occur, for example, at a time of severe international tension and also possibly, when one or more of the relevant states is led by an irresponsible leader. The extreme dangers inherent in such a combination of events is obvious. There is an ever present risk that any major conflict, even a limited non-nuclear war, will escalate to a general nuclear war. Moreover, the possibility of nuclear war by accident or miscalculation is always with us. The dangers of this situation are increased by advances in nuclear-weapon technology. They will also be multiplied if new nuclear-weapon powers emerge. And the likelihood is that new nuclear weapons will emerge, probably sooner than later, if no substantial progress on nuclear disarmament takes place.

The catastrophic consequences of a general nuclear war demand either that the probability of any war be reduced to an acceptable level (most reasonable men would say that this would have to be zero) or that nuclear weapons be abolished as part of a comprehensive programme of disarmament. Even though we do not underestimate the difficulties of the latter, we believe its achievement to be a simpler task than the former.

For all the reasons outlined above, we believe that the need for positive action in disarmament has never before been greater. The difficulty of achieving this objective is normally overrated. Time and energy spent on negotiating partial measures is time and energy diverted from negotiating real disarmament. And in this latter task we have precious little time to lose.

## Attributions

Below is a list of members of the SIPRI research staff responsible for the preparation of individual chapters and appendices:

*Part I:* Chapters 1, 2 and 5 (Frank Barnaby), Chapter 3 (Malvern Lumsden), Chapter 4 and Appendix 5 A (Olga Šuković), Appendix 4 A (Carl Erik Tottie) and Chapter 6 (Randall Forsberg).

*Part II:* Chapter 7 and Appendix 8B (Ron Huisken), Appendix 8C (Richard Booth), Chapter 8 and remaining appendices (Richard Booth, Randall Forsberg, Eva Grenbäck, Ron Huisken and Signe Landgren-Bäckström).

*Part III:* Chapter 9 (Bhupendra Jasani), Chapter 10 (Kosta Tsipis) and Chapter 11 (John Stares and Carl Erik Tottie).

*Part IV:* Jozef Goldblat.

The preparation of the Yearbook was directed and supervised by myself. The Yearbook was edited by Connie Wall, with the assistance of Mary Leiby, Brian Lilburn, Felicity Roos and Jill Schimpff.

## Acknowledgements

The Yearbook team wish to thank the Institute's librarians (Gunnel von Döbeln and Janet Meurling), the press cutters (William Jewson, Michal Lucki and Ernst Falta) and the secretarial staff for their assistance in preparing the Yearbooks. Ragnhild Jansson assisted in preparing the disarmament chronology and the appendices in Part IV.

February 1974

*Frank Barnaby*
Director

# CONTENTS

# TABLES AND CHARTS

CHARTS

**Chapter 8. World Armaments, 1973**


TABLES

CHART

Chapter 9. Reconnaissance satellites

TABLES

CHARTS

**Chapter 11. The automated battlefield**

TABLE

# ABBREVIATIONS, CONVENTIONS
# AND CONVERSIONS

## Abbreviations

| | |
|---|---|
| bn | billion (one thousand million) |
| cm | centimetre |
| db | decibel |
| FY | fiscal year |
| hr | hour |
| kg | kilogramme |
| km | kilometre |
| kt | kiloton |
| lb | pound |
| m | metre |
| mm | millimetre |
| mn | million |
| min | minute |
| mt | megaton |
| sec | second |

## Conventions

Some conventions used with particular tables only are given together with those tables.

| | |
|---|---|
| .. | Data not available |
| – | Nil or less than half the final digit shown; negligible; not applicable |
| ( ) | Greater degree of uncertainty about estimate |
| [ ] | Crude estimate |

**Country terminology**

For the convenience of the reader, we have tended to use the geographical rather than the formal official name of certain countries. In addition, several states have recently changed their official names. Examples are given here.

| | |
|---|---|
| North Viet-Nam | Democratic Republic of Viet-Nam (DRV) |
| South Viet-Nam | Republic of Viet-Nam |
| North Korea | Democratic People's Republic of Korea |
| South Korea | Republic of Korea |
| China | People's Republic of China |
| Taiwan | Republic of China |
| Congo | People's Republic of Congo |
| Zaïre | formerly Democratic Republic of Congo (Congo Kinshasa) |
| Egypt | Arab Republic of Egypt (formerly United Arab Republic) |
| Bangla Desh | formerly East Pakistan |
| Khmer Republic | formerly Cambodia |
| Sri Lanka | formerly Ceylon |
| Democratic Yemen | People's Democratic Republic of Yemen (formerly South Yemen) |
| Yemen | Arab Republic of Yemen |

**Conversions**

*Units of length*

1 millimetre=0.039 inch
1 inch=25.4 millimetres
1 metre=1.1 yard=3.28 feet
1 foot=30.480 centimetres
1 yard=3 feet=36 inches=0.91 metre
1 kilometre=0.62 statute mile=1 094 yards
1 statute mile=1.61 kilometres=1 760 yards
1 nautical mile=6 076 feet=1 852 metres

*Units of mass*

1 ton=1 000 kilograms (tonne)=2 205 pounds, avoirdupois=0.98 long ton=1.1 short ton
1 short ton=2 000 pounds=0.91 ton=0.89 long ton
1 long ton=2 240 pounds=1.1 ton=1.12 short ton
1 kiloton=1 000 tons
1 megaton=1 000 000 tons
1 kilogram=2.2 pounds
1 pound=0.45 kilograms

# Part I. 1973, the year in review

# 1. The main events of the year

*Square-bracketed references, thus* [1], *refer to the list of references on page 4.*

In 1945 Albert Einstein said that the atomic bomb "may intimidate the human race into bringing order into its international affairs, which, without the pressure of fear it would not do". World events during 1973 showed yet again that Einstein's desire to see at least some merit in the development of nuclear weapons has not been fulfilled. By the end of 1973 there was still little evidence that the degree of disorder in international affairs was, in a real sense, decreasing. The year did, however, begin auspiciously. The signing of the ceasefire agreement ending US involvement in Viet-Nam (see chapter 3), the cessation of US bombing in Cambodia, certain rapprochement between the Korean states, the entry into force of the treaty on the relations between the Federal Republic of Germany and the German Democratic Republic and the subsequent admission of the two countries to the United Nations, East-West multilateral discussions on European security and cooperation and on mutual force reduction (MFR) in Europe (see chapter 4), and the continuation of the second phase of the Strategic Arms Limitation Talks (SALT) (see page 361) were such hopeful signs for a new period of détente—seemingly formalized by the Nixon–Brezhnev agreements in June (see page 366)—that by mid-year world affairs were unusually and strangely quiet. But the lull was shattered on 6 October by the outbreak of the Middle East War. Among other things, this event once again pointed out how instability in other areas of the world can escalate to nuclear confrontation between the United States and the Soviet Union. As a further disturbance related to the Middle East War, the oil crisis was felt throughout the world. [1]

The demonstration of the capabilities of modern tactical weapons in the Middle East War will have far-reaching effects on military thinking and planning (chapter 2)—much more so than did the experiences in the Viet-Nam War. Further, this has come at a time when there is renewed debate on the potentialities of tactical nuclear weapons, particularly in Europe. In fact, the whole question of nuclear deterrence, tactical and strategic, is now being re-examined (chapter 5).

On 17 August the US Secretary of Defense announced that the Soviet Union had conducted flight tests of multiple independently targetable re-

1

entry vehicles (MIRVs).[1] Without doubt, the ongoing US MIRV programme and the reported new Soviet MIRVs (chapter 6) can seriously threaten world stability. The continuation of MIRV programmes is bound to raise the question: are the two powers racing for superiority in strategic weapons? In any event, the most remarkable factor in military technology in general is the way development and production of new weapons is forging ahead faster than ever— SALT, MFR and détente notwithstanding.

The furore over the French atmospheric nuclear-weapon tests conducted in the Pacific Ocean in July and August (chapter 13) once again illustrated the antagonism of world opinion to nuclear testing, particularly in the atmosphere. The tenth anniversary of the Partial Test Ban Treaty in August was a reminder that little progress has been made by the Conference of the Committee on Disarmament (CCD) in negotiating a comprehensive nuclear test ban (chapter 12). Similarly, no significant progress was made at the CCD during 1973 on the negotiations on the prohibition of the production of stockpiles of chemical weapons (chapter 12), the other topic of discussion. Ostensibly, the barrier to the negotiation of both a Comprehensive Test Ban Treaty (CTBT) and a CW treaty is the verification issue.

The general lack of progress at the CCD, the most important international forum for armscontrol and disarmament negotiations, but now overshadowed by the SALT and MFR negotiations, has renewed interest in other approaches. One such approach is the attempt to prohibit, first, the use of unnecessarily cruel and indiscriminate weapons and, second, acts of warfare directed against civilian populations. While these efforts should not be allowed to divert attention from the issue of the abolition of weapons of mass destruction, they do address a serious problem. The Hague Conventions of 1899 and 1907 prohibit the use of dum-dum bullets and the Geneva Protocol of 1925 prohibits the use of asphyxiating, poisonous and other gases and other chemical agents and bacteriological agents. However, since these early treaties, enormous improvements have been made in the effectiveness of a variety of inhumane weapons. Initiatives are now being taken to modernize the humanitarian law of war to take into account the advances in military technology. The issue of the use of napalm and other incendiary weapons has been put on the agenda of the UN. And an international forum of the Red Cross is considering the possibility of prohibiting the use of a wide range of antipersonnel weapons, including high-velocity bullets (which inflict wounds similar to dum-dum bullets), fragmentation weapons, and so on. Also considered will be such indiscriminate methods of warfare as the terror bombing of civilians, the large-scale destruction of food crops, the deliberate flooding of extensive areas, and so on.

[1] For a discussion of the development of the US MIRV programme, see reference [2].

2

Another approach to the problem of reducing the role of military force in international affairs is a reduction of the resources devoted to military purposes. This could take the form of cutting military expenditures directly without specifying the type of weapons or other costs to be involved (chapter 12). SIPRI has shown that world military expenditures are running at about \$207 billion per year[2] which is over 6 per cent of the gross national product of the countries of the world and equal to the total income of countries whose populations comprise more than half of mankind. The military expenditure of those countries which provide development aid is estimated to be approximately 6.7 per cent of their GNP, which is nearly 30 times greater than the official development aid they provide. The transfer of resources from military to peaceful uses could significantly raise standards of living and promote faster growth.

In this connection the enormous resources devoted to military research and development (R&D) should be mentioned. SIPRI estimates that about \$20 billion per year is being spent on military R&D, or about one-third of the entire world expenditure on all R&D. The use of these resources for appropriate research and development for peaceful purposes could have an enormous effect in contributing to progress and development in the underdeveloped parts of the world.

The dangers inherent in the present situation, particularly in the consequences of the onward rush of military technology, in which one revolution follows another, and in the probability of the proliferation of nuclear weapons involving more and more countries, are sufficient to justify the consideration of all approaches to disarmament. But the unimaginable consequences of a nuclear war, which would certainly eliminate civilization as we know it, demand nothing less than the abolition of nuclear weapons.

Today's military technology encompasses so many fields and spans such a diverse range of subjects, and so much is happening at such a rapid rate in each field, that an individual would find it an extremely arduous task to keep abreast, even superficially, of all the latest developments. This is particularly true for the US and Soviet arsenals which are in an entirely different league in comparison with those of the other powers. The virtually insuperable difficulty of coming to grips with the bewildering and ever increasing complexity of modern weapon systems is a major handicap for the world's disarmament negotiators.

The current practice of attempting to deal with disarmament piecemeal —the so-called partial arms control approach—by multilateral negotiations is inevitably a very lengthy process which enhances the difficulties created by the unrestrained onward rush of military technology, however "politically realistic" the partial method is perceived to be. What is clearly needed is a comprehensive approach to disarmament in which reductions in weapons of mass destruction are given priority.

[2] See table 8C.1, page 206.

## References

1. *Oil and Security,* SIPRI Monograph (Stockholm, Almqvist & Wiksell, 1974, Stockholm International Peace Research Institute).
2. *The Origins of MIRV,* SIPRI Research Report No. 9 (Stockholm, Almqvist & Wiksell, 1973, Stockholm International Peace Research Institute).

# 2. The military lessons of the Middle East War

The outbreak of the Middle East War took most nations by surprise. It had been generally assumed that the reconnaissance satellites of the United States and the Soviet Union would provide early warning of conflict between states in any region of the world. But the fact that the combined Syrian-Egyptian offensive on the Suez Canal and the Golan Heights was so unexpected indicates how intentions can be concealed, even though capabilities are known. The final stage of the preparations for the attack took place in the latter half of September, when both Egyptian and Syrian forces were concentrated near their respective ceasefire lines. The deployment of Syrian troops on the Golan frontier was first thought to be the result of an easing of tension with Jordan, which allowed troop concentrations along that Arab border to be reduced. Egyptian troop movements were thought to be part of large-scale war games, similar to previous operations of this type. Arab charges of Israeli troop concentrations near the Golan ceasefire line and along the Lebanese border were given little credibility. Thus, almost until the time war actually broke out, it was generally assumed that the relative ceasefire would continue for a long period and that the recent peace proposals were preoccupying both sides in the Middle East. In particular, Israeli preconceptions caused the country's leaders to ignore vital intelligence data which should have provided ample warning of attack.

US and Soviet reconnaissance satellites were, however, used to good effect to scan the entire battle area and to provide rapid and detailed information on the progress of the fighting. This information provided an unprecedented source of data for those engaged in diplomatic and political moves to control the crisis, an experience which should add a new dimension to future attempts at conflict resolution and crisis management.

The Middle East War involved a both qualitatively and quantitatively unprecedented use of modern weapons. Uniquely fierce battles took place on land and in the air, into which both sides poured a total of about 5 000 tanks and 2 000 aircraft. Losses in men and matériel on both sides were heavy. Over the three-week period of hostilities, aircraft were destroyed at the rate of more than one per hour and tanks were lost at a rate of more than one every 15 minutes. But most dramatic of all was the use of large numbers of a variety of types of missiles. The Viet-Nam War had already established air-to-air missiles as standard munitions in air combat operations and air-to-surface missiles as standard tactical weapons against troops and armour. In the Middle East War there was, in addition, a massive and effective use of anti-tank missiles and surface-to-air missiles and some use of surface-to-surface long-range missiles, ship-to-ship missiles, standoff bombs and "smart" bombs. This war was, therefore, unprecedently technological in character. Some types of missiles and tanks were used in combat for the first time.

Losses of US Air Force bombers during the Viet-Nam War gave some indication of the effectiveness of surface-to-air missiles (SAMs) and, therefore, the increasing vulnerability of aircraft. But this lesson was considerably reinforced during the Middle East War, in which Israeli planes were faced with a 20-mile belt of surface-to-air missiles, deployed along the west bank of the Suez Canal and defending an air space from ground level up to over 18 km. Similar anti-aircraft defence systems were used on the Golan Heights. Three types of radar-controlled Soviet SAMs were used together with anti-aircraft artillery—a combination which took a heavy toll of Israeli attack aircraft. SA-2 "Guideline" missiles were used against high-altitude aircraft, SA-3 "Goa" missiles against medium-altitude aircraft and SA-6 "Gainful" missiles against high- and low-flying aircraft.

The 10.6 m long SA-2, a two-stage (one using liquid propellant burning for about 5 seconds, the other solid propellant burning for about 22 seconds) guided weapon, is boosted to a speed of Mach 3.5, is capable of reaching an altitude of about 18 km and, when launched at the normal angle of 80 degrees, has a slant range of about 40 km. The missile is guided from the ground by radio-command signals. The attacking aircraft is tracked by radar and the radar signals are fed into a computer which generates radio signals to guide the missile. The weapon can carry a high-explosive warhead weighing about 130 kg (or alternatively a nuclear warhead) which is detonated by a command signal from the ground or by proximity or contact fuses. The SA-2 has been in service for at least 16 years and is deployed in very considerable numbers in the Soviet Union as a standard Soviet air-defence missile.

The SA-3, in production for about seven years, is also a two-stage missile but it is more compact than the SA-2—its length is only about one-half that of the latter. The missile is deployed as a mobile land-based system but it is also carried on Soviet cruisers and destroyers. The SA-3 can be used against aircraft up to a height of about 12 km with a slant range of about 24 km.

The older SA-2 and SA-3 missiles were used in some numbers in Viet-Nam but the SA-6 was used in combat for the first time during the Middle East War; it was the SA-6 missile which downed the largest number of Israeli aircraft. The missile is very compact, about 6 m long and only about 32 cm in diameter, and it is highly mobile. It is propelled by a solid-fuel ramjet system and, although it has been in production for at least seven years, the propulsion system is based on very advanced technology. The Mach-3 missile is highly effective at low altitudes but is also capable of reaching ceilings greater than 30 km, the altitude being limited by the type of radar employed for detecting and tracking the target. Like the SA-3, the SA-6 is ground-command guided but it also has a terminal seeker. The system is carried on two vehicles, one for the missiles and the other for the radar. The effectiveness of the missile is accounted for by the fact that the frequencies used to guide the missile are very difficult to counter, and, consequently, the jamming devices needed completely to counter the missile must have a very broad band capacity. In general, the major difficulty of countering a combination of types of SAMs and radar-guided anti-aircraft artillery is that each system operates in a frequency band different from the others. Effective electronic countermeasures must, therefore, provide jamming signals over a wide frequency range.

The Soviet SA-7 "Grail" anti-aircraft missile, first used in combat in Viet-Nam in 1972, was also used effectively against low-flying aircraft by the Syrians and Egyptians. This infrared-seeking missile can be shoulder-fired or fired from tracked vehicles. The highly mobile SA-6 and SA-7 missiles provided a protective anti-aircraft umbrella under which large formations of advancing Arab tanks could operate effectively against Israeli forces.

The Middle East War not only demonstrated the increasing vulnerability of aircraft but also that of tanks to highly mobile anti-tank missiles, particularly the Soviet "Sagger" and "Snapper" missiles and the US TOW and Maverick missiles.

"Snapper" and "Sagger" are wire-guided surface-to-surface anti-tank missiles, powered by solid-propellant rocket motors. "Snapper" is fired and guided by an operator who can, if necessary, be remote from the launcher: he sights the target through periscopic binoculars and uses a joystick to control the missile, keeping it on the line of sight to the target. The missile, about 1 m long, 14 cm in diameter and weighing about 22 kg, travels at speeds of more than 300 km/hr. "Sagger" is similar in operation but much smaller than "Snapper", that is, only 70 cm in length.

TOW (Tube-launched, Optically-tracked, Wire-guided) can be used either as a surface-to-surface or as an air-to-surface anti-tank guided weapon. The missile, about 120 cm long, 15 cm in diameter and weighing 18 kg, is equipped with two solid propellant motors. One motor ejects the missile from its launch tube, but burns out before the missile leaves the tube. The second motor ignites after the missile is well separated from the launch position to protect the operator against exhaust emissions. This motor very rapidly accelerates the missile up to its maximum speed (believed to be about 1 000 km/hr) and then burns out so that the missile leaves no significant visible trail. The operator's job is to keep the cross-wire of a telescope trained on the target until the missile hits it. A light source on the tail of the missile is automatically tracked by a sensor which measures the angle between the flight direction of the missile and the operator's line of sight. These angles are converted by a computer into guidance commands sent to the missile. TOW is manoeuvred by the control of aerodynamic surfaces, a method which gives the missile good manoeuvrability throughout its flight. The warhead is a high-explosive shaped-charge designed to penetrate the armour plate of all known types of tanks. TOW is adaptable for use with helicopters. The missiles can be effectively fired when the helicopter is flying at high speed and is manoeuvring.

Maverick is a sophisticated air-to-surface missile for use against tanks, gun positions and other concentrated targets. The missile, normally carried by strike aircraft, is about 250 cm long, 30 cm in diameter and weighs about 200 kg. The warhead is a 60 kg conical-shaped, high-penetrating, high-explosive charge. Maverick is guided by a small television system in the nose of the missile. The aircraft pilot chooses a target on a television monitor in his cockpit, locks the missile's electro-optical tracker onto the target and fires the missile which is then automatically guided to the target by the television tracker.

Events during the Middle East War will undoubtedly greatly stimulate further developments in a number of areas of military technology. For example, efforts underway to develop more advanced electronic countermeasures, improved stand-off weapons and remotely piloted aircraft will be seen as ways of overcoming missile air defences. There will be demands for more highly specialized air-superiority fighters and strike aircraft, for more refined air-launched stand-off anti-tank missiles and "smart" bombs and for ground-launched anti-tank missiles. Commanders will demand more highly developed sensors and computer equipment to command and control air and ground forces in the swift-moving three-dimensional milieu of the modern battlefield. Unified command of ground and air forces in airborne control centres will be called for. And the need has been perceived for greater intercontinental heavy airlift capabilities to replace the heavy and rapid expenditure of missiles and other munitions in modern warfare. But perhaps the most disturbing lesson of the Middle East War is that there are situations in which an advantage is to be gained in some circumstances from a massive surprise attack using the most sophisticated weapons. This increases the importance of very rapid gains in the early stages of combat. The desirability for speed is indicated by the Israeli demonstration that sustained air attacks can eventually destroy a modern anti-aircraft screen. Massive ground forces must, therefore, be used to gain their objectives before their protection against enemy aircraft can be destroyed. After this, air superiority becomes the paramount factor.

# 3. Military developments following the ceasefire agreements in Indo-China

*Square-bracketed references, thus [1], refer to the list of references on page 21.*

## I. *Viet-Nam*

### The Paris agreement on Viet-Nam

On 27 January 1973, in Paris, the Democratic Republic of Viet-Nam (DRV), with the concurrence of the Provisional Revolutionary Government of the Republic of South Viet-Nam (PRG), on the one side, and the United States, with the concurrence of the Republic of Viet-Nam (RVN), on the other, signed the Agreement on Ending the War and Restoring Peace in Viet-Nam. In protocols to the agreement additional procedures were agreed upon for the removal of mines in the territorial and inland waters of North Viet-Nam, the return of prisoners of war and the establishment of the International Commission of Control and Supervision and joint military commissions to supervise the ceasefire.

On 2 March, at an international conference in the presence of the Secretary-General of the United Nations, the foreign ministers of the USA, France, the Provisional Revolutionary Government of the Republic of South Viet-Nam, Hungary, Indonesia, Poland, the Democratic Republic of Viet-Nam, the United Kingdom, the Republic of Viet-Nam, the USSR, Canada and China signed the Act of the International Conference in which they *inter alia* solemnly acknowledged ''the commitments by the parties to the Agreement and the Protocols to strictly respect and scrupulously implement the Agreement and the Protocols''.

On 13 June a Joint Communiqué containing provisions for the implementation of the ceasefire agreement of 27 January was signed in Paris by the three Viet-Namese parties and the United States.

### The US withdrawal

In Article 2 of the Paris agreement the ceasefire was proclaimed as of 2400 hours GMT on 27 January 1973.

At the same hour, the United States will stop all its military activities against the territory of the Democratic Republic of Viet-Nam by ground, air and naval forces, wherever they may be based, and end the mining of the territorial waters, ports, harbors, and waterways of the Democratic Republic of Viet-Nam. The United States will remove, permanently deactivate or destroy all the mines in the territorial waters, ports, harbors, and waterways of North Viet-Nam as soon as this agreement goes into effect. The complete cessation of hostilities mentioned in this article shall be durable and without limit of time.

In Article 3 the parties undertake to maintain the ceasefire and ensure lasting and stable peace. Article 4 states that "the United States will not continue its military involvement or intervene in the internal affairs of South Viet-Nam". Article 5 stipulates the total withdrawal from South Viet-Nam, within 60 days, of

troops, military advisers, and military personnel, including technical military personnel and military personnel associated with the pacification program, armaments, munitions, and war material of the United States and those of the other foreign countries mentioned in Article 3(a).[1] Advisers from the above-mentioned countries to all paramilitary organizations and the police force will also be withdrawn within the same period of time.

According to Article 6, "The dismantlement of all military bases in South Viet-Nam of the United States and of the other foreign countries mentioned in Article 3(a) shall be completed within 60 days of this agreement". Thus the Paris agreement terminated the direct US military engagement in the Viet-Nam War. Between 1 January 1961 and 28 January 1973, more than two million US troops served in the theatre, and 45 941 of them were killed in action. (A further 10 298 deaths occurred from accidents, illness, drugs, murder and other noncombat causes.) [1] Total direct costs to the USA exceeded $140.8 billion between 1965 and 1973. [2a] US and allied forces consumed some 15 million tons of munitions between 1965 and 1973, of which the US air forces alone dropped 6.5 million tons. [3] The USA lost some 8 000 aircraft, including over 4 000 helicopters, at a cost of approximately $6 billion. [4] Although the number of US combat troops stationed in Viet-Nam had already been reduced to a relatively low level at the time of the ceasefire, the remaining contingents were withdrawn with dispatch, and air and naval forces in South East Asia were reduced to near "baseline" levels.[2]

**North Viet-Namese forces in South Viet-Nam**

No reference is made in the agreement to the withdrawal of North Viet-Namese forces from South Viet-Nam, although in article 7, the two South Viet-Namese parties undertook "not to accept the introduction of troops,

[1] Article 3(a) refers to "The United States forces and those of the other foreign countries allied with the United States and the Republic of Viet-Nam", namely the Republic of Korea, Thailand, Australia, New Zealand, the Philippines, the Republic of China and Spain. At the time of the ceasefire there were more troops from South Korea in South Viet-Nam than there were US troops.
[2] The USA maintains in South-East Asia three aircraft carrier task forces, that is, 79–80 ships and 37 000 men, on a rotating basis. [5] On at least one occasion such a task force has moved into the Tonkin Gulf. [6–7] In addition the USA maintains air bases in Thailand, the Philippines and Guam, all of which have been directly engaged in the war in Indo-China.

military advisers, and military personnel including technical military personnel, armaments, munitions, and war material into South Viet-Nam''.

On the other hand, Article 7 also stated that the two South Viet-Namese parties shall be permitted to make periodic replacements of

armaments, munitions and war material which have been destroyed, damaged, worn out or used up after the ceasefire, on the basis of piece-for-piece, of the same characteristics and properties, under the supervision of the joint military commission of the two South Viet-Namese parties and of the International Commission of Control and Supervision.

In spite of a number of press reports based on official US sources, other official US sources show little evidence of any substantial increase in the North Viet-Namese forces in the PRG areas compared with the "normal" complement in the pre-ceasefire period.[3] The very heavy fighting in the 10 months preceding the ceasefire led to considerable attrition of these forces which has probably been compensated for after the ceasefire, particularly in the first months. Although there is continued movement south, there is also continued attrition. [11]

Reports of 300–400 tanks moving into South Viet-Nam have been repeated at intervals, [12–13] but these reports seem to refer to the same tanks, a number of which a US official was quoted as saying is "as large or larger than what they employed last year". [12] However, the total inventory of heavy weapons does appear to be greater than at the time of the 1972 spring offensive. [9]

Nevertheless, there are a number of significant developments. The first of these is the building of an all-weather road stretching some 400 km south from the demilitarized zone to the central highlands. Some 20 000 engineering troops as well as civilian labour are said to be involved in its construction. This road will greatly improve communications with North Viet-Nam, as well as within the PRG areas. It has considerable political and strategic significance in that it potentially replaces the "Ho Chi Minh trail", the network of trails through Laos and Cambodia which was a major target of US bombing raids in these two countries. Second, at least 12 former US airfields are said to have been repaired and improved, with the one at Khe Sanh, at least, being defended by anti-aircraft missiles.[4] Some of these airfields are reported to be capable of accommodating jet aircraft.

[3] In 1968 the US Central Intelligence Agency (CIA) estimate of the strength of the North Viet-Namese Army in South Viet-Nam was 145 000. [8] In May 1972 the CIA estimate was 145 000–165 000; in January 1973, 120 500; and in April 1973, 142 000. [9] In February 1974 US sources estimated that during the year since the ceasefire 70 000 North Viet-Namese troops had moved south but that 40–50 000 had moved north. [10] The RVN reported in November 1973 that 38 630 North Viet-Namese and NLF soldiers had been killed since the ceasefire. [11] If these figures are correct they indicate a net reduction rather than a net increase in the number of North Viet-Namese troops in South Viet-Nam.
[4] The reported airfields are located at Khe Sanh and Dong Ha in the north, Ben Het, Polei Kleng, Dak To, Phuong Hoang and Duc Co in the central highlands, and Bo Duc, Loc Ninh, Katum, Minh Thanh and Thien Ngon northwest of Saigon. The USA and RVN protested about the airfields and the anti-aircraft missiles. [14]

**US military aid to the Republic of Viet-Nam**

US military aid to the Republic of Viet-Nam must be seen in the light of the massive arms build-up in the autumn of 1972 shortly before the cease-fire was expected. [15] This build-up included the supply of 32 C-130 transport aircraft which the RVN Air Force could not operate, and F-5 fighter-bombers borrowed from Iran, Taiwan and South Korea with the deliberate plan later to substitute up to 128 of the more sophisticated F-5E which had not then been produced. Also included were an additional 308 UH-1 and 24 CH-47 helicopters. [16a]

Before the ceasefire the USA also turned over to the RVN its military bases [9]—thereby avoiding the legal requirement to dismantle them— and considerable quantities of military equipment.[5] Although many of the bases have lapsed as military facilities, at least one major air base was maintained in each of the four military regions. US companies continue to provide major services, such as air transport and aircraft maintenance, on contract to the US Department of Defense. [9, 18]

The RVN also received a wide variety of complex communications systems, including the integrated communications centre in Saigon which had been used as a coordinating centre for all US military communications in South East Asia. This facility continues to be operated by a US company, on contract to the Department of Defense. [18]

Although the US military staff and advisers have formally been removed, a large Defense Attaché Office has been established, working out of four new Consulates established at Da Nang, Nha Trang, Bien Hoa and Can Tho, the headquarters of the four military regions.[6]

In brief, rather than dismantling and withdrawing its military infrastructure from Viet-Nam, the USA has greatly reduced it but maintained it in operational order. This infrastructure is being used to service RVN military, pacification and police operations[7] at a high level of activity.

---

[5] A "well informed US military source" estimated the value of the military equipment turned over to the RVN as $5 billion. [17]

[6] The US military command was relocated at Nakon Phanom air base in Thailand. The Defense Attaché Office (DAO), which moved into the command's former offices in Saigon, is subordinate to the new command in Thailand. The DAO staff budget is for 50 US military personnel, 1 200 US Department of Defense (DOD) direct-hire civilians, and 5 500 persons working for companies on contract to the DOD. [9] According to the National Liberation Front (NLF), the number of Americans remaining in South Viet-Nam in order to assist the RVN's military effort is considerably higher, and includes some 2 000 on the staff of the US Embassy and consulates, 3 500 military advisers to defence organs, 9 000 military advisers and personnel to various echelons of the RVN army, 6 000 involved in the training of air crews and the repair and maintenance of aircraft, 1 500 technical personnel manning electronic equipment and radar stations and training Viet-Namese counterparts, 300 advisers in intelligence services, 100 assisting in the transfer of military equipment, 300 employees of Air America, and 300 civil engineers at the military bases. [19]

[7] In place of Civilian Operations and Rural Development Support (CORDS), which has been terminated as a result of the Paris agreement, an office called the "Special Assistant to the Ambassador for Field Operations" (SAAFO) was created. CORDS was the major coordinator of the pacification programme. SAAFO had some 200 employees shortly after the ceasefire. [9] According to the NLF later in the year, there were 800 Americans advising in pacifica-

Some indication of the high level of military activity is given by the continued high level of US military expenditures for South East Asia. These amount to an estimated $2.9 billion for fiscal year 1974 [2b] and $1.9 billion requested for fiscal year 1975. [21–22] US expenditures for ammunition alone in Viet-Nam were reported as $276 million for the year since the ceasefire.[8] This is about 75 per cent of the amount spent in 1972, the year of the major offensive. [24]

## II. *Laos*

On 21 February 1973, the Agreement on the Restoration of Peace and the Realisation of National Concord in Laos was signed in Vientiane by representatives of the Vientiane government side and the Patriotic Forces side, the two parties in Laos. The political sections of the accords confirmed the existence of zones provisionally controlled by the two parties and envisaged a coalition government of provisional character and a consultative council for national conciliation. A protocol to the agreement was signed in Vientiane on 14 September 1973, defining *inter alia* the composition of the Provisional Government envisaged in the agreement. On 6 November the National Assembly in Vientiane supported the agreement and the protocol by a vote of 26 to 24.

Reaffirming the 1962 accords, Article 1 of the 1973 agreement stated that the United States, Thailand, other foreign states, as well as the Laotian parties concerned, must scrupulously respect and apply the declaration on the neutrality of Laos of 9 July 1962 and the 1962 Geneva Agreements on Laos. A ceasefire was proclaimed from 12 noon (Vientiane time) on 22 February 1973, when all military activity, including espionage by air or ground means, was to cease.

In Article 4 it was stipulated that within 60 days of the establishment of a Provisional Government all foreign troops, regular and irregular, were to be withdrawn and foreign military and paramilitary facilities were to be dismantled. "Special Forces" organized, armed, instructed and commanded by foreigners were to be dissolved, along with their bases, installations and positions.

According to a US Senate report,

tion operations and 5 300 others involved in activities related to pacification including economic, social and political organizations. [19] The police and prison systems in South Viet-Nam received $48 million in aid from the US Department of Defense between 1955 and 1973, as well as $83.7 million from the Agency for International Development (AID). These programmes were terminated as a result of the Paris agreement. However, according to Senator Edward M. Kennedy, at least $15.217 million is being spent by the USA on South Viet-Namese police activities in 1973–74, including $8.8 million in the Department of Defense budget for "public safety supplies". [20] According to the NLF, there were 1 500 Americans involved in assisting the RVN police. [19]

[8] This figure may be compared with the total expected RVN government revenues in calendar year 1973 of $335 million (not including US aid).

the Lao irregulars, certainly in the category of 'special forces', were organized, trained, equipped and controlled by CIA (although the Defense Department assumed funding responsibilities at the beginning of this fiscal year (1973)). They are the backbone of the Lao defence establishment and the only effective Lao armed force. To live with the provision of the agreement requiring the disbanding of 'special forces' controlled by foreigners . . . the irregulars were integrated into the Royal Lao Army by a directive issued on February 20 (the day before the ceasefire was signed) . . . [9]

The number of Lao irregulars concerned was 18 000. Many of the Lao irregulars were recruited from mountain tribes such as the Meo and the Lao Teung which have been decimated as a result of the war. [25] Since the military manpower base was inadequate to replace the depleted ranks, Thai troops, paid for by the United States, were brought in. The strength of the Thai irregulars reached 21 413 in September 1972. In March 1973 there were 27 Thai infantry batallions and three Thai artillery battalions (17 330 men) in Laos. [9] According to one report, a "substantial section" of this force has been transferred to Cambodia by the CIA. [26] The US government agreed with the Thai government to repatriate the Thai troops remaining in Laos by 1 July 1974. [27]

One US government estimate of the number of North Viet-Namese troops in Laos in early April 1973 was 61 610, of which 11 720 were infantry, 9 325 command and combat support, and 40 565 "infiltration support". [9] (Infiltration support presumably refers to the personnel required for ferrying supplies from North to South Viet-Nam and protecting these lines of communication from air and ground attack.) Some 30 000 Chinese engineering troops are reportedly continuing to construct roads in Northern Laos. [9]

## III. *The Khmer Republic (Cambodia)*

Following the ceasefire agreements in Viet-Nam and Laos, the focus of US bombing activity shifted to Cambodia (see table 3.1). In July 1973 the US Senate voted to stop US air operations over Cambodia as of 15 August. Already in April 1970, following the deposition of the Sihanouk government and the US and South Viet-Namese invasion, the US Congress had prohibited the introduction of US combat troops and advisers into Cambodia and limited expenditures and the number of US government employees there.

According to a US Senate report, US analysts who specialize in the study of the war in Cambodia agree that there are no more than approximately 5 000 North Viet-Namese combat troops in all of Cambodia, of whom probably 2 000 or at most 3 000, are directed against Cambodian government forces. US estimates claim that there are some 40 000–50 000

**Table 3.1. Monthly tonnage of bombs dropped on Indo-China preceding and following the ceasefire in Viet-Nam (27 January 1973) and Laos (22 February 1973)**

| Month | Air-craft | North Viet-Nam | South Viet-Nam | Laos | Cam-bodia | Total |
|---|---|---|---|---|---|---|
| January | FB | 4 251 | 13 004 | 14 186 | 1 608 | 33 049 |
| | B-52 | 11 096 | 27 910 | 10 364 | 3 558 | 52 928 |
| | | **15 347** | **40 914** | **24 550** | **5 166** | **85 977** |
| February | FB | – | – | 19 749 | 802 | 20 551 |
| | B-52 | – | – | 32 426 | 1 300 | 33 726 |
| | | – | – | **52 175** | **2 102** | **54 277** |
| March | FB | – | – | – | 9 847 | 9 847 |
| | B-52 | – | – | – | 24 309 | 24 309 |
| | | – | – | – | **34 156** | **34 156** |

FB=fighter-bombers of various types; B-52=heavy bomber.

*Source:* News release, US Department of Defense, July 1973.

men involved in the indigenous resistance movement against the government in Phnom Penh. [9]

As the network of roads in the PRG areas of South Viet-Nam is improved, the transport of people and goods from North Viet-Nam to South Viet-Nam by way of Cambodia is likely to diminish. Prince Sihanouk has said that as a result of the Paris agreement, his forces are not being supplied with new matériel from North Viet-Nam, although some ammunition is supplied from stocks in South Viet-Nam. [28]

Throughout the year there was a high level of military activity in Cambodia. On 19 October President Nixon sought a supplementary budget allocation of $200 million for military grant aid to Cambodia. [23] This is considerably more than the $133.3 million for military aid granted to Cambodia for fiscal year 1973. [9] By the end of the year, the US Administration had appropriated more than $700 million in additional funds for military aid to Cambodia. [46]

## IV. *The continuing war*

According to official US figures, between 1961 and the ceasefire, 927 124 North Viet-Namese and Liberation Front soldiers lost their lives in South Viet-Nam, as well as 184 546 RVN soldiers. [1] The US Senate Refugee Subcommittee estimates that some 415 000 South Viet-Namese civilians were killed between 1965 and the ceasefire. [29] The USA estimates that some 52 000 civilians were killed in the bombing of North Viet-Nam by 1968, [8b] and although only incomplete figures have since been published, the total may be perhaps half as much again. Although these figures are not reliable, they indicate a toll in the order of 1.5–2.0 million Viet-Namese war dead between the 1954 and 1973 agreements, including 10 000–20 000 between 1954 and 1960 and 100 000–200 000 between 1961 and 1964.

Experience in Viet-Nam indicates that there are approximately four wounded who survive for every one who dies. As of June 1973, there were some 80 000 amputees, 8 000 paraplegics and 40 000 blinded or deaf as a result of the war in the RVN alone. There were over three-quarters of a million orphaned children, of whom some 25 000 were in orphanages. By the time of the ceasefire, the cumulative total of displaced persons in South Viet-Nam was over 10 million in a population of some 18 million. [29] The proportion of war victims in the total population of South Viet-Nam between 1954 and 1973 can be compared with that of the very worst affected of the occupied countries during World War II. [30]

The RVN reported more than 50 000 combat deaths between February and November 1973, [11] which is more than the number suffered by the United States in its 12-year engagement. A US observer estimated that, since the ceasefire, civilian war casualties (including dead and wounded) amounted to some 6–8 000 per month. [29] There were 818 000 new refugees in 1973. [31]

The Paris agreement has considerable political significance in reaffirming the principles of the Geneva agreement of 1954, and in providing a legal foundation for solving the internal problems of South Viet-Nam. Article 1 of the Paris agreement states that the United States and all other countries "respect the independence, sovereignty, unity, and territorial integrity of Viet-Nam as recognized by the 1954 Geneva Agreement on Viet-Nam". The 1973 agreement recognized two South Viet-Namese parties, each with its own administration and armed forces. While the Paris agreement served to conclude the *de facto,* though undeclared, war between the United States and the Democratic Republic of Viet-Nam, it tacitly accepted the state of civil war between the government of the Republic of Viet-Nam and the Provisional Revolutionary Government of the Republic of South Viet-Nam. By the end of 1973, some 39 states had established diplomatic relations with the PRG [32] and 32 with the RVN.

The 1973 agreement contains a series of provisions intended to bring about national conciliation and free elections, as well as the return of detained civilians and refugees. These political provisions have yet to be implemented, and the civil war continues.[9]

[9] The National Council of National Reconciliation and Concord envisaged in the Paris agreement (Article 12) and which was, *inter alia,* to organize "genuinely free and democratic general elections under international supervision" (Article 9(b)) has never been formed. As a result, no general elections have been organized. The situation is thus reminiscent of that in 1956.

Article 8(c) of the Paris agreement states that "the question of the return of Vietnamese

The future of both South Viet-Nam and Cambodia remains unresolved. On 15 March 1973, President Nixon issued a warning to North Viet-Nam [33] and on 26 March 1973, as the last US prisoners of war were being repatriated, the US Department of Defense ordered the Air Force to prepare for an increased level of bombing. This increased level resulted in a budget request to triple the production of certain kinds of bombs in order to "provide for a possible Southeast Asia contingency". [16b, 34] On 30 November the US Secretary of Defense issued a reminder of the continuing presence of US military power in South East Asia. [35] On 4 February 1974, President Nixon sent to the US Congress the defence budget for fiscal year 1975, which included $450 million for the added costs of maintaining US men and bombers in Thailand, and $1.45 billion for military aid to the RVN, in addition to $562 million left over from previously approved funds. [21–22]

## V. *The proliferation of Viet-Nam-War-related weapon technology*

The Indo-China War led not only to a major investment in new weapon technology but also provided a proving ground to test new weapons.[10] There can be little doubt that this investment in limited war and COIN (counterinsurgency) technology by one of the world's major suppliers of arms will have a significant impact on military doctrines and procurement policies throughout the world.

Two kinds of proliferation are in evidence. The first is the profusion of new varieties of munitions, delivery platforms and target acquisition and guidance systems. Table 3.2 lists some weapon developments which were "stimulated or accelerated by the pressure of the war in Southeast Asia".[11] [38] A wide range of other weapons, either developed by govern-

personnel captured and detained in South Viet-Nam will be resolved by the two South Viet-Namese parties on the basis of the principles of Article 21(b) of the Agreement of the Cessation of Hostilities in Viet-Nam of July 20, 1954". There has been little success in resolving the issue of political detainees, of which there are said to be more than 200 000 in South Viet-Nam. [6, 20]

[10] According to the US Director of Defense Research and Engineering, as much as 12 per cent of the total US defence research and development budget was devoted to Indo-China-War-related projects. [36] The US Air Force alone spent $665 million on research and development for the war in Indo-China between 1965 and 1973. [37]

[11] *Flight International* gave the following evaluation of some of these developments: "Vietnam's contribution to aerospace development has been formidable. It has transformed the helicopter from the slow, noisy, vibrating and unreliable vehicle of the fifties to the fast, quiet, smooth and reliable machine it is today. Gen.Westmoreland demanded these qualities for stable weapon-aiming . . . The rigid motor was born on the field in Vietnam. So was the infrared sensor, to see convoys taking advantage of the night . . . So was laser targeting . . . So was the RPV, or remotely piloted vehicle, to wage war without losing any pilots at all, and to get 100 times the kill or intelligence per dollar. The C-5A, whence sprang the civil jumbo jets, is the result of Vietnam thinking. So are the light fighter and the A–X, in response

**Table 3.2. US weapon developments stimulated or accelerated by the war in Indo-China**[a]

*Tactical aircraft systems*
Cobra attack helicopter
A-37 attack aircraft
AC-119/123/130 gunships
OH-6/OH-58 helicopters

*Tactical missiles and ordnance*
M-16 rifle
M-72 light assault weapon
7.62 miniguns
Standard ARM missile
Talos ARM missile
Mk 36 destructor mine
BLU-61 bomb
Rockeye munition
Laser-guided weapons
Walleye/Hobo guided weapons
Fuel-air explosive munitions
CBU 24/49 cluster munitions
Wide Area Anti-Personnel Mines (WAAPM)
20 mm gun pods
2.75-inch rocket with warhead
New bomb fuses

*Combat vehicles*
M551 Sheridan vehicle

*Sensors, Command, Control and Communications, and Intelligence*
Loran D navigation system
PPS 4/5, TPS 58 surveillance radars
3 types Starlight Scopes
Laser rangefinder

[a] All these weapons have been adopted by US forces. Some other weapons were tested in Viet-Nam on an experimental basis only.

*Source:* Statement of John S. Foster, Jr., Director of Defense Research and Engineering, US House of Representatives Committee on Appropriations, *Department of Defense Appropriations for 1972,* Hearings, part 4 (Washington, US Government Printing Office, 1971) pp. 728–30.

ment laboratories or by private industry, were tested and employed in Viet-Nam by US and allied forces: examples range from CS gas munitions and herbicides to new kinds of small arms and ammunition, such as the 5.56 mm M-16 rifle and a 12-bore shotgun cartridge containing 20 flechettes.

New Soviet weapons did not appear in Viet-Nam in anything like the same profusion. Weapons like the "Grail" heat-seeking anti-aircraft missile and the "Sagger" wire-guided anti-tank weapon, both light infantry weapons, appeared in Viet-Nam only in 1972. The North Viet-Namese never acquired missiles fully able to defeat the B-52 bomber, which, since it

to the battle cry . . . for plain combat aircraft . . . The ceasefire will hit US production—bleakly in some areas. But the major part of America's military aerospace R&D is unlikely to be affected." [39]

was developed as a strategic nuclear bomber, must have been a major focus of Soviet anti-aircraft-missile development efforts.[12]

The "Styx" anti-ship missile, which sank the Israeli ship *Eilat* in 1967, and which might have threatened the ships of the US Seventh Fleet, never appeared in Viet-Nam. The Soviet weapons appearing in Viet-Nam were illustrative of what has been called the conservative Soviet design philosophy: improvements to simple, rugged, existing weapons, using proven, off-the-shelf components where possible. [42] The new technologies to emerge from the Viet-Nam War were those of the United States.

Many of the new weapon systems developed for the Viet-Nam War by the USA together form what has been termed collectively the "automated battlefield". These systems are described in chapter 11.

The second kind of proliferation is the spread of the new weapons and technologies to other countries. The spread of major weapon platforms, such as attack helicopters and gunships, can be seen from the SIPRI arms trade registers (appendix 8F).[13] A few examples of the spread of the new technologies are the following.[14]

1. Cluster bomb munitions have been developed in France (the Giboulée) and the UK (BL755) and supplied to several other countries. US-made munitions of this type were used by Israel in the recent conflict. The logic of a cluster of small bombs to give greater area coverage is commanding, because greater stand-off capability is demanded for aircraft engaged in attacking small point targets such as men or vehicles.

2. The technique of casting metal balls in a plastic shell, used in some US cluster bombs instead of the traditional fragmentation principle, has been adopted in the West German Diehl-DN-51 hand grenade.

3. The notched steel wire which breaks into small pieces, used in the US M-26 hand grenade and 40 mm grenade, is used in the Belgian PRB 423 hand grenade and in a new Swedish Bofors 40 mm grenade, which also contains metal balls.

4. The widespread use of the 40 mm grenade in Viet-Nam has led to the development of 40 mm grenade launchers for all the 5.56 mm rifles, and a number of larger automatic launchers for aircraft.

5. M-16 rifles, using the very high velocity 5.56 mm ammunition, have

---

[12] US sources report that during the 11-day concentrated bombing attacks in December 1972 on the Hanoi-Haiphong area, when over 700 B-52 sorties were flown (a sortie is one mission by one plane), 15 B-52s were shot down and six or seven damaged. One B-52 was lost previously and one subsequently. Since about 200 B-52s were operating over Indo-China, this represents about 7.5 per cent of the fleet. All are said to have been shot down by SA-2 "Guideline" missiles, though the DRV claims that one was shot down by a MiG-21 interceptor aircraft. The US estimates that on average 60–62 missile firings were required to shoot down each B-52. [2c, 40–41]

[13] The SIPRI arms trade registers do not include smaller items, such as small arms and ammunition.

[14] These are all weapons of the type likely to be considered by the Diplomatic Conference on the Geneva Conventions in its deliberations on means and methods of combat which may give rise to unnecessary suffering or indiscriminate effects (see chapter 12).

**Table 3.3. Current 5.56 mm weapons**

| Country of origin | Designation | Type | Number of rounds | Muzzle velocity *m/sec* | Muzzle energy *joules* | Cyclic rate of fire *shots/min* |
|---|---|---|---|---|---|---|
| Austria | Steyr | . . | . . | . . | . . | . . |
| Belgium | FN CAL | AR | 30 | 970 | 1 670 | 600 |
| | FN Minimi | LMG (belt-fed) | 100, 200 | | | 750–1 250 |
| FR Germany | HK 33 | AR | 20 | 970 | 1 670 | 650 |
| | HK 23 | LMG (prototype, belt-fed) | 50 | 985 | 1 740 | 800 |
| | HK 13 | LMG (magazine) | 20, 40, 100 | 985 | 1 740 | 800 |
| Israel | Galil | AR | 12, 35, 50 | 970 | 1 670 | 650 |
| | New Uzi | AR | . . | . . | . . | . . |
| Italy | Beretta AR-70 | AR, carbine, LMG | 30 | 970 | 1 670 | 630 |
| Switzerland | SG 530-1 | AR | 30 | 860 | 1 490 | 600 |
| UK | Parker Hale | . . | . . | . . | . . | . . |
| USA | AR15 (M16) | AR | 20 | 1 000 | 1 800 | 850 |
| | AR18 (AR180) | AR | 20 | 970 | 1 670 | 800 |
| | AR18S | SMG | . . | 820 | 1 300 | 800–830 |
| | Stoner 63 system | AR, SMG, LM, MMG, KVG | 30 | 1 000 | 1 800 | 650 |
| | Colt CAR 13 | HAR | 30 | 985 | 1 740 | 750 |
| | Colt CMG-2 | LMG | 150 | 1 000 | 1 800 | 650 |
| | Minigun | AC | . . | 950 | 1 625 | 4 000–10 000 |
| | Remington Model 760 | Slide-action rifle | . . | . . | . . | . . |

AR=Assault rifle; SMG=sub-machine gun; LMG=light machine gun; MMG=medium machine gun; FVG=fixed vehicle gun; HAR=heavy assault rifle; AC=aircraft cannon.

*Sources:* Hobart, F. W. A., "The Next NATO Rifle", *International Defence Review,* February 1971; "The Armalite AR-18: A Trials Report", *International Review,* June 1971; "The Infantry Light Machine Gun—7.62 or 5.56?", *International Defence Review,* June 1972; Weller, J., "The Galil Rifle—an Israeli Weapon System", *National Defense,* September–October 1973; *Jane's Weapon Systems 1972–73* (London, Sampson, Low, Marston & Co., Ltd., 1972).

been reported in many armed forces, including those of Lebanon, the Philippines, Portugal (in Angola) and the UK (in Aden and Indonesia). A great variety of similar weapons is now being produced by private manufacturers (table 3.3). Israel has adopted its own 5.56 mm calibre rifle, the *Galil,* which was used in the recent conflict.

The end of the overt US involvement in the war in Indo-China may lead to an increased rate of proliferation of many of the new weapons in several ways. First, the decline in contracts for the supply of US forces may stimulate US manufacturers to seek alternative markets. Second, a considerable amount of surplus matériel from Indo-China is being given as military assistance or sold (at one-third cost) to other governments.[15] Third, the USA is likely to focus its attention on other areas, such as

---

[15] For example, the South Korean forces evacuated from South Viet-Nam took with them 90 993 tons of matériel. $50 million worth of still usable items were available for sale on the open market. [17] The Philippines received 120 single-engine Beaver aircraft formerly used for target spotting in Viet-Nam. [43]

Europe, seeking to adapt the new technologies to other theatres.[16] Fourth, other armed forces are likely to seek to acquire the new technologies and other manufacturers to supply them. The processes are in turn likely to stimulate the development and spread of Soviet weapons.

In conclusion, it should be pointed out that light-weight weapons designed for jungle warfare may also be suitable for urban counterinsurgency. Rifles of the US 5.56 mm calibre have been reported in Northern Ireland, and anti-aircraft missiles of the Soviet SA-7 type were discovered in Rome, apparently to be used in an attack on a civil aircraft. The arms race in means of internal warfare is a further example of the proliferation of Indo-China-War-related technology.

## References

1. News release, US Department of Defense, Washington, 1 February 1973.
2. *Department of Defense Appropriations for 1974,* Hearings, part 1, US House of Representatives Committee on Appropriations (Washington, US Government Printing Office, 1973).
   (a) −, p. 149.
   (b) −, p. 72.
   (c) −, p. 265.
3. News release, US Department of Defense, Washington, July 1973.
4. *Impact of the Vietnam War,* Report prepared for the use of the US Senate Committee on Foreign Relations by the Foreign Affairs Division, Congressional Research Service, Library of Congress, 30 June 1971 (Washington, US Government Printing Office, 1971).
5. *Department of Defense Appropriations for 1974,* Hearings, part 2, US House of Representatives Committee on Appropriations (Washington, US Government Printing Office, 1973) pp. 322–23.
6. *Viet-Nam Courier,* No. 18, November 1973.
7. *White Paper on the Application of the Paris Agreement on Viet-Nam during the Past Year* (Hanoi, Ministry of Foreign Affairs, Democratic Republic of Viet-Nam, January 1974).
8. *Congressional Record,* 11 May 1972.
   (a) −, p. E5029.
   (b) −, p. E5063.
9. *Thailand, Laos, Cambodia, and Vietnam: April 1973,* Staff report prepared for the use of the Subcommittee on U.S. Security Agreements and Commitments Abroad, US Senate Committee on Foreign Relations, 11 June 1973 (Washington, US Government Printing Office, 1973).
10. *International Herald Tribune,* 14 February 1974.
11. *International Herald Tribune,* 20 November 1973.
12. *New York Times,* 17 March 1973.

[16] The United States invited 14 NATO countries to a two-week demonstration by 30 US manufacturers of "automated battlefield" equipment at Hohenfels in West Germany in May 1972. The objective was to "sell the equipment to NATO members" [44] and to "interest the Atlantic allies in what remote sensors can do to improve the combat efficiency of their forces, in hopes that the allies will decide to manufacture and employ them". [45] It was also reported that large-scale troop exercises with US and German battalions were planned to "determine which devices work best in the relatively congested areas of Europe". [44]

13. *New York Times,* 25 October 1973.
14. *New York Times,* 12 September 1973.
15. *World Armaments and Disarmament, SIPRI Yearbook 1973* (Stockholm, Almqvist & Wiksell, 1973, Stockholm International Peace Research Institute) p. 302.
16. *Department of Defense Appropriations for 1974,* Hearings, part 6, US House of Representatives Committee on Appropriations (Washington, US Government Printing Office, 1973).
    (a) −, pp. 1363–1416.
    (b) −, pp. 1610–46.
17. *Japan Times,* 14 March 1973.
18. "Aspin List Shows $260 Million in Southeast Asia Defense Contracts", Press Release from Congressman Les Aspin, US House of Representatives Armed Services Committee, 11 June 1973.
19. *South Viet Nam in Struggle* (Hanoi, The South Viet Nam National Front for Liberation, 1 January 1974).
20. Kennedy, Edward M., "Prisons and Political Prisoners in South Viet Nam", *Congressional Record,* 4 June 1973.
21. *FY 1975 Budget Briefing* (Washington, US Department of Defense, 4 February 1974).
22. *International Herald Tribune,* 5 February 1974.
23. *Emergency Military Assistance for Israel and Cambodia,* Hearings, US Senate Committee on Foreign Relations, 13 December 1973 (Washington, US Goverment Printing Office, 1973).
24. *International Herald Tribune,* 29 January 1974.
25. *Refugee and Civilian War Casualty Problems in Indochina.* A staff report prepared for the use of the Subcommittee to Investigate Problems Connected with Refugees and Escapees, US Senate Committee on the Judiciary (Washinton, US Government Printing Office, 1970).
26. *Daily Telegraph,* 11 August 1973.
27. *International Herald Tribune,* 18 January 1974.
28. *Le Monde,* 27 October 1973.
29. *Relief and Rehabilitation of War Victims in Indochina, Part IV: South Vietnam and Regional Problems,* Hearings, Subcommittee to Investigate Problems Connected with Refugees and Escapees, US Senate Committee on the Judiciary (Washington, US Government Printing Office, 1973).
30. Lumsden, M., "The Vietnamese People and the Impact of War", *Studies in Progress,* No. 3 (Copenhagen, Institute of Peace and Conflict Research, December 1969).
31. *Relief and Rehabilitation of War Victims in Indochina: One Year after the Ceasefire,* A Study Mission report prepared for the use of the Subcommittee to Investigate Problems Connected with Refugees and Escapees, US Senate Committee on the Judiciary (Washington, 1974).
32. *Sydvietnams PRR Bulletin* (Stockholm, Republiken Sydvietnams Provisoriska Revolutionära Regerings Informationsbyrå, 14 December 1973).
33. *New York Times,* 16 March 1973.
34. Decornoy, J., *Le Monde,* 8 December 1973.
35. *Le Monde,* 2–3 December 1973.
36. *Department of Defense Appropriations for Fiscal Year 1972,* Hearings, part 1, US Senate Committee on Appropriations (Washington, US Government Printing Office, 1971) p. 345.
37. *Department of Defense Appropriations for 1974,* Hearings, part 7, US House of Representatives Committee on Appropriations (Washington, US Government Printing Office, 1973) p. 961.

38. *Department of Defense Appropriations for 1972,* Hearings, part 4, US House of Representatives Committee on Appropriations (Washington, US Government Printing Office, 1971) pp. 728–30.
39. *Flight International,* Vol. 103, No. 3334, 1 February 1973.
40. *Aviation Week & Space Technology,* Vol. 98, No. 2, 8 January 1973.
41. Baldwin, H. W., "The Strategy of the Old Bombers", *New York Times,* 19 January 1973.
42. Mounter, L. A., "Soviet Design Philosophy . . . Research and its Impact on Weapons Systems Development", *US Army Research and Development News Magazine,* September–October 1973, pp. 14–15.
43. *International Herald Tribune,* 6 October 1973.
44. *International Herald Tribune,* 27 March 1972.
45. *Aviation Week & Space Technology,* 8 May 1972.
46. *Far Eastern Economic Review,* 11 February 1974, p. 21.

# 4. Mutual force reductions in Europe

*Square-bracketed references, thus* [1]*, refer to the list of references on page 46.*

## I. *Introduction*

On 30 October 1973, after five months of preparatory consultations, the representatives of 19 NATO and WTO states began negotiations in Vienna on the mutual reduction of forces and armaments and associated measures in Central Europe (MURFAAMCE).[1]

Although there are great differences between the positions of the two sides on many issues and the parties to the negotiations are far from reaching an agreement, the fact that they are dealing with such sensitive questions as the reduction of forces and armaments in the two opposing alliances marks, hopefully, the commencement of a new era for Europe, particularly as regards security. Although the recent crisis in the Middle East had some negative influence on political détente in Europe and shook relations between the Soviet Union and the United States, the atmosphere prevailing at the negotiations in Vienna is evidence that the participants are aware that some measures towards military détente must be taken.

The negotiations are expected to continue for several years. Since the proceedings and documents of the meetings are confidential it is difficult at this stage to evaluate the progress reached or discuss in detail the proposals put forward; this account of the negotiations is based on the limited number of documents available and on press reports. This chapter will also present the basic attitudes of the parties towards the question of the reduction of forces and armaments. Since it will not be possible here to deal with the broader political, strategic, economic and other aspects of this question, only certain issues directly related to the present negotiations on MFR will be considered.

## II. *NATO-WTO negotiations on MFR*

### Arrangements for the preparatory consultations

A fuller description of early proposals related to arms regulations and disarmament in Europe has been given in previous SIPRI publications [1–2]; here, a short review of events leading to the present negotiations on MFR in Vienna will be presented.

---

[1] Here *MFR* will be used rather than the longer acronym.

A variety of proposals were put forward by NATO and the WTO members concerning force reductions in Europe during the period 1967–72 and, in the first half of 1972, a number of important diplomatic developments occurred which gave renewed hope that progress in force reduction explorations might soon be made. The Federal Republic of Germany ratified the German-Soviet and German-Polish treaties. France, the United Kingdom, the United States and the Soviet Union agreed to sign, in early June, the Final Protocol to the Quadripartite Agreement on Berlin. President Nixon visited Moscow, where the SALT I agreements were signed.

These developments in East-West relations made it possible to seek to reduce the existing military confrontation in Europe. The ministers of the NATO countries agreed at the Bonn Meeting of the North Atlantic Council on 30–31 May 1972 "to enter into multilateral conversations concerned with preparations for a Conference on Security and Cooperation in Europe". They also agreed to "aim at negotiations on mutual and balanced force reduction and related measures" and therefore proposed "that multilateral explorations on mutual and balanced force reductions be undertaken as soon as possible, either before or in parallel with multilateral preparatory talks on the Conference on Security and Cooperation in Europe". [3]

After Henry Kissinger, then President Nixon's adviser on national security, visited Moscow in September 1972, it was announced that the Soviet Union had in principle accepted the Western position that a separate East-West conference on the reduction of military forces in Central Europe should be held the following year at about the same time as broad political talks on European security problems were being held. [4]

Following this agreement, the Western powers proposed exploratory talks on MBFR in Central Europe to begin on 31 January 1973, preferably in Geneva. The proposal was made in a note of 15 November 1972 sent by the United States, the Federal Republic of Germany, Canada, the United Kingdom and the Benelux countries to the Soviet Union, Poland, Czechoslovakia, Hungary and the German Democratic Republic. Several NATO states—Italy, Turkey and Greece on the southern flank, and Norway and Denmark in the north—which were not included in the exchange, were expected to participate on a rotating basis in the proposed conference. [5]

Although certain conditions were posed, on 18 January 1973 the WTO member states expressed readiness to participate in the proposed consultations on 31 January 1973 on mutual East-West reductions in military forces. Rather than limiting the participants in the talks to the Central European nations, as suggested by NATO, the Soviet Union proposed that the conference be open to any country in or outside the two organizations, even the neutral and nonaligned states. The Soviet Union and its Warsaw Treaty allies also asked that the negotiations take place in Vienna, rather than in Geneva, as suggested by NATO. [6]

The proposal for unlimited participation in the consultations on force reductions caused laborious and intricate negotiations to reach agreement among NATO powers before they approached the Soviet Union, only to reaffirm their position that the consultations should be limited to those states with military forces in the Central Region, with NATO participation by the United States, the United Kingdom, Canada, the Federal Republic of Germany, the Netherlands, Belgium and Luxembourg. Of the WTO members, NATO wanted the list to be limited to the Soviet Union, the German Democratic Republic, Poland, Czechoslovakia and Hungary.

Even earlier, NATO's "flank countries" had argued that it would be useless to reduce forces in Central Europe only to have the Soviet Union withdraw them to Murmansk or the Turkish frontier or the Bulgarian border with Greece. It was therefore agreed on the NATO side that Norway, Denmark, Greece and Turkey would have limited participation. They would be fully included in the preparation of NATO negotiating positions, but would not be full members of the conference. NATO was expecting similar restraint in numbers on the part of the Warsaw Treaty Organization.

The NATO formula had first been challenged during preparations in Helsinki for convening the European security conference, when Romania and some neutral and nonaligned countries expressed concern that they should be included in any conference on force reduction. To this end the Soviet Union responded by proposing that all interested states should participate. Moreover, at a meeting in Minsk on 12 January 1973, the Soviet Union had encouraged President Pompidou to reverse France's "Gaullist" attitude toward the negotiations and join them. [7] By proposing broader participation, the Soviet Union was also offering France an opportunity to participate, since it would not be a "bloc-to-bloc" negotiation any longer and since France had balked at negotiating under a NATO label. The Soviet proposal was not accepted, and France continued to refuse to participate in the negotiations.

The NATO Council decided on 24–25 January to reject suggestions from the Warsaw Treaty countries that the proposed talks on reducing forces in Europe should be open to all interested states. The North Atlantic Treaty allies made it clear to the WTO that they still wanted to limit the proposed negotiations on Central European force reductions to those countries directly involved in the area. But they suggested that participation in the troop-cut negotiations could be further discussed at the proposed preparatory consultations which were due to start on 31 January. According to the statement, [8] Vienna was not ruled out by NATO countries if satisfactory arrangements could be made there in time.

Although the WTO suggestion for unlimited participation in the consultations had not been accepted, the government of the Soviet Union informed the governments of NATO countries in a reply to their notes of 24–25 January 1973, that the Soviet delegates would be in Vienna on 31 January

1973 for preliminary consultations on the reduction of armed forces and armaments in Europe. At the same time it was stressed that the Soviet Union reserved the right to return to the question of participation of other interested European countries, including neutral states. [9]

## The preparatory consultations

On the appointed day, 19 nations began preparatory consultations in Vienna on the reduction of armed forces and armaments in Europe. Twelve NATO countries (all except France, Portugal and Iceland) and all the seven WTO countries were present at the opening meeting. It is noteworthy that in a statement to the press upon his arrival in Vienna, O. N. Khlestov, the Soviet delegation leader, referred to "talks on mutual reduction of armed forces and armaments in Europe". He also stated that "the Soviet Union attaches great importance to these consultations having in mind that an agreement about reduction of armed forces and armaments in Europe would promote the process of further lessening of tension on the European continent, the cause of strengthening the world peace". [10–11] After the short opening meeting the Dutch representative, acting as a spokesman for the Western countries, referred to these consultations as "talks on mutual and balanced force reductions in Central Europe" and made it clear that the attendance of all representatives did not prejudice the definition of their status or participation in any eventual conference. He also said that the 19 nations had agreed to hold informal meetings during the coming days to discuss such difficult questions as participation in the talks. [10]

After the opening meeting, the NATO and WTO countries began intensive, informal discussions on various questions of which there were differences of opinion, concerning the forthcoming negotiations. According to press reports, the main question discussed during the subsequent three and a half months was the participation of certain states in the negotiations, and some other procedural matters.

The NATO countries gave no indication that they would abandon their original plan, which was to limit full participation to the countries whose troops or national territories are involved. NATO participation was thus to be limited to the Benelux countries, Canada, the Federal Republic of Germany, the United Kingdom and the United States. At the outset of the consultations the question of the participation of Romania and Bulgaria was raised. NATO had expected them to be given special status, similar to that worked out for the five NATO flank countries, but, from the beginning, these two nations declined anything less than complete participation.

NATO has, to a large extent, created the problem itself. Its original plan for the MFR talks had been to exclude the flank countries—Denmark, Greece, Italy, Norway and Turkey—on the grounds that their troops were not present in the Central European area which NATO wanted to discuss. In a compromise reached in Brussels in the autumn of 1972, however, it was decided to give the flank countries special status; that is, they were to be permitted to present their views at the conference, but not actually to participate in the decision making.

As has already been noted, the WTO countries called for a conference of "all interested European parties" which would bring in its own flank countries, Romania and Bulgaria, and open the door to neutral and nonaligned countries. [12]

By the time Romania and Bulgaria were granted special status in the consultations, Hungary had also offered to participate under the same arrangement, which caused further delay in the discussion. The Western countries would not consent to grant Hungary special status on the grounds that it is situated in Central Europe and that Soviet forces are stationed there. The dispute over the status of Hungary was the subject of lengthy discussion between representatives of the USA and the Netherlands on the one side, and the USSR and Hungary on the other. [13]

After three and a half months of informal discussion, a compromise was reached on the question of the participants and on certain other procedural matters. The record of the second plenary meeting, held on 14 May 1973, stated that the representatives of the following states were potential participants in the possible agreements related to Central Europe: Belgium, Canada, Czechoslovakia, the Federal Republic of Germany, the German Democratic Republic, Luxembourg, the Netherlands, Poland, the Soviet Union, the United Kingdom and the United States. They were to make decisions on the basis of consensus. States which were to participate with special status were: Bulgaria, Denmark, Greece, Hungary, Italy, Norway, Romania and Turkey. All participants were to have a right to take part in and submit documents concerning the discussions. Proceedings and documents of the meetings were to be confidential except for those matters on which it was agreed in advance that another procedure was to be followed. [14]

Further, it was stated in the record that representatives of the above-mentioned potential NATO participants had stressed that the arrangements for the participation of Hungary in these consultations were without prejudice to the nature of its "participation in future negotiations, decisions, or agreed measures or to the security of any part" and that the nature and scope of Hungary's participation in future decisions, agreements or measures were to be examined and decided during the pending negotiations. In connection with the above unilateral statement of NATO countries, the Hungarian delegate stated that Hungary would participate in possible decisions, agreements or measures only if the appropriate conditions were fulfilled. [14]

It is noteworthy that the Dutch delegate, speaking on behalf of the NATO countries, further elaborated the NATO position at a press conference by stating that NATO would raise the question of Hungary's participation at a later date, claiming that Hungary, in fact, had a "unique status". [15]

After the acceptance of the arrangements on participants and rules of procedure and following further discussion on 28 June 1973, agreement was reached on the date and place, but not on an agenda, for negotiations on mutual force reductions in Central Europe. The communiqué defined the subject of the Vienna negotiations as "mutual reduction of forces and armaments and associated measures in Central Europe". It was decided that the negotiations would start on 30 October 1973 in Vienna. [16]

At the press conference after the final meeting the Dutch delegate, speaking on behalf of NATO states, stated that in spite of the omission of the word "balanced" in the communiqué, the NATO concept of "balanced" is satisfactorily covered by the statement that "specific arrangements will have to be carefully worked out in scope and timing in such a way that they will in all respects and at every point conform to the principle of undiminished security for each party". [17]

Speaking on behalf of WTO countries the Polish delegate stated that the socialist countries do not like the use of the word "balanced". This terminology is unacceptable because it is interpreted by the Western countries in such a manner that it violates the principle of symmetrical structure and thus the interests of the socialist countries. [18]

## The present negotiations

On 30 October 1973, as had previously been decided at the preparatory consultations, the representatives of the 19 NATO and WTO countries began their negotiations on MFR. During the first two days of the negotiations all the participants gave opening statements in which they expressed the views of their respective governments on the questions related to MFR in Central Europe.

Following the two plenary meetings, the negotiations have continued in strict confidentiality according to the rules of procedure set out in the Final Communiqué of 28 June 1973. The meetings, which are held in a business-like atmosphere, are open only to the participants and they are chaired in rotation by representatives of the decision-making participants in alphabetical order.

On 8 November 1973 the Soviet Union proposed, on behalf of Poland, the German Democratic Republic and Czechoslovakia, a draft agreement which was supported by other socialist countries. Romania has so far abstained from endorsing the proposal of the other WTO members, reiterating that the question of reduction of forces is an issue which is of interest to all European states and that it should be an all-European matter. The NATO countries' proposal was submitted on 22 November 1973 by the representative of the United States on behalf of the full participants to the negotiations from the NATO side and supported by other NATO members. Although these proposals are confidential and have not been published, some of the elements contained in them are known either because there were some leaks or because they express more or less the views of both sides which have already been expressed earlier in the opening statements or in some other official or semi-official statements. It is also known that while the proposal of the WTO countries is in the form of a draft agreement, the Western proposal is more in the form of an outline of basic principles.

According to press reports, the WTO countries have proposed a three-stage reduction of forces in Central Europe. In 1975, 20 000 troops would be withdrawn by both sides, that is, the Soviet Union, the German Democratic Republic, Poland and Czechoslovakia on one side, and the armed forces of the United States, the United Kingdom, the Federal Republic of Germany, the Netherlands, Belgium, Canada and Luxembourg on the other side. In 1976, the remaining troops would be reduced by 5 per cent, and in 1977 by 10 per cent. The WTO plan, further, envisages reduction of all armed forces, both foreign and national, and the reduction would be applied to all types of forces: to ground and air forces as well as to units equipped with nuclear weapons.

The NATO proposal calls for a cut during the first phase, of about 15 per cent each in US and Soviet forces stationed in Central Europe. According to some sources another 15 per cent cut in the subsequent phase, to be followed by the setting of a common ceiling for all NATO and WTO forces in the region at the level of about 700 000 men, is expected. This would represent, bearing in mind the Western estimates of existing forces, a 10 per cent reduction by NATO and a 20 per cent cutback by the WTO countries. [21] Certain elements contained in these proposals will be discussed below.

After a one-month recess (15 December 1973 – 15 January 1974) the negotiations were resumed and it is expected that they will continue for several years.


## III. *Military balance: some general remarks*

In order to analyse specific issues arising from the current negotiations on MFR, it is necessary to point out some of the factors which have broader implications, such as military strategy and balance. These two factors have been fully analysed in a SIPRI monograph [1] and in appendix 4A; only some general remarks on military balance will be made here.

The present military balance between NATO and WTO forces is, without doubt, of immense importance to the outcome of the current negotiations. Since the mutual force reduction negotiations are primarily concerned with conventional forces, this brief assessment will focus mainly on these forces. However, the military balance in Europe can be assessed not on the basis of NATO and WTO conventional forces alone, but also on how one views the relationship between strategic nuclear and conventional forces in an era of East-West nuclear parity. It is well known that the USA and the USSR have enough strategic nuclear weapons to inflict untold damage on each other. The threat posed by the enormously destructive nuclear forces of both East and West, along with the risk of escalation of any major conflict to the nuclear level, would appear more than sufficient to deter any aggression involving massive conventional forces. But on the other hand, awareness of the enormous destructive effects of nuclear weapons has led to changes in the military strategies of both alliances allowing for the possibility of waging local wars with conventional forces. As a result, increased emphasis has been put on the role of conventional forces in an era of relative balance in strategic nuclear weapons. Even though there is no agreement about the current state of balance or imbalance, it might perhaps be possible to say that there is a rough parity between NATO and WTO conventional forces, all factors taken into account, although it is impossible to express this total conventional balance in numbers and/or percentages.

There are several difficulties in comparing NATO and WTO forces. Some elements of the forces are quantifiable and constitute more or less adequate indicators of military strength in their respective fields. But there are also many other factors which must be taken into account to make a fair assessment of overall military strength. Theoretically these factors can be divided into the following categories: (*a*) other quantifiable elements which are roughly comparable, but for which available information does not permit exact estimates; (*b*) quantifiable elements which appear comparable and for which estimates are available, but which are not actually comparable when their constituent parts are considered; (*c*) quantifiable elements on each side, for which estimates may or may not be available but which have no counterpart on the opposing side; and (*d*) non-quantifiable factors with regard to which relative advantages can be assessed only very roughly, if at all. It is obvious that these factors cannot simply be added together to form an objective measure in mathematical terms of total military strength. Such factors include, for instance, figures for manpower and equipment of various kinds; considerations of geographical advantages, deployment, training and logistics support; and differences in doctrine, philosophy and the like.

Even if it were possible to give comparative values to all the relevant aspects of the forces to be compared—and it is not possible—the problem of assigning a relative weight to each aspect in the overall assessment would still remain. The importance attached to different elements of the forces must be based mainly on assumptions about developments in the event of a war. Such assumptions can be neither proved or disproved, nor, in most cases, shown to be more or less plausible or likely. Problems of this sort arise even when assessing the peacetime balance of forces, to which most comparisons are limited, but they are more difficult when the question of reinforcements is introduced. Finally, existing estimates of the forces of NATO and the WTO are primarily based on Western sources and, as such, inevitably reflect more or less one-sided assessments.

All these difficulties clearly show that any assessment of the military balance between NATO and the WTO involves comparisons of so many non-quantifiable and unpredictable factors that it is virtually impossible to make a meaningful overall evaluation. Consequently an assessment of parity is simply another way of saying that there are advantages and disadvantages on both sides.

With these general restrictions in mind the data on forces presented in appendix 4A are confined to the following elements: (*a*) ground forces (that is, divisions and division equivalents, combat and direct support troops (manpower) and tanks); (*b*) air forces; and (*c*) total military forces in peacetime. In addition to these factors, which are elaborated in detail in the SIPRI Monograph *Force Reductions in Europe,* some other factors should be mentioned which are even more difficult to compare but which are essential for an assessment of the balance, such as technical sophistication of weaponry and logistic and support infrastructure. Moreover, one must bear in mind not only these military and economic factors but also political factors and possibilities of different alignment in such cases. All these factors are non-quantifiable and difficult to assess. Thus the non-comparability of the forces, the unpredictability of a possible future war, and the consequent impossibility of arriving at generally accepted weights to assign to the various elements in an overall assessment preclude a comprehensive comparison of NATO and WTO conventional forces.

With these difficulties in mind it is unlikely that an agreement on MFR will be reached covering numerical balances only. The two sides will probably have to negotiate from a political point of view in order to determine first what figures could be used as points of departure for the subsequent discussions. This first step in the negotiations alone may require considerable time and diplomatic effort but seems to be necessary in order to provide military data in such a way as to support the basic political assumptions.

## IV. *Analysis of specific issues*

Bearing in mind the proposals of NATO and WTO countries put forward before the negotiations started and the views expressed by the participants at the beginning of the negotiations in Vienna, one can conclude that the major issues on which agreement will be sought are: (*a*) methods of reduction; (*b*) types of forces to be reduced; (*c*) the territory to be covered; and (*d*) "associated measures" which may be adopted.

## Methods of reduction

There are, in fact, several possible methods for the reduction of forces: (*a*) equal reductions for both sides (either by applying the same percentage of reduction or by reductions in absolute figures); (*b*) asymmetrical reductions but with the current "balance" maintained; (*c*) reductions which improve the current "balance" for one side or the other; and (*d*) reductions which produce a better balance than the existing one.

Differences exist between the two alliances on the question of the methods which should be applied to reduce existing forces. Different kinds of reductions have been proposed such as "balanced", "symmetrical", "asymmetrical" and so on.

The concept of so-called balanced reductions has caused difficulties. The United States and other NATO countries advocate that "mutual reduction should be reciprocal and balanced in scope and timing". This statement, which was included in the *Declaration on Mutual and Balanced Reduction,* agreed to at the Reykjavik meeting, was repeated in the documents from the subsequent meetings of NATO countries.

Although no official definition of the principle of "balanced reduction" exists, it is based, according to the interpretations given in the West, on several factors.

The NATO countries claim that there are significant, "objective" disparities affecting the current situation in Central Europe. According to Western estimates these disparities are in manpower, in the character of forces and in geography. As far as manpower is concerned, the NATO countries consider that the countries of the WTO have more ground personnel on active duty in Central Europe than does NATO. With respect to the character of the forces, the WTO forces maintain a concentration of heavy armour in Central Europe. A marked imbalance in tanks therefore exists in Central Europe. The West also claims that the WTO has superiority in air defence, in both radar detection and interceptors, and that it has about twice as many fighter aircraft as NATO.

This "imbalance" is even greater when mobilization and the reinforcement of existing forces are taken into account. It is assumed that the WTO would have an advantage here within the first few weeks and that subsequently NATO would be able to reinforce at an increasing rate.

Better reinforcement facilities are primarily based on the "geographical factor". Generally speaking, Western countries consider that the geographic advantage is clearly on the Soviet side for two basic reasons: first, because the proximity of Soviet territory to the Central Region makes it much easier for the Soviet Union, than for the USA, to reinforce its troops there and to maintain lines of communication with the base, and, second, because NATO countries lack sufficiently deep territory in Europe to provide for maximum manoeuvrability of forces and adequate defence.

The USA and USSR, which station significant forces in Central Europe, are located at vastly unequal distances from the area. The territory of the Soviet Union directly and immediately adjoins Central Europe. Soviet forces, located in Soviet territory, have ready access over the Polish plain to the very heart of the area. The USA, on the other hand, is located at a great distance from Central Europe and is separated from the area by the Atlantic Ocean. Thus, access to Central Europe is far more difficult for US forces. The geographic disparity has this consequence for mutual reductions: any Soviet forces withdrawn from Central Europe into the territory of the Soviet Union could return quickly and easily; US forces withdrawn to the United States would be an ocean away. This point applies equally to reinforcement capability. [22]

The perceived geographical advantage on the WTO side has been advanced as a major argument supporting NATO proposals for an asymmetrical approach with a view to preserving the current balance. Of course, asymmetrical reductions, while justified by geographical factors, would also reduce WTO superiority in certain quantitative elements of the forces. This could be seen either as improving the current situation from the NATO point of view, or as creating a new situation which would be more balanced than the present one.

The WTO countries, on the other hand, advocate that the reduction of armed forces and armaments in Europe should be based on the principles of "parity reduction" and undiminished security for both sides. They reject the principle of "balanced" reduction since, as it is interpreted by the West, it would lead to asymmetrical reductions which are clearly disadvantageous to the WTO position. The question of balanced reduction has been dealt with in a number of articles published by Soviet and East European scientists. The most detailed is one by Y. Kostko in which he criticizes the asymmetrical reduction of armed forces in Europe as proposed by the West. He concludes:

Analysis shows that all arguments about 'military inequality' in the spheres of conventional forces and of the necessity for 'asymmetrical' reduction do not stand up to criticism, all the more as in conditions of equality of strategic nuclear forces and of a reduction of the role of conventional forces the tipping of the scales cannot threaten 'the vital interests of security' of either side. In our opinion, if we are to approach the question of reduction of armed forces and armaments in Central Europe from realistic positions then the only possible principle is the principle of parity reduction. [23]

It has also been argued by the East that the principle of balanced reduction is based only or primarily on factors and elements which show a superiority on the part of WTO forces, while other elements, showing the opposite, are disregarded. Thus in a recent article in *Sprawy Miedzynaro-dowe* it is stated that the Western models of force reductions are based on biased material. This can be illustrated mainly by: (*a*) taking into consideration the entire military potential of the USSR and other member states on the WTO side, while the Western side is confined only to forces of the Federal Republic of Germany, Benelux and US forces in the Federal Republic of Germany; and (*b*) making a comparison of those forces and armaments in which the East outnumbers the West. Other factors which Western models do not take into consideration include: (*a*) the high degree of professionalism in the armies of the West; (*b*) the military potential of France and Spain which have to be taken into account because of their special relations with NATO; (c) the great military-industrial potential of Western Europe; (*d*) the highly developed infrastructure; and (*e*) nuclear weapons deployed in Europe, especially bearing in mind the fact that the SALT agreements do not cover such weapons maintained by the United Kingdom and France. [24]

Similarly, in a recent article in the Soviet journal *Mirovaya Ekonomika i Mezhdunarodnye Otnoshenia,* D. M. Proector argues that "all the 'asymmetrical' conceptions for troop reductions are not based on an objective and unbiased analysis of all components of reduction of forces in Europe." [25]

Since the necessity for "asymmetrical" reduction is based on the so-called geographical factor, Kostko points out that "it must be noted that with the reduction, i.e., the abolition of fighting units of foreign armed forces in Europe the "geographical factor" on the whole plays no particular part". He notes that

the Soviet Union . . . has enormously long land frontiers and is obliged to maintain considerable forces not only in the West but also in the East and the South for their defence. Hence, even if we proceed from the false premise of the 'atlanticists', we must take into account that the Soviet Union would have to transfer its troops to the West from, let us say, the Urals or Baikal and that these distances would in a sense exceed the distance, let us say, from New York to London.

Moreover, according to Kostko, the "geographical factor" would look quite different if we were to examine it from the position of the global alignment of forces between NATO and the WTO in the event of a major military conflict. [23]

Concerning the reference to the fact that, because of its geographical proximity, the Soviet Union could more quickly mobilize and transfer its divisions to Central Europe it is pointed out that "NATO's military command has at its disposal a wide range of transport facilities, an intricate network of airfields, the extensive communication system of Western Europe, all the various NATO transport aircraft and so on". [23]

Taking into account all these components, the WTO members consider that there is a balance between the armed forces and armaments of the two alliances and that any asymmetrical reduction would create one-sided military advantages and as such cannot represent a sound position for negotiations based on the principle of equal security. The elaboration of solutions adequate to the actual situation requires an exact estimate of the effectiveness of existing armed forces and armaments in Europe, their correlation, together with the feasibility of reinforcement which is dependent on the regions of deployment and on different conditions for movements of troops.

But although the West insists on so-called balanced reduction, the two sides have moved somewhat closer. This is illustrated by the Soviet-US communiqué of 29 May 1972 in which it is pointed out that "any agreement on this question should not diminish the security of any of the sides". This is more or less repeated in the US-Soviet communiqué of 24 June 1973 in which it is stated that both sides will contribute to the achievement of "mutually acceptable decisions on the substance of this problem, based on the strict observance of the principle of the undiminished security of any of the Parties".

The differences between the Soviet Union and the WTO countries on the one hand and the Western countries on the other, as to what kind of reductions they envisaged, became more obvious at the Vienna Force Reductions talks. While the representatives of Western countries used the term "mutual and balanced force reductions", the representatives of the WTO countries used the term "mutual reduction of forces and armaments in Europe".

During the preparatory consultations the concept of balanced reduction was questioned by the WTO countries and as a result of their opposition, the word "balanced" does not appear in the Final Communiqué of 28 June 1973 in which the subject of the negotiations is defined as "mutual reduction of forces and armaments and associated measures in Central Europe". But in a press statement about the Final Communiqué, made by the head of the Netherlands delegation on 28 June 1973 on behalf of NATO countries, it was said that in the view of these countries "the term 'balanced' comprehends the ideas that any future measures should be reciprocal, should provide for enhanced stability at a lower level of forces, and should not diminish the security of any party". Further in the agreed communiqué, it is stated that "specific arrangements will have to be carefully worked out in scope and timing in such a way that they will in all respects and at every point conform to the principle of undiminished security for each party." "This statement in fact", according to the head of the Netherlands delegation, "presents the NATO concept of 'balanced' as it has been defined in various NATO communiqués . . . We consider that the elements of the NATO concept of "balanced" are satisfactorily covered in the communiqué agreed today, and would also say that there is a substantial measure of agreement between the two sides as regards the underlying content of the 'balanced' concept, even though the Eastern authorities have been unwilling to accept the word itself''. [26]

At the Vienna negotiations on MFR, although both sides have accepted as a point of departure the principle of undiminished security and are advocating the reduction of forces in such a way as to lead to a more stable military balance at lower levels of forces, they differ in the way they interpret these principles, and as a result the differences between them on the question of the kinds of reduction they envisage have not been resolved.

Although the representatives of the NATO countries stopped using the term "balanced" reduction, their statements and proposals imply the concept of asymmetrical reductions. This concept is based, as has already been pointed out, on existing disparities in forces between the two sides, especially in Central Europe. The two-phase Western proposal called for cutback is to be effected remains to be settled by the participants in the talks, but the possibilities include reductions by equal percentages or by and WTO forces in Central Europe at 70 000 men. This would represent a 10 per cent reduction by NATO and a 20 per cent cutback by the WTO forces.

As far as the WTO countries are concerned, it became clear before the negotiations started that they advocated "parity" reductions. In his speech at the World Congress of Peace Forces held in Moscow on 26 October 1973 Leonid Brezhnev said that the exact method by which the cutback is to be effected remains to be settled by the participants in the talks, but the possibilities included reductions by equal percentages or by equal numbers. [27] This concept was further elaborated at the Vienna negotiations and it became clear that the WTO countries reject the West's plan for asymmetrical cuts. In the opening statement, the head of the East German delegation stated:

The aim of all participants should be to preserve the existing correlation of military forces on a lower level when reducing forces and armaments. This could be done by reducing forces and armaments by an equal percentage or an equal quantitative rate with the understanding that this reduction comprehends national and foreign forces and armaments including nuclear weapons and their delivery systems. [28]

This concept is further elaborated in the WTO proposal calling for a three-step reduction of forces in Central Europe, first by both sides withdrawing 20 000 troops in 1975, second by applying a further 5 per cent cut in 1976 and finally by making a 10 per cent cut in 1977.

The situation becomes even more complicated when these concepts are applied in practice because of the differing estimates of the existing forces of the two alliances in Central Europe. Up to now, judging on the basis of press reports, these difficulties and differences have not been resolved.

**Foreign and national forces—conventional and nuclear**

After the question of methods of reduction is settled, the next question will be which forces should be reduced. There are several possibilities. One would be the reduction of foreign forces, that is, forces stationed abroad. The second would be to reduce only national forces. The third and most desirable would be to reduce foreign as well as national forces.

The attitudes of the respective parties as they appear in official documents during the past few years as well as recent statements by leaders of some of the states participating in the negotiations show that at various times they had different opinions and that these differences still prevail.

Early official NATO communiqués did not specify what kind of force reductions were envisaged (for example *The Future Tasks of the Alliance* or the Reykjavik Deklaration of 1968). Both documents dealt with the reduction of forces only in general terms and without any particular specification of the term apart from emphasizing that reduction should be balanced in scope and timing. However, the *Declaration on Mutual and Balanced Force Reduction,* accepted in Rome in 1970, and the Brussels communiqué of 4 December 1970, made explicit reference to reductions of both foreign and indigenous forces. The former specified that "reduction should include stationed and indigenous forces and their weapons systems in the area concerned". The latter reconfirmed this by expressing the readiness of NATO countries "to examine different possibilities including the possible mutual and balanced reduction of stationed forces as part of an integral programme for the reduction of both stationed and indigenous forces." These statements were repeated or confirmed in subsequent communiqués and statements of NATO member countries.

But in spite of these official statements, pressure in the United States for unilateral withdrawal of US forces from Europe has prompted other diverging views. The following statement, from the *Report of the Special Subcommittee to NATO Commitments,* is indicative of such views:

The Subcommittee was amazed to learn that in discussions of MBFR other NATO nations had proposed various reductions in their own forces and that US representatives had been something less than adamant in opposing such an idea in the initial phase of negotiations. In view of the relatively greater cost of the burden borne by the US and in view of the more desirable impact of lessening tension, the subcommittee strongly believes that any initial reductions of an MBFR agreement should involve the withdrawal of American and Soviet forces. The tension is hardly going to be lessened for NATO partners by a withdrawal of Rumanian divisions, and likewise the concern of the Soviet Union by the reduction of Danish forces. What would contribute most to the lessening of tension is the reduction of Soviet and US forces. [29]

A look at the attitudes of other members of NATO towards the question of reductions of forces shows that the smaller NATO powers have in principle been positive towards reductions of indigenous forces. Some of them, such as Belgium and Denmark, are even contemplating certain measures in this regard independently of the results of the current negotiations on reduction of forces in Central Europe. According to press reports, both the USA and the UK expressed at the NATO meeting in December 1972 considerable concern about the tentative plans for certain member countries to reduce their armed forces. This does not mean that the differences within the Alliance cannot be overcome and that NATO countries will not be able to find a common approach to this problem.

A study of the attitude of the Soviet Union and the WTO member countries toward the question of reduction of foreign and indigenous forces shows that in the early stages the WTO members and especially the Soviet Union were talking only of "reduction of foreign armed forces". [30] Brezhnev stated in his address to the 24th Party Congress on 30 March 1971 that the Soviet Union "favours the reduction of armed forces and armaments" without qualifications while he was more specific in his speech on 11 June 1971, mentioning the reduction of both foreign and national forces. The subsequent WTO documents, notably the Prague Declaration on Peace, Security and Cooperation in Europe on 26 January 1972, repeatedly refer to "the question of reducing armed forces and armaments in Europe, both foreign and national".

This cursory analysis indicates that both sides were ready to discuss reductions of foreign as well as indigenous forces, while it remained unclear whether these reductions should be carried out simultaneously or successively.

At the Vienna negotiations the West has somewhat changed its attitude towards the question of which forces should be reduced. According to the statements and proposals of NATO countries the first phase of the negotiations should focus only on US and Soviet ground forces. The first phase of the Western plan called for cuts of about 15 per cent each by US and Soviet forces stationed in Central Europe, to be followed by the setting of a common ceiling for all NATO and WTO forces in the region.

By contrast, in the statements and proposals of the WTO countries, reduction of both national and foreign forces and armaments is envisaged. It seems that the proposal itself, however, does not specify what the proposed reduction would encompass—it is to be presumed that their plan envisages reduction of both "foreign and national troops". But it is interesting to point out that at a press conference the representative of Poland said that "it is too early to say now whether certain forces should come first" but he did not exclude partial US and Soviet troop withdrawals from Central Europe as a first step in East-West force reductions.

Another problem connected with the question of reduction of forces is that concerning what kinds of troops and armaments should be reduced, that is, whether the reduction will be confined only to ground forces and conventional weapons or whether it will also embrace air forces and tactical nuclear weapons.

In the opinion of the Soviet Union and other WTO members, reduction of armaments cannot be contemplated without proper reference to the nuclear weapons at the disposal of the NATO allies and in particular of US forces deployed in Europe. The reduction of conventional forces and weapons only partly contributes to strengthening security in Europe. The main threat to peace in Europe, according to the Soviet view, is represented by NATO nuclear weapons, particularly tactical nuclear weapons. These are stored all over Europe for use in compliance with the doctrine of flexible response. As long as this situation exists the Soviet Union may not feel secure enough to agree to any proposal providing for substantial reduction of its forces stationed in WTO countries. One of the messages of a scientific conference convened in Moscow on 24–25 January 1972 by the Soviet Committee for European Security of the USSR Academy of Sciences read:

The question of the disposition of tactical nuclear weapons in Europe should be specially considered.

According to foreign sources the USA have today accumulated on the territory of Western Europe a considerable amount of means of delivering the so-called tactical nuclear weapons; the number of nuclear warheads exceeds 7 200.

The withdrawal from the territory of European states the means of delivery of tactical atomic weapons and nuclear warheads . . . are the main conditions of the easing of military tension and an essential factor which will help Europe acquire a new platform for pursuing a policy based on the principles of collective security in Europe. [31]

On the other side it is also the firm position of the United States and its allies that, in view of Soviet geographical advantages which provide for easier redeployment of forces probably within a shorter period of time, continued reliance on nuclear weapons is a reasonable guarantee that reduction of forces would not operate to the military disadvantage of either side. In practice this means that NATO countries are very likely to object strongly to any proposal advocating total elimination of tactical nuclear weapons from the European theatre and carefully, if not hesitantly, to consider those calling for their reduction. [32]

It is further stressed that the supposed conventional force superiority of WTO could be best matched by an adequate supply and use of tactical nuclear weapons. This view is also held by the Special Subcommittee on NATO Commitments:

It has to be conceded that we have no assurance that conventional forces will hold out indefinitely. It may be that after a period of time in a general attack the only way to stop advancing WP forces would be with the use of tactical nuclear weapons. [29]

Even though it is obvious that the two sides in the negotiations have quite different approaches to the problem of tactical nuclear weapons, the possibility should not be excluded that during the negotiations there may be some agreement in the spectrum of reduction which will require the reduction also of these weapons. One must also bear in mind the possibility that during SALT II or later the two great powers may include the problems concerning tactical nuclear weapons in their negotiations.

These differences in approach to the problem of what kind of forces and armaments should be embraced by the forthcoming agreements on force reduction came to full expression at the Vienna negotiations. The NATO countries not only reject suggestions for including nuclear weapons in the negotiations but have restricted the subject matter of the negotiations even further by proposing that reductions should be confined to ground forces because they consider that the WTO countries have more ground troops in Central Europe than NATO does and according to their estimates the USSR has more than twice as many ground troops in that areas as the USA does. The NATO countries are particularly concerned about the armoured capability of the USSR in Central Europe, the reduction of which would enhance stability in Europe. On the other hand, NATO countries consider that the air forces and navies are not related only to Central Europe; because of the possibilities of their relocation and easy redeployment they should not be the subject of the present negotiations.

The WTO countries on the other hand are still advocating that reductions should not be confined only to ground forces but that they should embrace land and air forces as well as units equipped with nuclear weapons and their delivery systems. This is supported by the argument that the correlation of conventional forces cannot be separated from the correlation of tactical and strategic nuclear forces, and that the regional balance in Central Europe cannot be separated from the all-European and global balances. Apparently, according to reports in the Western press, proposals by the WTO countries deal only with "ground troops and [ignore] weapons and armaments", while in the Soviet press, these proposals are reported to embrace land, air and nuclear forces. [19]

## Territories to be covered by an MFR agreement

With respect to the territories where the reduction of forces and armaments should take place, disagreement between the two alliances has been partly resolved. The NATO Rome Declaration on Mutual and Balanced Force Reduction of May 1970, which invited interested states to hold exploratory talks on this question, emphasized that this should be done "with specific reference to the Central Region". This proposal was reconfirmed in subsequent NATO communiqués and declarations. On the other hand, WTO countries have mainly referred to the reduction of forces in Europe as a whole. This was the case in the Declaration on Peace, Security and Co-operation in Europe of 26 January 1972. But in time, the Soviet attitude regarding the territory concerned became more clearly defined. Thus in the joint communiqué of May 1972 on the visit of President Nixon to the Soviet Union, both sides expressed their belief that "the goal of ensuring stability and security in Europe would be served by a reciprocal reduction of armed forces and armaments, first of all in Central Europe". [34] A similar formulation is used in the joint US-Soviet communiqué of 24 June 1973 in which it is underlined that "they attach great importance to the negotiations on the mutual reduction of forces and armaments and associated measures in Central Europe". [35] Further, judging by the text of the final Vienna Communiqué it can be concluded that agreement was reached between the two sides that "during negotiations, mutual reduction of forces and armaments and associated measures in Central Europe would be considered".

But even if it is agreed that the reduction of forces and armaments should take place in Central Europe, the question remains of what is understood by the term "Central Europe". Both sides agreed that for the purpose of present negotiations this area includes the territories of the Benelux countries, Czechoslovakia, the Federal Republic of Germany, the German Democratic Republic and Poland, while there is no agreement as far as the territory of Hungary is concerned. As a result Hungary was granted special status in the Vienna consultations, but in the view of the Western participants the future status of Hungary remains to be determined. This means that Hungary could be included in the area covered by the forthcoming arrangements, if agreement is reached by consensus of all potential participants in any possible agreements related to Central Europe. This is also valid for any other state which might request to be included among the participatory states listed in the record of the plenary meeting of 14 May 1973.

Hungary is participating in the negotiations in Vienna with special status, but the representatives of NATO countries have reiterated their statement that "the question of how and to what extent Hungary will be included in future decisions, agreements or measures must be examined and decided during the pending negotiations".

Bearing in mind the attitudes of the two parties to the negotiations, it can be expected that reduction of forces and armaments will be gradual so that the first arrangements will cover the territories of the two German states, Poland, Czechoslovakia and the Benelux countries, and will either reduce only foreign or both foreign and national forces and armaments, while later arrangements might cover the territory of Hungary and Italy. Certainly the most desirable solution would be to cover the whole territory of Europe but at this stage of development of international relations this step is not likely to be taken and will require a longer period of time.

**So-called associated measures**

As has already been mentioned, in addition to reduction of armed forces and armaments, so-called associated measures are also the subject of the current negotiations in Vienna. The term "associated measures" was introduced into the Final Communiqué of 27 June 1973 when a compromise between the formula "mutual and balanced force reduction" which NATO participants used and the formula "mutual reduction of armed forces and armaments" used by the WTO participants was reached. It is considered that such measures will contribute to maintaining undiminished security and to enhancing stability in Central Europe. Up to now the meaning of this expression has not been clarified by the parties to the negotiations. Judging by the previous proposals on disarmament and arms regulations in Europe and by studies published on the matter, as well as by opening statements made by the participants to the negotiations, it can be concluded that this term includes three different kinds of measures: confidence-building measures, reduction or freezing of military budgets and verification procedures.

Up to the present, apparently, only NATO participants to the negotiations have expressed their opinion in more detail on so-called associated measures, while the WTO countries have abstained from making any comments on them.

The representatives of NATO countries talk about measures affecting military activities. According to their opinion, "activities of the forces in the area, if their purpose is ambiguous, or if they are carried out in such a scale or in such manner as to be perceived by other participants as a potential threat, could be destabilizing." Along with these measures relating to force activities, some arrangements should be made to reduce the danger of miscalculation of the intentions of either side and the fear of surprise attack. Although NATO participants have not specified these measures it is clear that by such measures they mean so-called confidence-building measures. These measures are usually understood to include advance notification of military manoeuvres, exchange of observers by invitation at military manoeuvres, prohibition of manoeuvres in border areas, inspection against surprise attack and similar measures.

Although the participants to the negotiations on MFR have up to now not included the reduction or freezing of military budgets in their proposals, the possibility of bringing this question into focus should not be excluded.

The proposal for the reduction or freezing of military budgets has been advocated for many years especially by the Soviet Union, and occasionally even by the United States. The reduction suggested, officially or unofficially, has ranged between 10 and 30 per cent.[2]

---

[2] The most recent proposal of the Soviet Union was made in a speech by Andrei Gromyko, Minister of Foreign Affairs, at the XXVIIIth Session of the General Assembly of the United

The experience of recent years has made it all too clear that the arms race not only threatens humanity with the possibility of total disaster, but also imposes an increasingly intolerable burden on the economic development of every country, regardless of a country's degree of advancement or its socio-economic system.

A look at the military expenditure of both alliances shows that enormous sums of money are spent on armaments. Furthermore, the military expenditures of NATO and the WTO countries have a tendency to increase from year to year. (See tables 8C.2 and 8C.6.) Moreover, there presently is a general understanding that NATO countries are contemplating various measures, including increases in military budgets, with a view to strengthening the organization, so as to compensate for a possible agreement on force reductions. At the regular NATO meeting in Brussels in December 1972 the ten nations of the "Eurogroup" within the Alliance agreed to increase their defence budgets in 1973 by at least $1.5 billion, in current prices. A similar process is taking place within WTO countries, in spite of a recent decision of the Soviet Union to reduce its defence budget. [36]

At the same time the governments of many of these countries are under pressure to take steps to decrease their military budgets and devote the money released to more urgent needs. Some analysts suggest that the economic pressure which is felt by both alliances will force them, sooner or later, to consider this possibility more seriously, while others believe that increases in spending made so far have not yet reached such a level as to jeopardize their economic development.

However, the prospects for an agreement on reducing or freezing military budgets as an independent measure under the circumstances presently prevailing in Europe are rather small. The possibility of such a measure being undertaken as a so-called associated measure should not, however, be excluded. It is also possible that a reduction of military budgets will depend on whether an agreement reached at the forthcoming negotiations stipulates reduction or only withdrawal of armed forces and armaments. The reduction of forces and armaments would certainly have some effect on the military spending of the countries concerned, but it is considered that such effects would be noticeable only if substantial reductions were made. On the other hand, the withdrawal of forces would have a much smaller effect on military spending since such a measure presupposes the redeployment elsewhere of the forces withdrawn.

If the question of reducing or freezing military budgets is discussed at the current negotiations, one of the central problems will be determining, for each country, the relationship between internal accounting procedures

Nations. Later the UN General Assembly adopted a resolution calling for a 10 per cent reduction of military budgets of the permanent members of the Security Council. [37] (See chapter 12.)

for the financing of military activities and the definition of military expenditure agreed upon. This will be essential for verification since, for many countries, a reasonably comprehensive definition of military expenditures will include activities not financed under the formal defence budget. A second major issue is likely to be whether military expenditures are to be presented in current or constant price terms. In the latter case the treatment of inflation becomes important. Bearing in mind the very complicated nature of the issues involved in such an undertaking it would be necessary to make a thorough analysis before suggesting possible approaches to the problem.

The third kind of measures which are more of a supplementary character are those related to verification procedures after an agreement on force reduction is reached. Although these questions have been raised only by NATO participants it can be assumed that all participants to the negotiations are interested in adequate assurance that the terms of an agreement on reduction were being faithfully carried out and that each party to a possible agreement would refrain from any action which would circumvent or undermine the agreement.

However, it is too early to deal in detail with these measures. Because of their supplementary character, they will be dealt with at a later stage in the negotiations when they will have been conditioned a great deal by the reductions agreed upon by the parties to the future agreements.

## V. *Conclusions*

On the basis of the agreement reached at the preparatory consultations and the proceedings of the current negotiations some conclusions can be drawn about the attitudes of states participating in the negotiations and about the measure of agreement which has been accomplished.

At the preparatory consultations, a number of principles were agreed upon as guidelines for the negotiations. (1) Participants are divided into two categories: those with decision-making power who are direct participants and whose territories are within the agreed area of Central Europe as well as those direct participants who have their troops within the mentioned area (Belgium, Canada, Czechoslovakia, the Federal Republic of Germany, the German Democratic Republic, Luxembourg, Netherlands, Poland, the USSR, the United Kingdom and the USA; and participants with a special status (Bulgaria, Denmark, Greece, Hungary, Italy, Norway, Romania and Turkey). (2) The subject matter of negotiations is defined as the "mutual reduction of forces and armaments and associated measures in Central Europe." This lengthy formula was a compromise between different formulas used by two sides. The essential elements in the agreed formula are that reductions would be mutual, focused on Central Europe and accompanied by "associated measures". Since no agenda was accepted, the agreement was reached that "any topic relevant to this subject matter may be introduced for negotiations by any of those states which will take the necessary decisions". (3) The general objective of the negotiations is defined as "a more stable relationship" and "the strengthening of peace and security in Europe". (4) "The principle of undiminished security for each party" is defined as a basic principle of the negotiations. (5) Such procedural rules as those concerning the confidentiality of meeting and documents, the rights of all participants to speak and circulate papers on the subject matter, official languages and so on shall apply to the negotiations themselves.

As far as the main, substantive issues are concerned, it is difficult at this stage of the negotiations to draw conclusions, especially when documents are confidential and meetings are open only to participants. Keeping this in mind, any conclusions are bound to be of a general character. First of all, as has been already mentioned, the views of the two sides in the negotiations are still far apart and it is difficult to say how much progress is being made in overcoming existing differences. Briefly, these differences exist concerning the methods which should be applied to reduce existing forces, what kind of forces and armaments should be reduced and what is the present balance of forces between NATO and the WTO. It is also not yet clear what the position of the WTO countries is towards "associated measures" and the question of verification. All these questions have to be decided if the current negotiations are to result in some meaningful measures aimed at achieving a more stable military balance at lower levels of forces with undiminished security not only for all participants in the negotiations but for all European states.

## References

1. *Force Reductions in Europe,* SIPRI Monograph (Stockholm, Almqvist & Wiksell, 1974, Stockholm International Peace Research Institute).
2. *SIPRI Yearbook of World Armaments and Disarmament 1969/70* (Stockholm, Almqvist & Wiksell, 1970, Stockholm International Peace Research Institute) pp. 64–91, and particularly pp. 388–424.
3. "Bonn Communiqué 1972", *Atlantic Community Quarterly,* Fall 1972, pp. 604–10.
4. *New York Times,* 21 September 1972.
5. *New York Times,* 17 November 1972.
6. *Le Monde,* 20 January 1973.
7. *Le Monde,* 13 January 1973.
8. *International Herald Tribune,* 25 January 1973.
9. *Krasnaya Zvezda,* 30 January 1973.
10. *International Herald Tribune,* 1 February 1973.
11. *Neue Zürcher Zeitung,* 2 February 1973.
12. *Borba,* 31 January 1973.
13. *International Herald Tribune,* 5–6 May 1973.

14. Record of Plenary Meeting of the Preparatory Consultations Held in Vienna on 14 May 1973.
15. *Financial Times*, 15 May 1973.
16. *Final Communiqué on the Preparatory Consultations*, Vienna, 28 June 1973.
17. *International Herald Tribune*, 29 June 1973.
18. *Archive der Gegenwart*, 28 June 1973, pp. 18008-9(C).
19. *Krasnaya Zvezda*, 2 December 1973.
20. *Financial Times*, 16 November 1973.
21. *International Herald Tribune*, 14 September 1973 and 23 November 1973.
22. Opening Statement of U.S. representative, Vienna, 31 October 1973.
23. Kostko, Yu., "'Ravnovesie Stracha' ili Obespechenie Podlinnoi Bezopasnosti", *Mirovaya Ekonomika i Mezhdunarodnye Otnoshenia*, No. 6, 1972, pp. 87–89.
24. Multan, W. and Twopik, A., "NATO Wobec Problemu Rozbrojenia w Europie", *Sprawy Miedzynarodowe*, No. 4, 1973, pp. 53–55.
25. Proector, D. M., "Evropeiskaya Bezopasnost: Nekhotorie Problemi", *Mirovaya Ekonomika i Mezdunarodnye Otnoshenia*, No. 9, 1973, p. 98.
26. *Press Statement on Final Communiqué* delivered on 28 June 1973 by Ambassador B. Quarles van Ufford, Head of the Netherlands delegation and spokesman for the 12 NATO countries, Vienna, 28 June 1973.
27. *Bulletin* No. 2, 27 October 1973, special issue of "Moscow News".
28. Statement made by Dr Ingo Oeser, Head of Delegation of the DR of Germany, Vienna, 30 October 1973.
29. *The American Commitment to NATO*, Report of the Special Committee on North Atlantic Treaty Organization Commitments of the Committee on Armed Services, House of Representatives, 92nd Congress, 2nd Session, 19 August 1972 (Washington, US Government Printing Office, 1972) p. 14986.
30. "WTO Memorandum, Budapest 21–22 June 1970", *Recueil de Documents*, No. 6 (Warsaw, Institut Polonais des Affaires Internationales, 1970) pp. 2063–66.
31. *European Security: Current Problems*, Scientific Conference, Moscow, 24–25 January 1972 (Moscow, USSR Academy of Sciences, 1972) pp. 152–53.
32. *World Armaments and Disarmament, SIPRI Yearbook 1973* (Stockholm, Almqvist & Wiksell, 1973, Stockholm International Peace Research Institute) pp. 124–25.
33. *International Herald Tribune*, 19 November 1973.
34. The American-Soviet Communiqué of 29 May 1972", *Survival*, July/August 1972, pp. 188–91.
35. "Joint Soviet-American Communiqué of 24 June 1973", *Moscow News*, Supplement to issue No. 26 (1173), 1973.
36. *Krasnaya Zvezda*, 14 December 1973.
37. *International Herald Tribune*, 26 September 1973.
38. Resolution 3093.A (XXVIII) of the UN General Assembly.

# Appendix 4A

## *The military balance between NATO and the WTO*

The regions in the tables below are defined, thus:

*Northern Region* (NATO): Denmark and Norway.
*Central Region:* Benelux, FR Germany, German DR, Czechoslovakia and
Poland.
*Southern Region:* Italy, Greece, Turkey, Hungary, Bulgaria and Romania.

It is to be noted that the northernmost part of FR Germany, although
under the NATO Northern Command, has been included in the Central
Region in this comparison. In table 4A.4 several of these regions are
somewhat extended.

The term "division equivalents" has been used in the tables as a common measure for regular divisions and other division-type units, as well
as to allow adjustment for those units which are not fullstrength. It does
*not* imply comparability between NATO and WTO divisions, which
differ in manpower and equipment. For a full discussion of the comparability of NATO-WTO data, of the definitions of regions and of the
sources used to prepare these tables, see *Force Reductions in Europe,*
SIPRI Monograph (Stockholm, Almqvist & Wiksell, 1974, Stockholm International Peace Research Institute) appendix A.

**Table 4A.1. NATO and WTO "division equivalents" in the European theatre**

| Regions | NATO (in NATO division equivalents) | WTO (in WTO division equivalents) |
|---|---|---|
| Northern Region | $1\frac{1}{3}$[a] | – |
| Central Region | 25[a] | 53[b] |
| Westernmost USSR (northern and central parts) | – | 14 |
| France | 4[c] | – |
| Southern Region | 36 | 25 |
| Westernmost USSR (southern part) | – | 3 |

[a] Thereof, 5 US and 2 French.
[b] Thereof, 27 Soviet.
[c] Another 2 French "division equivalents" are stationed in FR Germany and are included in the figure for the Central Region.

**Table 4A.2. NATO and WTO combat and direct support troops (manpower) in the European theatre**

*Thousands of men*

| Regions | NATO | WTO |
|---|---|---|
| Northern Region | 20 | – |
| Central Region | 620[a] | 700[b] |
| Westernmost USSR | | |
| (northern and central parts) | – | 200 |
| France | 100[c] | – |
| Southern Region | 530 | 280[d] |
| Westernmost USSR | | |
| (southern part) | – | 40 |

[a] Thereof, 125 US, 40 French.
[b] Thereof, 400 Soviet.
[c] Excluding those French troops stationed in FR Germany and included in the figure for the Central Region.
[d] Thereof, 50 Soviet.

**Table 4A.3. NATO and the WTO: numbers of battle tanks in the European theatre**

| Regions | NATO | WTO |
|---|---|---|
| Northern Region | 250 | – |
| Central Region | 6 000[a] | 13 350[b] |
| Westernmost USSR | | |
| (northern and central parts) | – | 3 550 |
| France | 500 | – |
| Southern Region | 2 150 | 5 100[c] |
| Westernmost USSR | | |
| (southern part) | – | 700 |
| Stockpiled in the Central Region | 5 000[d] | 4 300[e] |

[a] Including 1 350 US and 325 French stationed in FR Germany.
[b] Thereof, 6 850 Soviet.
[c] Thereof, 1 000 Soviet.
[d] Approximately 750 of which are for dual-based and immediate reinforcing formations. In addition, some 1 100 NATO tanks are estimated to be stockpiled in the Southern Region.
[e] 2 000 Soviet and 2 300 other. In addition, some 1 100 tanks are stockpiled in Bulgaria, Hungary and Romania (in the Southern Region).

**Table 4A.4. NATO and WTO tactical aircraft in the European theatre**[a]

| Regions | NATO | WTO |
|---|---|---|
| Northern Region | 180 | – |
| Central Region | 1 000[b] | 2 800[c] |
|   Extension of<br>    Northern and<br>    Central Regions | US and British aircraft<br>in Great Britain, US<br>aircraft in Spain:<br>600 | Westernmost USSR<br>(Northern and<br>Central parts):<br>800<br>Rest of European<br>  USSR (Northern and<br>  Central parts):<br>  750 |
| France | 350 | – |
| Southern Region | 600[d] | 900[e] |
| Westernmost USSR<br>  (Southern part) | – | 300 |
| Estimated maximum<br>  additional reinforce-<br>  ment, all regions | 3 500 | 500 |

[a] The table accounts for active aircraft only (i.e., not those in storage or reserve): including all fighter, fighter-bomber, light bomber, ground attack and reconnaissance aircraft, and dual purpose fighter-interceptor aircraft, trained and equipped for tactical purposes; and excluding strategic aircraft, pure air defence aircraft, army and navy aviation, tankers, transports, special purpose aircraft and aircraft used for training. Only fixed-wing aircraft are considered in this table.
[b] Thereof, 230 US.
[c] Thereof, 1 250 Soviet.
[d] Greek, Italian and Turkish forces only.
[e] Thereof, 300 Soviet.

**Table 4A.5. NATO and WTO combat aircraft, Europe and worldwide**[a]

| | Air defence exclusively | Dual purpose fighter-interceptors[b] | Tactical aircraft, excluding dual purpose fighter-interceptors[b] | Naval aircraft including marine corps (anti-ship, ASW, reconnaissance, patrol) |
|---|---|---|---|---|
| **NATO, Europe** | | | | |
| USA | – | – | 580 | 250 |
| Other NATO | 700 | 50–100 | 2 100 | 400 |
| **Total** | **700** | **50–100** | **2680** | **650** |
| **NATO, worldwide** | | | | |
| USA[c] | 585 | – | 2 500 | 2 100 |
| Other NATO | 760 | 50–100 | 2 150 | 450 |
| **Total** | **1 345** | **50–100** | **4650** | **2550** |
| **WTO, Europe** | | | | |
| USSR | 2 900[d] | 1 550 | 1 850 | 670[d] |
| Other WTO | – | 1 500 | 600 | 55 |
| **Total** | **2 900[d]** | **3 050** | **2 450** | **725[d]** |
| **WTO, worldwide** | | | | |
| USSR | 2 900 | [e] | 3 900 | 670 |
| Other WTO | – | 1 500 | 600 | 55 |
| **Total** | **2 900** | **1 500[e]** | **4 500** | **725** |

[a] This table accounts for active aircraft only (i.e., not those in storage or reserve). It does not include strategic offensive aircraft. The active inventory of the latter types, including long-range and medium-range bombers of various types, is estimated to be approximately as follows:

USA   460 (plus about 50 in active storage/reserve)
France   36 (plus about 20 in reserve)
USSR  840 (including 700 medium-range bombers which can be expected also be used in a tactical role, but excluding 300 medium-range bombers from the naval aviation, accounted for as naval aircraft).

It must be noted that these figures include aircraft of rather dissimilar performance which thus are not directly comparable.

[b] For a detailed definition, see table 4A.4, footnote *a*.
[c] Including Air National Guard.
[d] A small number of these aircraft are deployed outside Europe. The exact figure is not available.
[e] Sources did not show figures for this category as separate from that in the next column; see also figure in next column.

## Table 4A.6. Total NATO peacetime forces, by NATO country[a]

| Country | Regular forces | | | | Division equivalents | Battle tanks (in use; not in store or in reserve) | Active combat aircraft (incl strategic and naval aircraft) |
|---|---|---|---|---|---|---|---|
| | Army | Navy | Air Force | Total | | | |
| **Forces in Europe** | | | | | | | |
| Belgium | 65000 | 4600 | 20000 | 89600[b] | 1.7 | 300 | 140 |
| Britain[a] | 163500 | 79000 | 101500 | 344000[c] | 5[d] | 900 | 520 |
| Canada | 2800 | – | 2300 | 5100 | 0.3 | 30 | 50 |
| Denmark | 24000 | 6300 | 9500 | 39800 | 1 | 200 | 110 |
| France[a] | 320000 | 66400 | 100000 | 486800[e] | 6 | 820 | 690 |
| FRG | 334000 | 37000 | 104000 | 475000 | 12 | 2950 | 540 |
| Greece | 120000 | 18000 | 22000 | 160000 | 8 | 450 | 220 |
| Italy | 306500 | 44500 | 76500 | 427500 | 10 | 800 | 350 |
| The Netherlands | 70000 | 20000 | 22200 | 112200[f] | 2 | 450 | 190 |
| Norway | 18000 | 8000 | 9400 | 35400 | 0.3 | 50 | 130 |
| Turkey | 365000 | 40000 | 50000 | 455000 | 18 | 900 | 290 |
| *Total non-US* | *1789200* | *323800* | *517400* | *2630400* | *64.3* | *7850* | *3230* |
| *USA in Europe* | *200000* | *39000* | *50000* | *289000[g]* | *5[h]* | *1350* | *830* |
| *Total in Europe* | *1989200* | *362800* | *567400* | *2919400* | *69.3* | *9200* | *4060* |
| **Forces outside Europe** | | | | | | | |
| Canada | 30200 | 14000 | 33700 | 77900 | 0.7 | 70 | 110 |
| USA[i] | 601500 | 721400[k] | 641000 | 1963900 | 13[h] | 1100 | 5330 |
| **Total** | **2620900** | **1098200** | **1242100** | **4961200** | **83.0** | **10370** | **9500** |

[a] British and French forces deployed outside Europe (in all, some 35000 men) have been excluded as they are comparatively small, probably would not be withdrawn to Europe and, finally, in any case would be insignificant for this comparison. British forces in the Mediterranean (notably Cyprus) are included. For similar reasons, Portugal (some 204000 men) has been excluded from the comparison entirely. Apart from the bulk of its armed forces being in Africa it does not seem likely that Portuguese troops would be employed in Central or Southeastern Europe to any significant extent. In addition to the figures presented, Luxembourg has some 500 men, all army.
[b] 15000 in FR Germany.
[c] 63500 in FR Germany.
[d] Excluding about one division equivalent outside Europe.
[e] 50000 in FR Germany.
[f] 5000 in FR Germany.
[g] 210000 in FR Germany.
[h] The total of 18 division equivalents for the USA is calculated thus: 13 active army divisions, 3 marine corps divisions and 2 division equivalents from other independent units (independent brigades and regiments).
[i] Includes all US active forces except those in Europe. Excludes National Guard, although Air National Guard aircraft have been listed among active aircraft.
[k] Including 196000 marines.

**Table 4A.7. Total WTO peacetime forces, by WTO country**

| Country | Regular forces | | | | Division equiva-lents | Battle tanks (in use; not in store or in reserve) | Active combat aircraft (incl strategic and naval aircraft) |
|---|---|---|---|---|---|---|---|
| | Army | Navy | Air Force | Total | | | |
| Bulgaria | 120000 | 10000 | 22000 | 152000 | 8 | 1600 | 250 |
| Czecho-slovakia | 150000 | – | 40000 | 190000 | 8.5 | 2300 | 500 |
| GDR | 90000 | 17000 | 25000 | 132000 | 6 | 1400 | 320 |
| Hungary | 90000 | 500 | 12500 | 103000 | 4 | 800 | 110 |
| Poland | 200000 | 25000 | 55000 | 280000 | 11.5 | 2800 | 750 |
| Romania | 141000 | 8000 | 21000 | 170000 | 9 | 1700 | 250 |
| Total | 791000 | 60500 | 175500 | 1027000 | 47 | 10600 | 2180 |
| USSR, in Eastern European countries | 480000 | –[a] | 40000 | 520000 | 31 | 7850 | 1550 |
| Total | 1271000 | 60500 | 215500 | 1547000 | 78 | 18450 | 3730 |
| USSR, own territory[b] | 1570000 | 475000[a] | 510000 | 2905000[c] | 89[d] | 19300 | 6740[e] |
| **Total**[b] | **2841000** | **535500** | **725500** | **4452000** | **167** | **37750** | **10470** |

[a] Although several Soviet naval units are operating in the large oceans and the Mediterranean and some base facilities for the Baltic fleet are available, for example in Poland, the bulk of the Soviet Navy is based in harbours in the Soviet Union and all naval personnel are accounted for accordingly.
[b] Includes all Soviet forces (except those in East European countries), even those deployed in Asian USSR. According to Western assessments the USSR deploys about one quarter of its forces near the Sino-Soviet border, "more than one-half is oriented toward Western Europe, and the balance appears to be a strategic reserve". [30] This would imply that the USSR should have somewhat more divisions and other units in European USSR oriented toward Western Europe than they have deployed in the East European countries (excluding the national forces of these countries).
[c] Including Strategic Rocket Forces (separate service), 350000 men.
[d] Filling Soviet peacetime divisions to full strength would raise this number to approximately 130.
[e] Including 840 strategic aircraft and 2900 home defence aircraft.

**Table 4A.8. NATO and WTO troop proportions in the European theatre (all Europe, excl. Portugal)**

| | NATO | | | WTO | | |
|---|---|---|---|---|---|---|
| | Continental USA, active forces which might be dispatched in Europe | US troops in Europe | Non-US NATO troops | Non-USSR WTO troops | USSR troops in other WTO countries | European USSR troops |
| Men under arms, all services (*million*) | 0.3 (1.6)[a] | 0.3 | 2.6 | 1.0 | 0.5 | 1.0 |
| Division manpower (combat and direct support) (*thousand*) | 200 | 120 | 1 200 | 530 | 450 | 560 |
| Battle tanks | 1 100 | 1 350 | 7 850 | 10 600 | 7 850 | 9 250 |
| Division equivalents (NATO and WTO, respectively) | 9 (10) | 5 | 64 | 47 | 31 | 40 |
| Tactical aircraft[b] | 2 500 | 580 | 2 150 | 2 150 | 1 550 | 1 850 |

[a] First figure indicates reinforcements that might be dispatched from US active forces; figures in brackets are total inventory of active forces. National Guard and Reserves are not included.
[b] Excluding air defence interceptors, army and naval aviation and aircraft for training, in accordance with table 4A.4, footnote *a*. It includes, however, US Marine Corps aircraft. For the USSR. 700 medium bombers which could be used for tactical purposes are also excluded.


**Table 4A.9. NATO and WTO manpower, tanks and tactical aircraft in the Central European region (national and foreign)**

| Country | Men under arms, all services | Battle tanks | Tactical aircraft |
|---|---|---|---|
| Belgium | 74 600 | 300 | 110 |
| FR Germany | 823 600 | 5 250 | 780 |
| Luxembourg | 500 | – | – |
| Netherlands | 107 200 | 450 | 110 |
| Czechoslovakia | 275 000 | 3 500 | 800[a] |
| GDR | 462 000 | 6 400 | 1 000[a] |
| Poland | 325 000 | 3 400 | 1 000[a] |

[a] The figure given in sources for this region is 2 800 tactical aircraft. Here, based on our knowledge of divisions, we have reckoned the individual figures to be as above.

# 5. The nuclear deterrence debate

*Square-bracketed references, thus [1], refer to the list of references on page 71.*

The future role of nuclear weapons will be subject to detailed debate in the coming period for a variety of reasons. On the one hand, the USA has recently announced that it will emphasize counterforce capabilities in its strategic doctrines. Such emphasis will be made possible by continuing developments in military technology—improving the quality of strategic weapons and the accuracy of their delivery systems. In addition, the possibility of attaining strategic superiority looms in the background—an attractive prospect, albeit unattainable in the foreseeable future, to some influential groups in both of the major powers. There is also the possibility that a sixth nuclear-weapon power will soon emerge. On the tactical level, it has been proposed that accurately delivered low-yield nuclear weapons should replace the higher-yield nuclear arms now deployed, particularly in Europe. On the other hand, negotiations are in progress to limit strategic weapon developments. Further, the results of the mutual force reduction (MFR) negotiations may have significant consequences for nuclear policies in Europe.

As time goes on, the severe shortcomings of nuclear deterrent doctrines are becoming widely appreciated and these doctrines are becoming known for what they are—inhumane, irrational, positively dangerous and a bar to progress in disarmament. Although at first sight the proposals to revise the roles and capabilities of strategic and tactical nuclear weapons may seem more humane and useful than the policies they are to replace, on closer examination they contain major flaws and would not, if put into practice, be likely to reduce significantly the grave dangers to mankind inherent in the existence of nuclear arsenals.

## I. *The debate on strategic nuclear weapon development*

Until 1974, US and Soviet policies concerning strategic nuclear weapons relied primarily on the doctrine of "mutual assured destruction". The main feature of this deterrent doctrine is a certain ability to inflict massive destruction on the enemy population and industry in a retaliatory attack, following a massive nuclear strike by the enemy. During the course of the 1960s, it became increasingly apparent that both the United States and the Soviet Union had such a capability in their currently deployed forces. Recognition of the futility, wastefulness and danger of a substantial expansion of these forces, given the doctrine of assured destruction, was expressed in the first SALT agreements, which limited further deployment of both offensive and defensive strategic weapons.

In 1973, a number of articles and statements appeared in the United States calling for a revision in US strategic weapon policy. The essence of the change being suggested was to give much more emphasis than hitherto to the "counterforce" capabilities of the nuclear forces. Counterforce strategy does not replace deterrence: rather it supplements it with the additional capability to strike, either pre-emptively or in response to an attack, at the opponent's military targets, including hardened missile silos. Such a strategy requires a large number of accurate, powerful nuclear warheads targeted not against cities and industrial and transportation centres but against military installations. In addition, a counterforce strategy implies the capability of fighting a nuclear war if deterrence fails to prevent its outbreak.

An article [1] by Fred Iklé, now head of the US Arms Control and Disarmament Agency, illustrates the arguments put forward to support the change in strategy. Iklé claims that the doctrine of mutual assured destruction rests on three dogmas. First, US nuclear forces must be designed almost exclusively for retaliation in response to a Soviet nuclear attack, particularly an attempted pre-emptive strike. Second, US forces must be designed and operated in such a way that this retaliation can be swift, massive and prompt. Third, the threatened retaliation must be the killing of a major fraction of the Soviet population. Moreover, the same ability to decimate the US population must be guaranteed the Soviet government. Iklé argues that these requirements of stable deterrence are harmful to the prospect of disarmament and, more important, that they constitute a most perilous method of protection from nuclear catastrophe. His major criticism is that deterrence by mutual assured destruction disregards the very significant possibility of nuclear war breaking out by accident, miscalculation or madness: complete reliance is put into deterring war by "rational" decisions.

Iklé recommends a new strategy in which the potential accuracy of smart bombs and missiles, and current choices in weapon effects, should be used to enable both sides to avoid the killing of millions of civilians and yet to inflict assured destruction on military and industrial targets. He also recommends that strategic forces should be made as invulnerable as possible in order to break the "vicious circle" inherent in the present strategic doctrine, namely, that nuclear forces must be ready for immediate launching because they are vulnerable and that they are vulnerable because they must be ready.

He claims that these changes, although "avoiding the killing of hostages", would not make nuclear war more acceptable as an instrument of policy. Deterrence would remain effective. In fact, he argues that since the aggressors' conventional military power (the navy, army and air force) and its support facilities would be the first to suffer destruction, it would be even less tempting for the military to plan a nuclear war. And the risk of the destruction of population centres would still exist in the background.

Immediate objections were raised in the USA to the proposals for the adoption of a counterforce strategy. Most of the arguments against such a strategy are summarized in an article by Wolfgang Panofsky, [2] which rebuts the claims made by Iklé.

While accepting that the present strategic doctrine requires that strategic nuclear forces must be designed primarily for retaliation in response to a nuclear attack, Panofsky denies that this response, according to the present doctrine, need be rapid and massive. He points out that a successful first strike against a combination of nuclear forces (submarines, land-based missiles and bombers) is technically impossible now or in the foreseeable future. There is, therefore, no need for a rapid response to a nuclear attack. Moreover, nuclear forces can be used in a controlled way to produce many options against a nuclear strike and, therefore, it is incorrect to claim that the only possible response is instant and massive retaliation.

Panofsky points out that the destructiveness of the present nuclear arsenals is so great that deaths would number in the tens of millions even if only a fraction of one side's nuclear weapons were delivered on the opponent's territory. Therefore, even if a nuclear attack were confined to "military" targets, civilian casualties would still be very high. Moreover, it is impossible to be sure that an opponent would follow a similar "anti-military" strategy. And once the "barriers against use of nuclear weapons are broken, escalation toward full-scale nuclear war is exceedingly difficult to prevent".

Panofsky concludes that there is no technological way of escaping "the evil dilemma that the strategic forces on both sides must either be designed to kill people or else jeopardize the opponent's confidence in his deterrent".

No technological distinction exists or can be created between those nuclear weapons endangering the deterrent forces of the opponent in a first or pre-emptive strike (and thus decreasing stability) and weapons designed to attack the same forces by retaliation;

There is no demonstrable break between nuclear weapons designed for limited attacks and those designed for "strategic" retaliation;

Anti-military nuclear attacks of substantial size will almost certainly generate enormous civilian casualties;

Whatever plans or technological preparations the United States may make to fight a "controlled" nuclear conflict, there can be no certain method to protect the US population in case the opponent decides to respond with an anti-population attack;

Available casualty estimates understate the effects of large-scale nuclear war— such consequences as epidemics aggravated by maldistribution of medical care, fire, starvation, ecological damage and societal breakdown are well-nigh incalculable. [2a]

Similar objections were raised by Herbert York in a paper presented at the Pacem in Terris conference, held in Washington in October 1973:

. . . [S]uch counterforce strategies, as they are called, always turn out to require or at least justify, many more and generally larger weapons than are needed for the so-called counter-value, or deterrence strategy. In such a case, a failure in deterrence would generally result in many more deaths, especially in third countries, than would be the case for a force sized for deterrence only. This comes about partly due to an increase in collateral damage through fallout, and also because of the colocation of so many military targets with urban targets such as the military command posts in Washington, Omaha and Moscow; the transportation centres in St. Louis, Chicago, Kharkov and Kiev; the naval bases at New York, Boston, San Diego, Los Angeles, Leningrad, Sevastopol and Vladivostock, and so on.

Moreover, a policy to target only military installations would only be an administrative arrangement; it would not rely on anything intrinsic in the equipment. Hence such a policy, agreed to internationally or not, could be abandoned or abrogated on short notice, after first being used to justify a substantial increase in force levels. For these reasons, I believe the proposals for improving the present situation by going to a counterforce strategy are among the most dangerous proposals I know. [3]

In the face of considerable opposition within the US arms control community, illustrated by the views of Panofsky and York, US Secretary of Defense Schlesinger announced on 10 January 1974 that the USA actually intends to adopt a counterforce strategy as a strategic nuclear option and, to this end, is improving the accuracy of delivery of its nuclear weapon systems.

In order to assess the import of this announcement it is essential to observe, first, that in reality the United States has by now already had a counterforce capability and targeting policy for its strategic missiles for several years. A comparison between the number of Soviet urban centres worth a nuclear attack and the number and characteristics of nuclear warheads in the US strategic arsenals leads to the unavoidable conclusion that most of the US strategic nuclear weapons are targeted against military targets in the Soviet Union. The Soviet Union has at most 100 urban and industrial centres that would be targeted with nuclear warheads. The United States possesses at this time 1 200 160-kt MIRV warheads ($\sim 10^4$ sq. km foot-print) deployed on land-based ICBMs said to have an accuracy (CEP)[1] of 900 feet, 600 1–2-mt warheads on 600 ICBMs with somewhat less accuracy, 3 840 40-kt MIRV warheads ($5 \times 10^3$ sq. km foot-print) deployed on the Poseidon missiles with about 1 500 feet CEP, 528 200-kt MRV

[1] The "circular error probability" (CEP), a measure of accuracy of warhead delivery, is the radius of a circle centred on the target in which half of a large number of ICBM warheads fired at the target would fall.

warheads deployed on Polaris A-3 missiles, about 400 B-52 bombers capable of carrying several 1-mt bombs each, and several hundred fighter-bombers based on aircraft carriers and overseas bases on the perimeter of the Soviet Union capable of delivering nuclear weapons. Clearly even if the number of targets in the Soviet Union is not 100 but twice that, and even if one assumes an equal number of targets in the People's Republic of China, all the civilian targets do not exceed 400. Furthermore, even if we assume that each of these targets is double-targeted to allow for possible missile failure, the number of warheads aimed against them does not exceed 800. Not all the warheads in the US arsenal are, of course, available for launch at all times: only two-thirds of the ballistic missile submarines are on station at any time; therefore, on average, the total number of warheads available on them is 350 200-kt warheads, plus 2 560 40-kt warheads. On average probably only 90 per cent of the Minuteman ICBMs are ready for launch at any one time so there are 1 080 160-kt and 540 1-mt warheads loaded on Minuteman I, II and III available at any time. In addition a large fraction of the B-52s are available, adding several hundred 1-mt bombs to the arsenal. The total number of warheads ready to be launched at any instant is 4 500 on missiles and probably no less than 800 or so on B-52s. Since the number of warheads needed to destroy securely all the significant civilian targets in the Soviet Union and China is 800, over 4 000 nuclear warheads must have been targeted on military targets for the past several years.

A putative targeting schedule for the US strategic forces assumes that a portion of the 40-kt Poseidon missiles are targeted on soft time-urgent targets such as radar, airfields, and so on; the more accurate and powerful Minuteman II and III warheads are aimed at hard time-urgent targets such as missile silos; while urban and industrial targets are left for the B-52s, the balance of submarine-launched ballistic missiles, and the smaller but numerous fighter-bomber aircraft. Since most of the US missiles have multiple-target storage memories and performance indicators, the strategic force has considerable flexibility, recently augmented by the introduction of the command data-buffer system.[2] Therefore, in effect, the USA already possesses a counterforce nuclear arsenal which includes a variety of warheads and is controlled by a flexible command system.

What Schlesinger's announcement signaled is not a change in nuclear strategy but the decision of the US administration to announce what, up to now, was only tacitly admitted and played down in official pronouncements, that is, that the USA has been pursuing a counterforce nuclear strategy. What then is the purpose of this admission and what prompted the official announcement of it at this time?

[2] The command data-buffer system will enable an ICBM to be switched to a new target in a relatively short time (about 20 minutes). Without the system the process, which then entails reprogramming each missile's computer, would require up to 36 hours to complete.

In the past, new strategic postures have been promulgated in support of the procurement and deployment of a new weapon system under development or already developed. This is almost unavoidable since strategic weapon systems take many years to develop; therefore, to evolve a strategic posture first, and then begin development of the weapon it requires, is all but impossible. Consequently, strategies evolve based on the weapons that are under development at any one time. Choice of a specific strategy justifies the continued development of the weapon on which it is based and assures its procurement and deployment. For example, in the United States the need to overcome the Soviet ABM system was invoked to justify the need for MIRV warheads in 1968; but at that time MIRV was already developed after five years of work in government laboratories. The need to protect the nation from a Chinese attack was invoked in 1968 and the need to protect Minuteman silos from a Soviet attack was invoked in 1970 to justify the deployment of an ABM system that had been under study and development since 1955.

The strategy of mutual assured destruction designed to deter a nuclear attack was the rationale for the procurement and deployment of the strategic triad—Minuteman land-based missiles, B-52 bombers, and missile-carrying submarines. It was articulated in 1965, four years after the force levels of each of the three strategic systems had been decided. Such ex-post-development justifications of weapon systems by invoking an appropriate strategic posture that makes their deployment essential suggests that this otherwise superfluous announcement of a posture already in effect may be signaling the desire of the current administration in the USA to produce and deploy strategic weapon systems that could not be justified to the public and to the Congress in the context of the strategy of assured destruction or deterrence—the doctrine that up to now has been the officially declared strategic posture of the United States.

The counterforce strategy, as enunciated by Schlesinger, includes the humanitarian implication that the USA should acquire a "surgical strike" capability, that is, the ability to destroy a military target near or in an urban centre incisively without adverse effects to the civilian population. This posture, while acceptable to the public, requires warheads with very high accuracy and very small nuclear charge; such weapons are not currently deployed in the US arsenal. But mini-nuclear warheads and terminal guidance that endows warheads with pinpoint accuracy are two weapon developments that have reached a state of completion and are ready for procurement and deployment. The nuclear weapon laboratories of the US government have perfected small warheads in the low- or even fractional-kiloton region, and are pressing for their adoption in the US arsenal (see page 66). Project ABRES (Advanced Ballistic Re-Entry Systems), managed by the Space and Missiles Systems Organization (SAMSO) of the US Air Force, has succeeded in perfecting a terminal guidance system that, when incorporated in a manoeuvrable re-entry vehicle (MARV),[3] can guide it onto a prescribed target. Neither terminal guidance on MARV nor mini-nuclear warheads can be justified in the framework of an assured destruction posture; they can, however, be presented as essential weapons in a strategy of counterforce.

The introduction of MARV will eventually justify the development of yet another strategic weapon system that could not be justified by the strategy of deterrence, namely, the mobile land-based ICBM. It is almost certain that nuclear warheads on MARV will have the yield and accuracy to assure destruction of ICBMs in reinforced silos. It is then quite probable that, following procurement of a US MARV and invoking a projected acquisition of the same type by the Soviet Union, the US Air Force will request funds to deploy mobile ICBMs as a method of protecting the land-based component of US strategic forces. Indeed there must be considerable organizational pressure generated by the Ballistic Systems Division of the US Air Force, which is responsible for the development and procurement of land-based ballistic missiles, for the deployment of MARV and mobile ICBMs. With the termination of Minuteman III conversions, the Ballistic Systems Division has no mission to perform while its organization competitors, the Office of Special Projects in the Navy and Strategic Air Command in the Air Force, still have the Trident submarine and the B-1 supersonic bomber, respectively, to develop.

These intragovernmental organizational and bureaucratic pressures would have probably amounted to naught had the newly proclaimed strategic posture been completely devoid of political utility. The public declaration of the counterforce strategy of the United States will increase considerably the probability that Congress will fund the deployment of MARV and mobile ICBMs. The Soviet political and military leaderships, doubtless aware of this drift, must then decide between an accommodation in the SALT II negotiations that would forestall the deployment of these weapons on the one hand, and the task of countering the US move by developing their own MARV and mobile land-based ICBMs, on the other hand. The latter course is likely to be perceived as undesirable in the Soviet Union since it will mean the expenditure of precious resources for weapon production and the prospect that sometime in the future the Soviet silo-based ICBMs will be vulnerable to a pre-emptive strike. The political utility is, thus, that this may put the United States in a stronger negotiating position at the SALT II talks.

Once again the synergy of political utility and strong organizational and bureaucratic pressures in the United States will most probably induce a new cycle of strategic weapon procurement and deployment. It is presented to the public in the humanitarian form of counterforce strategy

---

[3] A MARVed warhead would be capable of changing direction in flight—an operation which no existing ICBM warhead can perform—to evade defensive missiles fired at it.

which, by obscuring the actual dangers resident in these new weapon systems, ensures their acceptance by the electorate and the Congress.

The formal adoption of the counterforce posture by the USA will tend to induce a number of serious ramifications.

1. By insisting on the capability for a "surgical strike" it tends to move strategic nuclear weapons closer to the tactical arena, and to blur further the distinction between tactical and strategic nuclear strikes. The elimination of this "firebreak", that has so far prevented the use of nuclear weapons in tactical operations, has been fervently pursued by the military in the past quarter century and adamantly opposed by those who believe that use of even small nuclear weapons for a "surgical strike" will inevitably lead to escalation and nuclear holocaust.

2. The introduction of MARV will provide the USA with undeniable first-strike capability against land-based missiles of other countries. It may be argued that this development may result in the eventual removal of these missiles from the active inventories of all nuclear powers. But the probability that this will occur in the near future is very small indeed: first, because China does not have sea-based missiles or strategic aircraft and, second, because, in the case of the Soviet Union, it will entail the dissolution of one entire branch of their armed forces, that is, the Strategic Rockets Division. It is reasonable to expect that this organization, with its powerful political backing, will resist successfully any efforts to negotiate it out of existence. Therefore, for the foreseeable future MARV will introduce an intense crisis instability by making Soviet land-based missiles vulnerable to a first strike.

3. It is almost certain that MARV will be used as an argument by the Ballistic Systems Division in the USA and the Strategic Rockets Division in the Soviet Union in favour of deploying mobile land-based ICBMs. Aside from the astronomical costs of such deployment and the danger to populations in territories adjacent to the routes that these mobile missiles will follow, any accurate estimate of their numbers will be so difficult to achieve by national means of inspection (satellites) that their inclusion in any future arms control agreement will stumble on the same issue of verification that has obstructed efforts to control MIRV.

But perhaps the greatest danger implicit in the posture of counterforce is the effort to make the "surgical strike" credible and acceptable. The fallacy of the claim that a nuclear weapon, no matter how accurate and small, can be used in or near an urban complex—where most of the militarily interesting targets actually lie—without detrimental effects to the civilian population has been shown in several recent studies. [4] Aside from the immediate blast effects, higher order effects and radiation will certainly take a heavy civilian toll whether the missile is actually targeted against an urban centre or an airfield a few miles away from it. The establishment of the "surgical strike" as an option available to the military appears to be a reckless and unnecessary escalation of the dangers inherent in the nuclear confrontation between the United States and the Soviet Union.

Rather than pursue this new policy, leading to a dangerous, destabilizing and costly continuation of the race in strategic nuclear arms, the United States should, in the second round of the SALT talks with the Soviet Union, seek both an end to qualitative improvements, and a reduction in the numbers of nuclear arms within the framework of the policy of assured destruction. It is true that this policy contains serious deficiencies. These are recognized by Herbert York, who observes that while deterrence may be the best strategy now available to the USA, "it is a terrible strategy, and our highest-priority, long-run objective should be to get rid of it altogether". [3] The main advantage of this policy is that, in contrast to the alternative now being proposed, it requires fewer rather than more nuclear weapons. The stockpile now relied on to fulfil the requirements of assured destruction is from 10 to 100 times as murderous and destructive as it need be to satisfy that purpose. "Therefore", York says, "our highest-priority objective for the immediate future should be to reduce greatly the current level of 'overkill' even while we still maintain the strategy of deterrence."

York observes that the best that is usually claimed for nuclear deterrence is that it "works" and that it is stable. The first of these claims is speculative and, in any event, unprovable. He believes that the current nuclear balance has been stable for some time, and that the SALT I agreements tend to assure that it will remain stable for the foreseeable future. Moreover, he believes that the present balance is stable in two different ways. First, it possesses what is called "crisis stability", that is, in a military crisis, one side cannot add much to its chances of survival by striking first, and so there is no strong inducement to do so. The current nuclear balance is also reasonably stable in the "arms race" sense; that is, there does not appear to be any way for one side to achieve an overwhelming advantage over the other side by quickly acquiring any feasible quantity of some weapon, and so again there exists no really strong inducement to do so.

In York's opinion, the problem with deterrence is that if for any political or psychological or technical reason deterrence should fail, the physical, biological and social consequences would be completely out of line with any reasonable view of the national objectives of the USA or the USSR.

Some authorities have proposed that we confront these awful possibilities by undertaking huge, complex programs designed to cope directly with a massive nuclear attack. Such programs usually include the installation of a so-called thick system of antiballistic missiles combined with very extensive civil defense and post-attack recovery programs. In detailed examinations, however, the main elements of such proposals have always been judged to be either technically unsound, or economically unfeasible, or socially and politically unacceptable, and so no such programs are currently underway or even being seriously considered.

In brief, for now and the foreseeable future, a nuclear exchange would result in the destruction of the two principles as nations regardless of who strikes first. This is what is usually meant by the phrase "Mutual Assured Destruction".

It is most important in any discussion about international affairs or the current military balance to have clearly in mind what the current technical situation means: the survival of the combined populations of the superpowers depends on the good will and the good sense of the separate leaderships of the superpowers. If the Soviet leadership, for whatever reason, or as a result of whatever mistaken information, chose to destroy America as a nation, it is unquestionably capable of doing so in less than half an hour, and there is literally nothing we could now do to prevent it. The only thing we could do is to wreak on them an equally terrible revenge. And, of course, the situation is the same the other way around.

No one can say when deterrence will break down, or even why it will. Indeed, if the leadership of all the nuclear powers always behave in a rational and humane way, it never will. But there are now five nuclear powers and there will be more someday, and if any of them ever makes a technical, political or military nuclear mistake for any reason, real or imagined, then there will be a substantial chance that the whole civilized world could go up in nuclear smoke. This is simply too frightful and too dangerous a way to live indefinitely; we *must* find some better form of international relationship than the current dependency on a strategy of mutual assured destruction. [3]

So far as the size of the force currently devoted to mutual assured destruction (the matter of "overkill") is concerned, York explains that informed opinions about how many weapons are really needed vary over an extremely wide range. For example, shortly after leaving the post of Special Assistant to the President for National Security Affairs, McGeorge Bundy wrote, "In the real world of real political leaders—whether here or in the Soviet Union—a decision that would bring even one hydrogen bomb on one city of one's own country would be recognized in advance as a catastrophic blunder; ten bombs on ten cities would be a disaster beyond history; and a hundred bombs on a hundred cities are unthinkable". For a very much higher estimate, York quotes calculations made in the early 1960s.

In order to quantify the question, it was assumed that "assured destruction" meant guaranteeing the deaths of 25% of the population and the destruction of a majority of its industrial capacity. From that, it was calculated that as many as 400 bombs on target might be needed.

As an intermediate estimate, we may turn to what the French and British have actually done to produce what they evidently think is a deterrent force. In each case the number of large bombs devoted to that purpose seems to be something less than one hundred. [3]

In York's view, Bundy was right: that from one to 10 are enough when the course of events is being rationally determined.

In the case of irrational behavior, there is no way of calculating what it would take. The case of irrational behavior is, therefore, of little interest in connection with the question of how big the deterrent force should be; rather, the matter of irrational behavior only enters into questions about when and how deterrence will fail, and about whether a policy based on deterrence is of any political value at all. [3]

Why is it, if one or 10, or maybe a few hundred bombs on target are all that are needed to deter, that the USA will possess more than 10 000? And why so much total explosive power? Similarly, why has the Soviet Union deployed a comparable nuclear force?

These numbers are *not* the result of a careful calculation of the need in some specific strategic or tactical situation. They are rationalizations after the fact.

One method for doing so is called "worst case analysis". In such an analysis, the analyst starts with the assumption that his forces have just been subjected to a massive preemptive attack. He then makes a calculation in which he makes a series of very favorable assumptions about the attacker's equipment, knowledge and behavior, and a similar series of very unfavorable assumptions about his own forces. Such a calculation can result in an arithmetic justification for a very large force indeed, provided that we really believe there is a chance that all the many deviations from the most probable situation will go in one way for them and in the other way for us.

An additional argument for possessing many more weapons than are needed for deterrence involves a notion called "Damage Limitation". The idea is that a part of our force should be reserved for attacking and destroying those enemy weapons that for some reason were not used in his first, preemptive strike. Besides the obvious technical difficulties with such a scheme, it is counterproductive for political reasons. In today's world, the internal politics of each of the two superpowers requires them to maintain strategic forces that are roughly equal in size. That in turn means that if one side builds a large force for "damage limiting" purposes, the other side will build a roughly equal force which will inevitably be "damage producing". Such a chain of events obviously leads from bad to worse. Furthermore, the kind of forces needed for this so-called "damage limiting" role are technologically identical to those needed for a first strike, and so such a strategy is obviously dangerous for that reason also.

In brief then, even if we accept for the time being the need for a policy of deterrence through mutual assured destruction, the forces now in being are enormously greater than are needed for that purpose. And again, if we recognize that deterrence can fail, and if we admit to ourselves the consequences of such a failure, then we see that greatly reducing the current degree of overkill is both possible and essential. [3]

York recommends that, as a first step towards a more sensible strategy, nuclear forces should be reduced by eliminating those elements that deliver the most megatons.

In each case, roughly 20% of the forces carry roughly 80% of the megatons. In the U.S. case, these are the several hundred long-range bombers and the 54 Titan missiles. In the Soviet case, these are the 300 very large SS-9 missiles plus a relatively small intercontinental bomber force. Ridding the world of all these weapons and, of course, prohibiting their replacement by newer versions, would decrease substantially the threat to the rural populations of the two protagonists. It

65

would also reduce the danger to residents of innocent countries five-fold. At the same time, the simultaneous elimination of these weapons through negotiation or even their unilateral elimination by one or both sides, would have little effect on the deterrent posture of either side.

There is another area where it should be easy to achieve a further two-fold reduction in potential fallout. Only one-half of our Minutemen are being converted to the new Minuteman III, and only 31 of our 41 Polaris boats are being converted to Poseidons. Simply abandoning the not-to-be converted residuals of these forces would eliminate about one-half the fallout potential of our missile forces. And precisely because these older weapons are less capable, their complete elimination would have only a marginal effect on our ability to deter. Similarly, we may be confident the Soviets also have some obsolescent weapons they could get rid of at the same time in order to keep things in formal balance. And beyond the elimination of these excessively murderous and obsolescent vehicles, we might also consider placing an upper limit on the explosive power of those remaining. For instance, we might set an upper limit in power equal to that of the Hiroshima bomb. The many thousands of bombs that would still remain in the strategic forces, even after the reductions I have suggested, would still seem to be many more than enough for deterrence through mutual assured destruction, even if each bomb were so limited in power.

The overkill capacity in the present forces is so large that even the rather substantial reductions I have suggested would not do much to the threat hanging over the inhabitants of the larger cities; most of them would still be killed in the event of a breakdown of deterrence. But, since there would be big decreases in death and destruction in rural areas and small towns, the prospects for some sort of national survival would be much improved. Perhaps most important, the number of deaths and the amount of genetic damage in innocent countries would be reduced more than ten-fold. And whether or not one believes the leadership of a nation has the right to place all of its own citizens at risk, it surely does not have that right with regard to third parties. [3]

## II. *Tactical nuclear weapon doctrine*

A number of articles have recently appeared discussing the implications of the possible acquisition of accurately delivered low-yield tactical nuclear weapons. But the strongest argument for an entirely new approach to tactical nuclear warfare based on the use of these weapons, particularly in Europe, was made in a paper by several members of the staff of the Los Alamos Scientific Laboratory. [5] The authors find the present NATO strategy of flexible response illusory, as it attempts to combine military and political measures to contain the more limited forms of aggression and seeks to deter the wider forms by threatening to inflict damage that the Soviet Union would find either unacceptable or out of proportion with any prospective gains. They question the ability of NATO forces to defend effectively against a massive attack. And they argue that the actual use of the nuclear deterrent forces would result in unacceptable damage to both NATO and WTO countries. As a consequence NATO relies on a military posture inadequate for effective defence and unusable if it fails to deter an attack.

Faced with this dilemma, how do our allies hope to prevent a war in Europe from proceeding beyond a defensive engagement on the battlefield to an exchange of high-yield nuclear weapons on a theater-wide scale? They see no alternative but to rely on the mutual restraint imposed by the possible involvement of the United States and the Soviet Union in a war of mutual destruction. [5a]

The fact that NATO members are under economic pressure to reduce their forces is seen as a factor which denies the stability of this situation. Another factor working in this direction is the enormous potential for collateral damage inherent in NATO's nuclear weapons and in the procedures designed for their use, even if only a defensive war is fought.

The most serious deficiency seen in the present NATO posture is the limited ability of NATO's existing forces to stop a determined attack. To do this, NATO would have to rely on mobilization and reinforcement, both time-consuming processes. During this time, an invading force may have penetrated deep into West German territory.

The authors argue that the discriminate use of nuclear weapons from the outset would enable NATO to conduct a successful defence.

Western policymakers should aim to replace, in Pact calculations, the uncertainty of an irrational NATO response with the certainty of an immediate, effective response to attempts to take NATO territory. Dealing with threats of irrational attacks to destroy all or part of NATO is a problem for our European allies to face without counting on U.S. strategic nuclear weapons. It is their survival that such attacks threaten. However, they should recognize that the existence of European retaliatory forces cannot be ignored by the Pact, and might provide an otherwise absent incentive for a pre-emptive disarming attack. [5b]

The authors do not deny that their proposed strategy is a radical departure from present plans to try in the first instance to defend Europe by conventional means, since it calls for the immediate use against the attackers of low-yield nuclear weapons for all but the most trivial incidents. But they argue that European reliance on the fact that any European conflict would rapidly involve a US-Soviet strategic nuclear exchange as the only deterrent that protects NATO is out-of-date now that the Soviet Union and the United States are in strategic nuclear parity.

A range of nuclear weapons, they say, should be designed for specific use in a possible European conflict situation. So far as the destructiveness of these weapons is concerned, "NATO's political leadership wants no weapon explosion to expose people or their cultural heritage to indiscriminate destruction. This collateral damage can be largely controlled by the choice of target area and target defeat criteria." But the military commander should have weapons capable of effective use for attaining his military objectives. "Delivery accuracy, range and responsiveness of the delivery system, weapon yield and fuzing, target acquisition, damage assessment and battlefield survivability of the system all play an obvious role in assuring effectiveness.''

The authors visualize a future NATO military posture based on the following considerations:

(1) The U.S. SIOP [Single Integrated Operational Plan] has some indeterminate residual value in deterring irrational forms of Warsaw Pact aggression or escalation, but this role should not be articulated in declared policy.

(2) No U.S. capability for other than defensive war should be retained on European soil.

(3) Any NATO forces deployed in Europe that are solely deterrent (i.e. punitive or retaliatory) should be provided and controlled by Europeans.

(4) The defensive capabilities of the NATO force should be tailored to the characteristics of each prospective battle area in which these capabilities may be exercised. The force should be constructed in each case around U.S.-supplied and U.S.-controlled nuclear weapons and should be designed to defend NATO at its borders.

(5) The design of the force should accommodate to economic pressures to reduce the cost of acquiring and maintaining forces. In particular, the size of the U.S. manpower commitment in Europe should be reduced. Since the NATO force will depend largely on nuclear weapons to defeat massed attacks by Warsaw Pact armor, our goal should be eventually to restrict the U.S. role to command and control of these weapons. The Europeans should be left to provide those elements of the force that would cope with other than massed armor attacks. This goal seems to be a clear application of the Nixon Doctrine to the defense of Europe. Also, emphasis should be placed on procuring weapons that minimize acquisition and maintenance costs.

(6) The force must be usable and effective without exceeding collateral-damage constraints. We offer two thoughts on the control of collateral damage, defined as unintended destruction which should be minimized or avoided if possible: (a) To make a nuclear-emphasis defense acceptable to our allies, the goals for minimizing expected collateral damage must be set at levels at least equal to and preferably even lower than would be associated with a conventional defense. (b) Concern about collateral damage stems largely from the presence of high-yield weapons (greater than a few kilotons) in our NATO stockpile and from vivid memories of wars as long engagements that ravaged the continent. We contend that a nuclear-defensive war by NATO, fought in proximity to the border with low-yield weapons and discriminating delivery systems, would result in a short conflict. Under such conditions, collateral damage is far less an issue, and the criteria set forth in (a) are reasonable.

(7) We are fated to pursue the brinkmanship game of strategic deterrence (assured destruction) in the NATO theater until NATO adopts this new defensive stance. The problem is far more one of policy and doctrine—and U.S. leadership—than it is one of technology. There are advantageous changes possible in both weaponry and forces, but the first step is a recognition that a new approach is necessary. As NATO comes to this realization, there is much to trade the Warsaw Pact in MBRF negotiations: our theater-range weapons for theirs, for example. We need not develop expensive new ''bargaining chips''; both sides have many of them already. Because Europe is the issue, this is a problem for the multilateral MBFR talks, not for bilateral SALT II negotiations. In any case, our negotiating position does not become worse by NATO's acquiring an effective defence. [5c]

According to the authors, the possibility of a limited nuclear war escalating out of hand can be minimized if the following steps are taken:

(1) We must construct a defensive force that can use low-yield nuclear weapons to stop the enemy before he becomes irreversibly committed through seizing a significant part of NATO territory, or through suffering nuclear retaliation that forces him to escalate.

(2) In conducting and terminating a conflict, the NATO objective must be to preserve or re-establish the pre-conflict border. Insistence on wider goals in an engagement supported by the USSR and the United States can lead to escalation involving a release of their strategic forces.

(3) We must exclude the planning option of using U.S. nuclear forces in Europe —primarily our Quick Reaction Alert (QRA) aircraft—which are capable of striking the territory of the USSR. To this end, such forces now in Europe should be removed. The United States should dissociate itself from allied forces possessing a comparable capability, and discontinue its declared policy of promising to defend NATO with U.S. CONUS-based and otherwise strategically-oriented nuclear forces. The importance of an undeclared policy in this regard is vital. Under these conditions, the President's options for defending NATO can be weighed separately from the problem of releasing forces meant only for deterrence, not for defense.

(4) Other steps doubtless need to be taken to relieve the President's concern over escalation, but they are more tenuous. For example, we should consider advertising the ground rules by which NATO would fight a war. These rules could cover such matters as number and yield of nuclear weapons in stockpile. In this regard NATO should consider a low maximum yield (in the neighborhood of a kiloton). [5d]

At first sight, this policy may seem attractive, particularly from the point of view of military tactics. *But there are fundamental weaknesses in any policy depending upon the use of tactical nuclear weapons.* Few would be confident that this or any other feasible policy would, in practice, prevent armed conflict involving the major powers from escalating to an all-out nuclear war so long as any nuclear weapons, regardless of type, are used. And there is no guarantee, or even likelihood, that the opponent will adopt similar tactics. In particular, the introduction of very low-yield (less than a kiloton) nuclear weapons would blur the present distinction between conventional and nuclear weapons. It is of *paramount importance* that an absolute "firebreak" should be maintained between nuclear and conventional war.

It is important that these objections to such a policy for the use of tactical nuclear weapons should be widely understood because strong pressures may arise in the near future for such a policy to be officially adopted, particularly in Europe.

## III. *Conclusions*

It is doubtful, at least in the long term, that nuclear weapons have had the political utility claimed for them, since their existence has indeed greatly decreased world security and most particularly the security of those countries actually having nuclear weapons.

No nuclear strategy, past or present, based on deterrence is credible to rational persons, particularly when the powers concerned are equally armed. Such strategies must be seen for what they are—mere rationalizations for the development and deployment of the weapons made available by military technology.

The commonly held view that the very destructiveness of nuclear weapons precludes the outbreak of thermonuclear war is incorrect. Even if "rational behaviour" is assumed, thermonuclear war is unlikely to occur only if it is believed that neither side can win. If one power perceives a chance of winning, then there is a risk that it will decide to strike while it has the advantage. Moreover, in the event of a serious crisis, the side placed at a disadvantage may, if it believes a nuclear war inevitable, attack first in the hope of reducing the damage it thinks it is bound to suffer.

At present, and for the foreseeable future, a general nuclear war could not be "won" by either side. As a result of timing and reliability considerations, small numbers of the most vulnerable components of the strategic forces—the bombers and the land-based ICBMs—would stand a chance of surviving an initial attack, even if attacking forces were much improved over existing ones. More important, despite the vast amount of money being spent on antisubmarine warfare research, nuclear submarines will almost certainly remain invulnerable to a mass attack. In addition to the strategic nuclear forces disposed by the two sides, there are of course the thousands of land- and sea-based medium- and short-range nuclear weapons, most with capabilities exceeding those of the Hiroshima and Nagasaki nuclear bombs. Because of the massive deployments of nuclear weapons of all types by both sides, the likelihood of either side escaping unscathed following an initial attack is virtually nil. But no one knows whether the present technological situation will continue for decades. There are various courses of development, some of which are now being pursued by both the USA and the USSR, which tend toward the acquisition of a first-strike capability. These are likely to produce periods of extreme instability and heightened risk of nuclear war.

Nuclear forces are also maintained on the grounds of deterring incursions or acts of political or economic blackmail. The requirement that the populations of not only the USA and the USSR but also other countries be placed in jeopardy of nuclear war cannot be justified by the potential deterrence of lesser conflicts. In addition to the possible erosion of the more "rational" reasons for the non-use of nuclear weapons, there is the great and ever present danger that nuclear war will come about by accident, miscalculation or madness. No nuclear strategy can deal effectively with this possibility.

President Nixon said in his State of the Union message: "We must never allow America to become the second strongest nation in the world''. This type of statement from the political leadership encourages those groups within societies which press for a continuation of the arms race and for maximum effort in military research to develop weapons to fight and ''win'' a nuclear war. Counterforce strategy can be seen as yet another step in this direction. In making nuclear war more ''flexible'', it makes it more thinkable, more tolerable and consequently more probable.

Because it cannot be said that efforts to acquire a first-strike capability will not eventually succeed, albeit in the long term, the only credible policy to reduce the probability of nuclear war to an acceptable level is far-reaching nuclear disarmament as a first step in a planned programme leading to general and complete disarmament. But perhaps the most immediate requirement is for the political decision-makers to understand and to recognize the urgent need for nuclear disarmament so that they will resist those vested interests within their societies which press for the application of all possible technological advances to weapon system development, for the deployment of all new weapons that are developed and for the maintenance and improvement of all existing weapon systems.

## References

1. Iklé, F. C., "Can Nuclear Deterrence Last Out the Century?", *Foreign Affairs*, Vol. 51, No. 2, January 1973, p. 267–85.
2. Panofsky, W. K. H., "The Mutual-Hostage Relationship Between America and Russia", *Foreign Affairs*, Vol. 52, No. 1, October 1973.
3. York, H., *Deterrence by Means of Mass Destruction*, Pacem in Terris, Conference III (Washington, October 1973).
4. *Kriegsfolgen und Kriegsverhütung* (Munich, Carl Hauser, 1972).
5. Bennett, W. S., Sandoval, R. R. and Shreffler, R. G., "A Credible Nuclear-Emphasis Defense for NATO", *Orbis*, Vol. XVII, No. 2, Summer 1973.
   (a) –, p. 464.
   (b) --, p. 465.
   (c) –, pp. 474–75.
   (d) –, pp. 471–72.

# Appendix 5A

## Strategic doctrines of NATO and the WTO

*Square-bracketed references, thus* [1], *refer to the list of references on page 94.*

## I. *US strategic doctrine*

During World War II a state of cooperation had been fostered between the United States and the Soviet Union. President Roosevelt, strongly supported by Secretary of State Cordell Hull, was convinced that a continuation of this cooperation could be a basis for a world peace without the familiar dangerous cycle of rival alliances, arms races and increasing tension leading to war. Roosevelt's aim was the post-war preservation of good working relations with the Soviet Union within the framework of the United Nations.

The Truman Doctrine, inaugurated in 1947, abruptly ended this key policy of attempted cooperation with the Soviet Union and initiated a basic change in attitude by the United States. It emphasized US determination to react forcefully whenever US interests were threatened and to accept confrontation rather than to seek solutions by negotiation. It heralded US involvement in any area where Western interests were threatened and the intention to act from a position of strength. Former ties with the Soviet Union were replaced by a policy of "containment".

### The US nuclear monopoly, 1945–53

The policy of containment was backed up primarily by the US monopoly of nuclear weapons. But most professional military strategists were of the opinion that the use of nuclear weapons alone could not defeat a nation which deployed vastly superior ground forces.

The signing of the NATO treaty in 1949 was, however, a recognition of the fact that the West European powers could not match the Soviet Union's conventional strength and of the desire of these powers to use US nuclear forces for the defence of Europe. An enemy was to be convinced of NATO's intention to use nuclear forces as strategic weapons in the event of an attack. Thus the concept of a relationship between conventional and strategic nuclear warfare was produced, whereby nuclear warfare subordinated the employment of conventional forces.

It was believed in 1949 that the dozen or so understrength Western divisions in Europe faced 25 divisions in Central Europe, out of a Soviet total of between 140 and 175 divisions at full battle strength. A huge build-up of forces would have been necessary if NATO had chosen to defend itself without nuclear weapons. The United States and West European countries were simply not willing even to attempt to match the Soviet Union's conventional forces. The European members of NATO considered economic reconstruction to be of greater importance than an increase in the level of conventional military forces. US nuclear superiority and the absence of an imminent Soviet threat further detracted from the impetus for a build-up. The NATO treaty had, in any case, been conceived not as a vehicle for redressing its prospective members' inferiority in conventional forces but as a way of clarifying US intentions regarding possible attempts by the Soviet Union to change the balance of power in Europe.

NATO is considered, by some, to have been born with a "complex" about conventional forces. The view was that Soviet levels of conventional forces could never be matched and US nuclear power made such an attempt unnecessary. This initial concept of the alliance—a clear statement of US intentions backed up by actual nuclear forces and potential conventional forces, the whole constituting a credible deterrent—survived, with minor revisions, until 1967 as the official policy of NATO. [1]

NATO strategy did not remain unchallenged for long. The nuclear monopoly of the United States was threatened in 1949 by the testing of a nuclear weapon by the Soviet Union. The commencement of the Korean War was a challenge to the deterrent credibility of existing nuclear forces, particularly as the war was seen by the West to be the result of a decision by the Soviet Union as part of a larger plan for expansion of its influence in the world.

When the decision was made by President Truman in 1950 to develop a hydrogen bomb, there was considerable discussion within the United States on the merits of developing a strategy of total nuclear deterrence. Until this time, US strategy had been based on fighting a nuclear war rather than deterring it. Military planning depended to a large extent upon conventional concepts, such as mobilization, of the type used in World War I and World War II. This ceased to be an acceptable strategy after the explosion of a Soviet nuclear weapon in August 1949 and the Soviet demonstration that nuclear weapons could be delivered against targets in the United States.

At its Lisbon meeting in 1952 the NATO Council approved force goals of 96 NATO divisions by 1954. The Lisbon goals, which met with considerable scepticism, confronted the member states with the huge costs involved in attempting to meet the Soviet levels of conventional forces. And the Lisbon meeting was the last occasion on which NATO considered but did not take the conventional option; the United States insisted on it 10 years later.

**The strategy of "massive retaliation", 1954–60**

Having studied the costs involved in carrying out the Lisbon proposals, the Eisenhower administration quickly abandoned the idea of matching Soviet forces locally and announced its "New Look" policy based on the strategy of "massive retaliation". The theory behind the New Look was developed in a study by the National Security Council, which maintained that each and every conflict above the level of a simple border incident or "brush fire" should lead to intervention with nuclear weapons. [2a] The principle was supported by Secretary of State John Foster Dulles who, in a speech in January 1954, announced that in order to get a "maximum deterrent at a bearable cost" the government had decided to

depend primarily upon a great capacity to retaliate, instantly, by means and at places of our choosing . . . We need allies and collective security, but our purpose is to make these relations more effective, less costly. This can be done by placing more reliance on deterrent power and less dependence on local defensive power. [3]

The policy of "massive retaliation" had an immediate effect on NATO planning. In late 1954 NATO commanders were authorized to base their plans on the prompt use of nuclear weapons, whether the aggressor had used them or not. Deputy Supreme Allied Commander, Field Marshal Montgomery stated this policy clearly:

I want to make it absolutely clear that we at SHAPE are basing all our operational planning on using atomic and thermonuclear weapons in our defence. With us it is no longer 'they may possibly be used'. It is very definitely: 'They will be used if we are attacked'. In fact we have reached the point of no return as regards the use of atomic and thermonuclear weapons in a hot war. [4]

Criticism of the New Look produced changes. Secretary of State Dulles suggested a modified doctrine on 29 November 1954:

Now you may ask does this mean that any local war would be automatically turned into a general war with atomic bombs being dropped all over the map? The answer is no. The essential thing is that we and our allies should have the means and the will to assure that a potential aggressor would lose from his aggression more than he could gain. This does not mean that the aggressor has to be totally destroyed. It does mean a capacity to inflict punishing damage. [5]

A basic premise of the New Look was that the Soviet Union would not achieve strategic parity with the United States until the end of the decade. In a statement to Congress in 1955, the Secretary of Defense explained that although there was no evidence that the Soviet Union would attack within the next few years, the United States must nevertheless be prepared for an attack resulting from a miscalculation by the Soviet Union. At the same time he postulated that the Soviet Union had not abandoned its plans for world domination and the United States must have the capacity to deter it from attack, or at least to blunt the impact of any such attack. This necessitated an effective retaliatory force together with advanced continental defence. Local aggressions were to be dealt with primarily by collective defence, although special US assistance might be necessary in specific situations. [6]

A new plan, the Radford Plan, which called for only 30 divisions, was submitted by the United States to NATO in 1957 and marked the formal abandonment of the Lisbon goal of 96 divisions. The plan was based on the assumption of a permanent inferiority on the part of NATO in conventional forces. The strength of the Soviet Union was still put at 175 divisions.[1] It was believed that the proposed 30 divisions of NATO troops could not hope to offer significant resistance without resort to nuclear weapons. Conventional land-based forces in Europe were intended primarily as a delaying mechanism in the event of a Soviet advance so that nuclear retaliation would have time to make itself felt. As part of the implementation of this strategy large numbers of tactical nuclear weapons were shipped into Europe. These were placed under the double veto system which required the consent of both the United States and the host country before they could be used.

This strategic concept gave conventional weapons a minor role. Conventional weapons were to be used to deal with minor incursions and to act as a screen to determine that a full-scale Soviet attack was taking place. There was some talk of a "pause" before nuclear weapons were to be used but the NATO logistic system left little doubt about the real emphasis of NATO strategy. None of NATO's conventional forces had supplies for more than two weeks. Any large-scale Soviet attack would, therefore, necessitate the use of nuclear weapons at a very early stage. "The pause", General Norstad, Supreme Allied Commander in Europe, observed, "will probably take place before the outbreak of hostilities." NATO doctrine described conventional weapons as the "shield" and nuclear weapons as the "sword" of the alliance.

The Soviet Union was catching up with nuclear developments faster than the United States had expected. In 1957 the Soviet Union tested an intercontinental ballistic missile (ICBM) and put a satellite into orbit around the Earth. This jolted the United States into the realization that the Soviet Union might have missiles which could deliver nuclear warheads onto targets in the United States. If this were so, then the Soviet Union had already surpassed the United States in the development of long-range missiles. According to Henry Kissinger it was in order to close the supposed "missile gap"[2] that the United States pressed its allies to permit the installation on their territories of intermediate-range ballistic missiles (IRBMs). Some of the allies considered the missiles vulnerable

---

[1] It should be noted that there are great differences in numbers of men and strength between NATO and WTO divisions. [7]
[2] For details on the so-called "missile gap" see references [8–9].

but the view of the United States prevailed. The United States argued that a Soviet attack on US bases in Europe would produce the unacceptable risk of a full-scale counteroffensive and that a coordinated attack against both domestic and overseas US bases would prove technically difficult. IRBMs were therefore stationed in Italy, Turkey and the United Kingdom. [10a]

The presence of these missiles in Europe tended to establish an inextricable link between the defence of Europe and that of the United States. An attack on Europe would damage the strategic balance and immediately threaten the survival of the United States. Thus strategic deployment rather than a decision taken at the moment of attack would determine the US response. [10b]

This emphasis on massive retaliation—and in particular on a strategic strike aimed at the enemy's power centre—involved certain implicit assumptions about the nature of future conflict: any attack would be total in character and directed either at the United States or at Europe; a reasonable measure of security could be obtained from the capacity to cause unacceptable damage in the enemy's own country.

The strategy of massive retaliation met with criticism from the date of its inception. As early as 1946, Bernard Brodie had suggested that the crucial factor concerning nuclear weapons was that they should not be used. [11] By the latter half of the 1950s other strategists argued that massive retaliation was hardly credible as a strategic doctrine. [12–15] The majority of critics noted the difficulty which Dulles had in defining the "major" aggression which was to trigger massive retaliation and the doctrine became hardly more plausible when it was advocated as a response to local and peripheral conflicts. [2b]

## The strategy of "flexible response", 1961–68

President Kennedy was also among those who questioned exclusive dependence on the strategy of massive retaliation. As Senator he had said:

Under every military budget submitted by the Administration, we have been preparing primarily to fight the one kind of war we least want to fight and are least likely to fight. We have been driving ourselves into a corner where the only choice is all or nothing at all, world devastation or submission—a choice that necessarily causes us to hesitate on the brink and leaves the initiative in the hands of our enemies. [16]

By the time the Kennedy administration took office, it had become clear that strategic nuclear forces aimed at the Soviet Union were ineffective or at least unusable in local conflicts, even in the critical European theatre. As crisis succeeded crisis, it became apparent that the United States was unwilling to invoke massive retaliation. The doctrine was not a credible response except in the most extreme circumstances. The Kennedy administration sought, therefore, to replace a strategy calling for a single all-out response to any attack with a strategy which included a number of options. The new policy, called "flexible response", was described by Secretary of Defense R. McNamara:

Our forces can be used in several different ways. We may have to retaliate with a single massive attack. Or, we may be able to use our retaliatory forces to limit damage done to ourselves, and our allies, by knocking out the enemy's bases before he has had time to launch his second salvos. We may seek to terminate a war on favorable terms by using our forces as a bargaining weapon—by threatening further attack.

In any case, our large reserve of protected firepower would give an enemy an incentive to avoid our cities and to stop a war. Our new policy gives us the flexibility to choose among several operational plans, but does not require that we make any advance committment with respect to doctrine or targets. We shall be committed only to a system that gives us the ability to use our forces in a controlled and deliberate way, so as best to pursue the interests of the US, our Allies, and the rest of the Free World. [17]

The new strategy was accompanied by considerable rearmament. The concern of the administration was that the United States should be able to meet the enemy at every level with forces so superior as to deter it from aggression, or at least offer a major chance of success if fighting broke out. This motivated rearmament over the entire strategic field. Minimum deterrence, which postulated the destruction of the major Soviet conurbations in the event of an attack on the United States, was given less weight than previously on the ground that it was sensitive to technological innovations and offered little deterrence to third parties. Alongside it the strategy of counterforce was developed. According to McNamara counterforce meant that the United States would develop weapons of retaliation for countering the weapons deployed by the Soviet Union on a total or selective basis according to the strategic situation; a reserve was also to be maintained to attack cities. Cities could thereby be used as "hostages"; the "pause" would be prolonged and the enemy given an opportunity to discontinue aggression before total war developed. A shift in emphasis can be traced from the extended deterrent to the possiblity of limiting the effects of total war.

The strategy also offered "assured destruction capability", a guaranteed capability to cause the enemy unacceptable damage even if he struck first. The strategy ensured that the first-strike capability of the enemy could never eliminate the defender's second-strike capability. How the new strategy was to be put into operation is unclear and official explanations are inconsistent. Secretary of Defense McNamara, criticizing the nuclear concepts of the United Kingdom and France, stated that the United States intended to confine its initial attacks to military targets:

The US has come to the conclusion that to the extent feasible, basic military strategy in a possible general nuclear war should be approached in much the same way that more conventional military operations have been regarded in the past. That is to say, principal military objectives . . . should be the destruction of the enemy's military forces, not of his civilian population. [18]

Throughout 1962 McNamara maintained that the United States had the capability to destroy all Soviet military targets even after absorbing a first blow. The corollary was, of course, that the United States would be able to overwhelm Soviet strategic forces by a first strike in response, for instance, to an attack on Europe. The administration considered tactical nuclear weapons in Europe too vulnerable to serve as reliable second-strike weapons.

It seems clear that the United States, which saw European national nuclear forces as irrelevant and tactical nuclear weapons as overvalued, considered now that Europe's optimum contribution lay in the field of conventional defence. McNamara said in January 1963: "The decision to employ tactical nuclear weapons should not be forced upon us simply because we have no other way to cope with a particular situation." [19]

The impotence of strategic nuclear weapons lies in their enormous destructive capacity. This makes them unsuitable for use in all but the most desperate circumstances. In minor confrontation, the side with the strongest conventional forces will have the advantage. Strategic nuclear forces were, however, of some significance in NATO thinking. They were supposed to deter aggression, including aggression limited to the European theatre. But if deterrence failed and war started with something less than an all-out attack, or if the Soviet Union used only conventional forces, how was the United States to respond? As McNamara noted: "One cannot fashion a credible deterrent out of an incredible action."

The realization that the doctrine of massive retaliation had shortcomings and that conventional options were expensive produced increased interest, especially among NATO military commanders, in the possibilities displayed by tactical nuclear weapons. The case for tactical nuclear weapons rested on several assumptions: that tactical nuclear weapons could be substituted for manpower; and that yields of weapons could be limited, thereby limiting damage and civilian casualties and preventing escalation of the conflict. These assumptions proved to be incorrect. Later studies showed that more manpower would be required to fight a tactical nuclear war; that the prospects for limiting collateral damage were poor due to weapon inaccuracy; and that the risk of escalation was increased by the absence of a natural firebreak between tactical and strategic use of nuclear warfare.

But tactical nuclear weapons were nevertheless retained for a number of reasons. (*a*) Several thousand tactical nuclear weapons including bombs, missiles and artillery shells were already in Europe. (*b*) The presence of these weapons was construed to contribute to the deterrence of conventional as well as nuclear aggression, and to the deterrence of a first use of tactical nuclear weapons by the Soviet Union. (*c*) They were thought to provide a hedge against the possibility of failure in other parts of the NATO posture.

In addition to tactical nuclear forces, the need for a major conventional option appeared obvious. The pursuit of counterforce strategy in the defence of Europe was declining. In fact, Secretary of Defense McNamara explicitly abandoned the notion of counterforce in his annual defence review before Congress in February 1965. He argued that specialization in conventional forces by Europe would enhance the credibility of the nuclear arsenal. Conventional forces, being less destructive, would reduce civilian casualties and a conventional option would solve the vexed question of who should decide on the use of nuclear weapons.

But the new strategic doctrine was not officially adopted by NATO until May 1967, and even then, only after much debate. Previously the European members of NATO had accepted US hegemony in defence questions as a necessary condition for an automatic nuclear response by the United States in the event of aggression in Europe. The doctrine of flexible response removed the automatic nuclear response. A nuclear reaction would now take place only after deliberation on the part of the United States and in stages. The European members were concerned to keep the commitment of the United States to their defence. They saw NATO as a means of ensuring US protection, by which they meant US nuclear protection. Europe strove for tangible guarantees which led to pressure on the United States to station troops in Europe. But large numbers of US troops could not be permanently maintained in Europe without the justification of a meaningful military role.

European concerns about the alliance were understandable, but they were not the only reason for evolving new strategy. By 1961 changing technology made a reassessment of NATO doctrine essential. Previously the security of Western Europe had been seen as guaranteed by US strategic dominance. The conventional superiority of the Soviet Union was not a threat in the face of the United States' capacity to conduct a counterforce disarming strategy. The US nuclear umbrella might be unpleasant but it was necessary and therefore tolerable. With the development of the Soviet nuclear capability, the question arose as to whether the United States was prepared to sacrifice North American cities in the event of a Soviet invasion of Europe. The "credibility of guarantees" became a central question in the alliance.

The problem was resolved not by a reassessment of the role of nuclear weapons but by searching for a device which would reduce allied misgivings about their dependence on the United States. Britain and France found their answer in creating their own independent nuclear force. In response, the United States proposed the creation of a "multilateral force" (MLF). At first glance MLF appeared to be a satisfactory solution, but it gradually became clear that the proposal raised virtually insoluble problems regarding political sovereignty and military command.

The strategy of flexible response, unlike that of massive retaliation, met with strong resistance among certain European states, notably France. Its major defect lay in the limited number of options which were available, in what is termed "truncated flexibility". It is inherent in the doctrine that there is a spectrum or hierachy of violence through which the enemy will proceed. In terms of Soviet policy this was seen as comprising a spectrum ranging from political agitation through insurgency, guerilla warfare, sub-theatre conventional warfare, and theatre conventional warfare to strategic nuclear warfare. NATO was, of course, concerned with theatre warfare. But for the doctrine to succeed it was essential that both sides be able to progress through the relevant part of the spectrum at similar speeds. This applied particularly to the conventional part of the spectrum and it therefore implied the necessity for a reasonable measure of equality in conventional force levels.

Any imbalance in conventional, tactical nuclear or strategic nuclear capabilities would tend to invalidate the theory of a strategy of flexible response and face the deficient side with practical decisions which allowed for no alternative options. NATO attempted to solve the problem of its deficiency in conventional forces by making a distinction between tactical and strategic nuclear weapons with regard to deterrent value, and suggesting that while strategic nuclear weapons may not represent a credible alternative to conventional forces, tactical nuclear forces are a reasonable substitute. The problems posed by the use of tactical nuclear forces made this situation only a temporary stopgap.

In the initial years of the strategy of flexible response the European members of NATO failed to implement it, probably as a result of both political reservations and economic pressures. However, in recent years there have been signs of a greater willingness to accept burdens implicit in the new strategy.

### The strategy of "realistic deterrence", 1969–the present

As indicated above, the strategy of flexible response was adopted by the Kennedy administration to replace the earlier strategy calling for an all-out response to any attack with a strategy which allow for more options. The new doctrine of "realistic deterrence" was designed for more effective interference in local conflicts in regions of special interest to the USA, an emphasis which reflected, among other things, greater concern with counterinsurgency operations. The Kennedy-Johnson counterinsurgency strategy led to US military engagement in different parts of the world and particularly in Viet-Nam.

The war in Viet-Nam resulted in a considerable increase of US military power and consequently also in US military expenditure. In spite of enormous military and manpower resources, the involvement of the USA in Viet-Nam and the application of the strategy of counterinsurgency did not give satisfactory results. The United States was faced not only with a military stalemate in Viet-Nam, but also with the moral condemnation of world public opinion and with economic difficulties as well as political opposition at home.

Confronted with these problems, the Nixon administration re-examined the doctrine of flexible response and attempted to adapt the strategy to the changed circumstances. Secretary of Defense M. Laird explained the new policy in connection with the presentation of the 1972 defence budet. [20] The "Nixon strategy for peace" had at its core a "doctrine of strength and partnership" to be developed parallel with a "strategy of negotiations". Together these added up to "realistic deterrence". He claimed that the economic, political, military and manpower realities had changed significantly during the preceeding five years and named seven factors which reflected these changes: (*a*) a growing Soviet military capability and momentum; (*b*) expanding Soviet influence around the world, as evidenced by the worldwide deployment of its growing naval forces; (*c*) an emerging Chinese nuclear threat; (*d*) the reordering of national priorities which had reduced the percentage of the GNP devoted to defence; (*e*) sharply rising US personnel costs and the move towards an all-volunteer military force, the so-called "zero-draft"; (*f*) a change in the world economic status of the NATO countries and the consequent need for burden sharing; and (*g*) the need among US Asian allies for regional support.

To what extent is the "new" strategy in fact new? Its authors claim that

The strategy of realistic deterrence is new. Those who would dismiss it as a mere continuation of past policies in new packaging would be quite mistaken. Past policy was responsive and reactive. Our new strategy is positive and active. Past policy focused on containment and accommodation. The new strategy emphasizes measured, meaningful involvement and vigorous negotiation from a position of strength. [20a]

But few would consider "negotiation from a position of strength" to be a new US doctrine. Furthermore, the main concepts of the strategy of flexible response remain: that is, strategic forces retain their central role as a deterrent against nuclear attack, and the need for the United States and its allies to maintain strong conventional capabilities is stressed. However, there are other elements which are new. In particular, the strategy is based on the following principles. (*a*) In deterring strategic nuclear war, primary reliance will be placed on US strategic deterrent forces. (*b*) In the event of theatre nuclear war in Europe the United States has primary responsibility but its allies are able to share the responsibility by virtue of their own nuclear capabilities. (*c*) In deterring theatre conventional warfare—for example, a major war in Europe—US and allied forces share the responsibility. (*d*) In deterring sub-theatre or localized warfare, the country or ally which is threatened would bear the primary burden, particularly in providing manpower. But in situations where US interests are threatened, the United States must be prepared to provide appropriate military and economic assistance. This would probably take the form of backup logistic support and sea- and air-combat support. In special cases, it could also include ground-combat support. [20b]

There is nothing intrinsically new in the total force approach. The United States had been trying to introduce a combination of US and allied means for "common defence" for some years, as is well illustrated by the existence of many defence pacts. But past results had not been satisfactory and had burdened the US defence budget. The strategy of "realistic deterrence" is an attempt to spread this burden.

The new strategy has been more or less accepted by the US allies in Asia and to some extent by its NATO partners. The strategy is already reflected in NATO military policy. The December 1971 meeting of the NATO Council dealt mainly with military posture, suggesting measures for modernizing the armed forces of the NATO countries. The measures are part of a 10-year plan known as Alliance Defense-AD-70. Under this plan, Eurogroup members of NATO are to increase their military budgets by between 5 and 15 per cent. The armed forces of the flank countries are to be strengthened. It has also been decided to form a NATO Naval On-Call Force, Mediterranean (NAVOCFORMED) consisting of the naval forces of Greece, Italy, Turkey, the United Kingdom and the United States. The plan highlights the need for greater conventional deterrence and points to specific inadequacies in existing NATO capabilities.

As a significant first step towards a more equitable partitioning of NATO defence costs, 10 European nations agreed among themselves to provide almost one billion dollars of additional expenditure over the next five years.[3] The sum is to be divided almost equally between improvements to their own forces and contributions to an additional infrastructure programme for better communications and aircraft shelters. The European members of NATO have, therefore, demonstrated that they accept some elements of the new US strategy.

The new strategy has done nothing to change US global policy. It has only changed some of the methods of realizing these goals, based on a more realistic interpretation of the nature of "the threat" and on the deployment of adequate forces to meet it. The allies have been given a greater and more coordinated role, and the role of negotiations in prevent-

---

[3] In fact, the real increase over this period may be greater than $1 billion: increases of $1.3 billion and $1.5 billion, at current prices, were budgeted in 1972 and 1973, respectively. [21]

ing armed conflict has been strengthened. "Realistic deterrence" relied on a policy of strength expressed in the term "assured destruction". The enemy is still to be deterred by the nuclear balance. To this extent realistic deterrence does not differ from the strategy of flexible response. But there are new notions which find expression in a potentially more flexible engagement of armed forces, not only those of the United States, but also those of its allies.

## II. *Soviet strategic doctrine*

### 1946–53

The Soviet Union emerged from World War II with the strongest tactical forces in Europe. Its position in Eastern and Central Europe was strengthened by the existence of the newly created socialist states and by its status as one of the occupying powers in Germany and Austria. It became clear at an early stage that the Soviet Union wished to play a role as a major power not only in Europe but also in a more global sense. Not surprisingly its strategy was basically influenced by its broader political aims.

In the early postwar years Soviet strategy had two main aims: to maintain large conventional forces as a deterrent against the Western nations and to break the US monopoly of nuclear weapons. Consequently the Soviet Union gave fresh attention to training and equipping its theatre forces for campaigns in Europe, giving priority to those already stationed in Eastern Europe. The priority given to conventional land and air forces did not, of course, mean that military strategists were indifferent to the military-technical revolution which ushered in the nuclear age. Well in advance of the expectations of the Western countries and much to their surprise, the Soviet Union exploded its first atomic bomb in August 1949 and four years later tested its first thermonuclear device.

In spite of important developments in Soviet military posture after 1949, theatre warfare in Europe still had first demand on Soviet military resources and planning. The main improvement of Soviet divisions stationed in East European countries lay in increasing their battlefield mobility and firepower. This was achieved by motorizing transport and strengthening armoured elements, by the introduction of an early generation of jet aircraft and by other measures.

Two other undertakings relating to conventional forces were initiated before the end of this period. The first was a naval programme which allowed for the development and modernization of the Soviet fleet. The programme included increased numbers of cruisers, destroyers and submarines. This programme might be considered as the initial response of a land power to superior enemy naval strength. The second undertaking lay in the reconstruction of the air-defence system. This programme was concentrated on the construction of jet fighters. By 1951 about 20 per cent of Soviet fighter units had been equipped with jets and by 1953 the changeover was almost complete. Efforts were also made to improve the Soviet electronics industry which was necessary for the creation of a nationwide radar warning network and other facilities of a modern air-defence system.

At the same time, efforts were being made to develop long-range bombers (such as the Bison jet bomber and the Bear turboprop bomber)[4] and to develop and improve Soviet strategic delivery capabilities, which were still oriented towards medium-range operations in Eurasia rather than towards intercontinental missions. Strategic missile deployments in the western border regions of the Soviet Union began in the late 1950s and early 1960s and consisted of medium- and intermediate-range ballistic missiles (MRBMs and IRBMs) for coverage of targets in the NATO European area.

A number of steps were also taken to rebuild the armed forces of the East European countries. Bilateral defence treaties were concluded to this end in 1948. This did not entail an alliance of the NATO type, but the armed forces of the East European countries were modified to conform to the Soviet military organizational pattern and they began to receive sizable quantities of Soviet arms and equipment. At the time of Stalin's death the process of reconstruction had not been completed but the forces of the East European countries had attained considerable strength and a basis had been laid for a future alliance. However, their strength and efficiency were still not such that the Soviet Union could depend on them and the Soviet Union "up to and beyond the end of the Stalin era counted essentially upon its own military forces to carry the burden of any military undertakings in Europe in which the Soviet Union might become involved". [22]

In general, early Soviet military strategy may be seen as evolving from the experiences of World War II. The armed forces were prepared for conflict using improved forms of traditional weapons, the armoured units and air forces being given a dominant role. The Soviet Union initiated the development of nuclear weapons, but it did not achieve operational nuclear capabilities in this period.

## 1953–64

During this period the Soviet Union took certain initiatives calculated to strengthen European security. There were several diplomatic achievements, such as the conclusion of the Austrian State Treaty and the Warsaw Treaty the holding of the Geneva summit meeting in 1955 and the commencement of negotiations for disarmament. Military strategy during the period was concerned with directing resources into supplying the armed forces first with strategic and subsequently with tactical nuclear weapons. The years

---

[4] These bombers became operational about 1956.

up to 1960/61 were dominated by the aspiration of reaching a balance in strategic nuclear weapons with the United States, while Soviet strategy continued to be based on the possession of large conventional forces. During the latter part of this period, which extended some years beyond the end of Khrushchev's term, each side had sufficient strategic nuclear weapons to deter the other and Soviet strategy was primarily based on nuclear weapons.

At the same time as Khrushchev became leader of the Party and of the state, nuclear weapons became a subject of serious theoretical and political debate. The debate resulted in the view that nuclear war would postpone the development of socialism. At the XXth Congress (1956) of the Communist Party of the Soviet Union it was concluded that "since the world socialist camp has become converted to a powerful political, economic and military force and since the forces of peace have gained worldwide strength, war is no longer a fatal inevitability". [23a]

This change in political doctrine took place in the same year as the Soviet Union introduced its first operational long-range bombers which could, for the first time, strike directly at the territory of the United States. Khrushchev was concerned to adapt Soviet military thinking to the revolution in the technology of warfare. The military reforms of the Khrushchev epoch affected not only the attitude of the Soviet Union towards Europe but also its global strategic posture. In his report to the Supreme Soviet in January 1960, Khrushchev announced the intention of reducing Soviet manpower under arms by one-third—from 3.6 million to 2.4 million men. This economically attractive policy was justified by the increased firepower that nuclear weapons had given to the Soviet Union. Khrushchev argued that, in any case, Soviet nuclear capability would deter all but a madman from starting a war. It was claimed that conventional armaments, including surface navies and air forces together with large standing armies, were rapidly becoming obsolete in the face of missiles and nuclear weapons. While implementing a considerable shift of resources to the strategic field Khrushchev gave theatre force dual capabilities for both conventional and nuclear warfare and left them to continue with a central role in the Soviet military posture.

Resistance to some of Khrushchev's reforms by military leaders who advocated traditional military concepts, together with the pressure of world events, notably the Berlin crisis of 1961, brought about various modifications in the military policy as outlined by Khrushchev in January 1960. Speaking at the XXIInd Party Congress in October 1961, Marshall Malinovski, Minister of Defence, gave a less optimistic picture of the Soviet defence outlook. He claimed that "in realistically appraising the situation" one must hold that the West was making serious preparations for a surprise nuclear attack. While he shared Khrushchev's view that a future war would "inevitably" be a nuclear-missile war and that the use of such weapons in the early stages would have a decisive influence on the war's outcome, he also brought in a traditional notion that final victory could be assured only by "combined action of all arms and services". [24]

The central issues in Soviet military theory and planning concerned the relationship between conventional theatre warfare in Europe and strategic operations on a global scale. The essential question was whether a future war would be

a land war with the employment of nuclear weapons as a means of supporting the operations of the ground forces [or] . . . a fundamentally new kind of war in which the main means of solving strategic tasks will be missiles and nuclear weapons. [23a]

The other controversial issue was whether Soviet military preparations should be aimed primarily at deterrence or at improving the Soviet capacity to fight a war if deterrence should fail. Two schools of military thought were engaged in this debate: the modernists, who stressed the need to discard the old doctrinal view and to exploit modern technologies of war; and the traditionalists, who argued for a moderate rate of military innovation and cautioned against extremes.

In spite of this debate it can be said that, beginning in the early 1960s and continuing throughout the remainder of this period and well into the next, a military strategy primarily based on nuclear weapons has dominated. This is demonstrated by, among other things, the massive deployment of nuclear weapons. Although this strategy continued to be valid after Khrushchev, it is best described in *Soviet Military Strategy* [23a] which was first published in 1962 and which was reissued in revised editions in 1963 and in 1968. Although the 1968 edition contains some changes the first edition of the book represents a theoretical generalization of the doctrine that has prevailed in the Soviet Union since the early 1960s.

The authors of the book claim that Khrushchev's report to the Supreme Soviet of 1960 and Malinovski's speech at the XXIInd Party Congress contain two important doctrinal turning points. They recognize a broad shift in Soviet strategic outlook from a primary preoccupation with conventional land warfare to a central focus on the problem of global strategic war. They also take the view that war is no longer inevitable but claim that it cannot be dismissed on account of "aggressive policies" and "intensified imperialist war preparations". [23b] In addition to the possibility of global strategic war they mention the possibility of an escalation from a local war, of "accidental" outbreak and of retaliation by the Soviet Union in the event of an attack on another WTO member.

The role of nuclear weapons is stressed:

In modern warfare, nuclear weapons can be employed for various missions: strategic, operational and tactical . . . It permits the execution of military missions in a considerably shorter time than was possible in past wars. [23c]

One of the important tenets in Soviet military doctrine is that a world war, if the "imperialists" initiate it, will inevitably assume the character of a nuclear war with missiles, that is, a war in which nuclear weapons will be the chief instruments of destruction, and missiles the basic vehicles for their delivery to targets. [23d]

The authors also point out the importance of preparing armed forces to cope with local wars outside the framework of a general war.

The armed forces of the socialist countries must be ready for small-scale local wars which the imperialists might initiate. Soviet military strategy must study the methods of waging such wars too, in order to prevent their expansion into a world war, and in order to achieve a rapid victory over the enemy. [23c]

No doctrine of local war is developed in the book but the authors give it greater recognition than does other Soviet literature. Wars of national liberation and revolutionary wars are also dealt with.

Conventional arms will find broad application in both local and world wars and their development is therefore important, but the leading role in any conflict is given to missiles. These, according to Soviet doctrine, can be divided into "strategic missiles" and "operational and tactical missiles". [23d] It is even expected that air forces will gradually be replaced by missiles, although aircraft still have a significant role and "some specific missions, for example striking mobile targets, could be executed more successfully by aircraft than by missiles". [23e] The navy will retain the tasks of destroying enemy attack carrier forces and of disrupting or destroying enemy maritime transportation. [23f]

The authors consider that the massive use of nuclear weapons for the purpose of achieving the annihilation or capitulation of the enemy in the shortest possible time poses a new question:

What, under these conditions, will constitute the main military-strategic goal of the war: defeat of the enemy's armed forces, as was the case in the past, or the annihilation and destruction of objectives in the enemy's rear, for the purpose of disorganizing it? Soviet military strategy gives the following answer to this question: both of these goals must be achieved simultaneously. [23g]

This strategy is to be backed up by four types of operations: (*a*) nuclear strikes by missiles; (*b*) military operations in ground theatres; (*c*) protection of the socialist countries and troop formations from enemy nuclear strikes; and (*d*) military operations in naval theatres to destroy enemy naval forces.

In summary, the military policy evolved under Khrushchev resulted in a shift from almost exclusive preoccupation with conventional warfare to new emphasis on the problem of intercontinental war. This shift in emphasis was accompanied by an appreciable reallocation of resources from theatre to strategic forces. Intercontinental bombers were introduced in the mid-1950s, followed by medium-range ballistic missiles at the end of this decade, and intercontinental ballistic missiles (ICBMs) in 1960. For some reason the Soviet Union failed to convert its advantage in missile technology into an operational ICBM inventory of superior size at an earlier time. A start was also made in building up a force of missile-launching submarines. These were similar in function although inferior in many respects to the US Polaris submarines. In addition, the Soviet Union embarked on R&D programmes in the anti-ballistic missile (ABM) field, although actual development of ABM defences awaited the decision of Khrushchev's successors.

While resources were shifted to strategic forces, there was also an important modernization of theatre forces during the Khrushchev era. They were left with enhanced capabilities for conducting theatre warfare on a nuclear basis and with a continuing role as a central element of Soviet military power. A major reorganization of the air-defence system was undertaken in the mid-1950s, followed by the introduction of surface-to-air missiles (SAMs). There were also changes in Soviet naval preparations during this period including, for example, improvements in amphibious landing capability.

During the same period that Soviet conventional forces were being strengthened, the theatre forces of Eastern Europe were gradually consolidated and proved. In 1955 the Warsaw Treaty was signed. This was in response to the Federal Republic of Germany's entry into NATO and marked the emergence of rival military alliances in postwar Europe. Until the end of the decade the contributions of the military forces of the other members of the WTO seem to have carried little weight in Soviet planning. Apart from the improvement of the joint air-defence arrangements, the Soviet Union made no major effort to weld the members of the alliance into an integrated military force.

In the early 1960s the importance of the Warsaw Treaty Organization to the common defence of the socialist countries began to be stressed. The military contribution of the other members played a greater role in Soviet military planning. The East European forces were given a more active role in theatre operations and joint training and re-equipment programmes were initiated. Modernization was seen largely in terms of improving conventional capabilities but in 1964 the Soviet Union began to furnish the other member countries with potential nuclear delivery systems in the form of tactical missiles with a range of about 150 miles. The nuclear warheads remained in the hands of the Soviet Union but the acquisition of delivery systems and participation in simulated nuclear exercises marked a significant step towards nuclear sharing at some future time.

## 1964–73

Although the strategy primarily based on nuclear weapons was still valid in the mid-1960s, the new Brezhnev–Kosygin leadership gradually introduced what was called "flexibility with caution". The governing assumptions and priorities on which the military policy of the current leadership appear to rest can be summarized thus:

(1) that general nuclear war must be avoided;

(2) that deterrence based on Soviet strategic nuclear power, both offensive and defensive, offers the best guarantee against nuclear war;

(3) that the Soviet Union must maintain its traditional strong conventional military posture both in order to back up its interests in the crucial political arena of Europe and to cope with problems created by the tension with the People's Republic of China; and

(4) that the Soviet Union must also continue to develop more mobile and versatile conventional forces, including naval capabilities, to support its interests in the third world and to sustain its role as a global competitor of the United States. [25]

Under the Brezhnev–Kosygin leadership, programmes in the strategic field have fallen largely into two categories: those aimed at a build-up of strategic delivery forces and those of ABM deployment. In the summer of 1966 an accelerated programme of ICBM development was set in motion. New missiles were introduced in dispersed and hardened sites including the SS-9 and SS-11, both of which are liquid-fuelled, and the SS-13, the Soviet Union's first solid-fuel ICBM. The Soviet Union also accorded special importance to the development of mobile land-based missiles. High priority was also given to missile-launching submarines.

Soviet conventional or general purposes forces have been improved with regard to range and mobility. These forces are maintained at a high degree of combat readiness and are supported by a system of mobilization and reinforcement that allows a rapid build-up. A policy has been put into action to transform the Soviet Navy from its role as a mere adjunct of land power into an instrument for global support of Soviet interests. Emphasis was placed primarily upon increasing and modernizing submarines to give the Soviet Union the world's largest undersea force. The submarine force has among others the two tasks of delivering strategic missiles and destroying seaborne supply lines. There was a significant renewal of surface ship construction and many existing cruiser and destroyer units were modernized to fire surface-to-surface and anti-aircraft missiles. A decision was also made to build naval helicopter carriers.

These technological improvements were, of course, accompanied by discussions of appropriate military doctrine. These discussions, while repudiating Khrushchev's military policy, did not represent any radical departure from the previous orientation of Soviet doctrine toward the problems of general nuclear war, although they placed more emphasis on the possibility of non-nuclear and limited warfare in various potential theatres, including Europe.

By 1965 it had become evident that Soviet strategy was growing less categorical in advancing the theory of nuclear-missile war. Since 1967 this has become even more apparent since some well-known military theorists and leaders have criticized the doctrine which gave strategic nuclear weapons such overriding importance. The importance of preparing Soviet forces for a wide range of operations below the level of general nuclear war began to be recognized more explicitly. General S. M. Shtemenko, Deputy Chief of General Staff of the Soviet military forces, stated in early 1965 that Soviet military doctrine did not "exclude" the possibility of non-nuclear warfare nor of warfare restricted to the use of tactical nuclear weapons "within the framework of so-called 'local' wars". [26] General Lomov even envisaged the possibility of a local war limited to conventional means or to tactical nuclear weapons in Europe, although he warned that "the probability of escalation into a nuclear world war is always great and might under certain circumstances become inevitable". [27a]

He insisted that Soviet forces should be prepared for operations "with conventional arms alone" or with "limited employment of nuclear weapons". [27b]

In July 1967 Marshall Iakubovski, Chief of Armed Forces of the Warsaw Treaty Organization, argued in an article that nuclear weapons should not be treated as "absolutes", especially in theatre operations. He noted that the past few years had seen the improvement of "the capability of the ground forces to conduct military operations successfully with or without the use of nuclear weapons". [28]

In addition to pressures for increased emphasis on conventional forces, the mid-1960s saw a reconsideration of the role of strategic nuclear weapons and consequently, the design of the nuclear forces. The doctrine of "minimum deterrence" was subjected to highly critical scrutiny by Colonel Rybkin. [29] Rybkin's point of view is interesting because it embodies pure "military" arguments. He claimed that defence was a problem for experts, that nuclear war could not be said to have lost all utility and therefore rationality, that "minimum deterrence" was not adequate for Soviet needs, and that nuclear war "by accident" (that is, by a political mistake) was a definite possibility which could not be countered simply by referring to some vague moral or political superiority. The study was an overt criticism of Khrushchev's problem. It also marked the beginning of formal, open discussions of the need for strategic superiority and hinted at the need to establish such superiority in peacetime. [30]

Debate was taking place on two levels. There was a dialogue between the military and the political leadership about what was needed to make Soviet deterrence credible and there were disputes within the military which ran on the familiar lines of interservice rivalry. The internal military disputes concerned, first, the balance between nuclear and conventional forces, and second, the proper mix of offensive and defensive strategic nuclear weapons. [31]

It can be claimed that the development of Soviet military power since 1966/67 has been marked by the "harmonic and even development of all types of forces, necessary for preparation of any kind of war". This development has been based on the judgement that the military balance has essentially lessened the possibility of direct military confrontation between the United States and the Soviet Union; that military-technical progress has led to a balance in strategic nuclear weapons and this in turn to the SALT agreements; and that, on the other hand, the importance of local war and of intervention by conventional forces has grown and that local war is also possible in Europe. Manoeuvres and exercises both by the Soviet Union and the WTO have confirmed, according to official statements, the capabilities of all kinds of armed forces to carry out combined offensive operations using conventional weapons. [32] Consonant with this last consideration has been a continued strengthening of Soviet conventional forces. At the same time there has been a steady deployment of new strategic weapons. While the Soviet Union, like the United States, has recognized the importance of negotiations and agreements on the limitation of strategic armaments, it has, just as the United States, not ceased to improve its offensive and defensive systems as permitted under the SALT agreements.

During the past few years the strategy calling for "harmonious development of all types of armed forces" appears to have gained complete acceptance. Soviet strategists have paid particular attention to the study of local wars and to the two questions of how they can be prevented from escalating and how a quick victory can be achieved. The opinion that every local war, particularly a local European war, must lead to world war has been replaced by the view that this will be the case only where a direct confrontation between the two major nuclear powers occurs. Military theory is increasingly taking the view that the use of nuclear weapons in war is unlikely; both sides would aim at avoiding their use.

Current Soviet military theory recognizes five basic types of wars as being possible at the present time:

(1) Wars between different social systems. These can include (*a*) general nuclear war between coalitions of states of two systems and (*b*) small-scale local wars which the "imperialists" might initiate against one or several socialist states. A general nuclear war is unacceptable for solving the basic contradictions of the present era. Such a war is unlikely but cannot be excluded and it is therefore necessary to maintain a balance in strategic nuclear weapons with the United States, this balance being a precondition of deterrence. Local wars are more likely and would primarily be conventional conflicts. Conventional operations would also be characteristic of the opening phases of a general war and the risks of a local war escalating are always present.

(2) Civil wars, by which are meant conflicts within a state with the pos-

sible involvement of interventionist forces. Civil wars can be subdivided into (*a*) wars between the proletariat and the bourgoisie in the struggle for socialism and (*b*) wars which are waged between the people and reactionary régimes, fascist, monarchist or other. Such wars are exemplified by the Spanish Civil War in 1936, the war in Greece in 1946 and by such wars as are today being waged in Laos and Cambodia. It is possible for these wars, which have the character of democratic revolutions, to grow into socialist revolutions as was the case in Cuba in 1960. Wars of liberation such as those in Indonesia, Indo-China and Algeria can also be placed in this category.

(3) Wars of newly created states against "imperialist" intervention. Such intervention would intend to impose a reactionary régime in order to increase the political and economic influence of the intervening country as in the case of the Anglo–French–Israel intervention in Egypt in 1956 or the Belgian intervention in the Congo in 1960.

(5) Wars of a special character. These would include conflicts between underdeveloped countries, such as boundary conflicts arising as a result of the artificial boundaries imposed by colonial rulers. Such conflicts have already arisen between India and Pakistan, between Yemen and Saudi Arabia and between Morocco and Algeria. [33]

This authoritative classification has been developed on socio-political grounds but it also provides the basis for the military classification of wars as either world nuclear-missile or local. It also provides a justification for the abandonment of the "absolute weapon" doctrine and shows the necessity of being able to wage all types of wars and most particularly, local conventional wars. [34]

## III. *Summary and conclusions*

In summary, there are three clearly discernible periods in the evolution of the strategic doctrines of the two alliances. In the first few years immediately after World War II, the doctrines of the United States and the Soviet Union were influenced primarily by the nature of the military forces available to each. The United States had, in addition to strong ground and naval forces, a monopoly of nuclear weapons, while Soviet strength was confined to large numbers of ground troops. As a result, the United States, on the one hand, relied on nuclear weapons to deter a westward expansion of the overwhelmingly superior conventional Soviet forces into Western Europe, and it extended the "nuclear umbrella" to this region through the creation of NATO in 1949. At the same time, it contributed to the re-equipment of West European forces and the re-establishment of West European defence industries. The Soviet Union, on the other hand, relied on its conventional superiority in the European theatre to deter Western aggression, including the possibility of surprise nuclear attack: following an immediate postwar demobilization of the majority of its troops, it doubled the number of forces in the period from 1948 to 1955. It also pursued the development of nuclear weapons intensively, exploding its first atomic weapon in 1949, and its first thermonuclear device in 1952. In addition, following the entry of the Federal Republic of Germany into NATO and the initiation of West German rearmament in 1953 and 1954, the Soviet Union undertook the establishment of the WTO, in an attempt to consolidate the eastern front. In sum, this first period may be considered a time of transition, marked by a considerable fear to attack on both sides; a movement toward the establishment of the two alliances; and a reliance on existing advantages in military strength (the nuclear advantage in the West and the conventional one in the East), accompanied by an initial attempt to ameliorate the corresponding weaknesses.

The second period—from the early 1950s to the early 1960s—is characterized by increased reliance on nuclear weapons on both sides, including, for a brief period on each side, exclusive reliance on nuclear armaments. This began with the adoption of the doctrine of massive retaliation by the Eisenhower administration in the United States. At the time this doctrine was most closely adhered to—in the mid-1950s—Soviet conventional forces were at their peak (in quantitative terms). Soviet development of nuclear weapons was proceeding rapidly and the Warsaw Treaty Organization was newly formed. It had also become clear that NATO would not actually attempt to match the WTO—or even the Soviet Union alone— in the number of conventional forces deployed in Europe. However, the United States retained a substantial advantage—an estimated ratio of about 10:1 in the number of nuclear weapons, as well as a monopoly of the means of delivery of these weapons to the territory of the opposing power (in the form of the earliest long-range and forward-based medium-range bombers). A doctrine which threatened all-out-nuclear retaliation as a response to any sort of aggression on the part of the enemy appeared a suitable US posture—which was both credible and appropriate with regard to the existing balance of forces. The Soviet Union, while moving towards the development and deployment of a credible intercontinental nuclear force, had no alternative but to rely on its conventional superiority in Europe in the early 1950s. However, following the introduction of its first intercontinental bombers in 1956, the USSR was able to place some emphasis on nuclear deterrence and to begin a reduction of some 50 per cent in the size of the armed forces over the period from 1955 to 1960. A debate on the respective roles of nuclear and conventional forces, pursued in the Soviet Union in the late 1950s, was brought to an end in early 1960 when Khrushchev announced the adoption of a new nuclear policy, the successful production of intercontinental ballistic missiles and a planned further reduction in the size of the armed forces. In both the United States and the Soviet Union, the announcements of virtually complete reliance on nuclear weapons for the prevention of a major confrontation were soon followed by some retraction, allowing a continued role for conventional forces. For both powers the second period is, nevertheless, dominated by the idea of nuclear deterrence.

The third period, extending from the early 1960s to the present time, has been marked in both East and West by a rejection of the nuclear-oriented doctrines of the 1950s, and an evolution of more flexible strategies. Again, it was the United States which took the first step in this direction. Factors which probably contributed to the development of the Kennedy–McNamara doctrine of "flexible response" in the early 1960s, and the eventual adoption of this doctrine by NATO in 1967, include: the lack of credibility in the "all or nothing" alternatives posed by the doctrine of massive retaliation; reaction against the dangers of a holocaust raised by this doctrine; and the steady build-up of Soviet strategic nuclear forces during the 1960s, in a manner which would eventually lead to nuclear parity between the two sides. The doctrine of flexible response implied greater reliance on increased conventional forces. In addition, it involved greater emphasis on tactical nuclear weapons.

President Nixon's doctrine of realistic deterrence and recent statements by Soviet military theorists have confirmed the common trend away from exclusive reliance on either nuclear or conventional forces and towards the development of a broad spectrum of armaments and support for a more complex strategy calling for the use of forces specifically appropriate to different types of conflicts.

**References**

1. Enthoven, A. and Smith, W., *How Much Is Enough? Shaping the Defense Program* (New York, Harper and Row, 1971) pp. 118–19.
2. Åkerman, N., *On the Doctrine of Limited War* (Lund, Berglingska Boktryckeriet, 1972).
   (a) –, p. 73.
   (b) –, pp. 69–71.
3. *US Department of State Bulletin,* Vol. XXX, No. 761, 25 January 1954.
4. *New York Times,* 30 November 1954, p. 13.
5. *Documents on American Foreign Relations,* 1954 (New York, Council on Foreign Relations, 1954) p. 18.
6. Huntington, S. P., *The Common Defense* (New York, Columbia University Press, 1961) pp. 70–84.
7. *Force Reductions in Europe,* SIPRI Monograph (Stockholm, Almqvist & Wiksell, 1974, Stockholm International Peace Research Institute) Appendix A.
8. York, H., *Race to Oblivion: A Participant's View of the Arms Race* (New York, Simon and Schuster, 1970).

9. Bottome, E. M., *The Missile Gap: A Study of the Formulation of Military and Political Policy* (Rutherford, Fairleigh Dickenson University Press).

10. Kissinger, H. A., *The Troubled Partnership* (New York, McGraw-Hill Book Company, 1965).
    (a) −, pp. 97–98.
    (b) −, p. 98.

11. Brodie, B., "War in the Nuclear Age", in B. Brodie, ed., *The Absolute Weapons* (New York, Harcourt Brace, 1946).

12. Kaufmann, W. W., "The Requirements of Deterrence" in W. W. Kaufmann, ed., *Military Policy and National Security* (Princeton, Princeton University Press, 1956).

13. Kissinger, H. A., *Nuclear Weapons and Foreign Policy* (New York, Random House, 1959).

14. Osgood, R. E., *Limited War: The Challenge to American Strategy* (Chicago, University of Chicago Press, 1959).

15. Wohlstetter, A., "The Delicate Balance of Terror", *Foreign Affairs*, Vol. 37, January 1957.

16. Kennedy, J. F., *The Strategy of Peace* (New York, Harper, 1960) p. 184.

17. McNamara, R. S. Address before the Fellows of the American Bar Foundation, Chicago, 17 February 1962, Department of Defense, Office of Public Affairs, *New Press Release No. 239–262*, pp. 6–7.

18. McNamara, R. S., Address at the Commencement Exercises, University of Michigan, 6 June 1962, Department of Defense, Office of Public Affairs, *New Press Release No. 980–63*, p. 9.

19. McNamara, R. S., *Statement before the House Armed Services Committee on Fiscal Year 1964–68 Defense Program and 1964 Defense Budget* (Washington, 30 January 1963) p. 29.

20. Laird, M. R., *Statement before the House Armed Services Committee on Fiscal Year 1972–76 Defense Program and 1972 Defense Budget* (Washington, 9 March 1971).
    (a) −, pp. 1–2.
    (b) −, p. 22.

21. *World Armaments and Disarmament, SIPRI Yearbook 1973* (Stockholm, Almqvist & Wiksell, 1973, Stockholm International Peace Research Institute) p. 212.

22. Wolfe, Th. W., *Soviet Military Power and European Security* (Rand Collection P-3429, October 1966) p. 10.

23. Sokolovskii, V. D. ed., *Soviet Military Strategy* (Santa Monica, Rand Corporation, 1963) [A translation of V. D. Sokolovskogo, ed., Voenaia Strategia (Moscow, Voennoe Izdatelstvo Ministarstva Obrony SSSR, 1962].
    (a) −, p. 367.
    (b) −, p. 312.
    (c) −, p. 297.
    (d) −, p. 299.
    (e) −, pp. 346–47.
    (f) −, pp. 420 and 348.
    (g) −, p. 305.

24. *Pravda*, 25 October 1961.

25. Wolfe, Th. W., *Soviet Power and Europe 1945–1970* (Baltimore & London, The Johns Hopkins Press, 1970) pp. 427–58.

26. Shtemenko, S. M., *Nedelia* No. 6, 31 January−6 February 1965.

27. Lomov, N. A., "The Influence of Soviet Military Doctrine on the Develop ment of the Military Art", *Kommunist Vooruzhenykh Sil* No. 21, November 1965.
    (a) –, pp. 16 and 18.
    (b) –, p. 22.
28. Marshal, I. I., Iakubovski, "Ground Forces", *Krasnaya Zvezda,* 21 July 1967.
29. Colonel Rybkin, "On the Essence of Nuclear-Missile War", *Kommunist Vooruzhenykh Sil,* No. 17, 1965, pp. 50–56.
30. Erickson, J., *Soviet Military Power* (London, RUSI, 1971) p. 9.
31. Zavyalov, I., "Soviet Military Doctrine", *Krasnaya Zvezda,* 30 March 1967.
32. D. M., "Neka novijsa gledišta vojne teorije SSSR-a i Varšavskog Ugovora", *Vojno Delo,* No. 2, 1972, p. 153.
33. Rybkin, E., "The Wars of the Modern Epoch and Their Influence on Social Processes", *Kommunist Vooruzhenykh Sil,* No. 11, 1970, pp. 10–17.
34. Drobac, M., and Grubišić, N., "Oružane snage i vojnostrategijske koncepcije u savremenim mednunarodnim adnosima", *Godišnjak 1971* (Institute za mevdjunarodnu politiky i privredu, Belgrade, 1972) pp. 133–35.

# Appendix 5B

## Chronological development of US and Soviet strategic nuclear forces

| Date | Soviet Union | United States |
|------|--------------|---------------|
| **1945** | | |
| 16 July | | First nuclear explosion at Alamogordo desert, New Mexico, is carried out by British and US scientists (yield 19 kilotons). |
| 6 August | | First nuclear bomb is dropped on Hiroshima (yield 12.5 kilotons). |
| 9 August | | Second nuclear bomb is dropped on Nagasaki (yield 22 kilotons). |
| **1946** | | |
| March | | US Strategic Air Command (SAC) is formed consisting of B-17 and B-29 medium bombers of World War II vintage. In mid-1946 the entire nuclear capability of SAC is one group located at Roswell Field, New Mexico. A few adequate overseas bases are available for emergency use. |
| 24 July | | USA conducts first underwater nuclear explosion at Bikini Island in the Pacific (yield about 20 kilotons). |
| **1948** | | |
| | | SAC receives first post-war bombers: B-36 heavy long-range bombers and improved B-50 medium bombers. Adequate bases are obtained in England and the Far East. SAC now provides first substantial but primitive strategic nuclear threat to the Soviet Union. |
| **1949** | | |
| 29 August | USSR explodes its first nuclear weapon near Semipalatinsk in Central Asia. | By this time the USA has already exploded eight nuclear devices with yields up to 50 kilotons, and has stockpiled a few hundred nuclear bombs with a total yield of about 10 megatons. |
| **1950** | | |
| 31 January | | President Truman orders commencement of full-scale programme to develop the thermonuclear weapon. |

97

| Date | Soviet Union | United States |
|------|--------------|---------------|
| **1951** | | |
| | | High-performance B-47 jet bombers (the first US jet bombers) enter service in SAC. |
| May | | USA achieves the first thermo-nuclear reaction at Eniwitok Atoll in the Pacific. |
| **1952** | | |
| 1 November | | First significant US thermonuclear explosion on Elugelab Island, Eniwitok Atoll (yield about 10 megatons). |
| **1953** | | |
| 12 August | First Soviet explosion of a thermo-nuclear device. | SAC now operates from a worldwide network of bases with an intercontinental modern bomber fleet capable of delivering nuclear weapons on targets in the Soviet Union at 2 610-nm ranges with one air-refuelling. The USA deploys a very sophisticated air-refuelling capacity. |
| **1954** | | |
| 1 March | | First US explosion of a true thermonuclear bomb at Bikini Atoll in the Pacific (yield about 15 megatons). |
| **1955** | | |
| | | USA begins intensive development of long-range strategic missiles with nuclear warheads. Within three years six programmes are initiated: Atlas (ICBM), Titan (ICBM), Thor (IRBM) and Jupiter (IRBM) in 1955; Minuteman (ICBM) in 1957; and Polaris (SLBM) in 1958. |
| June | | B-52B all-jet heavy bomber (Mach 0.95), a much larger version of the B-47, begins to replace B-36 in SAC. |
| 23 November | First Soviet thermonuclear explosion classified as being an "airburst" in the megation range comparable to the 1954 US tests. | |
| **1956** | | |
| | Soviet strategic turbo-prop Tu-20 "Bear" and turbo-jet Mya-4 "Bison" long-range bombers in service. | |
| **1957** | | |
| 15 February | | Completion of US B-47 production programme. A peak of 1800 B-47s in service with SAC is reached during the year. |

| Date | Soviet Union | United States |
|------|-------------|---------------|
| 31 May | | First US IRBM, Jupiter, successfully launched. |
| August | USSR achieves first long-range flight with ICBM. | |
| 4 October | USSR launches first satellite into orbit: Sputnik I (weight 83 kg). | |
| 3 November | USSR launches Sputnik II into orbit (weight 508 kg), carrying the dog Laika. | |

**1958**

| Date | Soviet Union | United States |
|------|-------------|---------------|
| 31 January | | USA launches its first satellite into orbit: Explorer I (weight 14 kg). |
| March | | US second and third satellites (weights 1.4 kg and 14.1 kg respectively) launched into orbit. |
| May | USSR launches Sputnik III (weight 1 326.5 kg). | |
| December | | US Atlas-A liquid-propelled ICBM successfully flight-tested with full thrust. |

**1959**

| Date | Soviet Union | United States |
|------|-------------|---------------|
| | Soviet "SS-4 Sandal" MRBM (range 1 040 nm) in service. | |
| 28 February | | USA launches first military satellite into orbit: Discoverer (weight 657.6 kg). |
| 15 September | | First successful firing of US solid-propellant missile (Mach 25) with intercontinental range. |

**1960**

| Date | Soviet Union | United States |
|------|-------------|---------------|
| | | USA deploys Hound Dog air-to-surface missiles (range 350 miles) on B-52 strategic bombers. |
| | | US B-58 supersonic (Mach 2) medium-range bomber in service. |
| | | US Atlas-A ICBM in service. |
| | | First US Polaris nuclear-powered submarine in service with Polaris A-1 SLBM (range 1 220 nm). |
| | | USA now has an arsenal of thousands of thermonuclear weapons and about 10 000 nuclear weapons. It is estimated that the world's nuclear arsenals contain the equivalent of some 30 000 megatons, mostly in US strategic weapons. |
| 22 June | | First US multiple satellite is launched. |

| Date | Soviet Union | United States |
|------|--------------|---------------|
| **1961** | Large Soviet air-to-surface missiles are identified at Soviet Aviation Day display. The "Kangaroo" missiles are carried by Tu-20 bombers. | USA deploys Quail air-launched bomber-defence air-to-surface missiles on B-52 strategic bombers. As missile build-up begins, the US SAC possesses nearly 1 700 intercontinental bombers, including 630 B-52s and 1 000 B-47s. |
| | Soviet "SS-5 Skean" IRBM (range 2 000 nm) in service. | |
| | | US Minuteman ICBM test-fired from operational underground silo. |
| | Soviet "SS-7 Saddler" ICBM (range 6 080 nm) in service. | |
| | Soviet "SS-N-4 Sark" SLBM (range 300 nm) in service in "G" class diesel-powered submarines. | |
| **1962** | | Last US B-bomber (the 744th) comes off lines. The B-52 has gone through a number of major model changes so that the final version, the B-52H, is very much more advanced than the original B-52A.[a] |
| | | US Titan-I liquid-propellant ICBM (range 6 255 nm) in service. |
| | | US Minuteman I solid-propellant ICBM (range 6 520 nm) in service. |
| | At this time, the USSR has about 100 Tu-20 "Bear" and 90 Mya-4 "Bison" long-range strategic bombers, in addition to 75 ICBMs. | By the end of the year, the USA has deployed 54 Titan, 90 Atlas and 150 Minuteman ICBMs, in addition to its large bomber force and growing SLBM force. |
| **1963** | | US IRBMs are withdrawn from Europe. |
| | | US Titan-II ICBM (capable of direct launching from its silo) in service, replacing Titan-I ICBM. Two squadrons of Titans, each with nine missiles, are based at each of three sites in the USA. |
| **1964** | Soviet "SS-N-5" SLBM (range 650 nm) in service in "H" class nuclear-powered submarines. The "SS-N-5" can be fired from a submerged position whereas the "SS-N-4" can only be fired from the surface. | Prototype US B-70 supersonic bomber (Mach 3) flight-tested; this aircraft would not be used operationally. |
| | | US Polaris A-3 SLBM (range 2 520 nm) with three MRVed missiles in service. |
| | | Development of US Poseidon MIRV (10–14 warheads, 40–50 kilotons each) and Minuteman MIRV (three warheads, 160–200 kilotons each) is approved. |

| Date | Soviet Union | United States |
|------|-------------|---------------|
| **1965** | | |
| | Soviet "SS-9 Scarp" ICBM (range 4 780 nm) in service. | US Atlas ICBMs are phased out. |
| | | For the first time, there are more missiles than bombers in the US strategic nuclear forces due to phase-out of B-47s and deployment of new Minuteman ICBMs. However, SAC bombers (630 B-52s) continue to carry about 80 per cent of the total megatonnage of the strategic nuclear forces. |
| **1966** | | |
| | Soviet "SS-11" ICBM (range 4 780 nm) in service. | US Minuteman-I ICBM (range 6 950 nm) in service. |
| | | US Polaris A-1 SLBM is phased out. There are now 28 US nuclear submarines armed with A-3s and 13 with A-2s. |
| **1967** | | |
| | Soviet fractional orbital bombardment system is flight-tested. | US land-based missiles are stabilized at 1 000 Minuteman ICBMs and 54 Titan-II ICBMs. |
| | | US decision to proceed with limited ABM deployment is announced. |
| **1968** | | |
| | Soviet "SS-13" ICBM (range 4 340 nm) in service. | |
| | USSR flight-tests MRV system for ICBM. | |
| **1969** | | |
| | Soviet ABM system around Moscow becomes operational. | |
| | Soviet "SS-N-6" SLBM (range 1 520 nm) in service in "Y" class nuclear-powered submarines. | |
| **1970** | | |
| | USSR continues to deploy nuclear submarines carrying SLBMs. | US FB-111 medium-range supersonic strategic bomber (Mach 2.2) in service in SAC. |
| | | US Minuteman-III MIRVed ICBM (range 6 950 nm) in service. |
| **1971** | | |
| | | US Poseidon submarine in service with MIRVed missiles (range 2 520 nm) to be carried on 31 "616" class submarines. |

| Date | Soviet Union | United States |
|------|--------------|---------------|
| **1972** | Soviet "SS-N-8" SLBM (range 2 606 nm) in service in new "D" class submarines. | USA deploys SRAM (short-range attack missile), air-to surface missile on B-52 (G–H models) and FB-111 strategic bombers to replace Hound Dog missiles. Each B-52 carries three SRAMs and each FB-111 four SRAMs. |
| **1973** | USSR reported to begin extended flight-test programme of MIRVed ICBMs. | |

| [a]*Model* | *First flight* | *Number built* |
|---------|-------------|--------------|
| B-52 A | 5 August 1954 | 3 |
| B-52 B | 25 January 1955 | 50 |
| B-52 C | 9 March 1956 | 35 |
| B-52 D | 4 June 1956 | 170 |
| B-52 E | 3 October 1957 | 100 |
| B-52 F | 6 May 1958 | 89 (last one completed November 1958) |
| B-52 G | 26 October 1958 | 193 (last one completed January 1961) |
| B-52 H | 6 March 1961 | 102 (last one completed June 1962) |

# 6. Developments in strategic nuclear weapons since SALT I

*Square-bracketed references, thus [1], refer to the list of references on page 119.*

## I. *Introduction*

The strategic weapon programmes which were underway in the United States and the Soviet Union at the conclusion of the first round of the Strategic Arms Limitation Talks (SALT) in May 1972, and new initiatives taken by both sides since that time, have now brought the two countries to a critical juncture in the strategic arms race. New generations of strategic weapons loom close and the systems that may follow these are already beginning to take shape in the plans of the weapon designers and the arguments of the strategists. At the same time, there are pressures on the two governments to achieve significant arms limitations and reductions in SALT II, both to build upon the limited success of SALT I in bringing the USA and the USSR to some mutual views and undertakings in the matter of controlling the arms race and to make up for the failure of SALT I to halt this race.

Of central importance to the likelihood of a new round in the strategic arms race and to prospects for preventing this are the recent Soviet development of MIRV technology, which was not surprising, and the redirection of US strategic weapon policy, which was.[1] The potential counterforce capability which Soviet MIRV developments might provide—particularly the capability to destroy a large fraction of US ICBMs in their silos—and the proposed new US programmes to improve further the existing capability of US forces to destroy a large portion of the Soviet ICBMs, as well as the likely interaction between these two developments,

[1] Signs of a possible change in US policy were in fact evident in the annual foreign policy statements of the President for 1970–72 [1–3] (for an assessment of these statements, see reference [4]); and the official announcement of the change, made in the posture statement of the Secretary of Defense in March 1974, [5] was preceded during 1973 and early 1974 by a number of articles and statements by administration spokesmen developing similar ideas (see for example references [6–11]). In addition, there were earlier proposals, and in some cases financial support, for some of the strategic weapon programmes which are proposed in the US fiscal year 1975 defence budget to support the new counterforce policy. These include the programmes to develop more accurate ICBMs with warheads of greater yield and to retain the option to deploy a larger number of Minuteman III missiles. [5, 12–14] However, the major change in US policy, involving a much more explicit attempt to acquire the capability to destroy the Soviet ICBM force, runs directly counter to earlier stated US policy: and a radical change of this sort was not generally foreseen outside the government until late 1973.

have stirred renewed concern with strategic weapon developments. Nuclear weapon doctrines and their relation to the capabilities of the forces are being examined afresh.

The intention of this chapter is to document recent developments in the deployed strategic weapons of the United States and the Soviet Union and in the new systems which are being evolved.[2] The chapter does not go into questions of strategy or policy: these are analysed in chapter 5. Some of the weapon developments which appear to be of particular significance in the light of the current debate are, however, singled out in the second part of this chapter. This is followed by a more detailed description of developments in particular weapon systems.

## II. *Main trends*

It is generally held that the main trend in US and Soviet strategic weapon developments is toward qualitative improvements rather than quantitative increases. The number of offensive nuclear-weapon delivery vehicles—bombers, intercontinental ballistic missiles (ICBMs), and submarine-launched ballistic missiles (SLBMs)—has tended to level off and, rather than deploying larger numbers of these aircraft and missiles, the USA and the USSR are replacing existing systems with newer and more effective ones.

This is particularly true of developments in the United States and rather less applicable—at least for the immediate present, if not for the near-term future—to Soviet programmes. The major increase in the number of US nuclear delivery vehicles took place in the first half of the 1960s, with the concurrent deployment of large forces of land- and sea-based ballistic missiles. The main growth in the Soviet ICBM force, on the other hand, took place in the second half of the 1960s, with the number of missile silos levelling out at about the same time as the first SALT negotiations began.[3] The build-up of the Soviet sea-based force began

---

[2] The scope of the chapter, in terms of the weapon systems discussed, is generally defined by the practice of US and Soviet government officials (particularly the former, as there is little information from the latter) in identifying their own and their opponent's strategic offensive and defensive systems. Even following their definitions, ambiguities arise relating to, first, whether shorter-range weapon systems should be included at all and, second, whether all existing units of certain longer-range systems should be counted. Two principles have been followed here: (*a*) to include all longer-range systems and to exclude shorter-range systems except when the latter are specifically assigned a strategic role by the country possessing them; and (*b*) to count all units of included types which are available for a strategic role on a longer-term basis, even if they are not specifically assigned this role at a particular time for one reason or another.

[3] Construction of the last 91 Soviet ICBM silos was initiated over the period from December 1970 to September 1971. [15–19] These silos stood empty, however, until late 1973, when a number of them began to be filled with modified "SS-11" missiles, accounting for the increase in the number of Soviet ICBMs from the 1 527 shown in table 6.1 for 1971 and 1972 to the 1 567 current level. The number of current Soviet ICBM launchers (1 527 with missiles plus 91 previously unfilled, for a total of 1 618), which has not changed since September 1971, is the maximum limit permitted to the Soviet Union under the SALT I agreements.

even later (in the late 1960s) and is still in progress. (See table 6.1.)

Despite the tendency of the number of strategic delivery vehicles on the two sides to level out—a trend at least temporarily sealed and codified by the SALT I agreements (table 6.2)—significant quantitative expansions in nuclear forces are continuing. The most important of these is, of course, that which results from MIRVed (multiple independently targetable re-entry vehicle) missile warheads, which are currently being deployed by the United States and developed by the Soviet Union. The US deployments involve the replacement of the majority of existing land- and submarine-based missiles by new MIRVed missiles (Minuteman III and Poseidon) in programmes which, between 1970 and 1977, will produce a five-fold increase (from about 2 000 to about 10 000) in the number of independent nuclear warheads that can be delivered by the missile forces. (The estimated numbers of warheads for 1970–74 are shown in table 6.1.) US development of MIRV was initiated in the early 1960s [20] and was publicly justified at the end of that decade by a requirement to penetrate possible future Soviet anti-ballistic missile (ABM) defences. ABM defences are limited by the SALT I ABM Treaty to a token number. US MIRV deployments had scarcely begun when the ABM Treaty was being negotiated; and it was widely recognized that these deployments would probably spur a similar development by the Soviet Union, giving rise to concern on both sides for the survivability of their ICBMs, and thence to pressures for development of alternative weapon systems. Installation of MIRVed missiles has nevertheless continued at a steady rate in the United States, both during and after SALT I.

The deployment of MIRVs has given the United States a very large quantitative lead over the Soviet Union in the number of deliverable nuclear warheads (see table 6.1). However, since the Soviet Union is currently developing MIRV technology and has deployed a larger number of land-based missiles, and missiles with a greater "throw-weight", it has the potential to close the gap and possibly exceed the USA in numbers of warheads.[4]

It is surprising that in the general assessment of the results of SALT I,

---

[4] Whether the USSR could match the USA in total force loadings depends of course not only on ICBM deployments, but also on bomber and SLBM deployments. The USSR now has launched or under construction more missile-carrying submarines than the USA (51 as against 41), but since 18 of these carry 12 rather than 16 missiles, the advantage in modern SLBMs is slight (744 to 656). If the USSR dismantles its older ICBMs and constructs the 11 additional submarines permitted under SALT I, equipping these with 16 missiles, it could still deploy the maximum allowed number of 950 SLBMs (including 30 older SLBMs on "H" class submarines). However, there has been no sign of development of MIRVs for the Soviet SLBMs. Consequently, the USSR could not match the number of MIRVed missile warheads now being deployed by the USA until after the expiration of the SALT I Interim Agreement on offensive missiles. Potential new missile deployments on both sides—including the planned US deployment of 240 MIRVed SLBMs on Trident submarines—as well as new constraints which may be negotiated in SALT II make it impossible to project the missile warhead balance beyond the late 1970s, a time at which the USA will still have a substantial lead. In bombers and bomber force loadings, the United States has a large edge, which it will retain for the foreseeable future.

**Table 6.1. US and Soviet strategic nuclear forces, 1965–74**

Mid-year (1 July) figures

| | | Intro-duced | Maximum range, nm | Payload | 1965 | 1966 | 1967 | 1968 | 1969 | 1970 | 1971 | 1972 | 1973 | 1974 |
|---|---|---|---|---|---|---|---|---|---|---|---|---|---|---|
| **Delivery vehicles** | | | | | | | | | | | | | | |
| *Strategic bombers* | | | | | | | | | | | | | | |
| USA | B-52C/D/E/F | 1956 | 10000 | 27 210 kg | (375) | (345) | (334) | (283) | (218) | (206) | (206) | (167) | (146) | (146) |
| | B-52G/H | 1959 | 10 860 | 34 015 kg | (283) | (283) | (283) | (283) | (283) | (283) | (283) | 282 | 274 | 274 |
| | B-58 | 1960 | (2 000) | 5 442 kg | 80 | 80 | 80 | 80 | 80 | – | – | – | – | – |
| | FB-111 | 1970 | 3 300 | 16 780 kg | | | | | | (28) | (76) | 76 | 76 | 76 |
| USSR | Mya-4 "Bison" | 1955 | 5 255 | 9 070 kg | 55 | 55 | 55 | 50 | 40 | 40 | 40 | 40 | 40 | 40 |
| | Tu-20 "Bear" | 1956 | 6 775 | 18 140 kg | 100 | 100 | 100 | 100 | 100 | 100 | 100 | 100 | 100 | 100 |
| | **Bomber total: USA** | | | | **(738)** | **(708)** | **697** | **646** | **581** | **517** | **565** | **525** | **496** | **496** |
| | **USSR** | | | | **155** | **155** | **155** | **150** | **140** | **140** | **140** | **140** | **140** | **140** |
| *Strategic submarines* | | | | | | | | | | | | | | |
| USA | With Polaris A-1 | 1960 | (unlimited) | 16×A-1 | 5 | 4 | – | – | – | – | – | – | – | – |
| | With Polaris A-2 | 1962 | (unlimited) | 16×A-2 | 13 | 13 | 13 | 13 | 13 | 8 | 8 | 8 | 8 | 6 |
| | With Polaris A-3 | 1964 | (unlimited) | 16×A-3 | 11 | 20 | 28 | 28 | 28 | 32 | 25 | 19 | 13 | 11 |
| | With Poseidon C-3 | 1970 | (unlimited) | 16×C-3 | – | – | – | – | – | 1 | 8 | 14 | 20 | 24 |
| USSR | With "SS-N-6" | 1967 | (unlimited) | 16×"SS-N-6" | – | – | – | (2) | (8) | (14) | (21) | (27) | 33 | 33 |
| | With "SS-N-8" | 1972 | (unlimited) | 12×"SS-N-8" | – | – | – | – | – | – | – | 1 | 3 | (9) |
| | **Submarine total: USA** | | | | **29** | **37** | **41** | **41** | **41** | **41** | **41** | **41** | **41** | **41** |
| | **USSR** | | | | **–** | **–** | **–** | **2** | **8** | **14** | **21** | **28** | **36** | **42** |
| *SLBMs (submarine-launched ballistic missiles)* | | | | | | | | | | | | | | |
| USA | Polaris A-1 | 1960 | 1 300 | 1×800 kt | 80 | 64 | – | – | – | – | – | – | – | – |
| | Polaris A-2 | 1962 | 1 520 | 1×800 kt | 208 | 208 | 208 | 208 | 208 | 128 | 128 | 128 | 128 | 96 |
| | Polaris A-3 | 1964 | 2 500 | 3×200 kt (MRV) | 176 | 320 | 448 | 448 | 448 | 512 | 400 | 304 | 208 | 176 |
| | Poseidon C-3 | 1970 | 2 500 | 10-14×40 kt (MIRV) | – | – | – | – | – | 16 | 128 | 224 | 320 | 384 |
| USSR | "SS-N-6" | 1967 | 1 300 | 1×1 mt | – | – | – | 32 | 128 | 224 | 336 | 432 | 528 | 528 |
| | "SS-N-8" | 1972 | 4 200 | 1×1 mt | – | – | – | – | – | – | – | 12 | 36 | 108 |
| | **SLBM total: USA** | | | | **464** | **592** | **656** | **656** | **656** | **656** | **656** | **656** | **656** | **656** |
| | **USSR** | | | | **–** | **–** | **–** | **32** | **128** | **224** | **336** | **444** | **564** | **636** |

*ICBMs (intercontinental ballistic missiles)*

| | | | | | | | | | | | | |
|---|---|---|---|---|---|---|---|---|---|---|---|---|
| **USA** | Titan I | 1961 | 1×5–10 mt | 54 | 54 | 54 | 54 | 54 | 54 | 54 | 54 | 54 | 54 |
| | Minuteman I | 1962 | 1×1 mt | 800 | 800 | 700 | 600 | 500 | 490 | 390 | 290 | (190) | (100) |
| | Minuteman II | 1966 | 1×2 mt | – | 80 | 300 | 400 | 500 | 500 | 500 | 500 | 500 | 500 |
| | Minuteman III | 1970 | 3×160 kt (MIRV) | – | – | – | – | – | 10 | 110 | 210 | (310) | (400) |
| **USSR** | "SS-7 Saddler" | 1961 | 1×5 mt | 150 | 150 | 150 | 150 | 150 | 150 | 139 | 139 | 139 | 139 |
| | "SS-8 Sasin" | 1963 | 1×5 mt | 70 | 70 | 70 | 70 | 70 | 70 | 70 | 70 | 70 | 70 |
| | "SS-9 Scarp" | 1964 | 1×20 mt | 42 | 108 | 162 | 192 | 228 | 288 | 288 | 288 | 288 | 288 |
| | "SS-11 mod. 1" | 1965 | 1×1 mt | – | (10) | (330) | (470) | (720) | (950) | 970 | 970 | 970 | 970 |
| | "SS-13" | 1967 | 1×1 mt | – | – | (10) | (20) | (30) | (40) | 60 | 60 | 60 | 60 |
| | "SS-11 mod. 3" | 1973 | 3×200 kt (MRV) | – | – | – | – | – | – | – | – | 20 | 40 |
| **ICBM total: USA** | | | | **854** | **934** | **1 054** | **1 054** | **1 054** | **1 054** | **1 054** | **1 054** | **1 054** | **1 054** |
| **USSR** | | | | **262** | **338** | **722** | **902** | **(1 198)** | **(1 498)** | **1 527** | **1 527** | **1 547** | **1 567** |
| **Total bombers and missiles: USA** | | | | **2 056** | **2 334** | **2 407** | **2 354** | **2 291** | **2 227** | **2 275** | **2 235** | **2 206** | **2 206** |
| **USSR** | | | | **417** | **493** | **877** | **1 084** | **1 466** | **1 862** | **2 003** | **2 111** | **2 251** | **2 343** |

**Independently-targetable nuclear warheads**

*Missile (ICBM and SLBM) warheads*

| | | | | | | | | | | | |
|---|---|---|---|---|---|---|---|---|---|---|---|
| **USA** | Maximum capacity (incl 14 warheads per Poseidon) | 1 318 | 1 526 | 1 710 | 1 710 | 1 710 | 1 938 | 3 594 | 5 042 | 6 490 | 7 502 |
| | Estimated actual total (incl 10 warheads per Poseidon) | 1 318 | 1 526 | 1 710 | 1 710 | 1 710 | 1 874 | 3 082 | 4 146 | 5 210 | 5 966 |
| | Estimated actual total (=maximum capacity) | 262 | 338 | 722 | 934 | 1 326 | 1 722 | 1 863 | 1 971 | 2 111 | 2 203 |

*Official US estimates of total warheads on bombers and missiles*

| | | | | | | | | | | |
|---|---|---|---|---|---|---|---|---|---|---|
| **USA** | .. | .. | 4 500 | 4 200 | 4 200 | 4 000 | 4 600 | 5 700 | 6 784 | 7 940 |
| **USSR** | .. | .. | 1 000 | 1 100 | 1 350 | 1 800 | 2 100 | 2 500 | 2 200 | 2 600 |

For sources and notes, see page 108.

## Sources and notes for table 6.1 (pages 106–107)

The estimates for 1974 are projected figures based on numbers operational and under construction in January 1974.

### USA

#### Strategic bombers

The figures for the total number of US bombers for 1967–74 are taken from the posture statements of the US Secretary of Defense. [5, 38–44] B-58 and FB-111 estimates are also taken from official sources. The division of B-52s between the older types with more limited capabilities (C, D, E, and F versions—in recent years, D and F only) and the newer G and H versions is derived from official data for the 1972–74 period and for 1966. The data for the latter year show that the number of "active" B-52G/Hs was then the same as in 1972 (255) and also provide the figure given in the table for the remaining B-52s. [45] Estimates for B-52C/D/E/F for other years are derived by subtraction, using the other figures shown in the table.

The difficulty in giving estimates for bombers lies mainly in finding figures for the period concerned which conform to a single definition as regards the status of the aircraft. The estimates given here are intended to represent the "total active inventory": this includes units in "active storage" and those assigned to other missions which could be returned to "unit equipped" status (that is, being assigned to a strategic bomber unit and having the requisite armament and equipment allocated), if that were desired. This definition was chosen because it appeared to provide figures most comparable with the only ones available for the Soviet Union, and with the definition generally (though not necessarily always) used in the Secretary of Defense's posture statement, and because it offered a better basis for constructing a continuous series than did any other alternative. The numbers of bombers actually assigned a strategic role at any given time were generally lower throughout the period covered, and especially during the B-52 bombing in South-East Asia, than the figures given here.

#### ICBMs

Estimates of the numbers of Minuteman I, II and III for the period 1967–72 have been taken from a publication of the US Congressional Research Service, [46] after comparison and corroboration with other

sources. The figures for 1966 are from an official source [38] and those for 1973 and 1974 rely heavily on a paper by the officer in charge of the Minuteman programme, within the USAF Space and Missiles Organization [27] (see also references [13] and [47]).

#### Strategic submarines and SLBMs

The estimates of the SLBM-carrying submarines are obtained directly from the dates of commissioning and, in the case of submarines converted from one type of missile to another, the dates on which the conversion overhauls were completed. [48–49] Following a convention also applied to ICBMs, submarines undergoing conversion are treated as retaining their former ability until the conversion is completed. The numbers of SLBMs are derived directly by multiplying the numbers of submarines equipped with a particular missile by 16 (the number of missiles per ship).

Official US estimates of the total number of strategic submarines and the total number of SLBM launchers after 1969 show the same, constant aggregate sum as that given here. As regards the numbers of particular types of missile, the numbers of submarines equipped with a particular type of missile, or the force loadings (warheads) on SLBMs, official US estimates diverge from this practice, however, and exclude vessels and launchers under conversion. Moreover, it appears that converted vessels are generally not counted in the new category until the date when they are assigned their first patrol, following conversion. For this reason, US estimates of SLBM force loadings (as well as ICBM force loadings, for ICBMs under conversion) tend to lag behind the estimates of ICBM and SLBM warhead capacity which appear in the last section of this table. Sufficient information was not available to construct continuous series of the numbers of "operational" ICBMs and SLBMs as defined in the occasional official estimates for individual types (that is, excluding units under conversion but including, for example, units in overhaul or otherwise temporarily non-operational).

#### Independently-targetable nuclear warheads

The numbers of missile warheads are derived directly from the data given in the preceding parts of the table relating to ICBMs and SLBMs: they are obtained by multiplying the number of missiles of each type by the number of independently-targetable warheads that type carries and summing the results. In the case of the MIRVed Poseidon C-3 it is not known exactly how many warheads are carried, and in this case, therefore, the calculations are based on assumptions. Two alternative calculations are presented. One uses figures which are widely accepted to represent the maximum number of warheads which can presently be carried on this missile (14). It is not known whether any of the deployed missiles actually carry the full potential complement of 14 warheads, but it is possible that some do so. In any case, the "maximum capacity" figures are undoubtedly larger than the actual number of force loadings. Missiles which do not carry the maximum number of warheads can carry penetration aids instead or they can provide extended range. A widely used figure for the second calculation, which should therefore provide estimates close to commonly accepted values for the actual number of warheads deployed on US ICBMs and SLBMs.

The official US estimates of total force loadings are taken from the annual posture statements. [5, 38-43] They differ from the estimates of the number of missile warheads in the following ways: (a) they include the nuclear warheads carried by the strategic bombers; (b) they exclude estimates of the warheads which can be carried by ICBMs and SLBMs under conversion; and (c) they presumably include the exact number of warheads carried by the "operational" ICBMs and SLBMs, rather than an approximation. It is not known whether the official estimates refer to independently-targetable warheads (that is, treating missiles with MRVs as having a single targetable warhead) or whether they treat each MRV warhead separately, or whether they are based on a consistent method of calculation from one year to the next. An alternative official estimate for 1972 specified the "independent force loadings" on bombers as numbering 2460 and on "operational" ICBMs and SLBMs as 3428, a total of 5 888. [50]

## USSR

### Comparability

There are two significant sources of non-comparability between the figures for the Soviet Union and those for the United States. First, it is not known whether any of the Soviet aircraft listed as strategic bombers are in fact assigned this role and it is doubtful whether they are equipped and deployed for carrying it out. Second, for both land-based missiles and

strategic submarines and their missiles, the figures shown for the Soviet Union represent the number of launchers estimated to have begun deployment by the dates indicated (in the case of silos, the number on which construction had begun, and in the case of submarines, the number launched) and not the number which may have been operational. Most of the published information relates to new starts; and rather than introduce time lags to allow for the period required to achieve operational status (generally one to two years), series have been constructed which follow the source material more closely.

One class of Soviet nuclear-powered submarine with ballistic missiles is excluded from the table—the "H" class, with "SS-N-5" missiles. Three "SS-N-5" missiles were refitted into each of 10 "H" class submarines in the period between 1963 and 1967. The "SS-N-5" has a much shorter range than any of the SLBMs included in the table (650 nautical miles), with the result that this SLBM system would be far more vulnerable to anti-submarine warfare countermeasures if it were deployed to cover targets in the United States. It is only rarely mentioned in discussions of the strategic forces of the two countries.

### Delivery vehicles

The estimates for the number of Soviet bombers are taken from the US posture statements, [5, 38-43] as are most of the figures for the total number of ICBMs. The numbers of "SS-9" are taken from an earlier SIPRI study: [51] and the numbers of "SS-11" and "SS-13" are interpolated, on the basis of the date they were introduced, the date and size of the ultimate total deployment and the US estimates of total ICBM numbers. Similarly, for the numbers of strategic submarines and related figures for SLBMs, an even rate of introduction was assumed up to the final deployment. This produced figures which appeared to be generally consistent with a variety of estimates which were made at the time these submarines were being deployed, but which tended to be revised up or down by a small number every few months.

### Independently-targetable nuclear warheads

The estimates of Soviet independently-targetable missile warheads are obtained by summing the numbers of missiles. The US estimates of total Soviet force loadings are taken from the posture statements. [5, 38-43]

**Table 6.2. SALT ceilings**

| Weapon system | USA | USSR |
|---|---|---|
| ICBM launchers | 1 000–1 054 | 1 408–1 618 |
| SLBM launchers | 710 | 950 |
| Ballistic missile submarines | 44 | 62 |
| ABMs | 2 sites, 100 missiles each | 2 sites, 100 missiles each |

the US advantage in MIRV technology was often cited as the main *qualitative* advantage on the US side offsetting the quantitative advantage in ICBMs and SLBMs permitted to the Soviet Union under the Interim Agreement on offensive strategic weapons. While the US lead of five years or more in the development of MIRV systems is undoubtedly a good indicator of a more general US technological advantage, the significance of the MIRV lead lies mainly in its quantitative impact. There are other areas of technology in which the United States has long held qualitative advantages which cannot easily be incorporated in an overall quantitative comparison of the forces. These include five important areas in which continuing advances have been made by the United States in the period since SALT I. The first is missile accuracy, which provides the capability to destroy ICBMs in hardened silos. The Minuteman III and Poseidon missiles currently being introduced into the US forces have an accuracy of about one-quarter of a nautical mile,[5] an improvement over the previous land- and sea-based missiles by a factor of two. Current Soviet ICBMs and SLBMs are generally credited with an accuracy of about one mile. Programmes to improve accuracies are underway in both the United States and the Soviet Union: but whereas improvements on the US side are clearly within reach, given the present state of US technology, [12, 23] the latest systems under development in the Soviet Union are reported not to have shown any significant improvement in accuracy.[6]

Second, all 1 000 modern US ICBM silos are "hardened" (reinforced with structures of concrete and steel) to withstand nuclear blast overpressure of about 300 pounds per square inch (psi). These silos are now being upgraded to a level of at least 900 psi [26] and possibly considerably more.[7] In the case of the Soviet Union, only two-thirds of the current ICBM force is believed to be emplaced in silos capable of withstanding

[5] There have been reports that the present accuracy of the Minuteman III is as good as 0.15 nautical miles (see, for example, references [21–22]).

[6] The "SS-N-8" is reported to be equipped with a stellar inertial guidance system which "has done little to improve the accuracy of the missile". [24] (The new guidance system may have contributed to maintaining previously achieved SLBM accuracy over a considerably extended range.) Similarly, although the new Soviet land-based missiles under development are said to be "designed for increased accuracy", [5] with new guidance systems and improved re-entry vehicle design, "US experts believe the accuracy of these missiles will probably not be sufficient to prevent a decline in Soviet hard-target capability". [25]

[7] The officer in charge of the Minuteman programme has reported that "With the higher hardness goals applying to all of our launchers, we are finding, as one might suspect, that

110

300 psi overpressure: silos of the other missiles, including the large "SS-9s", are estimated to have a 100 psi resistance or, in the case of the older "SS-7s" and "SS-8s", as little as 5 psi. [21–22] The 90 latest Soviet silos are believed to have been hardened to 600 psi [22] but there is no evidence of substantially increased hardening of the 1 527 earlier missile silos.

Third, a new US advantage in ICBMs, introduced within the past year, is that of "remote retargeting" of missiles from launcher control facilities. Even earlier, the United States had some lead in this area, since it could "preprogramme" Minuteman II missiles with up to eight alternative targets, as compared with the one to two targets which could be set in the earliest US ICBMs or in present Soviet missiles. For the Minuteman III, the number of alternative targets is essentially unlimited. This capability is useful in the event of a US counterforce attack against Soviet ICBMs, since it permits rapid and flexible replacement of first-round missiles which are observed to fail.

Fourth, continuing advances have been made by the United States in strategic bomber range and payload (including advances in the B-1 bomber, which is still under development). There have also been improvements in "escape time" and in the resistance of installed equipment to the effects of electromagnetic pulses, which increase the survivability of the bomber fleet in the event of an attack by Soviet nuclear forces.

Finally, US naval officials estimate that the United States has a considerable lead in the quietness and reliability of its strategic submarines. [28] This increases their invulnerability to antisubmarine warfare (ASW) efforts. Installment of "submarine quieting" equipment which will further improve the performance of the US strategic submarines is being undertaken at the same time as the fitting of the new MIRVed missile (Poseidon).

One new area of qualitative advantage on the Soviet side has been observed in the past two years. At the end of 1972 the Soviet Union tested a new SLBM ("SS-N-8") out to a range of 4 200 nautical miles—a vast improvement over its first longer-range SLBMs (the "SS-N-6", with a range of 1 500 nautical miles, equaling that of the US SLBMs introduced in 1962) and one which gave the Soviet Union a considerable advantage over the United States in SLBM range. However, when payload is taken into account, the Soviet advantage declines. The "SS-N-8" is believed to carry about the same payload as the US Polaris A-3; and the current US Poseidon C-3, which has the same range as the Polaris A-3 (2 500 nautical miles), is reported to weigh three times as much as, and to carry twice the payload of, the A-3. A reduction of the larger payload of the Poseidon would result in increased range: the potential range of the Poseidon has been kept secret, but published estimates range from more than 3 000 nautical miles to 4 300 nautical miles. [29–31]

a large number of the silos greatly exceed these goals". [27] Unofficial reports have put the hardness of the upgraded silos at 1 200 psi. [22]

The main effect of the on-going US programmes in offensive strategic weapons is to increase the invulnerability of the forces to Soviet attack or countermeasures and to improve their capability to attack Soviet land-based nuclear forces. This improvement in counterforce capability results mainly from the continuing increases in the number of missile warheads and in the accuracy of the delivery of these warheads—two areas in which the United States has a great advantage over the Soviet Union. The silo-hardening and "submarine-quieting" programmes, along with the development of a new, longer-range SLBM (Trident), account for the main increase in the invulnerability of the forces.

Unlike the US programmes, recent Soviet deployments have done little to increase the counterforce capabilities of Soviet strategic forces. However, the deployment of the new, longer-range Soviet SLBM will provide the USSR with a very considerable increase in the invulnerability of its submarine-based force to US ASW. The first generation of Soviet strategic submarines has been much more vulnerable to US ASW efforts than US submarines are to Soviet ASW, not only because of less advanced Soviet submarine and ASW technology, but also because of the geographic constraints within which the Soviet force must operate. This is more a matter of relative than absolute vulnerability, since locating and tracking a large number of submarines in the ocean is considered a virtually impossible task (see chapter 10). However, because of the limited range of the earlier SLBMs, Soviet strategic submarines had to pass through closely watched channels before coming within range of the US coasts. This requirement, combined with rapid US production of nuclear-powered "hunter-killer" submarines,[8] which are the only platforms with the quietness, speed and endurance needed to attempt submarine tracking, presented some risk that a significant portion of the Soviet sea-based force might be vulnerable to attack. With the longer-range missiles, the Soviet strategic submarines will be able to cover US targets without traversing areas where they are more subject to detection.

Soviet testing of new, large MIRVed ICBMs with a relatively large number of warheads (four to six) suggests a potential to develop a land-based missile force with counterforce capabilities comparable with those presently being introduced in the United States. The exploitation of this potential would require the development of greatly improved missile accuracies, as well as full use of the large potential throw-weight of the

[8] The United States now has 48 nuclear-powered hunter-killer submarines of newer classes introduced since 1962. [32] Production has been underway at a rate of more than five per year since 1967 and is scheduled to continue at this high level until at least 1980. By that time the number of newer types will be 82—a figure which should be set against the SALT limit of 62 strategic submarines for the Soviet Union. The Soviet Union currently has a large fleet of nuclear-powered submarines, but most of these are equipped primarily for counter-ship activities. There are at most 28 Soviet nuclear-powered hunter-killer submarines, of three classes designed before 1960, and no new vessels of this type are known to have been introduced in the past five years.

new missiles. Over the long term, a capability to destroy virtually all of the US ICBM force might be evolved. The Soviet lag in missile accuracy is, however, such that it would probably require a considerable time to develop this potential, particularly in view of the super-hardened silos under construction in the United States. The US programmes to improve ICBM guidance, warhead yield and warhead numbers, which have been proposed in the budget for fiscal year 1975 (July 1974—June 1975), if approved, would permit a much more rapid US acquisition of the capability to destroy the entire Soviet land-based missile force. The dangers of these developments are analysed in chapter 5.

## III. *Developments in specific weapon systems*

### Intercontinental ballistic missiles

The most dramatic developments in US and Soviet strategic forces which have taken place in the past two years are those discussed above relating to the land-based missiles, in particular the Soviet tests of three new ICBMs with MIRVed warheads and the proposed US programmes to improve the counterforce capabilities of its Minuteman missiles.

In all, four new Soviet ICBMs were observed on the testing grounds in 1973. These have been given the US designations "SS-X-16" to "SS-X-19". The "SS-X-18", which is believed to be a replacement for the very large "SS-9", is reported to have been tested with either five [5] or six [7] MIRV warheads of about one megaton each. The "SS-X-17" and "SS-X-19", believed to be competitive potential replacements for the "SS-11", have been tested with smaller MIRV warheads—four per missile in the case of the "SS-X-17" and six in the case of the "SS-X-19". Multiple re-entry vehicle tests of the "SS-X-16" have not been observed, although the warhead is believed to be a MIRV "bus".[9] The "SS-X-16" resembles the currently deployed "SS-13" and differs from all of the other Soviet ICBMs in that it is powered by a solid rather than a liquid propellant. This has given rise to the view that the "SS-X-16" may be a replacement for the "SS-13". However, the "SS-13" has been deployed in small numbers (60 out of a total of 1 550 Soviet ICBMs); and it has been suggested that the "SS-X-16" may be a prototype mobile ICBM rather than an "SS-13" replacement.

The MIRV tests conducted by the Soviet Union in 1973 were the first tests of a Soviet MIRV bus system. The earlier development of a system

[9] A MIRV "bus" is a warhead capable of dispensing individual nuclear-tipped re-entry vehicles at separate points and also capable of manoeuvring in the intervals between release of the re-entry vehicles, permitting the latter to be aimed at separate targets.

113

of this type in the United States required about two years from the first test to the first deployment of an operational system. It may be assumed than an equal period of development, and possibly a somewhat longer one, will be required for the Soviet Union. It had been expected that the first Soviet MIRV missiles—if and when such missiles appeared—would be deployed in 91 silos on which construction was initiated in late 1970 and which stood empty until late 1973. However, at the latter date, the Soviet Union began filling 60 of these silos with an improved "SS-11", tested earlier in 1973 with three multiple but not independently targetable warheads (MRVs). This MRV deployment would appear to preclude the most rapid possible deployment of a MIRVed "SS-11" follow-on missile and it raises a question as to the imminence of Soviet MIRV deployment of any sort.

The new Soviet missiles are larger than the currently deployed ones and are believed to have greater "throw-weight". The "SS-X-18" is estimated to have 30 per cent more throw-weight than the "SS-9", while the "SS-X-17" and "SS-X-19" are reported to have three to five times the throw-weight of the "SS-11". In addition, the "SS-X-17" and "SS-X-19" are said to have warheads shaped for high speed atmospheric re-entry, which would permit the development of considerably improved accuracy.

Two Soviet ICBM technology development programmes which were reported to be under way in late 1973 [33] have a bearing on the possibility of further development and deployment of the new ICBMs. One of these is a programme involving manoeuvring re-entry vehicles (MARVs). Since advanced MARV technology can provide pinpoint accuracy, by permitting guidance in the final stage of the flight path, this programme increases the likelihood that the new ICBMs will eventually be deployed in versions much more accurate than the existing ones. The second programme involves the development of "pop-up" techniques, in which missiles are ejected from their silos prior to the ignition of their rocket motors. The use of these techniques permits the emplacement of larger missiles in silos of a given size; and it appears that the additional volume that could be gained would be more than sufficient to allow backfitting of the new larger ICBMs into existing silos.

In the United States, the major ICBM activity in 1972 and 1973 was the continuation of the Minuteman III conversion programme which, like the Poseidon programme, involves the replacement of existing missiles with a new MIRVed version. Under the original programme, a total of 550 Minuteman III missiles, each capable of carrying three MIRV warheads, were scheduled to replace half of the existing 1 000-missile Minuteman I and II force over the period from 1970 to 1975. Funds for the final increment of Minuteman III missiles, to meet the deployment plan of 550, were allocated in 1973. In addition, in the budget for fiscal year 1975, there is a request for procurement of long lead-time components which would be required if a decision is made later to replace some or all the remaining 450 Minuteman II missiles with Minuteman III.

The retention of this option to procure additional MIRVed Minuteman III missiles is one of a number of programmes proposed in the FY 1975 budget to permit an increase in the counterforce capabilities of the US land-based missile force. These programmes include two new projects to improve ICBM accuracy: the "Minuteman III Guidance" project and the "MARV [Manoeuvring Re-entry Vehicle], Accuracy" portion of the ABRES (Advanced Ballistic Re-entry Systems) programme. In addition, funds have been requested for the expansion of the following projects which were already under way in 1973: one project to increase the numbers of re-entry vehicles (independently targetable warheads) deployed on Minuteman III missiles, and another to increase the yield of the individual warheads; continued development of the "Missile Performance Measurement System", which provides better data on missile operation during testing and thus permits improvements; continuation of work on the general ABRES project; and further development of the evasion capabilities of the manoeuvring re-entry vehicle (MARV) being designed as part of the ABRES project.

In addition to these programmes directed specifically at improvements in counterforce capabilities, a project to develop a new ICBM is proposed. If this project is approved, consideration is to be given to both mobile land-based and airborne launching platforms.

## Submarine-launched ballistic missiles and ballistic-missile submarines

The conversion of 31 of the 41 US strategic submarines from Polaris missiles, with single warheads or three MRVed warheads, to Poseidon missiles, capable of carrying 10–14 MIRVed warheads, continued in 1972 and 1973. The programme is now about two-thirds complete, 24 submarines having been converted by early 1974. Development of the Poseidon missile was initiated in 1965 and the first Poseidon-equipped submarine was operationally deployed in February 1971. There have been several postponements in the conversion schedule, which now runs to mid-1977. When the last conversion is completed, the number of independently targetable warheads carried by the Polaris/Poseidon fleet will have increased from 656 to an estimated 5 120.

Work on a follow-on SLBM, the C-4 Trident, entered engineering development in 1973, and funds for procurement of the first Trident submarine, which is to carry 24 ballistic missiles, were approved. It was originally planned that the Trident missile should be initially deployed in existing ballistic-missile submarines ("LaFayette" class), in advance of the availability of the Trident submarine. However, in the spring of 1973, it was announced that development of the missile would be extended for an additional year, so that the initial operating date—now 1978—would coincide with that of the new submarine; and plans for backfitting the missile to the current SLBM fleet were suspended.

Considerable opposition to the rapidity of the development of the Trident system was raised in the US Congress during the debate on the budget for fiscal year 1974. There was strong objection in particular to the commitment to the design of a new submarine at a time when foreseeable advances in ASW technology do not appear to pose any threat to the invulnerability to the present US ballistic-missile submarines, the last of which was completed in 1967. Improvements in the ASW-countermeasure capabilities of the current fleet, including the latest antisubmarine sensors and weapons as well as special ASW countermeasure devices and submarine-silencing, which are being incorporated during overhauls and Poseidon conversions, appear more than adequate to outmatch Soviet ASW equipment. The additional range—to provide more hiding space— offered by the Trident missile (4 000 nautical miles, compared with 2 500 nautical miles for Polaris A-3 or Poseidon) could be gained from deployment in the current fleet. Indeed, as observed above, a reduction of warheads on the Poseidon missile, which is about twice as large as the Polaris, could in itself produce a considerable increase in the range of this missile, obviating any perceived need for the Trident missile at the present time. A Senate amendment to cut funds for the Trident on grounds of this type lost by a narrow margin (47 to 49), however, and the only apparent consequence of the debate was the subsequent reintroduction of the plan to backfit the missile in existing submarines, although in addition to, rather than instead of, fitting it in the Trident submarine.

Among the new programmes requested in the US budget for fiscal year 1975 is yet another follow-on strategic submarine. This vessel, which is to be somewhat larger than the current Polaris/Poseidon submarines, will carry 16 of the new Trident missiles. The proposed submarine will be much smaller than the Trident submarine and will have a very quiet watercooled reactor of a new type developed for the experimental *Narwhal* submarine. As a result of its smaller size and quiet propulsion system, the proposed new submarine will probably be quieter than the Trident, and therefore even more invulnerable to Soviet ASW.

The major development of the past two years in Soviet sea-based strategic forces was the testing, mentioned above, of the new, longer-range "SS-N-8" SLBM in the autumn of 1972, followed by the deployment of this missile in new "D" class submarines, the first of which had been reported under construction earlier in 1972.

Construction of the earlier "Y" class submarine, with 16 "SS-N-6" missiles, as well as the new "D" class, with 12 "SS-N-8"s, has continued at the rate of five-six per year, with current construction apparently devoted entirely to the "D" class. According to US defence officials, a total of 33 "Y" class ships have been built, and all of the remaining 18–19 vessels launched or under construction are of the "D" class.

In September 1973, it was reported that a new Soviet class of strategic submarine, larger than either of the previous ones and with 16 launchers for larger, "SS-N-8"-sized missiles, had been sighted off the coast of Norway. No subsequent reports relating to this development have been found; and in the annual US military assessment of Soviet advances in strategic weapons which appeared in early 1974, the class was described as a possible, but not a definite development. [34] It was, however, reported that tests of a longer-range MRV version of the "SS-N-6" had been conducted and that deployment of the improved missile in "Y" class submarines might be expected.

With regard to improvements in US SLBM technology, two new projects associated with increasing counterforce capabilities have been proposed in the US FY 1975 budget. One is a programme intended specifically to work toward increases in the accuracy of existing SLBMs and the other is a project to develop a manoueuvring re-entry vehicle, capable of undertaking evasion tactics, for the Trident missile. In addition, a new navigation satellite system called the Global Positioning System (formerly Defense Navigation Satellite System) is under development to provide "a continuous, worldwide, all-weather positioning capability with an accuracy of tens of feet in three dimensions". [35] This system, for which the first launch is to take place in 1977 and limited global capability to be achieved by 1981, will also help to increase the accuracy of SLBMs.

Both the United States and the Soviet Union have recently encountered difficulties in tests of their new SLBMs. A high failure rate (58 per cent) in tests of the Poseidon missile in the summer of 1973 has led to a US programme to replace certain components of this missile during submarine overhauls over the next three years. And at the end of 1973, a planned three-week "SS-N-8" test series in the Soviet Union was abruptly ended after three days, apparently due to serious missile failures.

**Anti-ballistic missiles**

Both the United States and the Soviet Union have restricted deployment of anti-ballistic missiles (ABMs) to a single site, but both have also continued to work on more advanced ABM technology. No new ABM deployments have been observed in the Soviet Union since the time of the SALT I agreements, and the USSR still has 64 ABM launchers located in four groups around Moscow. The United States has continued with the deployment of 100 ABM launchers (30 for the longer-range Spartan missile and 70 for the shorter-range Sprint) around the Grand Forks, North Dakota, Minuteman ICBM site. The US ABM system is scheduled to be fully operational in June 1975.

## Strategic bombers, bomber-launched weapons and air-defence systems

The development of the B-1 strategic bomber, a long-range supersonic aircraft which can fly intercontinental missions without refuelling, is one of the major current US strategic weapon projects. The B-1 is designed for Mach 2.2 speeds at high altitudes, and high subsonic speed at low altitudes for flying past air defence systems at altitudes below radar acquisition ranges. It will carry a larger payload than the B-52 and more sophisticated electronic equipment. Development was initiated in 1970, the first prototype flight is scheduled for mid-1974 and the earliest expected date for a decision on series production is late 1976. If the system is procured, an order of 241 is now planned. The development cost of $2.8 billion and projected average unit price of $56 million make it the most expensive military aircraft ever undertaken.

The rationale for the development of the B-1 is to assure penetration of the Soviet air-defence system. The number of surface-to-air missiles deployed in the Soviet Union has apparently declined slightly recently, but remains very large (of the order of 9 000–10 000). The majority of these missiles are standard Soviet anti-aircraft missiles ("SA-2" and "SA-3") against which the United States has developed effective electronic countermeasure pods for tactical use. [36] Several other strategic weapon programmes in addition to the B-1 have, however, also been pursued by the USA as a counter to these defences. Two of these are the SRAM (Short-Range Attack Missile) and the SCAD (Subsonic Cruise Armed Decoy) programmes.

Operational deployment of SRAMs on US B-52G/H and FB-111 bombers (a maximum of 20 on the former and six on the latter) began in August 1972. Production of the full complement of 1 500 missiles for this deployment (including about 400 reserve missiles) is expected to be completed in late 1975. Additional procurement of SRAMs for deployment on the B-1 is expected if the B-1 is approved for production; and attempts are now being made to find ways to keep the production line open in the one- to two-year interval before the B-1 production decision.

SRAM is intended for use both as a defence suppression weapon— striking surface-to-air missiles, air-defence radars, and so on, to permit bomber penetration—and as a stand-off weapon, permitting the aircraft to attack targets of value located near the border without crossing the air-defence perimeter.

Development of the SCAD, which was also to have been deployed on

B-52G/H bombers, was terminated in mid-1973. One explanation given was that the projected unit cost of the weapon ($1.2 million) was too high. Another source reported that the increase in the total programme cost (estimated at $1.2 billion) as well as in the capability which this weapon could be expected to add to the B-52 was so great as to jeopardize support for development of the B-1. [37] The purpose of SCAD—a missile with a reported range over 500 km—was to divert air-defence forces from the bomber aircraft by simulating the radar characteristics of the aircraft. In addition, armed versions of the missile would attack certain targets.

At the time when the SCAD programme was terminated, increased attention was being given in the United States to the possible development of naval strategic cruise missiles; and it was speculated that all future strategic cruise missile developments would be centred on ship- or submarine-launched types. However, in the fiscal year 1975 budget, in addition to funds for a submarine-launched strategic cruise missile, support has been requested for an "Air Launch Cruise Missile" to be delivered by a modified tanker-type aircraft and/or possibly by the B-1. It has been suggested that this missile will serve as a replacement for SCAD, but no indication has been given of the differences in role or performance that can be expected.

No significant work on strategic bombers is under way in the Soviet Union. A supersonic medium-range bomber given the NATO code-name "Backfire" was developed in the late 1960s and was reported to be in series production by early 1974: but this bomber is incapable of intercontinental missions without air-refuelling and it does not appear to be intended primarily for a strategic role. [5] The Soviet Union is also reported to have a fleet of about 140 Mya-4 and Tu-20 bombers, but there is no evidence that these aircraft have actually been deployed as strategic bombers since the early 1960s.

The lack of a Soviet strategic bomber force has led to a gradual but steady decline in US air-defence systems over the past decade. The number of fighter-interceptor squadrons committed to continental US air defence declined from 40 in mid-1964 to 14 in 1970 and to 11 in 1972. The figure now scheduled for mid-1975 is six. At the same time, the number of air-defence missile batteries has decreased from 107 to 40 to 21, and these batteries are now scheduled to be entirely phased out by mid-1975. This has been accompanied by a slow-down of work on the SAM-D air-defence surface-to-air missile system, which is now being oriented more toward tactical deployment.

## References

1. *United States Foreign Policy for the 1970s: A New Strategy for Peace. A Report by President Richard Nixon to the Congress, February 18, 1970* (London, United States Information Service, 1970).

2. *President Nixon's Foreign Policy Report to the Congress, February 25, 1971* (n.p., United States Information Service, 1971).
3. *U.S. Foreign Policy for the 1970's: The Emerging Structure of Peace. A Report to the Congress by Richard Nixon, President of the United States, February 9, 1972* [Washington, 1972].
4. *Strategic Arms Limitation, Part II,* SIPRI Research Report No. 6 (Stockholm, Almqvist and Wiksell, 1972, Stockholm International Peace Research Institute).
5. *Report of the Secretary of Defense James R. Schlesinger to the Congress on the FY 1975 Defense Budget and FY 1975–1979 Defense Program, March 4, 1974* [Washington, 1974].
6. Iklé, F. C., "Can Nuclear Deterrence Last Out the Century?", *Foreign Affairs,* Vol. 51, No. 2, January 1973.
7. "News Conference by Secretary of Defense James R. Schlesinger at the Pentagon, Friday, August 17, 1973" [US Department of Defense news release (Washington, 1973)].
8. Cameron, J., "The Rethinking of U.S. Defense", *Fortune,* December 1973.
9. "Remarks by the Honorable James R. Schlesinger, Secretary of Defense, before National Jaycees, Twin Bridges Marriot Motel, Arlington, Va., Saturday, December 15, 1973", US Department of Defense news release no. 605–73 (Washington, 1973).
10. "Remarks by the Honorable James R. Schlesinger, Overseas Writers Association Luncheon, at International Club, Washington, D.C., Thursday, January 10, 1974" [US Department of Defense news release (Washington, 1973)].
11. "Arming to Disarm in the Age of Détente", *Time,* 11 February 1974.
12. Beecher, W., "Major War Plans are being Revised by White House", *New York Times,* 5 August 1972.
13. Getler, M., "More MIRV Missiles Sought", *Washington Post,* 5 January 1973.
14. Brownlow, C., "USAF Tightens Future Priorities", *Aviation Week and Space Technology,* Vol. 98, No. 11, 12 March 1973.
15. Beecher, W., "MIRV's in Soviet Believed in Place", *New York Times,* 23 April 1971.
16. Finney, J. W., "C.I.A. Said to Dispute Pentagon's View", *New York Times,* 5 May 1971.
17. Beecher, W., "U.S. Reassesses New Soviet ICBM Threat", *International Herald Tribune,* 28 May 1971.
18. Getler, M., "Russians Said to Build More ICBM Silos", *International Herald Tribune,* 9 August 1971.
19. "New ICBM Silos Seen in Soviet", *Washington Post,* 9 October 1971.
20. *The Origins of MIRV,* SIPRI Research Report No. 9 (Stockholm, Almqvist and Wiksell, 1973, Stockholm International Peace Research Institute).
21. Davis, L. E. and Schilling, W. R., "All You Ever Wanted to Know About MIRV and ICBM Calculations but Were Not Cleared to Ask", *Journal of Conflict Resolution,* Vol. 17, No. 2, June 1973.
22. Unpublished manuscript on strategic weapons, Center for Defense Information, Washington, 1973.
23. "U.S. Said to be Holding Back on Improvements to MIRV", *International Herald Tribune,* 14 July 1971.
24. "Soviets Test New MIRV Warhead ICBMs", *Aviation Week and Space Technology,* Vol. 100, No. 8, 25 February 1974.
25. Ulsamer, E., "The Soviet ICBM Threat is Mounting", *Air Force Magazine,* Vol. 56, No. 11, November 1973.
26. *New York Times,* 21 March 1971.

27. Martin, A. B., "The Land Based ICBM", paper presented at the American Institute of Aeronautics and Astronautics 10th Annual Meeting, Washington, 28–30 January 1974.

28. *Department of Defense Appropriations for 1974*, Hearings before a Subcommittee of the Committee on Appropriations, House of Representatives, 93rd Congress, 1st Session, part 2 (Washington, US Government Printing Office, 1973) p. 692.

29. Prina, L. E., "The Most Hunted Submarine", *Navy Magazine*, Vol. 14, No. 5, May 1971.

30. *SIPRI Yearbook of World Armaments and Disarmament 1968/69* (Stockholm, Almqvist and Wiksell, 1969, Stockholm International Peace Research Institute) p. 102.

31. "Navy Drafts Standard Hardware", *Electronics*, Vol. 41, No. 8, 15 April 1968.

32. *Tactical and Strategic Antisubmarine Warfare*, SIPRI Monograph (to be published).

33. Beecher, W., "Russians Reportedly Testing New Missile Guide System", *International Herald Tribune*, 2 October 1972.

34. *Statement by Admiral Thomas H. Moorer, USN, Chairman, Joint Chiefs of Staff, before the Defense Appropriations Subcommittee of the House Committee on Appropriations on February 26, 1974* [Washington, 1974].

35. *Statement of Honorable John L. McLucas, Secretary of the Air Force, before the Armed Services Committee, United States Senate, February 7, 1974* [Washington, 1974].

36. Miller, B., "Israeli Losses May Spur ECM Restudy", *Aviation Week and Space Technology*, Vol. 99, No. 18, 29 October 1973.

37. "Pentagon Halts Program That Cost $67-Million", *New York Times*, 7 July 1973.

38. *Statement of Secretary of Defense Robert S. McNamara before a Joint Session of the Senate Armed Services Committee and the Senate Subcommittee on Department of Defense Appropriations on the Fiscal Year 1968–72 Defense Program and 1968 Defense Budget, January 23, 1967* [Washington, 1967].

39. *Statement of Secretary of Defense Robert S. McNamara before the Senate Subcommittee on Department of Defense Appropriations on the Fiscal Year 1969–73 Defense Program and 1969 Defense Budget* (Washington, US Government Printing Office, 1968).

40. *Statement of Secretary of Defense Clark M. Clifford: The Fiscal Year 1970–74 Defense Program and 1970 Defense Budget* [Washington, 1969].

41. *Statement of Secretary of Defense Melvin R. Laird before a Joint Session of the Senate Armed Services Committee and the Senate Subcommittee on Department of Defense Appropriations on the Fiscal Year 1971 Defense Program and Budget, February 20, 1970* (Washington, US Government Printing Office, 1970).

42. *Statement of Secretary of Defense Melvin R. Laird before the House Armed Services Committee on the FY 1972–1976 Defense Program and the 1972 Defense Budget, March 9, 1971* (Washington, US Government Printing Office, 1971).

43. *Statement of Secretary of Defense Melvin R. Laird before the House Armed Services Committee on the FY 1973 Defense Budget and FY 1973–1977 Program, February 17, 1972* (Washington, US Government Printing Office, 1972).

44. *Statement of Secretary of Defense Elliot L. Richardson before the House Armed Services Committee on the FY 1974 Defense Budget and the FY 1974–1978 Program, Tuesday, April 10, 1973* (Washington, US Government Printing Office, 1973).

45. US Department of Defense, *Annual Report for Fiscal Year 1966* (Washington, US Government Printing Office, 1967).

56. Goldrich, R. L., *Statistics on U.S. Military Force Levels and Manpower Strengths, FY 1967–1973* (Washington, Library of Congress Congressional Research Service, 1973).

47. Yaffee, M. L., "US Reconfigures Minuteman ICBMs", *Aviation Week and Space Technology,* Vol. 99, No. 19, 5 November 1973.

48. Blackman, R. V. B., ed., *Jane's Fighting Ships 1972–73* (London, Sampson Low, Marston and Co., Ltd., 1972).

49. Moore, J. E., ed., *Jane's Fighting Ships 1973–74* (London, Sampson Low, Marston and Co., Ltd., 1973).

50. "Comparison of Strategic Forces of United States and Union of Soviet Socialist Republics", press release, U.S. Senate Committtee on Foreign Relations, 10 August 1972.

51. *SIPRI Yearbook of World Armaments and Disarmament 1969/70* (Stockholm, Almqvist & Wiksell, 1970, Stockholm International Peace Research Institute) p. 55.

# Part II. Developments in world armaments

**Chapter 7. The dynamics of world military expenditure**

Introduction / Pressures for increased expenditures on armaments / Military personnel costs / Summary and conclusions / The cost of acquiring, operating and maintaining weapons

**Chapter 8. World armaments, 1973**

Introduction / The acquisition of major weapons / The Middle East / NATO and the WTO / Significant developments in the rest of the world / Sources and methods / Estimating Soviet military expenditure / World military expenditure, 1973 / Register of indigenously designed weapons in development or production, 1973 / Register of licensed production of foreign-designed major weapons, 1973 / Register of world arms trade, 1972–73

# 7. The dynamics of world military expenditure[1]

*Square-bracketed references, thus [1], refer to the list of references on page 139.*

## I. *Introduction*

Since 1948, the quantity of resources devoted to military uses throughout the world has more than trebled. This enormous increase has not taken place steadily over the period: rather it has taken place mainly in distinct jumps. On three occasions since the end of World War II, military expenditure surged upwards in connection with a war or major crisis, and in each case the subsequent fall in expenditure, if one occurred at all, was relatively modest (chart 7.1).

Along with this increase in world military expenditure in absolute terms, there has been a dramatic increase in the share of world output devoted to military uses. In 1972, world military expenditure was valued at about $207 billion, which represented about 6.5 per cent of total world output. In many of the post-war years, the proportion was even higher—around 7–8 per cent. These are much higher proportions than those which prevailed in any other peacetime period in recent history: in the years preceding World War I, and in the inter-war years, the proportion was some 3–3.5 per cent.

The largest increases in military expenditure have occurred in the United States and the Soviet Union. Charts 7.2 and 7.3 show the military expenditures of these two countries since 1930 (fiscal year 1931 for the United States) and, for the United States, the proportion of GNP devoted to military uses over the same period. (Expenditures during the years of World War II—taken as 1939–45 for the Soviet Union and 1940–45 for the United States—have been omitted.) It is clear that in the immediate post-war period, the level of military expenditure in both countries was consider-

---

[1] This chapter is concerned with the level and trend of armaments, where this term is taken to mean destructive capacity or lethal power. The only convenient index of this is expenditure for military purposes. However, it should be borne in mind that the relationship between military expenditure and armaments is not perfect. Apart from the inflation factor, it is possible, particularly in view of the vast base of weapon technology which presently exists, for the level of armaments to rise without a commensurate rise in expenditure. The opposite is also true. Similarly, two countries with a comparable level of expenditure in any one year may have markedly different levels of armaments if one of the countries has only just attained this level of expenditure while the other has supported such a level for a number of years. In general, however, if all countries are considered together, expenditure and armaments will be strongly and directly related. These two terms have therefore been used interchangeably in this chapter.

**Chart 7.1. World military expenditure, 1948–72**

*US $ bn, at constant (1970) prices and exchange rates*

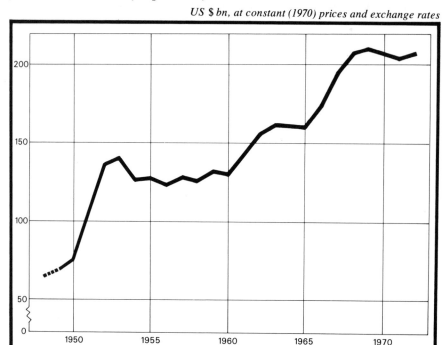

*Source:* The military expenditure tables in the *SIPRI Yearbooks 1968/69–1974*.

ably higher than in the pre-war period. This increase was evident even before the outbreak of the Korean War, although that conflict gave rise to a further jump in the general level of military expenditure, particularly in the United States. The expenditure figures in these charts are quoted in current prices and no allowance has been made for inflation, but the data available strongly suggests that the same conclusions concerning the general trend of military expenditures could be drawn, even if the movements in prices over the period could be accurately taken into account.

It is beyond the scope of this chapter to attempt to explain completely the reasons for this dramatic increase in military expenditure. The main purpose here is to describe some of the more important forces which have operated to sustain this level of militarization and which account for the persistent tendency of the level of world armaments to rise. These forces are considered under two main headings: technological factors, by which are meant the forces inherent in a process of extremely rapid technological change that tend to promote a rising level of armaments; and internal bureaucratic and economic pressures that operate to maintain large armed forces in peacetime. Since the United States and the Soviet Union account for approximately two-thirds of the total world military expenditure, it is reasonable to discuss these forces mainly with reference to these two coun-

**Chart 7.2. US expenditure for national security, 1931–73**

*A. Total, billions of dollars, at current prices*
*B. As a percentage of gross national product (GNP)*

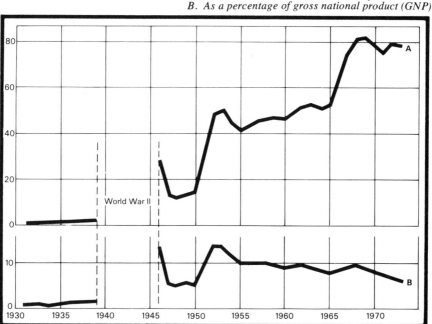

*Sources:* Pre-WWII, US Department of Defense News Release 1972. Post-WWII, *SIPRI Yearbooks 1968/69–1974.*

tries. A much less detailed account will be given of the factors operating to increase military expenditures in some other countries, although, of course, it is important to note that the long-term upward trend in the level of expenditures has been worldwide (table 7.1). Finally, the trends in expenditures for military personnel, and the way this factor contributes to the overall increase in military expenditures, will be discussed.

## II. *Pressures for increased expenditures on armaments*

### The United States and the Soviet Union

*Technological pressures*

A widely accepted explanation of the trend in armaments in the United States and the Soviet Union is that the "arms race" in which these two countries are engaged follows a characteristic pattern of action and reaction, or, in most cases, over-reaction. This implies that Soviet military activities are determined almost exclusively by those of the United States, and *vice versa*. The tendency to over-react arises because there is no precise answer to the question of how much (military capability) is enough, and where national security is concerned, uncertainty typically leads to a preference for too much rather than too little.

125

**Chart 7.3. Soviet budgetary outlays for defence, 1930–73**

*Billions of roubles, at current prices*

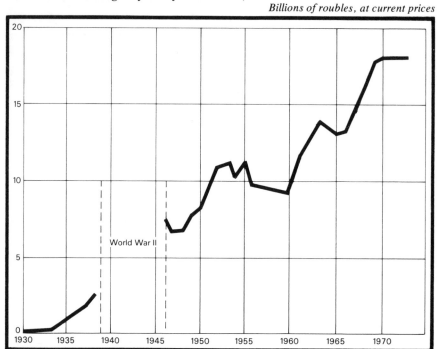

*Sources:* Pre-WWII, *Leagne of Nations Armaments Yearbooks 1933* and *1939/40*. Post-WWII, *SIPRI Yearbooks 1968/69–1974*.

While the action/reaction (or over-reaction) pattern is undoubtedly a factor influencing the US–Soviet arms race, there is little evidence to suggest that it is the most important one. In the early post-war years, when an atmosphere of fear and mistrust existed in relations between these two countries, the action/reaction process was a major force behind the arms race, but the fact that the level of armaments has not been noticeably influenced by the marked improvements in the international climate in recent years supports the conclusion that it is now of less importance. Instead, it seems that each side, rather than simply trying to match, or improve on, the capabilities of the other side, is now more concerned with exploiting to the full the technological opportunities available to it. This leads to much more rapidly increasing sophistication of weaponry: an action/reaction pattern would, in fact, represent a relatively constrained form of arms racing, since it only requires each side to "move ahead" of the other by one "step" at a time; but with each side exploiting technology for its own sake, this constraint is removed. There are a number of factors, such as those described below, which act to keep the technological process going and accelerating, and these are only reinforced, not controlled, by the action/reaction process.

The intense development and exploitation of technology for military purposes is essentially a post-war phenomenon. In the inter-war period,

**Table 7.1. Constant-price increases in military expenditure: by region, 1949–71**

| Region | Factor increase |
| --- | --- |
| NATO | 3.2 |
| WTO | 2.6 |
| Other Europe | 2.9 |
| Middle East | 14.6 |
| South Asia | 3.2 |
| Far East (excl China) | 7.2 |
| Oceania | 3.6 |
| Africa | 23.0 |
| Central America | 2.1 |
| South America | 2.0 |

*Source:* The military expenditure tables in the *SIPRI Yearbooks 1968/69–1974.*

military support for science and technology absorbed less than 1 per cent of the military budgets of the major powers, but the dramatic illustrations of the military potential of science and technology during World War II led to a phenomenal increase in such support. The shares of the major military budgets devoted to research and development (R&D) reached 10–15 per cent by the late 1950s and have remained at this level since, reflecting the widespread faith in the military and political utility of technological sophistication in weaponry. The United States and the Soviet Union have dominated this process.[2] In recent years the military R&D effort of each of these two countries has been equivalent to, or greater than, the *total* military expenditure of any other of the major powers, with the possible exception of China. [1]

The observable result of this effort—an unprecedented rate of technological change in the field of armaments—is reflected in the size of military budgets. Thus, the three-fold increase in world military expenditures in the post-war period has largely been due not to increases in the numbers of men under arms or to increases in the quantities of weapons deployed, but to qualitative improvements in weaponry, with each successive "generation" of weapons costing more to develop, to manufacture, and to operate and maintain (see appendix 7A).

The first and perhaps most important characteristic of the technological process that promotes a rising level of armaments is the extremely long lead-times or gestation periods of modern weapons. The development of a new missile or a new fighter aircraft to the stage at which it is ready for mass production and deployment may take up to 10 years. This time factor introduces an important qualitative change in the action/reaction pattern: participants in the "technological arms race"—primarily the United States and the Soviet Union—focus their attention not on which weapons the other side has already produced or is ready to produce, but on possible

[2] US military R & D expenditure increased from about $30 million in 1939 to $3 000 million in 1955 (in current prices).
[1] A similar increase has since occurred in the USSR.

future developments in the opponent's weaponry, and then undertake programmes designed to produce weapons to offset these anticipated developments. Thus the uncertainties surrounding the question of how much is enough are increased. Since the range of conceivable developments in the opponent's weaponry is essentially unlimited, there is a *prima facie* case for initiating programmes to protect oneself against as many conceivable developments as possible. The process is only exacerbated by the fact that technological advances make it possible to consider protection against increasingly remote contingencies.

The fallacy in this procedure is, of course, that the other side is following exactly the same pattern. Thus there is a high probability, given comparable technological opportunities and constraints, that both sides will independently pursue similar courses resulting in mutual, and therefore "justified", advances in weaponry. In fact, the United States and the Soviet Union do have roughly comparable weapons, for this reason. Any imbalances in weapon capabilities that do occur merely supply additional fuel to the process.

Another channel through which emphasis on technology promotes a rising level of armaments is the so-called "follow-on imperative". The development and production of modern military equipment is an extremely complex task requiring highly skilled, specialized resources. The technical and industrial teams engaged in these activities are regarded as national assets which, given the dynamic element in the technological process, cannot be allowed to disintegrate without risk to the nation's ability to keep abreast of foreign developments in weapon technology. In other words, these resources must be kept fully employed all the time, and this will automatically lead to the continual development of new weapon systems. An exacerbating phenomenon in this context is the fact that, as weapons become ever more complex, the technical and industrial capacity created at the peak of a programme grows larger. [2] The main reason for this is that, despite the growth in complexity, it is considered impossible in an environment of rapid technological change to make any commensurable increase in the length of the development process: to do so would be to risk the weapon becoming obsolete before it is deployed. Therefore, not only must these specialized resources be kept fully employed, but the increase in their size cannot be controlled.

*Internal bureaucratic and economic pressures*
After World War II, and to a greater extent after the Korean War, both the United States and the Soviet Union retained large military establishments. Inevitably this led to the emergence of powerful bureaucratic and economic forces which sought to resist any decline in these establishments and, of course, to promote their expansion. It is not possible to quantify these forces, only to describe them briefly in general terms, but it is

reasonable to suppose that they have indeed exerted an influence in maintaining and increasing the level of armaments.

An example of such economic pressures is the fact that many politicians in the United States can interpret a decision on whether or not to vote for the procurement of a particular weapon system in terms of substantial changes in the level of employment in their electoral districts. Obvious pressures against any reduction in the level of employment are therefore translated into pressures for the continued production of weapons. Similarly, as an example of bureaucratic pressures, it is perfectly natural for the military establishment, operating as a unified bureaucracy, to attempt to preserve its relative status in the government programme as a whole. Even at lower levels, the various components of the military establishment will attempt at least to preserve, and if possible to expand, their relative status.

Another important factor is the view that, because of the sheer complexity and variety of modern specialized weapon systems, only the military establishment itself is competent to decide the size and character of the national security effort: until recently this view apparently prevailed, at least in the United States. The fact that weapons are both complex and exist in bewildering variety can also be exploited to support claims for higher military spending. Thus, in the United States, debates on the defence budget rarely consider broad questions such as the adequacy of force levels in relation to the requirements of national security and international commitments. Rather these debates get lost in a mass of detail on particular new weapon systems or particular improvements to existing weapons and in equally narrow comparisons with Soviet capabilities, when such comparisons can be made, in order to show that the latter is ahead. This piecemeal review of the military programme contributes to the inflexibility—at least as far as reductions are concerned—of the overall size of the programme.

In summary, the action/reaction process, in its basic form, would seem at best only a partial explanation of the continuing rise in military capability. Other, probably more valid, explanations are to be found in the dynamics of the technological process itself, in the domestic factions that would benefit in some way from the military and in the broader political—mainly foreign-policy—objectives that are believed to be advanced by the maintenance of military forces. No attempt has been made to explore the ramifications of the role which armed force is given in the conduct of foreign relations. It may be observed, however, that in many cases, the political utility of military power is not measured against the requirement of "defence" proper or the achievement of well-defined military objectives. Instead, military power, measured in crude terms, is considered to contribute to the bargaining power of a country in its international dealings. In this light, it becomes an attractive commodity even in the absence of a plausible military threat or significant risk of armed conflict.

**Chart 7.4. Military expenditure in the third world, 1949–72**

*US $ bn, at constant (1970) prices and exhange rates*

*Source:* The military expenditure tables in the *SIPRI Yearbooks 1968/69–1974.*

## Other countries

Although the technological "arms race" has been, and is being, run primarily between the United States and the Soviet Union, the military "requirements" of these and other countries are highly interdependent. Therefore, the "pace-setting" role, in terms of weapon capabilities and the rate of change of these capabilities, played by these two countries has strongly influenced the level and trend of armaments and expenditures throughout the world.

As shown above, there are a number of forces operating in the United States and the Soviet Union which lead naturally to increases in armaments. Because of the vast amounts of resources available to these countries, the trends towards increased armaments can continue almost unchecked. Other developed countries, notably France and the United Kingdom, but also to a lesser extent countries such as FR Germany, Italy and Sweden,[3] have the capacity to produce a wide range of sophisticated conventional weapons. But because the resources available for military uses in these countries are much more limited than those available in the United

---

[3] The list could obviously be extended. Some indication of the relative status of different countries in this respect is provided in the production registers in appendix 8D below. See also reference [1].

**Table 7.2. Sizes of armed forces: by region, selected years, 1955–71**[a]

*Thousands of men*

|  | 1955 | 1960 | 1965 | 1971 |
|---|---|---|---|---|
| NATO | 5 460 | 5 884 | 5 696 | 5 733 |
| WTO | 6 903 | 4 434 | 4 271 | 4 362 |
| Other Europe | [700] | [1 100] | 795 | 780 |
| Middle East | [318] | 600 | 695 | 975 |
| South Asia | [500] | 844 | 1 196 | 1 477 |
| Far East (excl China) | [1 317] | 2 937 | 3 382 | 3 671 |
| China | 2 300 | 2 000 | 2 486 | 2 880 |
| Oceania | 59 | 60 | 73 | 101 |
| Africa | [68] | 133 | 315 | 702 |
| Central America | 158 | 148 | 240 | 235 |
| South America | 382 | 543 | 608 | 603 |
| **Total** | [20 465] | 20 683 | 22 243 | 24 399 |

[a] The figures for paramilitary forces have not been included but the estimates of these forces for 1969, for example, vary between 1.0 million and 1.4 million men worldwide. For many countries the data on regular armed forces in 1955 was incomplete: the world total for that year is probably somewhat conservative.

*Source:* See the section on sources in appendix 8A, pages 163–66.

States and the Soviet Union, the efforts of these other countries to develop and produce weapons comparable with those of the USA and the USSR have been restricted. On the one hand, they have had to limit the number of types of weapons that can be designed and produced simultaneously. And on the other, they have been subject to very strong pressures to export their weapons, not mainly, as in the case of the USA and the USSR, for political ends, but simply in order to alleviate the economic burden of developing and producing modern weapons.

The spread of sophisticated weaponry to non-arms-producing countries, and to underdeveloped countries in particular—with the attendant implications for the minimum level of conflict should it break out and the minimum cost of acquiring and operating effective armed forces[4]—has been a notable feature of the post-war armaments scene. It is also noteworthy that the trend in a growing number of third world countries is towards the establishment of indigenous defence industries. These two developments are reflected in the trend of military expenditure in the third world (see chart 7.4). Although the underdeveloped countries account for only a small fraction of total world military expenditure—less than 10 per cent in 1971[5]—the trend has been consistently upward.

[4] The cost is not only expressed in monetary terms. The operation of modern military equipment requires a heavy input of skilled manpower, a resource typically in short supply in underdeveloped countries. For example, the A-7, a USAF tactical fighter, requires 25 maintenance manhours per flying hour. To operate a squadron of 24 aircraft (assuming that each flies 50 hours per month) requires 559 men, nearly 80 per cent of them skilled technicians. The comparable figure for the F-4 Phantom varies between 694 for the single mission version and 996 for the dual mission version. [3]

[5] For the purpose of this calculation underdeveloped countries are defined as follows: all countries excluding NATO and Warsaw Treaty Organization members, other European countries, Japan, South Africa, Australia and New Zealand. The People's Republic of China is excluded because the figures for this country are very rough.

**Table 7.3. Military pay and allowances as a percentage of total military expenditure: selected developed countries, 1960–73[a]**

*Per cent*

| | 1960 | 1961 | 1962 | 1963 | 1964 | 1965 | 1966 | 1967 | 1968 | 1969 | 1970 | 1971 | 1972 | 1973 |
|---|---|---|---|---|---|---|---|---|---|---|---|---|---|---|
| USA | 28.3 | 25.3 | 25.9 | 24.9 | 26.2 | 29.1 | 28.0 | 26.6 | 25.7 | 27.4 | 29.8 | 30.4 | 30.1 | 31.1 |
| UK | 20.6 | 19.8 | 20.0 | 19.3 | 19.6 | 19.6 | 19.3 | 21.1 | 20.3 | 19.8 | 20.1 | 20.3 | 27.1 | 26.2 |
| FR Germany | .. | .. | .. | .. | .. | .. | 30.2 | 30.0 | 35.1 | 35.8 | 39.8 | 39.7 | 41.3 | 41.0 |
| Australia | 29.8 | 28.8 | 27.7 | 23.0 | 21.4 | 21.1 | 21.6 | 23.4 | 22.7 | 24.3 | 28.7 | 31.5 | 33.1 | 31.0 |
| Sweden | .. | .. | 27.0 | 30.0 | 29.0 | 31.0 | 30.0 | 31.0 | 32.0 | 38.0 | 37.0 | 38.0 | 38.0 | .. |
| Belgium | 58.4 | 56.7 | 54.0 | 53.5 | 51.3 | 58.0 | 59.1 | 61.0 | 58.3 | 58.5 | 56.2 | 59.1 | .. | .. |
| Finland | .. | 24.1 | 25.8 | 24.0 | 25.0 | 29.0 | 30.6 | 34.5 | 33.2 | 35.0 | 35.6 | 36.1 | .. | .. |

[a] The figures are primarily intended to illustrate trends. Comparisons between countries cannot be made due to differing accounting procedures.

## III. *Military personnel costs*

The above discussion has been concerned primarily with the rising level of armaments or the rising level of destructive capacity embodied in weapons and their associated equipment. This phenomenon has been one of the main forces behind the long-term rise in world military expenditure. A second major factor behind this rise is the trend in expenditure for military personnel.

In 1971, military personnel were estimated to number more than 24 million worldwide—an increase of almost 20 per cent over the 1955 figure (see table 7.2). However, virtually all of this increase took place in the underdeveloped countries. And because, in 1971, these countries accounted for less than 10 per cent of total military expenditure but for almost one-half of the world's military personnel, it follows that the trend in the size of the world's standing armies is not a particularly important factor in explaining the trend in world military expenditure.

What is important in explaining the trend in world military expenditure is the trend in personnel costs per man in the developed countries. In general, it would seem that cost per man has been rising faster in most developed countries than has total military expenditure. The share of personnel costs has therefore been rising except in countries where off-setting measures have been taken (see table 7.3).

Probably the main reason for the rising costs of personnel is the changing attitude towards conscription. This changing attitude can take one of two forms. If a country abandons conscription altogether in favour of maintaining an all-volunteer force, there will inevitably be a substantial increase in expenditure per man: such a transition requires substantial increases in military pay and allowances. Furthermore, there will be strong pressures for personnel expenditures, and therefore total expenditure, to rise more rapidly under a volunteer system than under a conscript system. However, from the point of view of explaining the long-term rise in world

**Table 7.4. Terms of conscription for army personnel in NATO countries: selected years, 1956–73**

*Numbers of months*

| | 1956 | 1960 | 1965 | 1973 |
|---|---|---|---|---|
| USA | 24 | 24 | 24 | *v* |
| Canada | *v* | *v* | *v* | *v* |
| Belgium | 18 | 12 | 12 | 12[a] |
| Denmark | 16 | 16 | 16 | 12[a] |
| France | 24[b] | 24[b] | 16 | 12 |
| FR Germany | 12 | 12 | 18 | 15 |
| Greece | 21[b] | 24 | 24 | 24 |
| Italy | 18 | 18 | 15 | 15 |
| Luxembourg | 12 | 12 | 9 | *v* |
| Netherlands | 18 | 18 | 18 | 16 |
| Norway | 16 | 16 | 12 | 12 |
| Portugal | 4 | 18 | 18 | 24 |
| Turkey | 24 | 24 | 24 | 20 |
| UK | 24 | 24 | *v* | *v* |

*v* denotes countries with a volunteer system.

[a] Belgium and Denmark have subsequently announced reductions in the period of conscription to 6 and 9 months, respectively.
[b] The legal draft was for a period of 18 months but conscripts were retained for the periods indicated.

*Sources: Western Europe and the New Economic Policy,* report to the Senate Foreign Relations Committee by Senator Mansfield (Washington, Ocotober 1971). *Economist,* 18 August 1973, p̄. 28.

military expenditure, the switch from conscript to volunteer forces is not particularly important: since 1960, only two countries with large military expenditures—the United States and the United Kingdom—have made this transition, with the USA ceasing the induction of conscripts only on 1 January 1973.[6] Moreover, in both of these countries, the increase in the share of personnel expenditures has been relatively modest. Such a tendency can be explained by the fact that total military expenditures have been rising as rapidly as the cost per man, or that there have been reductions in the number of military personnel.[7] In the United States, for example, the number of military personnel was reduced by more than one-third over the period 1969–73—the period of the transition to an all-volunteer army—while in the United Kingdom the stability of the share for military personnel between 1962 and 1973 is accounted for by a 55 per cent increase in total expenditure (in current price terms) coupled with a slow but persistent decline in the number of personnel.

Most countries of Western Europe, although they have not made the complete transition to an all-volunteer force, have changed their attitude towards conscription in another way: the concept of pure conscription—where the cost of the conscript is little more than his subsistence requirements—has gradually been abandoned in favour of higher pay and better

[6] In the USA, for FY 1973, the extra cost attributable directly to the all-volunteer force is estimated at $2.7 billion. [4]
[7] In addition, in a number of countries civilians have been employed for tasks formerly performed by military personnel.

standards generally. Because this pattern is more widespread, it is more useful than the transition to all-volunteer forces for explaining the rising share of personnel costs. A good, though indirect index of this changing attitude is the trend in the length of service required of conscripts. This trend in NATO countries for conscription into the army is shown in table 7.4: Greece and Portugal are the only exceptions to the trend towards shorter periods of conscription.

A second major factor behind the rising personnel costs has been the ever growing demand for skilled military personnel, or at least for personnel capable of acquiring the skills required to operate and maintain complex military equipment. This factor also reinforces the trend away from conscription: as military equipment becomes more complex, it takes longer to train men to use it efficiently, so that the period of time for which a conscript is an effective member of the armed forces is continuously falling.

## IV. *Summary and conclusions*

For various reasons—mainly stemming from the technological nature of the armaments process—there is an inherent tendency for military expenditure to rise, and rise rapidly. At the same time it would seem that resistance to rising—or at least rapidly rising—military expenditure is becoming more effective in many developed countries.[8] These somewhat conflicting trends have a number of visible manifestations. Most notable perhaps is the appreciable decline in the share (although not necessarily in absolute amounts) of capital expenditure—R&D and procurement—in the military budgets of many developed countries, mainly because of the rise in the share of personnel costs. With the exceptions of the United States and the Soviet Union, this decline has tended to limit both the range of weapon systems that can be developed and/or produced simultaneously and the number of units that can be purchased: this in turn reinforces the pressure to find export markets. These limitations are reflected in the growing trend towards international collaboration in the development and production of weapons, and in the tendency to seek second-best solutions to requirements for new tactical systems by making more extensive use of existing technologies rather than by developing totally new systems. Also important is the additional impetus that the above-mentioned conflict-

[8] In many countries this takes the form of a desire to keep the level of military expenditure constant in real terms. This is consistent with quite substantial increases in the level of expenditure in terms of current prices because of the manner in which military expenditure is typically adjusted for price changes. Particularly notable in this regard is that *all* increases in pay and allowances are usually treated as price increases.

ing trends have given to the substitution of equipment for manpower as a means of stabilizing the share of personnel costs in total expenditure. An outstanding example of this process is the keen interest presently being shown in the potentials of remotely piloted aircraft for a wide range of military functions. (See also chapter 11.)

# Appendix 7A

*The cost of acquiring, operating and maintaining weapons*

The emphasis in the post-war period on the development and exploitation of technology for military purposes has resulted in an enormous increase in the cost of weapon systems and related equipment.

Capital equipment with superior performance characteristics always costs more to develop and produce than did the equipment which it supersedes. In the military field, however, the increase in cost has, in general, exceeded the increase in performance by an appreciable margin (table 7A.1).

The primary military consideration is performance, not cost. A weapon is really useful only if its performance matches or exceeds that of weapons possessed by a potential enemy. In an attempt to secure superiority *vis-à-vis* an opponent's system and to minimize the likelihood of early obsolescence, a new weapon system is often required to have performance characteristics which are unattainable with existing technology. To develop new technology in specified areas and within a prescribed period of time is inevitably very costly.[1] It is often pointed out that the final 5 per cent of the performance parameters specified for a new weapon system account for a disproportionate share of the total cost of developing the system.

**Table 7A.1. Comparative increase from the 1950s to the 1960s in the cost and technical performance of military aircraft**[a]

*Factor increase*

| Cost | | Performance | | | | |
|------|------|---------|----------|-------|----------|-------------|
| R&D cost | Unit cost | Payload | Range or endurance | Speed | Avionics function | Delivery or navigation accuracy |
| 5.4 | 4.2 | 2.3 | 1.9 | 1.8 | 3 | 3 |

[a] The figures are averages based on a study of 13 major sets of old and new systems.

*Source: Cost Growth in Weapon Systems*, report to the Committee on Armed Services by the Comptroller General of the United States, 26 March 1973.

[1] In almost any undertaking, cost will be inversely related with time. This is particularly true for projects that seek to go beyond the existing technological frontiers because of the inherent difficulty of anticipating what technological problems will arise and how difficult their solution will be. A striking example is offered by the proposed development of the RB 211-24 turbofan engine for the long-range version of the Lockheed Tristar. Rolls-Royce has estimated the development costs of this new engine at $3 million for an evolutionary programme over four years or $20 million if it is to be available in one year or so. [5]

136

**Table 7A.2. Development costs of US fighter aircraft**[a]

| Year | Aircraft designation | Cost per prototype US $ *mn* |
|------|----------------------|------------------------------|
| 1946 | F-84  | 3.4  |
| 1947 | F-86  | 4.3  |
| 1953 | F-100 | 16.1 |
| 1956 | F-106 | 24.4 |
| 1972 | F-15  | 66.3[b] |

[a] All costs are expressed in constant (1962) prices.
[b] The RD&T costs for 20 test aircraft were estimated at $1 721.4 mn in 1972 ($86.1 mn per aircraft). The non-compensation component of the deflator for federal purchases was applied to convert this figure to 1962 prices.

*Source: Official Price List* (London, Aviation Studies Atlantic, periodical).

In addition, the continuous evolution of new technology will, in a comparatively short period of time, give rise to new developments which will sharply reduce the relative effectiveness of a particular weapon. Usually, therefore, there is a continuous effort to modify and improve a system in so far as its basic design permits: for example, through FY 1973, some $2.7 billion had been spent on modifications and improvements to the US B-52 strategic bomber.

**Table 7A.3. The effect of size and sophistication on the operating costs of US aircraft and ships**

*Figures in current (1972/73) prices*

| Type | Description | Direct operating cost[a] US $/hour | US $ thousand/ year |
|------|-------------|-----------------|---------------------|
| **Aircraft** | | | |
| A-37 A/B | Light strike aircraft | 128 | |
| T-38 | Supersonic trainer | 138 | |
| F-105 | Supersonic fighter-bomber | 553 | |
| F-4 | Supersonic fighter-bomber | 626 | |
| F-111 | Variable geometry fighter-bomber | 798 | |
| B-52 | Strategic bomber | 1 356 | |
| C-124 | Military transport | 355 | |
| C-133 | Military transport | 488 | |
| C-5 | Military transport | 963 | |
| **Ships** | | | |
| SS | Conventional submarine | | 103 |
| SSN | Nuclear hunter-killer submarine | | 213 |
| DD | Conventional destroyer | | 106 |
| DLG | Missile-armed destroyer | | 261 |

[a] Direct operating costs consist of (*a*) petrol, oil and lubricants (usually 25–35 per cent of total), (*b*) base material support, and (*c*) depot maintenance.

*Source: Department of Defense Appropriations, Fiscal Year 1972* and *Fiscal Year 1973*, Hearings, US Senate Committee on Appropriations (Washington, Government Printing Office, 1971, 1972).

**Chart 7A.1. Trends in the unit cost of selected types of weapon[a]**

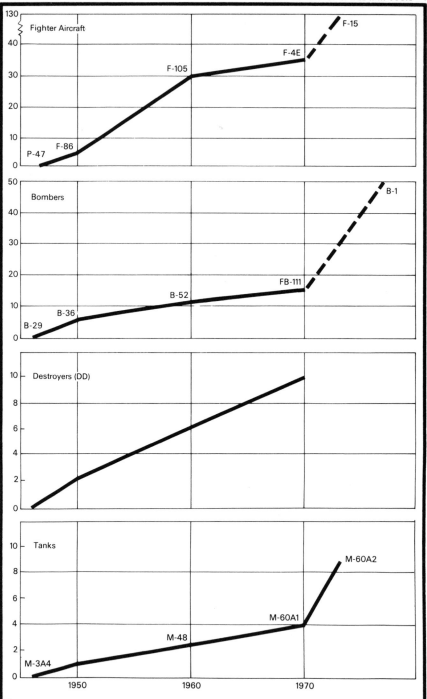

*Index numbers: WWII unit costs=1*

[a] Note the changes of scale.

All components of the cost of weapons have risen dramatically. Table 7A.2 shows the cost, in constant prices, of developing successive generations of US fighter aircraft. Chart 7A.1 gives indices of the cost of manufacturing successive generations of selected weapons in the United States. The indices are based on current price figures for the unit cost of weapons and should be interpreted in conjunction with the fact that the average price level in the United States approximately doubled over this period. Finally, table 7A.3 gives some indication of the effect of size and sophistication of the operating cost of weapons. All these data are for the USA but the direction, if not the strength, of the trend in costs is universal.

It is sometimes pointed out that it is no more valid to compare the cost of a World War II weapon with its present counterpart than it is to compare, say, the DC-3 of the 1930s with the DC-10 of the 1970s. In both cases the cost has increased enormously but there has been a compensating increase in technical performance. The unfortunate difference is that whereas there is no question that the DC-10 performs its particular function better than the DC-3, it is at least debatable whether, say, the F-15 will perform its air-superiority function better than did the P-51.

## References

1. *Resources Devoted to Military Research and Development: An International Comparison* (Stockholm, Almqvist & Wiksell, 1972, Stockholm International Peace Research Institute).
2. Kaldor, M., "European Defence Industries—National and International Implications", ISIO Monographs, First series, Number 8 (Institute for the Study of International Organisations, University of Sussex, 1972).
3. *Military Manpower Requirements Report for FY 1974*, US Department of Defense, February 1973, pp. 44–45.
4. Binkin, M. and Johnston, J., "All-Volunteer Armed Forces: Progress, Problems and Prospects", Report prepared for the Senate Armed Services Committee (Washington, Brookings Institution, June 1973).
5. *Flight International*, Vol. 103, No. 3346, 26 April 1973, p. 629.

# 8. World armaments, 1973

*Square-bracketed references, thus [1], refer to the list of references on page 158.*

*This chapter surveys the present state of world armaments and discusses the more significant developments in 1973. It incorporates material that, in previous editions of the SIPRI Yearbook, appeared as separate chapters relating to military expenditure, military research and development and the arms trade.*

*The chapter is supported by a large body of data, some of which appears for the first time in this Yearbook. The military expenditure figures and the register of the trade in major weapons with the third world, which have appeared in all of the SIPRI Yearbooks, have now been supplemented by registers showing the trade in major weapons between developed countries and the major weapons under development or in series production in all countries.*

*The data are contained in four appendices (8C-8F). These are preceded by a section on sources and methods (appendix 8A) and a special introduction to the military expenditure estimates for the Soviet Union, which have been substantially revised (appendix 8B).*

## I. *Introduction*

Since 1968, the level of world military expenditure has remained roughly stable at slightly over $200 billion annually.[1] The 1973 figure of $207 billion was about 1.5 per cent below the 1969 peak level of $210.5 billion.[2] The stability in the absolute level of expenditure has resulted in a decline in the proportion of world output devoted to military uses, from more than 8 per cent in 1968 to about 6.5 per cent in 1972. While a stable level of expenditure is to be preferred to a rising trend, the fact remains that an annual expenditure of $200 billion not only represents a colossal waste of resources but also permits the refinement and expansion of an already enormous capacity for destruction. Despite the levelling

---

[1] A similar levelling off in world military expenditure occurred over the years 1955–60 although at less than two-thirds of the current level.
[2] These estimates, in constant (1970) dollars, are taken from appendix 8C. SIPRI's estimates of total world military expenditure have recently been revised upward. The most important change is the new estimate of the dollar-equivalent of Soviet expenditure, the derivation of which is explained in appendix 8B.

off in world military expenditure, the technological arms race—the development of new and more lethal weapons—continues unabated.

Military research and development—the improvement of existing weaponry and the design and development of new weapons—currently absorbs about $20 billion annually and occupies the time of about 400 000 scientists and engineers throughout the world.[3] Unless one has studied the development of military technology over a period of time it is difficult to imagine what a scientific effort of this magnitude really implies. In 1972, the US Director of Defense Research and Engineering compiled a list of the major new weapon systems that had become operational in the United States over the period 1966–71. [2] The list included 11 items under the heading "strategic systems", 14 items under "tactical aircraft systems", eight items under "tactical missiles" and 18 items under "ordnance". When it is remembered that a similar list could probably be compiled for the Soviet Union, that the number of new items would be further increased if the rest of the world is taken into account and that "minor" systems and improvements to existing weapons are excluded, some idea is gained of what $20 billion invested annually over a period of years could achieve.

The stability of total world military expenditure disguises disparate trends in different countries and regions. Recent changes in the military expenditure of the 20 countries that each devoted the equivalent of $1 billion or more to military uses in 1972, and that together account for about 85 per cent of the world total, are shown in table 8.1. The relative changes in expenditure shown in this table are part of a gradual long-term trend towards a more even distribution of world military expenditure (table 8.2). While the world's military capability has been, and still is, heavily concentrated in a few large industrialized countries, it is clear that the degree of concentration has declined. In particular, the share of world military spending absorbed by the United States, the Soviet Union, France and the United Kingdom, taken together, has declined from 82 per cent in 1955 to 70 per cent in 1973. This does not reflect a reduction in the military capability of these four countries but rather indicates the magnitude of the increase in militarization elsewhere. The arms race has become a global phenomenon.

## II. *The acquisition of major weapons*

The activity which lies at the heart of the world's arms race is the continuous procurement of new weapons. The striking feature of the pattern of weapons acquisition is the complexity of the technical and economic

[3] These estimates are based on material assembled in the SIPRI publication *Resources Devoted to Military Research and Development*. [1]

**Table 8.1. Recent changes in the military expenditures of the major spenders**[a]

| | Military expenditure in 1972, US $ million, current prices and exchange rates | Percentage change | | |
|---|---|---|---|---|
| | | 1969–73 | 1971–72 | 1972–73 |
| **NATO:** | | | | |
| USA | 77 638 | −20.5 | 0.4 | −4.9 |
| FR Germany | 9 012 | 18.7 | 6.6 | 3.0 |
| UK | 8 135 | 11.0 | 9.2 | −2.6 |
| France | 7 300 | 3.6 | −1.0 | 5.2 |
| Italy | 3 706 | 31.0 | 10.4 | 0.0 |
| Canada | 2 260 | 5.0 | 0.2 | −0.7 |
| Netherlands | 1 550 | 17.3 | 3.3 | 5.3 |
| Belgium | 1 004 | 18.5 | 5.6 | 4.0 |
| **WTO:** | | | | |
| USSR | 63 000 | 1.3 | 0.0 | 0.0 |
| Poland | 2 506 | 22.6 | 7.2 | 3.0 |
| German DR | 2 249 | 30.7 | 5.9 | 8.8 |
| Czechoslovakia | 2 012 | 16.8 | 5.6 | −2.3 |
| **Other developed:** | | | | |
| Japan | 2 578 | 40.3 | 11.3 | 3.6 |
| Sweden | 1 452 | 0.9 | −0.1 | 0.0 |
| Australia | 1 420 | −5.5 | 1.6 | −2.6 |
| **Third world:** | | | | |
| China | 9 500 | .. | .. | .. |
| India | 2 232 | 24.9 | 14.4 | −5.3 |
| Egypt | 1 495 | 118.8 | −1.5 | 28.8 |
| Israel | 1 313 | 168.7 | −9.9 | 106.4 |
| Iran | 1 224 | 80.6 | 0.8 | 22.4 |
| Brazil | 1 094 | 3.8 | 0.7 | −4.8 |

*Source:* Appendix 8C.

[a] Major spenders are defined as countries having military expenditures of $1 billion or more (in current prices and exchange rates) in 1972. The percentage changes were calculated from the constant (1970) price and 1970 exchange-rate figures. China is included because that country is clearly a major spender. The estimates of Chinese expenditure, however, are too rough to warrant computing percentage changes in particular years.

relationships that link the military efforts of different countries. The United States and the Soviet Union are in a class of their own and essentially determine the military-technological environment for the rest of the world. Other countries accommodate themselves to this environment as their financial and technical resources permit.

Considerable differences in the availability of financial and technical resources result in a variety of means of acquiring weapons. These range from (a) outright importation, which can be least costly and technically demanding, through (b) licensed production, (c) indigenous design using imported major components (for example, engines and electronics), and (d) collaborative projects, to (e) wholly indigenous development and production. Completely indigenous undertakings generally require very

**Table 8.2. Distribution of world military expenditure: selected years, 1955–73**

*US $ billion at constant (1970) prices and exchange rates*

|  | 1955 | 1960 | 1965 | 1970 | 1973 |
|---|---|---|---|---|---|
| World military expenditure | 126.3 | 129.8 | 159.4 | 205.9 | 207.4 |
| Percentage distribution: |  |  |  |  |  |
| USA | *46.5* | *45.8* | *40.0* | *37.8* | *33.1* |
| USSR | *27.6* | *25.2* | *28.2* | *30.6* | *30.4* |
| France | *3.1* | *4.0* | *3.5* | *2.9* | *3.0* |
| UK | *5.1* | *4.5* | *3.9* | *2.8* | *3.1* |
| Other developed[a] | *12.4* | *14.1* | *14.8* | *14.1* | *15.9* |
| Third world | *5.2* | *6.6* | *9.5* | *11.7* | *14.4* |

[a] Other NATO and WTO, other Europe, Australia, New Zealand, Japan and South Africa.
*Source:* Appendix 8C.

large initial investments for the developmental stage of the work, as well as an advanced technological base. For this reason, the military research and development effort is heavily concentrated in a few countries. However, as a result of the pace-setting effect of developments in these countries, supported by export of designs (for licensed production), components and entire systems, the impact of indigenous developmental efforts can be observed down through the whole structure of alternative means of acquiring weapons.

## The development and production of major weapons

At the end of World War II, only five countries—the United States, the Soviet Union, the United Kingdom, Canada and Sweden—had any significant capacity to develop major weapons. In 1973 some 30 countries were engaged in this activity, and others were manufacturing weapons of foreign design under licence.[4]

As noted above, the distribution of indigenous weapon development and production efforts is very uneven. Sizeable nuclear weapon programmes are carried out only in the United States and the Soviet Union, with much smaller efforts also underway in France and China. In the case of conventional (non-nuclear) weapons, the number of countries with an indigenous development capacity is much larger, but the volume of work remains concentrated in the four main arms-producing countries—the USA, the USSR, the UK and France (table 8.3). The US programme is by far the largest, and also, in most cases, involves the most advanced technology. The Soviet programme is also comprehensive, but it appears to be characterized by long production runs of basic

[4] Some of these countries, notably France, FR Germany, Italy and Japan, were major arms producers before World War II but the majority have entered the field since then.

**Table 8.3. Numbers of indigenously designed major conventional weapons under developm**

| | Aircraft | | | | | Missiles[b] | | | | |
|---|---|---|---|---|---|---|---|---|---|---|
| | Super-sonic fighters/ trainers | Subsonic fighters/ trainers | Others with max. weight >10 000 kg[a] | Others with max. weight <10 000 kg | Heli-copters | Anti-air-craft | Anti-ship | Anti-sub-marine | Anti-tank | Othe |
| USA | 11 | 7 | 9 | 3 | 10 | 11 | 2 | 1 | 2 | 8 |
| USSR | 5 | 1 | 3 | .. | 3 | 5 | 7 | (1) | 1 | 1 |
| France | 7 | – | 1 | – | 5 | 6 | 1 | 1 | 5 | 3 |
| UK | 1 | 3 | 3 | 4 | 1 | 11 | 2 | – | 2 | 1 |
| Other developed | 5 | 14 | 9 | 22 | 9 | 10 | 7 | 1 | 7 | 2 |
| Third world | 4 | 2 | 1 | 10 | 2 | 1 | 1 | – | 1 | – |

*Source:* Appendix 8D.

[a] This category includes bombers, medium and heavy transports, maritime patrol and airborne ea warning aircraft.

[b] For the purposes of the table missiles were classified according to their target irrespective of launching platform. The category "other" comprises missiles intended for the destruction of large, fi ground targets such as cities, missile silos, radar installations, airfields and so on.

[c] The numbers refer to different classes of ships. Ships of less than 1 000 tons displacement are gener regarded as coastal patrol vessels.

designs, with the result that fewer different systems are in production at any one time.[5] Together, the United Kingdom and France are producing about as many different major conventional weapon systems as all of the remaining developed countries combined.

Although the programmes of countries other than the four main arms producers are comparatively small and are concentrated in low technology areas such as light aircraft and small warships, the volume of work in progress was very much greater in 1973 than it was 15 or even 10 years ago. In a number of developed and underdeveloped countries— including China, FR Germany, India, Israel and Japan—major long-term expansions in weapon development and production capacity are under way.[6] Moreover, unless some positive steps are made toward global disarmament, the horizontal and vertical proliferation of conventional weapon production capacity will almost certainly continue.[7]

The arms race in conventional weapons, and particularly the acquisi-

[5] The figures for the Soviet Union have a downward bias owing to the complete exclusion of systems in the design stage—that is, prior to the testing of a prototype—about which virtually no information is available.

[6] The expansion in underdeveloped countries is analysed in more detail in reference [3].

[7] The likelihood that the number of weapon-producing countries will increase even further is illustrated by the fact that four countries—Greece, Turkey, Iran and Pakistan—are presently establishing national aircraft industries, initially for the maintenance and overhaul of military aircraft, but with licensed production and indigenous design as longer-term objectives. Other countries such as Taiwan and South Africa have already followed this course.

n large-scale production in 1973

s^c

| [Nucl]ear-powered [sub]marines | Conventionally powered submarines | Surface ships >1000 tons displacement | Surface ships <1000 tons displacement | Armoured vehicles Main battle tanks | Light tanks | Others |
|---|---|---|---|---|---|---|
| – | 9 |  | – | 2 | – | 3 |
| – | 4 |  | 2 | 1 | – | 3 |
| 1 | 3 |  | 4 | 1 | 2 | 7 |
| 2 | 6 |  | 4 | 2 | 1 | 3 |
| 6 | 10 |  | 15 | 6 | 2 | 10 |
| 1 | 2 |  | 10 | 2 | 2 | 6 |

tion by more and more countries of the ability to develop and manu-facture their own major weapons, is a neglected phenomenon, despite the fact that it is these weapons that have been used in all the wars fought since World War II. For this reason it is worth pointing out that the financial and technical resources devoted to the development and production of conventional weapons are far greater than those absorbed by the nuclear programmes.

While the number of major conventional weapon programmes under way in 1973 (table 8.3) provides a good index of the volume of work, it nonetheless understates the intensity of the weapon technology ef-fort. Weapons have tended to become increasingly specialized so that many basic systems, particularly aircraft, are produced in multiple ver-sions, each with a specific task.[8] Similarly, there is a continuous ef-fort to incorporate the latest technological advances in a given basic design. Successive models of existing weapons, as well as completely new weapons, are almost invariably more sophisticated, more costly and more lethal than their predecessors. (See appendix 7A.)

The phenomenal growth in the investment costs of weapons has pro-duced powerful pressures in many countries to share these costs. The collaborative weapon programmes[9] under way in 1973 included five aircraft and eight missile systems (see apendices 8D and 8E). In addition, there were a number of national weapon programmes that involved close tech-nical liaison with another country. Another consequence of rising weapon costs is an increase in the tendency for some countries to specialize in

[8] As a result, weapon systems exist today which had no counterpart 10 years ago. Radar-jamming aircraft and missiles for defence against cruise missiles (so-called point-defence missile systems) are two examples.
[9] Collaboration is defined as the participation by two or more countries in the design and development of a weapon system, a process that requires the participating countries to agree on the roles the weapon is to fulfil and on its performance parameters.

particular areas of military technology, a phenomenon reflected in the substantial international trade in weapon components. Thus, for example, Dutch fire-control systems are found on West German submarines and on frigates being built in the United Kingdom for Brazil.

### The international trade in major weapons

*The trade between developed countries*

Supplies of major weapons to developed countries are dominated by the major arms-producing countries—the USA, the USSR, France and the UK. At the same time a distinguishing feature of the trade among developed countries is that it flows both ways: of the 27 developed countries that imported major weapons in 1973, 14 were also exporters (see appendix 8F[10]). This contrasts sharply with the pattern of the arms trade with the third world.

The reasons for this are fairly obvious. The ability to develop and manufacture weapons is more widespread among the developed countries but in general these countries have neither the resources nor the political incentive to maintain completely independent arms industries. The trade in weapons among the member countries of such groups as NATO, the WTO or the Commonwealth is comparatively free of military and political constraints, permitting economic considerations to play a larger role in determining the size and structure of national arms industries. The result is a considerable degree of specialization and exchange of technology.[11] Some of the trade has a compulsory element. Thus West German payments to the United States to help support the costs of the US forces stationed in Germany primarily take the form of purchases of weapons.

The most noteworthy importing country is Spain which, during 1972 and 1973, received or had on order a wide range of major weapons, including about 80 supersonic fighter aircraft. These imports supplement an expanding indigenous capacity for the development and manufacture of weapons, a trend reflected in the steady increase in Spain's military expenditure.

[10] Appendix 8F does not include the United States and the Soviet Union because imports of major weapons by these two countries are negligible in relation to their indigenous programmes. The United States is currently importing the VTOL Harrier strike aircraft from the United Kingdom, a temporary departure from a long-standing policy to produce everything indigenously. Some members of Congress have argued that the USA should be less rigid in this respect, but so far this view has not prevailed to any significant extent. The only major items that the Soviet Union is known to import are light jet trainers from Czechoslovakia and Poland.

[11] For this reason the trade in complete weapons between developed countries presents only a part of the total picture. Also important is the trade in major components of weapons, as mentioned above. While most industrialized and some underdeveloped countries can and do build basic weapon platforms such as ship hulls or airframes, only a comparatively small number of countries have the capacity to develop the engines, electronics and armaments required to transform these basic platforms into modern weapons.

**Chart 8.1. Value and distribution of the trade in major weapons with the third world in 1972 and 1973, by recipient and major supplier**

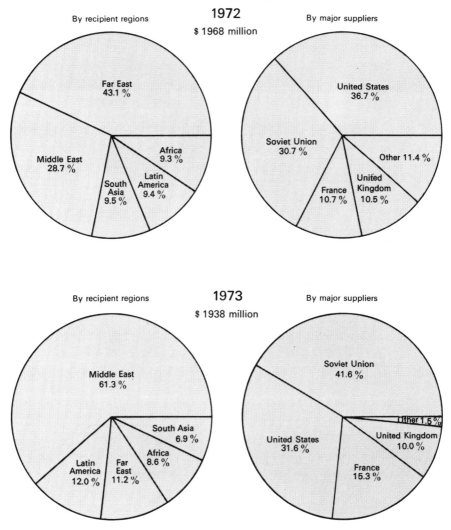

By recipient regions

**1972**

$ 1968 million

By major suppliers

Far East 43.1 %

Middle East 28.7 %

South Asia 9.5 %

Latin America 9.4 %

Africa 9.3 %

United States 36.7 %

Soviet Union 30.7 %

France 10.7 %

United Kingdom 10.5 %

Other 11.4 %

By recipient regions

**1973**

$ 1938 million

By major suppliers

Middle East 61.3 %

Latin America 12.0 %

Far East 11.2 %

Africa 8.6 %

South Asia 6.9 %

Soviet Union 41.6 %

United States 31.6 %

France 15.3 %

United Kingdom 10.0 %

Other 1.5 %

*The trade with the third world*

During both 1972 and 1973 the countries of the third world imported major weapons valued at about $1.9 billion (in constant 1968 prices).[12]

[12] The values are based on a list prepared by SIPRI of comparable 1968 prices for different types of major weapons. The figures do not, therefore, correspond to the actual monetary value of major weapon transactions in 1973. Similarly, they do not measure the size of the cash flow between suppliers and recipients in 1973 because most transactions involve credit arrangements of some kind and some are on a grant basis. The valuation system was designed primarily to provide an index of the quantity of resources absorbed in the arms trade with the third world. The figures are therefore useful for showing changes in the distribution of this trade and the trend in its value over time. Because SIPRI's

**Table 8.4. Regional distribution of exports of major weapons to the third world, 1972–73,**

| | Value of supplies, US $ million | | Percentage distribution | | | |
|---|---|---|---|---|---|---|
| | | | Middle East | | Far East | |
| | 1972 | 1973 | 1972 | 1973 | 1972 | 1973 |
| USA | 722 | 612 | *20.9* | *67.7* | *72.1* | *24.4* |
| USSR | 605 | 807 | *41.0* | *87.0* | *47.3* | *0.5* |
| France | 210 | 297 | *7.4* | *7.3* | *0.7* | *9.5* |
| UK | 208 | 194 | *61.0* | *45.2* | *5.2* | *13.1* |

*Source:* SIPRI worksheets.

There was, however, a significant shift in the regional distribution of these imports and in the rank order of the major suppliers (chart 8.1). The 1972 figure was bolstered by large supplies of weapons to Viet-Nam prior to the January 1973 ceasefire agreement. In 1973 the drop in supplies to Viet-Nam was fully offset by supplies to Israel, Egypt and Syria during and immediately after the October War. Also noteworthy was the 25 per cent increase in the value of major weapons supplied to Latin America.

The regional distribution of the arms exports of the four main suppliers is shown in table 8.4. Arms supplies to a particular region tend to vary erratically from year to year, but the observation can still be made that exports by France and the United Kingdom, particularly the former, tend to be more evenly distributed over the major regions of the world than is the case for either the United States or the Soviet Union. The latter two countries export weapons primarily for political or military reasons, economic considerations being of secondary importance. For France and the United Kingdom the motivations are reversed and both countries vigorously promote the sale of weapons on a global scale.

This is particularly true of France. Following the restrictions on oil supplies and the huge increases in the prices of oil, France was one of the first countries to attempt to secure barter arrangements with the major oil-producing countries in the Middle East, offering French technology and armaments in exchange for long-term supplies of oil. It seems reasonable to forecast a large increase in French arms sales to the Middle East. There is certainly no lack of demand for major weapons in this region and both of France's major competitors, the United States and the United Kingdom, are currently at some disadvantage, the former because of its long-standing support for Israel and the latter because it

historical arms trade registers are currently being revised and up-dated the publication in this Yearbook of time series data on the value of arms imports by third world countries was not possible.

**by major suppliers**

| Percentage distribution | | | | | | Number of countries receiving major weapons valued at $1 million or more | |
|---|---|---|---|---|---|---|---|
| South Asia | | Africa | | Latin America | | | |
| 1972 | 1973 | 1972 | 1973 | 1972 | 1973 | 1972 | 1973 |
| – | 3.5 | 0.8 | 0.3 | 6.2 | 4.1 | 16 | 20 |
| 8.5 | 5.4 | – | 3.6 | 3.1 | 3.5 | 8 | 10 |
| 10.6 | 12.7 | 54.6 | 29.8 | 26.7 | 40.5 | 17 | 16 |
| 18.0 | 14.5 | 4.7 | 8.6 | 10.9 | 18.5 | 13 | 14 |

embargoed arms supplies to the combatants in the recent war. The British embargo was lifted after the war but the fact that it was imposed during a time of crisis may make it more difficult for the United Kingdom to secure new orders for weapons from the countries of this region.

The tendency for more and more third world countries to acquire sophisticated weapons has persisted in recent years. For example, the number of third world countries possessing supersonic aircraft, which expanded from four in 1958 to 28 in 1968, had, by 1973, reached 39. A parallel trend is the growing willingness on the part of supplying countries to make their latest weapons available for export. Spectacular illustrations of this are the recent US decision to supply the F-14A to Iran and the reported Soviet export of the MiG-25 to Syria. These aircraft—which are the most sophisticated fighters available in the USA and the USSR—have been committed to export within two years of entering production for indigenous procurement.

## III. *The Middle East*

### The Arab-Israeli War

On 6 October 1973, a fourth war broke out between Israel and its Arab neighbours, Egypt and Syria. Despite its short duration—18 days—the war was extremely costly, with some 20 000 persons killed or seriously wounded.

Perhaps the only beneficial effect of the war was the renewed determination to find a solution to the Arab-Israeli conflict. The severity of the losses made both sides acutely aware of the need for a peaceful settlement of the dispute. Similarly the United States and the Soviet Union were reminded of the comparative ease with which a conflict be-

[13] The unit cost of this aircraft to Iran will be $30 million, including spares and supporting equipment. SIPRI's military expenditure tables list 41 countries whose total expenditure in 1972 (at current prices and exchange rates) was less than this figure.

149

tween third parties could bring them to a state of confrontation. The détente proclaimed by these two countries proved too immature to enable them to act decisively to bring about an early ceasefire, although ultimately their joint efforts were successful.

A second major international ramification of the war was that it provided the impetus for the major Arab oil-producing countries seriously to attempt to use control of oil supplies as a means of securing favourable changes in the political attitude of states towards the Arab-Israeli dispute. The security of oil supplies and, indeed, of raw material supplies in general has become a major issue in most countries of the world and may well become a main source of future conflict.[14]

In addition, the restrictions on oil supplies and the accompanying leap in oil prices have drastically altered the economic outlook of countries and may well generate fundamental changes in economic growth and development philosophies.

The war was also important internationally in the narrow military sense. Both sides employed a wide range of highly sophisticated conventional weapons and analyses of the relative performance of these weapons have been fed back into the weapon programmes of the major arms-producing countries.[15] Over the longer term it is possible that changes will be made in the tactical use of weapons as a result, for example, of the demonstrated vulnerability of the tank to modern anti-tank missiles. (See chapter 2.)

*Material losses in the war*

At the time of the outbreak of the war, both sides possessed large arsenals of sophisticated military equipment, to a large extent accumulated in the six years which separated this conflict from the previous one. Over this period both Israel and Egypt more than doubled the level of their military expenditures. The increase in Syria, nearly 90 per cent, was only slightly less dramatic.

Most of the weapons employed in the war—in the case of Egypt and Syria virtually 100 per cent—were imported, primarily from the United States in the case of Israel and from the Soviet Union in the case of Egypt and Syria. Over the period 1968 to 1972, Egypt and Syria imported at least 440 jet fighters, 2 000 tanks and other armoured vehicles as well as helicopters, medium bombers (for Egypt) and a wide range of missiles and munitions. Over the same period, Israel acquired at least 300 jet

[14] For example, the dispute over the ownership of the Paracel and Spratly Islands in the South China Sea appears to be at least partly motivated by the likelihood of oil reserves being discovered near these islands.
[15] In the United States, for example, the Department of Defense submitted to Congress in February 1974 a $6.2 billion supplementary budget, of which slightly more than $2 billion is said to be for programmes related to the experience gained as a result of the war.

**Table 8.5. Estimated material losses in the October 1973 Arab-Israeli War**[a]

|  | Aircraft | Tanks | Ships |
|---|---|---|---|
| Egypt/Syria | 450 | 1 900 | (13) |
| Israel | 105 | 800 + | (3) |
| **Total** | **555** | **(2 700)** | **(16)** |

[a] The aircraft totals consist predominently of jet fighters and fighter-bombers; losses of helicopters and other types of aircraft were of the order of 10 per cent of the total. The Israeli figure for tanks includes other types of armoured vehicles and the same is presumably true of the Arab figure. Only a few naval battles took place during the war and apparently only between missile-armed patrol boats; the figures are less certain than those for aircraft and tanks.

The Egyptian and Syrian forces were strengthed by contingents from many other Arab countries. Figures for losses suffered by these forces include 21 fighter and 125 tanks for Iraq and 20 tanks for Jordan. [4]

fighters (of which more than 100 were F-4 Phantoms), 500 tanks and other armoured vehicles plus helicopters and missiles.[16]

Losses during the war were extremely heavy. Of the combined initial inventories of the three major combatants, about one-third of the aircraft and one-half of the tanks were lost during less than three weeks of fighting. Some widely quoted estimates of matériel losses are listed in table 8.5.

The rate of loss of weapons and the consumption of munitions was so rapid that each side requested additional supplies within days of the outbreak of fighting. The Soviet airlift, reportedly begun on a minor scale on 7 October, rapidly escalated into a major air and sea re-supply effort to both Egypt and Syria. The United States began a major airlift of supplies to Israel on 14 October.

The scale of these respective re-supply efforts amounted to what might be termed instant rearmament for the major combatants. Losses of fighters and tanks appear to have been substantially made good even while the fighting was still in progress. Within three months of the cease-fire, each side possessed force levels substantially the same as those prevailing before the war.[17] It appears, however, that the respective major suppliers, particularly the United States, made the full replacement of losses conditional on progress towards a settlement.

*Financial cost*

The October War was also extremely expensive in financial terms. Israeli estimates of the cost to them of the first week and the first two weeks

[16] The figures are obtained from SIPRI's historical registers of the arms trade with the third world, due to be published in 1974. They exclude the large quantities of arms supplied in the second half of 1967 to replace losses in the Six Day War.

[17] Some of the weapons received were superior to any operated prior to the war. Egypt received 35–40 new long-range MiG-21MFs, and the "Scud" surface-to-surface missiles with an estimated range of 165–280 kilometres. Israel acquired new anti-tank and air-to-surface missiles (TOW and Maverick, respectively).

of the war were $1.9 billion and $4.1 billion, respectively. In December 1973 the Chairman of the American Israel Public Affairs Committee stated that provisional estimates of the military cost of the war totalled $6.0 billion. [5] It is not known how these war costs have been computed but other data, presented below, support figures of this general order of magnitude.

Israel's regular military budget for the financial year covering the period of the war was $1.5 billion (at current exchange rates). After the war a supplementary budget of $2.7 billion was announced, of which about 90 per cent ($2.4 billion) was said to be for defence purposes. In December 1973 the US Congress agreed to provide $2.2 billion in military assistance to Israel, $1 billion in the form of grants and $1.2 billion in credits repayable over 25 years. By the end of January 1974 approximately $1.6 billion of this assistance had been provided and this sum would be largely additive to the $2.4 billion supplementary budget. In addition, substantial funds were raised by Jewish organizations in many countries, particularly the United States.

Less information is available for the Arab countries. One source quotes a figure of $2.5 billion for the cost of the war to Egypt. [6] In Syria, military expenditure in the financial year covering the war period was reported to be almost double the budgeted figure, which suggests additional outlays directly attributable to the war of about $0.2 billion. The Soviet supplies provided during and immediately after the war have been estimated to value $2 billion. These supplies were reportedly paid for in cash by the Arab countries supporting Egypt and Syria, primarily Saudi Arabia, and could presumably be added to the figures above.

Summarizing these scattered figures, it seems likely that the total immediate cost of the war was in the region of $8–10 billion. The longer-term costs of the war, both direct and indirect, will be immeasurably larger.

**The Persian Gulf**

The military build-up in the Middle East is not exclusively related to the Arab-Israeli dispute. The other focal point is the Persian Gulf, a passage of critical importance for the shipment of oil. The countries bordering the Persian Gulf have dramatically increased their military expenditures in recent years, with Iran and Saudi Arabia in the vanguard. Over the decade 1963–73 the average *annual* rate of increase of military expenditure in Iran and in Saudi Arabia was 23 per cent.

There is every indication that the pace of the build-up in this region will accelerate even more. The largely successful use of oil as a "political weapon" and the recent huge increase in the price of oil have provided these countries with enormous bargaining power and essentially unlimited financial resources. Weapons received or on order in 1973 for these countries have contract values totalling billions of dollars. During 1973, for example, Iran had outstanding orders for about 800 Chieftain main battle tanks, 250 Scorpion light tanks, more than 200 F-4E/F-5E fighter aircraft and nearly 500 helicopters, some 200 of which will be Sea Cobra gunshps armed with TOWs, the latest US anti-tank missile. Early in 1974, Iran also ordered 30 F-14As at a total cost of some $900 million. The register in appendix 8F documents similar developments in the other countries of the region.[18] Moreover, most of these countries have embarked on ambitious programmes for using their oil revenues to industrialize their economies, and it appears almost certain that in some cases these programmes will include the development of arms industries. This is already the case in Iran.

**Conclusion**

If the proportion of gross domestic product devoted to military uses is used as an index, the Middle East has become the most militarized region in the world, a state of affairs which is incompatible with the demonstrated need to prevent instability in this region. In only two countries—Cyprus and Lebanon—has this proportion shown any long-term tendency to fall or even remain constant. Jordan could possibly be included in this group, but the proportion in that country has been consistently high with a minimum figure over the past decade of 12.8 per cent. Elsewhere the pattern over the past ten years has been for the proportion to increase substantially.

# IV. *NATO and the WTO*

NATO and the WTO totally dominate the world military scene. Four countries—the United States, the Soviet Union, the United Kingdom and France—provide the bulk of the world's capacity to design and produce weapons and, relatedly, virtually monopolize the international trade in arms, particularly with the third world. The combined military expenditures of the two alliances account for more than 80 per cent of the world total.

Total military expenditure in NATO is estimated at $98.4 billion for 1973, some 3 per cent less than in 1972. This fall is due mainly to a substantial drop in US expenditure; in the other NATO countries increases and decreases largely offset each other.

United States expenditure for 1973 is expected to show a fall of 4.9

---

[18] Kuwait, which acquired only a few patrol boats in 1973, is about to begin a $1.6 billion military re-equipment programme. [7]

per cent. The defence budgets relevant to the computation of expenditure for calendar year 1973—those for fiscal years 1973 and 1974—were subject to comparatively successful Congressional pressure to prevent substantial increases in military spending, so that in real terms, after adjusting for price changes, expenditure fell. The outlook for 1974 is that expenditure will be about the same as in 1973. The 8.8 per cent increase in national security expenditures proposed for fiscal year 1975 ($87.8 billion against $80.6 billion for fiscal year 1974) will substantially accommodate the probable increase in the price level.[19]

The outstanding feature of the fiscal year 1975 national security budget is the sizable increase proposed for expenditure on nuclear weapons. Most of the additional funds are absorbed by two on-going development programmes—the B-1 bomber and the Trident missile and submarine—which are moving into their most expensive phase, but the budget also calls for the initiation of a number of other projects in connection with the new "counterforce" strategy. (See chapters 5 and 6 above.)

For fiscal year 1974, US expenditures related to the conflict in Viet-Nam are estimated at $4.1 billion, with a similar figure forecast for fiscal year 1975.[20] Although small in relation to total military expenditure in the United States these outlays are still very large in absolute terms: only six countries in the world have total military expenditures that exceed this figure. The magnitude of US spending reflects the scale of the fighting which continues despite the ceasefire. Of the estimated US outlays for Viet-Nam in fiscal year 1974 some $2 billion is for major weapons and ammunitions: a clause in the ceasefire agreement permits the replacement of these items on a one-for-one basis (see chapter 3).

[19] It is worth pointing out in this context that SIPRI figures for military expenditure in constant prices are intended to provide a measure of the quantity of resources devoted to military uses and of the changes in this quantity over time. For this purpose, SIPRI's method of deflating total military expenditure by the consumer price index is deemed adequate. However, total military expenditure covers expenditure on a variety of activities to which different rates of inflation apply. Thus expenditure on a particular component of the total may rise in real terms even though the total remains constant or even falls, in real terms. The fiscal year 1975 US military budget is a case in point. Procurement outlays are slated to rise 8.6 per cent, which will almost certainly imply an increase in real terms since prices in manufacturing rise comparatively slowly. The same may also be true of R&D expenditures, which are slated to rise by 6 per cent, although no directly relevant price index exists for this activity. For a further discussion of these issues see the SIPRI publication *The Meaning and Measurement of Military Expenditure.* [8]

[20] In current price terms the prevailing level of total US military expenditure equals or exceeds that at the peak of the US involvement in Viet-Nam. The extent to which resources previously devoted to Viet-Nam have been diverted to other military programmes is difficult to determine. The primary reason for this is that during the years of withdrawal from Viet-Nam the USA was also preparing for the all-volunteer force, draft induction being formally ended on 1 January 1973. As expected, this programme proved extremely expensive, with military pay accounting for additional billions of dollars each year despite substantial reductions in the number of personnel. It could be argued that the so-called Viet-Nam "peace dividend" has been used to achieve an all-volunteer force. In general, however, there have been no significant increases in expenditure on such things as procurement or research and development that can be directly linked to declining US expenditures in Viet-Nam.

154

The major factor shaping current European attitudes toward military affairs is the Mutual Force Reduction (MFR) negotiations which began in Vienna in October 1973. Public support for military expenditure has been declining for some time in many European countries, a phenomenon reflected in the relatively modest increase in expenditure: between 1963 and 1973 total military expenditure by European NATO countries increased by 19.2 per cent. During 1973, therefore, many NATO and national defence officials argued that the fact that force reductions were under negotiation did not justify any unilateral relaxation of military efforts.

This sentiment is reflected in the military budget estimates for 1974 and 1974/75. The budgets for France, FR Germany and the Netherlands show increases that will substantially accommodate inflation. Similarly, the Canadian government has adopted a five-year plan under which military expenditure will increase by 7 per cent per annum, one official motive being to enable Canada to maintain its existing contribution to NATO. In Italy expenditure is to be held at roughly the existing level and will therefore probably fall somewhat in real terms. Only in the United Kingdom is expenditure being significantly cut back but this is due primarily to economic necessity rather than to any reassessment of the military situation.

The MFR negotiations have intensified the perennial debate within NATO on burden-sharing and particularly the issue of the net foreign-exchange cost to the United States of stationing its forces in Europe. This cost has averaged roughly $1 billion annually in recent years; estimates for fiscal year 1974 (ending in June 1974) range up to $1.5 billion. Mounting criticism of this annual deficit culminated in an amendment to the fiscal year 1974 Procurement Bill which requires that the foreign-exchange costs of US troops stationed in European NATO countries be reduced to zero, either by persuading the European countries to increase the value of their purchases from the United States (so-called "offset" purchases) or by withdrawing US forces.

Although the amendment does not take effect until mid-1975, US officials have attempted to use the prospect of unilateral reductions of US forces in Europe to reach more complete offset agreements, particularly in the case of FR Germany where some two-thirds of the foreign-exchange costs are incurred.[21] Initial negotiations were completely unsuccessful. One European response was to claim that any substantial increase in military outlays was politically and—given the impact of the large increases in the price of oil—economically impossible,

---

[21] Over fiscal years 1972 and 1973 FR Germany made offset purchases totalling just over $2 billion. For fiscal years 1974 and 1975 the USA initially requested $3.3 billion together with $310 million for the incremental budgetary cost to the United States of stationing its forces in Europe. The figure eventually agreed upon was $2.2 billion.

so that any additional payments to the United States would be at the expense of strengthening their own forces with the net result that NATO would be weakened. A second argument was that the US balance of payments was moving rapidly into a surplus as a result of the currency realignments which have taken place recently. This improvement, if it persists, together with the willingness of the United States to widen the definition of "offset" purchases, may well eliminate much of the balance-of-payments deficit that the USA incurs due to the stationing of forces in Europe, and thus satisfy the requirements of the amendment to the fiscal year 1974 Procurement Bill.

Whatever the outcome of these cost-sharing negotiations, it is clear that the possibility of unilateral reductions of US forces in Europe has influenced NATO's position at the MFR talks. NATO's current position is that initial force reductions should be confined to US and Soviet troops stationed in Central Europe. (See chapter 4.)

The total military expenditure of the WTO countries is estimated at $71.8 billion for 1973, a marginal increase over the 1972 level and less than 2 per cent higher than the 1970 figure. This small increase is largely due to increases in expenditure by Czechoslovakia, the German Democratic Republic and Poland. In the Soviet Union, which accounts for more than 85 per cent of the total, expenditure has remained constant over the period 1970–73 at an estimated $63 billion. In 1974 Soviet expenditure is budgeted to fall by 1.8 per cent.

These figures for the dollar-equivalent of Soviet military expenditure are substantially higher than those previously published by SIPRI. The basis for the new estimates is described in appendix 8B below. It is impossible to claim a high degree of accuracy for these figures but it is believed that they are more realistic than the earlier estimates.

The economic burden of military expenditure has shown a long-term tendency to fall or at least remain constant in most of the NATO and WTO countries.[22] The significant exceptions are Greece and Portugal in NATO and the German Democratic Republic in the WTO.[23] In the United States and the Soviet Union the burden is now smaller than in any year since the Korean War.[24]

[22] The economic burden of military expenditure is defined as the percentage of gross domestic product (for NATO countries) or net material product (for WTO countries) absorbed by this expenditure. These aggregates differ significantly, so that direct comparisons between the two cannot be made.

[23] The increase for the German Democratic Republic is difficult to account for; it is not reflected, for example, in the absolute size of the East German armed forces. Two explanations can be suggested. Firstly, East German military expenditure increased by 61 per cent in 1968 which suggests some connection with the 1967 price reforms; that is, there may have been an increase in the relative price of some or most military goods and services. However, this explanation does not cover the 43 per cent increase in military expenditure which occurred between 1968 and 1973. A second explanation may therefore be that the German Democratic Republic is gradually assuming more of the costs of the Soviet forces stationed in that country.

[24] The figure for the Soviet Union, 5.7 per cent in 1972, is based on the official defence

**Table 8.6.** **Annual average percentage change in the military expenditures of selected South American countries, 1965–72**

|  | Argen-tina | Bo-livia | Brazil | Chile | Colom-bia | Ecua-dor | Peru | Uru-guay | Vene-zuela |
|---|---|---|---|---|---|---|---|---|---|
| Percentage change | +3.2 | +2.3 | +5.1 | +11.0 | −1.9[a] | +4.1[b] | +7.9 | +11.5 | +6.1 |

*Source:* Appendix 8C.

[a] This is due to the large drop in budgeted expenditure for 1972. The average annual rate of growth in actual expenditure over the period 1965–71 was +10.0 per cent.
[b] 1965–71.

# V. *Significant developments in the rest of the world*

## Latin America

In January 1974 the Peruvian government proposed that Peru and its immediate neighbours freeze their military expenditure at existing levels in order to save resources for economic and social development. It is thought that the proposal will ultimately be extended to the whole Latin American region.

Freezing military expenditures at existing levels will, of course, only save resources if increases in military spending are anticipated: the evidence of past trends suggests that this is a reasonable assumption (table 8.6). The proposal's regional focus considerably reduces the technical problems associated with its implementation but the fact that many countries in the region have large outstanding commitments for new weapons and that two countries, Brazil and Argentina, are going ahead with the establishment of defence industries suggest that the adoption of the proposal will pose difficult problems.

## Japan

Japanese military expenditure continued to rise in 1973 although the size of the increase, 3.6 per cent, was relatively modest in comparison with the average annual increase of 8.8 per cent recorded for the years 1965–72. Despite this rapid growth, military expenditure continues to account for less than 1 per cent of Japan's gross domestic product. If Japan intends to keep the proportion of GDP devoted to military

budget. This was done for reasons of consistency since the calculations for all other countries are based on official figures, if these exist. Using SIPRI estimates of total Soviet military expenditure in rouble terms (see appendix 8B), the proportion becomes 7.4 per cent. Going one step further, if SIPRI's estimates of the dollar-equivalent of Soviet military expenditure are taken in conjunction with official Soviet estimates of the dollar-equivalent of Soviet national income, as distinct from Net Material Product, the figure becomes 14.8 per cent.

uses at this low level it may have to revise its current five-year defence build-up programme downwards, because comparatively slow rates of economic growth are forecast for the immediate future.

## Australia

In Australia, military expenditure will probably fall quite substantially in 1974. The Labour Government has dropped or deferred many of the major procurement plans that existed when it took office and is withdrawing the Australian forces stationed in Malaysia and Singapore. Australian forces in Viet-Nam were withdrawn at the end of 1972. The military budget for 1973/74 is only 2.6 per cent above that for the previous year, while inflation is currently running at about 13 per cent a year.

## India

Indian military expenditure fell substantially in 1973 after a sharp rise in 1972 due to the war with Pakistan. During 1973 the government re-emphasized its determination to make India self-sufficient in the production of weapons. In future, emphasis will be placed on wholly indigenous design, development and production of weapons, and collaborative and licence-production arrangements for the acquisition of weapons will be avoided.

## References

1. *Resources Devoted to Military Research and Development: An International Comparison* (Stockholm, Almqvist & Wiksell, 1972, Stockholm International Peace Research Institute).
2. *Statement by the Director of Defense Research and Engineering, Dr John S. Foster Jr., On the Fiscal Year 1973 Defense RDT&E Program, before the Armed Services Committee, US Senate, 17 February 1972* [Washington, 1972] Section 1, pp. 22–25.
3. *World Armaments and Disarmament, SIPRI Yearbook 1973* (Stockholm, Almqvist & Wiksell, 1973, Stockholm International Peace Research Institute) chapter 10.
4. *International Defence Review*, December 1973, p. 699.
5. Statement by I. L. Kenen, *Emergency Military Assistance for Israel and Cambodia*, Hearings, US Senate Committee on Foreign Relations, 13 December 1973 (Washington, US Government Printing Office, 1973) p. 114.
6. *Milavnews*, NL-145/11/73, p. 7.
7. *Milavnews*, NL-147/1/74, p. 16.
8. *The Meaning and Measurment of Military Expenditure*, SIPRI Research Report No. 10 (Stockholm, Almqvist & Wiksell, 1973, Stockholm International Peace Research Institute).

# Appendix 8A

## *Sources and methods*

*Square-bracketed references, thus [1], refer to the list of references on page 171.*

*This appendix describes the sources, objectives, scope and methodology of appendices 8C–8F. Following a general introduction of matter relevant to all of these, there are separate sections on the individual appendices. Detailed information is included on appendices 8D (indigenous arms production) and 8E (licensed production), which appear in the Yearbook for the first time this year. For appendices 8C (military expenditure) and 8F (arms trade), only the main points are noted: the sources and methods of these compilations have been described in full in previous editions of the SIPRI Yearbook, to which the reader is referred for further detail on all points except the estimates of the military expenditure of the USSR. The Soviet expenditure estimates have been revised this year and the sources and methods of the new figures are described in detail in appendix 8B.*

## I. *Introduction*

Previous editions of the *SIPRI Yearbook* have contained annually updated data on world military expenditure and on arms supplies to the third world. In addition to continuing these series (appendices 8C, 8E and 8F), this volume contains new surveys on major weapon development and production projects in all countries (appendices 8D and 8E) and on arms supplies to developed countries (appendices 8E and 8F).

### Purpose of the data

Together, the military expenditure tables and the arms production and trade registers form the nucleus of a comprehensive, quantitative survey of world armaments. The purpose of the military expenditure estimates is to provide an indication of the overall volume of military activity in different countries, and of the resources absorbed by this activity. The arms production and trade registers show the origin, flow, costs and main characteristics of the major weapons now being acquired in all countries. This data is essential to an analysis of the world arms race for several reasons. First, the growth in the lethal power of the world's armaments results not so much from increases in the number of men under arms or in the stock of weapons, as from the replacement of existing arms by new and more effective ones. This qualitative aspect of the arms race makes it necessary to look at the development and spread of new weapons, and not just at quantitative expansions. Second, since technological advances provide continual gains in productive efficiency, qualitative as well as quantitative "improvements" in the world's arsenals can be made even in the absence of rising military budgets. For this reason, aggregate measures such as military expenditure may obscure an on-going arms race, which becomes apparent only when trends in weaponry are examined. Third, to the extent that successive "generations" of weapons are more and more complex and costly, they give rise to pressures to maintain and increase the current high levels of military spending. In addition to absorbing a large fraction of military expenditure (about 30 per cent) directly, the introduction of new arms leads to higher costs in the other main areas of military spending—the pay of military personnel and the support of peacetime operations. In general, successive generations of weapons require increasingly skilled military operators and are increasingly costly to use and maintain in training, manoeuvres, standing deployments and other operations.

The arms production and trade registers give a reasonable indication of the nature and amount of weapon procurement activity under way in 1973. In addition, they reflect the initiation of an attempt to assemble sufficient data to permit a thorough analysis of the main longer-term trends in armaments: the rate of introduction of new weapons; trends in weapon costs and in developmental gestation periods; and similarities and differences in the arms procurement policies of different countries. The limited coverage of the data assembled thus far and the lack of historical data on weapon production and weapon exports to developed countries have made it impossible to undertake analysis along these lines this year. However, as noted below, collection of complementary data is being undertaken and it is hoped to provide a fuller analysis in future.

**Relation to previously published and forthcoming SIPRI data**

The military expenditure series (appendix 8C) continues the pattern established in previous editions of the *SIPRI Yearbook,* in providing data for a 21-year span, with the current year added and the earliest year shown in the previous *Yearbook* dropped. Comparable current price expenditure estimates going back to 1948 can be found in previous editions of the *Yearbook.* Constant-price figures can also be found in earlier *Yearbooks,* although the base year for the constant-price series was changed from 1960 to 1970 beginning with the *SIPRI Yearbook 1973.* Complete series of military expenditure as a percentage of gross domestic product (GDP) appear for the first time this year. GDP ratios for selected recent years were published in the 1973 *Yearbook*, but this indicator was not included in previous editions and is not available for the earliest years (1948–51).

As noted above, data on arms supplied to third world countries have also appeared in previous editions of the *Yearbook*, in the form of registers covering one or two years, for the period from 1968 to 1972. In addition, provisional third world arms trade worksheets for the period back to 1950 have been maintained at SIPRI; and tables showing the values of third world arms supplies for each year since 1950 have been published in previous *Yearbooks*, as well as in the separately published SIPRI study *The Arms Trade with the Third World*. The latter study also included some of the historical arms trade registers. The third world arms trade worksheets for the period from 1950 to 1972 have recently been finalized, and revised estimates of the value of the trade are now being calculated. The historical registers and the revised tables of values will appear in a separate SIPRI study, to be published in the autumn of 1974. Since the historical tables of values are under revision, they are not included in this edition of the *Yearbook* but they are scheduled to reappear next year. Estimates for 1972 and 1973 which will be consistent with the revised tables are given in chapter 8, page 147.

It should be noted that data on arms supplies to the third world, which were previously published in a single register, are now divided between two registers: appendix 8E, covering licensed production and appendix 8F, covering pure imports, with no indigenous production component. As in previous years, estimates of the value of the trade include both types of import.

In addition to covering third world arms supplies, appendices 8E and 8F include imports by developed countries. This means that, for the first time, a list of worldwide arms transfers is provided. In an attempt to give a more complete initial picture of recent transfers to developed countries, the first register of pure imports by developed countries (appendix 8F) has been extended to cover a two-year period (1972 and 1973), instead of being confined to the single year (1973) as in the case of the third world countries. Since sizable arms imports by any given country tend to occur intermittently, rather than in a steady stream, it would be misleading to draw far-reaching conclusions about the flow of arms even from a two-year survey. For this reason, no attempt has been made to give an aggregate picture of the volume of the trade among the developed countries, in the form of tables of values similar to those constructed for third world arms transfers. Registers of the trade among developed countries covering a longer period are now being compiled and it is planned to provide estimates of the value of the transfers when these registers are published.

The register of indigenously designed weapons in development or production (appendix 8D) is new this year. This register and that covering licensed production projects (appendix 8E) together provide a picture, which is probably very nearly complete, of the total current production of major weapon systems in all countries. This is the first time that a worldwide survey covering all the major weapons which are presently in some stage of the production process has been published by SIPRI or, to our knowledge, anywhere. Other weapon surveys appear periodically in reference books, trade journal articles and special studies. These are generally less broad in scope, giving instead greater depth of detail on particular sectors or particular aspects of weapons. Almost all include, and many concentrate primarily on, somewhat older weapon systems, which are still in service but no longer in production. Restrictions as to geographic region or type of weapon, or both, are common. Surveys with one or more such limitations which have been undertaken at SIPRI are: several studies relating to strategic nuclear weapon systems; a comprehensive list of antisubmarine warfare equipment and systems; and two surveys of weapon production in third world countries. SIPRI has also undertaken work relating to certain types of military equipment and arms which are not covered by appendices 8D and 8E. As a general rule, the appendices exclude small arms, ammunition and artillery; weapon system components; and unarmed military support systems and equipment. In-depth analysis of items which may be described as falling under one or another of these headings is given in SIPRI studies relating to chemical and biological warfare; the militarization of the deep ocean; the automation of land warfare; and reconnaissance satellites.

It is planned to update all of the present data series in future editions of the *Yearbook*. In the case of the indigenous-production register, the complete list is to be produced only at intervals, with notices given in the intervening years of items to be added to (for new starts) or dropped from (when production ceases) the previously published list.

## Countries and time period covered

The appendices cover all countries in the world. In each case, the countries are arranged alphabetically within the following regional groupings: NATO (North Atlantic Treaty Organization), WTO (Warsaw Treaty Organization), Other Europe, Middle East, South Asia, Far East, Oceania, Africa, Central America and South America. The military expenditure tables (appendix 8C) may serve as a guide to the countries included within the regional groupings for the other appendices. The absence of a country, or an entire region, from one or another of the arms production and trade registers means that no activity of the type indicated has been found for that area.

The arms production registers (appendix 8D and 8E) include only items believed to have been actually in production (for both), in development (appendix 8D) or on order (appendix 8E) during calendar year 1973. The arms trade register (appendix 8F) covers items on order or delivered in 1973 in the case of third world countries, and in 1972 or 1973 in the case of developed countries.[1] For the third world countries, the list includes some items which were already on order in 1972 and which were therefore included in the register for 1972 published in the *SIPRI Yearbook 1973.*

In the case of the military expenditure series, estimates for the current year (1974), where available, are included along with figures for earlier years. It should be noted that in each edition of the *Yearbook,* the figure for the current year represents estimated or budgeted outlays; the figure for the immediately preceding year is generally a revised estimate; and the figure for the next preceding year (in the present case, 1972) is, in general, a final figure for actual outlays in that year. The degree of uncertainty relating to current-year figures derives from the fact that unforeseen contingencies may result in actual expenditures which differ, occasionally very widely, from the budgeted amounts; and government accounting procedures can require a considerable time after the closing of the fiscal year to arrive at a final figure for the total amount paid out during that period.

The military expenditure estimates refer to the calendar year in all cases. For countries where the governmental fiscal year differs from the calendar year, conversion to a calendar-year basis is made on the assumption of an even rate of expenditure throughout the fiscal year.

## II. *Sources*

The sources of the data presented in the appendices are of five general types: official national documents; journals; newspapers; books, monographs and annual reference works; and documents issued by international intergovernmental organizations.

The official national documents include budgets; parliamentary or congressional proceedings, reports and hearings; statistics, white papers, annual reports and other documents issued by governments and agencies; and statements by government officials and spokesmen. These and the journals and newspapers contain information relating to both military expenditure and weapon production and trade. Comparatively few books or monographs are used, since the information in such works is generally

[1] For the purposes of aggregating arms trade and production data and military expenditure figures, developed countries are defined as those comprising North America, Europe except Greece and Turkey, South Africa, Japan, Australia and New Zealand. All other countries (Greece and Turkey, all of Africa except South Africa, the Middle East, South Asia, the Far East except Japan, and Latin America) are defined as third world countries.

too dated. An exception is annual reference works, which contain up-to-date information. The main official international documents which are used are those containing information relating to military expenditures. There are no surveys published by international intergovernmental organizations on weapon production or trade.

The following list shows the periodical publications which are examined regularly for relevant data:

**Journals**

Africa Diary (New Delhi)
Air et Cosmos (Paris)
Air Force Magazine (Washington)
Arab Report and Record (London)
Armed Forces Journal (Washington)
Armies and Weapons (Genoa)
Asian Recorder (New Delhi)
Aviation Week and Space Technology (New York)
China Report (New Delhi)
Congressional Quarterly Weekly Report (Washington)
Current Scene (Hong Kong)
Défense Nationale (Paris)
Economist (London)
Far Eastern Economic Review (Hong Kong)
Flight International (London)
Forces Armées Françaises (Paris)
Interavia (Geneva)
Interavia Airletter (Geneva)
International Affairs (London)
International Defense Business (Washington)
International Defense Review (Geneva)
New Times (Moscow)
News Review on China, Mongolia and the Koreas (New Delhi)
News Review on Japan, South East Asia and Australasia (New Delhi)
News Review on South Asia (New Delhi)
News Review on West Asia (New Delhi)
Official Price List (London, Aviation Studies Atlantic)
Peking Review (Peking)
US Naval Institute Proceedings (Annapolis, Md.)
Wehr und Wirtschaft (Munich)

**Newspapers**

Dagens Nyheter (Stockholm)
Daily Telegraph (London)

Financial Times (London)
Hindustan Times (New Delhi)
International Herald Tribune (Paris)
Japan Times (Tokyo)
Krasnaja Zvezda (Moscow)
Le Monde (Paris)
Neue Zürcher Zeitung (Zurich)
New York Times (New York)
Pravda (Moscow)
Standard Tanzania (Dar-es-Salaam)
Svenska Dagbladet (Stockholm)
Times (London)

## Annual publications

For data on military expenditure:

*AID Economic Data Book: Africa* (Washington, United States Agency for International Development)

*AID Economic Data Book: Far East* (Washington, United States Agency for International Development)

*AID Economic Data Book: Latin America* (Washington, United States Agency for International Development)

*AID Economic Data Book: Near East and South Asia* (Washington, United States Agency for International Development)

*Far Eastern Economic Review Yearbook* (Hong Kong, Far Eastern Economic Review)

*Military Balance* (London, International Institute for Strategic Studies)

"NATO defence expenditure", *NATO Review* (Brussels, NATO)

*Statesman's Year-Book* (London, Macmillan)

*Statistical Yearbook* (New York, United Nations)[2]

*World Military Expenditures* (Washington, United States Arms Control and Disarmament Agency)

For data on gross domestic product or net material product:[3]

*Yearbook of National Accounts Statistics* (New York, United Nations)[4]

For data on weapon production and trade:

"Forecast and Inventory", *Aviation Week and Space Technology* (New York, McGraw-Hill)

*International Air Forces and Military Aircraft Directory* (Stapleford, England, Aviation Advisory Services)[5]

[2] This source also contains information on gross domestic product.
[3] In addition to the source listed, two journals, *International Financial Statistics* and *IMF Survey*, both published by the International Monetary Fund (Washington), are used.
[4] This is supplemented by the monthly journal *Monthly Bulletin of Statistics*.
[5] This is supplemented by the monthly journal *Milavnews*.

*Jane's All the World's Aircraft* (London, Sampson Low, Marston & Co.)
*Jane's Fighting Ships* (London, Sampson Low, Marston & Co.)
*Jane's Weapon Systems* (London, Sampson Low, Marston & Co.)
"Military Aircraft of the World", *Flight International* (London, IPC Transport Press)
"World Missile Survey", *Flight International* (London, IPC Transport Press)

## III. *Definitions and restrictions*

The military expenditure estimates are intended to show the amount of money actually spent (outlays) for military purposes. It should be noted that in many countries there are alternative series for funds budgeted, appropriated (set aside) or obligated (committed to be spent). Since our objective is to show the volume of activity, series for actual expenditures have been chosen in preference to these alternatives. Even with this series, there may be some misrepresentation of the volume of activity—particularly for the United States and to a lesser extent for other major arms-producing countries—since payment for arms procurement may lag somewhat behind the actual production work. The expenditure series has the advantage, however, of being the only final measure of the actual amount of resources consumed.

Military expenditures are defined to include weapon research and development, to include military aid in the budget of the donor country and to exclude it from the budget of the recipient country, and to exclude war pensions and payments on war debts.

For calculating the ratio of military expenditure to national product, either gross domestic product (GDP) at purchasers' values or net material product (NMP) has been used, following the practice of the individual countries in identifying national product. GDP is defined as "the final expenditure on goods and services, in purchasers' values, less the c.i.f. [cost, insurance, freight] value of imports of goods and services". [1] NMP is defined as "the net (of depreciation) total amount of goods and productive series produced in a year expressed at realized prices". [2] The ratio of military expenditure to national product will generally be higher when NMP is used, since this measure excludes a variety of services which are included in GDP.

The three arms production and trade registers all cover what we have referred to as "major weapons"—that is, aircraft, ships, armoured vehicles and missiles. Strictly speaking, all of these except missiles are potential "weapon platforms", while missiles are part of "weapon systems". However, our use of the word "weapon" or "major weapon" by and large conforms with general practice. The great majority of the aircraft, ships and armoured vehicles entered in the registers are armed: as such they constitute either the central component of a weapon system which is generally identified by reference to that platform or else a major unitary fighting system. For production of indigenously designed weapons (appendix 8D) and for licensed production in developed countries (appendix 8E), only armed ships and armoured vehicles are included. However, all aircraft—including unarmed transports and utility planes—are covered. The reason for the different treatment of aircraft is two-fold. First, most aircraft can easily be converted to carry armaments and to form effective fighting platforms. This is not equally true of non-armoured vehicles and support ships. Second, the technology required to produce aircraft of any kind is generally more advanced than that required for vehicles and ships which may not differ significantly from widely produced civilian counterparts. The coverage of arms imports by all countries (appendix 8F) and licensed production in third world countries (appendix 8E) is extended to include unarmed ships and armoured vehicles as well as unarmed aircraft, the criterion for inclusion being simply delivery to the armed forces of the country concerned. This results in the listing of a very small number of items of the type not included in the indigenous production register.

As a result of the exclusion of small arms, ammunition and artillery, the coverage of weapon production and imports by third world countries is estimated to reflect only about one-half of the total procurement of military equipment in this region. In the case of the developed countries, which are generally equipped with more sophisticated weaponry, the proportion is probably considerably higher. The main aspect of the procurement activity in these countries which is not reflected in any way in the registers is that associated with infrastructure and support equipment, such as land-based radar systems, communication networks, data-processing facilities, and so on. The satellite systems produced by the United States and the Soviet Union for the purposes of reconnaissance, navigation and communication constitute the most advanced and expensive type of support equipment not covered by the registers: funds for the development and production of space systems are estimated to account for about 5 per cent of the annual US budget for procurement of weapons and equipment.

## IV. *Military expenditure tables (appendix 8C)*

For all but the most recent years, the estimates of the military expenditures of NATO countries are taken from official NATO data, the figures for Warsaw Treaty Organization countries other than the USSR are from national budgets, and the estimates for the remaining countries in the world are in general taken from the United Nations' *Statistical Yearbook*. The figures for the Soviet Union are SIPRI estimates, the methodology of which is explained in appendix 8B. For all countries, the estimates for the most recent years are based on budget figures derived from newspapers and journals and other sources described above.

In order to provide time series estimates of total world military expenditure at constant prices, two operations must be performed. First, all national expenditure must be converted into a common currency: the most widely used unit for such a purpose is the US dollar, which SIPRI has also adopted. For this purpose it is necessary to use constant exchange rates, preferably those prevailing in a "normal" year.[6] Second, it is necessary to adjust for the effect of changes in the level of prices.

For most countries we have used the official exchange rate in 1970 or, if this fluctuated during the year, the weighted average rate. For the Warsaw Treaty Organization countries, special purchasing power parities were used because these yielded more reasonable expenditure relationships both within the WTO and between these countries and the rest of the world. For WTO countries other than the USSR, and for Albania, purchasing power parities calculated by Benoit and Lubell were used. [3] For the USSR, SIPRI estimates of the rouble : dollar purchasing power parity have been calculated (see appendix 8B).

The adjustment for changes in prices was made by applying the consumer price index in each country. In many countries this is the only price index available: as an index of the general movement of prices, it is a reasonable one for showing the trend in the resources absorbed by the military, in constant prices. For further detail on this point, the reader is referred to the *SIPRI Yearbook 1972*. [4]


# V. *Register of indigenously designed weapons in development or production (appendix 8D)*

### Arrangement and classification of entries

Within the four broad categories (aircraft, missiles, ships and armoured vehicles), the systems produced by each country are arranged by function. Thus, aircraft are presented as follows: bombers, fighters, strike, other combat aircraft (for example, maritime patrol), reconnaissance aircraft and other electronic equipment platforms, transports, trainers, utility planes, armed helicopters, transport helicopters and utility helicopters. For all of these categories, except bombers, other combat aircraft, reconnaissance aircraft and armed helicopters, there is a further subdivision between

---

[6] A year in which most of the major currencies had a fixed parity with the dollar.

heavier and lighter types.[7] In the case of missile systems, a set of abbreviated descriptions of the launching platform and target is employed, and entries are listed first by launching platform (fixed land-based, towed, mobile, portable, fixed-wing aircraft, helicopter, ship, submarine) and, within these groups, by target (fixed land-based, tank, missile, fixed-wing aircraft, helicopter, ship, submarine). For ships, the following descriptive categories were evolved on the basis of the nomenclature employed by the majority of countries: strategic submarines (equipped with long-range strategic missiles), hunter-killer (counter-submarine) submarines (fast, nuclear-powered submarines without anti-ship missiles), anti-shipping submarines (equipped with anti-ship missiles), ordinary submarines, coastal submarines, aircraft carriers (over 30 000 tons displacement), cruisers (7 000–25 000 tons), destroyers (3 500–6 999 tons), frigates or escorts (1 350–3 499 tons), corvettes (500–1 300 tons) and patrol boats or missile boats (below 500 tons). In the few cases where national descriptive designations depart radically from this scheme—for example, the US use of "frigate" for ships displacing 7 000–10 000 tons or the French use of "corvette" for a 3 000-ton ship—these standardized descriptions have been inserted in square brackets in place of the official one.

An attempt has been made to place newer systems first and older ones second, within the various functional groupings.

## Aircraft, ship and armoured vehicle armament

No attempt has been made to describe the armaments carried on the combat aircraft since these are generally both too numerous for the space available and variable (that is, most combat aircraft can carry a variety of alternative weapon loads). For armoured vehicles, the main armament is indicated in the first of the columns of standardized data. In the case of ships, symbols indicating the nature and number of all armaments except the limited-capability antisubmarine mortars and rocket launchers are shown directly after the description. The order in which ship armaments are listed is as follows: missiles (ship-to-ship, ship-to-air, ship-to-submarine, submarine-to-submarine, submarine-to-surface), guns, antisubmarine torpedo tubes or torpedo launchers and ordinary torpedo tubes.

## System specifications

The data on speed, weight and range are maximum values in all cases except for ship displacement, which is standard. In some cases these

---

[7] In the case of transport aircraft, the following apply: heavy (over 200 000 kg), medium (50 000–200 000 kg), ordinary (10 000–30 000 kg) and light (6 000–10 000 kg). For fighter and strike aircraft, light types are defined as those weighing less than 11 000 kg. Most unarmed helicopters fall into one of the following categories: heavy lift (over 50 000 kg), medium transport (ca. 20 000 kg), transport (ca. 6 000–7 000 kg), utility (2 000–5 000 kg) or light utility (under 2 000 kg).

values are dependent on a number of variables. For example, in the case of aircraft the figure given for speed is the maximum speed under optimal conditions, which generally means that the aircraft carries no external payload and is flying at or near its maximum altitude.

## Programme history

The dates given for design, prototype test and production are initial dates only, except for data pertaining to the Soviet Union, where little official data relating to weapon system developments is published. In the case of the USSR, the dates shown in the prototype test column generally refer to the time when a system was first reported to have been observed. In most cases these dates probably post-date initial prototype tests by one to two years.

## Numbers to be produced

An attempt has been made to divide the total planned production number of each system, or the number on order, between units to be manufactured for domestic military acquisition and units manufactured for export. When such data was available, the numbers to be procured for domestic acquisition are shown first, followed by a slash and then the numbers for export. When a figure for total production was available but it was not known whether any of this production was intended for export, or what proportion was intended for export, a single figure neither preceded nor followed by a slash appears.

In the case of the Soviet Union and many third world countries, it has been impossible to obtain estimates for total planned production. For these countries, the number of units produced to date, if known, is shown, with a note indicating the special nature of the figure.

## Financial data

Data on research and development (R&D) costs refer to the total amount of money spent—or planned to be spent—on the development of the system over a period of years. Data on unit prices are average figures for the cost of an equipped item, excluding pro-rated R&D costs, spares and associated ground equipment.

The financial data should be used with great caution: they are intended to indicate general orders of magnitude only. It has not been possible to obtain standardized information, and in some cases the R&D costs and average unit prices have been calculated on a constant-price basis, with reference to some year in the early 1970s, while in other cases the figures represent actual funds expended over a period of years, with no allowance made for inflation. Projected costs for systems to be produced later in the 1970s have an even greater element of uncertainty added to the non-comparability arising from the fact that some figures are based on price levels in the early 1970s while others are computed on the basis of projected price levels.

**Foreign-designed components**

The last column of the register shows the use of foreign-designed power-plants (engines), armaments or electronic components, with the exporting country indicated in brackets. The type of imported electronic equipment is indicated by the following code: r=radar, n=navigation systems, f= (armament) fire-control systems, d=data processing equipment, s=sonars.

# VI. *Register of licensed production of foreign-designed weapons (appendix 8E)*

In general, the conventions and restrictions which apply to appendix 8D also pertain to appendix 8E. The arrangement of data and the column headings are similar, except in the case of the "Date" column in appendix 8E, which refers to the date on which the licence was granted.

# VII. *Arms trade registers (appendix 8F)*

The descriptive terminology used in appendix 8F differs slightly from that employed in appendices 8D and 8E, and generally follows the practice in previous SIPRI registers of the arms trade with the third world.

It should be noted that a special method for calculating the value of arms supplies to the third world has been devised, since the objective was to measure the total volume of supplies, rather than to aggregate the cash sums paid, the amounts of grant aid received, and so on. The methodology is explained in detail in all of the previous editions of the *Yearbook* and is described briefly in note 12, pages 147–48.

## References

1. *Statistical Yearbook* (New York, United Nations, 1970) p. XIX.
3. Wilczynski, J., "The Economics of Socialism", in C. Charter, ed., *Studies in Economics,* Number 2 (London, George, Allen and Unwin, 1970).
3. Benoit, E. and Lubell, H., "The World of National Defence", in E. Benoit, ed., *Disarmament and World Economic Interdependence* (Oslo, Universitets-förlaget, 1967).
4. *World Armaments, and Disarmament, SIPRI Yearbook 1972* (Stockholm, Almqvist & Wiksell, 1972, Stockholm International Peace Research Institute) pp. 78–79.

# Appendix 8B

*Estimating Soviet military expenditure*

*Square-bracketed references, thus [1], refer to the list of references on page 201.*

## I. *Introduction*

### The purpose of the study

In previous editions of the *SIPRI Yearbook* it has been argued that, while there were grounds for questioning the comprehensiveness of the Soviet defence budget, the available methods for calculating an adjusted rouble figure were too speculative. The official Soviet figures were therefore used. For the dollar-estimates of Soviet expenditure a purchasing power parity rate, rather than the official exchange rate, was employed because the evidence for this adjustment was rather stronger. Recently a considerable volume of new material on the subject has appeared, including material generated at SIPRI on Soviet expenditure on military research and development. A review of both the old and the new material was therefore considered appropriate in order to reassess our existing estimates of Soviet military expenditure in both rouble and dollar terms. The overall conclusions of this review are that additional refinements can be made to the rouble : dollar exchange rates and that adequate grounds exist for a considerable adjustment to the Soviet defence budget.

### The background to the problem

It is convenient to start by indicating briefly why the subject of Soviet military expenditure has received so much attention, even though a figure for defence expenditure is published annually in the Soviet Union. Perhaps the most persuasive reason is that if the published defence budget is converted to dollars at the official exchange rate, the level of Soviet expenditure relative to that of the United States and other countries is not consistent with other available evidence on the comparative size of their military establishments. For example, in 1972 the dollar-equivalent of Soviet military spending on this basis was $21.6 billion, while US spending amounted to $78.2 billion, or roughly $71 billion if the incremental cost of the Viet-Nam War is excluded. The difference is so great—almost four-fold—as to cast doubt on the defence budget, on the exchange rate used to convert this to dollars or on both.

172

Another reason is that occasional references in Soviet sources to the content of the budget allocation to defence suggest that its coverage is less broad than the concept of total military expenditure generally employed in international comparisons. For example, a 1965 Soviet source gives the following description:

Resources for the defense of the country are allocated in the estimate of the Ministry of Defense USSR, and are used for the maintenance of land forces, the navy, the air force, air defense forces, and rear-echelon and supply organs of all branches of the Armed Forces and types of troops. A number of economic organizations and industrial enterprises are under the control of the Ministry of Defense.

The estimate of the Ministry of Defense anticipates expenditures for:

Payments for armaments, ammunitions, equipment, fuel and lubricant supplies, food, clothing, personal equipment, and other articles needed to ensure the battle and political training and battle readiness of troops;

maintenance and personal support (*khozyaystvennobytovoye ustroyastvo*) of military units (*chasti*);

maintenance of military educational institutions (Suvorov and Nakhimov schools, secondary and higher educational institutions, and military academies), networks of hospitals, other medical institutions and sanatoria, officers' homes, clubs, sports installations, etc.;

issuance of monetary allowances (*dovol'stviye*) to servicemen and wages to workers and employees of military units and commands (*soyedineniya*);

financing capital construction and industrial enterprises of the Ministry of Defense USSR. [1]

In this passage there is no reference to military research and development (R&D), atomic energy, stockpiling, military aid or civil defence. In itself, a discrepancy between the official defence budget and the conventional notion of expenditure for military purposes is not significant. This occurs in many countries. But whereas in most other countries the items omitted from the military budget are relatively easy to locate elsewhere in the state budget, this is not the case for the Soviet Union. The foregoing comments apply to all the listed items except R&D. If military research and development is in fact excluded from the defence budget—and the weight of the evidence suggests that it is—this would constitute a significant departure from international practice.

Finally it has been questioned whether some of the categories of expenditure included under the defence budget are in fact wholly financed from this source. For example, there is good evidence that the bulk of the defence industry is not administratively subordinate to the Ministry of Defence. [1] In other words, the last item in the quotation above, "financing . . . industrial enterprises of the Ministry of Defense USSR", could be regarded as misleading insofar as it implies that the Ministry of Defence finances all the capital investment in defence industry.

A similar implication emerges if estimates of the cost of personnel, operations and maintenance and construction are aggregated and deducted from the official defence budget. This has been done by Abraham Becker for 1960. [2a] In that year the published defence budget was 9.3 billion roubles; and after deducting estimates of the above items Becker arrives at a residual of 0.2–3.1 billion roubles. It is at least questionable whether the upper figure in this range is sufficient to cover procurement, the remaining large item of expenditure stated to be financed under the defence budget. It would certainly appear too small to cover all of procurement, R&D and the military atomic energy programme.

In view of these various considerations, it seems reasonable to adopt the working hypothesis that the published defence budget does not cover all expenditures for military purposes. It can then be asked whether it is possible to estimate total Soviet expenditure for military purposes.

Before attempting to answer this question, it is useful to pose another —namely, why it is important to know the size of Soviet military expenditure. In answering this latter question it is necessary to distinguish between the magnitude of military expenditure in local currency and the magnitude in some external currency, such as US dollars.

The main reason for wanting to know the level of a country's military expenditure in local currency—in this case, roubles—is that this gives a rough idea of the amount of military activity: that is, it gives an indication of whether the overall size of the military establishment, and the quantity of resources it absorbs, is rising or falling over time. In addition, it is useful to have an indication of the economic burden of defence in order to be able to assess: (*a*) the extent to which economic constraints will inhibit an acceleration of military expenditure or maintenance of the existing rate of growth; and (*b*) the extent to which economic factors may figure in a country's attitude toward the desirability and feasibility of arms control and disarmament.

A distinct motivation is that the ability to verify the level of military spending is a prerequisite to any disarmament measure that may incorporate limitations on military budgets.

The reason for wanting to be able to convert the military expenditures of different countries to a common currency—usually dollars—is to permit an estimate to be made of the global diversion of resources to military uses, that is, of the global size of the military establishment. The Soviet Union accounts for a substantial fraction of world military outlays—a much larger portion than any other country about which there is similar doubt concerning the actual level of total military spending. It is for this reason that SIPRI is particularly concerned with the accuracy of the Soviet military expenditure estimates.

When the military expenditures of various countries are converted to a common currency, there is an unfortunate tendency in many quarters to use the estimates as a measure of relative military strength. It must be emphasized that this is not the intended function of the SIPRI military expenditure estimates. In particular, the attempt to derive a dollar-estimate of Soviet military spending does not imply a belief that the over-all military capacity of, for example, the United States and the Soviet Union can be assessed through a comparison of military expenditures.

This review begins by considering the alternative approaches to estimating the rouble value of total Soviet military outlays. Essentially, there are two alternative approaches: the "expenditure residual" approach, which examines the unspecified expenditures included in various parts of the state budget; and the "hardware" approach, which analyses Soviet statistics on industrial production in order to estimate the value of military hardware produced. The issue of Soviet expenditure for military R&D is common to both these approaches and is treated separately.

In section V this material is assessed and used to estimate the probable size of Soviet military expenditure over the period 1950 to 1973. Section VI considers the problem of the appropriate rouble : dollar exchange rate for military goods and services. The dollar-equivalent of Soviet military expenditure is estimated in section VII.

## II. *The expenditure residuals*

Every year the Soviet state budget contains large sums of money that are unitemized or unaccounted for. Given the hypothesis that the defence budget is "incomplete", these residuals have naturally attracted attention as potential sources of military expenditure. The following residuals are generally discussed in this connection:

1. The budgetary expenditure (BE) residual: for the state budget as a whole, the sum of expenditures under each of the main headings falls short of total outlays.

2. The national economy (NE) residual: the main budget heading "financing the national economy" contains a significant amount of expenditure in addition to that accounted for under the various sub-headings.

3. The industry and construction residual: under the budget heading "financing the national economy" there is a sub-heading for "industry and construction" within which a substantial residual is left after the individual line items are totalled.

The industry and construction residual is relatively large and is considered a possible source of finance for investment in defence industry [2b] and perhaps for some procurement or operational expenditures. [3] However, so little information is available on this category of expenditure that no attempt has been made to quantify these outlays. [2b]

**Table 8B.1. Gross budget residuals, 1950–68**                    *Billions of roubles*

| Year | BE residual | NE residual | Total |
|------|-------------|-------------|-------|
| 1950 | 4.24 | 1.43 | **5.67** |
| 1955 | 3.93 | 2.61 | **6.54** |
| 1956 | 4.45 | 2.35 | **6.80** |
| 1957 | 3.66 | 2.92 | **6.58** |
| 1958 | 3.27 | 5.02 | **8.29** |
| 1959 | 4.42 | 5.33 | **9.75** |
| 1960 | 3.68 | 4.17 | **7.85** |
| 1961 | 3.88 | 2.57 | **6.45** |
| 1962 | 3.24 | 4.99 | **8.23** |
| 1963 | 2.27 | 4.86 | **7.13** |
| 1964 | 3.93 | 4.70 | **8.63** |
| 1965 | 4.48 | 7.84 | **12.32** |
| 1966 | 6.50 | 5.30 | **11.80** |
| 1967 | 5.20 | . . | . . |
| 1968 | 9.50 | . . | . . |

*Source:* Anderson, S. and Lee, W. T., *Probable Trend and Magnitude of Soviet Expenditures for National Security Purposes* SSC-RM 5205-54 (Menlo Park, Calif., Stanford Research Institute, February 1969).

The BE and NE residuals are shown in table 8B.1. The series in two sources [2, 4] that agree very closely have been linked in order to obtain as long a series as possible. The budget residuals are not all potential military outlays. The known components of the BE residuals are (*a*) internal security, (*b*) loan service, and (*c*) grants to investment banks. Similarly, the NE residual is used to finance subsidies to agricultural procurement and, in some years, agricultural procurement itself. Table 8B.2 shows what remains of the residuals after deducting these various items, and then sums the two net residuals.

It has to be stressed that some of the adjustments made to obtain the net residuals involve uncertain estimates. The 1.5 billion rouble estimate for internal security, for example, is based on some official data for the mid-1950s supported by fragmentary evidence for later years. [2d] Similarly, the figures for procurement subsidies to agriculture are described in a study using this method as "one of the more uncertain entries". [4a] The grants to investment banks are apparently based on official data for the period 1955–62 (see table 8B.2). Whether this is true for more recent years is uncertain. One analyst, for example, refers only to "a variety of small outlays of a non-military character".[1]

These considerations, together with the possibility that not all the relevant adjustments for civil expenditures have been made, mean that the net residuals cannot be considered as precise measures of potential military outlays. In fact, in one Western study it is claimed that "iden-

[1] To account for these small outlays we have subtracted 0.5 billion roubles from the gross residual over the period 1963–68 (table 8B.2).

**Table 8B.2. BE and NE residuals adjusted for known components, 1955–69**

*Billions of roubles*

| | 1955 | 1956 | 1957 | 1958 | 1959 | 1960 | 1961 | 1962 | 1963 | 1964 | 1965 | 1966 | 1967 | 1968 | 1969 |
|---|---|---|---|---|---|---|---|---|---|---|---|---|---|---|---|
| **BE residual** | | | | | | | | | | | | | | | |
| Gross residual | 3.93 | 4.45 | 3.66 | 3.27 | 4.42 | 3.68 | 3.88 | 3.24 | 2.27 | 3.93 | 4.48 | 6.50 | 5.20 | 9.30 | .. |
| Loan service | 1.43 | 1.63 | 0.77 | 0.37 | 0.69 | 0.70 | 0.80 | 0.80 | 0.10 | 0.10 | 0.10 | 0.10 | 0.20 | 0.20 | .. |
| Grants to investment banks | 0.35 | 0.37 | 0.46 | 0.30 | 0.35 | 0.40 | 0.45 | 0.50 | (0.50) | (0.50) | (0.50) | (0.50) | (0.50) | (0.50) | .. |
| Internal security | 1.50 | 1.50 | 1.50 | 1.50 | 1.50 | 1.50 | 1.50 | 1.50 | (1.50) | (1.50) | (1.50) | (1.50) | (1.50) | (1.50) | (..) |
| Net residual | **0.65** | **0.95** | **0.93** | **1.10** | **1.88** | **1.08** | **2.08** | **0.44** | **(0.17)** | **(1.83)** | **(2.38)** | **(4.40)** | **(3.00)** | **(7.10)** | **(..)** |
| **NE residual** | | | | | | | | | | | | | | | |
| Gross residual | 2.61 | 2.35 | 2.92 | 5.02 | 5.33 | 4.17 | 2.57 | 4.99 | 4.86 | 4.70 | 7.84 | .. | | | .. |
| Procurement subsidies | (1.00) | (0.90) | (1.10) | (3.40) | (2.70) | (2.00) | (1.00) | (1.70) | (2.60) | (2.70) | (4.50) | .. | | | (6.50)[a] |
| Agricultural procurement | .. | 0.76 | 0.64 | 0.60 | 0.60[b] | .. | .. | .. | .. | .. | .. | .. | | | .. |
| Net residual | **(1.61)** | **(0.69)** | **(1.18)** | **(1.02)** | **(2,03)** | **(2.17)** | **(1.57)** | **(3.29)** | **(2.26)** | **(2.00)** | **(3.34)** | .. | | | .. |
| **Total** | **2.26** | **1.64** | **2.11** | **2.12** | **3.91** | **3.25** | **3.65** | **3.73** | **2.43** | **3.83** | **5.72** | .. | | | .. |

[a] The figure for 1969 is inserted because this was the first time that these subsidies were officially acknowledged and an estimate provided in the Soviet budget plan.

[b] In the years 1956–59 and 1966 the residual is said to include agricultural procurement. In other years this expenditure is included in the subheading "agriculture procurement" under "financing the national economy".

*Sources:* Becker, A., *Soviet Military Outlays Since 1955* RM-3886-PR (Santa Monica. Rand Corporation, July 1964). Becker, A., *Soviet National Income, 1958–1964* RM-464-PR (Santa Monica, Rand Corporation, August 1964). Anderson, S. and Lee, W. T., *Probable Trend and Magnitude of Soviet Expenditures for National Security Purposes* SSC-RM 5205-54 (Menlo Park, Calif., Stanford Research Institute, February 1969). Steel, R., "The State Budget for 1970", in *Economic Performance and Military Burden in the Soviet Union*, a compendium of papers submitted to the Sub-committee on Foreign Economic Policy of the Joint Economic Committee (Washington, 1970).

**Table 8B.3. The financial balance residual, 1956–65**

*Billions of roubles*

| | 1956 | 1957 | 1958 | 1959 | 1960 | 1961 | 1962 | 1963 | 1964 | 1965 |
|---|---|---|---|---|---|---|---|---|---|---|
| **Total public sector income** | 73.4 | 77.3 | 87.7 | 96.2 | 96.8 | 101.1 | 107.7 | 117.5 | 127.2 | 135.8 |
| **Investment** | | | | | | | | | | |
| Capital construction | 19.1 | 21.6 | 24.5 | 27.4 | 30.7 | 32.6 | 34.7 | 36.6 | 39.5 | 42.5 |
| Working capital | 8.0 | 4.7 | 8.5 | 11.1 | 6.1 | 8.4 | 8.1 | 9.5 | 12.2 | 6.9 |
| Warehouse stocks of equipment | – | – | – | – | 0.1 | 0.3 | 0.2 | – | 0.2 | 0.2 |
| **Capital repair** | 5.3 | 5.5 | 5.6 | 6.2 | 7.0 | 7.7 | 8.4 | 10.0 | 10.8 | 11.7 |
| **Subsidies, operating expenditures, and transfer payments** | | | | | | | | | | |
| Administration | 1.2 | 1.2 | 1.2 | 1.1 | 1.0 | 1.0 | 1.0 | 1.0 | 1.0 | 1.2 |
| Operational expenditures in agriculture | 2.8 | 2.5 | 2.0 | 1.0 | 1.2 | 1.5 | 1.6 | 1.8 | 2.0 | 2.1 |
| Outlays for foreign trade | 1.1 | 1.5 | 1.7 | 2.8 | 3.0 | 1.1 | 1.0 | 1.4 | 1.0 | 1.5 |
| Geological survey work | 0.7 | 0.8 | 0.8 | 0.9 | 0.9 | 0.9 | 1.0 | 1.2 | 1.2 | 1.3 |
| Purchases of domestic gold production | 0.5 | 0.5 | 0.5 | 0.5 | 0.6 | 0.1 | 0.2 | 0.2 | 0.2 | 0.2 |
| Wage reform subsidies | – | – | 0.2 | 0.8 | 0.9 | 1.2 | 1.0 | 0.6 | 0.2 | 0.9 |
| Subsidies for agricultural procurement price changes | 0.9 | 1.1 | 3.4 | 2.7 | 2.0 | 1.0 | 1.7 | 2.6 | 2.7 | 4.5 |
| Worker training and innovation incentives | 0.3 | 0.3 | 0.3 | 0.4 | 0.5 | 0.4 | 0.5 | 0.5 | 0.5 | 0.6 |
| Expenditures for state loan | 1.6 | 1.0 | 0.4 | 0.7 | 0.7 | 0.8 | 0.8 | 0.1 | 0.1 | 0.1 |
| Miscellaneous | 0.1 | 0.1 | 0.1 | 0.1 | 0.1 | 0.3 | 0.6 | 0.3 | 0.3 | 1.6 |
| **Social-cultural services** | 14.7 | 17.7 | 19.0 | 20.5 | 21.6 | 23.4 | 25.0 | 26.4 | 28.5 | 33.0 |
| **Defence and defence/space related** | | | | | | | | | | |
| Defence | 9.7 | 9.1 | 9.4 | 9.4 | 9.3 | 11.6 | 12.6 | 13.9 | 13.3 | 12.8 |
| Science | 1.4 | 2.1 | 2.0 | 2.3 | 2.5 | 2.8 | 3.2 | 3.8 | 4.2 | 4.6 |
| **Total identified expenditures** | **67.4** | **69.7** | **79.6** | **87.9** | **88.2** | **95.1** | **101.6** | **109.9** | **117.9** | **125.7** |
| **Residual**[a] | 5.3–6.0 | 6.9–7.6 | 7.4–8.1 | 7.6–8.4 | 7.6–8.6 | 4.9–6.0 | 4.8–6.1 | 6.1–7.6 | 7.8–9.3 | 8.5–10.1 |

[a] For an explanation of the range, see page 179.

*Source:* Anderson, S. and Lee, W. T., *Probable Trend and Magnitude of Soviet Expenditures for National Security Purposes* SSC-RM 5205-54 (Menlo Park, Calif., Stanford Research Institute, February 1969).

tification of the uses to which the residual monies are put is not possible within the budget framework as normally reported". [4b] This study therefore proceeds to set up an income and expenditure account for the state sector as a whole comprising, in addition to the budget, the retained funds of state enterprises and the financial flows in the banking system. The rationale for this procedure is that the data on the allocation of resources in the state sector as a whole is more complete than in the budget by itself. Table 8B.3, taken from this study, sum-

**Table 8B.4. The budget residuals and the financial balance residual, 1956–65**

*Billions of roubles*

| | 1956 | 1957 | 1958 | 1959 | 1960 | 1961 | 1962 | 1963 | 1964 | 1965 |
|---|---|---|---|---|---|---|---|---|---|---|
| Financial balance residual | 5.3–6.0 | 6.9–7.6 | 7.4–8.1 | 7.6–8.4 | 7.6–8.6 | 4.9–6.0 | 4.8–6.1 | 6.1–7.6 | 7.8–9.3 | 8.5–10.1 |
| Grants to investment banks | 0.4 | 0.5 | 0.3 | 0.3 | 0.4 | 0.4 | 0.5 | 0.5 | 0.5 | 0.5 |
| Internal security | 1.5 | 1.5 | 1.5 | 1.5 | 1.5 | 1.5 | 1.5 | 1.5 | 1.5 | 1.5 |
| Net financial balance residual | 3.4–4.1 | 4.9–5.6 | 5.6–6.3 | 5.8–6.6 | 5.7–6.7 | 3.0–4.1 | 2.8–4.1 | 4.1–5.6 | 5.8–8.3 | 6.5–8.1 |
| Percentage of defence budget | 34.9–42.1 | 50.6–57.9 | 59.5–67.0 | 61.8–70.4 | 61.2–72.0 | 25.8–35.3 | 22.0–32.2 | 29.4–40.2 | 43.6–62.4 | 50.7–63.2 |
| Sum of BE and NE residuals | 1.6 | 2.1 | 2.1 | 3.9 | 3.2 | 3.6 | 3.7 | 2.4 | 3.8 | 5.7 |
| Percentage of defence budget | 16.4 | 21.7 | 22.3 | 41.6 | 34.4 | 31.0 | 29.1 | 17.2 | 28.5 | 44.5 |

*Sources:* Becker, A., *Soviet Military Outlays Since 1955* RM-3886-PR (Santa Monica, Rand Corporation, July 1964). Becker, A., *Soviet National Income, 1958–1964* RM-464-PR (Santa Monica, Rand Corporation, August 1964). Anderson, S. and Lee, W. T., *Probable Trend and Magnitude of Soviet Expenditures for National Security Purposes* SSC-RM 5205-54 (Menlo Park, Calif., Stanford Research Institute, February 1969). Steel, R., "The State Budget for 1970", in *Economic Performance and Military Burden in the Soviet Union*, a compendium of papers submitted to the Subcommittee on Foreign Economic Policy of the Joint Economic Committee (Washington, 1970).

marizes total public sector income and attempts to provide a complete breakdown of public sector expenditure. As is the case with the budget, substantial residual expenditures emerge if total expenditure is deducted from total income.

In comparing the financial balance residual and the sum of the two budget residuals, several factors have to be taken into consideration. As can be seen from table 8B.3, this residual is net of agricultural procurement subsidies and loan service (expenditure for state loan), and also presumably of agricultural procurement. By implication the residual is gross of internal security and grants to investment banks.

An additional consideration is that the figures for total state income may be inflated due to double-counting. The public sector is known to have three broad sources of revenue: budget income, state enterprises and the banking system. It is thought that one item of revenue under state enterprises, the retained funds for "science", may be partially financed in the form of budgetary grants. [4c] To the extent that this is so, total state income and the residual will be inflated. To allow for this the analysts examining the financial balance give the residual obtained in table 8B.3 as a range, excluding and including an estimate of the retained funds of state enterprises for science.

To summarize, the budget residuals and the financial balance residual are apparently non-comparable only to the extent that the latter includes, and the former excludes, expenditure on internal security and grants to investment banks. Both these items have therefore been deducted from the financial balance residual.

Table 8B.4 compares the two residual series on this basis. As the table shows, the high-range estimate of the financial balance residual is higher than the sum of the budget residuals in all years. The same is true for the low-range estimate, except for the years 1961 and 1962.

The most likely explanation for this general relationship between the two residual series is that the financial balance residual includes some part of the industry and construction residual. This is because this residual is derived by subtracting fixed capital investment, increase of working capital and the current outlays of project design organizations from the budget allocation for industry and construction [2c] and all of these headings have their equivalent in table 8B.3. Another possible explanation is that the financial balance residual is acknowledged to include increments to state reserves, an item which appears in the official national income accounts and which, some Soviet sources have indicated, includes some armaments. This imparts an upward bias to the financial balance residual since increments to state reserves are known to have a civilian component. It is claimed that the financial balance residual is subject to various downward biases but it is possible that these are not fully offsetting.

# III. *Expenditures for military research and development (R&D)*

Statistics are published in the Soviet Union on national expenditures for "science"—a concept generally regarded as covering the activities referred to in the West as "research and development". The estimates of total national science expenditure comprise expenditures of three types: (*a*) the budget allocation for science, including both that in the state or All-Union budget and that in the budgets of the various Republics; (*b*) current outlays for science from "other"—unspecified—sources, some of which may be budgetary (other than the science item) but a major component of which is the retained funds of state enterprises used for scientific purposes; and (*c*) capital investment for science, which may also be channeled through the budget but for which the exact administrative or financial source has not been officially identified.

It has been presumed for some time that the total expenditure for science includes military R&D although, until recently, there was no explicit confirmation of this in any Soviet source. The primary basis for this presumption was simply that if military R&D was not included, then the Soviet civil R&D effort would appear inordinately large.[2] Recently, however, at least one explicit Soviet reference to military R&D as one of the activities covered by the national science expenditure statistics has appeared. This is cited below.

The overall expenditures for 'science' can be obtained from the Central Statistic Board of the USSR. However, not all these expenditures go to the development of science and technology. Thus only a part of the defence-related research is devoted to scientific and technical development. [5]

Thus it can now be assumed that the total expenditure for science includes at least some and perhaps most military R&D. The size of this expenditure, however, and its relationship to the published defence budget remain essentially open questions.

With respect to the size of expenditure for military R&D, one of the most influential studies has been Nancy Nimitz's "Soviet Expenditures for Scientific Research". [6] Nimitz found that, for data relating to the mid-1950s, more than one-half—the proportion varied between 60 and 75 per cent—of the All-Union budget allocation to science was excluded from a type-of-expenditure breakdown published in a 1958 Soviet source. There is no concrete information whatever on the content of this "residual" but its existence, together with the evidence that the defence budget did not include military R&D, suggested strongly that the residual contained at least some military R&D.

Data on the retained funds of state enterprises for scientific purposes can be estimated although, as mentioned above, there is some doubt as to whether these funds consist exclusively of retained profits or whether they are supplemented by budget grants and/or bank credits. Moreover, there is no evidence either for or against the proposition that these funds are used to finance military R&D. The same is true of the remainder of the "other"—unspecified—sources of science expenditures. A final point in this regard is that the Soviet concept of "science" is less comprehensive than the Western concept of research and development. Specifically, the science expenditures exclude much of the cost associated with the development and testing of prototypes which, at least in the United States, is considered to be R&D expenditure. As a result, R&D expenditures can be found, for example, under the budget heading "financing the national economy" which are not included in the expenditures for "science". [7]

In estimating the military proportion of total science outlays, Anderson *et al* take 50–80 per cent of the funds from "other" sources and 70–80 per cent of the All-Union budget expenditure for science. The authors

[2] In 1973, planned Soviet science expenditures amounted to roughly 15,5 billion roubles. This is equivalent to about $18 billion at the official exchange rate or $31 billion using a conservative dollar : rouble purchasing power parity ratio ($2:1 rouble). For comparison, civil R&D expenditures in the United States currently amount to about $20 billion.

**Table 8B.5. Selected Western estimates of Soviet expenditure on military R&D, 1955–65**

*Billions of roubles*

| | 1955 | 1956 | 1957 | 1958 | 1959 | 1960 | 1961 | 1962 | 1963 | 1964 | 1965 |
|---|---|---|---|---|---|---|---|---|---|---|---|
| **Anderson, S. *et al.*** | | | | | | | | | | | |
| All-Union Science | .. | 0.5–0.6 | 0.8–0.9 | 0.9–1.0 | 1.1–1.3 | 1.3–1.5 | 1.5–1.8 | 1.7–2.0 | 2.1–2.4 | 2.4–2.8 | 2.6–3.0 |
| "Other" Science | .. | 0.3–0.6 | 0.3–0.6 | 0.3–0.6 | 0.4–0.6 | 0.5–0.8 | 0.5–0.9 | 0.6–1.0 | 0.7–1.3 | 0.7–1.2 | 0.8–1.3 |
| Anderson, total | .. | 0.8–1.2 | 1.1–1.5 | 1.2–1.6 | 1.5–1.9 | 1.8–2.3 | 2.0–2.7 | 2.3–3.0 | 2.8–3.6 | 3.1–4.0 | 3.4–4.3 |
| Becker, total | 0.45 | 0.59 | 0.81 | 1.00 | 1.17 | 1.40 | 1.60 | 1.80 | .. | .. | .. |

*Sources:*
Anderson, S. and Lee, W. T., *Probable Trend and Magnitude of Soviet Expenditures for National Security Purposes* SSC-RM 5205–54 (Menlo Park, Calif., Stanford Research Institute, February 1969).
Becker, A., *Soviet Military Outlays Since 1955* RM-3886-PR (Santa Monica, Rand Corporation, July 1964).

note that "there is no empirical basis for the factors used", [4d] but it is worth pointing out that the percentage range adopted for the All-Union science expenditures is high compared with the proportion of this expenditure which Nimitz found to be unaccounted for.

Becker is more conservative but his approach is essentially the same: he takes Nimitz's figures for the unitemized portion of All-Union budget outlays for science, and assumes that the non-military elements in this portion are offset by the omission of the military component in "other" science outlays. Table 8B.5 summarizes the estimates of expenditure on military R&D given in these two sources.

No mention has yet been made of the expenditure for capital investment in science, as data on this expenditure first appeared after the studies analysed above were made. As mentioned above, there has been no indication of the source of the finance for capital investment. Nor is it known how this capital expenditure is allocated over the scientific institutions financed respectively (or mainly) by the All-Union budget, the Republican budgets and "other" sources.

## IV. *The "hardware" approach*

There are two partial alternatives to the financial residuals approach to estimating total Soviet military expenditures. They are partial in the sense that they refer only to the procurement of capital equipment for military and space purposes. The first of these alternatives utilizes the official national income accounts, specifically the item "increment of material working capital and reserves". As mentioned above, some

Soviet sources have indicated that the reserves component of this item includes armaments.

Becker considers the hypothesis that the bulk of military procurement is registered in the national accounts as increments to state reserves. However, he concludes that the paucity of data makes it impossible to derive any firm estimates. The later study by Anderson *et al* concurs with this conclusion. Thus, while state reserves do appear to have a military component they do not constitute a promising first step in computing total Soviet military outlays.

The second method of estimating expenditure for military/space procurement is to start with the production statistics. The Machine-Building and Metal-Working (MBMW) segment of the Soviet industrial classification provides a good coverage of the industries responsible for the production of military/space hardware. Moreover, some Soviet sources state explicitly that the production data for this industry includes armaments.

The gross value of output (GVO) in MBMW can be deduced from the official GVO index and the rouble figure for GVO which is published intermittently. Although the methodological basis of Soviet production statistics is still a subject of debate among Western scholars, there is some consensus on the steps to be taken in order to estimate the value of armaments production.

The first step is to convert GVO into net output by subtracting the value of intra-industry sales. This is done to eliminate the multiple counting of the value of parts and components at successive stages of production. The value of intra-industry sales is normally implicit in the Soviet input-output tables but, as these tables are only published at intervals, the values for intervening years have to be estimated by interpolation.

The resulting estimate for net output in MBMW has then to be allocated according to end-use. These end-uses are briefly described below.

1. A significant portion of net output constitutes the sale of intermediate products to non-MBMW sectors for the repair and maintenance of equipment. As with intra-industry sales, these values are implicit in the input-output tables and have to be interpolated for the years in which these tables do not appear.

2. Another major component of net output is the sale of final goods that constitute investment in machinery and equipment in the Soviet economy. The value of this component has to be estimated from a separate statistical series on "capital investment in equipment, instruments and implements". The values in this series include imports and transportation and distribution charges, all of which must be estimated and deducted in order to get the value of MBMW output involved.

3. A third component is the sale of final products to consumers, both public and private. Data is available on the value of consumer durables

**Table 8B.6. Estimates of the value of military/space hardware production in the Soviet Union: selected years, 1955–68**

*Billions of roubles*

|                        | 1955 | 1958 | 1959 | 1960 | 1962 | 1963 | 1965 | 1967 | 1968  |
|------------------------|------|------|------|------|------|------|------|------|-------|
| Boretsky[a]            | . .  | 1.85 | 2.68 | . .  | 5.62 | 6.42 | 6.31 | 9.28 | 10.69 |
| Becker[b]              | . .  | . .  | 5.00 | . .  | . .  | . .  | . .  | . .  | . .   |
| Greenslade[c]          | 3.92 | . .  | 3.91 | 4.96 | . .  | . .  | . .  | . .  | . .   |

[a] Residual in the value of net output in the machine-building industry.
[b] Residual in the value of net output in the MBMW industry.
[c] Greenslade gives estimates of value-added in the production of civil machinery, and points out that military production as a proportion of total value-added in the machinery sector is estimated at 50 per cent in 1955 and 40 per cent in 1959 and 1960.

*Sources:* Becker, A., *Soviet Military Outlays Since 1955* RM-3886-PR (Santa Monica, Rand Corporation, July 1964). Boretsky, M., "The Technological Base of Soviet Military Power", in *Economic Performance and the Military Burden in the Soviet Union,* a compendium of papers submitted to the Subcommittee on Foreign Economic Policy of the Joint Economic Committee (Washington, 1970). Greenslade, R., "Industrial Production Statistics in the USSR", in Treml, V. and Hardt, J. eds., *Soviet Economic Statistics* (Durham, North Carolina, Duke University Press, 1972) pp. 155–94.

purchased but these figures include turnover tax, transportation costs and various distribution mark-ups. As above, these must be estimated and deducted.

4. The remaining two components—changes in inventories and exports of machinery and equipment—are relatively small but, as in all other cases, the required data is not ready-made. In the case of exports, the proportion of total exports made up of machinery and equipment can only be roughly estimated and the figures have then to be converted from "foreign trade roubles" to domestic roubles.

When all these items are deducted from net output the residual should represent the value of military/space hardware produced. It should be apparent, even from this brief description, that the estimates of the residual value of MBMW output will be extremely rough. Moreover, some authors depart from the method described above in one way or another. Boretsky, for example, initially subtracts the metal-working portion of MBMW since he regards this activity as secondary from the viewpoint of the production of armaments. [8a] Another analyst, Greenslade, [9] proceeds on the basis of value-added in MBMW rather than net output.

Table 8B.6 compares the value of military/space hardware produced as estimated by three different analysts. For 1959, when the three estimates overlap, there is a marked divergence. In view of the manifold difficulties in estimating the residual, plus possible differences in definition and methodology, one must be extremely cautious in comparing alternative estimates. Boretsky's figures in table 8B.6 exclude the production of components for the repair and maintenance of all equipment including military equipment. In this respect, Becker's estimate seems to be comparable with Boretsky's, while Greenslade's figures are probably gross of components for repair and maintenance.[3]

There is also substantial disagreement over the rate of growth in the value of hardware production. Boretsky's figures, for example, imply an average annual growth rate of 10.5 per cent between 1962 and 1967, or 15.3 per cent between 1959 and 1965. Becker, Moorsteen and Powell, on the other hand, estimate the growth rate at 6.8 per cent between 1961 and 1966. [11]

In order to obtain an estimate for total military outlays, the figures for military/space procurement must be filled out with estimates for personnel costs, operations and maintenance and construction. For 1960, Becker [2] estimates these at 3.8 billion roubles, 1.9–3.8 billion roubles and 0.5–1.5 billion roubles, respectively. Subtracting these from the defence budget for 1960 (9.3 billion roubles) leaves a residual of 0.2–3.1 billion roubles which should cover procurement. Becker's estimate for procurement is 5 billion roubles, which suggests that some military expenditure is channeled outside the defence budget. Boretsky's estimate for procurement in that year, on the other hand, could be consistent with the proposition that there are little or no supplementary military outlays.[4]

The relationship between these figures and estimated total Soviet military expenditure will be considered in the next section where the latter series is developed.

## V. *Estimating total Soviet military expenditure*

In assessing the significance of the financial residuals and the expenditures for science for the relationship between the defence budget and total military outlays, there would appear to be two dominant considerations. On the one hand, the cumulative uncertainty regarding this relationship is very large. On the other hand, even the residual expenditures alone are large in relation to the defence budget, although the relationship is a fluctuating one. This is illustrated in table 8B.4.

These two considerations are, of course, offsetting and the most common procedure—since military R&D is regarded as the most critical omission from the defence budget—is to add a substantial slice of ex-

---

[3] In a paper entitled "Dimensions of Soviet Economic Power", submitted in 1962 to the Joint Economic Committee hearings, Boretsky estimated the "military acquisition" component of machine-building output at roughly 6.3 billion roubles and 9.2 billion roubles in 1958 and 1961, respectively. [10a] The large differences between these figures and those in table 8B.8 appear largely to be explained by the fact that in the earlier paper Boretsky did not deduct the value of sales of intermediate products. [8b]

[4] The use of the term "procurement" is not strictly accurate: Boretsky's estimates appear to include military exports and since the Soviet Union supplies most of the equipment for the rest of the WTO, these military exports could be a large item in some years.

penditures for science to the defence budget. This procedure is adopted, for example, by the US Arms Control and Disarmament Agency which adds one-half of total science expenditure (including capital investment) to the defence budget, [12] and by Stanley Cohn who adds the whole of the All-Union budget allocation for science. [13]

The risk that this procedure will exaggerate total military outlays is small, provided it can be assumed that the financial residuals contain a large element of military expenditure. For example, in 1965 the science allocation in the All-Union budget was 4.1 billion roubles or 72 per cent and 51–63 per cent of the budget residuals and the financial balance residual, respectively. Thus, even if one-half of the science allocation (2.05 billion roubles) was for non-military purposes this upward bias would be eliminated if only 36 per cent of the budget residuals or 25–31 per cent of the financial balance residual was in fact military expenditure. And while there is no proof that the residuals contain military expenditure, it is not unreasonable to assume that since these expenditures are unaccounted for they are used, at least in part, to support activities of a sensitive nature, for which military activities obviously qualify.

The general procedure outlined above is undeniably crude. The fact that it is widely employed is most probably due to the fact that even the most painstaking research offers little in the way of improvement. It does, however, seem worthwhile to attempt to take more explicit account both of what is known and what is not known—about the defence budget, the financial residuals and the expenditures for science—in deriving an estimate of total Soviet military outlays.

It is useful, first of all, to review briefly the main considerations. Descriptions in Soviet sources of the activities financed by the budget allocation to defence suggest a significant degree of non-comparability with the defence budgets of most other countries—in the sense of being less comprehensive—particularly with regard to expenditures for military R&D. In addition, there is no reference, either in descriptions of the defence budget or in any other part of the state budget, to such military activities as atomic energy, civil defence or military assistance, although the Soviet Union is known to engage in these activities. Finally, crude checks on the internal consistency of the defence budget based largely on manpower levels and estimates of the cost per man, suggest, at least for the early 1960s, that some military activities may be financed from sources other than the defence budget.

There are two factors which broadly support this presumption that the Soviet defence budget should be supplemented to render it comparable to the conventional notion of expenditure for military purposes. The first of these is the existence of various residual expenditures in the state budget (or the state sector as a whole) which are too large to be dismissed simply as collections of miscellaneous expenditures. The second is the expenditures for "science" which are arguably too large to consist purely of civil R&D.

Finally there are a number of considerations that complicate an evaluation of the possible relationship between the financial residuals and the expenditures for science, respectively, and total expenditures for military purposes. First, there is no evidence whatever that the financial residuals actually contain military expenditure. Second, while the expenditures for science probably include military R&D, it cannot be presumed that all military R&D is included since, for example, the Soviet definition of "science" is more narrow than the definition adopted in most other countries. Nor do Soviet sources give any indication as to the proportion of science expenditures going to military R&D, although the data used by Nimitz may be considered a partial exception. A third complication is that the financial residuals and the expenditures for sciences may overlap. As mentioned above, it is not known where the expenditures for science from "other" sources, or the expenditure for capital investment in science, originate, and one likely source for part of the former and most of the latter is the financial residuals.

This is a very meagre base from which to work and it explains, in a general way, why estimates of Soviet military expenditure range from the official defence budget, to the budget plus a substantial part of both the financial residuals and the expenditures for science, and occasionally even higher.[5] On balance, the available evidence would seem to support the proposition that the official defence budget omits, partially or completely, certain categories of military expenditure. In the first place it seems reasonable to supplement the defence budget with an estimate of expenditure for atomic energy, since Soviet sources do not include this as one of the activities financed by the Ministry of Defence. This is supported by the fact that none of the other nuclear powers finances its atomic energy programmes from the defence budget. Similar considerations apply to such relatively minor outlays as stockpiling and military aid. Finally, there is the evidence that the bulk of military R&D is excluded from the defence budget.

[5] An unofficial study by two Soviet economists estimated Soviet military outlays in 1969 at roughly 80 billion roubles. [14] This figure is roughly double the estimate one would arrive at by crudely (and extravagantly) applying the methods reviewed in this chapter. Specifically, in 1969 the published defence budget was 17.7 billion roubles; the BE and NE residuals in the state budget plan amounted to about 18 billion roubles [15]; and total outlays for science were 10 billion roubles. Therefore, total military outlays, including one-half of total science outlays, would be 40.7 billion roubles. This enormous discrepancy justifies scepticism of the figure of 80 billion roubles. Moreover, many Western experts consider the study to be methodologically incorrect. It is worth pointing out that the two Soviet economists believe that the dollar-equivalent of Soviet military expenditure cannot be significantly greater than US expenditure which amounted to $81.4 billion in 1969. They therefore appear to be implicitly discounting the view that the official exchange rate understates the purchasing power of the rouble relative to the dollar. Even at the official (1969) exchange rate, the dollar-equivalent of 80 billion roubles is $88.8 billion.

With respect to the adjustment for military R&D it seems worthwhile to seek some additional points of reference. The Soviet Union is one of four countries that design and manufacture the entire range of major armaments domestically, the other three being the United States, the United Kingdom and France. It seems reasonable to argue that relevant experience of these three countries could be used to make broad inferences about the Soviet Union. Specifically it is argued that the proportions of (*a*) the national research and development effort, and (*b*) total military outlays made up of military R&D in the Soviet Union should be comparable to those in the other three countries, particularly the United States.

Neither of these criteria can be rigorously applied for obvious reasons. With regard to the first it is generally accepted—even in the Soviet Union—that the overall level of technology in the Soviet Union is considerably lower than that in the major Western countries, particularly the United States. Since it can be assumed that the Soviet Union is endeavouring to overcome this deficiency, one could argue that non-military R&D will absorb a higher proportion of the total R&D effort than is the case in other countries. A countervailing argument is that the Soviet Union is engaged in a technological arms race with the United States and that given a lower technological base this requires a proportionally greater military R&D effort on the part of the Soviet Union.

In the United States, for the period 1960–70, the proportion of the national R&D effort accounted for by military R&D ranged between 50 per cent (in 1960) and 31 per cent (in 1970); in the UK over the same period the range was 41 to 30 per cent and in France it averaged about 25 per cent. [16a] Since we are placing the greatest weight on the US experience, military R&D in the Soviet Union might be expected to absorb between 30 and 50 per cent of the national R&D effort; proportions outside this range cannot, of course, be entirely excluded.

With regard to the second criterion, the proportion of R&D in total military expenditure, the experience of the USA, the UK and France suggests a range of 10–15 per cent. [16b] In view of the relatively low manpower costs in the Soviet Union the upper limit of this range could probably be extended to 20 per cent, despite the fact that Soviet military equipment is, generally speaking, less sophisticated or less R&D-intensive than, say, US equipment.

Since total Soviet military expenditure is a variable, this criterion cannot be rigorously applied. Conversely, to apply this criterion it is necessary to be explicit as to what categories of military expenditure, other than R&D, are assumed to be excluded from the official defence budget. As mentioned above, it is assumed here that the only other major category of military expenditure not financed by the defence budget is atomic energy, or the Soviet equivalent of the military activities conducted by the Atomic Energy Commission in the United States. In the

United States this expenditure has been relatively constant at about $2 billion over the past decade or so and, in the absence of any alternative hypotheses, a similar stability will be assumed for the Soviet Union. Using a rouble : dollar ratio of 0.5, a constant sum of 1 billion roubles will be added to the defence budget to account for this item. Finally, it is assumed that a number of small items such as military aid and stockpiling are also excluded from the defence budget and that these account for 5 per cent of total military outlays.

To illustrate the manner in which these criteria were applied, two extreme hypotheses will be considered as examples. At the conservative extreme, it could be assumed that all military R&D is included in the defence budget. It follows that military R&D will be included in the expenditures for science from "other" sources and in the expenditures for capital investment. Assuming that military R&D is made up of 50 per cent of "other" science expenditure and 75 per cent of capital investment expenditure, the resulting estimate for 1970 is 3.0 billion roubles. This figure represents 16 per cent of total military expenditure (if 5 per cent is added to the official defence budget) which is quite plausible. On the other hand 3.0 billion roubles represents only 26 per cent of the total national expenditures for science which, though not completely implausible, would appear too low. In addition, this procedure completely ignores the possibility that the financial residuals contain some military expenditure.

At the other extreme, it could be assumed that the defence budget excludes military R&D altogether. A military R&D estimate could then be built up, first, by pro-rating the expenditures for capital investment in science over the expenditures for science from the All-Union budget, the Republican budgets and "other" sources: since it is not known how the expenditures for capital investment are distributed this seems a convenient solution. Second, it could be assumed that military R&D is made up of 75 per cent of the adjusted All-Union budget allocation to science and 50 per cent of the expenditure from "other" sources (similarly adjusted). For 1970 this method results in an estimate for military R&D of 7.2 billion roubles which represents 26 per cent of total military outlays where the latter consists of the defence budget, plus R&D, plus 1 billion roubles for atomic energy, plus a 5 per cent allowance for military aid and stockpiling. As a proportion of total military outlays, 26 per cent for R&D would seem too high although it could be reduced simply by assuming that additional military expenditure is contained in the financial residuals. In 1970, the sum of the gross national economy and budgetary expenditure residuals was of the order of 20 billion roubles, providing ample flexibility in this direction. On the other hand, 7.2 billion roubles represents 62 per cent of total national science expenditure so that this estimate would be discounted on the basis of our first criterion.

The method adopted here for computing expenditure on military R&D falls between the two extreme methods discussed above, namely, it takes 50 per cent of the science allocation in the All-Union budget (adjusted for a proportionate share of the capital investment expenditure) plus 25 per cent of the science expenditure from "other" sources (similarly adjusted). To account for the possibility that the defence budget includes some R&D it is assumed that one-half of the military R&D financed from "other" sources is already in the budget.[6] This method yields a series for military R&D which accounts for 35–39 per cent of the national R&D effort over the period 1959–1970, and is therefore consistent with our first criterion. And, on the assumption that total Soviet outlays for national security consist of the defence budget plus (*a*) R&D, (*b*) an allowance for expenditure on atomic energy, and (*c*) an allowance for expenditure on military aid and stockpiling, it also satisfies our second criterion.

The method outlined in the previous paragraph was used to indicate the extent to which the official defence budget could reasonably be raised to provide an estimate of total Soviet national security outlays. Given the margin of uncertainty, it would seem inappropriate to attempt anything more specific.

For the period 1959 to 1970, this method suggests that the official defence budget could be raised by between 27 and 33 per cent. Since there is no smooth transition from the lower to the higher figure, (or *vice versa*), it seems reasonable to take the mid-point of 30 per cent. This figure was also applied to the years since 1970.

The same method was applied for the period 1950 to 1958 with two amendments; (*a*) the estimate for expenditure on atomic energy was reduced to 0.5 billion roubles; and (*b*) expenditure for capital investment in science was estimated on the basis of the relationship between this expenditure and total science expenditure over the period 1959–70. The result is that the defence budget could be raised by roughly 15 per cent over the period 1950–55 and by roughly 20 per cent over the period 1956–58. These figures are markedly lower than the 30 per cent figure suggested for the 1960s, but they are broadly consistent with the continuous growth in the expenditures for science (and the assumption that these include military R&D) and the significant restructuring of the Soviet armed forces, notably the large reduction in the number of military personnel from the peak figure of around five million in 1955, which took place over this period.

The estimates of total Soviet military outlays for the period 1950–73

---

[6] A point worth bearing in mind is the possibility that the cost of constructing and testing prototypes, to the extent that this is not included in the expenditure for science, may simply be incorporated in the price which the Ministry of Defence pays for its finished hardware.

190

**Table 8B.7. Estimated total Soviet military outlays, 1950–73**

*Billions of roubles*

| Year | Military outlays | Year | Military outlays |
|------|------------------|------|------------------|
| 1950 | 9.5  | 1962 | 16.5 |
| 1951 | 11.1 | 1963 | 18.1 |
| 1952 | 12.5 | 1964 | 17.3 |
| 1953 | 12.7 | 1965 | 16.6 |
| 1954 | 11.5 | 1966 | 17.4 |
| 1955 | 12.9 | 1967 | 18.8 |
| 1956 | 11.7 | 1968 | 21.7 |
| 1957 | 11.6 | 1969 | 23.0 |
| 1958 | 11.3 | 1970 | 23.3 |
| 1959 | 12.2 | 1971 | 23.3 |
| 1960 | 12.1 | 1972 | 23.3 |
| 1961 | 15.1 | 1973 | 23.3 |

are given in table 8B.7. It is of some interest to compare these figures with the estimates of the value of military hardware produced in the Soviet Union as is done in table 8B.8. Given the relatively low man-power costs in the Soviet Union it is reasonable to assume that pro-curement accounts for a higher proportion of total military expenditure than in the United States, although this would be offset to some degree by the larger number of military personnel in the former. This suggests that procurement may account for 30–35 per cent of total Soviet mili-tary expenditure. As table 8B.8 shows, the evidence, from the procure-ment estimates, for the validity of our estimates of total military ex-penditure is, strictly speaking, contradictory, but for most years they would support total expenditures of the same order of magnitude as those developed here.

## VI. *The exchange-rate problem*

Western scholars are virtually unanimous in their verdict that the official exchange rate—currently 0.829 roubles : US $1—is quite unrelated to the Soviet cost-price structure. Even under the best of circumstances an exchange rate is responsive only to the forces of supply and demand of goods and services traded internationally. Since, for most economies, the volume of domestic output exported or the volume of domestic ex-penditure on imports is only a small fraction of total output or ex-penditure, it should not be surprising to find that the official exchange-

**Table 8B.8. Alternative estimates of the value of military/space procurement as a proportion of total military outlays: selected years, 1955–68**[a]

*Per cent*

|  | 1955 | 1958 | 1959 | 1960 | 1962 | 1963 | 1965 | 1967 | 1968 |
|---|---|---|---|---|---|---|---|---|---|
| Boretsky | . . | *16.3* | *21.9* | . . | *34.0* | *35.4* | *38.0* | *49.0* | *49.0* |
| Greenslade | *30.3* | . . | *32.0* | *40.9* | . . | . . | . . | . . | . . |
| Becker | . . | . . | *40.2* | . . | . . | . . | . . | . . | . . |

[a] Figures are derived from data in the three sources below.

*Sources:* Becker, A., *Soviet Military Outlays Since 1955* RM-3886-PR (Santa Monica, Rand Corporation, July 1964). Boretsky, M., "The Technological Base of Soviet Military Power", in *Economic Performance and the Military Burden in the Soviet Union,* a compendium of papers submitted to the Subcommittee on Foreign Economic Policy of the Joint Economic Committee (Washington, 1970). Greenslade, R., "Industrial Production Statistics in the USSR", in Treml, V. and Hardt, J. eds., *Soviet Economic Statistics* (Durham, North Carolina, Duke University Press, 1972) pp. 155–94.

rate equivalent of two currencies is often not an accurate reflection of their respective internal purchasing power. This is likely to be particularly true if one is considering a particular class of goods and services— in the present case, military goods and services.

The problem can be formulated as follows: what would it cost if the USA were to duplicate the Soviet national security programme or, alternatively, what is the dollar-equivalent of the cost of acquiring, operating and maintaining Soviet soldiers, aircraft, tanks, ships, missiles and so on?

The general procedure in this situation is actually to price a representative sample of goods and services in each country. These various price ratios are then grouped into classes—for example, personnel, consumer goods and investment goods. A single ratio is then derived by weighting the ratios for the different classes of expenditure according to their importance in the total.

The components of Soviet military spending for which rouble : dollar ratios have been explicitly calculated are personnel pay and subsistence, R&D and procurement.

Western estimates of the cost per head of Soviet military personnel are already quite dated. The figure in widespread use is an estimate made for 1958 of 1 090 roubles per man. [2e] The annual cost to pay, feed and clothe a US soldier at that time was estimated at $3 859. [17] It is usually assumed that the Soviet figure can be extrapolated both forward and backward on the hypothesis that rising wages are offset by declining prices of consumer goods. The US figure, on the other hand, has been rising quite rapidly. Thus while the purchasing-power equivalent of a dollar for military personnel was 0.28 roubles in the late 1950s, it is generally assumed to have fallen in subsequent years. Benoit, for example, uses a rate of 0.2 roubles : US $1 for military personnel and internal transfers in 1962. [18]

For R&D (including military R&D) a purchasing power parity rate for 1960–62 has been computed by Davies, Barker and Fakiolas. [19] Their calculation is based on 1955/66 data for the earnings of R&D personnel and the prices of capital equipment used in R&D in both the United States and the Soviet Union. The price ratios for these two components of expenditure are weighted according to the Soviet distribution of R&D expenditure. This calculation, which is admitted to give nothing more than a general order of magnitude, results in an R&D exchange rate of 0.28–0.40 roubles : US $1. This range of conversion ratios was intended to measure the Soviet R&D effort, not the output of this effort. The US Department of Defense has used a conversion ratio which, in addition to reflecting price and wage differentials, also takes into account the relative productivities of R&D personnel. This ratio, 0.5 roubles per US dollar for recent years, therefore purports to give the dollar equivalent of the output of the Soviet R&D effort. It is evident that the productivity of R&D personnel is judged to be appreciably higher in the United States.

A relatively large number of estimates exist of an appropriate conversion rate for military hardware. The general assumption here is that the best available conversion rate for military hardware is that for producer durables.

The last occasion on which the Soviet authorities published data on the prices of producer durables was in 1955. Abraham Becker's study of the prices of producer durables in the USA and the USSR in 1955 is the basis of nearly all the subsequent estimates of relative prices in this field.[7] [20] If a conversion rate is required for a year subsequent to 1955, Becker's data has to be revised in the light of the relative movement in the prices of producer durables in both countries. The difficulty here is that the relevant Soviet price indices are generally considered to be inadequate for this purpose.

The most relevant index, the price index of output for the MBMW industry, is currently based on a fixed sample of fully specified goods produced in 1961. This index shows a falling average price level.[8] However, a large share—at least one-third—of MBMW output is classified as "new products" which carry "temporary" prices estimated to range 30–70 per cent above regular prices. It is quite possible, therefore, that the MBMW index actually misstates the direction of price change (see refer-

[7] Becker's study has some serious shortcomings, notably the exclusion of such important product groups as ships and aircraft from his sample and the fact that he could take little or no account of differences in quality.

[8] An earlier wholesale price index (1949=100) for this industry shows prices, exclusive of turnover tax, falling continuously for the period 1950–64: namely, 1950=52, 1958=45, 1964=42. Prices inclusive of turnover tax fell until 1958 and then remained constant through 1964. [21]

ence [22].[9] One estimate is that the wholesale prices of machinery rose by as much as 15–20 per cent from 1955 through the mid-1960s. [23a]

The final consideration here is the Soviet industrial price reforms of 1967. These reforms radically changed both the absolute level of industrial prices and the relative price structure. The prices of machinery and metal-working products were not changed, suggesting that profits—a major objective of the reforms—were already at the desired level in this sector. [23b]

Presumably, however, a zero overall change in the prices of MBMW products does not preclude relative price changes within this sector, particularly since the reforms included a revised formula for price-setting—the most important change being the inclusion of interest on capital as a component of price. In other words, these reforms would seriously limit, for the post-1967 period, whatever validity extrapolations of the 1955 relationships might have.

For 1955, Bornstein estimates the rouble : dollar ratio for producer durables at 0.6 roubles : US \$1, on US weights and 0.4 roubles : US \$1 on Soviet weights. [24a] These ratios were based directly on Becker's study.[10]

Boretsky arrives at two conversion rates for producer durables in 1964; 0.32 roubles : US \$1 and 0.36 roubles : US \$1. These rates are essentially extrapolations of Becker's data for 1955 on the basis of "a rather extensive reassessment and updating of all relevant information . . . on rouble versus dollar prices for machinery and related products". [8b] A significant innovation is that Boretsky attempts to take the phenomenon of temporary prices into account.

In an earlier study, Boretsky used a conversion factor of 0.36 roubles : US \$1 for converting the 1958 value of Soviet machinery output into dollars. [10b] The implication here is that Boretsky considers that price changes in the United States and the Soviet Union between 1958 and 1964 were roughly similar.[11]

---

[9] An additional consideration is that the use of a price index for civil equipment in this context implicitly assumes that the rate of quality change is the same for military and civil equipment, which it manifestly is not. In other words, this procedure begs the whole question of the effect of differential rates of quality change on the rate of price change.

[10] The existence of alternative weights is a variation of the familiar index number problem. The components of military expenditure—for example, personnel costs, R&D and procurement—can be further subdivided. Thus, personnel costs consist of basic pay plus a subsistence element, and producer durables consist of a wide range of different products. The distribution of expenditure or output over these sub-components will normally differ between countries and it is equally legitimate to weight the price ratios according to the distribution of either country. In the present case, we are seeking to estimate the dollar cost of the Soviet military effort, so it would seem appropriate to use Soviet-weighted price ratios where possible.

[11] The US Wholesale Price Index of finished goods was virtually constant over the period 1958–64. Boretsky cites Soviet sources as saying that, official price indices notwithstanding, no significant revision in the prices of machinery and equipment took place between 1955 and 1967. [8c]

In a recent publication, Becker has critically reviewed a large amount of material, both Soviet and Western and including all the studies discussed here, on trends in Soviet industrial prices and rouble : dollar ratios for machinery. [25] Regarding price trends in the MBMW industry, his conclusions reinforce the point made earlier that the official machinery price index actually misstates the direction of price change and that the treatment of new commodities is the essential reason for this. In a very tentative computation Beckers estimates a "true" output price index for the MBMW industry and uses this index in conjunction with his assessment of dollar : rouble ratios to compute a time series of these ratios for the period 1955–70. However, he places little faith in the accuracy of the ratio for any particular year and concludes by saying that the average rouble : dollar ratio for machinery over this period is estimated to fall in the range 0.38–0.44. [25a]

Finally, in an exhaustive survey of Soviet studies on rouble : dollar ratios, Treml and Gallik found that in all but one or two cases the ratios for machinery fell in the range 0.5–0.7. [26] Given the widely held opinion that the ratio for military equipment is lower than for civil equipment (Treml and Gallik cite a Soviet author who also holds this opionion [26a]) it would seem that Becker's estimate of 0.38–0.44 is not unreasonable.

In addition to conversion rates for the individual components of military/space expenditure, there are conversion rates for military/space expenditure as a whole and for GNP or Net Material Product (NMP).

Bornstein's rate for the defence sector as a whole in 1955 is 0.5 roubles : US $1 with US weights and 0.4 roubles : US $1 with Soviet weights. [24b] Benoit and Lubell use a rate of 0.42 roubles : US $1 in 1962. [18] Lee uses a rate that moves from 0.4–0.45 roubles : US $1 in 1955 to 0.45–0.50 roubles : US $1 in 1965 reflecting his judgement that the cost of developing and producing military hardware has risen more rapidly in the Soviet Union than in the United States. [27]

For GNP as a whole Bornstein's conversion rate for 1955 is 0.5 roubles : US $1 with Soviet weights (1.21 roubles : US $1 with US weights). [24b] Becker has computed the rouble : dollar ratios implicit in Soviet comparisons of the national income of various countries. The Soviet definition of national income (NMP), which excludes services, is used in these comparisons. Since services have relatively low rouble : dollar ratios, the conversion rates for national income will have an upward bias. Becker's rouble : dollar ratio for 1962 is 0.83 and this falls steadily to 0.75 in 1968. [25b]

The various conversion rates are collected in table 8B.9. A conspicuous feature is that the rouble : dollar ratios for military/space are significantly lower than those for GNP and NMP. A seemingly widely accepted explanation for this is that the military/space sector, and in par-

**Table 8B.9. Rouble : dollar conversion ratios**[a]

*Rouble-equivalent of US $1*

| | 1955 | 1956 | 1957 | 1958 | 1959 | 1960 | 1961 | 1962 | 1963 | 1964 | 1965 | 1966 | 1967 | 1968 |
|---|---|---|---|---|---|---|---|---|---|---|---|---|---|---|
| **Military personnel** | | | | | | | | | | | | | | |
| Pecker [2e] and US Sub-committee on Economic Statistics [17] | | | | | | | | | | | | | | |
| Benoit/Lubell [18] | | | | 0.28 | | | | | | | | | | |
| **R&D** | | | | | | | | | | | | | | |
| Davies, Barker, Fakiolas [19] | | | | | | 0.28–0.40 | 0.28–0.40 | 0.20  0.28–0.40 | | | | | | |
| **Military/space procurement** | | | | | | | | | | | | | | |
| Bornstein [24a] | 0.40 | | | | | | | | | | | | | |
| Boretsky [10c] | | | | 0.36 | | | | | | | | | | |
| Boretsky [8e] | | | | | | | | | | 0.32–0.36 | | | | |
| Becker [25b] | | Average rate 1955–70, 0.38–0.44 | | | | | | | | | | | | |
| **Total military/space** | | | | | | | | | | | | | | |
| Bornstein [24a] | 0.40 | | | | | | | | | | | | | |
| Benoit/Lubell [18] | | 0.40–0.45 | 0.40–0.45 | 0.40–0.45 | | | | | | | | | | |
| Lee [27] | | | | | 0.41–0.46 | 0.42–0.47 | 0.43–0.48 | 0.42  0.43–0.48 | 0.44–0.49 | 0.45–0.50 | 0.45–0.50 | | | |
| **GNP** | | | | | | | | | | | | | | |
| Bornstein [24b] | 0.60 | | | | | | | | | | | | | |
| **NMP** | | | | | | | | | | | | | | |
| Becker [25b] | | | | | | | | 0.83 | 0.81 | 0.78 | 0.78 | | 0.77 | 0.75 |

[a] Where there are alternatives, the Soviet-weighted ratio is given.

ticular the industrial enterprise producing armaments, enjoys a high priority in terms of resource allocation and R&D funds. The military/space sector is therefore more efficient or, alternatively, a rouble spent in this sector buys more than a rouble spent in, say, agriculture.[12]

On the other hand, Alec Nove argues that if the rouble : dollar ratio for industrial production were 0.5 or less, Soviet products would be extremely competitive on world markets. [28] Since this is not the case, Nove concludes that for equipment of the same performance and quality an average rouble : dollar ratio of 0.5 overstates the purchasing power of the rouble.[13]

In assessing this brief review of the exchange-rate problem it will be useful, first of all, to document the changes in the official exchange rate in the post-war period (all the rates are expressed in new roubles: 1 new rouble (1961)=10 old roubles).

Before March 1950 : 0.53 roubles : US $1
March 1950–1961 : 0.4 roubles : US $1
1961–1971 : 0.9 roubles : US $1
1972– : 0.829 roubles : US $1

There seems to be a consensus that, until the huge devaluation of 1961, the rouble was overvalued at the official exchange rate. The degree of overvaluation was substantial, of the order of 100 per cent. One source, for example, tentatively concludes that a proper conversion rate in 1950 would have been around 1 rouble : US $1. [29]

Similarly, a calculation made by Nove and Zaubermann suggests a conversion rate for GNP as a whole of 0.85–0.90 rouble : US $1 in 1955. [30] Finally, Bornstein's rate of 0.6 roubles : US $1 with Soviet weights in 1955 becomes 0.9 roubles : US $1 if one takes the average of his Soviet weighted and US weighted rates. The devaluation of 1961 could

---

[12] In a market economy the price system plays a critical role in the allocation of resources. In a Soviet-type economy the pattern of resource allocation is broadly determined by the central authority and prices are manipulated as one means of accomplishing this allocation. Soviet prices therefore do not necessarily reflect the relative scarcity of resources. Specifically, rouble estimates of military expenditure may understate the scarcity value of the resources employed.

[13] This brings out the point that in the calculation of purchasing power equivalent rates, the goods and services being compared are assumed to be qualitatively identical. In fact, however, only certain qualitative aspects are considered in a comparison of the prices of a particular item in two countries. For example, if a US machine tool were fully automated and its Soviet counterpart were not, this difference would be reflected in the respective prices for this machine. On the other hand, such factors as the rate and precision of output and the efficiency of equipment are not reflected. A corollary to this point is that even though Soviet and US military forces may be considered to be in rough numerical parity at the present time, it does not necessarily follow that the dollar-equivalent of Soviet military spending should match that of the USA. If, for example, US equipment is generally more sophisticated and technically efficient than Soviet equipment, then the dollar cost of acquiring this equipment and the manpower required to operate it will obviously be higher.

therefore be said to have eliminated the overvaluation which prevailed during the 1950s. Indeed, the implicit ratios calculated by Becker (table 8B.9) suggest that the official exchange rate now *undervalues* the rouble. As mentioned above, these rouble : dollar ratios are probably too high because of the exclusion of services.

The foregoing comments refer to the exchange rate appropriate for the conversion of GNP or NMP as a whole. For military/space activities alone, it would seem that, for the 1950s, the official exchange rate was roughly correct. After 1961, however, the official exchange rate is considered to undervalue significantly the military rouble.

In general there would seem to be no reason to doubt that the official rate of 0.829 roubles : US $1 understates the purchasing power of the rouble with respect to military goods and services. On the other hand, it is apparent that the purchasing power parity rates presented in table 8B.9 are derived from a rather fragile data base. In the case of producer durables the basic evidence was already 10 years old in 1965. In addition there are conflicting views on the relative movements in costs and prices in the USA and the Soviet Union. As already mentioned, Lee is of the opinion that the relevant costs and prices have risen more rapidly in the Soviet Union than in the USA. Stanley Cohn, on the other hand, using official data on movements in wages and prices, calculates a deflator for military expenditure which shows a fall of 8 per cent in the average price of military goods and over the period 1955–64 (1955= 100 : 1964=91.9).[14] [31] The US military price index—comparable to Cohn's deflator because all pay increases are regarded as price increases —increased by 29.2 per cent over the period 1955–64. In other words the average price level for military goods and services in the Soviet Union fell by more than 35 per cent relative to that in the USA. This means that if 0.4 was the appropriate rouble : dollar rate for military goods and services in 1955, the appropriate rate in 1964 was 0.26, or roughly half Lee's rate for the same year (0.4–0.5). In general, it is difficult to believe that, on the average, the prices of military goods and services have actually fallen in the Soviet Union. The point, however, is that no conclusive evidence to the contrary exists.[15]

There is no one answer, therefore, to the question of what is an appropriate conversion rate for Soviet military expenditure. And it is ob-

[14] The fact that Cohn employs official wage and price indices may give rise to some doubt as to the validity of his deflator. In particular, as noted above, there is considerable scepticism among Western scholars concerning the fall in the average price level of machinery products suggested by the official index. It is therefore worth pointing out that Cohn's assumption of personnel costs increasing at the same rate as civilian wages would be regarded by some as exaggerating the growth in these costs, thus offsetting, at least to some extent, the bias in the official machinery price index.

[15] Nancy Nimitz also expresses the opinion that the prices of military goods—though not military services—may have fallen significantly in the late 1950s. [32]

viously important if the rate selected is 0.4 roubles : US $1 rather than 0.55 roubles : US $1—such a choice will have the same effect as adding nearly 40 per cent to the Soviet defence budget to account for expenditures funded from other sources.

## VII. *The dollar-equivalent of Soviet military expenditure*

The estimates of total Soviet military expenditure can now be combined with the information on the rouble : dollar exchange rate to provide estimates of the dollar-equivalent of Soviet military expenditure. The SIPRI estimate of total world military expenditure is based on the dollar-equivalent military expenditure of all the countries in the world at constant 1970 prices and exchange rates. The first task is, therefore, to estimate a rouble : dollar ratio for military expenditure in 1970.

This can be done by selecting what appears to be the best ratio for each of the major categories of expenditure and then weighting these ratios by the distribution of military expenditure in 1970. In fact very little information is available on the distribution of Soviet military expenditure but a rough estimate can be made. The Department of Defense in the United States has estimated the distribution of Soviet expenditure in 1970 as follows: military personnel—28.2 per cent; operations and maintenance—21.5 per cent; procurement and other investment—29.7 per cent; R&D—20.6 per cent. [33]

The proportion for R&D is consistent with our hypothesis regarding this expenditure. Specifically, the calculations performed in section V suggest a figure of 19 per cent for R&D in 1970.

A possible means of checking the proportion for military personnel is to estimate the average cost per man in the Soviet Union and multiply this by the number of military personnel. The difficulty, of course, is that only one estimate of the average cost per man is available and this refers to 1958. It is widely assumed that this figure can be extrapolated both forwards and backwards. One argument supporting this assumption has already been mentioned. Another is presumably the fact that roughly 60 per cent of Soviet military personnel are conscripts who receive very low rates of pay. [34] Nonetheless, the assumption that the average cost per man has been constant is a rather extreme one and it would seem more realistic to allow for some increase.[16] This could be done

---

[16] At least one reason for this is that the Soviet military establishment must have experienced a growing demand for skilled—and therefore more expensive—personnel as the complexity of its equipment increased.

**Table 8B.10. Estimated dollar-equivalents of Soviet military expenditure, 1950–73**

*US $ bn*

| Year | Military expenditure | Year | Military expenditure |
|------|----------------------|------|----------------------|
| 1950 | 25.7 | 1962 | 44.6 |
| 1951 | 30.0 | 1963 | 48.9 |
| 1952 | 33.8 | 1964 | 46.7 |
| 1953 | 34.3 | 1965 | 44.9 |
| 1954 | 31.1 | 1966 | 47.0 |
| 1955 | 34.9 | 1967 | 50.8 |
| 1956 | 31.6 | 1968 | 58.6 |
| 1957 | 31.3 | 1969 | 62.2 |
| 1958 | 30.5 | 1970 | 63.0 |
| 1959 | 33.0 | 1971 | 63.0 |
| 1960 | 32.7 | 1972 | 63.0 |
| 1961 | 40.8 | 1973 | 63.0 |

for example by moving the average cost per man by the index of average annual money wages in Soviet industry. This index increased at an average annual rate of 2.5–3.0 per cent depending on the class of worker. The resulting estimate of average cost per man in 1970, when multiplied by the number of military personnel, gives a figure of roughly 5.0 billion roubles for personnel costs or about 21 per cent of the estimated total military outlays. Since we have no information on the method used by the US Department of Defense we shall employ the latter figure. Finally, we shall assume that procurement accounts for 35 per cent and operations and maintenance 25 per cent of total expenditure.

Regarding the rouble : dollar ratios it is proposed to use Becker's ratio of 0.38–0.44 for procurement, the Davies *et al.* ratio of 0.28–0.40 for R&D and 0.5 for O&M (this ratio was employed by Benoit and Lubell [18] for the combined expenditure on procurement, R&D, O&M and military construction). For military personnel, the rouble : dollar ratio in 1970 is 0.2 when the average cost per man in the Soviet Union is assumed to have increased in the manner described above.

The weighted average rouble : dollar ratio for total military expenditure in 1970 is a range of 0.35–0.40 or a mid-point of 0.375. It is worth mentioning that the average ratio is not particularly sensitive to small changes in the distribution of expenditure.

Table 8B.10 shows the dollar-equivalent of Soviet military expenditure at the constant 1970 rouble : dollar ratio of 0.37. The remaining problem is whether this expenditure series should be corrected for price changes. In the Soviet Union the consumer price index—the deflator used by SIPRI for all the other countries of the world—has remained virtually flat over most of the post-war period. There is a widespread opinion that this index—and indeed Soviet price indices in general—has a downward bias, that is, at the least, it overstates the extent to which the average price level has fallen and it may even misstate the direction of the change. However, with the exception of Becker's machinery price index mentioned in section VI above, no alternative price indices have been compiled. It will therefore be assumed that the figures in table 8B.10 represent expenditures in constant 1970 prices with the caveat that this assumption probably implies some overstatement.

## VIII. *Conclusions*

The estimates of the dollar-equivalent of Soviet military expenditures are subject to a wide margin of error, the product of uncertainties regarding both the rouble figure and the exchange rate. This is unfortunate but—given the available data—unavoidable. It follows that no great demands should be placed on these expenditure figures. In particular it is clear that any demonstration that the Soviet Union is spending $5 or $10 billion more or less than the United States cannot claim a degree of accuracy that would justify the use of such an expenditure relationship in assessments of the military situation or in decision-making on defence budgets. Indeed even accurate expenditure figures are of only marginal value in this role.

To reiterate, SIPRI is interested in the dollar-equivalent of Soviet military expenditure for the purpose of compiling an estimate of the quantity of resources devoted to military uses worldwide. The level and trend of this magnitude can be meaningfully discussed even if it is subject to substantial margins of error.

**References**

1. Gallik, D., *et al.*, *The Soviet Financial System* (Washington, US Department of Commerce, Bureau of the Census, June 1968) pp. 174–75.
2. Becker, A., *Soviet Military Outlays Since 1955* RM-3886-PR (Santa Monica, Rand Corporation, July 1964).
   (a) −, p. 12.
   (b) −, p. 34.
   (c) −, pp. 16.
   (d) −, p. 8–9.
   (e) −, p. 92.
3. Becker, A., *Soviet National Income, 1958–1964* RM-464-PR (Santa Monica, Rand Corporation, August 1964) p. 156.

4. Anderson, S. and Lee, W. T., *Probable Trend and Magnitude of Soviet Expenditure for National Security Purposes* SSC-RM 5205-54 (Menlo Park, Calif., Stanford Research Institute, February 1969).
   (a) −, p. 56.
   (b) −, p. 40.
   (c) −, p. 59.
   (d) −, p. 61.
5. Trapeznikov, S., "Scientific-Technical Development and the Efficiency of Science", *Voprosy Ekonomiki*, No. 2, 1973 p. 95.
6. Nimitz, N., *Soviet Expenditure for Scientific Research* RM-3384-OR (Santa Monica, Rand Corporation, 1963).
7. Nolting, L., "Sources of Financing the Stages of the Research, Development and Innovation Cycle in the USSR", *Foreign Economic Reports*, No. 3 (Washington, US Department of Commerce, September 1973).
8. Boretsky, M., "The Technological Base of Soviet Military Power" in *Economic Performance and the Military Burden in the Soviet Union*. A Compendium of Papers submitted to the Subcommittee on Foreign Economic Policy of the Joint Economic Committee (Washington, 1970).
   (a) −, pp. 227–29.
   (b) −, p. 214.
   (c) −, p. 202.
9. Greenslade, R., "Industrial Production Statistics in the USSR", in Treml, V. and Hardt, J. eds., *Soviet Economic Statistics* (Durham, North Carolina, Duke University Press, 1972) pp. 155–94.
10. Boretsky, M., "The Soviet Challenge to US Machine Building", in *Studies Prepared for the Joint Economic Committee Hearings on Dimensions of Soviet Economic Power* (Washington, December 1962).
    (a) −, p. 104.
    (b) −, p. 119.
11. Becker, A., Moorsteen, R. and Powell, R. P., "I. The Soviet Capital Stock: Extensions and Revisions, 1961–67", in Two Supplements to Moorsteen, R. and Powell, R. P., *The Soviet Capital Stock 1928–62* (New Haven, 1968, Yale University, Economic Growth Center).
12. *World Military Expenditures 1971* (Washington, 1972, US Arms Control and Disarmament Agency) p. 55.
13. Cohn, S., *The Economic Burden of Soviet Defense Outlays*, Joint Economic Committee Hearings on Economic Performance and the Military Burden in the Soviet Union (Washington, 1970) pp. 166–68.
14. Gol'tzov, A. and Ozerov, S., *Distribution of the National Income of the USSR* (Leningrad, 1971) (Unpublished).
15. Steel, R., "The State Budget for 1970", in *Economic Performance and Military Burden in the Soviet Union*, A Compendium of Papers submitted to the Subcommittee on Foreign Economic Policy of the Joint Economic Committee (Washington, 1970) p. 58.
16. *Resources Devoted to Military Research and Development* (Stockholm, Almqvist & Wiksell, 1972, Stockholm International Peace Research Institute).
    (a) −, (table B.7), p. 82.
    (b) −, (table B.4), p. 80.
17. *Comparisons of the United States and Soviet Economies*, Prepared by the Central Intelligence Agency in Cooperation with the Department of State and the Department of Defense for the Subcommittee on Economic Statistics of the Joint Economic Committee (Washington, 1960) p. 40.

18. Benoit, E. and Lubell, H., "The World Burden of National Defense", in Benoit, E., ed., *Disarmament and World Economic Interdependence* (Stockholm, Universitets förlaget, 1967) p. 40.

19. Davies, R. W., Barker, G. R. and Fakiolas, R., "Notes on Sources and Methods for the Soviet Statistics on Research and Development", Appendix II in C. Freeman and A. Young, *The Research and Development Effort in Western Europe, North America and the Soviet Union* (Paris, OECD, 1965).

20. Becker, A., *The Prices of Producer Durables in the United States and the USSR in 1955* RM-2432 (Santa Monica, Rand Corporation, 1959).

21. Bornstein, M., "Soviet Price Theory and Policy", *New Directions in the Soviet Economy*. Studies prepared for the Subcommittee on Foreign Economic Relations of the Joint Economic Committee Part II-A (Washington, 1966) pp. 66–69.

22. Bornstein, M., "Soviet Price Statistics", in V. Treml and J. Hardt, eds., *Soviet Economic Statistics* (Durham, North Carolina, Duke University Press, 1972).

23. Schroeder, G., "The 1966/67 Soviet Industrial Price Reform: A Study in Complications", *Soviet Studies*, Vol. XX, April 1969.
    (a) −, p. 466.
    (b) −, p. 467.

24. Bornstein, M., "A Comparison of Soviet and United States National Products", in *Comparisons of the United States and Soviet Economies,* papers submitted by panellists appearing before the Subcommittee on Economic Statistics of the Joint Economic Committee, Part II (Washington, 1960).
    (a) −, p. 386.
    (b) −, p. 385.

25. Becker, A., *Ruble-Price Levels and Dollar/Ruble Ratios of Soviet Machinery in the 1960s*, a report prepared for the Directors of Defense Research and Engineering, R-1063-DDRE (Santa Monica, Rand Corporation, January 1973).
    (a) −, p. 45.
    (b) −, p. 25.

26. Treml, T. and Gallik, D., *Soviet Studies on Ruble/Dollar Parity Ratios* (Washington, US Department of Commerce, May 1973) (Manuscript).
    (a) −, p. 33.

27. Lee, W., "Calculating Soviet National Security Expenditures", in *The Military Budget and National Economic Priorities*, hearings before the Subcommittee on Economy in Government of the Joint Economic Committee (Washington, 1969) p. 933.

28. Nove, A., "Soviet Defense Spending", *Survival*, October 1971.

29. Wyczalkowski, M., "The Soviet Price System and the Rouble Exchange Rate", *International Monetary Fund Staff Papers*, No. 1., September 1950, pp. 203–23.

30. Nove, A. and Zaubermann, A., "A Dollar Valuation of Soviet National Income?", *Soviet Studies*, Vol. X, No. 2, October 1958, pp. 146–50.

31. Cohn, S., "Soviet Growth Retardation" Trends in Resource Availability and Efficiency", in *New Directions in the Soviet Economy*, studies prepared for the Subcommittee on Foreign Economic Relations of the Joint Economic Committee, Part II-A (Washington, 1966) p. 130.

32. Nimitz, N., *Soviet National Income and Products* RM-3112-PR (Santa Monica, Rand Corporation, 1962).

33. *Statement by John S. Foster Jr., Director of Defense Research and Engineering during Hearings on Cost Escalation in Defense Procurement Contracts and Military Posture before the Committee on Armed Services* (Washington, March–June 1973) Part I, p. 526.
34. Brubaker, E., "The Opportunity Cost of Soviet Military Conscripts", in *Soviet Economic Prospects for the Seventies*, a compendium of papers submitted to the Joint Economic Committee (Washington, June 1973).

# Appendix 8C

*World military expenditure, 1973*

For sources and methods, see appendix 8A, page 159.

**Conventions**

[ ] = Rough estimates.

( ) = For military expenditure: estimates based on budget figures or using an estimated consumer price index, or both.

For GDP, NMP data: where sources other than *National Account Statistics* are used.

† = Year of independence.

− = No military expenditure.

**|** = GDP figures used for years after this symbol are not *strictly* comparable with those for preceding years.

## Table 8C.1. World summary: constant price figures

|  | 1952 | 1953 | 1954 | 1955 | 1956 | 1957 | 1958 | 1959 | 1960 | 1961 | 1962 |
|---|---|---|---|---|---|---|---|---|---|---|---|
| USA | 70 100 | 71 978 | 62 370 | 58 850 | 59 645 | 60 825 | 60 858 | 61 192 | 59 554 | 62 008 | 67 24 |
| Other NATO | 20 976 | 21 382 | 20 023 | 19 755 | 20 795 | 21 071 | 19 401 | 20 924 | 21 760 | 22 537 | 24 5 |
| **Total NATO** | **91 076** | **93 360** | **82 393** | **78 605** | **80 440** | **81 896** | **80 259** | **82 116** | **81 314** | **84 545** | **91 81** |
| USSR | 33 800 | 34 300 | 31 100 | 34 900 | 31 600 | 31 300 | 30 500 | 33 000 | 32 700 | 40 800 | 44 60 |
| Other WTO*a* | 2 050 | 2 200 | 2 150 | 2 600 | 2 600 | 2 700 | 2 900 | 3 150 | 3 350 | 3 700 | 4 17 |
| **Total WTO** | **35 850** | **36 500** | **33 250** | **37 500** | **34 200** | **34 000** | **33 400** | **36 150** | **36 050** | **44 500** | **48 77** |
| Other Europe | 2 100 | 2 065 | 2 055 | 2 040 | 2 050 | 2 190 | 2 235 | 2 300 | 2 295 | 2 465 | 2 67 |
| Middle East | 375 | 410 | 460 | 575 | 750 | 780 | 925 | 1 005 | 1 015 | 1 070 | 1 18 |
| South Asia | 940 | 865 | 870 | 935 | 930 | 1 010 | 1 015 | 1 010 | 1 030 | 1 075 | 1 34 |
| Far East (excl. China) | 1 550 | 1 825 | 1 875 | 1 840 | 1 960 | 2 275 | 2 550 | 2 625 | 2 650 | 2 800 | 3 039 |
| China | [3 000] | [2 500] | [2 500] | [2 500] | [2 500] | [2 750] | [2 500] | [2 800] | [2 800] | [3 300] | [3 80 |
| Oceania | 753 | 746 | 672 | 687 | 672 | 620 | 610 | 625 | 624 | 626 | 64 |
| Africa | 145 | 140 | 140 | 175 | 200 | 250 | 255 | 270 | 310 | 440 | 64 |
| Central America | 245 | 270 | 230 | 255 | 285 | 330 | 340 | 355 | 355 | 374 | 41 |
| South America | 1 060 | 1 165 | 1 165 | 1 200 | 1 425 | 1 530 | 1 585 | 1 315 | 1 320 | 1 285 | 1 33 |
| **World total** | **137 094** | **139 846** | **125 610** | **126 312** | **125 412** | **127 631** | **125 674** | **130 571** | **129 763** | **142 480** | **155 67** |

*a* At current prices and Benoit-Lubell exchange rates.

## Table 8C.2. NATO: constant price figures

|  | 1952 | 1953 | 1954 | 1955 | 1956 | 1957 | 1958 | 1959 | 1960 | 1961 | 1962 | 1963 |
|---|---|---|---|---|---|---|---|---|---|---|---|---|
| **North America:** | | | | | | | | | | | | |
| USA | 70 100 | 71 978 | 62 370 | 58 850 | 59 645 | 60 825 | 60 858 | 61 192 | 59 554 | 62 008 | 67 241 | 66 280 |
| Canada | 2 659 | 2 822 | 2 508 | 2 576 | 2 643 | 2 477 | 2 306 | 2 153 | 2 143 | 2 202 | 2 294 | 2 134 |
| **Europe:** | | | | | | | | | | | | |
| Belgium | 594 | 590 | 605 | 503 | 489 | 511 | 505 | 510 | 519 | 525 | 558 | 611 |
| Denmark | 192 | 253 | 249 | 244 | 235 | 248 | 242 | 236 | 264 | 269 | 328 | 332 |
| France | 4 469 | 4 994 | 4 217 | 3 922 | 5 118 | 5 312 | 4 905 | 5 004 | 5 158 | 5 316 | 5 513 | 5 418 |
| FR Germany | 3 207 | 2 565 | 2 603 | 2 968 | 2 816 | 3 407 | 2 535 | 4 047 | 4 375 | 4 612 | 5 854 | 6 580 |
| Greece | 162 | 155 | 166 | 170 | 221 | 194 | 190 | 197 | 209 | 202 | 206 | 211 |
| Italy | 1 459 | 1 317 | 1 438 | 1 428 | 1 464 | 1 515 | 1 547 | 1 614 | 1 678 | 1 734 | 1 903 | 2 121 |
| Luxembourg | 12 | 14 | 16 | 17 | 11 | 12 | 11 | 11 | 7 | 7 | 9 | 9 |
| Netherlands | 654 | 694 | 789 | 827 | 893 | 834 | 734 | 654 | 720 | 839 | 892 | 905 |
| Norway | 222 | 279 | 285 | 238 | 231 | 245 | 228 | 241 | 230 | 250 | 276 | 288 |
| Portugal | 101 | 116 | 125 | 132 | 132 | 136 | 140 | 157 | 163 | 261 | 296 | 290 |
| Turkey | 287 | 320 | 328 | 351 | 331 | 321 | 332 | 381 | 401 | 434 | 450 | 463 |
| UK | 6 958 | 7 263 | 6 694 | 6 379 | 6 215 | 5 859 | 5 726 | 5 719 | 5 893 | 5 886 | 5 997 | 6 057 |
| **Total NATO** | **91 076** | **93 360** | **82 393** | **78 605** | **80 440** | **81 896** | **80 259** | **82 116** | **81 314** | **84 545** | **91 817** | **91 699** |
| **Total NATO (excl. USA)** | **20 976** | **21 382** | **20 023** | **19 755** | **20 795** | **21 071** | **19 401** | **20 924** | **21 760** | **22 537** | **24 576** | **25 419** |
| **Total NATO Europe** | **18 317** | **18 560** | **17 515** | **17 179** | **18 152** | **18 594** | **17 095** | **18 771** | **19 617** | **20 335** | **22 282** | **23 285** |

*US $ mn, at 1970 prices and 1970 exchange rates (Final column, X, at current prices and exchange rates)*

| 963 | 1964 | 1965 | 1966 | 1967 | 1968 | 1969 | 1970 | 1971 | 1972 | 1973 | 1972X |
|---|---|---|---|---|---|---|---|---|---|---|---|
| 6 280 | 64 096 | 63 748 | 76 043 | 87 730 | 90 103 | 86 274 | 77 854 | 71 776 | 72 087 | 68 586 | 77 638 |
| 5 419 | 25 858 | 25 775 | 25 998 | 27 132 | 26 363 | 26 302 | 26 710 | 28 017 | 29 395 | 29 805 | 35 834 |
| **699** | **89 954** | **89 523** | **102 041** | **114 862** | **116 466** | **112 576** | **104 564** | **99 793** | **101 482** | **98 391** | *113 472* |
| 8 900 | 46 700 | 44 900 | 47 000 | 50 800 | 58 600 | 62 200 | 63 000 | 63 000 | 63 000 | 63 000 | *63 000* |
| 4 403 | 4 397 | 4 456 | 4 859 | 5 266 | 6 386 | 7 030 | 7 580 | 8 035 | 8 500 | 8 764 | *8 500* |
| **3 303** | **51 097** | **49 356** | **51 859** | **56 066** | **64 986** | **69 230** | **70 580** | **71 035** | **71 500** | **71 764** | *71 500* |
| 2 764 | 2 916 | 2 938 | 3 038 | 3 032 | 3 133 | 3 269 | 3 362 | 3 397 | 3 494 | 3 500 | *4 160* |
| 1 326 | 1 541 | 1 771 | 2 113 | 2 804 | 3 229 | 3 762 | 4 697 | 5 240 | 5 490 | 8 370 | *5 981* |
| 2 000 | 2 003 | 2 166 | 2 169 | 1 941 | 2 006 | 2 150 | 2 238 | 2 573 | 2 900 | 2 680 | *2 920* |
| 3 067 | 3 567 | 4 098 | 4 060 | 4 461 | 4 952 | 5 518 | 5 999 | 6 560 | 6 550 | 6 400 | *6 757* |
| 4 300] | [4 800] | [5 500] | [6 000] | [6 500] | [7 000] | [8 000] | [8 500] | [9 000] | [9 500] | [10 000] | [9 500] |
| 680 | 770 | 907 | 1 102 | 1 283 | 1 378 | 1 333 | 1 294 | 1 282 | 1 297 | 1 261 | *1 571* |
| 720 | 865 | 977 | 1 034 | 1 289 | 1 529 | 1 898 | 1 882 | 1 805 | 2 035 | 2 250 | *2 137* |
| 431 | 452 | 474 | 488 | 538 | 597 | 589 | 621 | 605 | 650 | 660 | *683* |
| 1 406 | 1 408 | 1 726 | 1 700 | 2 043 | 2 011 | 2 138 | 2 188 | 2 445 | 2 460 | 2 130 | *3 047* |
| **1 696** | **159 374** | **159 436** | **175 604** | **194 819** | **207 287** | **210 463** | **205 925** | **203 735** | **207 358** | **207 406** | *221 728* |

*US $ mn, at 1970 prices and 1970 exchange rates (Final column, X, at current prices and exchange rates)*

| 64 | 1965 | 1966 | 1967 | 1968 | 1969 | 1970 | 1971 | 1972 | 1973 | 1974 | 1972X |
|---|---|---|---|---|---|---|---|---|---|---|---|
| 096 | 63 748 | 76 043 | 87 730 | 90 103 | 86 274 | 77 854 | 71 776 | 72 087 | 68 586 | (68 446) | 77 638 |
| 221 | 1 983 | 2 035 | 2 185 | 2 060 | 1 944 | 2 040 | 2 051 | 2 055 | 2 041 | (2 022) | · 2 260 |
| 652 | 636 | 647 | 678 | 709 | 709 | 755 | 765 | 808 | 840 | .. | *1 004* |
| 342 | 363 | 358 | 358 | 381 | 375 | 368 | 403 | 401 | (402) | [378] | *488* |
| 568 | 5 658 | 5 821 | 6 133 | 6 127 | 6 045 | 6 014 | 6 010 | 5 952 | 6 264 | (6 202) | *7 300* |
| 306 | 6 232 | 6 108 | 6 351 | 5 637 | 6 142 | 6 188 | 6 638 | 7 080 | 7 290 | (6 833) | *9 012* |
| 219 | 237 | 257 | 332 | 387 | 439 | 474 | 501 | 534 | 523 | .. | *574* |
| 172 | 2 254 | 2 439 | 2 381 | 2 426 | 2 378 | 2 506 | 2 836 | 3 131 | 3 116 | (2 850) | *3 706* |
| 11 | 11 | 11 | 9 | 8 | 8 | 8 | 8 | 9 | 10 | .. | *12* |
| 984 | 959 | 935 | 1 034 | 1 023 | 1 070 | 1 103 | 1 154 | 1 192 | 1 255 | (1 244) | *1 550* |
| 292 | 338 | 336 | 347 | 367 | 388 | 389 | 398 | 398 | (415) | [414] | *490* |
| 316 | 316 | 333 | 409 | 430 | 399 | 436 | 456 | 450 | 386 | .. | *591* |
| 501 | 532 | 517 | 521 | 551 | 541 | 579 | 677 | 703 | 754 | [774] | *712* |
| 274 | 6 256 | 6 201 | 6 394 | 6 257 | 5 864 | 5 850 | 6 120 | 6 682 | 6 509 | [6 175] | *8 135* |
| **954** | **89 523** | **102 041** | **114 862** | **116 466** | **112 576** | **104 564** | **99 793** | **101 482** | **98 391** | ·· | *113 472* |
| **858** | **25 775** | **25 998** | **27 132** | **26 363** | **26 302** | **26 710** | **28 017** | **29 395** | **29 805** | ·· | *35 834* |
| **637** | **23 792** | **23 963** | **24 947** | **24 303** | **24 358** | **24 670** | **25 966** | **27 340** | **27 764** | ·· | *33 574* |

## Table 8C.3. NATO: current price figures

| | Currency | 1952 | 1953 | 1954 | 1955 | 1956 | 1957 | 1958 | 1959 | 1960 | 1961 |
|---|---|---|---|---|---|---|---|---|---|---|---|
| **North America:** | | | | | | | | | | | |
| USA | mn dollars | 47 598 | 49 377 | 42 786 | 40 371 | 41 513 | 44 159 | 45 096 | 45 833 | 45 380 | 47 808 |
| Canada | mn dollars | 1 875 | 1 970 | 1 771 | 1 819 | 1 888 | 1 829 | 1 740 | 1 642 | 1 654 | 1 715 |
| **Europe:** | | | | | | | | | | | |
| Belgium | mn francs | 19 965 | 19 815 | 20 707 | 17 067 | 17 065 | 18 356 | 18 312 | 18 686 | 19 161 | 19 561 |
| Denmark | mn kroner | 676 | 889 | 885 | 920 | 936 | 1 012 | 988 | 986 | 1 113 | 1 180 |
| France | mn francs | 12 531 | 13 865 | 11 710 | 11 020 | 14 690 | 15 600 | 16 569 | 17 926 | 19 162 | 20 395 |
| FR Germany | mn marks | 7 898 | 6 195 | 6 287 | 7 383 | 7 211 | 8 962 | 6 853 | 11 087 | 12 115 | 13 175 |
| Greece | mn drachmas | 2 655 | 2 767 | 3 428 | 3 688 | 4 939 | 4 477 | 4 469 | 4 735 | 5 110 | 5 034 |
| Italy | bn lire | 521 | 480 | 543 | 551 | 584 | 611 | 647 | 667 | 710 | 749 |
| Luxembourg | mn francs | 436 | 488 | 565 | 614 | 395 | 439 | 429 | 402 | 263 | 290 |
| Netherlands | mn guilders | 1 253 | 1 330 | 1 583 | 1 699 | 1 854 | 1 845 | 1 656 | 1 505 | 1 728 | 2 013 |
| Norway | mn kroner | 831 | 1 067 | 1 141 | 953 | 967 | 1 049 | 1 024 | 1 107 | 1 058 | 1 179 |
| Portugal | mn escudos | 1 691 | 1 975 | 2 100 | 2 224 | 2 297 | 2 391 | 2 485 | 2 820 | 3 023 | 4 922 |
| Turkey | mn lire | 725 | 827 | 934 | 1 077 | 1 159 | 1 266 | 1 470 | 2 153 | 2 405 | 2 718 |
| UK | mn pounds | 1 561 | 1 681 | 1 569 | 1 567 | 1 615 | 1 574 | 1 591 | 1 589 | 1 657 | 1 709 |

## Table 8C.4. NATO: military expenditure as a percentage of gross domestic product

| | 1952 | 1953 | 1954 | 1955 | 1956 | 1957 | 1958 | 1959 | 1960 | 1961 |
|---|---|---|---|---|---|---|---|---|---|---|
| **North America:** | | | | | | | | | | |
| USA | 13.6 | 13.4 | 11.6 | 10.0 | 9.8 | 9.9 | 10.0 | 9.4 | 8.9 | 9.1 |
| Canada | 7.7 | 7.8 | 7.0 | 6.6 | 6.1 | 5.6 | 5.2 | 4.6 | 4.3 | 4.3 |
| **Europe:** | | | | | | | | | | |
| Belgium | .. | 4.8 | 4.8 | 3.8 | 3.5 | 3.6 | 3.6 | 3.5 | 3.4 | 3.3 |
| Denmark | 2.7 | 3.4 | 3.2 | 3.2 | 3.0 | 3.1 | 2.9 | 2.6 | 2.7 | 2.6 |
| France | 8.6 | 9.1 | 7.3 | 6.4 | 7.7 | 7.3 | 6.8 | 6.6 | 6.4 | 6.2 |
| FR Germany | 5.8 | 4.2 | 4.0 | 4.1 | 3.6 | 4.1 | 3.0 | 4.4 | 4.0 | 4.0 |
| Greece | 6.5 | 5.2 | 5.5 | 5.2 | 6.0 | 5.1 | 4.8 | 4.9 | 4.9 | 4.3 |
| Italy | 4.5 | 3.8 | 4.0 | 3.7 | 3.6 | 3.5 | 3.4 | 3.3 | 3.3 | 3.1 |
| Luxembourg | 2.4 | 2.9 | 3.3 | 3.2 | 1.9 | 1.9 | 1.9 | 1.8 | 1.1 | 1.1 |
| Netherlands | 5.6 | 5.6 | 6.0 | 5.7 | 5.7 | 5.2 | 4.7 | 4.0 | 4.1 | 4.5 |
| Norway | 4.0 | 5.1 | 5.0 | 3.9 | 3.5 | 3.6 | 3.5 | 3.6 | 3.2 | 3.3 |
| Portugal | .. | 4.0 | 4.2 | 4.2 | 4.0 | 4.0 | 4.0 | 4.3 | 4.2 | 6.4 |
| Turkey | 5.1 | 4.9 | 5.4 | 5.1 | 4.7 | 4.1 | 3.8 | 4.5 | 4.7 | 5.0 |
| UK | 10.0 | 10.0 | 8.8 | 8.2 | 7.8 | 7.2 | 7.0 | 6.6 | 6.5 | 6.3 |

## Table 8C.5. WTO: current price figures

| | 1952 | 1953 | 1954 | 1955 | 1956 | 1957 | 1958 | 1959 | 1960 | 1961 | 196 |
|---|---|---|---|---|---|---|---|---|---|---|---|
| Bulgaria | 139 | .. | .. | .. | .. | 133 | 149 | 141 | 154 | 187 | 222 |
| Czechoslovakia | .. | 988 | 918 | 1 227 | 1 071 | 1 094 | 1 047 | 1 035 | 1 035 | 1 118 | 1 282 |
| German DR | .. | .. | .. | .. | .. | .. | 487 | .. | .. | .. | 815 |
| Hungary | .. | .. | .. | .. | .. | 110 | .. | 144 | .. | 205 | 288 |
| Poland | 415 | 647 | 666 | 791 | 754 | 634 | 704 | 898 | 936 | 1 068 | 1 156 |
| Romania | .. | .. | .. | .. | .. | .. | 405 | 381 | 365 | .. | 414 |
| USSR[a] | 33 800 | 34 300 | 31 100 | 34 900 | 31 600 | 31 300 | 30 500 | 33 000 | 32 700 | 40 800 | 44 600 |
| **Total WTO** | [35 850] | [36 500] | [33 250] | [37 500] | [34 200] | [34 000] | [33 400] | [36 150] | [36 050] | [44 500] | 48 777 |

[a] At SIPRI-estimated exchange rates (see pages 191 ff.).

*Local currency, current prices*

| | 1963 | 1964 | 1965 | 1966 | 1967 | 1968 | 1969 | 1970 | 1971 | 1972 | 1973 | 1974 |
|---|---|---|---|---|---|---|---|---|---|---|---|---|
| 81 | 52 295 | 51 213 | 51 827 | 63 572 | 75 448 | 80 732 | 81 443 | 77 854 | 74 862 | 77 638 | 78 462 | (84 600) |
| 10 | 1 712 | 1 813 | 1 659 | 1 766 | 1 965 | 1 927 | 1 899 | 2 061 | 2 132 | 2 238 | 2 391 | (2 560) |
| | | | | | | | | | | | | |
| 1 | 23 596 | 26 241 | 26 606 | 28 169 | 30 396 | 32 676 | 33 892 | 37 502 | 39 670 | 44 140 | 49 075 | . . |
| 51 | 1 651 | 1 764 | 1 974 | 2 080 | 2 249 | 2 591 | 2 640 | 2 757 | 3 195 | 3 386 | 3 711 | (3 820) |
| 84 | 22 849 | 24 280 | 25 300 | 26 732 | 28 912 | 30 200 | 31 700 | 33 200 | 35 000 | 36 800 | 41 460 | (46 250) |
| 13 | 19 924 | 19 553 | 19 915 | 20 254 | 21 408 | 19 310 | 21 577 | 22 573 | 25 450 | 28 720 | 31 597 | (32 130) |
| 12 | 5 385 | 5 647 | 6 290 | 7 168 | 9 390 | 11 003 | 12 762 | 14 208 | 15 480 | 17 211 | 19 478 | . . |
| 1 | 1 031 | 1 118 | 1 212 | 1 342 | 1 359 | 1 403 | 1 412 | 1 562 | 1 852 | 2 162 | 2 385 | (2 465) |
| 5 | 348 | 462 | 477 | 497 | 413 | 374 | 391 | 416 | 442 | 517 | 575 | . . |
| 6 | 2 307 | 2 661 | 2 714 | 2 790 | 3 200 | 3 280 | 3 682 | 3 968 | 4 466 | 4 974 | 5 651 | (6 358) |
| 1 | 1 465 | 1 570 | 1 897 | 1 947 | 2 097 | 2 300 | 2 502 | 2 774 | 3 022 | 3 239 | 3 621 | (3 895) |
| 4 | 5 724 | 6 451 | 6 680 | 7 393 | 9 575 | 10 692 | 10 779 | 12 538 | 14 699 | 16 046 | 15 528 | . . |
| 0 | 3 157 | 3 443 | 3 821 | 3 996 | 4 596 | 5 159 | 5 395 | 6 237 | 8 487 | 9 961 | 12 483 | (14 975) |
| 4 | 1 870 | 2 000 | 2 091 | 2 153 | 2 276 | 2 332 | 2 303 | 2 444 | 2 800 | 3 272 | 3 481 | [3 800] |

*Per cent*

| 1963 | 1964 | 1965 | 1966 | 1967 | 1968 | 1969 | 1970 | 1971 | 1972 |
|---|---|---|---|---|---|---|---|---|---|
| 8.8 | 8.0 | 7.5 | 8.4 | 9.4 | 9.2 | 8.6 | 7.8 | 6.9 | 6.6 |
| 3.7 | 3.6 | 3.0 | 2.8 | 3.0 | 2.6 | 2.4 | 2.4 | 2.3 | 2.2 |
| | | | | | | | | | |
| 3.4 | 3.4 | 3.2 | 3.1 | 3.1 | 3.2 | 2.9 | 2.9 | 2.8 | . . |
| 3.0 | 2.8 | 2.8 | 2.7 | 2.7 | 2.8 | 2.5 | 2.3 | 2.5 | 2.3 |
| 5.6 | 5.3 | 5.2 | 5.0 | 5.0 | 4.8 | 4.4 | 4.1 | 3.9 | 3.7 |
| 5.2 | 4.6 | 4.3 | 4.1 | 4.3 | 3.6 | 3.6 | 3.3 | 3.4 | 3.5 |
| 3.9 | 3.7 | 3.6 | 3.7 | 4.5 | 4.8 | 4.9 | 4.9 | 4.8 | 4.7 |
| 3.3 | 3.3 | 3.3 | 3.4 | 3.1 | 3.0 | 2.7 | 2.7 | 3.0 | 3.1 |
| 1.3 | 1.5 | 1.4 | 1.4 | 1.2 | 1.0 | 0.9 | 0.8 | 0.9 | 0.9 |
| 4.4 | 4.3 | 3.9 | 3.7 | 3.9 | 3.7 | 3.6 | 3.5 | 3.5 | 3.4 |
| 3.5 | 3.4 | 3.7 | 3.5 | 3.4 | 3.6 | 3.6 | 3.5 | 3.4 | 3.3 |
| 6.5 | 6.7 | 6.3 | 6.3 | 7.2 | 7.5 | 6.9 | 7.2 | 7.6 | . . |
| 4.6 | 4.6 | 4.8 | 4.3 | 4.4 | 4.6 | 4.4 | 4.3 | 4.5 | 4.3 |
| 6.2 | 6.1 | 6.0 | 5.7 | 5.8 | 5.5 | 5.1 | 4.9 | 5.1 | 5.4 |

*US $ mn, at Benoit–Lubell exchange rates*

| 63 | 1964 | 1965 | 1966 | 1967 | 1968 | 1969 | 1970 | 1971 | 1972 | 1973 | 1974 |
|---|---|---|---|---|---|---|---|---|---|---|---|---|
| 233 | 224 | 199 | 207 | 228 | 228 | 261 | 279 | 316 | [341] | 364 | . . |
| 271 | 1 200 | 1 188 | 1 282 | 1 459 | 1 553 | 1 682 | 1 753 | 1 906 | 2 012 | 1 965 | . . |
| 815 | 815 | 826 | 973 | 1 062 | 1 711 | 1 873 | 1 990 | 2 124 | 2 249 | 2 448 | 2 625 |
| 349 | 346 | 284 | 292 | 313 | 381 | 440 | 567 | 565 | 560 | 567 | 928 |
| 300 | 1 376 | 1 457 | 1 583 | 1 658 | 1 903 | 2 104 | 2 242 | 2 337 | 2 506 | 2 580 | 2 856 |
| 435 | 436 | 502 | 522 | 546 | 610 | 670 | 749 | 787 | 832 | 840 | . . |
| 00 | 46 700 | 44 900 | 47 000 | 50 800 | 58 600 | 62 200 | 63 000 | 63 000 | 63 000 | 63 000 | 61 900 |
| 803 | 51 097 | 49 356 | 51 859 | 56 066 | 64 986 | 69 230 | 70 580 | 71 035 | [71 500] | 71 764 | . . |

### Table 8C.6. WTO: current price figures

| | Currency | 1952 | 1953 | 1954 | 1955 | 1956 | 1957 | 1958 | 1959 | 1960 | 1961 |
|---|---|---|---|---|---|---|---|---|---|---|---|
| Bulgaria | mn leva | 161 | .. | .. | .. | .. | 154 | 173 | 163 | 179 | 21 |
| Czechoslovakia | mn korunas | .. | 8 400 | 7 800 | 10 430 | 9 100 | 9 300 | 8 900 | 8 800 | 8 800 | 9 50 |
| German DR | mn marks | .. | .. | .. | .. | .. | .. | 1 650 | .. | .. | . |
| Hungary | mn forints | .. | .. | .. | .. | .. | 1 912 | .. | 2 500 | .. | 3 56 |
| Poland | mn zlotys | 6 600 | 10 300 | 10 600 | 12 600 | 12 000 | 10 100 | 11 200 | 14 300 | 14 900 | 17 00 |
| Romania | mn lei | .. | .. | .. | .. | .. | 3 817 | 3 597 | 3 446 | .. | |
| USSR | mn roubles | 10 900 | 11 020 | 10 030 | 11 210 | 9 730 | 9 672 | 9 400 | 9 370 | 9 300 | 11 60 |

### Table 8C.7. WTO: military expenditure as a percentage of net material product

| | 1952 | 1953 | 1954 | 1955 | 1956 | 1957 | 1958 | 1959 | 1960 | 1961 |
|---|---|---|---|---|---|---|---|---|---|---|
| Bulgaria | 6.2 | .. | .. | .. | .. | 4.8 | 5.0 | 3.9 | 4.0 | 4.6 |
| Czechoslovakia | .. | 6.5 | 6.3 | 7.8 | 6.8 | 6.6 | 6.0 | 5.8 | 5.4 | 5.6 |
| German DR | .. | .. | .. | .. | .. | .. | 2.7 | .. | .. | .. |
| Hungary | .. | .. | .. | .. | .. | 1.8 | .. | 2.0 | .. | 2.4 |
| Poland | 3.2 | 4.5 | 4.2 | 5.6 | 4.8 | 3.4 | 3.5 | 4.1 | 4.0 | 4.1 |
| USSR[a] | 13.4 | 12.9 | 10.9 | 11.4 | 9.1 | 8.6 | 7.4 | 6.9 | 6.4 | 7.6 |

[a] An alternative series for the Soviet Union shows the SIPRI estimates of the dollar-equivalent of Soviet military expenditure as a percentage of official Soviet estimates of the dollar-equivalent of Soviet National Income for 1962–1972:

### Table 8C.8. Other Europe: constant price figures

| | 1952 | 1953 | 1954 | 1955 | 1956 | 1957 | 1958 | 1959 | 1960 | 1961 | 1962 | 1963 |
|---|---|---|---|---|---|---|---|---|---|---|---|---|
| Albania[a] | .. | .. | .. | .. | .. | .. | .. | .. | .. | [60] | [68] | [69] |
| Austria | 30 | 29 | 3 | 12 | 60 | 99 | 113 | 112 | 104 | 101 | 106 | 129 |
| Finland | 56 | 62 | 64 | 86 | 82 | 80 | 83 | 98 | 103 | 119 | 167 | 133 |
| Ireland | 35 | 42 | 38 | 35 | 33 | 32 | 31 | 33 | 35 | 37 | 37 | 38 |
| Spain | 308 | 298 | 324 | 310 | 332 | 352 | 315 | 296 | 349 | 356 | 415 | 427 |
| Sweden | 646 | 724 | 758 | 781 | 786 | 804 | 813 | 847 | 833 | 875 | 940 | 1 002 |
| Switzerland | 303 | 270 | 237 | 255 | 229 | 306 | 328 | 316 | 297 | 346 | 382 | 398 |
| Yugoslavia | 678 | 593 | 584 | 512 | 475 | 464 | 499 | 540 | 514 | 571 | 564 | 568 |
| **Total Other Europe** | [2 100] | [2 065] | [2 055] | [2 040] | [2 050] | [2 190] | [2 235] | [2 300] | [2 295] | 2 465 | 2 679 | 2 764 |

[a] Figures for Albania are at current prices and Benoit–Lubell exchange rates.

### Table 8C.9. Other Europe: current price figures

| | Currency | 1952 | 1953 | 1954 | 1955 | 1956 | 1957 | 1958 | 1959 | 1960 | 1961 |
|---|---|---|---|---|---|---|---|---|---|---|---|
| Albania | mn leks | .. | .. | .. | .. | .. | .. | .. | .. | .. | [24 |
| Austria | mn schillings | 476 | 443 | 47 | 188 | 1 001 | 1 714 | 1 986 | 1 989 | 1 893 | 1 89 |
| Finland | mn marks | 107 | 121 | 124 | 163 | 170 | 184 | 206 | 246 | 267 | 3 |
| Ireland | mn pounds | 7.5 | 9.4 | 8.6 | 8.1 | 7.9 | 8.1 | 8.3 | 8.6 | 9.2 | |
| Spain | mn pesetas | 7 540 | 7 431 | 8 210 | 8 167 | 9 330 | 10 881 | 11 067 | 11 115 | 13 375 | 13 93 |
| Sweden | mn kronor | 1 786 | 2 026 | 2 147 | 2 264 | 2 389 | 2 557 | 2 706 | 2 820 | 2 898 | 3 1 |
| Switzerland | mn francs | 880 | 775 | 688 | 750 | 682 | 930 | 1 009 | 972 | 924 | 1 09 |
| Yugoslavia | mn new dinars | 1 822 | 1 674 | 1 627 | 1 593 | 1 580 | 1 590 | 1 785 | 1 956 | 2 077 | 2 47 |

*Local currency, current prices*

| 2 | 1963 | 1964 | 1965 | 1966 | 1967 | 1968 | 1969 | 1970 | 1971 | 1972 | 1973 | 1974 |
|---|------|------|------|------|------|------|------|------|------|------|------|------|
| 258 | 270 | 260 | 231 | 240 | 264 | 264 | 303 | 324 | 366 | [397] | 422 | .. |
| 900 | 10 800 | 10 200 | 10 100 | 10 900 | 12 400 | 13 200 | 14 300 | 14 900 | 16 200 | 17 100 | 16 700 | .. |
| 764 | 2 764 | 2 764 | 2 800 | 3 300 | 3 600 | 5 800 | 6 350 | 6 747 | 7 200 | 7 625 | 8 300 | 8 900 |
| 998 | 6 050 | 6 005 | 4 926 | 5 064 | 5 433 | 6 611 | 7 644 | 9 848 | 9 811 | 9 715 | 9 850 | 16 117 |
| 400 | 20 700 | 21 600 | 23 200 | 25 200 | 26 400 | 30 300 | 33 500 | 35 700 | 37 200 | 39 900 | 41 066 | 45 468 |
| 900 | 4 100 | 4 110 | 4 735 | 4 927 | 5 146 | 5 751 | 6 319 | 7 067 | 7 424 | 7 845 | 7 922 | .. |
| 700 | 13 900 | 13 300 | 12 800 | 13 400 | 14 500 | 16 700 | 17 700 | 17 900 | 17 900 | 17 900 | 17 900 | 17 600 |

*Per cent*

| 52 | 1963 | 1964 | 1965 | 1966 | 1967 | 1968 | 1969 | 1970 | 1971 | 1972 |
|----|------|------|------|------|------|------|------|------|------|------|
| 0 | 4.8 | 4.2 | 3.5 | 3.3 | 3.4 | 3.1 | 3.2 | 3.1 | 3.5 | [3.5] |
| 3 | 6.3 | 6.1 | 5.9 | 5.6 | 5.3 | 5.1 | 4.9 | 4.8 | 5.0 | 5.0 |
| 7 | 3.6 | 3.4 | 3.4 | 3.8 | 3.9 | [5.9] | [6.1] | [6.1] | [6.4] | [6.5] |
| 2 | 3.7 | 3.5 | 2.9 | 2.7 | 2.6 | 2.9 | 3.0 | 3.6 | 3.3 | 3.0 |
| 3 | 4.5 | 4.4 | 4.4 | 4.4 | 4.4 | 4.5 | 4.8 | 4.8 | 4.4 | 4.2 |
| 7 | 8.2 | 7.3 | 6.6 | 6.5 | 6.4 | 6.8 | 6.8 | 6.2 | 5.9 | 5.7 |
| 5 | 23.4 | 20.2 | 18.1 | .. | 17.3 | 18.0 | 17.4 | 16.5 | 15.4 | 14.8 |

*US $ mn at 1970 prices and 1970 exchange rates (Final column, X, at current prices and exchange rates)*

| 64 | 1965 | 1966 | 1967 | 1968 | 1969 | 1970 | 1971 | 1972 | 1973 | 1974 | 1972X |
|----|------|------|------|------|------|------|------|------|------|------|-------|
| 71 | 73 | 69 | 69 | 77 | 106 | 120 | 128 | 141 | (148) | .. | 141 |
| 163 | 135 | 155 | 157 | 157 | 162 | 160 | 154 | 154 | (170) | .. | 191 |
| 131 | 134 | 131 | 128 | 147 | 134 | 142 | 155 | 165 | (168) | [175] | 193 |
| 42 | 43 | 41 | 42 | 43 | 45 | 51 | 57 | (66) | .. | .. | 80 |
| 435 | 431 | 509 | 550 | 570 | 592 | 603 | 623 | 663 | (691) | .. | 843 |
| 054 | 1 118 | 1 128 | 1 098 | 1 100 | 1 159 | 1 190 | 1 174 | 1 173 | 1 170 | 1 154 | 1 452 |
| 432 | 435 | 458 | 446 | 425 | 453 | 467 | 485 | 468 | 467 | (461) | 602 |
| 588 | 569 | 547 | 542 | 614 | 618 | 629 | 621 | 664 | 626 | .. | 658 |
| 916 | 2 938 | 3 038 | 3 032 | 3 133 | 3 269 | 3 362 | 3 397 | 3 494 | [3 500] | .. | 4 160 |

*Local currency, current prices*

| 62 | 1963 | 1964 | 1965 | 1966 | 1967 | 1968 | 1969 | 1970 | 1971 | 1972 | 1973 | 1974 |
|----|------|------|------|------|------|------|------|------|------|------|------|------|
| [270] | [275] | 282 | 288 | 272 | 272 | 304 | 420 | 475 | 508 | 558 | 589 | .. |
| 076 | 2 608 | 3 408 | 2 957 | 3 474 | 3 661 | 3 775 | 4 006 | 4 135 | 4 166 | 4 417 | 5 250 | .. |
| 460 | 383 | 417 | 446 | 456 | 471 | 589 | 549 | 597 | 692 | 791 | 899 | 1 047 |
| 10.5 | 10.8 | 12.9 | 14.0 | 13.7 | 14.4 | 15.5 | 17.3 | 21.3 | 25.8 | (32.4) | .. | .. |
| 173 | 19 218 | 20 920 | 23 471 | 29 407 | 33 850 | 36 780 | 39 016 | 42 067 | 47 019 | 54 172 | 63 000 | .. |
| 500 | 3 839 | 4 173 | 4 646 | 4 990 | 5 072 | 5 176 | 5 596 | 6 150 | 6 518 | 6 908 | 7 347 | 7 963 |
| 264 | 1 362 | 1 521 | 1 586 | 1 746 | 1 770 | 1 726 | 1 889 | 2 014 | 2 232 | 2 295 | 2 496 | 2 680 |
| 701 | 2 862 | 3 321 | 4 305 | 5 070 | 5 382 | 6 406 | 6 980 | 7 864 | 8 948 | 11 180 | 12 800 | .. |

**Table 8C.10. Other Europe: military expenditure as a percentage of gross domestic product**

| | 1952 | 1953 | 1954 | 1955 | 1956 | 1957 | 1958 | 1959 | 1960 | 1961 |
|---|---|---|---|---|---|---|---|---|---|---|
| Austria | 0.6 | 0.5 | 0.1 | 0.2 | 0.8 | 1.3 | 1.5 | 1.4 | 1.2 | 1.0 |
| Finland | 1.3 | 1.5 | 1.4 | 1.6 | 1.5 | 1.5 | 1.6 | 1.7 | 1.7 | 1.8 |
| Ireland | 1.7 | 1.9 | 1.7 | 1.6 | 1.5 | 1.5 | 1.5 | 1.4 | 1.4 | 1.4 |
| Spain | . . | . . | 2.4 | 2.2 | 2.2 | 2.2 | 1.9 | 1.8 | 2.2 | 2.0 |
| Sweden | 4.4 | 4.9 | 4.9 | 4.8 | 4.7 | 4.6 | 4.7 | 4.6 | 4.0 | 4.0 |
| Switzerland | 3.9 | 3.3 | 2.7 | 2.8 | 2.4 | 3.0 | 3.2 | 2.9 | 2.5 | 2.7 |
| Yugoslavia[a] | 19.3 | 14.8 | 12.6 | 10.3 | 9.9 | 7.9 | 9.0 | 8.0 | 7.2 | 7.4 |

[a] Percentage of gross material product.

**Table 8C.11. Middle East: constant price figures**

| | 1952 | 1953 | 1954 | 1955 | 1956 | 1957 | 1958 | 1959 | 1960 | 1961 | 1962 | 19 |
|---|---|---|---|---|---|---|---|---|---|---|---|---|
| Cyprus | . . | . . | . . | . . | . . | . . | . . | . . | . .† | . . | . . | . . |
| Egypt | 127.3 | 125.7 | 165.7 | 249.8 | 288.4 | 257.5 | [243.3] | [245.9] | [263.3] | [290.3] | [330.5] | 368 |
| Iran | 71.5 | 67.2 | 77.6 | 107.1 | 125.6 | 151.4 | 242.9 | 271.3 | 215.9 | 216.0 | 213.8 | 217 |
| Iraq | 40.0 | 75.6 | 74.9 | 66.6 | 93.8 | 102.3 | 110.2 | 128.7 | 147.3 | 153.4 | 163.8 | 190 |
| Israel | 43.6 | 34.8 | 31.6 | 33.9 | 68.1 | 96.5 | 108.6 | 121.2 | 144.1 | 144.1 | 162.3 | 201 |
| Jordan | (36.7) | (39.3) | (39.9) | (40.6) | (48.4) | (50.1) | (58.5) | (72.9) | (68.3) | (66.6) | (71.3) | (72 |
| Kuwait[a] | . . | . . | . . | . . | . . | . . | . . | . . | . . | 17.1 | 19.0 | 22 |
| Lebanon | 7.2 | 9.3 | 10.0 | 12.1 | 16.3 | 15.8 | 17.6 | 16.1 | 17.1 | 20.4 | 28.9 | 24 |
| Saudi Arabia | . . | . . | . . | . . | . . | . . | . . | . . | . . | (87.8) | (111.1) | 137 |
| Syria | 19.5 | 26.5 | 24.9 | 27.2 | 47.0 | 39.1 | [69.4] | 68.2 | 68.7 | 70.1 | 79.4 | 82 |
| Yemen[a] | . . | . . | . . | . . | . . | . . | . . | . . | . . | . . | [4.2] | [8 |
| **Total Middle East** | [375.0] | [410.0] | [460.0] | [575.0] | [750.0] | [780.0] | [925.0] | [1 005.0] | [1 015.0] | [1 070.0] | 1 184.3 | 1 326 |

[a] At current prices and 1970 exchange rates.
[b] 1970.

**Table 8C.12. Middle East: current price figures**

| | Currency | 1952 | 1953 | 1954 | 1955 | 1956 | 1957 | 1958 | 1959 | 1960 | 19 |
|---|---|---|---|---|---|---|---|---|---|---|---|
| Cyprus | mn pounds | . . | . . | . . | . . | . . | . . | . . | . . | . . | . |
| Egypt | mn pounds | 40.3 | 37.1 | 46.9 | 70.7 | 83.4 | 77.6 | [73.3] | [74.1] | [79.8] | [8 |
| Iran | mn rials | 2 545 | 2 544 | 3 468 | 4 956 | 6 205 | 7 960 | 12 771 | 15 699 | 13 756 | 14 18 |
| Iraq | mn dinars | 11.8 | 19.4 | 18.8 | 17.1 | 25.8 | 29.7 | 31.0 | 35.8 | 42.4 | 4 |
| Israel | mn pounds | 48.4 | 49.4 | 50.3 | 56.6 | 121.6 | 183.4 | 212.1 | 242.6 | 293.6 | 31 |
| Jordan | mn dinars | 9.1 | 9.9 | 10.2 | 10.5 | 12.8 | 13.4 | 15.9 | 20.1 | 19.1 | 1 |
| Kuwait | mn dinars | . . | . . | . . | . . | . . | . . | . . | . . | . . | . |
| Lebanon | mn pounds | 17.6 | 21.2 | 21.7 | 26.7 | 38.0 | 39.1 | 45.6 | 43.0 | 47.8 | 5 |
| Saudi Arabia | mn rials | . . | . . | . . | . . | . . | . . | . . | . . | . . | 33 |
| Syria | mn pounds | 70 | 87 | 76 | 82 | 161 | 140 | [234] | 237 | 251 | 26 |
| Yemen | mn rials | . . | . . | . . | . . | . . | . . | . . | . . | . . | . |

*Per cent*

| 1963 | 1964 | 1965 | 1966 | 1967 | 1968 | 1969 | 1970 | 1971 | 1972 |
|---|---|---|---|---|---|---|---|---|---|
| *1.3* | *1.5* | *1.2* | *1.3* | *1.3* | *1.2* | *1.2* | *1.1* | *1.0* | *0.9* |
| *1.9* | *1.8* | *1.7* | *1.6* | *1.6* | *1.7* | *1.4* | *1.4* | *1.5* | *1.4* |
| *1.3* | *1.4* | *1.4* | *1.3* | *1.3* | *1.2* | *1.2* | *1.3* | *1.4* | *1.5* |
| *2.0* | *1.9* | *1.8* | *2.0* | *2.1* | *2.0* | *1.9* | *1.9* | *1.8* | *1.8* |
| *4.2* | *4.1* | *4.2* | *4.1* | *3.9* | *3.7* | *3.7* | *3.6* | *3.6* | *3.5* |
| *2.7* | *2.8* | *2.7* | *2.7* | *2.6* | *2.4* | *2.4* | *2.3* | *2.3* | *2.0* |
| *6.2* | *5.4* | *5.4* | *5.1* | *5.2* | *5.7* | *5.3* | *5.0* | *4.4* | *4.6* |

*US $ mn, at 1970 prices and 1970 exchange rates (Final column, X, at current prices and exchange rates)*

| 64 | 1965 | 1966 | 1967 | 1968 | 1969 | 1970 | 1971 | 1972 | 1973 | 1974 | 1972X |
|---|---|---|---|---|---|---|---|---|---|---|---|
| .2 | 8.7 | 7.4 | 8.1 | 6.8 | 7.1 | 7.9 | .. | .. | .. | .. | 8^b |
| 2.6 | 501.1 | 516.3 | 717.9 | 740.3 | 835.9 | 1 262.6 | 1 441.6 | 1 419.7 | (1 828.7) | [2 295.0] | 1 495 |
| 0.6 | 323.3 | 446.7 | 561.0 | 636.2 | 748.3 | 841.1 | 1 094.6 | 1 103.9 | [1 725.0] | .. | 1 224 |
| .1 | 268.1 | 273.5 | 264.6 | 321.4 | 382.6 | 418.9 | 407.9 | 383.8 | [392.0] | .. | 454 |
| 2.5 | 287.6 | 364.6 | 561.8 | 730.1 | 958.2 | 1 345.0 | 1 383.5 | 1 246.8 | (2 575.0) | [2 335.0] | 1 313 |
| .9) | (71.2) | (84.9) | 114.8 | 136.1 | 136.4 | 117.6 | 87.3 | 104.5 | [101.0] | [130.0] | 118 |
| .9 | 30.5 | 35.0 | 54.3 | 63.3 | 68.9 | 73.1 | 80.6 | 86.3 | 313.6 | .. | 94 |
| .4 | 30.7 | 35.1 | 38.9 | 43.7 | 42.8 | 42.6 | 43.1 | 61.5 | (65.3) | [73.0] | 70 |
| .8 | 140.2 | 257.3 | 379.3 | 396.5 | 412.3 | 430.0 | (538.8) | (844.4) | (1 082.2) | .. | 964 |
| .2 | 99.9 | 81.8 | 90.7 | 140.4 | 144.8 | 142.8 | 137.9 | (213.5) | (256.2) | [229.5] | 226 |
| .5] | [9.4] | [10.2] | [13.0] | [14.0] | [15.0] | [15.0] | .. | .. | .. | .. | [15]^b |
| .7 | 1 770.7 | 2 112.8 | 2 804.4 | 3 228.8 | 3 762.3 | 4 696.6 | [5 240.0] | [5 490.0] | [8 370.0] | .. | 5 981 |

*Local currency, current prices*

| 962 | 1963 | 1964 | 1965 | 1966 | 1967 | 1968 | 1969 | 1970 | 1971 | 1972 | 1973 | 1974 |
|---|---|---|---|---|---|---|---|---|---|---|---|---|
| . | .. | 2.7 | 3.3 | 2.8 | 3.1 | 2.7 | 2.9 | 3.3 | .. | .. | .. | .. |
| 8.0] | 110.0 | 143.0 | 178.0 | 200.0 | 280.0 | 300.0 | 350.0 | 549.0 | 650.0 | 650.0 | 881.0 | 1 168.0 |
| 56 | 14 487 | 16 606 | 22 826 | 31 364 | 40 030 | 45 734 | 55 720 | 63 712 | 86 315 | 92 738 | [160 000] | .. |
| 8.2 | 58.3 | 66.1 | 80.6 | 83.9 | 83.8 | 104.1 | 134.3 | 149.6 | 150.9 | 149.4 | [160.0] | .. |
| 6.3 | 511.3 | 700.0 | 825.4 | 1 130.5 | 1 771.5 | 2 351.0 | 3 162.5 | 4 707.0 | 5 423.5 | 5 516 | 13 665 | 14 895 |
| 0.6 | 21.1 | 21.1 | 21.5 | 26.0 | 35.7 | 42.2 | 45.6 | 42.0 | 32.5 | 42.0 | [45.0] | [65.0] |
| 6.8 | 7.9 | 7.1 | 10.9 | 12.5 | 19.4 | 22.6 | 24.6 | 26.1 | 28.8 | 30.8 | 112.0 | .. |
| 0.6 | 68.9 | 76.6 | 90.1 | 105.9 | 121.9 | 135.9 | 139.1 | 138.4 | 142.3 | 212.9 | 246.2 | (300.2) |
| 8 | 541 | 531 | 561 | 1 050 | 1 579 | 1 688 | 1 798 | 1 935 | 2 485 | 3 990 | (5 235) | .. |
| 9 | 297 | 346 | 365 | 316 | 366 | 587 | 600 | 617 | 625 | (975) | 1 400 | 1 500 |
| 5.3] | [10.6] | [10.6] | [11.7] | [12.7] | [16.3] | [17.5] | [18.8] | [18.8] | .. | .. | .. | .. |

213

**Table 8C.13. Middle East: military expenditure as a percentage of gross domestic product**

| | 1952 | 1953 | 1954 | 1955 | 1956 | 1957 | 1958 | 1959 | 1960 | 1961 |
|---|---|---|---|---|---|---|---|---|---|---|
| Cyprus | .. | .. | .. | .. | .. | .. | .. | .. | .. | .. |
| Egypt | .. | .. | .. | .. | .. | .. | .. | .. | 5.6 | 6.0 |
| Iran | .. | .. | .. | .. | .. | .. | .. | .. | 4.2 | 4.1 |
| Iraq | .. | 5.6 | 4.7 | 4.1 | 5.7 | 6.5 | 6.0 | 6.7 | 7.1 | 6.9 |
| Israel | 4.4 | 3.6 | 2.8 | 2.5 | 4.6 | 5.9 | 5.9 | 5.9 | 6.6 | 5.9 |
| Jordan | .. | .. | .. | .. | .. | .. | .. | 21.5 | 19.4 | 15.7 |
| Kuwait | .. | .. | .. | .. | .. | .. | .. | .. | .. | .. |
| Lebanon | .. | .. | .. | .. | .. | .. | .. | .. | .. | .. |
| Saudi Arabia | .. | .. | .. | .. | .. | .. | .. | .. | .. | .. |
| Syria | .. | .. | .. | .. | .. | .. | .. | .. | .. | .. |

**Table 8C.14. South Asia: constant price figures**

| | 1952 | 1953 | 1954 | 1955 | 1956 | 1957 | 1958 | 1959 | 1960 | 1961 | 196: |
|---|---|---|---|---|---|---|---|---|---|---|---|
| Afghanistan | .. | .. | .. | .. | .. | .. | .. | .. | .. | .. | |
| Bangla Desh | .. | .. | .. | .. | .. | .. | .. | .. | .. | .. | |
| India | 551.1 | 548.2 | 585.6 | 610.2 | 607.1 | 730.4 | 723.2 | 674.2 | 677.6 | 728.0 | 1 0 |
| Nepal | .. | .. | .. | .. | .. | .. | .. | .. | [3.1] | [3.0] | |
| Pakistan | 350.9 | 276.0 | 240.9 | 281.3 | 274.0 | 226.8 | 235.7 | 277.3 | 290.1 | 287.4 | 2 |
| Sri Lanka | 3.2 | 4.4 | 7.2 | 6.6 | 7.9 | 10.4 | 14.5 | 15.8 | 16.0 | 16.2 | |
| **Total South Asia** | **[940.0]** | **[865.0]** | **[870.0]** | **[935.0]** | **[930.0]** | **[1 010.0]** | **[1 015.0]** | **[1 010.0]** | **[1 030.0]** | **[1 075.0]** | **[1 3** |

[a] 1971.

**Table 8C.15. South Asia: current price figures**

| | *Currency* | 1952 | 1953 | 1954 | 1955 | 1956 | 1957 | 1958 | 1959 | 1960 | 196 |
|---|---|---|---|---|---|---|---|---|---|---|---|
| Afghanistan | *mn afghanis* | .. | .. | .. | .. | .. | .. | .. | .. | 552 | [56 |
| Bangla Desh | *mn taka* | .. | .. | .. | .. | .. | .. | .. | .. | .. | . |
| India | *mn rupees* | 1 878 | 1 926 | 1 969 | 1 932 | 2 110 | 2 665 | 2 797 | 2 699 | 2 774 | 3 04 |
| Nepal | *mn rupees* | .. | .. | .. | .. | .. | .. | .. | .. | [14.6] | [1 |
| Pakistan | *mn rupees* | 935 | 817 | 705 | 787 | 793 | 718 | 771 | 878 | 978 | 98 |
| Sri Lanka | *mn rupees* | 13.8 | 19.0 | 30.2 | 27.5 | 32.8 | 46.0 | 66.2 | 71.9 | 71.3 | 7 |

**Table 8C.16. South Asia: military expenditure as a percentage of gross domestic product**

| | 1952 | 1953 | 1954 | 1955 | 1956 | 1957 | 1958 | 1959 | 1960 | 1961 |
|---|---|---|---|---|---|---|---|---|---|---|
| India | [1.7] | [1.7] | [1.8] | [1.7] | [1.7] | [2.1] | [2.0] | [1.9] | [1.9] | 1.9 |
| Nepal | .. | .. | .. | .. | .. | .. | .. | .. | .. | .. |
| Pakistan | [4.0] | [3.6] | [3.1] | [3.4] | [3.1] | [2.5] | [2.6] | [2.8] | 2.8 | 2.6 |
| Sri Lanka | 0.3 | 0.4 | 0.6 | 0.5 | 0.6 | 0.8 | 1.1 | 1.1 | 1.1 | 1.1 |

| 1963 | 1964 | 1965 | 1966 | 1967 | 1968 | 1969 | 1970 | 1971 | 1972 |
|---|---|---|---|---|---|---|---|---|---|
| . . | 2.4 | 2.4 | 1.9 | 1.9 | 1.5 | 1.4 | 1.5 | . . | . . |
| 6.2 | 7.0 | 7.7 | 8.2 | 11.2 | 11.5 | 12.4 | 18.0 | . . | . . |
| 3.7 | 3.8 | 4.7 | 5.9 | 6.8 | 6.8 | 7.4 | 7.4 | 8.4 | 7.5 |
| 8.3 | 8.2 | 9.2 | 8.9 | 8.9 | 9.9 | 12.0 | . . | . . | . . |
| 6.7 | 8.0 | 7.9 | 9.8 | 14.7 | 16.6 | 19.4 | 24.4 | 22.4 | 18.6 |
| 16.3 | 14.2 | 12.8 | 15.2 | 18.3 | 22.6 | 20.7 | 20.0 | 14.5 | 17.5 |
| 1.2 | 1.0 | 1.5 | 1.5 | 2.2 | 2.4 | 2.5 | 2.5 | 2.2 | . . |
| . . | 2.4 | 2.6 | 2.7 | 3.2 | 3.2 | 3.0 | 2.8 | . . | . . |
| 6.0 | 5.4 | 5.0 | 8.3 | 11.3 | 11.0 | 10.7 | 9.9 | . . | . . |
| 7.5 | 7.5 | 7.9 | 6.7 | 5.8 | 10.6 | 10.0 | 9.6 | 8.3 | 11.3 |

*US $ mn, at 1970 prices and 1970 exchange rates (Final column, X, at current prices and exchange rates)*

| | 1964 | 1965 | 1966 | 1967 | 1968 | 1969 | 1970 | 1971 | 1972 | 1973 | 1972X |
|---|---|---|---|---|---|---|---|---|---|---|---|
| | 46.5 | 44.4 | 43.3 | 37.3 | 31.4 | 46.0 | 32.7 | 28.3 | . . | . . | 36ª |
| | . . | . . | . . | . . | . . | . . | . . | . . | 23.1 | (23.5) | 34 |
| .5 | 1 607.6 | 1 567.6 | 1 480.1 | 1 373.2 | 1 429.0 | 1 511.9 | 1 558.2 | 1 743.9 | 1 995.5 | 1 929.0 | 2 232 |
| .0] | [3.7] | [3.8] | 4.1 | 5.0 | 5.4 | 5.5 | 5.2 | 5.9 | 6.2 | (6.4) | 7 |
| .6 | 333.3 | 537.7 | 627.8 | 511.0 | 525.2 | 571.1 | 623.0 | 766.3 | 819.5 | (652.3) | 582 |
| .7 | 12.3 | 12.8 | 13.5 | 14.0 | 14.9 | 15.1 | 18.9 | 29.0 | 28.1 | [40.0] | 29 |
| ).0] | 2 003.4 | 2 166.3 | 2 168.8 | 1 940.5 | 2 005.9 | 2 149.6 | 2 238.0 | 2 573.4 | [2 900.0] | [2 680.0] | 2 920 |

*Local currency, current prices*

| | 1963 | 1964 | 1965 | 1966 | 1967 | 1968 | 1969 | 1970 | 1971 | 1972 | 1973 |
|---|---|---|---|---|---|---|---|---|---|---|---|
| ] | [666] | 909 | 1 023 | 1 088 | 1 177 | 1 224 | 1 750 | 1 470 | 1 600 | . . | . . |
| | . . | . . | . . | . . | . . | . . | . . | . . | . . | 250 | 360 |
| | 7 306 | 8 084 | 8 651 | 9 027 | 9 535 | 10 170 | 10 840 | 11 747 | 13 581 | 16 518 | 18 571 |
| .7] | [23.7] | [25.5] | [28.3] | 35.2 | 41.9 | 45.9 | 49.0 | 52.6 | 59.0 | 66.7 | 76.5 |
| | 1 029 | 1 208 | 2 059 | 2 575 | 2 240 | 2 307 | 2 588 | 2 975 | 3 831 | 4 461 | 4 345 |
| .9 | 59.6 | 59.7 | 62.0 | 65.4 | 69.1 | 78.0 | 85.0 | 112.9 | 177.4 | 182.7 | [290.0] |

| 1963 | 1964 | 1965 | 1966 | 1967 | 1968 | 1969 | 1970 | 1971 | 1972 |
|---|---|---|---|---|---|---|---|---|---|
| 3.8 | 3.6 | 3.6 | 3.4 | 3.0 | 3.1 | 3.0 | . . | . . | . . |
| . . | [0.6] | [0.5] | [0.6] | [0.6] | [0.7] | [0.6] | [0.6] | . . | . . |
| 2.4 | 2.6 | 4.0 | 4.4 | 3.5 | 3.3 | 3.5 | [3.7] | [4.5] | . . |
| 0.8 | 0.8 | 0.8 | 0.8 | 0.8 | 0.7 | 0.7 | 0.9 | 1.3 | . . |

## Table 8C.17. Far East: constant price figures

|  | 1952 | 1953 | 1954 | 1955 | 1956 | 1957 | 1958 | 1959 | 1960 | 1961 | 1962 | 196. |
|---|---|---|---|---|---|---|---|---|---|---|---|---|
| Burma[a] | 46.6 | 64.7 | 77.4 | 70.8 | 74.8 | 79.2 | 85.1 | 86.0 | 89.3 | 85.4 | 90.5 | 1( |
| Indonesia | .. | 253.0 | 224.0 | 182.0 | 179.0 | 222.0 | 281.0 | 285.0 | 336.0 | 373.0 | 252.0 | 17 |
| Japan | 769.6 | 870.4 | 843.6 | 795.3 | 785.8 | 778.6 | 786.3 | 804.1 | 798.3 | 826.9 | 905.4 | 9( |
| Khmer Rep. | .. | ..† | .. | .. | .. | .. | .. | 49.2 | 41.5 | 41.7 | 43.8 | 4 |
| Korea, North | .. | .. | .. | .. | .. | .. | .. | .. | .. | [225.0] | [250.0] | [2! |
| Korea, South | 53.5 | 119.1 | 141.3 | 113.6 | 110.1 | 141.6 | 167.6 | 175.4 | 172.5 | 179.6 | 207.3 | 17 |
| Laos | .. | .. | .. | .. | .. | .. | .. | .. | .. | .. | 64.9 | 4 |
| Malaysia | 50.9 | 68.5 | 64.4 | 57.8 | 52.7 | 54.9 | 57.3 | 50.6 | 46.6 | 39.4 | 39.8 | 5 |
| Mongolia[a] | .. | .. | .. | .. | .. | .. | .. | .. | .. | [15.0] | [15.0] | [1 |
| Philippines | 48.5 | 49.6 | 47.4 | 46.4 | 46.7 | 47.8 | 50.0 | 51.8 | 51.5 | 66.3 | 51.3 | 5 |
| Singapore | .. | .. | .. | .. | .. | .. | .. | .. | .. | .. | .. | . |
| Taiwan | .. | 91.9 | .. | 153.2 | 157.8 | 174.3 | 285.8 | 304.3 | 281.6 | 296.8 | 340.5 | 34 |
| Thailand | 64.2 | 65.8 | 65.5 | 56.3 | 50.4 | 91.2 | 76.3 | 81.9 | 80.2 | 84.6 | 88.6 | 9 |
| Viet-Nam, North | .. | .. | ..† | .. | .. | .. | .. | .. | .. | [225.0] | [250.0] | [32 |
| Viet-Nam, South | .. | .. | ..† | .. | .. | .. | 308.8 | 305.3 | 279.1 | 286.5 | 439.4 | 4! |
| Total Far East | [1 550.0] | [1 825.0] | [1 875.0] | [1 840.0] | [1 960.0] | [2 275.0] | [2 550.0] | [2 625.0] | [2 650.0] | [2 800.0] | 3 038.5 | 3 06 |

[a] At current prices and 1970 exchange rates.
[b] 1971.

## Table 8C.18. Far East: current price figures

|  | Currency | 1952 | 1953 | 1954 | 1955 | 1956 | 1957 | 1958 | 1959 | 1960 | 1961 |
|---|---|---|---|---|---|---|---|---|---|---|---|
| Burma | mn kyats | 222.3 | 308.9 | 369.6 | 338.0 | 357.3 | 378.3 | 406.5 | 410.8 | 426.3 | 40 |
| Indonesia | mn new rupiah | .. | 3.9 | 3.6 | 3.9 | 4.4 | 6.1 | 11.1 | 14.1 | 21.7 | 3 |
| Japan | bn yen | 131.0 | 157.5 | 162.0 | 151.3 | 149.5 | 152.3 | 153.8 | 159.3 | 163.3 | 17! |
| Khmer Rep. | mn riels | .. | .. | .. | .. | .. | .. | .. | 1 656 | 1 495 | 1 61( |
| Korea, North | mn won | .. | .. | .. | .. | .. | .. | .. | .. | .. |  |
| Korea, South | bn won | 0.8 | 2.7 | 4.4 | 5.9 | 7.1 | 11.3 | 12.8 | 14.0 | 14.8 | 1( |
| Laos | mn kips | .. | .. | .. | .. | .. | .. | .. | .. | .. |  |
| Malaysia | mn dollars | 160.9 | 210.1 | 184.4 | 160.5 | 148.1 | 160.6 | 166.2 | 142.3 | 131.3 | 11( |
| Mongolia | mn tugriks | .. | .. | .. | .. | .. | .. | .. | .. | .. | [6( |
| Philippines | mn pesos | 174.6 | 171.8 | 162.3 | 157.2 | 161.6 | 169.1 | 182.4 | 186.9 | 193.4 | 20! |
| Singapore | mn dollars | .. | .. | .. | .. | .. | .. | .. | .. | .. |  |
| Taiwan | bn dollars | .. | 1.5 | .. | 2.8 | 3.2 | 3.8 | 6.3 | 7.4 | 8.1 | ! |
| Thailand | mn baht | 844.4 | 961.0 | 943.6 | 855.2 | 816.7 | 1 566.7 | 1 389.7 | 1 420.5 | 1 378.4 | 1 47! |
| Viet-Nam, South | bn piastres | .. | .. | .. | .. | .. | .. | 6.0 | 6.1 | 5.5 | ! |

## Table 8C.19. Far East: military expenditure as a percentage of gross domestic product

|  | 1952 | 1953 | 1954 | 1955 | 1956 | 1957 | 1958 | 1959 | 1960 | 1961 |
|---|---|---|---|---|---|---|---|---|---|---|
| Burma | 4.4 | 5.8 | 6.7 | 5.9 | 6.0 | 6.0 | 6.4 | 6.1 | 6.0 | 5.7 |
| Indonesia | .. | .. | .. | .. | .. | .. | .. | .. | 5.4 | 6.3 |
| Japan | 2.1 | 2.2 | 2.1 | 1.8 | 1.5 | 1.4 | 1.3 | 1.2 | 1.1 | 0.9 |
| Khmer Rep. | .. | .. | .. | .. | .. | .. | .. | .. | .. | .. |
| Korea, South | .. | 5.7 | 6.6 | 5.1 | 4.7 | 5.8 | 6.2 | 6.4 | 6.0 | 5.7 |
| Malaysia | .. | .. | .. | 3.2 | 2.9 | 3.1 | 3.4 | 2.6 | 2.2 | 1.9 |
| Philippines | 2.3 | 2.0 | 1.8 | 1.7 | 1.6 | 1.6 | 1.6 | 1.5 | 1.4 | 1.4 |
| Singapore | .. | .. | .. | .. | .. | .. | .. | .. | .. | .. |
| Taiwan | .. | 6.5 | .. | 9.3 | 9.3 | 9.4 | 14.1 | 14.3 | 12.9 | 13.2 |
| Thailand | 2.7 | 3.0 | 2.8 | 2.4 | 2.1 | 3.4 | 2.9 | 2.8 | 2.6 | 2.5 |
| Viet-Nam, South | .. | .. | .. | .. | .. | .. | .. | .. | 6.6 | 7.0 |

*US $ mn, at 1970 prices and 1970 exchange rates (Final column, X, at current prices and exchange rates*

| | 1965 | 1966 | 1967 | 1968 | 1969 | 1970 | 1971 | 1972 | 1973 | 1974 | 1972X |
|---|---|---|---|---|---|---|---|---|---|---|---|
| 97.7 | 107.0 | 105.2 | 101.8 | 104.3 | 114.1 | 121.9 | 126.3 | 125.8 | .. | .. | 111 |
| 57.0 | 75.0 | 79.0 | 171.0 | 221.0 | 284.0 | 301.0 | 336.0 | .. | .. | .. | 336 |
| 56.4 | 1 095.6 | 1 169.2 | 1 253.1 | 1 338.0 | 1 453.9 | 1 594.8 | 1 769.3 | 1 969.3 | 2 040.1 | (2 041.8) | 2 578 |
| 45.7 | 41.4 | 42.9 | 45.1 | 47.2 | 49.9 | 124.8 | 195.2 | [152.3] | (59.3) | .. | [119] |
| 0.0] | [350.0] | [350.0] | [465] | 630 | 700 | (745) | 735.8 | (487.9) | .. | .. | 488 |
| 52.0 | 170.6 | 208.1 | 231.2 | 272.8 | 314.7 | 324.6 | 383.7 | 427.2 | (445.6) | [510.3] | 432 |
| 41.0 | 41.2 | 41.4 | 38.7 | 36.7 | 36.2 | 38.0 | 38.6 | 34.0 | [31.2] | .. | 17 |
| 75.1 | 105.0 | 129.6 | 120.2 | 124.6 | 184.8 | 253.6 | 265.2 | 270.2 | [275.0] | .. | 311 |
| 5.0] | [15.0] | [15.0] | [20.0] | [20.0] | [20.0] | [25.0] | 42.3 | 47.8 | .. | .. | 48 |
| 9.0 | 53.5 | 65.2 | 72.2 | 85.4 | 102.2 | 116.3 | 122.8 | (96.2) | .. | .. | 105 |
| . | ..† | .. | 25.7 | 32.6 | 97.4 | 104.4 | 141.5 | 199.2 | (163.8) | .. | 228 |
| 70.8 | 395.6 | [439.4] | [471.9] | [508.2] | [561.6] | 482.5 | 595.2 | (627.9) | .. | .. | 678 |
| 46.9 | 103.7 | 112.1 | 128.9 | 154.4 | 180.9 | 210.5 | 248.0 | 259.0 | [281.7] | .. | 275 |
| 0.0] | [450.0] | [500.0] | [500.0] | [500.0] | [500.0] | [585.0] | .. | .. | .. | .. | [600] |
| 0.2 | 1 094.4 | 781.9 | 815.9 | 877.0 | 918.5 | 972.0 | 957.5 | 903.0 | [680.0] | [750.0] | 431 |
| 6.8 | 4 098.0 | [4 060.0] | 4 460.7 | 4 952.2 | 5 518.2 | 5 999.4 | [6 560.0] | [6 550.0] | [6 400.0] | .. | 6 757 |

*Local currency, current prices*

| | 1963 | 1964 | 1965 | 1966 | 1967 | 1968 | 1969 | 1970 | 1971 | 1972 | 1973 | 1974 |
|---|---|---|---|---|---|---|---|---|---|---|---|---|
| 1.9 | 477.7 | 466.3 | 510.7 | 502.2 | 485.9 | 498.1 | 544.9 | 582.2 | 603.1 | 600.9 | .. | .. |
| 7.4 | 91.4 | 57.7 | 308 | 3 700 | 21 600 | 63 100 | 86 000 | 102 200 | 119 000 | .. | .. | .. |
| 8.5 | 238.0 | 272.0 | 300.5 | 337.0 | 375.5 | 422.5 | 483.0 | 570.3 | 671.3 | 781.0 | 903.9 | 1 053.6 |
| 6 | 1 764 | 1 964 | 1 846 | 1 893 | 1 992 | 2 204 | 2 479 | 6 930 | 18 650 | [18 225] | 17 800 | .. |
| . | .. | .. | .. | .. | [1 200] | 1 617 | 1 798 | 1 918 | 1 891 | (1 254) | 1 282 | .. |
| 0.5 | 20.5 | 24.9 | 29.9 | 40.7 | 50.0 | 65.4 | 84.9 | 101.6 | 136.3 | 170.1 | 184.8 | 220.4 |
| 2 | 3 312 | 4 935 | 7 391 | 8 463 | 8 531 | 8 511 | 8 672 | 9 131 | 9 375 | 10 330 | [12 400] | .. |
| 2.0 | 154.9 | 217.0 | 303.0 | 379.5 | 366.6 | 379.3 | 558.0 | 783.6 | 832.8 | 875.1 | [975.0] | .. |
| 0] | [60] | [60] | [60] | [60] | [80] | [80] | [80] | [100] | 169 | 191 | .. | .. |
| 7.6 | 219.2 | 227.0 | 259.6 | 330.8 | 391.1 | 464.6 | 571.2 | 686.1 | 746.8 | (700.7) | .. | .. |
| . | .. | .. | .. | .. | 78.9 | 100.8 | 300.0 | 322.5 | 445.5 | 640.8 | 647.3 | .. |
| 0.8 | 11.2 | 12.0 | 12.8 | [14.5] | [16.1] | [18.7] | [21.7] | 19.3 | 24.5 | 27.1 | .. | .. |
| 0.0 | 1 643.0 | 1 778.0 | 1 921.0 | 2 575.2 | 2 575.2 | 3 151.7 | 3 768.7 | 4 420.0 | 5 312.5 | 5 770.0 | [7 000.0] | .. |
| 9.5 | 9.5 | 19.4 | 30.4 | 35.2 | 52.8 | 72.0 | 92.0 | 133.0 | 155.0 | 183.0 | [200.0] | [320.0] |

*Per cent*

| | 1963 | 1964 | 1965 | 1966 | 1967 | 1968 | 1969 | 1970 | 1971 | 1972 |
|---|---|---|---|---|---|---|---|---|---|---|
| | 6.1 | 6.0 | 6.1 | 6.0 | 5.5 | 5.1 | .. | .. | .. | .. |
| | 2.8 | 0.8 | 1.3 | 1.2 | 2.5 | 3.0 | 3.2 | 3.1 | 3.2 | .. |
| | 1.0 | 0.9 | 0.9 | 0.9 | 0.9 | 0.8 | 0.8 | 0.8 | 0.8 | 0.9 |
| | 6.9 | 7.1 | 6.1 | 5.9 | .. | .. | .. | .. | .. | .. |
| | 4.2 | 3.6 | 3.7 | 4.0 | 4.1 | 4.2 | 4.1 | 3.9 | 4.3 | 4.4 |
| | 2.4 | 3.1 | 4.0 | 4.8 | 4.4 | 4.4 | 5.9 | 7.9 | 8.1 | .. |
| | 1.2 | 1.1 | 1.1 | 1.3 | 1.4 | 1.5 | 1.7 | 1.6 | 1.5 | 1.2 |
| | .. | .. | .. | .. | .. | 2.0 | 2.2 | 5.9 | 5.4 | 8.3 |
| | 12.8 | 11.7 | [11.3] | [11.5] | [11.2] | [11.1] | 11.4 | 8.8 | .. | .. |
| | 2.4 | 2.4 | 2.3 | 2.1 | 2.4 | 2.7 | 2.9 | 3.3 | 3.7 | 3.7 |
| | 9.4 | 16.8 | 21.2 | 16.0 | 15.8 | 20.1 | 17.2 | 17.1 | 15.5 | 16.2 |

**Table 8C.20. Oceania: constant price figures**

|  | 1952 | 1953 | 1954 | 1955 | 1956 | 1957 | 1958 | 1959 | 1960 | 1961 | 1962 |
|---|---|---|---|---|---|---|---|---|---|---|---|
| Australia | 654.0 | 636.0 | 577.0 | 598.0 | 583.0 | 534.0 | 525.0 | 537.0 | 534.0 | 542.0 | 564.0 |
| New Zealand | 99.0 | 109.8 | 94.7 | 89.2 | 89.3 | 86.2 | 85.0 | 88.0 | 89.8 | 84.4 | 82.4 |
| **Total Oceania** | **753.0** | **745.8** | **671.7** | **687.2** | **672.3** | **620.2** | **610.0** | **625.0** | **623.8** | **626.4** | **646.4** |

**Table 8C.21. Oceania: current price figures**

|  | *Currency* | 1952 | 1953 | 1954 | 1955 | 1956 | 1957 | 1958 | 1959 | 1960 | 1961 |
|---|---|---|---|---|---|---|---|---|---|---|---|
| Australia | *mn dollars* | 368.0 | 373.0 | 342.0 | 362.0 | 372.0 | 351.0 | 349.0 | 365.0 | 376.0 | 391.0 |
| New Zealand | *mn dollars* | 47.4 | 55.0 | 49.5 | 48.1 | 49.6 | 48.8 | 50.4 | 53.7 | 55.5 | 53.1 |

**Table 8C.22. Oceania: military expenditure as a percentage of gross domestic product**

|  | 1952 | 1953 | 1954 | 1955 | 1956 | 1957 | 1958 | 1959 | 1960 | 1961 |
|---|---|---|---|---|---|---|---|---|---|---|
| Australia | *4.6* | *4.3* | *3.6* | *3.6* | *3.4* | *3.0* | *2.9* | *2.8* | *2.6* | *2.7* |
| New Zealand | *3.1* | *3.3* | *2.7* | *2.5* | *2.4* | *2.2* | *2.2* | *2.2* | *2.1* | *1.9* |

*US $ mn, at 1970 prices and 1970 exchange rates (Final column, X, at current prices and exchange rates)*

| 1964 | 1965 | 1966 | 1967 | 1968 | 1969 | 1970 | 1971 | 1972 | 1973 | *1972X* |
|------|------|------|------|------|------|------|------|------|------|------|
| 670.0 | 797.0 | 985.0 | 1 173.0 | 1 262.0 | 1 213.0 | 1 162.0 | 1 159.0 | 1 177.0 | 1 146.8 | *1 420* |
| 100.0 | 110.0 | 116.6 | 109.8 | 116.0 | 120.1 | 131.5 | 123.3 | 119.6 | 114.6 | *151* |
| **770.0** | **907.0** | **1 101.6** | **1 282.8** | **1 378.0** | **1 333.1** | **1 293.5** | **1 282.3** | **1 296.6** | **1 261.4** | *1 571* |

*Local currency, current prices*

| 1963 | 1964 | 1965 | 1966 | 1967 | 1968 | 1969 | 1970 | 1971 | 1972 | 1973 |
|------|------|------|------|------|------|------|------|------|------|------|
| 431.0 | 496.0 | 613.0 | 781.0 | 959.0 | 1 060.0 | 1 048.0 | 1 043.0 | 1 103.0 | 1 185.0 | 1 265.0 |
| 55.5 | 68.2 | 77.6 | 84.5 | 84.3 | 92.9 | 100.9 | 117.8 | 122.0 | 126.5 | 131.0 |

*Per cent*

| 1963 | 1964 | 1965 | 1966 | 1967 | 1968 | 1969 | 1970 | 1971 | 1972 |
|------|------|------|------|------|------|------|------|------|------|
| *2.5* | *2.7* | *3.1* | *3.6* | *4.1* | *4.2* | *3.7* | *3.3* | *3.2* | *. .* |
| *1.7* | *2.0* | *2.1* | *2.1* | *2.1* | *2.1* | *2.1* | *2.2* | *2.0* | *. .* |

## Table 8C.23. Africa: constant price figures

| | 1952 | 1953 | 1954 | 1955 | 1956 | 1957 | 1958 | 1959 | 1960 | 1961 | 19 |
|---|---|---|---|---|---|---|---|---|---|---|---|
| Algeria^a | .. | .. | .. | .. | .. | .. | .. | .. | .. | .. | |
| Burundi | .. | .. | .. | .. | .. | .. | .. | .. | .. | .. | |
| Cameroon | .. | .. | .. | .. | .. | .. | .. | .. | 11.3† | 14.4 | |
| Central African Republic | .. | .. | .. | .. | .. | .. | .. | .. | 0.01† | 1.1 | |
| Chad | .. | .. | .. | .. | .. | .. | .. | .. | ..† | 0.04 | |
| Congo | .. | .. | .. | .. | .. | .. | .. | 0.4 | 0.5† | 2.5 | |
| Dahomey^a | .. | .. | .. | .. | .. | .. | .. | .. | ..† | 2.2 | |
| Ethiopia | .. | .. | .. | .. | .. | .. | .. | .. | 24.9 | (27.3) | |
| Gabon | .. | .. | .. | .. | .. | .. | .. | .. | ..† | 1.2 | |
| Ghana | .. | .. | .. | 8.9 | 14.3 | 17.5† | 17.9 | 18.7 | 30.6 | 41.9 | |
| Guinea^a | .. | .. | .. | .. | .. | .. | ..† | .. | .. | 4.0 | |
| Ivory Coast | .. | .. | .. | .. | .. | .. | .. | .. | ..† | 4.7 | |
| Kenya | .. | .. | .. | .. | 6.5 | 6.9 | 6.0 | 5.5 | 3.1 | 1.1 | |
| Liberia | .. | .. | .. | .. | .. | .. | .. | .. | .. | .. | |
| Libya | .. | .. | .. | .. | .. | .. | .. | (6.1) | (5.9) | (7.3) | |
| Malagasy Rep. | .. | .. | .. | .. | .. | .. | .. | .. | 1.9† | 9.7 | |
| Malawi | .. | .. | .. | .. | .. | .. | .. | .. | .. | | |
| Mali^a | .. | .. | .. | .. | .. | .. | .. | .. | ..† | 4.1 | |
| Mauritania | .. | .. | .. | .. | .. | .. | .. | .. | ..† | 2.6 | |
| Mauritius | .. | .. | .. | .. | .. | 0.5 | 0.5 | 0.5 | 0.4 | 0.3 | |
| Morocco | .. | .. | .. | .. | 32.7† | 44.5 | 52.2 | 51.6 | 52.1 | 59.4 | |
| Niger | .. | .. | .. | .. | .. | .. | .. | .. | ..† | 1.4 | |
| Nigeria | (4.8) | 7.4 | [7.6] | 7.3 | 7.3 | 8.6 | 20.1 | 23.8 | 26.3† | 25.6 | |
| Rhodesia, S. | .. | .. | .. | .. | .. | .. | .. | .. | .. | .. | |
| Rwanda^a | .. | .. | .. | .. | .. | .. | .. | .. | .. | .. | |
| Senegal | .. | .. | .. | .. | .. | .. | .. | .. | ..† | 3.3 | |
| Sierra Leone | .. | .. | .. | .. | .. | .. | .. | .. | 2.6 | 2.3† | |
| Somalia | .. | .. | .. | .. | .. | .. | .. | .. | ..† | 4.4 | |
| South Africa | 103.1 | 88.5 | 83.3 | 86.7 | 96.8 | 100.4 | 75.5 | 70.6 | 80.2 | 127.6 | 2 |
| Sudan | 6.8 | 8.4 | 10.3 | 11.7 | 13.0† | 17.5 | 19.9 | 21.8 | 24.6 | 25.1 | |
| Tanzania | .. | .. | .. | .. | .. | .. | .. | .. | ..† | | |
| Togo | .. | .. | .. | .. | .. | .. | .. | .. | ..† | (0.3) | |
| Tunisia | .. | .. | .. | .. | 3.6† | 6.1 | 10.4 | 16.1 | 18.6 | 20.7 | |
| Uganda | .. | .. | .. | 3.0 | 3.2 | 3.1 | 2.9 | 2.9 | 1.6 | 0.2 | |
| Upper Volta | .. | .. | .. | .. | .. | .. | .. | .. | (1.6)† | (1.9) | |
| Zaïre | .. | .. | .. | .. | .. | .. | .. | .. | ..† | .. | |
| Zambia | .. | .. | .. | .. | .. | .. | 7.4 | .. | 10.1 | 15.2 | |
| **Total Africa** | **[145.0]** | **[140.0]** | **[140.0]** | **[175.0]** | **[200.0]** | **[250.0]** | **[255.0]** | **[270.0]** | **[310.0]** | **[440.0]** | **[6** |

^a At current prices and 1970 exchange rates.
^b 1971.
^c 1970.

*US $mn, at 1970 prices and 1970 exchange rates (Final column, X, at current prices and exchange rates)*

| | 1964 | 1965 | 1966 | 1967 | 1968 | 1969 | 1970 | 1971 | 1972 | 1973 | 1972X |
|---|---|---|---|---|---|---|---|---|---|---|---|
| 1 | 99.3 | 99.3 | 105.3 | 99.7 | 99.7 | 99.7 | 99.7 | 99.7 | 99.7 | .. | 108.2 |
| 4) | (1.6) | 2.4 | 2.5 | 3.0 | 3.2 | 3.3 | 3.4 | (3.3) | .. | .. | 3.4[b] |
| 2 | 16.3 | 16.4 | 17.5 | 18.7 | 19.2 | 19.9 | 20.2 | 20.5 | 24.6 | [24.6] | 30.1 |
| 2 | 2.7 | 2.3 | 2.4 | 3.3 | 4.2 | 5.5 | 4.9 | 4.9 | [4.0] | .. | 4.8 |
| ) | 2.1 | 3.7 | 6.0 | 6.1 | 6.3 | 8.9 | 13.9 | [11.9] | [10.4] | .. | [12.3] |
| 5) | 5.3 | 5.3 | 7.4 | .3 | 7.7 | 8.5 | [10.1] | .. | .. | .. | [10.1][c] |
| 5 | 4.1 | 4.5 | 4.3 | 4.5 | [4.5] | [5.0] | [5.4] | .. | .. | .. | [5.4][c] |
| 5 | 50.8 | 54.0 | 49.0 | 41.5 | 38.8 | 38.9 | 35.8 | 36.4 | 39.9 | (44.4) | 40.9 |
| 7 | 2.1 | 2.6 | 3.0 | 2.9 | 2.9 | 3.2 | [3.1] | .. | .. | .. | [3.1][c] |
| # | 33.4 | 29.7 | 28.5 | 47.0 | 51.7 | 47.0 | 42.2 | 41.0 | 37.1 | .. | 34.6 |
| ) | 5.0 | 11.5 | 13.2 | 14.0 | 14.1 | 14.0 | [15.0] | .. | .. | .. | [15.0][c] |
| 5 | 12.7 | 14.7 | 14.5 | 15.5 | 16.3 | 16.8 | 22.9 | [24.2] | 25.3 | .. | 27.4 |
| #† | 6.7 | 10.8 | 13.6 | 16.4 | 16.7 | 16.1 | 17.7 | 17.5 | 18.6 | (25.4) | 20.5 |
| | 3.3 | 3.5 | 3.4 | 3.8 | 3.1 | 3.3 | 3.8 | 4.2 | .. | .. | 4.2[b] |
| #) | 20.3 | 25.9 | 49.2 | 136.2 | 215.6 | [321.7] | [364.0] | [388.5] | .. | .. | [378.9][b] |
| 8 | 9.8 | 10.7 | 11.0 | 11.6 | 12.4 | 12.5 | 12.1 | .. | .. | .. | 12.1[c] |
| | (1.0)† | (1.1) | (1.4) | (1.5) | 1.5 | 1.6 | 1.5 | 1.6 | .. | .. | 1.8[b] |
| 7 | 4.9 | 4.6 | [4.8] | [5.2] | [5.4] | [5.6] | [6.0] | .. | .. | .. | [6.0][c] |
| ) | 4.9 | 4.4 | 4.2 | 6.1 | 7.8 | 7.9 | [8.0] | .. | .. | .. | [8.0][c] |
| 4 | 0.3 | 0.3 | 0.3 | 0.3† | [0.3] | [0.3] | .. | .. | .. | .. | [0.3][c] |
| | 74.5 | 65.1 | 68.2 | 73.7 | 86.3 | 92.9 | 87.7 | 93.5 | 103.9 | (116.4) | 121.9 |
| ) | 5.6 | 6.4 | 2.9 | 3.0 | 3.6 | 3.2 | [4.0] | .. | .. | .. | [4.0][c] |
| 5 | 44.8 | 51.9 | 44.0 | 152.9 | 262.9 | 493.6 | 409.5 | 244.6 | 351.8 | .. | 446.2 |
| | 16.0 | 19.3 | 18.7 | 21.1 | 22.2 | 22.7 | 26.3 | 25.7 | 30.2 | [41.1] | 29.3 |
| 5 | .. | 2.5 | 4.8 | 3.9 | 4.1 | 4.0 | 3.9 | .. | .. | .. | 3.9[c] |
| 2 | 10.9 | 14.6 | 14.5 | 15.6 | 16.3 | 16.6 | 16.7 | 16.9 | .. | .. | 17.5[b] |
| 5 | 2.6 | 2.6 | 2.3 | 2.4 | 2.7 | 2.9 | [3.0] | [3.2] | (3.4) | .. | 3.6 |
| 4 | 6.6 | 5.5 | 7.2 | 8.4 | 8.9 | 9.1 | 11.2 | 11.3 | .. | .. | 11.4[b] |
| 7 | 291.3 | 298.6 | 323.6 | 360.2 | 379.2 | 391.8 | 363.5 | 396.5 | 426.2 | 497.7 | 446.1 |
| 9 | 40.7 | 49.9 | 54.1 | 54.2 | 66.0 | 72.1 | 93.3 | 124.5 | (114.1) | .. | 129.2 |
| ) | 5.7 | 8.3 | 10.4 | 13.0 | 14.3 | 15.9 | 16.9 | 25.5 | 31.3 | (35.4) | 35.6 |
| 9 | (2.7) | (2.7) | 2.3 | 2.5 | 2.7 | 2.8 | 3.1 | 3.0 | 3.5 | .. | 4.3 |
| 3 | 20.1 | 16.3 | 18.6 | 17.3 | 21.1 | 20.2 | 22.5 | 18.9 | 24.3 | .. | 28.5 |
| 2 | 7.6 | 13.1 | 17.5 | 20.0 | 24.5 | 24.2 | 22.3 | 20.3 | 31.2 | .. | 35.0 |
| 4 | 5.3 | 3.5 | 3.9 | 5.2 | 5.2 | 4.0 | 4.0 | .. | .. | .. | 4.0[c] |
| 2 | 34.4 | 86.9 | 78.1 | 65.8 | 51.1 | 63.0 | 84.0 | 66.1 | .. | .. | 69.4[b] |
| 7 | 8.5† | 22.5 | 21.4 | 23.7 | 26.2 | 19.1 | 19.9 | .. | .. | .. | 19.9[c] |
| 0] | [865.0] | 977.4 | 1 034.0 | 1 288.5 | 1 528.7 | 1 897.8 | 1 881.8 | [1 805.0] | [2 035.0] | [2 250.0] | [2 136.9] |

## Table 8C.24. Africa: current price figures

| | Currency | 1952 | 1953 | 1954 | 1955 | 1956 | 1957 | 1958 | 1959 | 1960 | 1961 |
|---|---|---|---|---|---|---|---|---|---|---|---|
| Algeria | *mn dinars* | .. | .. | .. | .. | .. | .. | .. | .. | .. | .. |
| Burundi | *mn francs* | .. | .. | .. | .. | .. | .. | .. | .. | .. | 19 |
| Cameroon | *mn francs* | .. | .. | .. | .. | .. | .. | .. | .. | 2 186 | 2 841 |
| Central African Republic | *mn francs* | .. | .. | .. | .. | .. | .. | .. | .. | 1 | 203 |
| Chad | *mn francs* | .. | .. | .. | .. | .. | .. | .. | .. | .. | 7 |
| Congo | *mn francs* | .. | .. | .. | .. | .. | .. | .. | 70 | 90 | 500 |
| Dahomey | *mn francs* | .. | .. | .. | .. | .. | .. | .. | .. | .. | 610 |
| Ethiopia | *mn dollars* | .. | .. | .. | .. | .. | .. | .. | .. | 41.5 | 46 |
| Gabon | *mn francs* | .. | .. | .. | .. | .. | .. | .. | .. | .. | 245 |
| Ghana | *mn cedis*.. | .. | .. | 4.0 | 6.7 | 8.3 | 8.5 | 9.1 | 14.9 | 21.9 | |
| Guinea | *mn sily* | .. | .. | .. | .. | .. | .. | .. | .. | .. | 98 |
| Ivory Coast | *mn francs* | .. | .. | .. | .. | .. | .. | .. | .. | .. | 990 |
| Kenya | *mn pounds* | .. | .. | .. | .. | 1.8 | 2.0 | 1.8 | 1.6 | 0.9 | 0 |
| Liberia | *mn dollars* | .. | .. | .. | .. | .. | .. | .. | 1.0 | .. | .. |
| Libya | *mn dinars* | .. | .. | .. | .. | .. | .. | .. | 1.4 | 1.4 | 1 |
| Malagasy Rep. | *mn francs* | .. | .. | .. | .. | .. | .. | .. | .. | 396 | 2 094 |
| Malawi | *mn kwachas* | | . | .. | .. | .. | .. | .. | .. | .. | |
| Mali | *mn francs* | .. | .. | .. | .. | .. | .. | .. | .. | .. | 2 271 |
| Mauritania | *mn rupees* | .. | .. | .. | .. | .. | .. | .. | .. | .. | 99 |
| Mauritius | *mn rupees* | .. | .. | .. | .. | .. | 2.0 | 2.0 | 2.0 | 1.7 | 1 |
| Morocco | *mn dirhams* | .. | .. | .. | .. | 116 | 165 | 198 | 198 | 211 | 244 |
| Niger | *mn francs* | .. | .. | .. | .. | .. | .. | .. | .. | .. | 295 |
| Nigeria | *mn nairas* | 1.6 | 2.6 | [2.8] | 2.8 | 3.0 | 3.6 | 8.4 | 10.4 | 12.2 | 12 |
| Rhodesia, S. | *mn dollars* | .. | .. | .. | .. | .. | .. | .. | .. | .. | .. |
| Rwanda | *mn francs* | .. | .. | .. | .. | .. | .. | .. | .. | .. | |
| Senegal | *mn francs* | .. | .. | .. | .. | .. | .. | .. | .. | .. | 740 |
| Sierra Leone | *mn leones* | .. | .. | .. | .. | .. | .. | .. | .. | 1.5 | 1 |
| Somalia | *mn shillings* | .. | .. | .. | .. | .. | .. | .. | .. | .. | 22 |
| South Africa | *mn rands* | 46.9 | 41.5 | 39.5 | 42.4 | 48.4 | 51.7 | 40.2 | 38.0 | 44.0 | 71 |
| Sudan | *mn pounds* | 1.5 | 1.8 | 2.4 | 2.8 | 3.0 | 4.1 | 5.0 | 5.4 | 6.1 | 6 |
| Tanzania | *mn shillings* | .. | .. | .. | .. | .. | .. | .. | .. | .. | |
| Togo | *mn francs* | .. | .. | .. | .. | .. | .. | .. | .. | .. | 66 |
| Tunisia | *mn dinars* | .. | .. | .. | .. | 1.4 | 2.5 | 4.4 | 6.6 | 7.4 | 8 |
| Uganda | *mn shillings* | .. | .. | .. | 12.9 | 15.0 | 14.7 | 14.2 | 14.0 | 7.5 | 1 |
| Upper Volta | *mn francs* | .. | .. | .. | .. | .. | .. | .. | .. | 311 | 403 |
| Zaïre | *mn zaires* | .. | .. | .. | .. | .. | .. | .. | .. | .. | .. |
| Zambia | *mn kwachas* | .. | .. | .. | .. | .. | .. | 3.4 | .. | 4.8 | 7 |

[a] GDP figure used excludes Eastern states.

[b] GDP at factor cost.

*Local currency, current prices*

| 1963 | 1964 | 1965 | 1966 | 1967 | 1968 | 1969 | 1970 | 1971 | 1972 | 1973 |
|---|---|---|---|---|---|---|---|---|---|---|
| 450 | 490 | 490 | 520 | 492 | 492 | 492 | 492 | 492 | 492 | . . |
| 99.9 | 118.9 | 181.9 | 199.8 | 239.0 | 268.0 | 291.9 | 300.0 | (300.0) | . . | . . |
| 3 860 | 3 865 | 3 978 | 4 365 | 4 773 | 4 991 | 5 240 | 5 609 | 5 921 | 7 700 | [8 535] |
| 247 | 579 | 547 | 588 | 827 | 1 109 | 1 451 | 1 351 | 1 468 | 1 227 | . . |
| 367 | 441 | 820 | 1 426 | 1 476 | 1 540 | 2 277 | 3 850 | [3 500] | [3 150] | . . |
| 990 | 1 235 | 1 235 | 1 910 | 2 218 | 2 133 | 2 336 | [2 800] | . . | . . | . . |
| 968 | 1 145 | 1 261 | 1 194 | 1 256 | [1 250] | [1 375] | [1 500] | . . | . . | . . |
| 67.8 | 90.4 | 107.3 | 108.6 | 92.7 | 86.8 | 88.4 | 89.5 | 91.1 | 94.1 | (114.0) |
| 620 | 494 | 625 | 740 | 740 | 740 | 860 | [860] | . . | . . | . . |
| 21.9 | 22.2 | 25.4 | 25.5 | 39.0 | 47.2 | 46.8 | 43.1 | 43.1 | 44.4 | . . |
| 148.7 | 123.5 | 284.0 | 325.4 | 344.8 | 348.9 | 345.5 | [370.0] | . . | . . | . . |
| 2 000 | 2 700 | 3 200 | 3 300 | 3 600 | 4 000 | 4 300 | 6 350 | [6 675] | 7 000 | . . |
| 0.7 | 2.1 | 3.5 | 4.7 | 5.7 | 5.8 | 5.6 | 6.3 | (6.4) | (7.3) | (10.7) |
| 2.4 | 2.6 | 2.8 | 2.8 | 3.3 | 2.8 | 3.3 | 3.8 | 4.2 | . . | . . |
| 4.7 | 5.4 | 7.3 | 15.0 | 43.0 | 71.0 | [115.0] | [130.0] | [135.0] | . . | . . |
| 2 211 | 2 330 | 2 650 | 2 800 | 2 990 | 3 220 | 3 380 | 3 370 | . . | . . | . . |
| . . | 0.7 | 0.8 | 1.0 | 1.1 | 1.1 | 1.2 | 1.2 | 1.5 | . . | . . |
| 2 621 | 2 697 | 2 553 | [2 675] | [2 875] | [2 975] | [3 115] | [3 350] | . . | . . | . . |
| 210 | 224 | 200 | 197 | 296 | 395 | 414 | [444] | . . | . . | . . |
| 1.5 | 1.5 | 1.5 | 1.5 | 1.5 | 1.6 | [1.5] | [1.6] | . . | . . | . . |
| 379 | 354 | 320 | 332 | 356 | 419 | 464 | 444 | 493 | 568 | (665) |
| 840 | 1 235 | 1 480 | 740 | 780 | 902 | 885 | [1 100] | . . | . . | . . |
| 19.6 | 23.4 | 28.2 | 26.0 | 86.8 | 150.8 | 311.3 | 292.5 | 198.3 | 293.5 | . . |
| . . | 10.2 | 12.6 | 12.6 | 14.4 | 15.5 | 15.9 | 18.8 | 18.9 | 22.9 | [32.5] |
| 63.9 | . . | 250 | 480 | 391 | 414 | 400 | 390 | . . | . . | . . |
| 1 975 | 2 715 | 3 705 | 3 800 | 4 050 | 4 250 | 4 500 | 4 639 | 4 823 | . . | . . |
| 1.5 | 1.7 | 1.8 | 1.7 | 1.8 | 2.1 | 2.3 | [2.5] | [2.6] | (2.9) | . . |
| 32.0 | 38.7 | 36.9 | 46.4 | 53.8 | 59.6 | 64.3 | 80.0 | 81.0 | . . | . . |
| 118.7 | 170.7 | 181.6 | 203.8 | 234.3 | 251.0 | 267.2 | 260.7 | 301.7 | 345.4 | (438.3) |
| 9.2 | 12.2 | 14.6 | 16.1 | 17.9 | 19.6 | 24.1 | 32.5 | 43.9 | (45.0) | . . |
| 17.1 | 33.2 | 51.2 | 67.6 | 86.5 | 98.5 | 110.5 | 120.7 | 188.9 | 254.6 | (306.9) |
| 228.6 | 682.2 | 678.4 | 583.5 | 629.2 | 670.2 | 734.8 | 849.1 | 897.2 | 1 104.4 | . . |
| 7.1 | 8.6 | 7.4 | 8.8 | 8.4 | 10.5 | 10.5 | 11.8 | 10.5 | 13.8 | . . |
| 19.5 | 39.2 | 76.7 | 101.9 | 120.3 | 142.5 | 157.5 | 159.2 | 167.4 | 250.0 | . . |
| 1 294 | 1 313 | 860 | 960 | 1 235 | 1 235 | 1 045 | 1 110 | . . | . . | . . |
| 3.3 | 6.2 | 15.3 | 15.9 | 18.3 | 21.8 | 30.5 | 42.0 | 34.7 | . . | . . |
| 8.0 | 4.2 | 12.0 | 12.6 | 14.6 | 17.9 | 13.3 | 14.2 | . . | . . | . . |

**Table 8C.25. Africa: military expenditure as a percentage of gross domestic product**

| | 1952 | 1953 | 1954 | 1955 | 1956 | 1957 | 1958 | 1959 | 1960 | 1961 |
|---|---|---|---|---|---|---|---|---|---|---|
| Algeria | .. | .. | .. | .. | .. | .. | .. | .. | .. | .. |
| Burundi | .. | .. | .. | .. | .. | .. | .. | .. | .. | .. |
| Cameroon | .. | .. | .. | .. | .. | .. | .. | .. | .. | .. |
| Central African Republic | .. | .. | .. | .. | .. | .. | .. | .. | .. | 0.6 |
| Chad | .. | .. | .. | .. | .. | .. | .. | .. | .. | .. |
| Congo | .. | .. | .. | .. | .. | .. | .. | .. | .. | [1.5] |
| Dahomey | .. | .. | .. | .. | .. | .. | .. | .. | .. | 1.6 |
| Ethiopia | .. | .. | .. | .. | .. | .. | .. | .. | .. | 1.9 |
| Gabon | .. | .. | .. | .. | .. | .. | .. | .. | .. | 0.7 |
| Ghana | .. | .. | .. | 0.6 | 0.9 | 1.1 | 1.1 | 1.0 | 1.6 | 2.1 |
| Guinea | .. | .. | .. | .. | .. | .. | .. | .. | .. | [2.0] |
| Ivory Coast | .. | .. | .. | .. | .. | .. | .. | .. | .. | 0.6 |
| Kenya | .. | .. | .. | .. | .. | .. | .. | .. | .. | .. |
| Liberia | .. | .. | .. | .. | .. | .. | .. | .. | .. | .. |
| Libya | .. | .. | .. | .. | .. | .. | .. | .. | .. | .. |
| Malagasy Rep. | .. | .. | .. | .. | .. | .. | .. | .. | 0.3 | [1.5] |
| Malawi | .. | .. | .. | .. | .. | .. | .. | .. | .. | .. |
| Mali | .. | .. | .. | .. | .. | .. | .. | .. | .. | [3.1] |
| Mauritania | .. | .. | .. | .. | .. | .. | .. | .. | .. | 2.3 |
| Mauritius | .. | .. | .. | .. | .. | 0.3 | 0.3 | 0.3 | 0.3 | 0.2 |
| Morocco | .. | .. | .. | .. | 1.7 | 2.3 | 2.4 | 2.4 | 2.3 | 2.7 |
| Niger | .. | .. | .. | .. | .. | .. | .. | .. | .. | [0.4] |
| Nigeria | 0.1 | 0.2 | [0.2] | 0.2 | 0.2 | 0.2 | 0.4 | 0.5 | 0.5 | 0.5 |
| Rhodesia, S. | .. | .. | .. | .. | .. | .. | .. | .. | .. | .. |
| Rwanda | .. | .. | .. | .. | .. | .. | .. | .. | .. | . |
| Senegal | .. | .. | .. | .. | .. | .. | .. | .. | .. | 0.5 |
| Sierra Leone | .. | .. | .. | .. | .. | .. | .. | .. | .. | .. |
| Somalia | .. | .. | .. | .. | .. | .. | .. | .. | .. | [2.2] |
| South Africa | 1.5 | 1.1 | 1.0 | 1.0 | 1.1 | 1.1 | 0.8 | 0.8 | 0.8 | 1.3 |
| Sudan | .. | .. | .. | .. | 1.0 | 1.2 | 1.5 | 1.5 | 1.6 | 1.7 |
| Tanzania | .. | .. | .. | .. | .. | .. | .. | .. | .. | .. |
| Togo | .. | .. | .. | .. | .. | .. | .. | .. | .. | 0.2 |
| Tunisia | .. | .. | .. | .. | .. | .. | .. | .. | 2.2 | 2.3 |
| Uganda[b] | .. | .. | .. | 0.5 | 0.5 | 0.5 | 0.5 | 0.5 | 0.2 | 0.03 |
| Upper Volta | .. | .. | .. | .. | .. | .. | .. | .. | (0.7) | [0.8] |
| Zaïre | .. | .. | .. | .. | .. | .. | .. | .. | .. | .. |
| Zambia | .. | .. | .. | .. | .. | .. | 1.2 | .. | 1.1 | 1.8 |

[a] GDP figure used excludes Eastern states.
[b] GDP at factor cost.

*Per cent*

| 1963 | 1964 | 1965 | 1966 | 1967 | 1968 | 1969 | 1970 | 1971 | 1972 |
|---|---|---|---|---|---|---|---|---|---|
| (3.5) | [4.1] | [3.4] | [3.6] | [3.0] | (2.7) | [2.5] | [2.2] | .. | .. |
| (1.4) | .. | .. | .. | .. | (1.7) | (1.7) | .. | .. | .. |
| 2.6 | 2.4 | 2.3 | 2.3 | 2.3 | 2.1 | 2.0 | 1.9 | .. | . |
| 0.7 | 1.5 | (1.3) | (1.3) | (1.7) | 2.2 | [2.7] | 2.4 | .. | .. |
| 0.6 | 0.7 | .. | .. | .. | .. | .. | .. | .. | .. |
| (2.7) | [3.3] | [3.0] | [4.1] | [4.4] | (4.0) | (3.9) | [3.7] | .. | .. |
| 2.4 | 2.7 | 2.8 | 2.5 | .. | .. | .. | .. | .. | .. |
| 2.7 | 3.1 | 3.3 | 3.2 | 2.7 | 2.3 | 2.2 | 2.0 | 1.9 | .. |
| 1.4 | 1.0 | 1.2 | 1.3 | 1.3 | 1.0 | 1.0 | [0.9] | .. | .. |
| 1.8 | 1.6 | 1.6 | 1.4 | 2.2 | 2.3 | 2.0 | 1.7 | .. | .. |
| (2.7) | .. | .. | .. | .. | (4.9) | (4.6) | .. | .. | .. |
| 1.0 | 1.1 | 1.3 | 1.3 | 1.3 | 1.2 | 1.2 | 1.5 | [1.5] | .. |
| 0.2 | 0.6 | 1.0 | 1.1 | 1.3 | 1.2 | 1.1 | 1.1 | (1.0) | (1.0) |
| 0.9 | 0.9 | 0.9 | 0.9 | 1.0 | 0.8 | 0.8 | 0.9 | .. | .. |
| 1.9 | 1.4 | 1.4 | 2.3 | 5.5 | 6.4 | [9.1] | [9.8] | [8.9] | .. |
| (1.5) | 1.5 | 1.6 | 1.5 | 1.6 | 1.5 | 1.5 | 1.4 | .. | .. |
| .. | 0.5 | 0.4 | 0.5 | 0.5 | 0.5 | 0.5 | 0.4 | 0.5 | .. |
| [3.2] | 3.1 | .. | .. | .. | .. | .. | .. | .. | .. |
| 3.8 | 3.2 | [2.7] | [2.4] | [3.3] | 4.2 | 4.0 | [3.8] | .. | .. |
| 0.1 | 0.2 | 0.2 | 0.2 | 0.2 | 0.2 | [0.1] | [0.2] | .. | .. |
| 3.2 | 2.8 | 2.4 | 2.6 | 2.6 | 2.7 | 2.9 | 2.6 | 2.7 | [2.8] |
| [1.0] | [1.5] | [1.6] | 0.8 | 0.8 | 0.9 | 0.9 | .. | .. | .. |
| 0.7 | 0.7 | 0.9 | [0.8] | [2.8][a] | 5.2[a] | 8.7[a] | .. | .. | .. |
| .. | 1.5 | 1.7 | 1.7 | 1.9 | 1.8 | 1.6 | 1.7 | 1.5 | 1.7 |
| (1.3) | .. | (4.1) | (4.1) | .. | 2.5 | 2.2 | 1.8 | .. | .. |
| 1.1 | 1.4 | 1.9 | 1.9 | 2.1 | 2.0 | 2.1 | 2.0 | 2.2 | .. |
| [0.7] | 0.7 | 0.7 | 0.6 | 0.6 | 0.7 | 0.6 | [0.7] | .. | .. |
| (2.9) | [3.5] | [3.2] | [4.0] | [4.6] | (4.9) | (5.1) | [6.1] | .. | .. |
| 1.8 | 2.4 | 2.3 | 2.4 | 2.5 | 2.5 | 2.4 | 2.1 | 2.2 | 2.2 |
| 2.0 | 2.6 | 3.0 | 3.2 | 3.5 | 3.5 | 4.1 | 5.2 | .. | .. |
| 0.3 | 0.6 | 0.8 | 1.0 | 1.2 | 1.2 | 1.3 | 1.3 | 1.9 | 2.3 |
| 0.7 | 1.8 | 1.6 | 1.1 | 1.1 | 1.1 | 1.1 | 1.2 | .. | .. |
| 1.8 | 2.0 | 1.5 | 1.7 | 1.6 | 1.8 | 1.6 | 1.6 | 1.3 | .. |
| 0.4 | 0.8 | 1.3 | 1.7 | 1.9 | 2.2 | 2.1 | 1.9 | 1.8 | .. |
| (2.4) | [2.4] | 1.5 | 1.6 | [1.9] | 1.6 | .. | .. | .. | .. |
| 1.7 | 3.2 | 5.6 | 5.2 | 5.9 | 3.0 | 3.5 | 3.9 | 2.7 | .. |
| 1.9 | 0.8 | 1.8 | 1.6 | 1.6 | 1.8 | 1.1 | 1.2 | .. | .. |

225

**Table 8C.26. Central America: constant price figures**

|  | 1952 | 1953 | 1954 | 1955 | 1956 | 1957 | 1958 | 1959 | 1960 | 1961 | 196? |
|---|---|---|---|---|---|---|---|---|---|---|---|
| Costa Rica | 2.2 | 2.2 | 2.4 | 2.4 | 2.4 | 2.7 | 2.6 | 2.6 | 2.6 | 2.5 | 2.6 |
| Cuba[a] | .. | .. | .. | .. | .. | .. | .. | .. | .. | 175 | 200 |
| Dominican Rep. | .. | .. | .. | .. | .. | .. | 39.9 | 49.2 | 39.9 | 39.1 | 37.8 |
| El Salvador | 6.3 | 7.2 | 6.5 | 7.2 | 7.6 | 8.6 | 8.0 | 6.7 | 6.5 | 6.8 | 9.5 |
| Guatemala | 6.9 | 6.7 | 7.4 | 8.6 | 9.4 | 10.0 | 10.5 | 10.5 | 10.2 | 10.0 | 9.9 |
| Haiti | 5.6 | 7.0 | 6.5 | 6.4 | 6.5 | 7.0 | 8.2 | 8.5 | 8.7 | 8.9 | 9.5 |
| Honduras | 4.6 | 4.2 | 4.2 | 3.9 | 5.8 | 5.7 | [5.7] | 5.8 | 5.2 | 8.9 | 8.9 |
| Jamaica | .. | .. | .. | .. | .. | .. | .. | .. | .. | .. | 1.2 |
| Mexico | 71.5 | 80.4 | 64.2 | 73.4 | 83.2 | 98.6 | 96.5 | 96.7 | 106.6 | 113.9 | 127.5 |
| Nicaragua | .. | .. | .. | .. | .. | .. | .. | .. | .. | 8.5 | 9.2 |
| Panama | .. | .. | .. | .. | .. | .. | .. | .. | .. | .. | 0.6 |
| Trinidad & Tobago | .. | .. | .. | .. | .. | .. | .. | .. | .. | .. | .. |
| **Total Central America** | **[245.0]** | **[270.0]** | **[230.0]** | **[255.0]** | **[285.0]** | **[330.0]** | **[340.0]** | **[355.0]** | **[355.0]** | 373.6 | 416.7 |

[a] At current prices and 1970 exchange rates.   [b] 1970.   [c] 1971.

**Table 8C.27. Central America: current price figures**

|  | Currency | 1952 | 1953 | 1954 | 1955 | 1956 | 1957 | 1958 | 1959 | 1960 | 1961 |
|---|---|---|---|---|---|---|---|---|---|---|---|
| Costa Rica | mn colones | 9.8 | 9.9 | 11.2 | 11.6 | 12.0 | 13.6 | 13.2 | 13.3 | 13.6 | 13 |
| Cuba | mn pesos | .. | .. | .. | .. | .. | .. | .. | .. | .. | 175 |
| Dominican Republic | mn pesos | .. | .. | .. | .. | .. | .. | 34.5 | 42.6 | 33.4 | 31 |
| El Salvador | mn colones | 12.7 | 15.4 | 14.5 | 16.4 | 17.4 | 19.2 | 19.0 | 15.6 | 15.3 | 15. |
| Guatemala | mn quetzales | 6.0 | 6.0 | 6.7 | 8.0 | 8.8 | 9.3 | 9.8 | 9.8 | 9.4 | 9.2 |
| Haiti | mn gourdes | 22.9 | 26.3 | 25.7 | 25.9 | 27.2 | 29.7 | 35.0 | 34.4 | 33.3 | 35 |
| Honduras | mn lempiras | 6.5 | 6.1 | 6.4 | 6.4 | 9.3 | 8.9 | [9.1] | 9.3 | 8.2 | 14 |
| Jamaica | mn dollars | .. | .. | .. | .. | .. | .. | .. | .. | .. | .. |
| Mexico | mn pesos | 435.0 | 479.0 | 405.0 | 533.0 | 632.0 | 792.0 | 862.0 | 883.0 | 1 021.0 | 1 111 |
| Nicaragua | mn cordobas | .. | .. | .. | .. | .. | .. | .. | .. | .. | 49. |
| Panama | mn balboas | .. | .. | .. | .. | .. | .. | .. | .. | .. | .. |
| Trinidad & Tobago | mn dollars | .. | .. | .. | .. | .. | .. | .. | .. | .. | .. |

**Table 8C.28. Central America: military expenditure as a percentage of gross domestic product**

|  | 1952 | 1953 | 1954 | 1955 | 1956 | 1957 | 1958 | 1959 | 1960 | 1961 |
|---|---|---|---|---|---|---|---|---|---|---|
| Costa Rica | 0.6 | 0.6 | 0.6 | 0.6 | 0.6 | 0.6 | 0.5 | 0.5 | 0.5 | 0.5 |
| Cuba[a] | .. | .. | .. | .. | .. | .. | .. | .. | .. | .. |
| Dominican Republic | .. | .. | .. | .. | .. | .. | 4.8 | 6.1 | 4.6 | 4.5 |
| El Salvador | .. | .. | .. | .. | .. | .. | 1.4 | 1.2 | 1.1 | 1.1 |
| Guatemala | 0.9 | 0.8 | 0.9 | 1.0 | 1.0 | 1.0 | 0.9 | 0.9 | 0.9 | 0.9 |
| Haiti | [1.7] | [2.0] | [1.8] | [1.8] | [1.7] | [1.9] | [2.2] | [2.3] | [2.3] | [2.4] |
| Honduras | 1.3 | 1.0 | 1.1 | 1.0 | 1.4 | 1.3 | [1.3] | 1.2 | 1.1 | 1.8 |
| Jamaica | .. | .. | .. | .. | .. | .. | .. | .. | .. | .. |
| Mexico | 0.7 | 0.8 | 0.6 | 0.6 | 0.6 | 0.7 | 0.7 | 0.6 | 0.7 | 0.7 |
| Nicaragua | .. | .. | .. | .. | .. | .. | .. | .. | .. | 1.7 |
| Panama | .. | .. | .. | .. | .. | .. | .. | .. | .. | .. |
| Trinidad & Tobago | .. | .. | .. | .. | .. | .. | .. | .. | .. | .. |

[a] Percentage of net material product.

US $ *mn, at 1970 prices and 1970 exchange rates (Final column, X, at current prices and exchange rates)*

| 3 | 1964 | 1965 | 1966 | 1967 | 1968 | 1969 | 1970 | 1971 | 1972 | 1973 | *1972X* |
|---|---|---|---|---|---|---|---|---|---|---|---|
| .5 | [2.4] | [2.1] | [2.9] | [3.0] | [3.9] | [4.2] | [4.2] | .. | .. | .. | *[4.2]ᵇ* |
|  | 200 | 220 | 220 | 230 | 250 | 300 | 250 | 290 | 290 | .. | *290ᶜ* |
| 8 | 38.7 | 36.9 | 34.7 | 32.8 | 33.5 | 32.6 | 31.3 | 31.0 | 29.7 | .. | *33.0* |
| 2 | 8.5 | 9.5 | 9.8 | 10.0 | 12.1 | 29.5 | 10.0 | 13.2 | 12.2 | .. | *12.5* |
| 9 | 13.6 | 15.4 | 15.8 | 17.5 | 16.4 | 16.0 | 28.7 | 18.6 | 19.0 | 18.3 | *19.0* |
| 7 | 8.6 | 8.0 | 7.1 | 7.4 | 7.3 | 7.2 | 7.2 | 6.6 | 7.0 | .. | *8.0* |
| 2 | 6.8 | 6.3 | 6.7 | 6.6 | 6.8 | 14.9 | 8.6 | 11.1 | .. | .. | *11.4ᶜ* |
| 4 | 4.6 | 5.3 | 5.3 | 5.6 | 5.7 | 5.7 | 5.8 | 5.5 | .. | .. | *5.9ᶜ* |
| 0 | 156.7 | 157.2 | 163.1 | 190.2 | 197.8 | 214.3 | 218.0 | 210.8 | 256.1 | (265.4) | *281.2* |
| 3 | 8.7 | 9.1 | 9.6 | 10.9 | 10.4 | 10.9 | 11.8 | .. | .. | .. | *11.8ᵇ* |
| 6 | 0.7 | 0.6 | 0.5 | 0.9 | 0.9 | 1.3 | 1.6 | 2.0 | 2.0 | .. | *2.0* |
|  |  |  |  |  |  |  |  |  |  |  | |
| 7 | 2.6 | 2.6 | 2.5 | 2.6 | 2.5 | 2.6 | [3.5] | .. | .. | .. | *[3.5]ᵇ* |
| 3 | **451.9** | **473.6** | **488.0** | **537.5** | **597.3** | **589.2** | **620.7** | **605.0** | **[650.0]** | **[660.0]** | *[682.5]* |

*Local currency, current prices*

| ? | 1963 | 1964 | 1965 | 1966 | 1967 | 1968 | 1969 | 1970 | 1971 | 1972 | 1973 |
|---|---|---|---|---|---|---|---|---|---|---|---|
| 4.1 | 14.4 | [14.0] | [15.5] | [17.0] | [17.5] | [24.0] | [26.5] | [27.5] | .. | .. | .. |
| 0.0 | 200.0 | 200.0 | 220.0 | 230.0 | 250.0 | 300.0 | 250.0 | 290.0 | 290.0 | .. | .. |
| 3.1 | 34.0 | 37.0 | 35.0 | 32.4 | 31.2 | 32.5 | 31.0 | 31.3 | 31.9 | 33.0 | .. |
| 1.7 | 21.3 | 20.0 | 22.6 | 23.0 | 23.7 | 29.5 | 71.8 | 24.9 | 33.1 | 31.2 | .. |
| 9.3 | 10.2 | 12.7 | 14.3 | 14.7 | 16.3 | 15.7 | 15.6 | 28.7 | 18.5 | 19.0 | 21.0 |
| 7.5 | 35.7 | 38.8 | 36.8 | 35.4 | 35.8 | 35.8 | 35.8 | 35.8 | 36.6 | 40.1 | .. |
| 4.5 | 15.4 | 12.0 | 11.4 | 12.4 | 12.3 | 12.9 | 28.9 | 17.2 | 32.8 | .. | .. |
| 0.7 | 2.1 | 2.9 | 3.4 | 3.5 | 3.8 | 4.1 | 4.3 | 4.8 | 4.9 | .. | .. |
| 8.0 | 1 388.0 | 1 589.0 | 1 651.0 | 1 789.0 | 2 148.0 | 2 285.0 | 2 548.0 | 2 723.0 | 2 720.0 | 3 512.0 | 4 409.0 |
| 3.2 | 54.3 | 53.2 | 57.2 | 62.4 | 72.4 | 70.9 | 75.0 | 82.9 | .. | .. | .. |
| 0.5 | 0.5 | 0.6 | 0.6 | 0.5 | 0.8 | 0.9 | 1.3 | 1.6 | 2.0 | 2.0 | .. |
| . | 2.8 | 4.3 | 4.3 | 4.3 | 4.5 | 4.7 | 5.1 | [7.0] | .. | .. | .. |

*Per cent*

| 2 | 1963 | 1964 | 1965 | 1966 | 1967 | 1968 | 1969 | 1970 | 1971 | 1972 |  |
|---|---|---|---|---|---|---|---|---|---|---|---|
|  | 0.4 | [0.4] | [0.4] | [0.4] | [0.4] | [0.5] | [0.5] | [0.4] | .. | .. | |
|  | 6.1 | 5.0 | 5.7 | 6.1 | .. | .. | .. | .. | .. | .. | |
|  | 3.4 | 3.4 | 3.7 | 3.0 | 2.8 | 2.8 | 2.4 | 2.1 | 2.0 | .. | |
|  | 1.3 | 1.1 | 1.1 | 1.1 | 1.1 | 1.3 | 3.0 | 1.0 | 1.2 | 1.1 | |
|  | 0.8 | 1.0 | 1.1 | 1.1 | 1.1 | 1.0 | 0.9 | 1.5 | 0.9 | 0.9 | |
| ] | 2.3 | [2.2] | [2.0] | [1.8] | [1.9] | 1.8 | 1.7 | 1.5 | .. | .. | |
|  | 1.8 | 1.3 | 1.1 | 1.1 | 1.0 | 1.0 | 2.2 | 1.2 | 1.5 | .. | |
|  | 0.4 | 0.5 | 0.5 | 0.5 | 0.5 | 0.5 | 0.4 | 0.4 | 0.4 | .. | |
|  | 0.7 | 0.7 | 0.7 | 0.7 | 0.7 | 0.7 | 0.7 | 0.6 | 0.6 | 0.7 | |
|  | 1.7 | 1.4 | 1.3 | 1.4 | 1.5 | 1.4 | 1.4 | 1.4 | .. | .. | |
|  | 0.1 | 0.1 | 0.1 | 0.1 | 0.1 | 0.1 | 0.1 | 0.2 | 0.2 | 0.2 | |
|  | 0.2 | 0.4 | 0.3 | 0.3 | 0.3 | 0.3 | .. | .. | .. | .. | |

### Table 8C.29. South America: constant price figures

| | 1952 | 1953 | 1954 | 1955 | 1956 | 1957 | 1958 | 1959 | 1960 | 1961 | 1962 | 1963 |
|---|---|---|---|---|---|---|---|---|---|---|---|---|
| Argentina | 364.8 | 398.2 | 428.9 | 341.3 | 428.8 | 450.3 | 467.3 | 368.5 | 406.3 | 396.7 | 380.3 | 382 |
| Bolivia | .. | 8.2 | .. | 5.6 | 4.1 | 4.7 | [5.1] | [5.6] | [7.1] | 7.7 | 7.7 | 9 |
| Brazil | 409 | 408 | 394 | 450 | 545 | 603 | 619 | 500 | 462 | 417 | 449 | 44( |
| Chile | 80.1 | 125.0 | 79.7 | 119.2 | 114.0 | 122.3 | 114.2 | 91.9 | 98.4 | 100.6 | 101.3 | 91 |
| Colombia | 53.7 | 71.3 | 84.1 | 83.2 | 81.1 | 72.6 | 66.7 | 54.9 | 62.1 | 73.7 | 116.3 | 128 |
| Ecuador | 8.9 | 14.2 | 19.0 | 22.0 | 23.4 | 22.4 | 21.6 | 18.9 | 25.4 | 24.4 | 23.2 | 20 |
| Guyana | .. | .. | .. | .. | .. | .. | .. | .. | .. | .. | .. | . |
| Paraguay | .. | .. | .. | .. | .. | .. | .. | .. | .. | 5.8 | 5.7 | [7 |
| Peru | 59.9 | 59.3 | 55.8 | 59.6 | 97.7 | 88.0 | 99.4 | 88.2 | 86.3 | [101.8] | [101.1] | 13 |
| Uruguay | .. | .. | .. | .. | .. | .. | .. | .. | .. | 23.3 | 24.8 | 34 |
| Venezuela | 57.5 | 57.5 | 73.9 | 92.5 | 103.4 | 138.8 | 159.2 | 154.3 | 139.7 | 134.1 | 128.5 | 153 |
| **Total South America** | [1 060.0] | [1 165.0] | [1 165.0] | [1 200.0] | [1 425.0] | [1 530.0] | [1 585.0] | [1 315.0] | [1 320.0] | 1 285.1 | 1 337.9 | 1 40( |

[a] 1970.

### Table 8C.30. South America: current price figures

| | Currency | 1952 | 1953 | 1954 | 1955 | 1956 | 1957 | 1958 | 1959 | 1960 | 1961 |
|---|---|---|---|---|---|---|---|---|---|---|---|
| Argentina | mn new pesos | 33.2 | 37.8 | 42.5 | 38.1 | 54.2 | 71.2 | 98.3 | 171 | 236 | 26: |
| Bolivia | mn pesos | .. | 1.7 | .. | 4.7 | 9.7 | 23.9 | [26.4] | [35.1] | [48.9] | 5' |
| Brazil | mn cruzeiros | 9.3 | 11.3 | 13.0 | 17.8 | 26.2 | 34.6 | 40.8 | 43.9 | 69.6 | 5< |
| Chile | mn escudos | 6.0 | 11.7 | 13.2 | 34.3 | 51.7 | 73.1 | 82.2 | 91.1 | 109 | 11' |
| Colombia | mn pesos | 150 | 214 | 275 | 272 | 283 | 289 | 306 | 272 | 317 | 41( |
| Ecuador | mn sucres | 113 | 181 | 250 | 295 | 298 | 289 | 282 | 247 | 336 | 33( |
| Guyana | mn dollars | .. | .. | .. | .. | .. | .. | .. | .. | .. | . |
| Paraguay | mn guaranis | .. | .. | .. | .. | .. | .. | .. | .. | .. | 63( |
| Peru | mn soles | 522 | 562 | 551 | 618 | 1 066 | 1 039 | 1 265 | 1 259 | 1 340 | [1 68 |
| Uruguay | mn pesos | .. | .. | .. | .. | .. | .. | .. | .. | .. | 18' |
| Venezuela | mn bolivares | 212 | 210 | 270 | 338 | 381 | 496 | 601 | 607 | 540 | 53 |

### Table 8C.31. South America: military expenditure as a percentage of gross domestic product

| | 1952 | 1953 | 1954 | 1955 | 1956 | 1957 | 1958 | 1959 | 1960 | 1961 |
|---|---|---|---|---|---|---|---|---|---|---|
| Argentina | 3.0 | 2.9 | 2.9 | 2.2 | 2.5 | 2.6 | 2.5 | 2.3 | 2.3 | 2.2 |
| Bolivia | .. | 0.5 | .. | 0.3 | 0.4 | 0.8 | [0.8] | [0.9] | [1.1] | 1.2 |
| Brazil | 2.3 | 2.4 | 2.2 | 2.3 | 2.6 | 2.9 | 2.8 | 2.2 | 2.0 | 1.7 |
| Chile | 2.3 | 3.3 | 2.2 | 3.3 | 3.1 | 3.2 | 2.7 | 2.2 | 2.6 | 2.5 |
| Colombia | 1.6 | 2.0 | 2.2 | 2.1 | 1.9 | 1.6 | 1.5 | 1.2 | 1.2 | 1.3 |
| Ecuador | 1.3 | 1.9 | 2.4 | 2.7 | 2.6 | 2.4 | 2.3 | 1.9 | 2.4 | 2.2 |
| Guyana | .. | .. | .. | .. | .. | .. | .. | .. | .. | .. |
| Paraguay | .. | .. | .. | .. | .. | .. | .. | .. | .. | 1.6 |
| Peru | 2.5 | 2.5 | 2.1 | 2.1 | 3.2 | 2.9 | 3.1 | 2.7 | 2.4 | [2.6] |
| Uruguay | .. | .. | .. | .. | .. | .. | .. | .. | .. | 1.1 |
| Venezuela | 1.5 | 1.4 | 1.6 | 1.9 | 1.9 | 2.1 | 2.4 | 2.4 | 2.1 | 2.0 |

*US $mn, at 1970 prices and 1970 exchange rates (Final column, X, at current prices and exchange rates)*

| | 1965 | 1966 | 1967 | 1968 | 1969 | 1970 | 1971 | 1972 | 1973 | 1972X |
|---|---|---|---|---|---|---|---|---|---|---|
| 1.7 | 391.7 | 441.4 | 480.2 | 406.2 | 431.2 | 449.8 | 452.5 | 488.5 | 340.8 | *834* |
| 7.0 | 20.0 | 18.4 | 16.9 | 15.0 | 16.5 | 17.8 | 16.5 | 23.4 | [18.7] | *23.2* |
| 2 | 697 | 595 | 820 | 820 | 904 | 853 | 978 | 985 | [937] | *1 094* |
| 5.4 | 98.0 | 120.7 | 128.2 | 136.2 | 143.0 | 176.7 | 226.5 | 203.4 | (70.5) | *281* |
| 1.0 | 133.0 | 133.9 | 137.2 | 180.4 | 168.0 | 202.7 | 235.9 | 116.7 | (89.8) | *122.4* |
| 3.7 | 26.6 | 24.7 | 26.2 | 29.1 | 37.0 | 37.9 | 33.8 | [41.4] | (46.3) | *[39.2]* |
| . | 0.5 | 1.1† | 2.3 | 2.1 | 2.4 | 3.3 | .. | .. | .. | *3.3ª* |
| 7.6] | [8.2] | 9.3 | 9.9 | 10.4 | 11.1 | 12.0 | 13.1 | 15.1 | (14.4) | *17.3* |
| 6.1 | 135.4 | 134.7 | 171.4 | 171.8 | 183.5 | 192.8 | 207.6 | 230.0 | (247.7) | *263* |
| 3.4 | 37.5 | 35.9 | 41.9 | 31.5 | 43.3 | 44.0 | 38.7 | 80.4 | .. | *75.4* |
| 8.9 | 178.5 | 184.9 | 209.2 | 208.5 | 197.6 | 198.0 | 239.2 | 270.5 | 279.8 | *294* |
| **7.8** | **1 726.4** | **1 700.0** | **2 043.4** | **2 011.2** | **2 137.6** | **2 188.0** | **[2 445.0]** | **[2 460.0]** | **[2 130.0]** | **[3 046.8]** |

*Local currency, current prices*

| | 1963 | 1964 | 1965 | 1966 | 1967 | 1968 | 1969 | 1970 | 1971 | 1972 | 1973 |
|---|---|---|---|---|---|---|---|---|---|---|---|
| 25 | 402 | 452 | 647 | 962 | 1 354 | 1 329 | 1 521 | 1 799 | (2 438) | 4 170 | 4 434 |
| 61 | 75 | 147 | 178 | 175 | 179 | 168 | 188 | 212 | 203 | 307 | 441 |
| 15 | 195 | 389 | 924 | 1 157 | 2 066 | 2 574 | 3 492 | 3 926 | 5 446 | 6 517 | [7 170] |
| 35 | 179 | 245 | 358 | 542 | 681 | 917 | 1 257 | 2 054 | 3 163 | 5 053 | 8 000 |
| 64 | 965 | 1 072 | 1 218 | 1 467 | 1 627 | 2 263 | 2 321 | 2 998 | 3 789 | 2 148 | 2 036 |
| 29 | 307 | 370 | 428 | 413 | 456 | 527 | 714 | 767 | 742 | [980] | 1 221 |
| .. | .. | .. | 0.8 | 1.9 | 4.3 | 4.1 | 4.6 | 6.5 | .. | .. | .. |
| 30 | [815] | [870] | [975] | 1 132 | 1 227 | 1 292 | 1 414 | 1 514 | 1 727 | 2 176 | 2 336 |
| 85] | 2 614 | 2 824 | 3 286 | 3 575 | 4 994 | 5 957 | 6 769 | 7 463 | 8 587 | 10 193 | (12 000) |
| 21 | 365 | 509 | 900 | 1 500 | 3 300 | 5 600 | 9 300 | 11 000 | 11 998 | 43 964 | .. |
| 09 | 613 | 650 | 742 | 782 | 885 | 894 | 867 | 891 | 1 113 | 1 294 | 1 400 |

*Per cent*

| | 1963 | 1964 | 1965 | 1966 | 1967 | 1968 | 1969 | 1970 | 1971 | 1972 |
|---|---|---|---|---|---|---|---|---|---|---|
| 2 | 2.2 | 1.8 | 1.8 | 2.1 | 2.3 | 1.9 | 1.9 | 1.9 | .. | .. |
| 1 | 1.3 | 2.3 | 2.5 | 2.2 | 2.0 | 1.6 | 1.7 | 1.8 | 1.5 | .. |
| 7 | 1.6 | 1.7 | 2.5 | 2.2 | 2.9 | 2.6 | 2.6 | 2.2 | 2.3 | 2.2 |
| 4 | 2.1 | 1.9 | 2.0 | 2.2 | 2.1 | 2.1 | 1.9 | 2.2 | 2.6 | .. |
| 9 | 2.2 | 2.0 | 2.0 | 2.0 | 2.0 | 2.3 | 2.1 | 2.3 | .. | .. |
| 0 | 1.8 | 1.9 | 2.1 | 1.8 | 1.8 | 1.9 | 2.3 | 2.1 | 1.7 | [1.9] |
| | .. | .. | 0.2 | 0.5 | 1.0 | 0.9 | 0.9 | 1.2 | .. | .. |
| 4 | [1.7] | [1.7] | [1.7] | 1.9 | 2.0 | 2.0 | 2.0 | 2.0 | 2.1 | 2.2 |
| 4] | 3.2 | 2.9 | 2.9 | 2.6 | 3.2 | 3.2 | 3.3 | 3.2 | 3.3 | .. |
| 2 | 1.6 | 1.6 | 1.7 | 1.5 | 2.0 | 1.5 | 1.9 | 1.8 | 1.6 | 3.3 |
| 7 | 1.9 | 1.8 | 2.0 | 2.0 | 2.1 | 2.1 | 2.0 | 1.9 | 2.1 | .. |

# Appendix 8D

*Register of indigenously designed weapons in development or production, 1973*

For sources and methods, see appendix 8A, pp. 159–71.

## Abbreviations and conventions

.. = Information not available
( ) = Uncertain data. All future dates (post 31 December 1973) are in brackets
+ = At least the figure given and probably more
\* = Number produced by 1973
− = Nil or not applicable
[ ] = Standardized rather than official descriptions
No. = Total number planned or on order

*Powerplant*
*for aircraft*
J = Jet
T = Turboprop (fixed wing), turboshaft (helicopter)
P = Piston

*for missiles*
S = Solid propellant
L = Liquid propellant
SL = Storable liquid
J = Jet

*for ships*
N = Nuclear
GT = Gas turbine
ST = Steam turbine

*Aircraft descriptions*
VTOL = Vertical take-off and landing
STOL = Short take-off and landing
VSTOL = Vertical or short take-off and landing
VG = Variable geometry
recce = Reconnaissance
hel. = Helicopter
transp. = Transport
A/S or ASW = Antisubmarine warfare
AEW = Airborne early warning
ECM = Electronic countermeasures
com.&con. = Command and control
car.-b. = Aircraft-carrier based
car./l.-b. = Aircraft-carrier based or land-based

*Missile launch platform and target descriptions*
fixed = Fixed land-based
towed = Towed ground-based
SP = Self-propelled ground-based
mobile = Mobile ground-based
portable = Portable (man-carried)
miss. = Missile
air. = Fixed-wing aircraft
hel. = Helicopter
sub. = Submarine

*Missile warheads*
N = Nuclear
kt = Kiloton (1000 tons of TNT equivalent)
mt = Megaton (1 000 000 tons of TNT equivalent)
HE = High explosive

*Ship armament*
S-A = Ship-to-air missile
S-S = Ship-to-ship missile
S-Sub. = Ship-to-submarine missile
Sub.-S = Submarine-to-ship or -surface missile
Sub.-Sub. = Submarine-to-submarine missile
TT = Torpedo tubes
A/STT = Antisubmarine torpedo tubes

*Foreign-designed components*
P = Powerplant
A = Armament
E = Electronic equipment
E-d = Computer/data processing equipment
E-f = Fire-control system (for armaments)
E-g = Guidance system (for missiles)
E-n = Navigation equipment
E-r = Radar
E-s = Sonar

# Part 1. Aircraft

| Country | Designation, description | Power-plant | Weight, kg | Speed, km/hr or Mach no. | Design begun | Proto-type flight | In pro-duction | No.: domestic/export or total | R&D cost, $ mn | Unit price, $ mn | Foreign-designed Powerplant, Electronics or Armaments |
|---|---|---|---|---|---|---|---|---|---|---|---|
| **NATO** | | | | | | | | | | | |
| Canada | CX-84  VSTOL light strike/ASW | T | 7 200 | 570 | .. | 1965 | .. | ./.. | | .. | P (USA) |
| | Buffalo  STOL transport | T | 18 600 | 815 | 1962 | 1964 | 1966 | .. | | (2) | P (USA) |
| | Caribou  STOL transport | P | 12 925 | 350 | 1956 | 1958 | 1962 | (307) | | (0.8) | P (USA) |
| | Twin Otter  STOL utility | T | 5 670 | 340 | 1964 | 1965 | (1965) | (340) | | 0.6 | – |
| France | G8  VG fighter/strike | J | 20 000 | M 2.5 | .. | 1971 | no | .. | | .. | .. |
| | Avion de Combat Futur  fighter/strike | J | (24 000) | (M 2.5) | (1972) | (1976) | (1979) | .. | (1 000) | (12) | .. |
| | F1  fighter/strike | J | 14 900 | M 2.2 | 1964 | 1966 | 1972 | 105/69 | | 5[a] | .. |
| | F1 International  fighter/strike | J | 15 200 | M 2.5 | .. | (1974) | (1976) | .. | | .. | E-r (UK) |
| | Mirage III  fighter/strike | J | 13 500 | M 2.2 | .. | 1956 | 1958 | (1 250) | | 3 | .. |
| | Mirage 5  strike/fighter | J | 13 500 | M 2.2 | .. | 1967 | (1969) | –/(350) | | .. | .. |
| | Super Etendard  strike/fighter car.-b. | J | 11 500 | M 1.0 | .. | (1975) | (1976) | 100/– | | 3.4 | E-n (USA) |
| | Atlantic  maritime patrol | T | 43 500 | 660 | 1958 | 1961 | 1965 | 40/47 | | 7.5 | P (UK) Co-prod. (Bel. FRG It. Neth. UK) |
| | Puma  medium transport helicopter | T | 6 700 | 270 | .. | 1965 | 1968 | 130/120 | | 1.1 | Co-prod. (UK) |
| | Alouette 316C  utility helicopter | T | 2 250 | 220 | .. | .. | 1971 | .. | | 0.1 | – |
| | SA360  utility helicopter | T | 2 730 | 310 | .. | 1973 | (1975) | .. | | .. | .. |
| | Gazelle  light utility helicopter | T | 1 700 | 260 | 1968 | 1967 | 1971 | (342) | | (0.2) | Co-prod. (UK) |
| | Lama  light utility helicopter | T | 1 750 | 120 | 1964 | .. | (1970) | –/(65) | | .. | .. |
| | VAK 191B  VTOL light strike | J | 9 000 | .. | (1969) | 1971 | no | .. | (180) | .. | P (UK) |
| | Do 231M  VTOL medium transport | J | 66 900 | 900 | (1973) | .. | no | .. | (30) | .. | P (UK) |
| | Do 24/72  rescue flying boat | T | 18 600 | (400) | .. | .. | .. | .. | | .. | P (USA) |
| | Do 28D-2  STOL utility | P | 3 650 | 320 | 1972 | 1966 | 1968 | 145/14 | | .. | P (USA) |
| | Bo 115  attack helicopter | T | .. | .. | 1972 | .. | no | .. | | .. | .. |
| | Bo 105  utility helicopter | T | 2 100 | 250 | 1962 | 1967 | 1971 | (150/–) | (25) | 0.3 | P (USA) |
| | Do 132  light utility helicopter | T | 1 650 | 230 | .. | (1972) | .. | ./.. | | .. | P (Can.) |
| **International:** | | | | | | | | | | | |
| FRG (42.5%) UK (42.5%) It. (15%) | Panavia 200 MRCA  fighter/strike/recce | J | .. | M 2.0+ | 1969 | (1974) | (1977) | 807 | (1 000) | 8.0 | E-r (USA) |

[a] Including spares but excluding R&D.

| Country | Designation, description | Power-plant | Weight, kg | Speed, km/hr or Mach no. | Design begun | Proto-type flight | In production | No.: domestic/export or total | R&D cost, $ mn | Unit price, $ mn | Foreign-designed Powerplant, Electronics or Armaments |
|---|---|---|---|---|---|---|---|---|---|---|---|
| Fr. (50%) UK (50%) | | | | | | | | | | | |
| | *Jaguar* strike/jet trainer | J | 13 500 | M 1.7 | 1964 | 1969 | 1972 | 400 | (380) | 3.7 | .. |
| USA (67%) UK (33%) | | | | | | | | | | | |
| | *AV-16A* (US)/*Super Harrier*(UK) VSTOL strike | J | .. | (M 1.0+) | 1973 | .. | no | .. | (800) | 4.5 | .. |
| Fr. (50%) FRG (50%) | | | | | | | | | | | |
| | *Alpha* jet trainer/light strike | J | 7 000 | 1 000 | 1969 | 1973 | 1976 | 390/33 | .. | 1.1 | P (USA) |
| Italy | *G91Y* light fighter/strike | J | 8 700 | 1 050 | 1965 | 1966 | 1971 | 75/– | .. | (1.6) | P (UK It.) |
| | *MB326* light strike/jet trainer | J | | | | | | | | | P (UK) |
| | *326K* | | 5 440 | 890 | .. | 1970 | (1972) | –/.. | .. | 0.4 | |
| | *326GB* | | 5 215 | 800 | .. | 1967 | yes | 43/– | | | |
| FR Germany | *G222* transport | T | 26 000 | 530 | .. | 1970 | (1974) | 44/– | .. | 5 | P (USA) |
| | *P166S* search/surveillance | P | 3 950 | 400 | .. | 1968 | (1971) | 20/– | | | P (USA) |
| | *S210M* light utility | P | 1 850 | 340 | .. | 1970 | yes | .. | | | P (USA) |
| | *SM1019* light utility | P | 1 270 | 250 | 1969 | 1969 | 1972 | 100/– | | | P (USA) |
| | *SF 260M* light utility | P | 1 360 | 340 | .. | 1969 | yes | –/116 | | | P (USA) |
| | *AM-3C* light utility | P | 1 700 | 280 | .. | 1967 | (1970) | 40/60 | | | P (USA) |
| | *S 208M* light utility | P | 1 350 | 300 | .. | 1967 | 1968 | 44/– | | | P (USA) |
| | *A129* attack helicopter | T | 2 600 | 290 | (1972) | .. | no | .. | | | P (USA) |
| | *A106* light ASW helicopter | T | 1 400 | 125 | 1965 | .. | (1972) | (24)/– | | | P (Fr.) |
| | *A109* utility helicopter | T | 2 300 | 275 | 1969 | 1971 | yes | .. | | | P (USA) |
| | *SV-20A* utility helicopter | T | 4 535 | 325 | | | b | .. | | (1) | P (Can.) |
| Netherlands | *F.27Mk400M* transport | T | 20 410 | 485 | .. | 1955 | 1958 | 40 | .. | .. | P (UK) |
| Portugal | .. STOL light transport | T | 6 000 | (420) | (1972) | .. | no | .. | .. | .. | P (Fr.) |
| UK | *Buccaneer S.Mk2* strike/recce | J | 28 120 | 1 040 | .. | 1963 | 1964 | 126/16 | .. | (8.0) | – |
| | *Harrier* strike/fighter | J | 11 340 | (M 1.1) | (1959) | 1966 | 1968 | 105/118 | .. | (2.5) | – |
| | .. carrier-based version | | | | (1972) | .. | no | (25)/.. | (85) | 3.0 | – |
| | *Strikemaster* light strike | J | 5 215 | 835 | 1964 | 1967 | yes | –/115 | .. | 0.6 | – |
| | *Nimrod* maritime patrol | J | 87 100 | 925 | 1973 | 1967 | 1968 | 49/– | .. | 10.2^c | – |
| | .. airborne early warning | | | | 1972 | .. | no | .. | (60) | .. | |
| | *Mainlander* STOL transport | | 28 400 | .. | 1972 | .. | no | .. | | | – |
| | *Andover* transport | T | 20 180 | 450 | 1959 | 1960 | 1961 | 31/31 | .. | .. | P (USA) |
| | *Skyvan* STOL light transport | T | 6 575 | 326 | .. | 1970 | 1970 | –/43 | .. | (0.8) | – |
| | *Hawk* jet trainer/light strike | J | (7 080) | M 0.9 | (1971) | (1974) | (1976) | 175/– | (125) | (1.2) | P (UK Fr.) |

| | | Aircraft / version | Weight | Speed | Yr | Yr | Yr | Prod. (home/exp.) | Number | Cost | Notes |
|---|---|---|---|---|---|---|---|---|---|---|---|
| | P | *Defender* utility/light strike | 3 150 | 290 | : | (1971) | 1972 | –/– | : | 0.3 | P (Fr.) |
| | T | *Jetstream 200* trainer | 5 670 | 460 | 1968 | (1970) | 1972 | 26/– | : | : | P (USA) |
| | P | *Bulldog* primary trainer | 1 065 | 240 | (1968) | 1969 | (1971) | 132/124 | (78) | (1.2) | Co-prod. (Fr.) |
| | T | *Lynx* multi-purpose helicopter | 4 130 | 295 | 1970 | 1971 | (1974) | 60/40 | : | : | – |
| USA | J | *B-1* strategic bomber | 176 815 | M 2.2 | 1972 | (1974) | (1976) | 241/– | >2 000 | 45.2 | – |
| | J | *F-111* fighter-bomber | 40 816 | M 2.5 | 1965 | : | : | 106/– | : | : | – |
| | | F-111F latest production version | | | | | yes | | | | – |
| | | EF-111A ECM version | | | | | no | | | | – |
| | J | *F-15A Eagle* fighter | 24 490 | M 2.3 | : | 1972 | 1973 | 749/50 | 1 600 | 7 | – |
| | | TF-15A 2-seat trainer | | | | | 1973 | [e] | | | – |
| | J | *F-14A Tomcat* fighter/strike car.-b. | 28 570 | M 2+ | 1970 | 1970 | 1971 | 303/30 | 1 100 | 11.4 | – |
| | J | *F-14B* with advanced engine | | M 2+ | | 1973 | no | | | | – |
| | J | *XFV-12A* VTOL light fighter car.-b. | 8 845 | M 2 | 1973 | (1974) | no | | | 3[d] | – |
| | J | *F-4 Phantom II* fighter-strike | 25 397 | M 2.2 | : | : | 1966 | 660/– | : | : | – |
| | | F-4J carrier-based version | | : | | | 1973 | –/175 | | | – |
| | | F-4F export version | | M 2.2 | | | yes | –/102 | | | – |
| | | RF-4E recce version | 26 304 | M 2.2 | 1972 | : | 1967 | : | : | : | – |
| | | F-4E | 26 304 | M 2+ | : | (1974) | no | 753/. | | | – |
| | J | *Lightweight fighter* | | M 1.6 | | | (1974) | | | | – |
| | | YF-17 competitive prototype | 9 525 | | 1972 | 1972 | 1972 | 20/307 | | : | – |
| | | YF-16 competitive prototype | 7 938 | M 1.6 | : | 1972 | 1973 | –/124 | | : | – |
| | J | *F-5E/F Tiger II* light fighter | 10 922 | M 1.6 | 1955 | 1959 | 1962 | –/737 | | 1.8 | – |
| | | F-5E first production version | | | | 1972 | 1972 | | 60 | | – |
| | | F-5F 2-seat version | | | | | (1975) | | >300 | | – |
| | J | *F-5A Freedom Fighter* light fighter | 9 379 | 740 | : | : | 1968 | 729/– | | 0.6 | – |
| | J | *A-10A* strike | 20 206 | | : | 1972 | 1968 | | | 1.5[f] | – |
| | J | *A-7 Corsair II* strike | 19 050 | M 1[g] | 1966 | 1968 | 1968 | | | 3.5 | – |
| | | A-7E carrier-based version | | | | 1968 | 1968 | 706/– | | | P (UK) |
| | | A-7D close air support | | | | 1968 | 1968 | 645/– | | | P (UK) |
| | J | *A-6 Intruder* strike car./land-based | 27 397 | M 1.1 | : | 1970 | 1970 | | | 6.0 | – |
| | | A-6E latest production version | 26 576 | M 1.1 | 1967 | 1968 | 1969 | 192/– | | | – |
| | | EA-6B ECM version | | | | | 1972 | 64/– | | | – |
| | J | *A-4 Skyhawk* strike car./land-based | 11 100 | | : | 1972 | 1972 | | | | – |
| | | A-4N improved export version | | M 1 | | 1970 | 1970 | –/. | | | – |
| | | A-4M latest production version | | | 1967 | 1967 | (1968) | 141/– | | | – |
| | J | *A-37B Dragonfly* light strike | 6 350 | 843 | 1968 | 1973 | 1973 | 453 | | | – |
| | T | *OY-10E Bronco* light strike | 6 563 | 452 | : | : | 1973 | | | | – |
| | T | *P-3 Orion* ASW patrol | 64 410 | 761 | 1968 | : | 1968 | : | | | – |
| | | P-3F export 3C, simpler electronics | | | | | 1973 | –/4 | | | – |
| | | P-3C latest production version | | | | 1968 | 1968 | 202/– | | | – |

[b] Project abandoned late 1973.
[c] Including R&D.
[d] Design price.
[e] Included in total for F-15A.
[f] 1970 prices.
[g] Level flight.

| Country | Designation, description | Power-plant | Weight, kg | Speed, km/hr or Mach no. | Design begun | Proto-type flight | In production | No.: domestic/export or total | R&D cost, $ mn | Unit price, $ mn | Foreign-designed Powerplant, Electronics or Armaments |
|---|---|---|---|---|---|---|---|---|---|---|---|
| | S-3A Viking ASW carrier-based | J | 23 827 | 880 | 1969 | 1972 | 1972 | 186/– | .. | .. | – |
| | E-4A AABNCP-Advanced Airborne National Command Post com.&con. | J | .. | .. | .. | 1973 | .. | 6/– | .. | .. | – |
| | E-3A AWACS-Airborne Warning and Control System AEW/com.&con. | J | 147 392 | 926 | .. | 1972 | (1975) | 46/– | .. | .. | – |
| | E-2C Hawkeye AEW carrier-based | T | 23 391 | 602 | 1972 | 1971 | 1971 | 34/– | .. | .. | – |
| | U-2 EP-X reconnaissance | J | 1 733 | 795 | 1972 | 1973 | .. | .. | .. | .. | – |
| | C-5A Galaxy heavy transport | J | 346 770 | 1 018 | 1963 | 1968 | 1968 | 81/– | .. | 7.8[g] | – |
| | AMST-Advanced Medium STOL Transport | | | | 1972 | (1975) | (1977) | .. | .. | .. | – |
| | YC-15 competitive prototype | J | 86 407 | 805 | | | 1973 | 16/– | .. | .. | – |
| | YC-14 competitive prototype | T | 72 570 | .. | | | 1972 | 5/– | .. | .. | – |
| | C-130 Hercules medium transport | T | 79 380 | 618 | | | | 10/– | .. | .. | – |
| | KC-130R tanker | | | | | .. | 1973 | | .. | .. | |
| | LC-130R wheel-ski version | | | | | .. | 1972 | | .. | .. | |
| | EC-130Q airborne comm. relay | | | | | .. | | | .. | 10.6 | |
| | C-130H latest standard version | | | | | .. | yes | 78[a]/20 | .. | 4.6 | |
| | C-9B Skytrain II medium transport | J | 49 887 | 926 | | .. | 1971 | 33/– | .. | .. | |
| | CT-39 Sabreliner light transport | J | 8 498 | 906 | | .. | 1971 | 103/– | .. | .. | |
| | T-43A navigation trainer | J | 52 608 | 926 | | 1973 | 1973 | 19/– | .. | .. | |
| | T-37C basic jet trainer | J | 3 632 | 578 | | .. | no | –/734[j] | .. | .. | |
| | Beechcraft Baron B55 light utility | P | 2 313 | 380 | | 1960 | 1965 | –/12 | .. | .. | |
| | T-41D primary trainer | P | 907 | 221 | | .. | .. | –/7 | .. | .. | |
| | T-2C/D Buckeye jet trainer car./l.-b. | J | 5 977 | 840 | | 1968 | 1968 | 243/12 | .. | <.5 | |
| | AAH-Advanced Attack Helicopter | T | | .. | 1971 | (1975) | (1978) | .. | .. | .. | |
| | AH-1 Cobra attack helicopter | T | | .. | | .. | .. | .. | .. | .. | |
| | AH-1Q Cobra/Tow | | 4 309 | 352 | .. | 1973 | 1974 | 21/–[k] | .. | .. | |
| | AH-1J Sea Cobra | T | 4 535 | 333 | | .. | 1969 | 69/202 | .. | .. | |
| | XCH-62 HLH-Heavy Lift Helicopter | | 67 135 | .. | 1971 | (1975) | no | .. | .. | .. | |
| | UTTAS-Utility Tactical Transport Aircraft System medium transp. hel. | | | | | (1974) | no | .. | .. | .. | |
| | YUH-61A competitive prototype | T | 7 189 | .. | | .. | .. | .. | .. | .. | |
| | YUH-60A competitive prototype | .. | .. | .. | | .. | .. | .. | .. | .. | |
| | OH-58A Kiowa light utility helicopter | T | 1 360 | 222 | 1965 | 1968 | 1968 | 2 200/– | 100 | .. | |
| | COH-58A export version | | | | | | | –/74 | .. | .. | |
| | H-53 multi-purpose helicopter | T | 10 000 | 254 | | | | 70/– | .. | .. | |
| | CH-53E Sea Stallion shipb. transp. | | 10 286 | 315 | 1971 | (1974) | (1976) | 6/– | .. | .5 | – |
| | UH-53D executive transport | | 10 286 | 315 | | .. | 1973 | .. | .. | 5 | – |
| | RH-53D mine countermeasures | | 10 286 | 315 | 1970 | 1972 | 1972 | 30/– | .. | .. | – |

| Country | Designation and description | Type | Unit price | Year | Max speed | First flight | In prod. | No. ordered | Comments |
|---|---|---|---|---|---|---|---|---|---|
| | CH-47C *Chinook* transport helicopter | T | 20 865 | .. | 306 | 1967 | 1968 | 51'/26 | — |
| | UH-1 *Iroquois* utility helicopter | T | .. | 1968 | .. | .. | .. | .. | — |
| | UH-1N latest production version | | 4 762 | .. | 203 | .. | 1969 | 236/– | — |
| | UH-1H AF version | | 4 309 | .. | 204 | .. | 1967 | 1 243/118 | — |
| | NH-1H rescue version | .. | 4 309 | (1971) | 204 | .. | yes | 40/– | .. |
| | LAMPS MkIII—*Light Airborne Multi-Purpose System* hel. | | .. | .. | .. | 1972 | no | .. | .. |
| | *Bell Model 301* tilt rotor research vehicle | .. | .. | 1973 | .. | 1973 | .. | 2/– | — |
| **Warsaw Treaty Organization** | | | | | | | | | |
| Czechoslovakia | A-159 light fighter | J | (3 800) | .. | (730) | .. | no | ./. | (Co-prod. (Pol.)) |
| | L-39Z light strike | J | 3 800 | .. | 750 | 1968 | (1973) | ./. | P (USSR) |
| | L-39 jet trainer | J | 3 540 | .. | 655 | 1968 | 1972 | (3 000) | P (USSR) |
| | L-29 jet trainer/light strike | J | .. | (1971) | .. | 1959 | 1963 | ./. | .. |
| | HC-4 utility helicopter | T | .. | .. | .. | .. | no | .. | .. |
| Poland | *Grot* light fighter | J | 3 800 | .. | 720 | 1960 | no | .. | (Co-prod. (Czech.)) |
| | *Iskara* jet trainer/light strike | J | .. | .. | .. | 1960 | 1962 | .. | .. |
| Romania | IS-23A STOL light utility | P | 2 100 | (1969) | 205 | 1967 | yes | .. | P (USSR) |
| | IS-24 light utility | P | 1 900 | .. | 220 | (1971) | yes | .. | P (USA) |
| USSR | TU-... "*Backfire*" bomber | J | 123 350 | (1969) | M 2.5 | (1971) | no | .. | — |
| | MiG-25 "*Foxbat*" fighter | J | 29 120 | .. | M 3.1 | 1965 | (1969) | .. | — |
| | .. recce version | | .. | .. | .. | .. | (1970) | .. | — |
| | .. interceptor version | | .. | .. | .. | .. | (1970) | .. | — |
| | MiG-23 "*Flogger*" fighter | J | 12 700 | .. | M 2.3 | 1967 | no | .. | — |
| | "*Fencer A*" fighter-bomber version | | .. | .. | .. | 1973 | yes | .. | — |
| | MiG-21MF "*Fishbed J, K*" light fighter | J | 9 400 | .. | M 2.1 | 1967 | (1968) | .. | — |
| | SU-15 "*Flagon A*" fighter | J | 16 000 | .. | M 2.5 | 1967 | (1969) | .. | — |
| | SU-20 "*Fitter B*" STOL strike | J | 13 500 | .. | M 1.6 | 1967 | no | .. | — |
| | Yak-36 "*Freehand*" VTOL strike | J | (60 000) | .. | <M 1 | 1967 | yes | .. | — |
| | Il-38 "*May*" ASW | T | .. | .. | 645 | 1967 | yes | .. | — |
| | An-22 "*Cock*" heavy transport | T | 250 000 | .. | 680 | 1965 | (1967) | .. | — |
| | Il-76 "*Candid*" medium transport | J | 157 000 | .. | 850 | 1971 | (1972) | .. | — |
| | .. "*Hind*" attack helicopter | .. | .. | .. | .. | 1973 | no | .. | — |
| | Mi-12 "*Homer*" heavy lift helicopter | T | 105 000 | .. | 260 | 1969 | (1972) | .. | — |
| | Ka-25 K "*Hormone*" ASW/transp.hel. | T | 7 300 | .. | 220 | 1961 | (1964) | .. | — |

a Orders from 1972 on.  
e Design price.  
j Initial order only.  
k FY 1975 order only.  
l Recent orders only (1973–74).

| Country | Designation, description | Power-plant | Weight, kg | Speed, km/hr or Mach no. | Design begun | Proto-type flight | In pro-duction | No.: do-mestic/ export or total | R&D cost, $ mn | Unit price, $ mn | Foreign-designed Powerplant, Electronics or Armaments |
|---|---|---|---|---|---|---|---|---|---|---|---|
| **Other Europe** | | | | | | | | | | | |
| Finland | *LEKO-70* trainer | P | 1 150 | 240 | (1973) | (1974) | no | .. | .. | .. | P (USA) |
| International: Yugoslavia, Romania | *Jurom* fighter | J | .. | .. | .. | (1972) | no | .. | .. | .. | P (UK) |
| Spain | *Super Saeta* light strike | J | 3 700 | 700 | .. | 1970 | yes | 25/10 | .. | .. | P (Fr.) |
| | *Casa-401* STOL transport | T | 24 500 | 470 | (1972) | .. | no | .. | .. | .. | P (USA) |
| | *Aviocar* STOL light transport | T | 6 300 | 400 | 1964 | 1970 | yes | 50/28 | .. | 0.65 | P (USA) |
| Sweden | *Project 80* fighter | J | .. | .. | 1973 | .. | (1984) | .. | .. | .. | .. |
| | *JA.37* fighter | J | .. | (M 2.0) | (1968) | .. | (1978) | 120/– | (212) | .. | P (USA Swe.) E-d E-n (USA) A (Switz.) |
| | *AJ.37* strike/reconnaissance | J | 16 000 | M 2.0 | 1962 | 1967 | 1970 | 175/– | .. | (4.3) | P (UK) |
| | *J35* fighter/attack | J | 15 000 | M 2.0 | 1955 | .. | yes | (550/63) | .. | (1.5) | P (USA) E-r (UK) |
| | *SAAB 105G* jet trainer/light strike | J | 6 500 | 960 | .. | 1972 | no | –/20 | .. | 1.6 | P (USA) |
| | *MFI-17* light utility | P | 1 100 | 260 | .. | 1969 | (1972) | ./.. | .. | .. | P (USA) |
| Switzerland | *C-3605* utility | T | 3 715 | 430 | 1967 | 1968 | (1970) | 23/– | .. | .. | P (USA) |
| | *Turbo Porter* STOL light utility | T | 2 200 | 260 | 1957 | 1959 | (1960) | ./.. | .. | .. | P (Can.) |
| | *Swiss Trainer* trainer | P | 720 | .. | (1965) | 1971 | yes | ./.. | .. | .. | P (USA) |
| Yugoslavia | *Jastreb* light strike | J | 4 665 | 820 | .. | 1970 | yes | 150/– | .. | (0.17) | P (UK) |
| | *Galeb 3* jet trainer/light strike | J | 4 810 | 800 | 1969 | 1970 | yes | 150/– | .. | .. | P (UK) E-n (UK) |
| | *Galeb 2* jet trainer/light strike | J | 4 180 | 810 | 1957 | 1961 | 1963 | ./.. | .. | (0.16) | P (UK) |
| **Middle East** | | | | | | | | | | | |
| Israel | *Barak* STOL fighter | J | .. | M 2.5 | 1968 | 1971 | (1975) | 24 | .. | .. | P (USA) |
| | *Arava* STOL light transport | T | 6 125 | 320 | 1966 | 1969 | 1972 | 70 | .. | .. | P (Can.) |
| | *Westwind* light transport | J | 9 390 | 870 | .. | .. | 1971 | 20 | .. | .. | P (USA) E (USA) |
| **South Asia** | | | | | | | | | | | |
| India | *HF-24 Marut* light fighter | J | 10 925 | M 1.0 | 1956 | 1961 | 1963 | 80 | .. | .. | P (UK) E (UK) A (Fr. UK) |
| | *HJT-16 Kiran* jet trainer/light strike | J | 4 200 | 690 | 1961 | 1964 | 1968 | (150) | .. | .. | P (UK) E (UK) |

**Far East**

| | | | | | | | | | | |
|---|---|---|---|---|---|---|---|---|---|---|
| **China**[a] | | | | | | | | | | |
| .. (*Tu-16*) medium bomber | J | 68 000 | 945 | .. | .. | 1970 | 110 | .. | .. | .. |
| *F-9* light fighter | J | 10 000 | M 2.0 | .. | .. | 1971 | 200 | .. | .. | .. |
| *F-6* (MiG-19) light fighter | J | 8 700 | M 1.3 | .. | .. | 1963 | 1 200/200 | .. | .. | .. |
| .. jet transport | T | .. | .. | 1972 | .. | (no) | .. | .. | .. | P (Can.) |
| "Whirlwind" (Mi-4) medium transp. hel. | P | 7 200 | 210 | .. | .. | 1959 | 400 | .. | .. | .. |
| .. helicopter | T | .. | .. | 1972 | .. | (no) | .. | .. | .. | P (Can.) |
| **Japan** | | | | | | | | | | |
| *FST-2* light strike | J | 9 450 | M 1.6 | 1967 | 1971 | (1974) | 68/- | .. | .. | P (Fr. UK) E-n (UK) |
| *T-2* jet trainer/light strike | | | | | | (1973) | (70)/- | | | P (Fr. +UK) |
| *PS-1* ASW flying boat | T | 43 000 | 545 | 1959 | 1967 | (1972) | 14/- | | (16) | P (USA) |
| *C-1* transport | J | 38 700 | 815 | 1966 | 1970 | 1973 | (23)/- | (50) | (14) | P (USA) |
| *MU-2 E/K* utility | T | 4 560 | 550 | 1967 | 1967 | (1969) | 24/.. | | (1.2) | P (USA) |
| *FA-300* trainer/light utility | P | .. | .. | 1970 | .. | yes | .. | | | P (USA) |
| *XMH* high speed research helicopter | T | 3 450 | 252 | 1968 | 1970 | no | .. | | | P (USA) |
| **Taiwan** | | | | | | | | | | |
| *XT-CH-IA Chunghsing* trainer | T | 4 175 | 410 | 1970 | 1973 | (no) | .. | .. | .. | P (USA) E (USA) |

**Oceania**

| | | | | | | | | | | |
|---|---|---|---|---|---|---|---|---|---|---|
| **Australia** | | | | | | | | | | |
| *Nomad* STOL utility | T | 3 630 | 320 | 1965 | 1971 | 1973 | (70) | .. | .. | P (USA) |
| .. STOL transport | .. | .. | .. | 1973 | .. | no | .. | .. | (0.3) | A (Switz. Belg.) |
| **New Zealand** | | | | | | | | | | |
| *CT 4* trainer | P | 1 066 | 295 | .. | 1972 | 1972 | ../(53) | .. | (0.01) | P (USA) |

**South America**

| | | | | | | | | | | |
|---|---|---|---|---|---|---|---|---|---|---|
| **Argentina** | | | | | | | | | | |
| *Pucara* light strike | T | 6 200 | 485 | 1966 | 1970 | 1973 | (55) | .. | .. | P (Fr.) E (UK) |
| **Brazil** | | | | | | | | | | |
| *JA50GII* light transport | T | 7 350 | 490 | 1960 | 1963 | 1966 | 38 | .. | .. | P (Fr.) E (UK) |
| *EMB-110 Bandeirante* utility | T | 5 100 | 420 | 1965 | 1968 | 1972 | (99) | 8 | .. | P (Can.) E (UK Fr.) |
| *EMB-120* utility | T | .. | 520 | 1972 | 1974 | no | .. | (6) | .. | P (Can.) E (UK Fr.) |
| *Neiva Bi* trainer | P | 2 400 | 350 | 1972 | .. | (1974) | .. | .. | .. | P (USA) |
| *Neiva T-25* trainer | P | 1 700 | 280 | 1963 | 1966 | 1971 | (150) | .. | .. | P (USA) |
| *Aerotec T-23* primary trainer | P | 840 | 185 | 1961 | 1965 | 1968 | (90) | .. | .. | P (USA) |

[a] Aircraft of Soviet origin are shown with the Soviet designation in brackets. They are listed as indigenous weapons because China has been almost totally isolated from Soviet technology since 1960.

## Part 2. Missiles

| Country | Designation, description | Power-plant | War-head, kg (if nuclear, kt/mt) | Range, km | Design begun | Proto-type flight | In pro-duction | No.: domestic/export or total | R&D cost, $ mn | Unit price, $ mn | Foreign-designed Powerplant or Electronics |
|---|---|---|---|---|---|---|---|---|---|---|---|
| **NATO** | | | | | | | | | | | |
| Canada | *Sea Sparrow*[a] ship-to-air./miss./ship | S | HE | : | : | : | (1972) | ./. | : | : | E-f (Neth.) |
| France | *S-3* fixed-to-fixed | S | (1 mt) | 3 500 | (1971) | : | no | (27)/– | : | : | |
| | *Pluton* mobile-to-fixed | S | 15 kt | 120 | : | (1969) | (1972) | 120/– | : | : | – |
| | *Harpon* mobile/air.-to-fixed/tank | S | (2.6) | 3 | : | : | yes | ./. | : | : | – |
| | *SS/AS-11* mobile/air.-to-fixed/tank | S | (2.6) | 3 | : | : | 1962 | (160 000) | : | : | – |
| | *SS/AS-12* mobile/air.-to-fixed/tank | S | 30 | 6 | : | : | yes | 1 800 | : | : | – |
| | *Entac* mobile-to-tank | S | 4 | 2 | : | : | (1957) | (140 000) | : | : | – |
| | *Acra* mobile-to-tank | b | HE | 3 | 1963 | : | no | ./. | : | : | |
| | *Crotale* mobile-to-air. | S | 15 | 13 | 1964 | 1965 | 1968 | (250)/(250) | : | (5) | |
| | *AS.20* air.-to-fixed/ship | S | 30 | 7 | : | : | yes | (8 000+) | : | : | |
| | *AS.30* air.-to-fixed/ship | S | 230 | 12 | : | : | yes | (8 500) | : | : | |
| | *AS.30L* air.-to-fixed/ship | S | 115 | : | : | : | (yes) | ./. | : | : | |
| | *R.530* air.-to-air. | S | 27 | 18 | 1958 | : | (1963) | (4 000) | : | : | |
| | *Super 530* air.-to-air. | S | HE | (40) | : | (1975) | 1977 | (1 000) | : | : | |
| | *R 550* air.-to-air. | S | HE | 10 | 1968 | 1972 | (1974) | ./. | : | : | |
| | *Masurca* ship-to-air. | S | HE | (40) | : | : | (1965) | ./. | : | : | E-d (USA) |
| | *Hirondelle* ship-to-air./miss. | : | HE | : | : | : | (1976) | ./. | : | : | |
| | *Exocet* ship-to-ship | S | (150) | (38) | (1967) | (1958) | 1972 | (650) | : | (0.27) | E-d (UK) |
| | *Malaphon* ship-to-sub. | S | : | 13 | 1956 | : | yes | ./– | : | : | |
| | *M-2* sub.-to-ship | S | (500 kt) | (3 000) | : | : | (1971) | ./– | : | : | |
| | *M-3* sub.-to-ship | S | (1 mt) | (3 000) | : | : | (1975) | ./– | : | : | |
| FR Germany | *Cobra* portable-to-tank | S | 2.5 | 2 | 1957 | : | 1960 | (150 000) | : | : | P (Switz.) |
| | *Mamba* portable-to-tank | S | 2.7 | 2 | : | 1972 | (1974) | ./. | : | : | |
| | *Jumbo* air.-to-fixed | S | HE | : | (1972) | : | no | ./. | : | : | P (Nor.) |
| | *Viper* air.-to-air. | S | HE | : | : | 1973 | (1975) | ./. | : | : | E-g (Fr.) |
| | *Kormoran* air.-to-ship | S | 250 | : | 1964 | (1969) | (1975) | 200/– | 30 | : | |
| **International:** | | | | | | | | | | | |
| FRG, France | *HOT* mobile/hel.-to-tank | S | 6 | 4 | 1964 | : | 1972 | ./. | (44) | : | |
| FRG, France | *Milan* portable-to-tank | S | 3 | 2 | 1963 | : | 1972 | 10 000 | : | : | |

| Country | Missile / version | | | | | | | | | |
|---|---|---|---|---|---|---|---|---|---|---|
| Belgium, UK | *Atlas* portable-to-tank | S | HE | .. | (1969) | no | ./. | .. | .. | .. |
| NATO consortium | *SAM 80* fixed-to-air. | .. | HE | .. | 1973 | no | ./. | .. | .. | .. |
| FRG, France | *Roland* mobile-to-air. | S | 6.5 | 6.2 | | | | | | |
| | *I* clear weather version | | | | 1964 | (1972) | ./. | (94) | 0.02^c | .. |
| | *II* all weather version | | | | .. | no | ./. | | | .. |
| France, UK | *Martel* air.-to-fixed | S | HE | (60) | 1963 | 1973 | ./. | .. | .. | .. |
| | *AS.37* anti-radar version | | | | (1968) | | ./. | | | |
| | *AJ.168* TV-guided version | | | | (1973) | | ./. | | | |
| Belgium, Denmark, Italy, Netherlands, Norway, USA | *Sea Sparrow system*^d ship-to-air./miss. | S | HE | .. | | no | ./. | .. | .. | − |
| France, Italy | *Otomat* ship/air.-to-ship | J | (200) | (80) | 1969 | 1973 | ./. | .. | 0.2^e | .. |
| Italy | *Spada system* fixed-to-air. | S | HE | (9) | (1974) | no | ./. | .. | .. | E-f (Switz.) |
| | *Indigo* mobile-to-air. | S | 21.4 | 2.3 | 1962 | (1972) | ./. | .. | .. | .. |
| | *Mosquito* portable-to-tank | S | 4 | (3) | .. | yes | ./. | .. | .. | .. |
| | *Sparviero* portable-to-tank | S | 4 | .. | (1972) | no | ./. | .. | .. | .. |
| | *Aspide* air./fixed-to-air. | S | (35) | 11 | 1969 | (1976) | ./. | .. | .. | .. |
| | *Airtos* air.-to-ship | S | 35 | 20 | (1969) | no | −/. | .. | .. | .. |
| | *Marte system*^f hel.-to-ship | .. | HE | .. | 1969 | (1973) | ./. | .. | .. | .. |
| | *Albatross system*^g ship-to-air./miss. | .. | HE | .. | 1966 | 1973 | ./. | .. | .. | .. |
| | *Sea Killer* ship-to-ship | | | | | | | | | |
| | *1* original production version | S | HE | (10) | 1963 | (1968) | ./. | .. | .. | .. |
| | *2* improved version | S | 70.4 | 25 | 1965 | (1972) | −/. | .. | 0.15^h | E-f (Switz.) |
| | *3* under development | S | 150 | (45) | (1972) | (1974) | ./. | .. | .. | .. |
| Norway | *Penguin* ship-to-ship | S | 120 | (28) | (1961) | 1969 | ./. | .. | 0.01^i | .. |
| UK | *Thunderbird 2* fixed-to-air. | S | HE | .. | 1956 | 1964 | ./. | .. | .. | .. |
| | *Swingfire* mobile-to-tank | S | HE | 4 | 1958 | (1968) | ./. | .. | .. | .. |
| | *Vigilant* portable-to-tank | S | 5.4 | 1.3 | 1956 (1957) | 1960 | (15 000) | (2.5) | .. | .. |
| | *Rapier* mobile-to-air. | S | HE | (6) | 1963 | 1967 | ./(1 600) | .. | .. | − |
| | *Tigercat* towed/fixed-to-air. | S | HE | (3.5) | .. | (1969) | ./. | .. | .. | .. |
| | *Blowpipe* portable-to-tank. | S | HE | .. | 1966 | (1973) | ./. | (25) | .. | .. |
| | *Hellcat* air.-to-mobile/ship | S | HE | (3.5) | .. | (1968) | ./. | .. | .. | .. |

^a With US Sparrow missile.
^b Gun-launched.
^c Cost per missile.
^d Referred to in the USA as "Improved point defense surface missile system".
^e With US Sparrow or Italian Aspide missile.
^f With Italian Sea Killer 1/2 missile.
^g With NATO Sea Sparrow or Italian Aspide missile.
^h Cost per missile.
^i Cost per missile.

| Country | Designation, description | Power-plant | War-head, kg (if nuclear, kt/mt) | Range, km | Design begun | Proto-type flight | In production | No.: domestic/export or total | R&D cost, $ mn | Unit price, $ mn | Foreign-designed Powerplant or Electronics |
|---|---|---|---|---|---|---|---|---|---|---|---|
| | *Red Top* air.-to-air. | S | 31 | (12) | 1957 | : | : | ./.– | : | : | : |
| | *Goshawk* air.-to-air. | S | HE | : | 1973 | (1974) | (1975) | ./.– | 50 | : | Cross licence (USA) |
| | *Mongoose* air.-to-air. | S | 10 | : | 1972 | : | : | ./.– | : | : | : |
| | *Skua* air.-to-ship | S | (35) | (15) | (1970) | : | : | ./.– | : | : | : |
| | *Seadart* ship-to-air. | S/L | HE | (30) | (1962) | (1965) | 1972 | ./.– | : | : | : |
| | *Seacat* ship-to-air. | S | HE | (3.5) | (1958) | : | (1962) | ./.– | : | (0.02)[j] | : |
| | *Sea Wolf* ship-to-miss./air./ship | S | (14) | : | (1967) | : | (1976) | ./.– | (68) | (0.04)[k] | : |
| | *SLAM—Submarine-Launched Airflight Missile*[l] sub./ship-to-air./ship | S | HE | : | 1968 | (1972) | : | ./.– | : | (0.6) | : |
| | *Swordfish* sub-to-ship | : | HE | : | (1972) | : | : | ./.– | : | : | : |
| USA | *LGM-30G Minuteman 3* MIRV fixed-to-fixed | S | 3 × 170 kt | 13 000 | : | 1968 | 1970 | 500–/–[m] | : | : | — |
| | *BGM-71A TOW—Tube-Launched Optically tracked, Wire-guided* fixed/hel.-to-tank | S | HE | 3 | 1962 | 1965 | 1968 | ./.– | : | : | — |
| | *Site Defense* fixed-to-miss. | : | N | : | 1971 | : | no | 0 | : | : | — |
| | *Safeguard system* fixed-to-miss. | | | | | | | | | | |
| | *LIM-49R Spartan* high altitude | S | N-mt | 185 | 1965 | 1968 | 1970 | ./.– | : | : | — |
| | *Sprint* low altitude | S | N-kt | 45 | 1963 | 1965 | 1970 | ./.– | : | : | — |
| | *MGM-52C Lance* SP/towed-to-fixed | SL | N/HE | 110 | 1962 | 1965 | 1971 | ./.– | : | : | — |
| | *MGM-31A Pershing IA"* mobile-to-fixed | S | N | : | 1957 | : | 1962 | ./.– | : | : | — |
| | *SAM-D—Surface-to-Air Missile Development* mobile-to-air. | S | N/HE | : | 1965 | 1970 | no | ./.– | : | : | — |
| | *MIM-23B Improved Hawk* mobile-to-air. | S | HE | 41 | : | 1971 | 1972 | ./.– | : | : | — |
| | *MIM-72A Chaparral*° mobile-to-air. | S | HE | : | 1965 | 1965 | 1966 | ./.– | : | : | — |
| | *FGM-77A Dragon* portable-to-tank | S | HE | 1 | 1964 | 1968 | 1971 | ./.– | : | : | — |
| | *XFIM-92A Stinger* portable-to-air. | S | 3 | 3 | (1970) | : | no | ./.– | : | : | — |
| | *AGM-69A SRAM—Short-Range Attack Missile* air.-to-fixed | S | 170 kt | 160 | 1963 | 1969 | 1971 | 1 500/–[p] | : | : | — |
| | *AGM-86 SCAD—Subsonic Cruise Armed Decoy* air.-to-fixed | : | N | (500– 1 000) | (1970) | : | [q] | 0 | : | : | : |
| | Guided unpowered bombs ("smart bombs") air.-to-fixed | : | : | : | (1972) | : | : | ./.– | : | : | : |
| | *Fat Albert* with larger warhead | – | HE | : | (1972) | : | no | ./.– | : | : | — |
| | *GW Mkl Walleye* original version | – | HE | : | : | : | 1966 | ./.– | : | : | — |

240

| Designation | Launch | Warhead | Range | | | | | | Cost |
|---|---|---|---|---|---|---|---|---|---|
| *Terminal Homing Flight Test Vehicle* (Hornet) air./fixed-to-fixed | S | HE | 4 | 1970 | 1970 | r | .. | | — |
| *AGM-78A Standard ARM-Anti-Radiation Missile* air.-to-(fixed) radar | S | HE | 25 | 1966 | 1967 | 1968 | ./. | .. | — |
| *AGM-45A Shrike* air.-to-(fixed) radar | S | HE | 16 | 1962 | | 1963 | .-. | .. | — |
| *AGM-65A Maverick* air.-to-fixed/tank | S | 59 | .. | 1966 | 1969 | 1971 | .-. | .. | — |
| *XAIM-97A[s] Seekbat* air.-to-air. | S | .. | .. | 1972 | .. | no | .-. | .. | — |
| *Agile* air.-to-air. | .. | .. | .. | 1968 | no | no | .-. | 300 | — |
| *AIM-54 Phoenix* air.-to-air./miss. | S | HE | 165 | 1962 | 1965 | 1970 | ./. | .. | — |
| *AIM-9 Sidewinder IA/IC* air.-to-air. | S | 11 | | | | | ./. | .. | — |
| *9L* new 1A version in development | | | | 1972 | | no | | | — |
| *9HJ* advanced IA versions | | | 3.5 | | | 1971 | | | |
| *9D/G* longer-range IC versions | | | 18 | | | 1965 | | | |
| *AIM-7 Sparrow III* air.-to-air. | S | | 30 | | | | .. | | — |
| *Bravo* with anti-radar sensor | | | | 1972 | | no | | | |
| *7F* with longer range | | | 45 | yes | | yes | | | |
| *7E* recent production version | | | 22 | | | | | | |
| *AGM-53 Condor* air.-to-ship/fixed | S | HE | 92 | 1965 | 1970 | 1972 | ./. | .. | — |
| *RGM-66D Standard[t]* ship-to-(fixed/ship) radar | S | .. | | | | no | ./. | .. | — |
| *SSM (ARM)* semi-active homing | | | | 1972 | | | | | |
| *Active SSM* active homing | | | | 1973 | | | | | |
| *Aegis[u]* ship-to-air./ship | S | .. | | 1969 | 1973 | no | ./. | .. | — |
| *Standard* ship-to-air./miss./ship | S | HE | | 1964 | | 1967 | ./. | .. | — |
| *RIM-67A ER-Extended Range* | | | 56 | | | | | | |
| *RIM-66A MR-Medium Range* | | | 20 | | | | | | |
| *Harpoon* (anti-shipping) | .. | HE | | | | | ./. | .. | — |
| *AGM-84A* air.-to-ship | J | .. | | 1968 | 1970 | 1974 | | | |
| *RGM-84A-I* ship-to-ship | J+S | .. | | 1968 | 1970 | 1974 | | | |
| *Encapsulated* sub.-to-ship | J+S | | | 1970 | .. | no | | | |
| *Trident MIRV* sub.-to-fixed | S | N | | | | | ./. | .. | — |
| *2* larger, longer-range version | | | 10 000 | (1972) | .. | no | | | |
| *1 (Poseidon C-4)* current version | | | 7 000 | (1972) | .. | no | | | |
| *UGM-73A Poseidon C-3* MIRV sub.-to-fixed | S | (10× 50 kt) | 4 630 | 1965 | 1968 | 1969 | ./ | .. | — |
| *UUM-44A Subroc* sub.-to-ship | S | N | 56 | 1958 | 1964 | 1965 | ./ | .. | — |

j Cost per round.
k Missile plus launch container.
l With UK Blowpipe missile.
m Figure corresponding to number to be deployed.
n Limited production for testing purposes.
o System incorporating US Sidewinder IC missiles.
p Number to be produced for B-52 and FB-111 deployment: additional missiles to be procured for B-1 if ordered into production.

q Further development and production cancelled mid-1973 and replaced by development of "Air Launched Cruise Missile".
r For research only, leading to improvements in unpowered guided bombs and other missiles.
s With modified US Standard missile.
t With developed US Standard MR missile.
u With developed US Standard MR missile.

| Country | Designation, description | Power-plant | War-head. kg (if nuclear, kt/mt) | Range, km | Design begun | Proto-type flight | In pro-duction | No.: do-mestic/export or total | R&D cost, $ mn | Unit price, $ mn | Foreign-designed Powerplant or Electronics |
|---|---|---|---|---|---|---|---|---|---|---|---|
| **Warsaw Treaty Organization** | | | | | | | | | | | |
| USSR[a] | "SSX-18" MIRV fixed-to-fixed | SL | 6× 1 mt | .. | .. | 1973 | no | ./– | .. | .. | – |
| | "SS-11" replacement MIRV fixed-to-fixed | SL | | | | | no | ./– | .. | .. | – |
| | "SSX-19" competitive prototype | | .. | .. | .. | 1973 | | | | | |
| | "SSX-17" competitive prototype | | .. | .. | .. | 1972 | | | | | |
| | Improved "SS-11" MIRV fixed-to-fixed | SL | 3× (200 kt) | 10 500 | .. | 1970 | 1972 | 40[b]/– | .. | .. | – |
| | "SSX-16" fixed/(mobile)-to-fixed | S | (1 mt) | .. | .. | (1973) | no | ./– | .. | .. | – |
| | "SS-12 Scaleboard" mobile-to-fixed | SL | N | (725) | .. | 1967 | (1970)[c] | ./– | .. | .. | – |
| | "Sagger" mobile-to-tank | S | 11.5 | 2.5 | .. | 1965 | yes[d] | ./. | .. | .. | – |
| | "SA-6 Gainfull" mobile-to-air. | SL | 80 | 35[e] | .. | 1967 | 1970[f] | ./. | .. | .. | – |
| | Improved "SA-2 Guideline" mobile-to-air. | SL | 130[g] | 40 | .. | 1967[h] | yes | ./. | .. | .. | – |
| | "SA-7 Grail" portable-to-air. | S | 1.8 | 2.5 | .. | 1971[i] | yes | ./. | .. | .. | – |
| | "AS-6" air.-to-ship/fixed | L | .. | (550) | .. | 1972[j] | no | ./. | .. | .. | – |
| | "AS-5 Kelt" air.-to-ship/fixed | .. | .. | 160 | .. | 1968 | 1970 | ./. | .. | .. | – |
| | "SS-N-13" ship-to-ship/fixed | .. | .. | (650) | .. | 1973 | no | ./. | .. | .. | – |
| | "SS-N-11" ship-to-ship | .. | .. | (45) | .. | 1973[k] | yes | ./. | .. | .. | – |
| | "SS-N-10" ship-to-ship | .. | .. | (55) | .. | 1969 | yes | ./. | .. | .. | – |
| | "SS-N-9" ship-to-ship | .. | .. | (92) | .. | 1969[m] | yes | ./. | .. | .. | – |
| | "SA-N-4" ship-to-hel. | .. | .. | n | .. | 1969[o] | yes | ./. | .. | .. | – |
| | "SA-N-3 Gobler" ship-to-air. | .. | .. | 725 | .. | 1967[p] | yes | ./. | .. | .. | – |
| | "SS-N-8" sub-to-fixed | S | (1 mt) | 7 780 | .. | 1972 | (1973)[q] | ./. | .. | .. | – |
| | "SS-N-6" sub-to-fixed | S | (1 mt) | 2 780 | .. | 1967 | 1967 | ./. | .. | .. | – |
| | "SS-N-7" sub-to-ship | .. | HE | (55) | .. | 1967[r] | yes | ./. | .. | .. | – |
| **Other Europe** | | | | | | | | | | | |
| Sweden | Rb 70 mobile-to-air. | S | .. | (5) | 1969 | (1973) | no | ./.. | (20) | .. | ' |
| | Bantam portable/mobile/air./hel.-to-tank | S | 1.9 | 2 | 1956 | .. | (1962) | ./.. | .. | .. | .. |
| | Rb 05A air.-to-ship/fixed | L | .. | .. | 1960 | (1968) | 1971 | ./– | .. | .. | .. |
| | Rb 04E air.-to-ship | S | .. | .. | (1969) | (1972) | yes | ./– | .. | .. | E-g (Fr.) |
| Switzerland | Micon fixed-to-air. | .. | .. | (30) | 1959 | .. | (yes) | ./.. | .. | .. | .. |

| Region / Country | Missile | Role | | Warhead | | | | | | |
|---|---|---|---|---|---|---|---|---|---|---|
| **Middle East** | | | | | | | | | | |
| Israel | *Jericho* | fixed-to-fixed | S | HE/N | 11 | .. | 1966 | 1968 | no | ./- |
| | *Shafrir* | air-to-air. | S | HE | .. | 5 | 1965 | .. | 1969 | ./. |
| | *Gabriel* | ship-to-ship | S | HE | 180 | 41 | 1966 | .. | 1970 | ./. |
| **Far East**[u] | | | | | | | | | | |
| Japan | *Tan Sam* | fixed-to-air. | .. | HE | (3 500) | .. | 1964 | .. | no | ./. |
| | *KAM-9* | mobile/ship-to-tank/ship | .. | HE | .. | .. | .. | .. | 1974 | ./. |
| | *KAM-3D* | portable-to-tank | .. | HE | 1.8 | .. | 1956 | .. | (1962) | ./. |
| | *ASM-1* | air-to-fixed/ship | S | HE | 136 | (40) | .. | .. | no | ./. |
| | *AAM-1* | air-to-air. | S | HE | .. | .. | .. | .. | (1968) | 68/- |
| | *AAM-2* | air-to-air. | .. | HE | .. | .. | .. | .. | (1975) | 330/- |
| **Oceania** | | | | | | | | | | |
| Australia | *Ikara* | ship-to-sub. | S | HE | (20) | .. | .. | .. | (1961) | ./. [v] |
| **Africa** | | | | | | | | | | |
| South Africa | .. | air-to-air. | S | HE | .. | .. | 1966 | .. | 1971 | ./. |
| **South America** | | | | | | | | | | |
| Brazil | .. | fixed-to-tank | .. | HE | 3 | .. | 1967 | 1970 | 1972 | ./. |
| | *Avibras MAS-1* | air-to-fixed | .. | HE | .. | .. | .. | .. | 1973 | ./. |

[a] In addition to the missiles listed, several of the older air-to-air missiles may still be in production, including "Ash" (deployed on Tu-28P), "Atoll" (deployed on MiG-21 and Yak-28P) and "Anab" (deployed on Yak 28P, Su-9 and Su-11). A new air-to-air missile is reported to have been deployed on the MiG-25.

[b] Number deployed as of end 1973.

[c] Reported to make up increasing proportion of 300 Soviet nuclear short-range ballistic missiles.

[d] In addition to original production, this missile is now entering service on a new vehicle (BMP 8-man APC) first seen in 1967.

[e] Max. range at low-medium altitude. Early assessments gave longer range at high altitude, but high altitude capacity later questioned.

[f] Reported first deployed in Egypt in 1971.

[g] One version (Mk 4) shown in 1967 with white-painted nose may have nuclear warhead.

[h] Improved versions reported in production.

[i] Reported to have been deployed in Egypt in 1971 and Viet-Nam in 1972. May have been in service in Soviet and other Warsaw Treaty Organization services earlier.

[j] Reported seen on Tupolev "Backfire" and Tu-16 "Badger".

[k] Deployed on "Osa" class patrol vessels.

[l] Deployed on "Krivak" and "Kresta II" class ships.

[m] Deployed on "Nanuchka" class patrol vessels.

[n] Limited range.

[o] Deployed on "Krivak", "Grishna" and "Nanuchka" class ships.

[p] Deployed on "Moskva" and "Kresta II" class ships. Earlier referred to as improved "SA-N-1" or "SA-3".

[q] Deployed on "D" class submarines.

[r] Deployed on "Y" class submarines.

[s] Deployed on "C" class submarines.

[t] Switzerland may contribute to R&D costs.

[u] China is known to have produced a first-generation intermediate-range ballistic missile with a nuclear warhead—apparently copied from an early Soviet missile—and has tested longer-range missiles. In addition, China has manufactured anti-aircraft missiles of Soviet design (for example, "Ash" and "Atoll"). No detailed information is available on missiles currently under development or in production.

[v] RN version subsequently developed by Australia and UK.

# Part 3. Ships

| Country | Class, description, armaments | Power-plant | Displace-ment, tons | Speed, knots | Laid down | Launched | Commissioned or completed | No.: domestic/export or total | Aircraft capacity | Unit price, $ mn | Foreign-designed Powerplant, Electronics or Armaments |
|---|---|---|---|---|---|---|---|---|---|---|---|
| **NATO** | | | | | | | | | | | |
| Belgium | *E71* frigate S-A, 100 mm, A/STT | GT | 1 500 | 28 | 1974 | .. | (1976) | 4/– | .. | .. | P (UK) A (NATO) |
| Canada | *Iroquois* destroyer (S-S), S-A, 127 mm, A/STT | GT | 4 050 | 27 | 1969 | 1970 | 1972 | 4/– | 2 hel. | .. | E-f (Neth.) E-r (It.) A (It.) |
| Denmark | .. missile boat (S-S), 76 mm or 57 mm | GT | 240 | 40 | 1971 | .. | (1975) | 8/– | – | .. | P (UK) |
| France | *Le Redoubtable* strategic submarine 16Sub.-S | N | 7 500 | (25) | 1964 | 1967 | 1971 | 5/– | – | .. | – |
| | *Agosta* patrol submarine 4TT | D | 1 200 | 20 | 1972 | .. | (1976) | 4/– | – | .. | – |
| | *Tourville* [destroyer] S-S, S-Sub., 3×100 mm, 2A/STT | GT | 4 580 | 31 | 1970 | 1972 | (1975) | 3/– | 2 hel. | .. | A-hel. (UK) |
| | *C-70* [destroyer] | GT | 3 950 | 30 | 1972 | .. | .. | | | .. | P (UK) A-hel. (UK) |
| | *C-70 A/S* S-S, S-Sub., 2×100 mm, 10TT | | | | | .. | .. | 12/– | 2 hel. | .. | |
| | *C-70 A/A* S-A, 2×10 mm, 10TT | | | | | .. | .. | 12/– | 2 hel. | .. | |
| | *A69* [corvette] 100 mm, 2×40 mm, 4TT | D | 950 | 24 | 1971 | .. | (1974) | 14/– | – | .. | P (FRG) E-r (UK) |
| | *S148* missile boat S-S, 76 mm, 40 mm | D | 234 | 38 | 1971 | .. | 1973 | –/20 | – | .. | P (FRG) A (It. Swe.) |
| | .. missile boat S-S, 57 mm, 40 mm | D | 234 | 38 | .. | 1972 | 1972 | –/4 | – | (14) | P FRG) A (Swe.) |
| | .. hydrofoil missile boat S-S | .. | 56 | 50 | .. | .. | .. | | – | .. | .. |
| FR Germany | *Type 209* submarine 8TT | D | 1 000 | 22 | .. | .. | .. | –/12 | – | .. | E-f (Neth.) |
| | *Type 206* submarine 8TT | D | 500 | 17 | (1969) | 1971 | 1972 | 18/– | – | .. | Co-design (UK) |
| | *Type 143* missile boat S-S, 76 mm, 2TT | D | 360 | 38 | (1972) | .. | .. | 10/– | – | (27)a | E-f (Neth.) A (Fr. It.) |
| | .. patrol boat | D | 240 | 40 | .. | .. | .. | –/2 | – | .. | .. |
| International: FR G, Italy, USA | *PHM-Patrol Hydrofoil Missile* hydro-foil missile boat S-S, 76 mm | GT | 220 | .. | 1973 | (1974) | .. | .. | – | .. | E-r (Neth.) |
| Italy | *Sauro* patrol submarine | D | .. | .. | (1973) | .. | .. | 2/– | – | (18) | .. |
| | .. corvette S-S, 76 mm, 40 mm | .. | 550 | .. | .. | .. | .. | | – | .. | .. |
| | .. missile boat S-S, 76 mm | D | 230 | 42 | .. | .. | .. | 6/– | – | .. | .. |

| | | | | | | | | | | | |
|---|---|---|---|---|---|---|---|---|---|---|---|
| | *Swordfish* hydrofoil missile boat S-S, 76 mm | GT | 60 | 50 | (1971) | 1973 | 1973 | ·· | - | ·· | P (UK) |
| Netherlands | *Tromp* destroyer S-A, 2×119 mm, 6A/STT | GT | 4 300 | (30) | 1971 | ·· | (1975) | 2/- | 1 hel. | ·· | P (UK) A (USA) |
| | .. frigate S-S, S-A | GT | (3 000) | (30) | ·· | ·· | (1978) | 4/- | 1 hel. | ·· | ·· |
| Norway | *Snögg* missile boat S-S, 40 mm, 4TT | D | 100 | 32 | ·· | ·· | 1970 | 6/- | - | ·· | P (FRG) |
| Turkey | *Berk* frigate 4×76 mm, 6TT | D | 1 450 | 25 | 1967 | 1971 | 1973 | 2/- | 1 hel. | ·· | P (It.) |
| | .. missile boat S-S | D | (360) | (38) | 1973 | ·· | ·· | ·· | - | ·· | ·· |
| UK | *Swiftsure* hunter-killer submarine 5A/STT | N | 3 500 | (30) | 1969 | 1971 | 1973 | 5/- | - | (75) | ·· |
| | *Oberon* submarine 8TT | D | 1 610 | (18) | 1957 | 1959 | 1961 | 13/14 | - | (12) | ·· |
| | *500-ton* submarine 8TT | D | 500 | 17 | (1972) | ·· | ·· | -/3 | - | ·· | Design (UK FRG) |
| | *Through-deck cruiser* aircraft/hel. cruiser S-S, S-A | GT | 22 000 | (30) | 1973 | ·· | (1979) | 3/- | 9 hel. | (195) | A (Fr.) |
| | *Type 42* destroyer S-A, (S-S), 114 mm | GT | 3 500 | 30 | 1970 | 1972 | 1973 | 6/1 | A/S hel. | (43) | ·· |
| | *Vosper Mk10* destroyer S-S, 2×114 mm | GT | 3 300 | 30 | 1972 | ·· | (1976) | -/2 | hel. | (43) | E-r (Neth. It.) |
| | *Vosper Mk10* frigate S-A, S-Sub.. 114 mm | GT | 3 300 | 30 | (1973) | ·· | (1977) | -/2 | A/S hel. | (43) | E-r (Neth. It.) |
| | *Type 22* frigate (S-S), S-A, 114 mm | GT | 3 000 | 30 | ·· | ·· | (1978) | -/- | A/S hel. | (23) | A (Aust. Swe.) |
| | *Type 21* frigate S-A, 114 mm, 6TT | GT | 2 500 | 34 | 1969 | 1971 | 1974 | 8/- | A/S hel. | (23) | A (Fr.) |
| | *Leander* frigate S-S, S-A, 2×144 mm | GT | 2 500 | 30 | 1973 | ·· | ·· | -/2 | hel. | ·· | P (FRG) E-r E-f (It.) A (Fr. It.) |
| | .. missile boat S-S, 76 mm | D | 150 | 30 | ·· | ·· | ·· | -/3 | - | ·· | P (FRG) E-r (It.) A (It.) |
| | .. patrol boat 76 mm | D | 150 | 30 | (1972) | (1974) | ·· | -/3 | - | ·· | ·· |
| | *B.H.F.* air cushion missile boat S-S | GT | 10 | 60 | ·· | ·· | ·· | -/4 | - | ·· | ·· |
| | *VT2* air cushion missile boat S-S | GT | (65) | (60) | ·· | ·· | ·· | ·· | - | ·· | ·· |
| USA | *SSBN.. Trident* strategic submarine 24Sub.-S, A/STT | N | 15 000 | 30 | ·· | ·· | (1978) | 10/- | - | 789 | - |
| | *SSN-688 Los Angeles* hunter-killer submarine Sub.-Sub., 4A/STT | N | 6 900 | 40 | 1972 | 1973 | 1974 | 30/- | - | 200 | - |
| | *SSN-685 Lipscomb* hunter-killer submarine Sub.-Sub., 4A/STT | N | 5 000 | 25 | 1971 | 1973 | 1974 | 1/- | - | 175 | - |
| | *SSN-637 Sturgeon* hunter-killer submarine Sub.-Sub., 4A/STT | N | 3 860 | 30 | 1963 | 1966 | 1967 | 37/- | - | 80 | - |
| | *CVN-68 Nimitz* aircraft carrier 3S-A | N | 91 400 | 30+ | 1968 | 1972 | (1974) | 3/- | 90 | 770 | - |
| | *SCS-Sea Control Ship* aircraft/hel. cruiser | GT | 14 000 | 25 | (1975) | ·· | (1977–1978) | 8/- | 3 VTOL 14 hel. | 125 | - |

*a* Including development costs and sub-systems.

| Country | Class, description, armaments | Power-plant | Displace-ment, tons | Speed, knots | Laid down | Launched | Commissioned or completed | No.: domestic/export or total | Aircraft capacity | Unit price, $ mn | Foreign-designed Powerplant, Electronics or Armaments |
|---|---|---|---|---|---|---|---|---|---|---|---|
| | DLGN-38 Virginia [cruiser] 2S-A/Sub., 2×127 mm, A/STT | N | 10 000 | 30+ | .. | .. | (1975) | 3/- | 2 hel. | 200–250 | – |
| | DLGN-36 California [cruiser] 2S-A, S-Sub., 2×76 mm, A/STT | N | 10 150 | 30+ | 1970 | 1971 | 1973 | 2/- | - | 190 | – |
| | DD963 Spruance destroyer 2S-A, S-Sub., 2×127 mm, A/STT | GT | 6 900 | 30+ | .. | .. | (1974) | 30/- | 1 hel. | 100 | – |
| | DE-1052 Knox escort S-A, S-Sub., 127 mm, 4A/STT | GT | 3 011 | 27 | 1965 | 1966 | 1969 | 46/- | 1 hel. | 20 | – |
| | PF-Patrol Frigate frigate | GT | 3 500 | .. | (1976) | (1975) | (1977) | 50/- | .. [VTOL/hel.] | 45b | – |
| | SES-Surface Effect Ship air cushion frigate | GT | (2 000) | (80) | .. | .. | (1980s) | .. | [VTOL/hel.] | c | – |
| | LHA-1 Tawara amphibious assault | T | 39 300 | 24 | 1971 | 1973 | (1975) | 5/- | VTOL/hel. | 170 | – |
| **Warsaw Treaty Organization** | | | | | | | | | | | |
| DR Germany | Hia patrol boat 4×37 mm | GT | 300 | 25 | .. | .. | 1963 | 14*/- | - | .. | A (USSR) E (USSR) |
| | Condor coastal minesweeper 2×25 mm | D | 245 | 24 | .. | .. | (1969) | 25*/- | - | .. | A (USSR) |
| Poland | Wisla patrol boat 2×40 mm, 4TT | GT | 70 | 30+ | .. | .. | .. | 4/- | .. | .. | A (USSR) E (USSR) |
| | Polnocny amphibious assault | D | 780 | 18 | .. | .. | .. | 22*/69 | .. | .. | .. |
| USSR | "Stretched" D strategic submarine 16Sub.-S | N | .. | .. | (1973) | .. | .. | 1*/- | - | .. | - |
| | D strategic submarine 12Sub.-S | N | (8 000) | 25 | .. | 1972 | .. | 3*/- | - | .. | - |
| | Y strategic submarine 16Sub.-S | N | 8 000 | 25 | .. | 1967 | (1969) | 33/- | - | .. | - |
| | P anti-shipping submarine 6Sub.-S | N | .. | (30) | .. | (1971) | (1969) | 1*/- | - | .. | - |
| | C anti-shipping submarine 8Sub.-S | N | 4 300 | (30) | .. | 1967 | (1969) | 11*/- | - | .. | - |
| | Kuril aircraft carrier 2 S-A, (2S-Sub.), 57 mm | .. | (45 000) | (30) | 1970 | 1972 | (1975–1976) | 2*/- | 35 VTOL 35 hel. | .. | - |
| | Kara cruiser 2S-S, 2 S-A, 2×76 mm, 10A/STT | GT | (9 000) | 34 | .. | (1971–1972) | (1974) | 3/- | 1 hel. | .. | - |
| | Kresta II cruiser 2S-S, 2S-A, 2×57 mm | ST | 7 500 | 33 | .. | 1969 | (1971) | 8*/- | 1 hel. | .. | - |
| | Krivak escort S-S, 2S-A, 2×76 mm | GT | 3 400 | (32–35) | .. | (1969–1970) | (1971) | 5*/- | - | .. | - |

|  | Prop. | Displ. | Speed |  |  |  | Price |  |  | Suppliers |
|---|---|---|---|---|---|---|---|---|---|---|
| *Grisha* [corvette] S-A, 2×57 mm, 4A/STT | GT | 750 | .. | .. | 1970 | 1972 | 5*/- | .. | .. | – |
| *Nanuchka* [corvette] 2S-S, 2×57 mm | D | 600 | 30 | .. | 1971 | .. | .. | .. | – | – |
| **Other Europe** | | | | | | | | | | |
| **Spain** | | | | | | | | | | |
| *Baleares* frigate S-A, S-Sub., 2×127 mm, 2×40 mm, 4A/STT, 2TT | GT | 3 000 | (28) | 1968 | 1970 | (1974) | 5/- | .. | .. | E-r Es (USA) A (USA) |
| corvette 100 mm, 2×40 mm | D | 1 200 | 24 | .. | .. | .. | –/4 | .. | .. | P (FRG) E-r (UK) A (Fr.) |
| **Sweden** | | | | | | | | | | |
| *A 14* submarine 8(A/S)TT | D | 980 | 20 | 1973 | .. | .. | 5/- | .. | .. | .. |
| corvette 57 mm, 40 mm | GT | (700) | .. | .. | .. | .. | 2/- | (20) | .. | .. |
| *Spica II* patrol boat 57 mm, 6TT | GT | 235 | 40 | .. | 1972 | 1973 | 12/- | (8) | .. | P (UK) E-r (Den.) |
| minelayer/depot ship 3×40 mm | D | 2 650 | 15 | 1972 | .. | .. | 2/- | (8) | .. | .. |
| **Yugoslavia** | | | | | | | | | | |
| *Heroj* submarine 6TT | D | 1 000 | 16 | (1973) | 1968 | .. | 3/- | .. | .. | P (UK) |
| patrol boat | GT | .. | .. | .. | .. | .. | .. | .. | – | .. |
| **Middle East** | | | | | | | | | | |
| **Israel** | | | | | | | | | | |
| *SAAR IV* missile boat S-S, 76 mm | D | 415 | 32 | .. | 1973 | 1973 | 2 | .. | – | P (FRG) A (It.) |
| **South Asia** | | | | | | | | | | |
| **India** | | | | | | | | | | |
| *Ajay* patrol boat guns | D | 120 | 18 | 1968 | 1969 | .. | .. | .. | – | .. |
| **Far East** | | | | | | | | | | |
| **China**[d] | | | | | | | | | | |
| submarine S-S, TT | N | .. | .. | 1969 | .. | .. | .. | .. | – | .. |
| (*R*) submarine TT | D | 1 100 | 15 | .. | .. | .. | 4/year | .. | – | .. |
| destroyer S-S, guns | D | 3 500 | (30) | 1973 | .. | .. | .. | .. | .. | .. |
| *Kiangnan* frigate guns | D | 1 350 | 30 | 1968 | .. | .. | 5 | .. | .. | .. |
| (*OSA*) missile boat S-S | D | 165 | 32 | .. | .. | 1965 | 40 | .. | – | .. |
| (*Komar*) missile boat S-S | D | 70 | 40 | .. | .. | 1965 | 30 | .. | – | .. |
| *Shanghai II, III, IV* patrol boat TT, guns | D | 120 | 30 | 1965 | .. | .. | 200 | .. | – | .. |
| *Huchwan* air cushion patrol boat TT | D | 45 | 55 | 1966 | .. | .. | 90/12 | .. | – | .. |
| **Japan** | | | | | | | | | | |
| *Uzushio* submarine 6TT | D | 1 850 | 20 | 1968 | 1970 | 1971 | 6/- | .. | – | .. |
| *Haruna* destroyer S-Sub., 2×127 mm, 6A/STT | GT | 4 700 | 32 | 1970 | 1972 | 1973 | 2/- | .. | 3 hel. | A (USA) |

b At 1973 prices.

c Price two to three times greater than for a conventionally powered ship of the same size.

d Ships of Soviet origin are shown with Soviet designations in brackets. They are listed as indigenous because China has been almost totally isolated from Soviet technology since 1960.

* Number produced to date.

| Country | Class, description, armaments | Power-plant | Displace-ment, tons | Speed, knots | Laid down | Launched | Commissioned or completed | No.: domestic/export or total | Aircraft capacity | Unit price, $ mn | Foreign-designed Powerplant, Electronics or Armaments |
|---|---|---|---|---|---|---|---|---|---|---|---|
| | *DD 168* destroyer S-A, S-S, S-Sub., 2×127 mm, 6A/STT | GT | 3 850 | 32 | 1973 | .. | .. | 1/– | 1 hel. | .. | A (USA) |
| | *Chikugo* escort S-Sub., 2×76 mm, 2×40 mm | D | 1 470 | 25 | 1968 | 1970 | 1970 | 10/– | – | .. | A (USA) |
| | .. patrol boat 2×40 mm 4TT | D | 100 | 40 | 1970 | .. | 1971 | 4/– | – | .. | .. |
| Indonesia | *Mewar* patrol boat guns | D | 147 | 21 | .. | .. | 1972 | 3 | – | .. | .. |
| **South America** | | | | | | | | | | | |
| Argentina | *Guipo I* air cushion patrol boat | .. | .. | .. | .. | 1971 | .. | .. | – | .. | P (USA) |
| Brazil | *Pedro Teixeira* corvette | D | 700 | 16 | 1970 | .. | 1973 | 2 | 1 hel. | .. | .. |
| | *Roraima* patrol boat guns | D | 340 | 14 | .. | .. | 1973 | 3 | – | .. | .. |

# Part 4. Armoured vehicles

| Country | Designation, description | Main armament mm | Combat weight, tons | Road speed, km/hr | Design begun | Prototype test | In production | No.: domestic/export or total | R&D cost, $ mn | Unit price, $ mn | Foreign-designed Powerplant, Electronics or Armaments |
|---|---|---|---|---|---|---|---|---|---|---|---|
| **NATO** | | | | | | | | | | | |
| France | AMX-30 main battle tank | 105 | 36 | 65 | 1957 | .. | 1966 | (1 000)/(350) | .. | .. | .. |
| | AMX-13 light tank | 105 | 15 | 64 | 1946 | .. | yes | ../(4 000) | .. | .. | .. |
| | Even 90 light tank | 90 | 85 | 68 | .. | .. | (1972) | ./.. | .. | .. | .. |
| | VXB 170 armoured personnel carrier/air defence | 20 | 11.3 | 80 | 1965 | .. | (1972) | (240)/.. | .. | .. | .. |
| | AMX-10P armoured personnel carrier | 20 | .. | 65 | (1965) | 1971 | 1972 | ./.. | .. | .. | .. |
| | AMX 10RC anti-tank vehicle | 105 | .. | .. | .. | .. | yes | ./.. | .. | .. | .. |
| | M3/VTT armoured personnel carrier | .. | 5.5 | 90 | .. | .. | (no) | ./.. | .. | .. | .. |
| | M4 armoured personnel carrier/anti-tank | 90 | 9.5 | 80 | (1968) | (1972) | (no) | ./.. | .. | .. | .. |
| | M6 armoured personnel carrier/anti-tank | 90 | .. | 80 | .. | (1973) | no | ./.. | .. | .. | .. |
| | M8 armoured personnel carrier/anti-tank | 105 | .. | 80 | .. | (1973) | no | ./.. | .. | .. | .. |
| FR Germany | Leopard II main battle tank | 110 | .. | .. | .. | (1973) | no | ./.. | .. | .. | E (FRG/UK) |
| | Leopard I main battle tank | 105 | 40 | 65 | 1957 | .. | 1965 | (4 000) | (25) | 0.25 | A (UK) |
| | FMBT-80 main battle tank (competitive prototype)[a] | 105 | (45) | 100 | .. | (1974) | no | ./.. | .. | .. | .. |
| | Marder armoured personnel carrier | 20 | 28.2 | 70 | 1959 | 1972 | 1970 | 2 000/.. | .. | .. | .. |
| | Spähpanzer 2 armoured car | 20 | 193 | 90 | .. | 1972 | (1974) | 408/.. | .. | (0.3) | .. |
| | UR416 armoured personnel carrier | 90 | 6.3 | 80 | .. | 1973 | (no) | ../106 | .. | .. | .. |
| **International** | | | | | | | | | | | |
| FR Germany, United Kingdom | FMBT-80 main battle tank | (120) | .. | .. | 1972 | .. | no | ./.. | .. | .. | .. |

[a] See FR Germany-UK entry under the heading International.

| Country | Designation, description | Main armament mm | Combat weight, tons | Road speed, km/hr | Design begun | Proto-type test | In production | No.: domestic/export or total | R&D cost, $ mn | Unit price, $ mn | Foreign-designed Powerplant, Electronics or Armaments |
|---|---|---|---|---|---|---|---|---|---|---|---|
| Italy | Type 6616 armoured reconnaissance car | 20 | 7 | 100 | .. | 1973 | no | ./.. | .. | .. | A (FRG) |
| United Kingdom | Chieftain main battle tank | 120 | 53 | 48 | (1958) | 1960 | 1963 | (800)/800 | .. | (0.5) | .. |
| | Vickers Mk3 main battle tank | 105 | 36 | 53 | .. | (1972) | (no) | ./.. | .. | .. | .. |
| | Falcon anti-aircraft tank | 30 | 16 | 48 | .. | 1970 | yes | ./.. | .. | .. | A (Fr.) |
| | Scorpion light tank[b] | 76 | 8 | 80 | 1964 | .. | 1971 | ./130 | .. | (0.16) | .. |
| | Fox armoured car | 30 | 5.7 | 100 | .. | .. | 1972 | ./.. | .. | .. | – |
| | Ferret Mk5 missile armoured car | .. | 5.4 | 80 | .. | .. | 1972 | ./.. | .. | .. | – |
| United States | XM-1 main battle tank | 105 | 50 | 80 | 1972 | 1976 | 1977 | 3 312/.. | .. | 0.8 | – |
| | M-60 main battle tank | 120 | 52 | 48 | .. | .. | 1962 | ./.. | .. | 0.4 | A (UK) |
| | M-60A1 current production version | | | | | | | | | | |
| | M-60A3 improved vehicle & equipment | | | | 1971 | – | (1974) | | | | |
| | XM 723 MICV-Mechanized Infantry Combat Vehicle | 20–30 | 8.8 | 72 | 1967 | 1974 | no | ./.. | .. | .. | – |
| | M113A1 armoured personnel carrier | 12.7 | 10.8 | 64 | .. | 1964 | (1965) | ./.. | .. | .. | – |
| | XM800 ARSV-Armoured Reconnaissance Scout Vehicle | 20 | 7 | .. | 1972 | | no | ./.. | .. | .. | – |
| | .. wheeled competitive prototype | | | | | 1973 | | | | | |
| | .. tracked competitive prototype | | | | | 1973 | | | | | |

**Warsaw Treaty Organization**

| Country | Designation, description | Main armament mm | Combat weight, tons | Road speed, km/hr | Design begun | Proto-type test | In production | No.: domestic/export or total | R&D cost, $ mn | Unit price, $ mn | Foreign-designed Powerplant, Electronics or Armaments |
|---|---|---|---|---|---|---|---|---|---|---|---|
| Czechoslovakia | JPzG13 light tank | 83.4 | 16 | .. | .. | .. | .. | ./.. | .. | .. | .. |
| | OT 64 armoured personnel carrier | .. | 12 | .. | .. | .. | (1963) | ./.. | .. | .. | .. |
| | BMP-76PB armoured personnel carrier | 76 | 12–14 | 51 | .. | 1967 | yes | ./.. | .. | .. | .. |
| USSR | BRDM-2 (BTR-40PB) armoured reconnaissance car | 14.5 | 7 | 80 | .. | 1966 | yes | ./.. | .. | .. | – |
| | .. armoured personnel carrier[c] | 76 | 10 | .. | .. | 1973 | (no) | ./.. | .. | .. | .. |
| | "T-62 M-1970" ("T-64") main battle tank[d] | 115 | 36 | .. | .. | 1973 | yes | ./.. | .. | .. | .. |

| Designation | | | | | | | | | |
|---|---|---|---|---|---|---|---|---|---|
| **Other Europe** | | | | | | | | | |
| **Austria** | | | | | | | | | |
| *Panzerjäger K* anti-tank gun | 105 | 17 | 63 | 1965 | (1968) | (1972) | (115)/.. | .. | A (Fr.) |
| *4K 4FA* armoured personnel carrier | 20 | 12.5 | 60 | 1956 | (1958) | (1961) | ./. | .. | A (Switz.) |
| **Sweden** | | | | | | | | | |
| *STRV 103* main battle tank | 105 | 39 | (50) | (1956) | .. | (1966) | ./. | .. | P (UK) A (UK) |
| *Ikv 91* light tank | 90 | 15.5 | 67 | 1968 | (1970) | (1973) | ./. | .. | .. |
| *EPbv* artillery-fire control vehicle | .. | 13 | (80) | .. | .. | (1972) | ./. | (0.12) | .. |
| **Switzerland** | | | | | | | | | |
| *Pz 68* main battle tank | 105 | 38 | 55 | 1966 | .. | (1967) | 170/.. | .. | P (FRG) A (UK) |
| *Gepard* anti-aircraft tank system | 35 | .. | .. | .. | (1969) | (1973) | ./.550 | (1.5) | P (FRG) E-r (FRG Neth.) |
| **Middle East** | | | | | | | | | |
| **Israel** | | | | | | | | | |
| *Sabra* medium tank | 105 | 40 | .. | 1970 | .. | 1971 | ./. | .. | P (USA) |
| **South Asia** | | | | | | | | | |
| **India** | | | | | | | | | |
| .. light tank | .. | .. | .. | 1970 | .. | .. | ./. | .. | .. |
| **Far East** | | | | | | | | | |
| **China[e]** | | | | | | | | | |
| *T-59 (T-54)* main battle tank | 100 | 32 | .. | .. | .. | 1968 | ./. | .. | — |
| *T-62* light tank | 85 | 21 | .. | .. | .. | 1968 | ./. | .. | — |
| *T-60 (PT-76)* light amphibious tank | 85 | .. | .. | .. | .. | yes | ./. | .. | — |
| .. tracked armoured car | .. | 11 | .. | .. | .. | yes | ./. | .. | — |
| .. wheeled armoured car (BTR-40) | .. | .. | .. | .. | .. | yes | ./. | .. | — |
| .. wheeled armoured car (BTR-152) | .. | .. | .. | .. | .. | yes | ./. | .. | — |
| **Japan** | | | | | | | | | |
| *ST-B* main battle tank | 105 | 38 | 60 | 1966 | 1969 | (1972) | (280)/.. | 0.6 | |
| **South America** | | | | | | | | | |
| **Brazil** | | | | | | | | | |
| *EE-11 Urutu* amphibious armoured personnel carrier | .. | 105 | 95 | 1970 | 1970 | 1972 | ./. | .. | P (USA) |
| *EE-9 Cascavel* armoured personnel carrier | 37 | 9 | .. | 1970 | 1971 | 1972 | ./. | .. | .. |

[b] Six derivative vehicles have also been developed.

[c] Believed to be airdroppable paratroop fire support vehicle. First seen in November 1973 parade in Moscow.

[d] Version of "T-62" with improved vehicle.

[e] Armoured vehicles of Soviet origin are shown with the Soviet designation in brackets. They are listed as indigenous weapons because China has been almost totally isolated from Soviet technology since 1960.

# Appendix 8E

*Register of licensed production of foreign-designed major weapons, 1973*

For sources and methods, see appendix 8A, page 159. For abbreviations and conventions, see the list in appendix 8D, page 230.

## Part I. Aircraft

| Country | Licenser | Date | Designation, description | Power-plant | Weight kg | Speed km/hr or *Mach* no. | Nature of licence, technical changes by licensee | In production | No.: domestic/export or total | Unit price $ mn |
|---|---|---|---|---|---|---|---|---|---|---|
| **NATO** | | | | | | | | | | |
| Belgium | France | .. | *Mirage 5* fighter/strike | J | 13 500 | M 2.2 | Assembly, partial indigenous manufacture | 1969 | 106/– | .. |
| Canada | USA | .. | *F-5* light fighter | J | 9 300 | M 1.4 | Indigenous manufacture, improved electronics | 1967 | 135/75 | .. |
| FR Germany | USA | (1960) | *F-104* fighter/strike | J | 14 060 | M 2.4 | Recent manufacture wholly indigenous, design changes for multi-purpose capability | 1961 | (970)/– | .. |
| | USA | 1969 | *CH-53* medium transport hel. | T | 10 285 | (254) | Indigenous manufacture except avionics | 1971 | 110/– | .. |
| Italy | USA | (1966) | *F-104* fighter/strike | J | 14 060 | M 2.2 | .. | 1968 | 205/– | (2.2) |
| | USA | (1973) | *CL-1200* fighter | J | .. | M 2.4 | Co-production with USA | no | .. | (4.0) |
| | USA | (1966) | *SH-3D* A/S helicopter | T | 9 525 | 265 | Indigenous manufacture except radar imported | 1967 | (24)/10 | .. |
| | USA | .. | *AB204AS* A/S helicopter | T | 4 310 | 195 | Indigenously developed A/S version of US aircraft | yes | ../.. | .. |

| Country | Supplier | Year | Aircraft & type | | Weight | Speed | Comments | Year | Nos. | Value |
|---|---|---|---|---|---|---|---|---|---|---|
| | USA | .. | *AB212AS* A/S helicopter | T | (5 000) | (205) | Indigenously developed A/S version of US aircraft, power plant imported (Can.) | (1975) | 28/.. | (2.1) |
| | USA | .. | *AB206B-1* utility transp. hel. | T | 1 520 | 220 | Indigenous manufacture | 1972 | .. | (0.4) |
| | USA | 1968 | *CH-47C* transport helicopter | T | 17 780 | 285 | Co-production of components with USA | 1970 | 26/(20) | .. |
| | USA | .. | *AB205* utility helicopter | T | 4 310 | 220 | Indigenous manufacture | yes | ../.. | .. |
| | USA | .. | *S-61R* utility helicopter | T | 9 525 | 265 | Indigenous manufacture | 1973 | 20 | .. |
| United Kingdom | USA | 1966 | *SH-3 Sea King* A/S helicopter | T | 9 300 | (215) | Wholly indigenous manufacture, indigenous avionics | 1969 | 56/68 | 1.7 |
| | USA | 1966 | *Commando* transport version | T | 9 525 | 208 | Indigenous manufacture | 1972 | ../24 | .. |
| **Warsaw Treaty Organization** | | | | | | | | | | |
| Poland | USSR | 1959 | *An-2* utility bi-plane | P | 5 500 | 260 | Indigenous manufacture | 1960 | 5 000[a] | .. |
| | USSR | 1964 | *Mi-2* utility helicopter | T | 3 550 | 210 | Indigenous manufacture | 1966 | ../.. | .. |
| Romania | UK | 1968 | *Islander* light utility transport | P | 2 860 | 290 | Indigenous manufacture | 1969 | 215 | .. |
| | France | 1971 | *Alouette III* utility helicopter | T | 2 250 | 220 | Assembly, some indigenous manufacture | 1971 | 50/- | .. |
| **Other Europe** | | | | | | | | | | |
| Finland | Sweden | 1966 | *Draken* fighter/strike | J | 15 000 | M 2.0 | Assembly only | (1974) | 12/- | .. |
| Switzerland | France | 1969 | *Alouette III* utility helicopter | T | 2 250 | 220 | .. | (1971) | 60/- | .. |
| Yugoslavia | UK, France | 1971 | *Gazelle* light utility helicopter | T | 1 700 | 310 | Assembly only | 1973 | .. | .. |
| **South Asia** | | | | | | | | | | |
| | USSR | 1964 | *MiG-21FL* fighter | J | 9 400 | M 2.0 | *60% indigenous manufacture* | 1966 | 196/- | 2.0 |
| | USSR | 1970 | *MiG-21M* fighter/strike | J | 9 400 | M 2.0 | .. | 1973 | 150 | .. |
| | United Kingdom | 1956 | *Gnat* light fighter | J | 3 010 | 1 118 | Indigenous manufacture | 1959 | 215*/- | .. |
| | United Kingdom | 1959 | *HS748* transport | T | 5 580 | 820 | Indigenous manufacture | 1964 | 45*/- | 1.5 |
| | France | 1964 | *Alouette III* utility helicopter | T | 2 250 | 195 | Indigenous manufacture | 1965 | 156*/- | .. |
| | France | 1970 | *SA-315 Cheetah* light helicopter | T | 2 200 | 120 | Assembly | 1972 | 100/- | .. |
| Pakistan | France | 1971 | *Alouette III* utility helicopter | T | 2 250 | 195 | Assembly | 1972 | (20*) | .. |

*Note*: For abbreviations and conventions, see the list on page 230.

* Number produced to date.

| Country | Licenser | Date | Designation, description | Power-plant | Weight kg | Speed km/hr or Mach no. | Nature of licence, technical changes by licensee | In production | No.: domestic/ export or total | Unit price $ mn |
|---|---|---|---|---|---|---|---|---|---|---|
| **Far East** | | | | | | | | | | |
| Japan | USA | 1969 | *F-4E* fighter | J | 24 765 | M 2.4 | Some imported components, mainly indigenous manufacture | 1972 | 118/- | (3.6) |
| | USA | 1959 | *P-2J* maritime patrol | T | 34 000 | (370) | Indigenous manufacture, substantial modification of US design | 1969 | 101/- | (8.8) |
| | USA | (1962) | *SH-3A/D* A/S helicopter | T | 9 300 | 265 | Assembly | yes | (80*)/- | .. |
| | USA | (1961) | *KV-107II/IIA* transport hel. | T | 8 620 | 270 | Indigenous manufacture | (1962) | (90*)/7 | (2.3) |
| | USA | .. | *B204B* utility helicopter | T | 4 310 | 195 | .. | 1965 | 90*/- | (1.1) |
| | USA | .. | *B205* utility helicopter | T | 4 310 | 220 | .. | (1972) | 11*/- | (1.1) |
| | USA | 1967 | *OH-6J* light helicopter | T | 1 225 | 240 | Assembly | yes | 118/- | (0.4) |
| Taiwan | USA | 1973 | *F-5E Tiger II* fighter | J | 9 900 | M 1.6 | Limited indigenous manufacture | no | 100/- | .. |
| | USA | 1968 | *Pazmany PL-1B* primary trainer | P | 600 | 185 | Indigenous manufacture | 1968 | 50*)/- | .. |
| | USA | 1969 | *Bell 205-A1* helicopter | T | 4 765 | 180 | Indigenous manufacture | 1969 | 118*)/- | .. |
| Thailand | USA | 1972 | *Pazmany PL-2* primary trainer | P | 655 | 210 | Indigenous manufacture | 1972 | 14*/- | .. |
| Viet-Nam, South | USA | 1971 | *Pazmany PL-2* primary trainer | P | 655 | 210 | Indigenous manufacture | 1971 | 11*/- | .. |
| **Oceania** | | | | | | | | | | |
| Australia | USA | 1971 | *B206B-1* utility transport hel. | T | 1 520 | 220 | Ultimately wholly indigenous manufacture | yes | 75/- | .. |
| **Africa** | | | | | | | | | | |
| South Africa | Italy | 1965 | *MB-326M (Impala)* trainer/light strike | J | 5 215 | 800 | 70% indigenous manufacture | 1967 | 200*/- | .. |
| | Italy | 1973 | *MB-326K* light strike | J | 5 445 | 890 | Assembly, subsequent manufacture | (1974) | 100/- | .. |
| | France | 1971 | *Mirage F-1* fighter | J | 14 900 | M 2.2 | Component manufacture, initial assembly in France | (1977) | 100/- | .. |
| | France | 1973 | *SA-330 Puma* utility helicopter | T | 6 700 | 270 | Assembly, subsequent manufacture | 1973 | 20/- | .. |

**South America**

| Country | | Year | Type | | | | Note | | | |
|---|---|---|---|---|---|---|---|---|---|---|
| Argentina | USA | 1965 | Cessna 182 monoplane | P | 1 340 | 255 | Indigenous manufacture | 1967 | 500* | .. |
| | USA | 1971 | Cessna 150 trainer | P | 730 | 190 | Assembly, subsequent manufacture | 1973 | .. | — |
| | USA | 1973 | Piper Cherokee light plane | P | 975 | 215 | Assembly, subsequent manufacture | 1973 | 1 000 | .. |
| | USA | 1973 | Piper Seneca light plane | P | 1 815 | 300 | Assembly, subsequent manufacture | 1973 | 340 | .. |
| | USA | 1973 | DH-6A light helicopter | T | 1 160 | 215 | 22% indigenous manufacture | (1974) | 120 | .. |
| Brazil | Italy | 1970 | MB-326GB trainer/light strike | J | 5 215 | 800 | Assembly, partial indigenous manu-facture (air frame) | 1971 | 112 | .. |
| | Italy | 1973 | SH-4 utility helicopter | P | 860 | 130 | Assembly, subsequent manufacture | (1974) | .. | .. |
| Colombia | USA | 1968 | Piper light aircraft | P | .. | .. | Assembly, subsequent manufacture | 1969 | (100*) | .. |

*Note:* For abbreviations and conventions, see the list on page 230.
* Number produced to date.

# Part 2. *Missiles*

| Country | Licenser | Date | Designation, description | Power-plant | Warhead weight, kg (if nuclear, kt/mt) | Range, km | Nature of licence, technical changes by licensee | In production | No.: domestic/ export or total | Unit price $ mn |
|---|---|---|---|---|---|---|---|---|---|---|
| **NATO** | | | | | | | | | | |
| International: | | | | | | | | | | |
| European NATO Consortium (leader, FRG) | | | | | | | | | | |
| | USA | .. | *Sidewinder*, air-to-air | S | He | .. | Consortium manufacture, improved homing system | yes | .. | .. |
| European NATO Consortium (leader, Norway) | USA | .. | *Bullup* air-to-ship/fixed | S | 113.4 | 11 | .. | yes | .. | .. |
| Italy | USA | .. | *Sparrow III* air./ship/ fixed-to-air./miss. | S | 30 | (25) | Probably indigenous manufacture | yes | .. | .. |
| Turkey | FR Germany | .. | *Cobra 2000* portable-to-tank | S | 2.5 | 2 | .. | yes | .. | .. |
| **Other Europe** | | | | | | | | | | |
| Sweden | USA | .. | *Falcon* air-to-air | S | .. | .. | .. | yes | .. | .. |
| **South Asia** | | | | | | | | | | |
| India | France | 1970 | *SS-11* mobile-to-tank | S | He | 3 | Assembly; indigenous manufacture in 1974 | 1971 | .. | .. |
| | France | 1970 | *Harpon* mobile-to-tank | S | He | 3 | .. | 1971 | .. | .. |
| | USSR | 1964 | *Atoll* air-to-air | S | He | 1 | .. | 1967 | .. | .. |
| Pakistan | FR Germany | 1965 | *Cobra 2000* portable-to-tank | S | 2.7 | 2 | Assembly | 1966 | .. | .. |
| **Far East** | | | | | | | | | | |
| Japan | USA | 1972 | *Nike-J* fixed-to-air | S | He | (140) | .. | (1933) | (36)/– | (3.0) |
| | USA | 1972 | *Hawk* mobile-to-air | S | He | (11) | .. | (1973) | (30)/– | (2.5) |
| | USA | .. | *Sparrow III* air.-to-air. | S | 30 | (25) | .. | (1973) | 600/– | .. |
| **South America** | | | | | | | | | | |
| Brazil | FR Germany | 1973 | *Cobra 2000* portable-to-tank | S | 2.7 | 2 | .. | 1974 | .. | .. |
| | FR Germany | 1973 | *Roland I/II* mobile-to-air. | S | He | 6.5 | Final assembly | no | .. | .. |

Part 3. *Ships*

| Country | Licenser | Date | Class, description | Dis-place-ment, *tons* | Speed, *knots* | Nature of licence, technical changes by licensee | Laid down | Launched | Commis-sioned or completed | No.: do-mestic/ export or total | Unit price $ *mn* |
|---|---|---|---|---|---|---|---|---|---|---|---|
| **Other Europe** | | | | | | | | | | | |
| Spain | France | .. | *Daphne* submarine 12TT | 970 | 16 | Extensive French assistance | 1968 | 1970 | 1974 | 4/– | .. |
| **South Asia** | | | | | | | | | | | |
| India | United Kingdom | 1965 | *Leander* frigate S-S, 1 hel. | 2 450 | 30 | 53 per cent indigenous manufacture | 1966 | 1968 | 1972 | 6/– | .. |
| **South America** | | | | | | | | | | | |
| Argentina | FR Germany | 1969 | *Type 209* submarine 8TT | 1 000 | 22 | Final assembly only | 1969 | 1972 | .. | 2/– | .. |
| | United Kingdom | 1970 | *Type 42* S-A, 2×114 mm, 1 hel. | 3 500 | 30 | Assembly | 1970 | .. | .. | 1/– | .. |
| | FR Germany | 1970 | patrol boat guns | 240 | 40 | Assembly | 1970 | .. | .. | 1/– | .. |
| Brazil | United Kingdom | 1970 | *Niteroi* destroyer S-S, 2×114 mm, 1 hel. | 3 300 | 30 | Assembly | .. | .. | .. | 1/– | (43) |
| | | | *Niteroi* frigate S-A, S-Sub., 1×114 mm, 1 hel. | 3 300 | 30 | Assembly | .. | .. | .. | 1/– | (43) |
| Colombia | Italy | 1971 | *Midget* submarine | 78 | 14 | Assembly | 1972 | .. | .. | 2/– | .. |

# Part 4. Armoured vehicles

| Country | Licenser | Date | Designation, description | Main armament, *mm* | Combat weight, *tons* | Road speed, *km/hr* | Nature of licence, technical changes by licensee | In production | No.: domestic/ export or total | Unit price, $ *mn* |
|---|---|---|---|---|---|---|---|---|---|---|
| **NATO** | | | | | | | | | | |
| Italy | FR Germany | .. | *Leopard* main battle tank | 105 | 40 | 65 | Indigenous manufacture | (1973) | 600/– | .. |
| | USA | .. | *M113* armoured personnel carrier | – | 10 | 65 | Indigenous manufacture | yes | (4 500) | .. |
| **Other Europe** | | | | | | | | | | |
| Spain | France | 1972 | *AMX-30* main battle tank | 105 | 36 | 65 | Assembly only | yes | 180/– | 0.6 |
| **South Asia** | | | | | | | | | | |
| India | United Kingdom | 1965 | *Vijayanta* main battle tank | 105 | 37 | 48 | 68 per cent indigenous manufacture: powerplant imported | 1966 | 500/– | .. |
| **Africa** | | | | | | | | | | |
| South Africa | France | 1960 | *Panhard AML 245 "Eland"* | .. | 5.5 | 90 | Local development of AML 245 | 1967 | 750ᵃ/50 | .. |

ᵃ Including earlier production of basic AML 245.

# Appendix 8F

*Register of world arms trade, 1972–73*

For sources and methods, see appendix 8A, page 159.

## Abbreviations and conventions

| | |
|---|---|
| . . | = Not available |
| ( ) | = Uncertain data |
| + | = At least the number given and probably more |
| batt | = battery (of missiles) |
| Displ | = Displacement of naval vessels, in tons |
| 1969– | = 1969 and subsequent years |
| Mk | = Mark |
| Srs | = Series |
| t | = Tons |
| u.c. | = Unit cost |
| AAM | = Air-to-air missile |
| A-A missile | = Air-to-air missile |
| AC | = Armoured car |
| AD | = Air defence |
| AF | = Air Force |
| APC | = Armoured personnel carrier |
| ASM | = Air-to-surface missile |
| ASW | = Antisubmarine warfare |
| ATM | = Anti-tank missile |
| COIN | = Counterinsurgency |
| ECM | = Electronic countermeasures |
| LOH | = Light observation helicopter |
| LST | = Landing-ship, tank |
| MAP | = (US) Military Assistance Program |
| MBT | = Main battle tank |
| SAM | = Surface-to-air missile |
| SAR | = Search and rescue/sea-air rescue |
| SLAM | = Submarine-launched air missile |
| SSM | = Surface-to-surface missile |
| STOL | = Short take-off and landing |
| USAF | = United States Air Force |
| USN | = United States Navy |
| VG | = Variable geometry |
| VIP | = Very important person |
| V/STOL | = Vertical or short take-off and landing |
| WEU | = Western European Union |

| Recipient | Supplier | Number | Item | Description | Comment | Ordered | Delivered |
|---|---|---|---|---|---|---|---|
| **NATO** | | | | | | | |
| *North America:* | | | | | | | |
| Canada | UK | 100 | Short Blowpipe | Anti-aircraft missile system | $28 mn | May 1973 | 1974–76 |
| | USA | 50 | Bell model 212 CUH-IN | Utility helicopter | | Sept 1969 | 1971–72 |
| | | 74 | Bell COH-58A Kiowa | LOH | $23.7 mn | May 1970 | 1971–72 |
| | | 8 | Boeing-Vertol CH-47C Chinook | Helicopter | $30 mn incl spares and support equipment | Aug 1973 | 1974–75 |
| *Europe:* | | | | | | | |
| Belgium | France | 2 | Dassault Falcon | Transport | | .. | 1973 |
| | | 10 | Fouga Magister | Trainer | Refurbished | .. | 1972 |
| | | 63 | Dassault Mirage 5BA | Fighter/strike | | 1968–69 | 1970–73 |
| | | 27 | Dassault Mirage 5BR | Tactical reconnaissance | U.c.: $1.49 mn for first 88 | | |
| | | 16 | Dassault Mirage 5BD | Trainer | | | |
| | France/ | 33 | Dassault-Bréguet/ Dornier Alpha-Jet | Trainer | U.c.: $1.9–2.3 mn | 1973 | 1977 |
| | FR Germany | 55 | Krauss Maffei Leopard | Main battle tank | In addition to 334 previously purchased | July 1973 | .. |
| | FR Germany | 80 | Rheinstahl 90 mm tank destroyer | | About $25 mn, incl spare parts etc. | Dec 1972 | 1975 |
| | Switzerland | 55 | Oerlikon-Contraves 5PFZ Gepard | Anti-aircraft tank | | 1973 | .. |
| | UK | .. | BAC Swingfire | A-T missile system with missiles | To equip 43 Striker launching vehicles | May 1973 | .. |
| | USA | 12 | Lockheed C-130H Hercules | Transport | Subject to parliamentary approval | 1971 | 1972–73 |
| | | .. | LTV MGM-52A Lance | S-S missile system | | June 1973 | .. |
| Denmark | Canada | 15 | Canadair CF-104 Starfighter | Fighter/bomber | | 1971 | Aug 1973– |
| | | 7 | Canadair CF-104D Starfighter | Trainer | U.c.: $265 000 | | |

| Recipient | Supplier | Number | Item | Description | Comment | Date of order | Date of delivery |
|---|---|---|---|---|---|---|---|
| | Sweden | 5 | Saab-Scania TF-35 Draken | Trainer | | Nov 1973 | (1974–77) |
| | USA | 3 | Lockheed C-130H Hercules | Transport | $13.0 mn. In addition to 46 previously purchased | April 1973 | 1975 |
| | | 8 | NA F-100F | Trainer | $19.2 mn incl spares; $3.9 mn refurbished incl modification: ex-USAF. Initial batch | 1973 | .. |
| | | .. | Hughes TOW | A-T missile | | Aug 1973 | .. |
| France | USA | 1 | McDonnell-Douglas DC-8 | ECM aircraft | $8.7 mn | (1973) | 1976 |
| | | 10 | Piper Navajo | Light aircraft | | .. | 1973 |
| FR Germany | France | 20 | Fast missile patrol boat, type 148 | Displ.: 234 t | $220 mn | Oct 1970 | 1973–75 |
| | | .. | Aérospatiale Exocet | S-S missile | | Mid-1973 | .. |
| | | 320 | Aérospatiale AS-30 | A-S missile | | | .. |
| | Switzerland | 3 | Contraves Skyguard-M | Autonomous S-A missile system | Prototypes | 1971 | .. |
| | | 408 | Oerlikon-Contraves 5 PFZB | Anti-aircraft tank system | | 1971: 12; (1973): 396 | 1974: 12; 1976: 393 |
| | UK | 22 | Westland Sea King Mk 41 | SAR helicopter | $85.3 mn incl spares, crew training and infrastructure | June 1969 | 1973–74 |
| | USA | 175 | McDonnell-Douglas F-4F Phantom II | Fighter | | 1971 | 1973 |
| | | 26 | LTV MGM-52A Lance | S-S missile | Initial $99 mn order subject to parliamentary approval | Nov 1973 | .. |
| | | .. | Raytheon Sparrow III | A-A missile | On order | | .. |
| | | 100 | Hughes TOW launcher } | A-T missile system | | (May) 1972 | 1972– |
| | | 3 000 | Missile | | | | |
| Greece | USA | 36 | McDonnell-Douglas F-4 Phantom | Fighter | $150 mn, incl spares and ground equipment. Extensive US credit | March 1972 | By 1974 |
| | | 8 | Cessna A-37 | COIN aircraft | | .. | 1973 |
| | Canada | 2 | Canadair CL-215 | Amphibian | | Mid-1973 | .. |
| | FR Germany | 4 | Submarine | Displ: 1 000 t | $28 mn. WEU approved Jan 1971 | 1967 | 1972–73 |

| Recipient | Supplier | Number | Item | Description | Comment | Date: number of items Ordered | Delivered |
|---|---|---|---|---|---|---|---|
| Iceland | Denmark | 1 | Patrol vessel | Displ: 1 800 t | | Sept 1973 | .. |
| Italy | France | 18 | Dassault-Bréguet 1150 Atlantic | ASW aircraft | $111 mn | Nov 1968 | June 1972–74 |
| | FR Germany | 200 | Krauss-Maffei Leopard | Main battle tank | $273 mn; incl licensed production of additional 600 | Jan 1971 | 1972 |
| | USA | 14 | Lockheed C-130H Hercules | Transport | $60 mn | Mid-1970 | May 1972–June 1973 |
| | | 2 | McDonnell-Douglas DC-9 | VIP transport | | (1970) | 1973 |
| | | .. | LTV MGM-52A Lance Missile | S-S missile system | $48 mn | 1973 | .. |
| | | 130 | Hughes TOW launcher | A-T missile system | $51.5 mn | 1972 | 1973 |
| | | 5 000 | Missile | | | | |
| | | 2 | Landing ship, tank, "Suffolk County" class | Displ: 4 164 t | Commissioned 1957–58. Leased | July 1972 | July 1972 |
| | | 2 | Submarine, "Guppy III" type | Displ: 1 975 t | Commissioned 1948–49. On loan | .. | Aug 1972 |
| Luxembourg | USA | 6 | Hughes TOW launcher | A-T missile system | | Aug 1973 | .. |
| | | 60 | Missile | | | | |
| Netherlands | France | 9 | Dassault-Bréguet BR 1150 Atlantic | ASW aircraft | $60 mn incl spares | July 1968 | July 1969–Jan 1972 |
| | Switzerland | 5 | Oerlikon-Contraves 5 PFZ-C 35 mm gun | Anti-aircraft tank system | | 1968 | 1974 |
| | UK | 1 | Westland Wasp | ASW helicopter | Under construction in 1973 | .. | .. |
| | USA | .. | Hughes TOW | A-T missile system | Initial contract worth $15 mn | 1971 | By 1975 |
| | | .. | | A-T missile system | Second contract | Feb 1973 | .. |

| | | | | | Comment | | |
|---|---|---|---|---|---|---|---|
| Norway | Canada | 13 | Canadair CF-104 Starfighter | Fighter/bomber | Ex-CAF. $10 mn incl cost of conversion to interceptor | 1972 | 1972 |
| | | 22 | Canadair CF-104 Starfighter | Fighter | $13.4 mn incl spares and cost of conversion to F-104G standard | .. | March 1973–May 1974 |
| | UK | 10 | Westland Sea King Mk 43 | SAR helicopter | $24 mn | Dec 1970 | 1972 |
| | USA | 2 | Dassault Falcon | Transport | Second-hand | (1973) | (1974) |
| Turkey | USA | 40 | McDonnell-Douglas F-4 Phantom | Fighter | $200 mn, incl spares and training | Aug 1972 | By 1976 |
| | | 42 | Northrop F-5E Tiger II | Fighter | Agreement includes assembly and licensed production | April 1972 | By 1975 |
| | | .. | Hughes TOW | A-T missile | On order | .. | .. |
| | | 250 | M-48 Patton | Tank | | 1972 | .. |
| | | 2 | Fast patrol boat, "Ashville 1968" class | Displ: 225 t | Commissioned 1969 | .. | Feb–June 1973 |
| | FR Germany | 4 | Submarine | Displ: 1 000 t surface | Being built | .. | .. |
| UK | France | 300 | Aérospatiale MM-38 Exocet | Naval S-S missile | | .. | 1973– |
| | Sweden | 10 | Bofors STRV 103 | Main battle tank (S-tank) | On loan for evaluation | .. | (1973) |

**Warsaw Treaty Organization**

| | | | | | | | |
|---|---|---|---|---|---|---|---|
| Bulgaria | USSR | 4 | Coastal minesweeper, "Vanya" type | Displ: 250 t | | .. | 1971–72 |
| Czecho-slovakia | USSR | .. | Mi-8 | Helicopter | | .. | 1973 |
| | | .. | T-62 | Main battle tank | | .. | (1972) |
| GDR | USSR | .. | SA-7 | SAM, mounted on BRDM-2 AC | | .. | (1973) |
| | USSR | Some | T-62 | Main battle tank | | .. | 1972 |
| Hungary | USSR | Some | T-62 | Main battle tank | | .. | 1972 |

| Recipient | Supplier | Number | Item | Description | Comment | Ordered | Delivered |
|---|---|---|---|---|---|---|---|
| Poland | USSR | .. | SA-7 | SAM mounted on BRDM-2 AC | | .. | (1973) |
| **Other Europe** | | | | | | | |
| Albania | China | 25–30 | MiG-21 | Fighter | | .. | 1972–73 |
| Austria | France | 10 | Aérospatiale SA-316C Alouette III | Helicopter | | Early 1973 | 1973 |
| | Sweden | 20 | Saab 105 OE | Light strike trainer | Repeat order $15.5 mn+. In addition to 20 previously purchased | .. | 1970–72 |
| Finland | Sweden | 6 | Saab 35BS Draken | | $1.05 mn; leased for training while awaiting delivery of 12 being assembled | April 1972 | 1972 |
| | | 12 | Saab 35S Draken | Fighter/bomber | $49 mn incl weapons, ground support and assembly in Finland | April 1970 | 1974–75 |
| | USSR | 2 | Mi-8 | Helicopter | | .. | 1973 |
| Ireland | France | 2 | Aérospatiale Alouette III | Helicopter | Additional purchase | .. | 1973 |
| | | 12 | Reims/Cessna FR172H | Light patrol aircraft | | 1972 | 1973 |
| | | 4 | Panhard AML-90 | Armoured car | | .. | 1972 |
| | | 30 | Panhard AML-VTT | Armoured personnel carrier | | .. | 1972 |
| | Italy | .. | Aermacchi MB-326 | Trainer/light ground attack aircraft | | 1973 | .. |
| | Sweden | 15 | Unimog | Armoured car | | .. | Feb 1972 |
| Spain | France | 4 | Dassault Mirage IIIDE | Trainer | $90 mn incl spares and training | Feb 1970 | 1970–72 |
| | | 26 | Dassault Mirage IIIEE | Fighter/bomber | | | |
| | | 15 | Dassault Mirage F-1C | Fighter | In production | Early 1972 | 1974– |

| Country | No. | Weapon | Description | Comments | Order | Delivery |
|---|---|---|---|---|---|---|
| | Several | Missile patrol boat, "La Combattante II" type | Displ: 234 t | | Feb 1973 | .. |
| FR Germany | 1 | Lürssen, Bremen-Vegesack patrol vessel | Displ: 400 t | Prototype of 6—other 5 to be built in Spain | 1973 | .. |
| Italy | 5 | Agusta-Bell 47 G-2 | Helicopter | From surplus stock | .. | 1973 |
| | 4 | Agusta-Bell 212AS | ASW and strike helicopter | | .. | 1973 |
| USA | 7 | Beechcraft Baron | Trainer | | .. | 1972 |
| | 1 | Piper PA-31P Pressurized Navajo | For use as trainer | | .. | 1972 |
| | 6 | Piper Turbo Aztec E | Trainer | Additional order | .. | Summer 1972 |
| | 6 | Boeing-Vertol CH-47C Chinook | Transport helicopter | $18 mn | .. | Dec 1972–74 |
| | 6 | HS Harrier | V/Stol fighter | $30 mn; 6 built to AV-8A standard, 2 to TAV-8A standard | Aug 1973 | 1976 |
| | 2 | HS Harrier | V/Stol trainer | | | |
| | 6 | Lockheed C-130 A/B Hercules | Transport | Ex-USAF | .. | 1973 |
| | 8 | Bell AH-IG Huey-Cobra | Anti-shipping strike helicopter | | .. | 1973 |
| | 5 | Hughes 500M | ASW helicopter | $1 mn initial batch | .. | 1973 |
| | 7 | Hughes 500M | ASW helicopter | Second batch | .. | 1973 |
| | 16 | Bell UH-1H Iroquois | Helicopter | | .. | 1972–73 |
| | 16 | Bell OH-58 Kiowa | Helicopter | | .. | 1972–73 |
| | 4 | Lockheed P-3A Orion | ASW aircraft | Ex-USN | .. | July 1973 |
| | 36 | McDonnell-Douglas F-4C Phantom | Fighter | $55 mn; ex-USAF, replacing F-104G returned to USA | (1970) | 1972 |
| | 6 | Sikorsky SH-3D Sea King | ASW helicopter | Additional order | .. | 1972: 2 / 1973: 4 |
| | 5 | Destroyer, "Fletcher" class | Displ: 2 080 t | Sold while on loan for u.c.: $153 000. Completed 1943–44 and transferred on loan 1957–60 | .. | 1972–73 |
| | 2 | Destroyer, modernized "Gearing" class | Displ: 2 425 t | Commissioned 1945. Of total of 5 due to be transferred, other 3 rejected by Spanish Navy in Feb 1973 | .. | Aug 1972 |
| | 1 | Helicopter carrier | Displ: 11 000 t | Sold for $500 000 while on loan; completed 1943 and originally transferred Aug 1967 | .. | 1972–73 |

| Recipient | Supplier | Number | Item | Description | Comment | Date: number of items | |
|---|---|---|---|---|---|---|---|
| | | | | | | Ordered | Delivered |
| | | 1 | Ocean minesweeper, "Agile" class | Displ: 665 t | | .. | April 1972 |
| | | 2 | Submarine, "Guppy IIA" class | Displ: 1 840 t | Transferred on loan | .. | Oct 1972 |
| Sweden | Finland | 1 | Icebreaker, similar to "URHO" class | Displ: 8 000 t | Under construction | .. | .. |
| | FR Germany | 1 | Oiler | Displ: 145 t | Built 1965 | .. | 1972 |
| | Japan | 7 | Kawasaki/Boeing Vertol KV-107/II-5 | | Engines fitted in Sweden | .. | Oct 1972–73 |
| | Norway | 1 | Fast missile patrol boat, similar to "Snögg" class | Displ: 145 t | ($1.2 mn) with Penguin SSM; may be first of class of 16 in total | .. | 1972 |
| | UK | 58 | Scottish Aviation Bulldog 101 (SK 61) | Trainer | For Air Force | June 1969 | July 1971– |
| | | 20+ | Scottish Aviation Bulldog 101 (SK-61) | Liaison aircraft | For Army | July 1971 | March 1973 |
| | USA | 2 | Lockheed C-130 E Hercules | Transport | | (1969) | 1972 |
| | | 2 | Gates Learjet | Target tug aircraft | Bought by Swedair, to operate under contract to the Swedish Government as target tugs for ground-to-air artillery training | Nov 1972 | Mid-1973 |
| Switzerland | France | .. | Aérospatiale AS-30 | A-S missile | | .. | 1971–73 |
| | Sweden | .. | Bofors Bantam | A-T missile | Still in production for the Army | .. | .. |
| | UK | 30 | HS Hunter | Fighter | ($23.2 mn); refurbished | (Jan 1971) | 1972–74 |
| | | 30 | HS Hunter | Fighter | ($42 mn); additional refurbished aircraft | March 1973 | 1974 |
| Yugoslavia | Poland | 1 | Hydrographic vessel | Displ: 1 475 t | | .. | 1972 |

## Middle East

| Country | Supplier | Number | Designation | Description | Comments | Date of order | Date of delivery |
|---|---|---|---|---|---|---|---|
| Abu Dhabi | USA | 2 | Lockheed C-130 Hercules | Transport | | Mid-1973 | 1975 |
| | UK | .. | Short Tigercat | S-A missile | | 1971 | 1973 |
| | | 10 | Patrol boat | Displ: .. | | 1972 | 1973–74 |
| | France | 12 | Dassault Mirage 5 | Fighter | $15 mn. Pakistan AF will provide training and technical aid | July 1972 | 1973–74 |
| | | 2 | Dassault Mirage 5D | Trainer | | | |
| | | 2 | Aérospatiale SA-330 Puma | Helicopter | | .. | July 1973 |
| Dubai | UK | .. | Scorpion | Light tank | A small number on order | .. | .. |
| Egypt | USSR | .. | MiG-17 | Fighter | 1973 war replacement; incl 35–40 "Super MiGs" longer range MiG-21 | Oct 1973 | 1973 |
| | | .. | MiG-19 | Fighter | | | |
| | | .. | MiG-21 | Fighter | | | |
| | | 40–60 | Su-7 | Fighter | | | |
| | | | SS-1C "Scud" | S-S missile | 2 brigades. Capable of carrying nuclear warhead. Manned by Soviet personnel | .. | Sept–Oct 1973 |
| | | .. | SA-4 "Ganef" | S-A missile | | Oct 1972 | (1973) |
| | | .. | SA-6 "Gainful" | S-A missile | Vehicle-mounted and shoulder-fired versions | (Late 1972) | 1972–73 |
| | | .. | SA-7 "Grail" | S-A missile | | | 1973 |
| | | .. | AT-1 "Snapper" | A-T missile | | .. | 1972–73 |
| | | .. | AT-3 "Sagger" | A-T missile | | .. | 1972–73 |
| | | 600 | Armoured vehicle | | 1973 war replacement. Incl T-62 tanks | Oct 1973 | 1973 |
| | | .. | Amphibious vehicle | | To launch "Sagger" ATM | .. | 1972–73 |
| | UK/Saudi Arabia | 6 | Westland Sea King | Helicopter | Ordered by Saudi Arabia on behalf of Egypt. | Mid-1973 | .. |
| | | 24 | Westland Commando | Helicopter | | | |
| Iran | USA | 108 | McDonnel-Douglas F-4 Phantom | Fighter | Armed with Sparrow and Sidewinder AAM. In addition to 72 previously purchased | .. | By 1974 |
| | | 141 | Northrop F-5E Tiger II | Fighter | U.c: $1.9 mn. Delivery delayed for incorporation of changes requested by Iran | April 1972 | March 1974– |
| | | 4 | Lockheed P 3F Orion | ASW aircraft | | (Aug) 1972 | 1974– |
| | | 287 | Bell 214A Isfahan | Helicopter | Developed with Iranian funding | Dec 1972 | 1974–79 |
| | | 202 | Bell AH-1J Sea Cobra | Helicopter | | | |

| Recipient | Supplier | Number | Item | Description | Comment | Date: number of items Ordered | Delivered |
|---|---|---|---|---|---|---|---|
| Iran | | 6 | Boeing 707-320 | Tanker transport | $62.5 mn, incl spares | Late 1972 | 1973–74 |
| | | .. | Lockheed C-130 Hercules | Transport | | 1972 | .. |
| | | 30 | Beech F33 Bonanza | Cabin monoplane | $2 mn+incl spares, service support, training and shipping | July 1972: 18 (Feb) 1973: 12 | Aug 1972– Jan 1973: 18 Late 1973: 12 |
| | | 3 | NA-Rockwell Aero Commander 690 | Light aircraft | For Air Force. Cost: $2.5 mn | .. | 1972–73 |
| | | 6 | NA-Rockwell Aero Commander Shrike | Light aircraft | For Navy | | |
| | | 2 500 | Hughes Maverick | A-S missile | To arm F-4 Phantom. Sales agreement includes participation of Iranian industry in missile projects | Mid-1973 | .. |
| | | .. | Hughes TOW | A-T missile | Cost of first order $15 mn | Nov 1971 | 1971–73 |
| | | .. | Raytheon Hawk | S-A missile | Improved version under US Foreign Military Sales Program FY 1973 | Early 1973 (1972) | .. |
| | UK | .. | BAC Swingfire | A-T missile | On order to arm Scorpion light tanks | .. | .. |
| | | 800 | Chieftain Mk5 | Tank | $346 mn incl spares, training and support equipment | 1971 | 1971 |
| | | .. | Scorpion | Light tank | $72 mn for several hundred Scorpion and Fox. Scorpion to be armed with Swingfire ATM | Aug 1972 | .. |
| | | .. | Fox | Armoured car | | | |
| | | 4 | Hovercraft, "Wellington" (BH.7) class | Displ: 50 t max | $13 mn approx. To be armed with missiles | March 1971 | 1973–75 |
| | | 2 | Store ship | Displ: .. | 300 ft. | 1972 | 1974 |
| | Italy | 91 | Agusta-Bell 206 Jet Ranger | Helicopter | | Early 1973 | .. |
| | Netherlands | 10 | Fokker-VFW F.27 Friendship | Transport | | Feb 1973: 6 Sept 1973: 4 | End 1973– mid-74 End 1974– mid-75 |

| | | | | | | |
|---|---|---|---|---|---|---|
| Iraq | USSR | | | | | |
| | .. | MiG-21 M | Fighter | | (April 1972) | Spring 1973 |
| | .. | MiG-21 | Fighter | | Oct 1973 | 1973 |
| | .. | Su-7 | Fighter | | (April 1972) | Spring 1973 |
| | 12 | Tu-22 | Bomber | 1973 war replacement | .. | Oct 1973 |
| | Czecho-slovakia | | | | | |
| | .. | Mi-6 | Helicopter | Not certain whether on visit or transferred to Iraqi AF | (April 1973) | Spring 1973 |
| | .. | Aero L-39 Z | Trainer/strike | Part of $75 mn arms deal | Spring 1973 | 1973– |
| Israel | USA | | | | | |
| | 42 | McDonnell-Douglas F-4 Phantom | Fighter | $500 mn incl 80 Skyhawk | Dec 1971 | 1972–73 |
| | 48 | McDonnell-Douglas F-4 Phantom | Fighter | $220 mn incl 36 Skyhawk. Agreement in March for 24 extended to cover 48 | Sept 1973 | By 1977 |
| | .. | McDonnell-Douglas F-4 Phantom | Fighter | 1973 war replacement. Ex-USAF | Oct 1973 | 1973 |
| | 80 | McDonnell-Douglas A-4N Skyhawk | Fighter | | Dec 1971 | 1972–mid-74 |
| | 36 | McDonnell-Douglas A-4 Skyhawk | Fighter | Agreement in March for 24 extended to cover 36. Partly surplus A-4E | Sept 1973 | By 1977 |
| | .. | McDonnell-Douglas A-4 Skyhawk | Fighter | 1973 war replacement. Ex-US Marine Corps | Oct 1973 | 1973 |
| | 8 | Boeing-Vertol CH-47C Chinook | Helicopter | | .. | Dec 1973– |
| | 12 | Sikorsky S-61R | Helicopter | | (Oct 1973) | Dec 1973– |
| | : | Sikorsky S-65 | Helicopter | | : | 1973 |
| | 12 | Lockheed C-130 Hercules | Transport | In airlift during 1973 war | (Oct 1973) | Oct 1973 |
| | 2 000 | Sidewinder | A-A missile | | : | |
| | : | Sparrow | A-A missile | | | |
| | : | Shrike | A-S missile | In airlift during 1973 war | : | Oct 1973 |
| | 200 + | Hughes Maverick | A-S missile | | | |
| | : | Raytheon Hawk | S-A missile | | | |
| | : | Hughes TOW | A-T missile | | | |
| | (150) | M-60 | Tank | By air and sea; 1973 war replacement | : | Oct 1973– |
| | : | M-48 | Tank | By air and sea; 1973 war replacement | : | Oct 1973– |
| | : | Patrol boat, "Firefish III" type | Displ: 6 t | Being built; capable of being remote-controlled | : | : |

| Recipient | Supplier | Number | Item | Description | Comment | Date: number of items | |
|---|---|---|---|---|---|---|---|
| | | | | | | Ordered | Delivered |
| Israel | UK | .. | Short Blowpipe | Submarine-launched air missile | 4 launchers on each of 3 submarines | (Mid-1973) | .. |
| | | 3 | Submarine | Displ: 500 t | Being built to FR German design. To be armed with Blowpipe SLAM | April 1972 | .. |
| Jordan | USA | 24 | Northrop F-5E Tiger II | Fighter | MAP | (April) 1972 | (1973)– |
| | | 6 | Northrop F-5B | Trainer | | (April) 1972 | 1972–73 |
| | | .. | Lockheed C-130B Hercules | Transport | US surplus, refurbished | .. | 1973 |
| | | 200 | M-113 | Armoured personnel carrier | | 1972 | 1974 |
| | UK | .. | HS Hunter | Fighter | Refurbished | .. | 1973 |
| Kuwait | UK/ Singapore | 8 | Vosper Thornycroft 38 ft. type | Displ: .. | Being built by Vosper Thornycroft, Singapore | July 1972 | .. |
| Lebanon | France | 6 | Aérospatiale Alouette | Helicopter | | Jan 1972 | (1973) |
| | Italy | 6 | Agusta-Bell 212 | Helicopter | | Mid-1972 | (1973) |
| Oman | USA | 1 | DHC-2 Beaver | STOL transport | Second-hand, formerly civil | .. | Early 1973 |
| | UK | 8 | BAC 167 Strikemaster | Trainer/strike | | Late 1971 | 1973 |
| | | 2 | Short Skyvan | STOL transport | | Aug 1972 | (1973) |
| | Canada | 2 | DHC-4 Caribou | STOL transport | | Early 1973 | (1973) |
| | Ireland | 3 | Vickers Viscount | Transport | Ex-Aer Lingus | Early 1973 | (1973) |
| Qatar | UK | 2 | HS Hunter | Fighter | In addition to 4 fighters and 2 trainers previously purchased | (Late 1972) | (1973) |

| | Supplier | No. | Item | | Description | | |
|---|---|---|---|---|---|---|---|
| Saudi Arabia | USA | 30 | Northrop F-5E Tiger II | Fighter | $130 mn. F-5E modified for low-altitude reconnaissance and strike missions. May order 70 more F-5Es | Oct 1971 | 1974 |
| | | 20 | Northrop F-5B | Trainer | | Oct 1971 | 1973 |
| | | 4 | Lockheed C-130 Hercules | Transport | Equipped for aerial tanker operations | Aug 1972 | .. |
| | | .. | Raytheon Hawk | S-A missile | Improved missile and digital data processing | Late 1973 | .. |
| | UK | | BAC maintenance, construction and training for Saudi Arabian AF | | $630 mn | May 1973 | .. |
| | | 10 | BAC 167 Strikemaster | Trainer/strike | | Dec 1972 | 1973 |
| | | 6 | Westland Sea King | Helicopter | Ordered on behalf of Egypt | (July) 1973 | 1974 |
| | | 24 | Westland Commando | | | | |
| | France | 34 | Dassault Mirage IIE | Fighter | Order may also include Crotale SAMs | Late 1973 | .. |
| | | 4 | Dassault Mirage IIID | Trainer | | | |
| | | .. | AMX-30 | Tank | | 1972 | 1972–73 |
| Syria | USSR | .. | MiG-17 | Fighter | 1973 war replacement | Oct 1973 | 1973 |
| | | .. | MiG-21 | Fighter | | (May 1972) | 1973 |
| | | .. | MiG-21 | Fighter | 1973 war replacement | Oct 1973 | 1973 |
| | | .. | Su-7 | Fighter | | (May 1972) | (1973) |
| | | .. | Mi-8 | Helicopter | | (May 1972) | 1973 |
| | | 20 + | Frog 7 | Artillery rocket | | | |
| | | .. | V-750 VK (SA-2) "Guideline" | S-A missile | | (May 1972) | 1973 |
| | | .. | SA-3 "Goa" | S-A missile | | (May 1972) | 1973 |
| | | .. | SA-6 "Gainful" | S-A missile | | (May 1972) | 1973 |
| | | .. | SA-7 "Grail" ("Strela") | S-A missile | | (May 1972) | Nov 1972–1973 |
| | | .. | SS-N-2 "Styx" | Naval S-S missile | To arm "Osa" class patrol boats | (May 1972) | Dec 1972–73 |
| | | .. | AT-1 "Snapper" | A-T missile | | (May 1972) | 1972–73 |
| | | .. | AT-3 "Sagger" | A-T missile | | (May 1972) | 1972–73 |
| | | 340 | T-62 / T-54 | Tank | 1973 war replacement | Oct 1973 | 1973 |
| | | 3 + | Patrol boat, "Osa" class | Displ: 165 t | Ex-USSR. Armed with "Styx" SSM | (May 1972) | Dec 1972: 2 / 1973: 1 + |
| Democratic Yemen | USSR | 12 | MiG-21 | Fighter | | 1971 | 1973– |

| Recipient | Supplier | Number | Item | Description | Comment | Ordered | Delivered |
|---|---|---|---|---|---|---|---|
| **South Asia** | | | | | | | |
| Bangladesh | USSR | 10 | MiG-21 MF | Fighter | Military assistance | March 1972 | 1973 |
| | | 2 | MiG-21 UTI | Trainer | | | |
| | | 1 | An-24 | Transport | | .. | 1973 |
| | | (3) | An-26 | Transport | | .. | 1973 |
| India | UK | 6 | Westland Sea King | Helicopter | | 1972 | 1973–74 |
| | | 40 systems | Short Tigercat | S-A missile | | Oct 1971 | 1972–73 |
| | France | .. | Short Seacat | Naval S-A missile | To arm "Leander" class frigates | .. | .. |
| | | 8 | Aérospatiale Alouette III | Helicopter | To arm "Leander" class frigates | .. | 1972– |
| Pakistan | USA | 10 | Sikorsky | Helicopter | On order | .. | .. |
| | | 300 | M-113 | Armoured personnel carrier | $13 mn; embargoed until 14 March 1973 | Oct 1970 | 1973 |
| | UK | 6 | Westland Sea King | Helicopter | U.c.: $2.16 mn; for ASW Ex-UK | Oct 1972 | .. |
| | | 2 | Frigate, "Whitby" class | Displ: 2 560 t | | (Early 1973) | .. |
| | France | 28 | Dassault Mirage 5 | Fighter | In addition to 24 previously purchased. Is reportedly negotiating for more | 1970 | 1972–73: 20 |
| | | 2 | Dassault Mirage III | Trainer | | | .. : 10 |
| | Iran | 40 | Northrop F-5 Freedom Fighter | Fighter | To receive when Iran re-equips with F-5E. May also get NA F-86s, Lockheed C-130s and helicopters | Mid-1973 | 1974– |
| Sri Lanka (Ceylon) | USA | 10 | Cessna 150 | Cabin monoplane | Gift, 6 for training, 4 for transport | Nov 1972 | 1973 |
| **Far East** | | | | | | | |
| Brunei | USA | 1 | Bell 212 Twin-Pac | Helicopter | | Mid-1973 | Jan 1974 |

| Recipient | Supplier | No. | Designation | Description | Comments | Date of order | Date of delivery |
|---|---|---|---|---|---|---|---|
| Indonesia | USA | 14 | NA F-51 Mustang | Fighter | MAP | .. | Spring 1973 |
| | | 16 | Lockheed T-33 | Trainer | | 1972 | Mid-1973 |
| | | 10 | Sikorsky S-55 | Helicopter | | .. | 1972–73 |
| | | 1 | Frigate, "Claud Jones" class | Displ: 1 450 t | Commissioned 1959, modernized 1973. Cost $145 000 | Feb 1973 | 1973 |
| | Australia | 16 | Avon Sabre | Fighter | Gift; worth $11.9 mn, incl training, spares and ancillary equipment. Ex-Australian AF | (March 1972) | Feb 1973 |
| | | 4 | GAF Nomad | STOL transport | Gift; a further 2 may be provided Ex-Australian AF | 1973 | 1974–75 |
| | | 2 | Douglas C-47 | Transport | Gift; ex-Australian AF | (1973) | 1973 |
| | | 2 | Patrol boat, "Attack" class | Displ: 146 t full load | Gift | (1972) | 1973–74 |
| | | 6 | Patrol boat, 51 ft. | Displ: .. | Gift | (1972) | .. |
| Japan | USA | 3 | Beechcraft C-90 King Air | Trainer | | Late 1972 | Summer 1973 |
| | | 14 | McDonnell-Douglas RF-4E Phantom | Tactical reconnaissance aircraft | | April 1973 | 1974–75 |
| | USA | 82 | Douglas Nike-Hercules | S-A missile | Included in purchase of US missile and air-defence control systems in Okinawa. Total contract $25.6 mn incl launchers and other ground facilities, manual AD warning and control facilities, and spare parts | Oct 1972 | 1973 |
| | | 144 | Raytheon Hawk | | | | |
| | | .. | General Dynamics Tartar | S-A missile | $31 mn. For new guided-missile destroyer | July 1973 | .. |
| Khmer Republic | USA | 24 | Cessna A-37 | COIN aircraft | Promised after cessation of US bombing | Aug 1973 | .. |
| | | 36 | NA T-28D | Trainer/strike | Mainly supplied in 1973 | Aug 1973: 15 | 1972–73 |
| | | 32 | Bell UH-1 Iroquois | Helicopter | | .. | 1972–73 |
| | | 4 | Douglas C-47 | Transport | | .. | 1973 |
| | | 20 + | Fairchild C-123 | Transport | Previously operated in Viet-Nam | .. | Aug 1973 |
| | | 8 | DHC-3 Otter | STOL transport | Probably part of batch of 82 aircraft transferred from Viet-Nam | .. | (Aug 1973) |
| | | (35) | Cessna L-19 Bird Dog | Cabin monoplane | | .. | (Aug 1973) |

| Recipient | Supplier | Number | Item | Description | Comment | Date: number of items | |
|---|---|---|---|---|---|---|---|
| | | | | | | Ordered | Delivered |
| | | 14 | Helio Stallion AU-24 | Coin aircraft | Supplied as aid under USAF "Credible Chase" COIN programme | .. | Spring 1973 |
| | | 30 | Armoured personnel carrier | | | .. | 1973 |
| | | 21 | River patrol boat | Displ: .. | | .. | 1973 |
| Korea, North | USSR | .. | SA-7 | S-A missile | | .. | 1972–73 |
| | | .. | Frog 7 | Artillery rocket | | .. | 1972–73 |
| | | .. | T-55 | Tank | | .. | 1972–73 |
| Korea, South | USA | 40 | Northrop F-5E Tiger II | Fighter | | Nov 1972 | .. |
| | | 2 | Coastal minesweeper | Displ: 320 t | Being built | .. | .. |
| | | 1 | Patrol boat | Displ: 70 t full load | | .. | 1973 |
| Laos | USA | 7 | Cessna T-41D | Trainer | MAP | .. | (1972–73) |
| | | 24 | Sikorsky S-58 | Helicopter | MAP; transferred from Viet-Nam | .. | (1972–73) |
| | | .. | Douglas C-47 | Transport | MAP; transferred from Viet-Nam | .. | (1972–73) |
| | | 6 | Cessna 185 Skywagon | Cabin monoplane | MAP | .. | (1972–73) |
| Malaysia | USA | 14 | Northrop F-5E Tiger II | Fighter } | $35 mn incl spares and technical support | July 1972 | 1975–76 |
| | | 2 | Northrop F-5B | Trainer } | | | |
| | France | 4 | Aérospatiale Alouette III | Helicopter | | Aug 1970 | 1973 |
| | | 4 | Fast patrol boat, "La Combattante II" type | Displ: 234 t | $22.5 mn incl Exocet SSM. Plans to order a further 3 armed with guns | Aug 1970 | 1973 |
| | | .. | Aérospatiale MM-38 Exocet | Naval S-A missile | 2 launchers on each fast patrol boat | Aug 1970 | 1973 |
| | Canada | 5 | DHC-4 Caribou | STOL transport | | ..:4 / 1973:1 | 1972:4 / ..:1 |

| Recipient | Supplier | No. | Item | Description | Comments | Date of order | Date of delivery |
|---|---|---|---|---|---|---|---|
| Philippines | USA | .. | Bell UH-1 Iroquois | Helicopter | Acquired for development purposes with $8 mn Ex-Im Bank loan. Used for troop transport | .. | 1973 |
| | | 4 | Lockheed L 100-20 Hercules | Civil transport | | .. | 1973 |
| | | .. | DHC-2 Beaver | STOL transport | Acquired for development purposes. Viet-Nam surplus, purchased for cost of shipping. Armed with machine guns. | .. | 1973 |
| | Italy | 6 | Inshore patrol craft | Displ: 33 t full load | | 1971 | .. |
| | | 48 | SIAI-Marchetti SF.260 | Trainer | Incl 16 for COIN | Late 1972 | May 1973–May 1974 |
| Singapore | USA | 40 | McDonnell-Douglas A-4 Skyhawk | Fighter | Ex-US Navy. Initial 8 refurbished in USA, remainder in Singapore | Mid-1972 | 1973:12 1974:28 |
| | UK | 22 | HS Hunter F.74 | Fighter | Refurbished | 1971 | 1972–73 |
| | | 5 | HS Hunter T.75 | Trainer | | | |
| | | 6 | Short Skyvan | STOL transport | Cost $3.6 mn; 3 specially equipped for search and rescue duties | Nov 1972 | 1973–74 |
| | New Zealand | .. | BAC Rapier | S-A missile | On order | Aug 1972 | .. |
| | | 4 | AESL Airtourer | Monoplane | Cost $157 000. Has option for 2 more | July 1971 | 1973 |
| Taiwan | USA | 2 | Submarine, "Guppy II" type | Displ: 1870 t | Completed 1945–46. Modernized. On loan for ASW practice. Negotiated since 1970 | Oct 1972 | 1973 |
| | | 5 | Destroyer, "Gearing" class | Displ: 2 425 t | Completed 1945–46. 4 modernized, 1 used for spares. | .. | 1972:2 1973:3 |
| | Israel | .. | Rafael Shafir | A-A missile | | Mid-1973 | .. |
| Thailand | USA | 30 | McDonnell-Douglas A-4 Skyhawk | Fighter | U.c.: $350 000. Ex-US Navy. Half to be refurbished in USA, remainder in Thailand | May 1973 | .. |

| Recipient | Supplier | Number | Item | Description | Comment | Date: number of items | |
|---|---|---|---|---|---|---|---|
| | | | | | | Ordered | Delivered |
| | | .. | Northrop F-5E Tiger II | Fighter | MAP | .. | By 1975 |
| | | 16 | NAR OV-10 C Bronco | COIN aircraft | $5.8 mn; in addition to 16 previously delivered | (June 1972) | 1973 |
| | | 13 | Fairchild AU-23 Peacemaker | COIN aircraft | Supplied under USAF "Credible Chase" COIN programme | .. | (1973) |
| | | 16 | Fairchild-Hiller FH-1100 | Helicopter | For Army | .. | (1973) |
| | | 3 | Frigate, "Corvette" type | Displ: 900 t | New; third being built. Cost of second $5.9 mn grant aid construction | June 1969: 1 June 1971:1 ..:1 | 1972–73: 2 ..:1 |
| | UK | 1 | Frigate, "Yarrow" type | Displ: 1 780 t | $15.6 mn. Armed with Seacat SAM | Aug 1969 | 1973 |
| | | .. | Short Seacat | Naval S-A missile | 1 quadruple launcher on frigate, "Yarrow" type | Aug 1969 | 1973 |
| | Italy | 12 | SIAI-Marchetti SF.260 MT | Trainer | | Late 1972 | 1973 |
| | New Zealand | 24 | AESL CT 4 Airtrainer | Monoplane | $1.3 mn | Mid-1972 | 1973–74 |
| Viet-Nam, South | USA | 72–78 | Northrop F-5 E Tiger II | Fighter | To replace F-5 A delivered in Nov 1972 airlift | .. | 1973–75 |
| | | 20 | Boeing-Vertol CH-47 Chinook | Helicopter | | .. | 1973 |
| **Oceania** | | | | | | | |
| Australia | Canada | 1 | DHC-4 Caribou | Trainer | | (1972) | .. |
| | France | 6 | Dassault Mirage IIID | Trainer | $12.2 mn | 1970 | 1973 |
| | New Zealand | 37 | N.Z. Aerospace Industries CT-4 Airtrainer | Trainer | $4.6 mn | (Oct) 1973 | (1974–76) |
| | UK | 2 | HS 748 | Trainer/transport | $4.8 mn | .. | (1973) |
| | | 10 | Westland Sea King | Helicopter | $53.6 mn incl spares and ground support | 1972 | 1974–75 |

| Supplier | Number | Designation | Description | Comments | Date of order | Date of delivery |
|---|---|---|---|---|---|---|
| USA | 1 | Destroyer, "Daring" class | Displ: 2 800 t | Purchased while on loan | .. | 1972 |
| | 2 | Submarine, "Oberon" class | Displ: 1 610 t | ($44.7 mn) | 1972 | (1975: 1) (1976: 1) |
| | 12 | Boeing-Vertol CH-47C Chinook | Transport helicopter | $44.2 mn | March 1972 | 1973–74 |
| | 24 | General Dynamics F-111C | VG fighter/bomber | $466 mn | Oct 1963 | 1973 |
| **New Zealand** | | | | | | |
| UK | 10 | BAC 167 Strikemaster Mk 88 | Strike/reconnaissance trainer | $9.3 mn incl spares, training etc. | Nov 1970 | 1972– |
| | 1 | Westland Wasp. | Helicopter | Under construction | .. | Aug 1972 |
| | 1 | Frigate, "Leander" class | Displ: 2 450 t | | Aug 1968 | 1974 |
| | 4 | Patrol craft, "Lake" class | Displ: 105 t | Under construction | .. | |
| USA | .. | Bell UH-1 Iroquois | Helicopter | | .. | 1970–72 |
| **Africa** | | | | | | |
| *North Africa* | | | | | | |
| **Libya** | | | | | | |
| UK | .. | Short Seacat | Naval S-A missile | 2 triple launchers on Vosper Mk 7 frigate | Feb 1968 | 1973 |
| | 1 | Frigate, Vosper Mk 7 | Displ: 1 325 t | New. Armed with Seacat SAM | Feb 1968 | 1973 |
| France | 58 | Dassault Mirage 5 | Fighter | $144 mn+. Some alleged by Israel to have been transferred to Egypt; denied by Libya and France | Jan 1970 | 1971–73: 90 |
| | 32 | Dassault Mirage III E | Fighter | | | |
| | 10 | Dassault Mirage III R | Reconnaissance | | | |
| | 10 | Dassault Mirage III B | Trainer | | | |
| | .. | Matra R-550 Magic. | A-A missile | On order | | |
| France/ S. Africa | 3 batt | Matra/Thomson-CSF Crotale | S-A missile | | Mid-1973 | 1973 |
| Egypt | .. | S-A missile | | | .. | Spring 1973 |
| **Morocco** | | | | | | |
| USA | .. | Lockheed C-130 Hercules | Transport | U.c.: $4.8 mn in 1975, incl engines, avionics and some training | Mid-1973 | 1975 |

| Recipient | Supplier | Number | Item | Description | Comment | Ordered | Delivered |
|---|---|---|---|---|---|---|---|
| | | | | | | | Date: number of items |
| | France | 2 | Patrol boat | Displ: 440 t full load | | Late 1973 | .. |
| | Canada/ Italy | 5 | Fairchild C-119 Packet | Transport | Ex-Canadian AF. Refurbished by SIAI-Marchetti | (1973) | .. |
| Tunisia | USA | 1 | Destroyer, converted "Edsall" class | Displ: 1 590 t | Completed 1943 | .. | Oct 1973 |
| | France | .. | Aérospatiale SS. 12 (M) | S-S missile | To arm 1 patrol boat | (Oct) 1973 | Nov 1974 |
| | | 1 | Patrol Boat, "P 48" type | Displ: 250 t | Armed with SS.12 SSM | (Oct) 1973 | Nov 1974 |
| | | 1 | Corvette, "A 69 Aviso" type | Displ: 950 t | | 1972 | (1974) |
| | | 1 | Coastal minesweeper, "Acacia" class | Displ: 320 t | Ex-USA, ex-France. On loan until completion of corvette | May 1973 | (1973) |
| *Sub-Saharan Africa* | | | | | | | |
| Cameroun | France | 6 | Fouga Magister | Trainer | French surplus, refurbished | .. | 1973 |
| | | 1 | Aérospatiale SA-330 Puma | Helicopter | For VIP transport | .. | (1973) |
| Ethiopia | USA | .. | Northrop F-5 Freedom Fighter | Fighter | Part of $30 mn FY 1974 military aid | .. | (1973–74) |
| Ghana | UK | 8 | Britten Norman BN-2 Islander | Transport | $1.8 mn incl avionics, spares and special interior conversions | April 1973 | 1973 |
| | | 6 | Scottish Aviation Bulldog 120 | Transport | $480 000 incl spares and services | March 1973 | 1973 |
| | | 6 | Short Skyvan 3 M | Transport | $4.9 mn incl spares | Oct 1973 | Mid-1974 |
| | France | 4 | Aérospatiale Alouette III | Helicopter | On order | .. | .. |
| | Netherlands | 5 | Fokker-VFW F.27 Friendship Mk 400 M | Transport | | | |
| | | 1 | Fokker-VFW F.27 Friendship Mk 600 | Transport | | Oct 1973 | 1974 |

| Country | Supplier | Number | Item | Description | Comment | | June 1973 |
|---|---|---|---|---|---|---|---|
| Guinea | China | 4 | Patrol boat, "Shanghai" class | Displ: 100 t full load | With 40 advisors to assist with training | .. | .. |
| Ivory Coast | France | 3 | Aérospatiale SA-330 Puma | Helicopter | On order | .. | .. |
| Kenya | (USA) | 1 + | Piper Navajo | Transport | | .. | (1973) |
| Malagasy | Mexico | 1 | Transport ship | Transport | Being built | .. | .. |
| Malawi | UK | 3 + | Gunboat | Displ: .. | On order | .. | .. |
| Nigeria | USA Switzerland | 3 | Piper Navajo | Transport | $1 mn incl spares. Sold by Piper International, Geneva | (May 1973) | 1973 |
|  | UK | 20 | Scottish Aviation Bulldog 120 | Transport | $1.85 mn incl spares, support equipment and training | (May) 1973 | 1973– |
|  |  | 2 | Fast patrol boat | Displ: 105 t | $3 mn +; being built | 1971 | .. |
|  | FR Germany | 4 | Dornier Do 28 | Monoplane | | Mid-1973 | .. |
|  |  | 4 | MBB Bo 105 | Helicopter | | Mid-1973 | .. |
|  | Netherlands | 1 | Fokker-VFW F.28 | Transport | $15.7 mn incl 2 for Nigerian Airways | (May) 1972 | Feb 1973 |
| Rhodesia | (South Africa) | .. | Aérospatiale SA-330 Puma | Helicopter | | .. | (1973) |
| Rwanda | France | .. | Aérospatiale Alouette III | Helicopter | | .. | (1973) |
|  | Italy | 6 | Aermacchi MB.326 6B | Trainer/strike | | 1972 | .. |
| Senegal | UK/ Singapore | 12 | Patrol boat, Vosper 45 ft type | Displ: .. | Being built by Vosper Thornycroft, Singapore | .. | .. |
| Sierra Leone | Sweden | 10 | Saab-Scania MFI-15 | Light aircraft | | Late 1972 | April 1973: 2 |
|  | USA/Sweden | 2 | Hughes 300 | Helicopter | Supplied by Saab, Scandi-navian distributor for Hughes | (Late 1972) | 1973 |

279

| Recipient | Supplier | Number | Item | Description | Comment | Ordered | Delivered |
|---|---|---|---|---|---|---|---|
| Somalia | USSR | .. | MiG-15 | Fighter | | .. | |
| | | .. | MiG-17 | Fighter | | | |
| | | .. | MiG-21 | Fighter | | | |
| | | .. | Il-28 | Bomber | 120 aircraft reportedly being delivered 1973–74 | | 1973–74 |
| | | .. | Mi-4 | Helicopter | | | |
| | | .. | Mi-8 | Helicopter | | | |
| | | .. | An-24 | Transport | | | |
| | | .. | An-26 | Transport | | | |
| | | .. | Il-18 | Transport | | | |
| | | .. | Armoured personnel carrier | | | .. | 1973 |
| | | .. | Motor torpedo boat, "P 6" class | Displ: 50 t | | .. | 1973 |
| Tanzania | UK | 1 | HS 748 | Transport | For VIP transport | Mid-1973 | .. |
| | China | 12 | Shenyang F-4 (MiG-17) | Fighter | | .. | 1973 |
| | | 12 | Shenyang F-6 (MiG-19) | Fighter | | .. | 1973–74 |
| | Italy | 2 | Agusta-Bell 206A Jet Ranger | Helicopter | | .. | 1973 |
| | (Italy) | 2 | Bell 47 G | Helicopter | | .. | 1973 |
| Uganda | USSR | 7 | Helicopter | Helicopter | According to Kenyan sources. Denied by Soviet Union | (April 1973) | Nov 1973 |
| | | 58 | Light tank | | | | |
| | | 62 | Armoured car | | | | |
| | France/Libya | .. | Aérospatiale SS.11 Savien | Anti-tank missile | ACs armed with SS.11. Delivered via Libya which pays most of cost | (Oct) 1972 | 1973– |
| | | 80 + | | Armoured car | | | |
| | Italy | 6 | Agusta-Bell 205 Iroquois | Helicopter | | .. | 1973 |
| | | 2 | Agusta-Bell 206 A Jet Ranger | Helicopter | | .. | 1973 |
| | (Libya) | 8 + | (Northrop F-5) | Fighter | According to Radio Uganda at least 8 fighter-bombers were provided by a friendly country | .. | Early 1973 |

*Date: number of items* (column group over Ordered / Delivered)

| Country | Supplier | Number | Weapon | Category | Comments | Date of order | Date of delivery |
|---|---|---|---|---|---|---|---|
| Zaire | USA | .. | Lockheed C-130 Hercules | Transport | | (July 1973) | 1973 |
| | France | 17 | Dassault Mirage 5 | Fighter | Plus option for further 17. Has a total requirement for 40+ | Sept 1972 | 1974–75 |
| | | 23 | Aérospatiale SA-330 Puma | Helicopter | On order; an addition to 7 delivered in 1971 | .. | .. |
| | Italy | 6 | Aermacchi MB. 326 | Trainer/striker | In addition to previous 17 | (July 1973) | .. |
| | | 12 | SIAI-Marchetti SF.260 | Cabin monoplane | In addition to 12 delivered 1970 | Sept 1972 | .. |
| Zambia | Italy | 25 | Agusta-Bell 205 Iroquois | Helicopter | | Early 1973 | 1973– |
| **South Africa** | | | | | | | |
| South Africa | UK | 7 | Westland Wasp | Helicopter | Under Simonstown Agreement | Nov 1971 | 1973:3 1974:4 |
| | France | 16 | Dassault Mirage F-1C2 | Fighter | Part of licensed agreement. To be manufactured in France (see appendix 8E.) | June 1971 | .. |
| | | 32 | Dassault Mirage F-1A2 | Fighter | Increasing share of Atlas-built components | June 1971 | .. |
| | | 4 | Dassault Mirage III R | Reconnaissance | With other supplementary deliveries | Mid-1972 | (1973) |
| | | 1 | Submarine, "Daphne" class | Displ: 850 t | Reportedly being built; in addition to previous 3 | .. | .. |
| | Italy | .. | Piaggio P.166 | Transport | | 1971 | 1973– |
| | | 40 | Aermacchi Aerfer AM 3 C | Monoplane | U.c.: $120 000 fully equipped | 1971 | Early 1973– |
| | | .. | Silvercraft SH-4 | Helicopter | | 1973 | |
| | | 6 | Aermacchi MB.326 K | Trainer/striker | Initial supply of improved version, prior to start of licensed production. A further 15 as knocked-down parts | .. | 1974– |
| **Central America** | | | | | | | |
| Cuba | USSR | (30) | MiG-21 | Fighter | | .. | 1972–73 |
| Honduras | USA | 5 | Cessna-T-41D | Trainer | | .. | Dec 1973 |

281

| Recipient | Supplier | Number | Item | Description | Comment | Date: number of items Ordered | Delivered |
|---|---|---|---|---|---|---|---|
| Jamaica | USA | 3 | Patrol boat | Displ: 104 t | | .. | 1974– |
| | UK | 1 | Britten Norman BN-2 Islander | Transport | $600 000 | Sept 1973 | .. |
| | | .. | Military vehicle | | | | |
| Mexico | USA | 5 | Bell 205 A-1 | Helicopter | | Nov 1972 | 1973 |
| | | 5 | Bell 206 B Jet Ranger | Helicopter | | Nov 1972 | April 1973 |
| | | 19 | Minesweeper, "Auk" class | Displ: 890 t | $28 000. 10 to be used for spares | Feb 1972: 10 1973: 10 | 1972–73 |
| | | 1 | Minesweeper, "Admirable" class | Displ: 650 t | | .. | .. |
| | | 1 | Small auxiliary floating dry dock | Displ: .. | On lease; FY 1973 transfer | .. | .. |
| | UK | 21 | Fast patrol boat | Displ: .. | $28 mn loan. Designed in consultation with Mexico. Fitted with arms in Mexico | (April) 1973 | By late 1976 |
| | Israel | 5 | IAI Arava | STOL transport | $15 mn incl initial spares. Israel to set up overhaul facilities in Mexico | April 1973 | .. |
| Nicaragua | Israel | 14 | IAI Arava | STOL transport | | .. | 1973– |
| El Salvador | Israel | 25 | (IAI Arava) | STOL transport | | Sept 1973 | .. |
| **South America** | | | | | | | |
| Argentina | USA | 6 | Hughes 500 M | Helicopter | On order for Navy | .. | .. |
| | | 3 | Lockheed L-188 Electra | Transport | On order for Navy | 1973 | Jan 1973 |
| | | 1 | Destroyer, "Gearing" class | Displ: 2 425 t | Completed 1945; modernized $229 500. FY 1973 ship sale | .. | .. |
| | UK | 2 | Westland WG 13 Lynx | Helicopter | For use on Vickers type 42 frigates | (May 1970) | After Oct 1975 |
| | | .. | HS Sea Dart | Naval S-A missile | 1 twin launcher on two Vickers type 42 frigates | (May 1970) | .. |

| Supplier | No. | Designation | Description | Comments | Date of order | Date of delivery |
|---|---|---|---|---|---|---|
|  | 1 | Frigate, Vickers Type 42 | Displ: 3 500 t | $72 mn, incl $24 mn for missile system and gas turbines. Second assembled in Argentina | May 1970 | .. |
| France | 10 | Dassault Mirage III E | Fighter | Armed with Matra R.530 AAM | Oct 1970 | Sept 1972–73 |
|  | 2 | Dassault Mirage III B | Trainer | | (Oct 1970) | 1972–73 |
|  | : | Matra R. 530 | A-A missile | To arm Mirage | March 1973 | .. |
|  | 20 | Aérospatiale SS.11 | S-S missile | For Navy use on Alouette III | | .. |
|  | 30 | Aérospatiale AS.12 | A-S missile | | | .. |
| FR Germany | 2 | Submarine, type 205 | Displ: 1 000 t | Being built in FR Germany | Jan 1969 | |
|  | 2 | Fast patrol boat | Displ: 240 t | Being built in FR Germany and Argentina | 1970 | |
| Bolivia | | | | | | |
| USA | 3+ | NA F-86F Sabre | Fighter | MAP | : : | Late 1973 |
|  | 8 | Cessna 185 Skywagon | Cabin monoplane | | : : | Sept 1973 |
|  | 2 | Cessna Turbo Centurion | Cabin monoplane | | : : | Sept 1973 |
|  | 1 | Cessna 414 | Cabin monoplane | | : : | Late 1973 |
|  | 1 | Beech King Air | Transport | | : : | Late 1973 |
| Canada | 13 | Canadair T-33 A/N | Trainer | $4 mn; incl spares and technical support. Refurbished | Feb 1973 | 1973 |
| Brazil | | | | | | |
| USA | 36 | Northrop F-5E Tiger II | Fighter | $70 mn+. Agreement may involve future coproduction | Mid-1973 | From 1975 |
|  | 6 | Northrop F-5B | Trainer | | | |
|  | 22 | Bell UH-1H | Helicopter | To support oil drilling operations | : | Jan 1973: 8 |
|  | 8 | Sikorsky S-58 T | Helicopter | | Mid-1973 | Late 1973 |
|  | 2 | Sikorsky S-61 | Helicopter | On order. For ASW operations | : | : |
|  | 1 | Submarine, "Guppy II" type | Displ: 1 870 t | Completed early 1940s; modernized | : | March 1973 |
|  | 1 | Destroyer, "Allen M Sumner" class | Displ: 2 200 t | Completed mid-1940s; modernized | : | July 1973 |
| UK | 6 | HS 748 | Transport | | Oct 1973 | July 1974– |
|  | 5 | HS 125, Srs 400 | Transport | $12.5 mn | May 1972: 1 (Oct) 1973: 1 | 1972–73: 4 |
|  | 3 | Submarine, "Oberon" class | Displ: 1 619 t | | 1969: 2 Aug 1972: 1 | 1972–73: 2 1974: 1 |
|  | 4 | Frigate, Vosper Mk 10 "Nitheroi" class | Displ: 3 500 t | Plus 2 built in Brazil. Cost of 6: $283 mn. 2 general purpose, 2 ASW versions | Sept 1970 | 1976–79 |

| | | | | | | Date: number of items | |
|---|---|---|---|---|---|---|---|
| Recipient | Supplier | Number | Item | Description | Comment | Ordered | Delivered |
| Brazil | | .. | Short Seacat | Naval S-A missile | 2 triple launchers on 6 Vosper Mk 10 frigates | Nov 1970 | (1976–79) |
| | France | 12 | Mirage III E | Fighter | Armed with Matra R.530 AAM | May 1970 | 1972: 2 1973: 14 |
| | | 4 | Mirage III D | Trainer | | | |
| | | .. | Matra R.530 | A-A missile | To arm Mirage III | (May 1970) | (1972–73) |
| | | 20 | Aérospatiale MM-38 Exocet | Naval S-S missile | 2 twin launchers on 2 Vosper Mk 10 general purpose frigates | Nov 1972 | (1976–79) |
| | France/ FR Germany | (40) | Aérospatiale/MBB Roland 1/2 | S-A missile | 4 systems each with 10 missiles. Clear-weather and all-weather versions; partial assembly | Oct 1972 | 1972–73 |
| | | 4 | Tank | | Armed with Roland SAM. AMX-30 from France or Spz Neu (Marder) from FR Germany | Oct 1972 | (1972–73) |
| | Italy | .. | Silvercraft SH-4 | Helicopter | A number imported prior to start of licensed production | .. | 1973 |
| | Australia | .. | GAF/HSD Ikara | ASW missile | $26 mn; 1 launcher on 4 Vosper Mk 10 ASW frigates | Feb 1972 | (1976–79) |
| Chile | UK | 8 | HS Hunter | Fighter | Ex-UK Navy, refurbished | 1972 | 1973 |
| | | 6 | HS Sea Vampire T.22 | Trainer | Armed with Seacat SAM. Exocet SSM and helicopter | Dec 1972 | 1973 |
| | | 2 | Frigate, "Leander" class | Displ: 2 500 t | | Oct 1969 | .. |
| | | 2 | Submarine, "Oberon" class | Displ: 1 610 t | 1 quadruple launcher on each "Leander" class frigate | Oct 1969 | .. |
| | | .. | Short Seacat | Naval S-A missile | | (Oct 1969) | .. |
| | France | 10 | Aérospatiale SA-330 Puma | Helicopter | For Army | Late 1971 | 1973– |
| | | 3 | Convair PBY-5A | Naval bomber | Ex-French, after use in Pacific | 1973 | 1973 |
| | | 20 | Aérospatiale MM-38 Exocet | Naval S-S missile | 4 launchers on order for each "Leander" class frigate | .. | .. |

| Country | Supplier | No. | Designation | Type | Comments | Order date | 1972–73 |
|---|---|---|---|---|---|---|---|
| Colombia | France | 14 | Dassault Mirage 5 | Fighter | | Dec 1970 | .. |
| | | 2 | Dassault Mirage 5 R | Reconnaissance | | | .. |
| | | 2 | Dassault Mirage 5 D | Trainer | | | .. |
| | FR Germany | 2 | Submarine, type 209 | Displ: 1 000 t | Being built | .. | .. |
| Ecuador | France | 6 | Aérospatiale Aloette III | Helicopter | | Late 1971 | .. |
| Guyana | UK | 3 | Vosper Thornycroft Patrol craft | Displ: .. | 110 ft | 1970 | .. |
| Paraguay | Brazil | 20 | Aerotec T-23 Uirapuru | Trainer | | March 1972 | .. |
| Peru | USA | 24 | Cessna A-37 | COIN aircraft | Subject to satisfactory credit arrangements | .. | .. |
| | | 14 | Bell 212 Twin-Pac | Helicopter | $11.5 mn, incl spares and technical support | (Oct) 1973 | 1973–74 |
| | USSR | 3 | Mi-8 | Helicopter | Gift | .. | May 1973 |
| | UK | 2 | Destroyer, "Ferré" class (T-54/55) | Displ: 2 800 t | Completed 1953–54 | 1969 | 1973 |
| | | .. | | Tank | | .. | Late 1973 |
| | France | 8 | Dassault Mirage 5 | Fighter | | Sept 1973 | .. |
| | FR Germany | 2 | Submarine, type 209 | Displ: 1 000 t | | May 1972 | .. |
| | Netherlands | 1 | Cruiser | Displ: 9 529 t | Completed 1953. $7.5 mn | Feb 1973 | 1973 |
| Uruguay | USA | 1 | Fairchild FH.227 | Transport | | .. | 1973 |
| Venezuela | USA | 12 | NA Rockwell T-2D Buckeye | Trainer | Initial funding $5.2 mn. Purchased through US Navy | April 1972 | 1973 |
| | | 1 | Submarine, "Guppy II" type | Displ: 1 870 t | Completed early 1940s | .. | May 1973 |
| | UK | 6 | Fast patrol boat, Vosper Thornycroft 121 ft class | Displ: 150 t approx. | $16 mn. 3 armed with Otomat SSM | April 1972 | Late 1974 |
| | France | 7 | Dassault Mirage III E | Fighter | | Nov 1971 | 1973–74 |
| | | 6 | Dassault Mirage 5 | Fighter | | | |
| | | 2 | Dassault Mirage III B | Trainer | | | |

| Recipient | Supplier | Number | Item | Description | Comment | Date: number of items | |
|---|---|---|---|---|---|---|---|
| | | | | | | Ordered | Delivered |
| | | 142 | AMX-30 | Tank | | July 1972 | 1972–73 |
| | | 20 | AMX-155 | Self-propelled howitzer | $60 mn | | |
| | France/ Italy | 40 | Matra-OTO Melara Otomat | S-S missile | To arm 3 Vosper patrol boats | June 1972 | 1974 |
| | FR Germany | 2 | Submarine | Displ: 2 200 t | | (Aug) 1973 | .. |

# Part III. Advances in weapon technology

# 9. Reconnaissance satellites

*Square-bracketed references, thus [1], refer to the list of references on page 302.*

## I. *Introduction*

Reconnaissance by satellites became an internationally recognized activity when the SALT I agreements were signed in May 1972. The articles in the two SALT I agreements which deal with the problems of verification stipulate that "for the purpose of providing assurance of compliance with the provisions [of the agreements] each party shall use national technical means of verification at its disposal". Reconnaissance by means of satellites was envisaged as the basic element of the "national technical means" of verification to provide assurance of compliance.

In 1972 the Soviet Union orbited 29 photographic reconnaissance satellites, providing them with a total of 279 days of observation time.[1] In the same year the United States orbited eight photographic reconnaissance satellites, giving them a total observation time of 265 days. With this extensive use of reconnaissance satellites an analysis of their recent activities gives a good indication of their potential. The various types and roles of satellites launched since the beginning of the US and Soviet programmes have been described in the *SIPRI Yearbook 1973*. [1] Therefore, only satellite activities during 1972 and 1973 will be considered here.

## II. *US reconnaissance activities*

During 1972, the United States orbited eight photographic reconnaissance, two electronic reconnaissance and two early-warning satellites.

The USA has three types of photographic reconnaissance satellites which usually orbit at perigee[2] heights of between 150 and 200 km. The area-surveillance satellite carries a wide-angle, low-resolution camera for searching a large area of a particular country for objects or events of potential interest. When the satellite is within communication range of one of the US Air Force ground stations, the exposed film, which has been processed aboard the satellite, is scanned electronically and the resulting

[1] The observation time for a particular year was calculated by adding the number of days for which satellites were in orbit during the year. When two or more satellites were in orbit simultaneously, the number of days during which overlap occurred were subtracted from the total, giving the observation time.
[2] The orbital path of a satellite is generally elliptical. The shortest distance between the Earth and the satellite during the orbit is called the perigee height, and the longest distance the apogee height.

electrical signals are transmitted to the station by radio. Area-surveillance satellites are usually launched using Long-Tank Thurst-Augmented Thor (LTTAT) rockets. The second type, the "close-look" satellite, re-photographs areas of particular interest located by the area-surveillance satellite. The film, contained in a capsule, is ejected from the satellite and recovered for processing. The close-look satellite carries a high-resolution camera with a very long focal-length lens. Such a camera has a relatively narrow field of view. These satellites are larger than those used for area surveillance and they are launched using Titan-3B rockets. The third type, the new generation "Big Bird" satellite, is designed to perform both the area-surveillance and the close-look types of mission. These satellites are launched using Titan-3D rockets.

Electronic reconnaissance satellites are launched into orbits with perigee heights of about 300–500 km and have considerably longer orbital lives.[3] As the satellite passes over an area of interest, radar signals and other sources of electromagnetic radiation are recorded on tapes: the tapes can then be played back, and the recorded information transmitted to ground receiving stations.

Early-warning satellites use infrared techniques to detect the launch of enemy missiles. These satellites orbit at very high perigee heights, usually greater than 30 000 km, and have very long orbital lives, greater than one million years.

Of the eight US photographic satellites launched in 1972, three were the new generation Big Bird satellites which are now performing an increasing share of the total reconnaissance activities of the United States. In 1972 these satellites provided 158 out of a total 265 days of photographic reconnaissance satellite observation time.

In 1973 the United States launched five photographic reconnaissance satellites and two early-warning satellites, but no electronic reconnaissance satellites. Out of a total of 286 days of US observation time in 1973, 222 days were provided by three Big Bird satellites.

Such orbital characteristics as the orbital inclination, the period[4] and the perigee and apogee heights of all reconnaissance satellites launched in 1972 are shown in the *SIPRI Yearbook 1973*. [1] The characteristics of those launched in 1973 are shown below in tables 9.1 and 9.2.

**The role of area-surveillance, close-look and Big Bird satellites**

The times during which various types of US photographic reconnaissance satellites were in orbit in 1972 and 1973 are shown in chart 9.1. Although

---

[3] The number of days for which a satellite orbits the Earth before it either decays or is recovered is called the orbital life.

[4] The orbital inclination is the angle between the orbital plane of the satellite and the equatorial plane of the Earth. The period is the time required for a satellite to orbit the Earth once.

Big Bird satellites are now being used on a regular basis, several older generation area-surveillance and close-look reconnaissance satellites are still being launched. From the timing of these satellites it can be seen that the older generation satellites are launched either when no Big Bird satellite is in orbit or towards the end of the lifetime of a Big Bird satellite, that is, possibly when there is an urgent need for observation in the absence of a Big Bird satellite. After a Big Bird satellite has decayed, there is usually an interval of at least 25 days before the next one is launched. This delay may suggest that Big Bird satellites are so costly that only two or three such satellites can be launched per year.

In chart 9.1 the dates of the Chinese and French nuclear tests carried out during 1972 and 1973, the dates of the SALT I agreements and the 1973 outbreak of war in the Middle East are indicated. It is interesting to note the clusters of satellites launched around the time of these events, showing that the nuclear tests and the Middle East War could have been observed by the satellites of both the United States and the Soviet Union. For example, the United States launched a close-look satellite, 1972-16A, on 17 March 1972 and on 18 March the People's Republic of China carried out a nuclear test. Such tests may also have been detected by US Vela[5] and early-warning satellites but the advantages of photographic reconnaissance satellites, particularly close-look satellites, are considerable.

Other examples of older generation satellites used by the United States are two area-surveillance satellites launched on 19 April and 25 May 1972. The first of these satellites was launched two weeks, and the second only one day, before the SALT I agreements were signed. In addition, a close-look type satellite was launched on 20 May 1972, but it failed to achieve an orbit. [2] This succession of satellites may have been used to gather up-to-date intelligence on the inventory of Soviet weapons.

However, the use of these older generation satellites is decreasing because the Big Bird satellites perform both close-look and area-surveillance missions (as well as other missions). They are equipped with high-resolution cameras, carry six recoverable film capsules and their photographs are usually returned to the Earth at two- to three-week intervals. [3] The spacecraft is also believed to be equipped with large antennae so that photographs taken during an area-surveillance mission can be transmitted to the Earth. It can be seen from chart 9.1 that no US area-surveillance satellite was launched in 1973, suggesting that these missions are now probably carried out by Big Bird satellites. Also, it is believed that the Big Bird satellites carry ultra-high-frequency equipment to provide

---

[5] Between the end of 1963 and April 1970, Vela satellites were launched to detect nuclear explosions in the atmosphere and in space. They were launched in pairs in near-circular orbits. No new Vela satellite has been launched since April 1970. The detection of nuclear tests is now probably carried out by the early-warning satellites. [1]

**Chart 9.1. US and Soviet photographic reconnaissance satellites launched during 1972 and 1973**

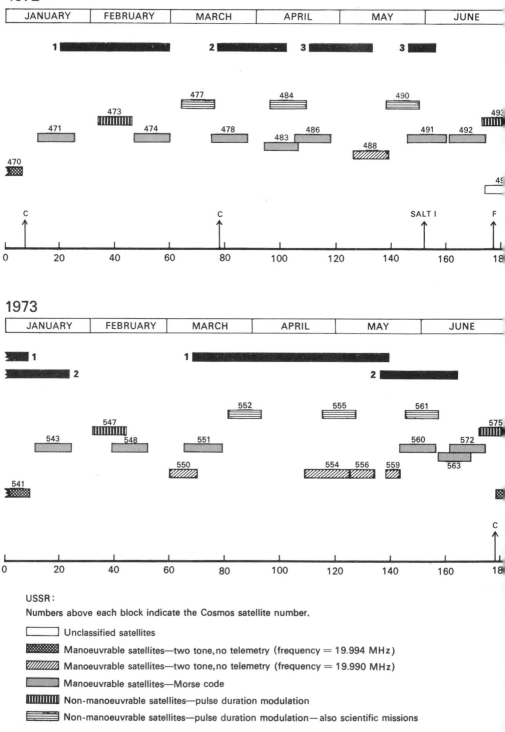

USSR:

Numbers above each block indicate the Cosmos satellite number.

☐ Unclassified satellites

▨ Manoeuvrable satellites—two tone, no telemetry (frequency = 19.994 MHz)

▨ Manoeuvrable satellites—two tone, no telemetry (frequency = 19.990 MHz)

▨ Manoeuvrable satellites—Morse code

▥ Non-manoeuvrable satellites—pulse duration modulation

▤ Non-manoeuvrable satellites—pulse duration modulation—also scientific missions

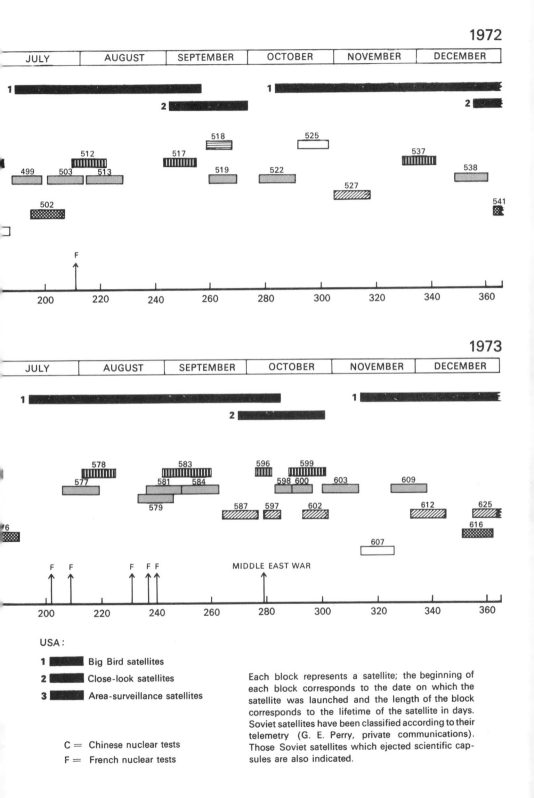

USA:

**1** Big Bird satellites

**2** Close-look satellites

**3** Area-surveillance satellites

C = Chinese nuclear tests
F = French nuclear tests

Each block represents a satellite; the beginning of each block corresponds to the date on which the satellite was launched and the length of the block corresponds to the lifetime of the satellite in days. Soviet satellites have been classified according to their telemetry (G. E. Perry, private communications). Those Soviet satellites which ejected scientific capsules are also indicated.

communications with Strategic Air Command aircraft operating in the polar region. [3–4]

Additional atmospheric nuclear tests have recently been carried out, one by the People's Republic of China on 27 June 1973 and a series by France beginning on 21 July 1973. A Big Bird satellite launched by the United States on 13 July orbited for 91 days until 12 October, and a close-look satellite, launched on 27 September 1973 with an orbital life of 31 days, decayed on 28 October. These two satellites could have observed both the preparation and the actual outbreak of the 1973 Middle East War. The third Big Bird satellite, launched on 10 November, may have been intended to monitor compliance with the ceasefire agreements in the Middle East.

### The role of early-warning satellites

Early-warning satellites, the ballistic missile early-warning system (BMEWS) and the integrated missile early-warning system (IMEWS) are included among the reconnaissance satellites because, apart from providing early warning of an ICBM attack, they also provide a capability to monitor missile tests. The United States launched two early-warning satellites in 1973. In conjunction with over-the-horizon (OTH) radars,[6] these satellites can be used to verify the restrictions on missile testing stipulated in the SALT I ABM Treaty. Both OTH radar and early-warning satellites, when used with other types of radar system, can be used to indicate when and where missile tests are taking place and to provide information on the type of tests being conducted.

The orbital characteristics of two US early-warning satellites launched in 1973 are shown in table 9.2. The IMEWS-4 was probably launched to supplement the IMEWS-2 launched on 5 May 1971. The infrared sensors on the IMEWS-2 are believed to be losing their sensitivity, [5] and tests are being carried out to determine the cause. New infrared sensors are probably also being tested. [6] The early-warning satellites launched prior to the IMEWS-4 were intended only as development models for test and evaluation.

## III. *Soviet reconnaissance activities*

A major difference between the photographic reconnaissance satellites of the United States and those of the Soviet Union is the orbital lives of the satellites. Since about 1970, the United States has launched, on average,

---

[6] A characteristic of OTH radar is that its range is not restricted by the Earth's curvature, since use is made of the ionosphere for reflecting radar signals.

seven satellites per year, with relatively long orbital lives. On the other hand, since 1968, the Soviet Union has continued to launch an average of about 30 13-day Cosmos satellites per year. Although this rate is considerably greater than that of the United States, the available satellite observation time is similar for both countries; in 1972 the United States and the Soviet Union had satellite observation times of 265 and 279 days, respectively; in 1973 they had 277 and 284 days, respectively.

### The role of 13-day Cosmos satellites

The periods for which Soviet Cosmos photographic reconnaissance satellites were in orbit during 1972 and 1973 are shown in chart 9.1. Soviet satellites which are equivalent to the US close-look satellites may be identified by their manoeuvring capability. The long focal-length lens of a camera mounted on a close-look satellite results in a smaller area of the Earth being photographed on each pass. Therefore, the satellite ground tracks[7] must be closely spaced so that complete coverage of an area of particular interest can be achieved. It would, therefore, be advantageous if the satellite were able to manoeuvre and obtain such coverage more precisely. Cosmos 251, launched on 31 October 1968, was the first Soviet reconnaissance satellite which manoeuvred. A further characteristic of this satellite was that on the 12th day of its flight it ejected two objects. Similar objects were ejected by many other Soviet reconnaissance satellites on the day preceding the recovery of the main satellite. [7] Such objects are believed to be either vernier control rockets, used to make small adjustments in the orbital period of the spacecraft so as to bring it directly over targets of interest, or discarded scientific packages. [8] Cosmos 208, launched in 1968, was the first Soviet satellite to eject a scientific capsule. Of a total of 29 satellites launched in 1968, four ejected either vernier control rockets or scientific packages. In 1972, 23 of the 29 Soviet satellites ejected such objects; and in 1973, the proportion was 27 out of 35 satellites. It is possible that satellites which eject such objects, and manoeuvre, are close-look satellites.

A Soviet area-surveillance satellite was launched at the beginning (7 April 1972) and at the end (21 June 1972) of a series of close-look satellites launched during May and June 1972. This sharp increase in numbers of Soviet reconnaissance satellites may be related to the SALT I agreements signed on 26 May 1972.

The Chinese nuclear tests of 18 March 1972 and 27 June 1973 (the latter in the two- to three-megaton range) were presumably monitored by Soviet satellites launched in March 1972 and June 1973, respectively. During the months of June and July 1972 and August 1973, several nuclear tests were

---

[7] The ground track is defined as the projected path traced out by a satellite over the surface of the Earth.

**Chart 9.2. Ground tracks of the non-manoeuvrable Cosmos 596 satellite over the Middle East. (The figures in brackets indicate the number of orbits.)**

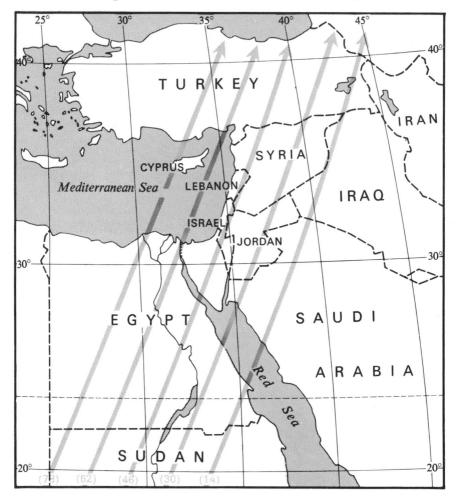

carried out by France: several Cosmos satellites were launched during these periods (see chart 9.1).

One of the most striking uses of reconnaissance satellites was during the Middle East War which began on 6 October 1973. The Soviet Union orbited a succession of Cosmos reconnaissance satellites during the periods immediately before and after the war. [9–10] Cosmos 596, 597 and 598 were launched on 3, 6 and 10 October, respectively. Each of these satellites was recovered only six days after it was launched, although the orbital lives of such satellites are usually 13 days. The first of these satellites was non-manoeuvrable and probably carried a low-resolution camera for surveying large areas. Within six days the orbital path of the satellite was such that no further useful information could be obtained from the

294

**Chart 9.3. Ground tracks of the manoeuvrable Cosmos 597 satellite over the Middle East. (The figures in brackets indicate the number of orbits.)**

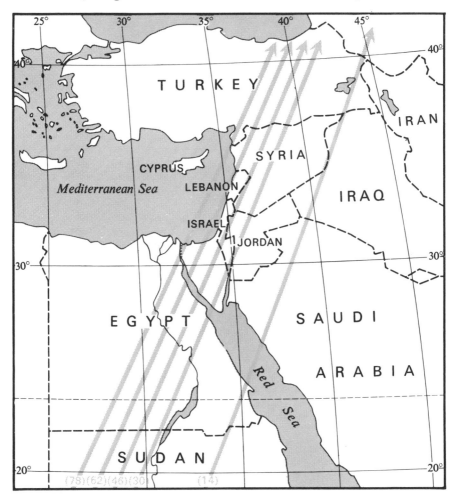

Middle East area and therefore the satellite was recovered. Just before recovery of this satellite, Cosmos 597, which was already in orbit, was maneouvred. The ground tracks of these satellites are shown in charts 9.2 and 9.3. An interesting feature of the third satellite, Cosmos 598, was that it was launched from Plesetsk at an orbital inclination of 72.9°, an orbit that is not used very frequently. An advantage of such an inclination is that the Middle East can be photographed at the end of the first day of the mission rather than at the beginning of the third day. During the flights of these satellites, near real-time surveillance was obtained by raising their altitudes as they passed over the Middle East, so that they could be within transmitting range of the ground station at Yevpatoria. [9] The characteristics of the Soviet photographic reconnaissance satellites are shown in table 9.3.

Unlike the United States, the Soviet Union has continued to launch electronic reconnaissance satellites. It is difficult to identify with certainty which Soviet satellites perform electronic reconnaissance activities, but it is thought that, of the large number of satellites in the Cosmos series, those with an orbital inclination of about 71° and orbital periods of 92 minutes and 95 minutes may be electronic reconnaissance satellites. Soviet satellites launched at an inclination of about 74° with an orbital period of 95 minutes may also fall within this group. [1] Twelve such satellites were launched in 1973; their orbital characteristics are given in table 9.4.

It has recently been suggested that a number of Soviet electronic reconnaissance satellites with an orbital inclination of 71° and an orbital period of 92 minutes may be weather satellites, but this interpretation is not generally accepted. [11] The purpose of weather satellites is to predict when targets of interest are free of cloud so that these areas can be photographed by photographic reconnaissance satellites. Weather satellites are also being used by the United States, but only two or three are launched per year. [12] Many more Soviet weather satellites are launched because they have relatively short orbital lives of about six months.

## IV. *Future developments*

An analysis of satellites launched during the past few years shows that since 1968 the Soviet Union has launched an average of about 30 photographic reconnaissance satellites per year whereas the rate for the United States has been about seven per year since 1971. As can be seen from chart 9.4, which shows the yearly launch rates of photographic reconnaissance satellites for the United States and the Soviet Union since the beginning of their programmes, these rates are now fairly constant. The rate of satellite launches by the Soviet Union seems high. One reason for this may be the lack of a Big Bird-type satellite capable of staying in orbit for longer periods of time and performing a variety of missions. The first Big Bird satellite was launched in 1971 by the United States and now, after two years, these satellites are performing most of the reconnaissance missions; during 1973, no area-surveillance satellite was launched.

The number of reconnaissance satellites launched each year seems high, particularly if the satellites are used only for verifying the implementation of the SALT I agreements and possibly for monitoring such events as those described above. Both the USA and the USSR use nearly the same length of time (about 280 days per year) for reconnaissance activities. One explanation may be that a number of photographic reconnaissance satel-

**Chart 9.4. US and Soviet photographic reconnaissance satellites: number launched per year**

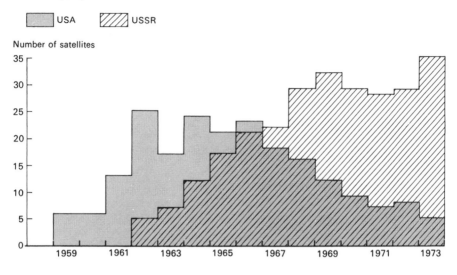

lites are now being used for ocean surveillance to monitor the location of naval fleets and shore facilities. For monitoring mobile objects such as ships, photographs returned to Earth after 10 or 12 days, as would be the case with the Soviet older generation satellites, are less useful. Thus it is possible that some of the new generation of Soviet photographic reconnaissance satellites may be carrying equipment for near real-time image read-out systems so that the images of the photographs processed on the spacecraft are transmitted back to Earth by radio. Such a system is already employed by the United States. [1] Although it is difficult to identify positively those Soviet satellites which perform ocean-surveillance missions, there is evidence that some satellites launched from Plesetsk with an orbital inclination of about 81° are used to survey the Arctic Sea. For example, Cosmos 541 was launched at the end of 1972 at an orbital inclination of 81°, probably to check ice pack conditions on the Arctic Sea routes. This satellite was recovered on 8 January and a few days later five icebreakers and four cargo vessels embarked for Murmansk from the Yenisei river estuary. Their safe arrival was attributed to successful air reconnaissance, since the Arctic sea routes are normally closed for about six months a year. [13]

As regards US satellites, it is believed that some of the older generation satellites which are launched soon after Big Bird satellites may be carrying infrared equipment for ocean-surveillance purposes. [14] The infrared equipment carried by some of the US reconnaissance satellites is similar to that used in the Earth Resources Technology Satellite (ERTS 1). Photographs taken by cameras on ERTS 1 from a height of 900 km even show such details as small pleasure boats. The resolution would improve by a factor of six if photographs are taken from a height of about 150 km, the perigee height of most US photographic reconnaissance satellites. Such infrared devices are still in the development stages but, when they are fully developed, it may be possible to detect nuclear submarines travelling at considerable depths, [15–16] since the water used to cool the core of the nuclear reactor of a submarine is expelled into the sea and the temperature of the expelled water may be sufficiently higher than that of the surrounding water so that it can be detected by satellite infrared sensors.

Although the time interval between the location of an area of interest by an area-surveillance satellite and obtaining high-resolution photographs using close-look satellites has been reduced by the use of large Big Bird satellites, this time interval is still long since the film from a Big Bird satellite must first be recovered and processed for analysis. Development of real-time close-look reconnaissance by Big Bird satellites has already begun in the United States under a project code-named 1010. [17] The aim is to convert the high-resolution image on a photograph into electronic signals using a new-generation scanning system and then to transmit the signals back to the Earth via a data-relay satellite. A similar project is being developed to provide the United States with real-time oceanic surveillance. [18] The availability of such techniques will give almost instantaneous surveillance of areas of potential interest.

# V. *Tables of US and Soviet reconnaissance satellites*

## Conventions

| | |
|---|---|
| A-2 | Vostok up-rated second stage |
| A/A-D | Atlas Agena-D |
| B-1 | Modified Sandal intermediate-range missile with an added upper stage |
| BMEWS | Ballistic missile early-warning system |
| C-1 | Skean intermediate-range missile plus upper stage |
| Cape Ken | Cape Kennedy |
| IMEWS | Integrated missile early-warning system |
| PL | Plesetsk |
| T-3C | Titan-3C |
| T-3D | Titan-3D |
| T-3B/A–D | Titan-3B Agena D |
| T-3D/A–D | Titan-3D Agena-D |
| TT | Tyuratam |
| Van | Vandenberg |

**Table 9.1. US photographic reconnaissance satellites launched in 1973**

| Satellite name and designation[a] | Launch site and vehicle | Launch date and time GMT | Orbital inclination deg | Period min | Perigee height km | Apogee height km | Lifetime days | Whether film capsule recovered[b] |
|---|---|---|---|---|---|---|---|---|
| USAF[c] (1973-14A) | Van T-3D/A-D | 9 Mar 2038 | 95.7 | 88.76 | 152 | 270 | 71 | Yes |
| USAF (1973-28A) | Van T-3B/A-D | 16 May 1634 | 110.49 | 89.39 | 136 | 352 | 28 | Yes |
| USAF[c] (1973-46A) | Van T-3D | 13 Jul 1955 | 96.22 | 88.77 | 156 | 269 | 91 | Yes |
| USAF (1973-68A) | Van T-3B/A-D | 27 Sep 1717 | 110.48 | 89.67 | 131 | 385 | 31 | Yes |
| USAF[c] (1973-88A) | Van T-3D | 10 Nov 1955 | 96.94 | 88.85 | 159 | 275 | 91 | Yes |

[a] The designation of each satellite is recognized internationally and is given by the World Warning Agency on behalf of the Committee on Space Research.
[b] Uncertainty about the data and recovery of satellites is indicated by question marks.
[c] "Big Bird" satellites.

**Table 9.2. US electronic and early-warning satellites launched in 1973**

| Satellite name and designation[a] | Launch site and vehicle | Launch date and time GMT | Orbital inclination deg | Period min | Perigee height km | Apogee height km | Lifetime years |
|---|---|---|---|---|---|---|---|
| BMEWS-6 (1973-13A) | Cape Ken A/A-D | 6 Mar 1200 | 10.1 | 1 441.0 | 42 259 | 32 100 | >10[6] |
| IMEWS-4 (1973-40A) | Cape Ken T-3C | 12 Jun 0936 | 0.53 | 1 431.9 | 35 533 | 35901 | >10[6] |

[a] See footnote *a* to table 9.1.

**Table 9.3. Soviet photographic reconnaissance satellites launched in 1973**

| Satellite name and designation[a] | Launch site and vehicle | Launch date and time GMT | Orbital inclination deg | Period min | Perigee height km | Apogee height km | Lifetime days | Whether recovered[b] |
|---|---|---|---|---|---|---|---|---|
| Cosmos 543[c] (1973-02A) | TT A-2 | 11 Jan 1005 | 64.98 | 89.62 | 203 | 309 | 12.9 | ? |
| Cosmos 547 (1973-06A) | TT A-2 | 1 Feb 0838 | 64.97 | 89.63 | 203 | 310 | 11.8 | ? |
| Cosmos 548[c] (1973-08(A) | PL A-2 | 8 Feb 1376 | 65.38 | 89.55 | 205 | 300 | 12.7 | Yes |
| Cosmos 550[d] (1973-11A) | PL A-2 | 1 Mar 1243 | 65.42 | 89.73 | 206 | 317 | 9.8 | ? |
| Cosmos 551[c] (1973-12A) | TT A-2 | 6 Mar 0922 | 65.00 | 89.52 | 206 | 296 | 13.8 | ? |
| Cosmos 552[d] (1973-16A) | PL A-2 | 22 Mar 1005 | 72.84 | 89.68 | 204 | 312 | 11.8 | ? |

299

| Satellite name and designation[a] | Launch site and vehicle | Launch date and time GMT | Orbital inclination deg | Period min | Perigee height km | Apogee height km | Life-time days | Whether recovered[b] |
|---|---|---|---|---|---|---|---|---|
| Cosmos 554[c] (1973-21A) | PL A-2 | 19 Apr 0907 | 72.85 | 89.50 | 194 | 304 | 16 | Destroyed, in orbit |
| Cosmos 555[d] (1973-24A) | PL A-2 | 25 Apr 1048 | 81.33 | 89.02 | 216 | 233 | 11.9 | ? |
| Cosmos 556[c] (1973-25A) | PL A-2 | 5 May 0658 | 81.33 | 88.97 | 218 | 225 | 8.9 | ? |
| Cosmos 559[d] (1973-30A) | PL A-2 | 18 May 1102 | 65.41 | 89.79 | 204 | 325 | 4.8 | ? |
| Cosmos 560[c] (1973-31A) | PL A-2 | 23 May 1033 | 72.85 | 89.68 | 203 | 314 | 12.8 | Yes |
| Cosmos 561[d] (1973-33A) | PL A-2 | 25 May 1341 | 65.41 | 89.51 | 206 | 295 | 11.7 | ? |
| Cosmos 563 (1973-36A) | PL A-2 | 6 Jun 1131 | 65.40 | 89.53 | 206 | 298 | 11.7 | ? |
| Cosmos 572[c] (1973-35A) | TT A-2 | 10 Jun 1019 | 51.66 | 89.32 | 206 | 281 | 12.9 | Yes |
| Cosmos 575 (1973-43A) | PL A-2 | 21 Jun 1326 | 65.41 | 89.25 | 204 | 271 | 11.7 | Yes |
| Cosmos 576[d] (1973-44A) | PL A-2 | 27 Jun 1200 | 72.86 | 89.88 | 204 | 332 | 11.8 | Yes |
| Cosmos 577[c] (1973-48A) | PL A-2 | 25 Jul 1131 | 65.39 | 89.45 | 207 | 289 | 12.7 | ? |
| Cosmos 578 (1973-51A) | PL A-2 | 1 Aug 1410 | 65.38 | 89.41 | 200 | 292 | 11.7 | Yes |
| Cosmos 579[c] (1973-55A) | PL A-2 | 21 Aug 1229 | 65.41 | 89.27 | 196 | 382 | 12.7 | ? |
| Cosmos 581[c] (1973-59A) | TT A-2 | 24 Aug 1117 | 51.62 | 89.40 | 208 | 288 | 12.8 | Yes |
| Cosmos 583 (1973-62A) | TT A-2 | 30 Aug 1033 | 64.92 | 89.52 | 204 | 298 | 13 | ? |
| Cosmos 584[c] (1973-63A) | PL A-2 | 6 Sep 1048 | 72.85 | 89.95 | 205 | 336 | 13.8 | ? |
| Cosmos 587[c] (1973-66A) | PL A-2 | 21 Sep 1312 | 65.42 | 89.55 | 205 | 300 | 12.8 | Yes |
| Cosmos 596[d] (1973-70A) | TT A-2 | 3 Oct 1258 | 65.41 | 89.42 | 206 | 287 | 5.8 | Yes |
| Cosmos 597[c] (1973-71A) | PL A-2 | 6 Oct 1229 | 65.42 | 89.45 | 206 | 290 | 5.8 | ? |
| Cosmos 598[c] (1973-72A) | PL A-2 | 10 Oct 1048 | 72.84 | 89.94 | 208 | 334 | 5.8 | ? |
| Cosmos 599 (1973-73A) | TT A-2 | 15 Oct 0853 | 64.94 | 89.32 | 202 | 280 | 12.9 | ? |
| Cosmos 600[c] (1973-74A) | PL A-2 | 16 Oct 1214 | 72.83 | 59.97 | 205 | 340 | 6.8 | ? |
| Cosmos 602[c] (1973-77A) | PL A-2 | 20 Oct 1019 | 72.88 | 89.97 | 210 | 335 | 8.8 | ? |
| Cosmos 603[c] (1973-79A) | PL A-2 | 27 Oct 1117 | 72.86 | 90.15 | 205 | 357 | 12.8 | ? |

| Satellite name and designation[a] | Launch site and vehicle | Launch date and time *GMT* | Orbital incli- nation *deg* | Period *min* | Perigee height *km* | Apogee height *km* | Life- time *days* | Whether recov- ered[b] |
|---|---|---|---|---|---|---|---|---|
| Cosmos 607[c] (1973-87A) | PL A-2 | 10Nov 1243 | 72.84 | 89.98 | 204 | 341 | 12.8 | ? |
| Cosmos 609[c] (1973-92A) | TT A-2 | 21 Nov 1005 | 69.95 | 90.07 | 241 | 314 | 12.9 | Yes |
| Cosmos 612 (1973-95A) | PL A-2 | 28 Nov 1146 | 72.82 | 90.05 | 206 | 346 | 12.8 | ? |
| Cosmos 616 (1973-102A) | PL A-2 | 17 Dec 1200 | 72.86 | 89.90 | 206 | 332 | 10.8 | ? |
| Cosmos 625 (1973–105A) | PL A-2 | 21 Dec 1229 | 72.83 | 89.77 | 204 | 321 | 12.78 | ? |

[a] See footnote a to table 9.1.
[b] See footnote b to table 9.1.
[c] Manoeuvrable satellites which also ejected hardware.
[d] Satellite ejected hardware but did not manoeuvre.

**Table 9.4. Possible Soviet electronic reconnaissance satellites launched in 1973**

| Satellite name and designation[a] | Launch site and vehicle | Launch date and time *GMT* | Orbital incli- nation *deg* | Period *min* | Perigee height *km* | Apogee height *km* | Life- time |
|---|---|---|---|---|---|---|---|
| Cosmos 544 (1973-03A) | PL C-1 | 20 Jan 0336 | 74.03 | 95.23 | 510 | 548 | 8 years |
| Cosmos 545 (1973-04A) | PL B-1 | 24 Jan 1146 | 71.00 | 92.20 | 269 | 495 | 6 months decayed |
| Cosmos 549 (1973-10A) | PL C-1 | 28 Feb 0434 | 74.02 | 95.23 | 513 | 545 | 8 years |
| Cosmos 553 (1973-20A) | PL B-1 | 12 Apr 1200 | 70.96 | 92.22 | 272 | 494 | 7 months decayed |
| Cosmos 558 (1973-29A) | PL B-1 | 17 May 1326 | 70.98 | 92.26 | 269 | 501 | 6 months |
| Cosmos 562 (1973-35A) | PL B-1 | 5 Jun 1131 | 70.98 | 92.13 | 270 | 487 | 6 months |
| Cosmos 580 (1973-57A) | PL B-1 | 22 Aug 1131 | 71.00 | 92.22 | 273 | 493 | 6 months |
| Cosmos 582 (1973-60A) | PL C-1 | 28 Aug 1005 | 74.04 | 95.27 | 519 | 543 | 8 years |
| Cosmos 608 (1973-91A) | PL B-1 | 20 Nov 1229 | 70.97 | 92.29 | 270 | 503 | 8 months |
| Cosmos 610 (1973-93A) | PL C-1 | 27 Nov 0014 | 74.04 | 95.27 | 515 | 546 | 7 years |
| Cosmos 611 (1973-94A) | PL B-1 | 28 Nov 1005 | 70.97 | 92.06 | 270 | 481 | 7 months |
| Cosmos 615 (1973-99A) | PL B-1 | 13 Dec 1117 | 71.02 | 95.70 | 270 | 834 | 18 months |

[a] See footnote a to table 9.1.

**Sources**

1. *Table of Earth Satellites* (Farnborough, England, Royal Aircraft Establishment): monthly reports for 1973.
2. Perry, G. E. (Private communications).

**References**

1. *World Armaments and Disarmament, SIPRI Yearbook 1973* (Stockholm, Almqvist & Wiksell, 1973, Stockholm International Peace Research Institute) pp. 60–101.
2. "USAF Launches Two Recon-Sats", *Aviation Week & Space Technology,* Vol. 96, No. 23, 5 June 1972, p. 14.
3. *Aviation Week & Space Technology,* Vol. 98, No. 16, 16 April 1973, p. 9.
4. Johnsen, K., "Air Force Assigns Top Priority To 3-Segment Satcom Program", *Aviation Week & Space Technology,* Vol. 98, No. 9, 26 February 1973, p. 19.
5. "Warning Satellite", *Aviation Week & Space Technology,* Vol. 98, No. 25, 18 June 1973, p. 17.
6. "Additional Warning Satellites Expected", *Aviation Week & Space Technology,* Vol. 98, No. 20, 14 May 1973, p. 17.
7. Perry, G. E., "Cosmos Observation", *Flight International,* Vol. 100, No. 3251, 1 July 1971, pp. 29–32.
8. Perry, G. E., "Recoverable Cosmos Satellites with Scientific Missions", *Space Flight,* Vol. 16, February 1974, p. 69.
9. Perry, G. E., "Looking Down on the Middle East War", *Flight International,* Vol. 105, No. 3389, 21 February 1974, pp. 240-1-245.
10. "Soviet Aid Sparks Arab Gains", *Aviation Week & Space Technology,* Vol. 99, No. 16, 15 October 1973, p. 12.
11. "Weather Flights Support Soviet's Recon Satellites", *Aviation Week & Space Technology,* Vol. 98, No. 12, 19 March 1973, p. 51.
12. "USAF Admits Weather Satellite Mission", *Aviation Week & Space Technology,* Vol. 98, No. 11, 12 March 1973, p. 18.
13. "USSR's Cosmos Pace Quickened", *Aviation Week & Space Technology,* Vol. 98, No. 7, 12 February 1973, pp. 50–51.
14. Klass, P. J., "Soviets Push Ocean Surveillance", *Aviation Week & Space Technology,* Vol. 99, No. 11, 10 September 1973, pp. 12–13.
15. Taylor, J. W. R. and Monday, D., *Spies in the Sky* (Ian Allan Ltd., Shapperton, Surrey, U.K., 1972) p. 118.
16. Klass, P. J., *Secret Sentries in Space* (New York, Random House, 1971) p. 146.
17. *Aviation Week & Space Technology,* Vol. 96, No. 20, 8 May 1972, p. 9.
18. "Navy Plans Satellite/Aircraft Ocean Surveillance", *Aviation Week & Space Technology,* Vol. 99, No. 8, 20 August 1973, p. 66.

# 10. Antisubmarine warfare

*Square-bracketed references, thus* [1], *refer to the list of references on page 324.*

## I. *Introduction*

Since its inception during World War I, antisubmarine warfare (ASW) has been perceived as a tactical (theatre) naval operation aimed at preventing hostile submarines from successfully attacking one's own surface ships. ASW is a defensive reaction to ever evolving counter-shipping weapon systems. The systems and tactics employed in ASW therefore change as a function of the evolution of submarines and the weapons deployed on them. During World War II, for example, straight-running torpedoes with ranges of a few thousand metres were the main offensive weapons employed by diesel-powered submarines. Consequently World War II ASW systems and tactics were designed to maintain a submarine-free zone of comparable width around a convoy of surface ships. Contemporary counter-shipping submarines employ ordnance of considerably longer range and greater sophistication: homing torpedoes with ranges of 10–20 km and cruise missiles with ranges of 20–400 km or more. To counter the threat to surface ships created by these new projectiles, ASW technology has had to be modified drastically. A second and even more decisive factor that dictated fundamental changes in the tactics and hardware employed in modern ASW was the introduction of the use of nuclear reactors to propel submarines. Submarines with conventional diesel and electrical battery engines had limited underwater endurance, were detectable by radar while driven by diesel engines since they had to travel with their snorkels above the surface, and travelled at speeds of only 10–20 km/hour. By comparison, the introduction of nuclear-power reactors on submarines meant improvements in speed, endurance and quietness. This rendered the World War II generation of ASW equipment obsolete and created the need for an entirely new research and development field to support the development of consecutive generations of ASW systems designed to cope with the nuclear submarines.

Perhaps the most momentous development in the field of underwater warfare was the introduction about 15 years ago of the ballistic missile-carrying nuclear-powered submarine (SSBN). Unlike torpedo- or cruise missile-carrying counter-shipping submarines, the ballistic missile submarine has a strategic rather than a tactical role. Its operations are therefore not confined to the vicinity of a convoy or a task force; rather it roams submerged in the millions of cubic kilometres of ocean from where it can be within range of its strategic inland targets. It does not seek to approach, but rather avoids, surface ships, since its main operational requirement is to remain undetected and thereby ensure the availability of its ballistic missiles at any instant.

The deployment of SSBNs, first by the United States, then by the Soviet Union and Britain, and more recently by France, introduced a new set of technical and political problems into undersea warfare. Missile-carrying submarines form the sea-based component of a country's deterrent force. It would thus be highly provocative and certainly strategically destabilizing to attack them (or even to have the capability to attack them), even if 100 per cent success were guaranteed: the response would almost certainly be nuclear retaliation with land-based missiles or long-range aircraft.

The deployment of ABM (anti-ballistic missile) systems to protect urban areas was prohibited by the SALT I agreements, the reason being that such systems impede the ability of ballistic missiles to attack urban areas and hence erode the countervalue role of these missiles. Similarly, an ASW system designed to attack missile-carrying submarines could threaten the second-strike capability of these submarines, and would thus be as undesirable as an urban ABM system: both ABM and ASW systems undermine the credibility of deterrence as a viable strategic posture. The institutionalization of deterrence as the mutual strategic posture of the Soviet Union and the United States (and presumably also of France, Britain and China) appears to proscribe any military operation that could threaten the stability of strategic weapon systems on which the credibility of deterrence is based. Antisubmarine warfare is carried on in an ever changing, inhomogeneous and as yet little understood environment—the ocean. The efficiency of the weapon systems employed cannot be predicted with any accuracy, and the operational procedures themselves are ill-defined and multipurpose. Therefore ASW is not amenable to the same analytical approach that one could use in the case of ABM systems. Also unlike ABM operations, ASW does not address a single task nor is it practised by only two nations. Consequently the division into tactical and strategic components is burdened by a multiplicity of political considerations and technical difficulties, the latter caused by the well-understood desire of the military to deploy the best possible systems available, irrespective of the potential political implications.

This chapter will examine in some detail, first, the technical infrastructure of antisubmarine warfare as dictated by the properties of the ocean environment (section II); and second, the systems and operations employed in tactical situations on the one hand, and the corresponding systems and operations necessary in counter-SSBN activities on the other (sections III, IV and V). The interactions between tactical and counter-SSBN ASW, both technical and political, and their potentially detrimental effects on the stability of deterrence are identified and examined in a more detailed analysis in another SIPRI publication. [1] Classes of measures, both technical and political, that could minimize the interaction between tactical and counter-SSBN operations, and consequently preserve the invulnerability of the sea-based deterrent, a result in consonance with the tenor of the SALT I agreements, are also identified in this more detailed work.

## II. *Underwater acoustics*

### The ocean environment

#### *Propagation of sound in seawater*

The basic operation in any type of antisubmarine warfare is the detection of a submarine in the vast ocean environment. Since electromagnetic radiation is rapidly attenuated by seawater, high search-rate equipment used for the detection of submerged submarines cannot employ electromagnetic waves (as does radar, for example) but must instead rely on sound, a form of mechanical energy transmitted well by an elastic medium such as seawater. The physics of sound transmission in water and the acoustic properties of the oceans thus determine the performance characteristics and dictate the inherent limitations of underwater acoustic systems used in antisubmarine warfare.

The velocity of a sound wave in the ocean depends on temperature, salinity and pressure. Pressure is a function of depth, salinity varies as a function of location on the globe, and water temperature varies as functions of time (for example, according to changing weather conditions and seasonal changes), depth (thermal layers are formed naturally in the oceans) and geographic location. Thus the velocity of sound varies from point to point on the globe, from point to point vertically in the ocean, and from day to day.

The significant and persistent effect of the presence of natural thermal layers of ocean waters and of the continuous variation in the velocity of sound with depth is that the paths of sound waves in the ocean are not straight lines: instead they undergo refraction according to Snell's law. Sound wave paths further depart from straight line trajectories as sound is reflected from the discontinuities of the ocean medium at the surface and the ocean bottom. A combination of scattering from these interfaces, and refraction of sound paths caused by the continuous variations of the velocity of sound, gives rise to "shadow zones"—large volumes of the ocean in which sound from a source near the surface does not penetrate, regardless of the intensity of the sound source. A submarine located in such a zone can remain undetected even if very near the detection device.

*Oceanic noise*

The motion of the ocean waters, atmospheric and volcanic activities, and the presence of marine animals and ships in the oceans are sources of sound which contribute to the *ambient noise* of the ocean environment. In addition, this ambient noise is intensified by sea-surface noise at high wind speeds.

The performance of underwater acoustic systems designed to detect submarines in such an inhomogeneous, variable and noisy environment is often unpredictable and certainly variable both in space and time. This reflects an inherent property of the ocean that cannot be overcome by technological advances, and is not amenable to analytical treatment in any but its broadest details.

*Passive and active acoustic submarine detection*

Two properties of a submarine moving submerged in the ocean make it susceptible to detection by acoustic means. First, the submarine emits a spectrum of acoustic energy generated by the cavitation and turbulence caused by its motion. Superimposed on that spectrum are distinct monochromatic sounds caused by rotating machinery on board. This acoustic energy propagates as a sound wave in the ocean and can be detected from great distances by a listening device placed in the water (a hydrophone). Secondly, the hull of the submarine constitutes a density discontinuity in the ocean medium and, as such, reflects sound waves incident upon it. These reflected sound waves can also be detected by a listening device.

Acoustic detection methods are either passive or active. Passive methods rely on sensitive hydrophones that can detect the sounds emitted by a submarine in motion, and elaborate processors to distinguish them from the ambient noise. Active methods make use of a sound generator—that can be any equipment from a sonar transducer, described below, to a small explosive charge—and hydrophones that detect the sound reflected from the hull of the submarine. Such active systems, known as sonar, can be bi-static (the sound source and the hydrophone are not at the same point in the ocean) or mono-static.

Sonar consists of a sound generator that emits into the ocean pulses of acoustic energy ranging in duration from a few milliseconds to a second or more, and a listening hydrophone capable of detecting the echoes of these pulses reflected by the submarine hull. In both passive and active systems, however, the acoustic signal that indicates the presence of a submarine is accompanied by background oceanic noise. Submarine detection, then, always involves a decision whether the sound received by a hydrophone includes such a signal or not. This implies the existence of a detection threshold below which the acoustic signal from a submarine cannot be resolved from the background noise. In fact, detection is rarely certain, and, in spite of the enormous efforts devoted to developing submarine-detection equipment of exquisite sophistication and manageable size, when one speaks of the ability of a system to detect a submarine one speaks in terms of probabilities rather than of accurately predictable performance. What may be true 90 per cent of the time in a given sea-state at a given latitude may be true only 10 per cent of the time in a different sea-state or at a different location.

The exact nature of an echo pulse resulting from the scattering of a sound wave by the hull of a submarine depends on the state of the motion of the craft, because it is modulated by the *Doppler shift*. The Doppler shift changes the frequency of a wave reflected by a moving vessel in proportion to its radial speed.

Modern active detection systems are often quoted as having detection ranges no longer than 20 km or so, while passive mobile systems are said to be able to detect a submarine 100 km or more away. [2] The unpredictable behaviour of sound in the ocean makes it very difficult to state the ranges of these detection devices with any accuracy. One has to contend with the fact that most of the time a device will behave in an expected manner only under certain conditions. Training and experience of operators is often as important in a tactical situation as the built-in characteristics of a detector.

**Underwater acoustic devices**

*Emitters and receivers*

Emitters and hydrophones are electromechanical devices (transducers) capable of transforming electrical into acoustic energy or *vice versa*. The hydrophone receives acoustic energy and transforms it into an electrical signal, while the emitter transforms electrical power into acoustic power of the desired frequency.

The intensity of the emitted acoustic power produced by a sonar is of central importance in the detection of submarines. The working principle of the acoustic transducers employed in high power emitters is based on the magnetostrictive or piezoelectric properties of certain materials or on the electric-motor principle used in ordinary loudspeakers. Piezoelectric radiators can produce a sound field of megawatt level. In addition, such transducers can have high directivity resulting in an overall equivalent pressure level of about 150 db[1] one yard from the transducer. It is worth noting at this point that low frequency radiation is preferable since it is attenuated less by seawater.

---

[1] A decibel (db) expresses the ratio of the two intensities on a logarithmic scale. Usually acoustic intensities are expressed in decibels with respect to an agreed reference unit of intensity.

*Underwater sound processors*

The purpose of an underwater acoustic submarine detection system is to detect the presence of sound signals characteristic of submarines, to localize their source and to determine whether this source is indeed a submarine or not.

These operations—detection, localization and identification—require different signal processing techniques and equipment that are not necessarily compatible with each other. For example, to detect a signal at the longest possible range, the receiving system must be designed to use the full signal energy; on the other hand, to determine whether a signal is indeed generated by a submarine (and not by a whale, for example) it is almost always necessary to determine the spectral structure of the signal, a process that may utilize only a fraction of the total signal energy.

To make optimal use of the signal characteristics (amplitude, structure, and so on) and at the same time discriminate against the ubiquitous (but non-uniform in space and time) noise field, a complex and highly sophisticated array of electronics is needed to process the sound signal received by the hydrophone. Most of these systems employ one- or two-dimensional arrays of hydrophones as their receiving elements. By introducing appropriate electrical delays at the output of each hydrophone and then adding together the resulting signals, such an array can be made to scan the ocean around it, just like a searchlight, either emitting a narrow "beam" of sound and waiting for the returning echo, or listening at a narrow sector of the ocean for a period of time. The resulting high directivity helps distinguish the signal from the noise.

# III. *Submarine acoustic detection systems and their platforms*

The major portion of this section is devoted to the description of various deployed acoustic submarine detection systems. Although ASW involves several operations (detection, classification, localization and destruction), the most difficult and most important is the initial detection of a submarine hiding in the ocean. The importance of detection is reflected here by the emphasis given to detection systems as compared with the less detailed treatment of the various ASW platforms (aircraft, surface ships, and so on), and weapon systems (such as torpedoes or mines) in use. For a comprehensive account of all currently deployed ASW systems, see reference [1].

The detection of a submarine in the ocean is effectively carried out by acoustic means. Other means such as radar and lowlight television cameras are also used, but are of tertiary importance since modern nuclear submarines seldom rise to the surface where they could be detected by these devices. Additional detectors, such as infrared sensors that can detect a temperature rise in the ocean water due to the presence of a nuclear submarine, and the Magnetic Anomaly Detector (MAD) that detects local distortions of the geomagnetic field caused by the hull of a submarine, are also used in modern ASW. But they either have short ranges (MAD is effective at about 1 km from the submarine) or poor resolution (an infrared sensor could probably detect the upwelling of warm water caused by a hovering nuclear submarine, but not the layered hot effluents produced by a submerged craft in motion).

Passive and active acoustic systems can be either mobile or fixed. Mobile systems use aircraft (either fixed-wing aircraft or helicopters), surface ships or submarines as platforms. In each case the system has a different configuration and the mode in which it is used determines its technical details.

### ASW systems based on fixed-wing aircraft

One of the most effective methods of ASW employs aircraft that can deploy detection equipment to localize a submarine, and weapons to destroy it. These fixed-wing aircraft, either land-based or carrier-based, can search the oceans and detect submerged submarines by using passive and active sonobuoys. A sonobuoy is a hydrophone, or an emitter-hydrophone combination, that dangles from an air-droppable floating buoy. The depth at which the hydrophone descends after the buoy has hit the surface of the water can often be pre-set to suit local ocean conditions and can be as much as a few hundred metres. After the sonobuoy is dropped into the ocean, underwater sounds detected by the hydrophone are relayed by a small radio transmitter on the buoy to the aircraft flying overhead. The aircraft carries a substantial number of such buoys and can seed them into the ocean as it patrols a given area. If a hydrophone intercepts the characteristic sounds emitted by a moving submarine, the aircraft can release several buoys in the area and attempt to localize the submarine by comparing the intensity of the signals picked up and transmitted by the various sonobuoys. When a submarine is located in this manner within an area of 1 sq km or so, the aircraft can use MAD equipment to pinpoint its exact position. A homing acoustic torpedo can then be released by the aircraft to search for the submarine, home on to it and destroy it with a conventional or nuclear explosive charge.

The United States, Britain and France, among other nations, deploy ASW patrol aircraft. Two such aircraft recently introduced by the USA, the land-based Orion P-3C and the carrier-based Viking S-3A (which is just entering service), give good illustrations of the performance characteristics and functions of ASW fixed-wing aircraft. The Orion is a four-engine turbo-prop aircraft with a crew of 12. It has a patrol endurance of

11 hours, a maximum speed of 475 knots and a patrol speed of about 200 knots. It is equipped with radar, lowlight TV, electronic countermeasure equipment, MAD and the new sonobuoy system known as DIFAR (Directional Low Frequency Analyzer and Ranging).[2] The system employs a passive directional sonobuoy for wide-area search, that can detect a submarine at a great distance (passive sonobuoy ranges are reported to go up to 10 km). In addition, it can determine the direction from which the submarine sound is coming, and also establish and transmit to the aircraft the frequency characteristics of the submarine signal. In principle, information from only two such buoys is enough to fix the position of the submarine. In addition to the passive directional buoys, the Orion P-3C employs active sonobuoys that can determine the range of the submarine from the buoy by generating a sound pulse with a small explosive charge, and by intercepting the portion of this pulse reflected by the submarine hull. The range of active sonobuoys is said to be about 3 km or more in good ocean conditions. The Orion can carry up to 87 passive and active buoys either in the fuselage or stored externally.

Each Orion carries two DIFAR processors. The aircraft has both inertial guidance and Doppler-shift radar to navigate either while cruising or during tactical operations. It is capable of performing in all weather conditions and can be used for a multiplicity of tasks (patrol, escort, coordination of an ASW operation, and so on). It is considered to be effective against the quiet, deep diving nuclear submarines that will be deployed in the 1970s and 1980s.

The great improvement in Orion's ASW capabilities over older US ASW aircraft derives from the installation of a new avionics system known as ANEW. This system coordinates all information received from all sonobuoys, keeps track of the position of the aircraft with respect to the dropped buoys, monitors the other detection devices, and displays all sensor information on a large electronic display. ANEW is based on a Univac computer with a 64 000 30-bit word memory, 16 input/output channels and a four microsecond add time. The computer can handle about four million bits of information per second. It coordinates communications, navigation and signals from ASW sensors; it monitors and launches weapons and maintains, in real time, sonobuoy positions, target location, aircraft position and track; and it evaluates and displays the sensor information. In addition, this computer monitors continuously the condition of the various systems, performs its own diagnostics and makes decisions, based on radio frequency signal intensities, on optimal use of sonobuoys and ultimately of weapons. Thus, ANEW allows for efficient use of the increased amount of information collected by the sonobuoys and leaves the human operators much more time to make tactical decisions.

[2] For sources of data on this ASW system and others described below, the reader is referred to reference [1].

The United States had, by 1973, deployed about 100 Orions, and plans to acquire about 140 more. Several innovations are already under way and will be incorporated into existing Orion P-3Cs when completed. One is a new communications system that will permit transmission of sonar information received by one aircraft to other aircraft or surface vessels, in order to improve coordination during ASW operations. Another is an addition to the DIFAR processor that will permit utilization of CASS (Command Activated Sonobuoy System) and DICASS (Directional CASS) sonobuoys. Both CASS and DICASS are self-powered, active, localization sonobuoys that can be turned on and off upon command over a radio link from the overflying aircraft. Turning the sonobuoy on and off prolongs the life of its battery power supply and therefore extends its useful life. (The DIFAR sonobuoys, which do not possess this facility, have a mean life of about 80 hours.) DICASS has the added advantage over CASS of providing a directional signal which enables the aircraft to locate the submarine with fewer sonobuoys and in a shorter period of time. Thus, although the unit cost of both the DIFAR ($650) and CASS-DICASS type sonobuoy is considerably higher than the $85 price of the simpler non-directional LOFAR buoys [3] used until recently by the USA, the overall cost of operating Orion P-3C patrols may not be much higher since these newer expensive buoys are more efficient.

The carrier-based S-3A Viking ASW aircraft is a twin-engine jet with a crew of four, an operational combat range of 2 000 nautical miles, a maximum speed of 440 knots, and a sea-level loiter speed of 160 knots. The aircraft is equipped with a miniaturized and more compact ANEW system which performs the same set of functions as the P-3C version. Instead of the lowlight TV, the S-3A will carry a forward-looking infrared sensor. The first S-3A Vikings are scheduled to enter operational service at the beginning of 1974 and the 190 complement will probably be completed in 1978. These aircraft are designed to offer long-range protection against cruise-missile submarines to task forces and aircraft carriers, but are not suitable for lengthy ocean patrol and surveillance. [4–6]

Britain, France and the Soviet Union have also developed land-based long-range ASW aircraft. Britain has introduced into service a four-engined jet known as Nimrod which apparently has capabilities similar to those of the Orion P-3C—a range of 5 000 nautical miles, a speed of 180–500 knots and an endurance of 12 hours. The French aircraft Atlantic—also used by FR Germany, Italy and the Netherlands—is a propeller-driven craft equipped to detect non-nuclear submarines. It has a mission range of 3 600 nautical miles, a patrol speed of 170 knots and an endurance of up to 18 hours. The Soviet Union has deployed the Beriev M-12 and Ilyushin Il-38 (NATO code names "Mail" and "May") for employing air-droppable sonobuoys in submarine-surveillance operations.

The avionics and sonobuoy systems deployed on the Orion and Nimrod are examples of a new generation of aircraft-based ASW systems. They incorporate the most recent advances in electronic technology but no new detection principle or system. As such, they can be easily duplicated by other nations with advanced electronics industries.

## Helicopter-mounted ASW systems

The installation of cruise surface-to-surface missiles on submarines altered the fundamental parameter of tactical ASW operations, that is, the range from which the submarines can launch weapons against their targets. Different types of cruise missiles have effective ranges of from 20 to 400 km or more. To counter submarines equipped with such weapons, modern ASW operations incorporate a wide and varied use of helicopters, either based on escort vessels such as destroyers and frigates, or on special aircraft carriers. A helicopter has the unique advantage of being able to hover over a point in the ocean sufficiently long to lower a sonar by cable into the water and listen for submarine sounds. In addition, it has the ability to land and take off from an area not much larger than its own dimensions. Thus it is invulnerable to and undetectable by its quarry, is not affected by weather conditions and does not contribute to the ambient noise field of its sonar. The cruising speed of a helicopter (up to five times faster than any submarine) allows it to search extensive areas of the ocean either by means of its dipping sonar or by sowing sonobuoys. A helicopter carrying a dipping sonar with a 5-km range and averaging 10 minutes between dips can examine a corridor 10 km wide and 100 km long, in one hour. A small number of such helicopters can effectively "sanitize" the area around a task force or a carrier moving at 40 km/hour.

In addition to the Magnetic Anomaly Detector, dipping sonar, the same types of passive and active sonobuoys carried by fixed-wing aircraft, acoustic homing torpedoes, and data link to its surface platform, an ASW helicopter could carry counter-cruise missile equipment such as radar, mechanical or electronic decoys, and air-to-air and air-to-surface missiles. Thus it can be an effective defensive system against counter-shipping submarines equipped with cruise missiles. Neither the endurance of a helicopter, nor the range of its sonar, allows it to undertake any ASW role other than the protection of surface ships from counter-shipping submarines.

The defensive capabilities of shipborne helicopters are reflected in their wide use by a number of maritime powers. Since the mid-1960s the Soviet Union has deployed a shipborne seven-ton helicopter ("Hormone") with a three-hour search endurance. Under the first phase of the LAMPS (Light Airborne Multi-Purpose System) programme the United States is converting about 100 Sea Sprite two-man crew helicopters to antisubmarine and counter-cruise missile operations. [7] These helicopters will be based aboard destroyers, escorts and frigates and will be equipped with the latest submarine detector and avionics package available. In another LAMPS programme an entirely new helicopter and avionics-detection device system is under study.

Britain has adopted the Sea King, the Westland version of the US Sikorsky SH-3 helicopter, for ASW operations. This is a land- or carrier-based helicopter with approximately five hours' endurance and equipped with a 350-kg active-ranging dipping sonar that has a reported range of 4–6 km, 12 sonobuoy launchers, MAD, and radar and electronic gear for counter-cruise missile operations. Various versions of the Sea King are employed in tactical ASW operations by Argentina, Brazil, Canada, India, Iran, Italy, Japan, Spain and the United States. The latest version carries a low-frequency long-range dipping sonar with an angular resolution of about 10 degrees (equivalent to roughly 1 000 metres, 10 km away). Ongoing development programmes in the USA aim at further reducing the weight of helicopter-borne sonars and eventually replacing them with an airborne towed array system (AIRTASS) that will increase the range and sensitivity of the detector.

France has introduced a modified version of the Super-Frelon helicopter to ASW operations. It is a five-man crew helicopter with four hours' endurance and a range of over 700 km. It is equipped with a 230-kg dipping sonar designed for shallow water (about 50 metres maximum) operations.

### Surface ships and their sonars

The utility of fast surface vessels as sonar platforms has been rapidly diminishing as submarine speed and quietness have increased and the ranges of torpedoes and cruise missiles have become considerably greater than the effective detection range of hull-mounted active sonars. The range of active sonars generally deployed on US surface ASW ships, for example, does not exceed 15 km under good ocean conditions and can drop to as little as 2 km in warm, noisy waters. [8] As a result, the USA and other nations have undertaken major programmes for improving or replacing the currently deployed surface ship sonar systems. Under programme PAIR (Performance and Integration Retrofit), existing sonar detectors on US ships are equipped with an integrated digital processing system that incorporates the most advanced signal-processing methods and computer-generated displays. In addition, project PADLOC (Passive-Active Detection and Localization) provided existing ASW surface ships with a passive sonar detection set consisting of three hydrophones which can determine the range and bearing of the target by triangulation. [9]

A parallel effort of the US Navy is the installation, to date on about 120 ships, of a new bow-mounted active sonar, about three times larger and heavier than the earlier type. This new sonar consists of 576 transducers in a cylindrical array mounted in a bulbous dome. It is an efficient, complex, multi-mode sonar that can operate either in a direct path or bottom bounce mode, or can take advantage of the convergence zones[3] when ocean conditions permit. It is clear, however, that neither the sophisticated signal processing nor the increased power of hull-mounted sonars can effectively overcome the noise created by a speeding surface craft, especially in high-sea states. Neither is detection of submarines hiding in the shadow zones of the ocean much improved by such efforts. These problems seem to have been countered effectively by removing the listening hydrophones from the hull of the ship and instead towing them at some distance from the ship. By varying the length of the tow cable, the sonar can be lowered below the thermocline layer where detection of submarines is not obstructed by the refractive effects of ocean layers. A further development along this line is the use of entire arrays of hydrophones that can be towed at considerable depths thus avoiding both the thermal inversion layers of the ocean and the ship noises. [9] The Soviet Union has deployed variable depth sonar on many of its new surface ships; this sonar is apparently used both for detection and for antisubmarine weapon launching control. Both Britain and France have similar hull-mounted and towed variable depth sonars deployed on surface ASW ships.

A joint US-French research programme is under way to study the use of such towed arrays at great depths. In another joint programme, between the USA and the UK, the applicability of long-range active planar array sonar mounted on a surface ship is being investigated.

**Hunter-killer submarines**

By far the most effective weapon against a quiet deep-diving nuclear submarine is another submarine, since it can be equally if not more quiet, can occupy the same portion of the ocean as its quarry (thus avoiding the abbreviation of sonar range caused by the oceanic inversion layers and the ever changing seasonal thermocline), and is large enough to accommodate extensive sonar arrays, their power sources and elaborate processors, and antisubmarine weapons. Thus a submarine is an integrated ASW system that can detect, follow, localize and destroy another submarine. Since cavitation noises decrease with increasing depth, a deep-diving submarine is quieter than a similar craft travelling at the same speed but at a lesser depth (or equally as noisy at a higher speed). Reduction of noise levels at high speeds and the ability to dive deeply are primary characteristics of

---

[3] The same combination of refraction and reflection of sound waves that gives rise to shadow zones (see page 305) also causes the formation of convergence zones of sound intensification. In these zones, which are 5–10 km wide and occur at intervals of about 70 km in the tropics and about 40 km in northern waters, sound from an underwater source is 15–20 db more intense than in neighbouring ocean areas.

hunter-killer submarines. The diesel-electric conventional submarines, although they may be quieter than a nuclear submarine when they move submerged, powered by their electrical motors, do not present a real threat to nuclear submarines because of their limited underwater endurance and slower speeds. Thus current non-nuclear submarines are not only more vulnerable to surface-ship or airborne ASW systems because they are forced to travel semi-submerged most of the time, but are also extremely vulnerable to the faster and deeper-diving nuclear submarines.

Only the United Kingdom, the United States and the Soviet Union possess nuclear hunter-killer submarines (SSNs). Britain has seven such craft with four more under construction. The Soviet Union deploys 28 SSNs of various types (with speeds between 25 and 35 knots submerged) and an additional 40 nuclear submarines carrying countershipping cruise missiles (SSGNs) and therefore capable of a dual role (countershipping and ASW). The Soviet Union apparently plans to continue construction of advanced type SSGNs ("Charlie" and "Papa" class) during the next few years. The United States has 58 deployed SSNs mostly of the "Permit" and "Sturgeon" classes (speeds of 30 and 32 knots, respectively) with six more of the latter under construction. [1] In addition, the USA has started producing a new class of 6 900-ton hunter-killer submarine (the "Los Angeles" SSN-688 class) which is expected to have a submerged speed of 40 knots and a maximum depth of 300 fathoms (550 metres). The US Navy plans to order 32 such submarines by 1967 and the total number may reach 43. Further in the future, the USA is planning to replace all SSNs other than the "Los Angeles" class with a new craft, designated as CONFORM, that will combine the technological advances attained with the SSBN-688 class with those of the experimental "quiet" *Libscomb* SSN-685 submarine now under construction. If this plan is achieved, the US Navy may have 68 CONFORM submarines by the early 1980s, since their declared goal is 100 SSNs by that date. [10] France and the People's Republic of China do not have SSNs at this time.

Submarine-mounted sonar systems are undergoing constant improvement and refinement. The basic sonar equipment of US hunter-killer submarines, which consists of an active/passive sonar, underwater communications equipment, and a sophisticated computer-supported processing unit, has been improved by the introduction of an active detection and ranging set. The system has been further improved by the introduction of the DIMUS (Digital Multi-Beam Steering System) which improved the resolution and effective range of the system by enabling the passive sonar to form a narrow listening beam. This system is said to be able to detect submarines up to about 160 km away and to possess classification capabilities, which, for example, enable it to recognize the acoustic "fingerprint" of an unknown submarine.

An entirely new system known as DNA (Digital multi-beam, Narrow band processing, Accelerated active search rate sonar) has been developed for installation on the new "Los Angeles" class submarines, and in time will probably replace the older sonars on the "Sturgeon" and "Permit" class ships. DNA is designed as an integral part of the submarine hull, and employs the latest processing techniques for active and passive detection. It also controls the launching and targeting of "Subroc", an antisubmarine missile-carried depth charge with a nuclear warhead. The follow-up submarine-based sonar system under development is probably a submarine-towed sonar array that will also incorporate acoustic countermeasures. Yet another towed array has been developed in the USA for missile-carrying submarines and is now being installed concurrently with the Poseidon conversion. It incorporates a 12-beam processor and display unit and the latest digital techniques in signal processing. It is designed to give the SSBNs increased ability to detect SSNs which at this time represent the only potential threat to the missile-carrying submarines.

As nuclear submarines become increasingly quiet (it is reported that the US Polaris emits less than one milliwatt of acoustic energy unidirectionally in the ocean), an ever intensifying effort is under way to develop more powerful and sophisticated acoustic underwater detection systems, an effort which in turn motivates construction of ever faster, quieter and deeper-diving hunter-killer submarines.

## Large fixed arrays

Long-range surveillance of the ocean depths by acoustic means can be achieved with systems that possess high discrimination gain, that is, systems that can distinguish the faint sound signal of a distant submarine from the ambient noise of the ocean. Such gains can be attained by adding coherently signals received at hundreds or perhaps thousands of hydrophones deployed in an ocean basin. These hydrophones can either be deployed as a dispersed array of upward-listening devices moored at different depths over a very large area, or can be concentrated in a two-dimensional array a few hundred metres long. In both cases the hydrophones are in communication with a large shore-based computer that can add these signals after introducing appropriate time delays. In the dispersed array the computer guesses that the submarine is located at a specific point in the ocean and adds the signals after inserting appropriate delays in each one of them. If the guess is correct the resultant signal will resemble the sound from a submarine; if the guess is wrong, the resulting signal will be noise. The computer can make many such guesses every minute and thus locate the submarine and subsequently, by utilizing appropriate programmes, track it as it moves through the ocean. In the case of the concentrated array, the computer forms a narrow listening beam by integrating the signals from the hydrophones of the array after it has introduced the proper set of delays in each hydrophone output. A very large computer can in this fashion form several beams simultaneously so that no signal is lost as the various narrow listening beams "sweep" the ocean. Such arrays can detect the presence of a submarine hundreds of kilometres away.

Under a programme that was initiated in the 1950s the United States has emplaced such surveillance arrays (bottom-mounted, upward listening, interconnected sonars) on the continental shelf along the eastern seaboard of North America. This system, known as "Caesar", is now in its fifth generation. A similar system, "Colossus" (involving 5–15 sonars per linear mile), was installed on the west coast of the United States in the mid-1960s. Some of the arrays are said to be along the Aleutian Islands chain and the Kuriles-Kamchatka trench. Similar systems, code-named "Barrier" and "Bronco", have been installed along the coastlines of other countries. To date there are 21 shore stations receiving data from such underwater surveillance arrays. The US Navy is now installing a similar array in the Gulf of Mexico. Late in 1969 an attempt was made to moor a listening hydrophone, three metres in diameter, north of Hawaii in 3 000 fathoms of water. The attempt was unsuccessful, but it was probably repeated successfully later.

Still another surveillance system, known as AFAR, was established north of the Azores Islands. It consists of sonars mounted on three or more 130-metre high submerged towers arranged in a triangle of about 35 km on each side. The installation can monitor submarine traffic through the Straits of Gibraltar and can localize submarines by triangulation methods.

Plans for still another bottom-anchored active array of monumental dimensions are under way. The "Suspended Array System" (known as SAS) [11] involves a high tripod tower resting at 3 000 fathoms which will be so large that each leg of the tripod will be 10 km away from the other two legs. Acoustic transducers mounted on this tripod will be of such size and power that just one such installation will be capable of surveying an entire ocean. The cost of the system is estimated at over $1 billion. [12]

Another system now under active development in the USA, known as the Moored Surveillance System (MSS), is a system incorporating characteristics of both fixed arrays and short-lived air-droppable sonobuoys. It will consist of air-droppable, long-life sonobuoys that will automatically moor to the bottom of the ocean and transmit information to satellite-borne or airborne receivers. Equipped with elaborate sonar and communications systems, each buoy will occupy a known fixed position in the ocean so that by correlating data from several buoys, triangulation techniques can be used to localize submarines. The sonobuoys will have a useful lifetime of 90 days, can be moored in up to 3 000 fathoms of water and will have a controlled sensor depth. This system is intended as part of the US effort to achieve total surveillance of the oceans through an extended detection system that would collect data about the movements of submarines, and transmit it in real time to central processing and operation stations via communications satellites. [12]

## IV. *Tactical antisubmarine warfare*

Tactical antisubmarine warfare consists of a series of operations that can be divided into four phases—detection, classification, localization and destruction of a hostile submarine. Such operations can be initiated to protect a convoy of supply ships, an expeditionary force or a task force of warships from submarine attack. The means by which these operations are carried out are largely independent of the particular task at hand, but are generally a function of the geographic circumstances.

Tactical ASW operations of most national navies are designed to prevent hostile submarines from using the oceans to the detriment of the nation's security in times of war. These tasks involve patrolling coastlines, protecting surface vessels engaged in naval operations and protecting merchant ships performing supply operations. In peacetime, ASW operations are confined to training, monitoring, testing and intelligence gathering. A distinction is necessary between those conventional operations and the ASW tasks facing the US and Soviet navies (and to a lesser extent the British Navy as well). In the case of these powers one must distinguish not only between peacetime and wartime operations, but also between the class of tasks that ASW forces will face in a conventional protracted war and in a nuclear conflict.

### Tactical ASW operations

Two distinct types of operation can be employed in tactical ASW. One involves the effort to deny the opponent submarines access to large portions of the ocean. This is an offensive operation that attempts to secure entire areas against submarine counter-shipping activities by attacking all submarines that try to enter a given ocean basin (area defence). Patrols by land-based fixed-wing aircraft and helicopters and by roving hunter-killer submarines often lying in ambush outside nuclear submarine bases, and ocean surveillance by fixed arrays are designed to support the operational requirements for area defence. The other type of operation aims at defending a particular point in the ocean occupied by a convoy, a task force or even a single ship such as a carrier, by organizing carrier-based ASW fixed-wing aircraft, ASW helicopters, surface ASW vessels and hunter-killer submarines into protective screens (point defence).

The US Navy intends to employ both area and point defence in times of hostilities, a conclusion that emerges from an examination of the ASW systems deployed and the tactics practised. The establishment of air and naval patrols along the Greenland-Iceland-Scotland passages to the North Atlantic indicates an area-defence approach that intends to deny all Soviet submarines access to the entire Atlantic Ocean. [13] In line with this area-defence approach is the intent to destroy as many Soviet submarines as possible as they exit from the only year-round operational ports of Murmansk and Petropavlosk where the density of submarines is greatest. Area defence uses long-range land-based patrol aircraft (such as the P-3C), hunter-killer submarines and surface ships to patrol the entry points to an ocean or the exits from hostile submarine bases. This tactic derives from World War II experience and seems really suitable only for the northern approaches to the Atlantic Ocean. The Soviet Navy does not seem to practise area defence since its primary tactical objectives are to protect its operations in the Norwegian and Mediterranean seas and to prevent hostile submarines from approaching Soviet shores. The US Navy justifies the continuous practice of area-defence system tactics with the claim that, in time of war, area defence of the North Atlantic will be essential. It is clear, on the other hand, that in time of war, or even threat of war, the northern passages to the Atlantic can be sealed with antisubmarine minefields rather than with the enormously expensive barrier of SSNs, land-based patrol aircraft and surface ships assisted by ocean-surveillance arrays [14] now deployed. The "Captor", a mine specifically designed for that purpose, can detect the presence of a submarine within approximately 3 km and release a homing torpedo, capable of destroying the submarine on contact. [11]

Wide-area surveillance from fixed-wing aircraft, large fixed arrays and SSNs are part of the area-defence operations but can also be employed by the USA to monitor the number of Soviet SSBNs in the Atlantic Ocean. Since, however, knowledge of the exact number of such submarines present in the Atlantic at any one instant is not essential to US defences, and since it is not clear that such monitoring provides the USA with an accurate number anyway, it is remarkable that enormous sums of money and considerable expenditure of scientific and trained manpower are devoted to such marginal defence needs. Consequently, the inference can be drawn that the deployment of such ASW platforms as land-based patrol aircraft and mid-ocean fixed arrays is not intended for the purpose of intelligence gathering: either it is intended primarily for acquiring operational experience and tactical flexibility that could be used pre-emptively against Soviet SSBNs during a period of crisis, or it reflects special subservice entrenched interests within the Navy. Any other use of area defence as presently practised by the USA appears to be cost-ineffective both in the context of tactical ASW operations during war, and surveillance operations during peacetime.

Point defence against cruise missile-carrying counter-shipping submarines employs helicopters based on sea-going platforms, carried-based ASW fixed-wing aircraft, surface ships and hunter-killer submarines. It is a strictly defensive operation that does not seek hostile submarines far away from the surface ships that it protects, but sanitizes a wide area of the ocean around these ships. Fixed-wing aircraft provide very long-range surveillance while helicopters form a second screen against submarines, and provide over-the-horizon counter-cruise-missile capability to the surface ships both by detecting such missiles and by attacking them with air-to-air rockets. The SSNs provide more secure long-range acoustic detection capability and act as weapon-launching platforms. Point-defence capabilities can be saturated by a concerted attack by a large number of hostile hunter-killer submarines. It is unlikely, however, that an area-defence barrier based on land-based fixed-wing aircraft rather than antisubmarine minefields could inflict such a severe attrition upon the attackers that the efficacy of point-defence task forces would be substantially improved.

# V. *Anti-strategic submarine warfare (ASSW)*

Although detection, localization and classification of missile-carrying submarines can be achieved with the same acoustic systems and the same platforms used in tactical operations, the tactics and purpose of these submarines are distinctly different from those of counter-shipping submarines and ASW operations against them therefore have entirely different scales and goals. First of all, a missile-carrying submarine avoids surface traffic; point-defence ASW is thus irrelevant in this case. Even more importantly, while the purpose of detecting and localizing an attack submarine is to destroy it, the ultimate purpose of anti-strategic submarine warfare (ASSW) is not always the destruction of a missile-carrying submarine. More often than not the last stage of ASSW could be protracted trailing of the quarry rather than the launching of a weapon against it. By necessity then, counter-missile-submarine operations cannot be examined in connection with a study of operations against counter-shipping submarines since the tactics and requirements are very different indeed.

## Requirements of counter-SSBN antisubmarine warfare

Each Soviet or US missile-carrying submarine represents about 2 per cent of each country's sea-based deterrent force. (France has two missile-launching submarines and three more under construction; Britain has four Polaris-type craft deployed; the People's Republic of China has no nuclear or missile-carrying submarine.) SSBNs have at the present time no role other than that of acting as firing platforms for submarine-launched ballistic missiles (SLBMs). Therefore any ASW operations against SSBNs can be seen at present only as efforts to destroy a country's sea-based nuclear deterrent. Such efforts can proceed only along three lines: (*a*) to attempt a pre-emptive surprise first strike in order to destroy *all* the missile-carrying submarines of an adversary nation, or group of allied opponents; (*b*) to launch a damage-limiting attack on an opponent's submarine force in order to limit the possible damage sea-based missiles can visit upon one's own country; or (*c*) to attrite the opponent's submarine force by a series of destructive encounters made over a relatively extended period of time such that during peacetime these encounters could be mistaken for accidents. Although this last approach is not a very credible alternative, it is conceivably useful as a prelude to an overt first strike or a damage-limiting operation.

A simultaneous attack against the entire SLBM force of an opponent with the intent of annihilating it within a number of minutes is in practice possible only during peacetime, although technically it may be possible during war as well; however, no participant in a nuclear exchange, or even in a conventional war, would permit circumstances to arise which would allow for such an attack, as will be explained below. The operational requirements for such a first-strike attack are: (*a*) knowledge of the location of *every* strategic submarine of the opponent in real time, continuously and securely for extended periods (weeks if not months) while the submarines are on station, in transit or in port; and (*b*) the undeniable ability to deliver a lethal weapon against each such submarine almost simultaneously (within minutes) with a very high confidence of kill. These requirements for a surprise first strike against all of a country's SSBNs can be fulfilled only by continuous trailing of the opponent's ballistic missile submarines at sea. It is the method that can ensure, first, that *all* the relevant submarines are accessible to a destructive blow and, second, that this blow can be administered to all submarines simultaneously. [15] If either of these requirements is not fulfilled the opponent will be given the opportunity to launch at least a number of sea-based missiles, an unacceptable circumstance in the context of a pre-emptive first strike. A first strike requires not only very high confidence in the ability to destroy the entire SLBM force of an opponent but in addition assumes a simultaneously and equally completely successful attack against the opponent's land-based nuclear strategic forces, if they exist. Such a strike is conceivable only in the context of a surprise attack during peacetime. During a conventional war or a nuclear exchange no country will allow its missile-carrying submarines to be trailed, the key operational requirement of a surprise attack.

A damage-limiting counter-SLBM operation differs from a first strike in important ways: in the latter operation one allows no possibility for damage to one's own urban centres while in the former, one can expect *a priori* a measure of destruction of one's own cities. This removes the operational requirements of (*a*) total and (*b*) simultaneous destruction of the opponent's SLBM force from the damage-limiting case. Therefore a damage-limiting attack that aims at the destruction of as many of the opponent's missile-carrying submarines as possible at a given time requires knowledge of the location of, and ability to destroy only a fraction of these submarines. Such an operation could stretch over a long period of time. It can be launched as a surprise attack during peacetime, or it can commence during war. Damage-limiting ASSW operations thus seem to be the most probable, the most destabilizing and, in the long run, the most dangerous ASW operations.

### ASW systems capable of supporting a damage-limiting or a pre-emptive first-strike attack

It was pointed out in the previous section that the only method that could fulfil the operational requirements for a first strike is the uninterrupted trailing of an opponent's missile-carrying submarines. No other method that can be supported either by existing ASW systems or by any foreseeable technical development can achieve the high confidence required for a first strike. The trailing of nuclear submarines can be practised either by hunter-killer submarines such as those already deployed by the USA, the Soviet Union and Britain, or by special surface or subsurface platforms, designed specifically for the purpose of trailing. Most probably more than one trailer is necessary per missile-carrying submarine if the trail is to be securely maintained. These trailers do not have to be as large or complex as the SSNs now deployed. A craft capable of keeping up with an SSBN in all sea states, equipped with a few homing torpedoes and a high-resolution active sonar, could be an effective trailer provided it could be supplied *en route* and therefore had long endurance, or that it could be readily relieved by another such craft. There is no such system either deployed or under development at the present time. Long-range surveillance systems would have to be used to detect the missile-carrying submarines and monitor their movement until a trailer was attached to them.

The requirements for a damage-limiting attack can be fulfilled by the existing deployed ASW area-defence and SSN systems. According to unofficial estimates, the United States could, under favourable conditions, detect and localize most of the Soviet missile-carrying submarines on station or in transit most of the time, using presently available area-defence ASW systems. The deployment of the Moored Sonobuoy System (MSS) and the very large SAS surveillance array will enhance this capability. On the other hand, the Soviet Union possesses enough hunter-killer submarines to be able to trail a substantial number of the Polaris craft during peacetime. As the Soviet naval planners re-assess the relative danger resident in US missile submarines as compared with aircraft carriers, it is probable that they will assign a larger and larger portion of their hunter-killer submarines to the task of trailing the Polaris. Thus the capability for either the Soviet Union or the United States to launch a successful damage-limiting attack against each other's or any other nation's sea-based deterrent is certain.

# VI. *Conclusions*

SLBM forces remain the most stable component of deterrence in the foreseeable future. A first strike against them is impossible with the currently deployed ASW systems; the British and French forces have been and will remain, because of their small size, limited missile range and constrained geographic basing, vulnerable both to US and Soviet SSN forces. In a WTO-NATO confrontation these two forces might be secure because they would not have the undivided attention of Soviet SSNs; but in any other confrontation their strategic value would be marginal. The US and Soviet SLBM fleets cannot be seriously threatened as deterrent forces at the present time or in the foreseeable future. Only a highly specialized force consisting of numerous trailers (several per SSBN) could threaten them. Even this threat can be eliminated with the stationing of SSBNs near one's own coastlines.

On the other hand, systems developed and deployed explicitly for use in area-defence ASW operations offer at the present time the option of a destabilizing damage-limiting attack on either the Soviet or the US submarine missile forces. This threat can be eliminated by the introduction of submarine missiles with ranges greater than 7000 km, that will allow SLBMs of both great powers to loiter in their respective coastal waters while well within range of their targets. The Soviet Union appears already to have deployed one operational submarine with such missiles. The United States already possesses the capability to equip 31 of the 41 Polaris submarines with such long-range missiles by off-loading the Poseidon and thereby gaining in range. Furthermore the USA will be developing the C-4 missile that can fit into the Poseidon tubes. By 1977 or 1978, if its development is appropriately funded, this missile will have the required range, without loss of MIRV capability, to permit deployment of the Polaris submarine in safe sanctuaries.

There are of course several steps that can be taken as measures to reduce the danger from damage-limiting attacks to the SLBM fleets of the USA and the USSR. Such measures would include: (*a*) restricting the appertures (for passive) and frequencies and power levels (for active) ocean-surveillance arrays so that their capability is restricted to coastal monitoring, for example about 1 000 km; (*b*) prohibiting the implantation of large ocean surveillance arrays in mid-oceanic regions; (*c*) prohibiting the development and deployment of surface ships or aircraft capable of tracking submarines uninterruptedly for long periods of time; and (*d*) setting an upper limit to the ratio of the number of SSNs of one country to the number of SSBNs of the other. Clearly these measures asymmetrically affect US practices. However, this is a byproduct of the fact that only the USA has deployed area-defence ASW capability. While it would be desirable to ensure the stability of all the SLBM forces by such a series of arms-limitation agreements, it appears that the only realistic way to achieve this highly desirable result is, ironically, to introduce a new weapon, the 7 000–10 000 km submarine ballistic missile. The disadvantage of this solution is that it does not increase the security of the British and French SLBM forces. The size and geographic basing of the British and French SLBM forces are such that only a further series of arms-limiting measures can endow them with pragmatic utility and decrease their susceptibility to annihilation. The treaty banning ABMs established the credibility of these forces as deterrents to a nuclear attack against Britain and France. It will, however, take international arms control agreements that would drastically reduce ASW operations in the Atlantic to increase the survivability of the French and British nuclear ballistic missile-carrying submarines. [16]

## References

1. *Tactical and Strategic Antisubmarine Warfare,* SIPRI Monograph (Stockholm, Almqvist & Wiksell, 1974, Stockholm International Peace Research Institute).
2. *Congressional Quarterly,* Vol. 31, 31 March 1973, p. 713.
3. *Undersea Technology,* Vol. 12, No. 11, November 1971.
4. *Statement of Admiral Elmo R. Zumwalt, Jr., U.S. Navy Chief of Naval Operations before the Committee on Armed Services, United States Senate, concerning FY 1974 Military Posture and Budget of the United States Navy, 12 April 1973* [Washington, 1973].
5. *Navy International,* Vol. 77, No. 8, August 1972, p. 20.
6. *Undersea Technology,* Vol. 10, No. 11, November 1969, p. 50.
7. *Statement of the Honorable John W. Warner, Secretary of the Navy, before the Committee on Armed Services, United States Senate, concerning the FY 1974 Program and Budget of the United States Navy and Marine Corps, 12 April 1973* [Washington, 1973].
8. *Space/Aeronautics,* No. 2, February 1969, pp. 43 ff.
9. *The ASW Market* (New York, Frost & Sullivan, Inc., July 1972).
10. Information provided by the Center for Defense Information, Washington, D.C.
11. *Statement of the Honorable Peter Waterman, Acting Assistant Secretary of the Navy for Research and Development, before* [the] *Committee on Armed Services, United States House of Representatives, concerning Research, Development, Test and Evaluation, Navy, Fiscal Year 1974, 22 May 1973* [Washington, 1973].
12. *Undersea Technology,* Vol. 13, No. 11, pp. 18 ff.

13. *The Department of Defense Program of Research, Development, Test and Evaluation, FY 1974, Statement by the Director of Defense Research and Engineering to the 93rd Congress, First Session, 28 March 1973* [Washington, 1973] pp. 6–20 ff.
14. *U.S. Naval Institute Proceedings*, Vol. 98, No. 9, September 1972, pp. 31 ff.
15. Garwin, R. W., in K. Tsipis, A. Cahn and B. Feld, eds., *The Future of the Sea-based Deterrent* (Boston, Mass., The MIT Press, 1973).
16. *Expenditure Committee (Defence and External Affairs Sub-committee), Minutes of Evidence, Wednesday, 13 February, 1973, Session 1972–73 Mr. Francois Duchene* (London, HMSO).

# 11. The automated battlefield

*Square-bracketed references, thus* [1] *refer to the list of references on page 359.*

## I. *Introduction*

Automation is, today, a familiar concept, at least in the industrialized countries of the world. In fact, so many aspects of everyday life are automated, to a greater or lesser degree, that automation is almost taken for granted. In the home, for example, automatic, pre-programmed washing machines and cookers, and thermostats to control the central heating, are well known. In towns and cities, traffic density can be registered and traffic lights operated automatically by means of pressure sensors in or on the road surface. In shops, offices and factories, both goods and people can be watched by television cameras. And in industry, many repetitive, tedious or dangerous tasks are performed by automatic systems. The motives for automating are numerous, the most important probably being cost-effectiveness and efficiency: the employment of a machine to perform a particular task is generally much cheaper than the employment of a man or woman to perform the same task, and the trend towards automation greatly reduces the need for direct human involvement; a machine is usually capable of performing a particular task much faster than a man or woman; and automation also makes possible the performance of certain tasks, such as the handling of radioactive materials, which could not otherwise be carried out at all, simply because they present insurmountable difficulties or unacceptable dangers for a human being.

But automation is by no means confined to the civilian field. Armed combat is one of the most dangerous, as well as increasingly costly, activities involving human beings, and so, again mainly for reasons of efficiency and cost-effectiveness, the trend in the military field too has been towards automation. In the past, military automation was rather unsophisticated, being mainly restricted to the deployment of booby-trapped weapons, such as mines, which were triggered by the victim without further direct involvement of the aggressor. Later, automation was advanced by the introduction of automatic fire-control systems, for example, anti-aircraft artillery that could be aimed at targets by radar. Later still came the development of homing devices which, fitted to projectiles, enabled them to reach their targets more reliably. And many recent developments in military technology have been directed towards improving such automated systems. In recent years, however, expressions such as "automated warfare", "the automated battlefield" and "the electronic battlefield" have appeared more and more in public debates. Such expressions would indicate that, just as the trend in automation in the civilian field is towards full automation, where robots perform all domestic chores and carry out all industrial operations, so too is the trend in the military sector, in this case towards full automation of warfare, where battles are fought between opposing "armies" of automatic machines and weapons.

At present, full automation, in either field, is a situation belonging more to the world of science fiction than to reality. In either case, it is clear that increasing automation will bring a multitude of problems which will have to be solved. In the civilian field, for example, there is the question of whether human beings or machines will actually be in control, and the problem of how best to utilize the increased leisure time that will be available. In the military sector there is also the question of whether men or machines will be in control of a war, but in addition a range of philosophical questions will present themselves. It is thus important to be aware of the trends towards automation, and more important to be aware of how far these trends have progressed so that the problems may be realized in good time. But while the trends towards full automation in civilian life are taking place in full public view and can be examined, analysed and assessed by almost anyone who cares to take the trouble, the technological developments in the military field which lead towards full automation of warfare are almost always obscured by a shroud of secrecy, so that it is difficult to discover just how far the trend has progressed.

In its widest sense, including ground, sea and air combat, automated warfare is an extremely complex field indeed, and the development of the automatic systems involved draws on advances in many branches of science and technology, such as electronics, telecommunications, computers, chemistry and so on. Automated warfare is also a very dynamic field. In all branches of military technology, the development of a new offensive weapon system is followed by the development of a new defensive system effective against it, and this is further followed by the development of yet another offensive system designed to overcome the defence. In the field of automated warfare, the momentum of the technological arms race is perhaps even greater than that in other military fields: most of the automatic systems rely on electronics at least to some extent, for example, for the collection and analysis of data concerning the enemy, for guiding weapons to their targets and so on, and the development of new electronic offensive systems gives rise to the development of electronic countermeasures against them, which in turn gives rise to the development of new electronic counter-countermeasures, and so on into ever increasing complexity.

Quite apart from the more general problems associated with automation of warfare as mentioned above, the increasingly technological nature of warfare brings other dangers. The use of massive quantities of very sophisticated equipment and weapons in warfare is bound to impose a considerable strain on the capacities of industrialized countries: more and more of a country's resources, in terms of skilled scientific and technological manpower, of productivity and so on, might be devoted to the military field. At the same time, the trend towards military automation could prove disadvantageous to underdeveloped countries which would be unable to keep up with the ever increasing sophistication of military technology; the result in this case would be a widening of the gap between the various types of powers.

Of the many fields of warfare in which automation has been or could be applied, this chapter will deal mainly with only one—the automated ground combat systems that have been developed, essentially during the past decade. Some of the systems involved in automated ground combat—the term "automated battlefield" will be used hereafter to include all such systems—have been used in the war in South East Asia, and this application has given rise to controversial public debate. It is important to bear in mind that the experience gained from using automated battlefield systems and devices in South East Asia is not necessarily relevant in all aspects to other regions or situations. However, it may serve as a basis for some assessments concerning the likelihood of the application of such systems and devices in other parts of the world, and in other environments and situations.

## II. *Automated battlefield systems and devices*

In order to examine the components of an automated battlefield, it is convenient to consider a battle sequence as being made up of four phases. The first is the location and identification of the enemy, the intelligence-gathering phase. Once the enemy is located, a decision is made on the appropriate course of action to be taken, the decision-making phase. Third comes the action phase, in which weapons are actually fired against the enemy targets. And finally, it is necessary to assess the results of the action against the targets in order to decide whether or not the sequence should be repeated. The last phase is called impact monitoring.

Under ordinary combat conditions, all the operations in this sequence are carried out directly by men: soldiers locate and identify the enemy visually; officers make the appropriate decisions based on the information provided to them; soldiers fire the weapons against the targets; and the results of the action are also assessed visually. Automation of one or more phases of this sequence leads to a partially or fully automated battlefield, and indeed it is possible to envisage a battlefield situation in which the whole process from start to finish is fully automated. In such a situation, the presence of enemy troops, vehicles and so on would be detected by means of artificial sensing devices planted on the battlefield. The information collected by these sensors would be transmitted back to a central control station where it would be analysed by computers. The computers would then make the decisions on what action to take and control the firing of weapons against the targets. When the action is over, sensing devices on the battlefield would again collect information to enable an assessment to be made of the result of the action.

This scheme is, to a certain extent, fictional, in that a *fully* automated battlefield is not yet a reality. Although it is known that a number of the automatic systems required for an automated battlefield are available, and in use, at the present time, a great deal of secrecy surrounds the development and use of these systems, and a great deal of information concerning individual components and devices is classified. So, as mentioned above, it is very difficult to assess precisely just how close present-day technology is to making a fully automated battlefield feasible in practice. In the following sections, the technological developments and current "state of the art" of the four phases of the automated battlefield are described and assessed. The descriptions will be rather general: they will cover the general capabilities of the systems and devices involved in the four main phases of the battle sequence as well as some of the general problems which have not yet been solved. Most of the information available on this issue and used in this chapter concerns systems developed in the United States, where the techniques are considered to be well ahead of the counterparts in other countries.

### The intelligence-gathering system: sensors

Intelligence gathering, the first phase of the automated battlefield, can be examined in two parts. The first is the identification and location of the enemy targets by means of artificial sensors; this part of the system will be described in the section below. The other part, the transmission of information collected by the sensors back to a control station for analysis and decision-making, will be described in the next section.

The identification and location of enemy targets on the automated battlefield is achieved by means of artificial sensing devices—which will here be called sensors—planted on the battlefield. Under ordinary combat circumstances the enemy is located by means of one or more of the natural human senses—sight, hearing and so on. The sensors on the automated battlefield can be sensitive either to the same physical stimuli as the human senses, for example light or sound, although usually with greater sensitivity, or to physical stimuli which are not directly detectable by a human being, such an infrared radiation, magnetic fields, electromagnetic waves and so on. Thus, in the context of the automated battlefield, sensors may

**Table 11.1. Characteristics of some sensors suitable for use on the automated battlefield**[a]

| Name of sensor | Type | Method of delivery | | Detecting range (m) for | |
|---|---|---|---|---|---|
| | | Hand-emplaced | Air-dropped | Men | Vehicles |
| Acoustic Buoy (ACOUBUOY) phase II | Acoustic | Yes | Parachute/ free fall[b] | . . | 200–1 600 |
| Anti-intrusion Alarm Unit (AAU) | Acoustic | Yes | – | . . | . . |
| Commandable microphone (Commike) | Acoustic | – | Parachute | 30 | 300 |
| RCA prototype[d] | Acoustic | (Yes) | – | 30 | – |
| SPIKEBUOY | Acoustic | – | Free fall | (30) | (300) |
| Air-delivered Seismic Intrusion Detector (ADSID) phase I | Seismic | – | Free fall | 30 | 300 |
| Air-delivered Seismic Intrusion Detector (ADSID) phase III | Seismic | Yes | Free fall | 30 | 300 |
| Ground-emplaced Seismic Intrusion Detector (GSID) | Seismic | Yes | – | 30 | 300 |
| Micro Seismic Intrusion Detector (MICROSID) | Seismic | Yes | – | 30 | 100 |
| Miniature Seismic Intrusion Detector (MINISID) | Seismic | Yes | – | 30 | 90 |
| TOBIAS Intruder Alarm System | Seismic | Yes | – | 50–300 | . . |
| Acoustic Seismic Intrusion Detector (ACOUSID) | Seismic/ acoustic | – | Parachute | 30 | 300 |
| Seismic Hand-emplaced Acoustic Intrusion Detector (SHAID) | Seismic/ acoustic | Yes | – | 20 | Seismic 100 acoustic 300–400 |
| Balanced Pressure System (BPS) | Pressure | Yes | – | (100) | (100) |
| Wire Intrusion Detector (WID) | Pressure | Yes | – | Length of wire | |
| Electromagnetic Intrusion Detector (EMID) | Electro-magnetic field | Yes | – | 20 | 40 |
| Engine Detector (EDET) | Radio frequency | (Yes) | Yes[e] | – | 150–250 |
| Commandable Audio Engine Detector (CAEDET) | (Radio frequency) | (As EDET) | | – | . . |
| Noiseless Button Bomblet (NBB) | Radio frequency | Yes | . . | Direct contact | |
| Infrared Intrusion Detector (IID) | Active infrared | Yes | – | 100–120 | 100–120 |

330

| Size cms | Weight kg | Lifetime (of batteries) days | Transmitter range | Remarks |
|---|---|---|---|---|
| 91.4×12.1 (diam) | 11.8 suspended 14.5 buried | 60[c] | Line of sight | Suspended or buried configurations |
| 43.5×7.6 (incl batt) | 4 (incl batt) | 30–45 | No own transmitter | Uses transmitter contained in MINISID III |
| 94×12.1 (diam) | 11.8 | 20–30 | Line of sight | Suspended, commandable |
| As packet of cigarettes | . . | . . | Line of sight | Able to discriminate footsteps |
| 167.6×12.7 (diam) | 18.2 | (30–45) | Line of sight | Buried |
| 78.7×7.6 (diam) | 11.4 | <90 | Line of sight | Cost: $1 900 |
| 50.8×7.6 (diam) | 5.9 | 100 | Line of sight | Cost: $975 |
| 23×11×13 | 2.7 | 45 | . . | |
| (Very small) | 2 | <90 | Line of sight | |
| 20.6×20.6×7.6 | 3.6 | 30–45 | Line of sight | |
| 3.8×3.8×5.1 | 0.17 | 3 | "Many miles" | Wire-connected. British made |
| 134.6×7.6 (diam) | 18.1 | 45 | Line of sight | Suspended, commandable. Cost: $3 500 |
| 79×13 | 9 | 45 | Line of sight | |
| . . | . . | 12–18 months | (8 km) | |
| . . | . . | 30 | – | Wire connected, for local use by patrols |
| 18×18×8 | 7 | 45 | . . | |
| 94×12.1 (diam) | 12.7 | 30[f] | . . | Vehicles with electrical ignition only |
| . . | . . | . . | . . | Should provide more data than EDET and also acoustic capability |
| <2.5 cm³ | 30×10⁻³ | 2 000 activations | 100 m | Emits radio frequency when moved. Signals picked up by Automatic Radio Frequency Buoy (ARFBUOY) receiver/transmitter |
| . . | 43.6 | 1 year | . . | Wire connected |

331

| Name of sensor | Type | Method of delivery | | Detecting range (m) for | |
|---|---|---|---|---|---|
| | | Hand-emplaced | Air-dropped | Men | Vehicles |
| Infra-Red Intrusion System (IRIS) | Active infrared | Yes | – | 50–200 | 50–200 |
| Passive Infrared Intrusion Detector (PIRID) | Passive infrared | Yes | – | Line of sight | |
| Chemiluminescence monitor | Chemical | Yes | – | – | 30–150 |
| Chemiluminescence monitor (projection) | Chemical | Yes | – | – | 50–150 |
| Condensation nuclei detector | Chemical | Yes | – | – | 100–400 |
| Condensation nuclei detector (projection) | Chemical | Yes | – | – | 100–400 |
| Honeywell ionization detector | Chemical | (Yes) | –[e] | – | 20–35 |
| Honeywell ionization detector (projection) | Chemical | (Yes) | –[e] | – | 50–150 |
| XM3 personnel detector | Chemical | (Yes) | –[g] | . . | – |
| Airborne magnetometer | Magnetic | – | –[g] | . . | . . |
| Magnetic Intrusion Detector (MAGID) phase III | Magnetic | Yes | – | 3–4 | 20–25 |

[a] This table is by no means a complete list of automated battlefield sensors: the intention here is only to give a few typical examples of the different types.
[b] Spike configuration.
[c] Operating at 1 per cent duty cycle.
[d] Under development.
[e] May also be deployed on airborne platforms.
[f] At 40 activations per hour.
[g] May also be dangled by cable from a helicopter.

be defined as devices which improve on, or supplement, the capabilities of the human senses as means for detecting an enemy.

The range of types of sensor which can be used in a battlefield situation is very wide. At one end of the scale, there are devices which are really little more than sophisticated "trip wires": they can be used, for example, in front of defence positions or by an individual patrol camping at night to give advance warning of the presence or approach of an enemy. Examples of such devices are long, fluid-filled pipes, or long uninsulated oxide-covered wires which, when buried in the ground, respond to changes in pressure on the ground above them. Thus when a person or a vehicle passes over such a sensor, the pressure change induces an electrical signal which can be transmitted by wire to a receiver in the defence position or the patrol's camp. The operating range of such devices is limited by their physical dimensions, and because the signals generated by the

| Size cms | Weight kg | Lifetime (of batteries) days | Transmitter range | Remarks |
|---|---|---|---|---|
|  ..  |  ..  |  ..  | – | Wire connected. British made |
| Sensor: 8×2 Processor: 11×13×16 | 1.6 | 45 | No own transmitter | Uses transmitter contained in MINISID |
| 56 634 cm³ | 18.2 |  ..  |  ..  | Detects vehicle exhaust |
| 3 277 cm³ | 1.1 |  ..  |  ..  | Detects vehicle exhaust Cost: $2 000 |
| >1 230 cm³ | 2.3 |  ..  |  ..  | Detects vehicle exhaust |
| 1 230 cm³ | 1.1 |  ..  |  ..  | Detects vehicle exhaust Cost: $300 |
| 8 495 cm³ | 7 |  ..  |  ..  | Detects vehicle exhaust |
| 3 277 cm³ | 1.1 |  ..  |  ..  | Could be developed to discriminate between diesel and gasoline exhaust. Cost: $600 |
|  ..  |  ..  |  ..  |  ..  | Detects ammonia. Also known as "People Sniffer" |
|  ..  |  ..  | – | – | Developed in 1972 for cache detection |
| 31.7×6.4 (diam) | 1.8 | >45 | No own transmitter | Uses transmitter contained in MINISID. Cost: $280 |

pressure changes are transmitted by wire, the receiver must in most cases be located fairly close—say, within a 100-metre radius. (There are reports, however, of sensors that can be physically connected to receivers over distances of several miles.) Other, seemingly more sophisticated sensors which rely on wires for the transmission of information back to receiver, or which must be man-attended, are also only really suitable for rather local use. Such sensing devices will not be considered further in this chapter.

Of much more interest in the context of the automated battlefield are sensors that can be remotely deployed and that can transmit information concerning enemy locations or movements over long distances by radio. Such sensors can be designed to respond to a wide range of physical stimuli originating from enemy troops or vehicles, such as sound, seismic disturbances, radio frequency waves, infrared radiation, visible light, chemicals, magnetic fields and so on. The sensors can be either passive, in which case they simply detect signals originating from some external source (for example, a microphone picking up sound), or active devices which themselves emit a signal and then monitor interferences or reflection of this signal due to some external object (the classic example being a radar).

Sensors can be deployed on the battlefield in many ways. They can be deployed on the ground, buried in the ground or hung from foliage in forests, and they can be either hand-emplaced, air-dropped or fired into position from artillery or mortars. Some sensors can be carried on Earth-orbiting satellites or on manned or unmanned aircraft[1] and can thus "watch" the battlefield from the air.

But whatever their sensitivity to specific physical stimuli, or mode of deployment, there are a number of general problems and limitations associated with the design and use of sensors on the battlefield. Because they transmit their information by radio, sensors must incorporate a radio transmitter and must carry a power supply to operate it. But because they are deployed in territory in which an enemy is located, they must be capable of being hidden. Thus there is a design conflict between size and operating efficiency. A small sensor may have the advantage of being easily hidden or camouflaged, but it will only be able to incorporate a small power supply, and thus both the area from which the sensor can collect information and the distance over which it can transmit this information by radio will, in general, be limited. A larger device may be able to collect information from a larger area and to transmit this information over longer distances, but because of its size, there will be a greater risk of its being discovered and inactivated by an enemy. Another factor associated with available power supply is the operating life of the sensor. Sensors with long operating lifetimes will need larger power supplies and so in principle will be larger than sensors which only operate for short periods.

Another general problem of sensors is their limited ability to discriminate between similar signals from different sources. For example, a sensor able to detect seismic disturbances in the ground may not be able to distinguish between the vibrations produced by passing troops or vehicles and those made by "noise" sources such as wild animals, and will certainly not be able to distinguish between friendly and unfriendly troops or vehicles. To a certain extent, some discriminating ability can be designed into some types of sensors, but the sensors with this ability are likely to be much more complex, and hence probably much larger, than the less sophisticated devices, and so the chances of their being discovered by the enemy are rather high.

In summary, sensors for use on the automated battlefield should have the following characteristics: they should be as small or as easily camouflaged as possible; they should be able to detect signals from as wide an area as possible; they should be able to transmit their collected information over as long a distance as possible; they should have as long an

---

[1] Two types of unmanned air vehicles are commonly recognized. Those whose flight is directed and controlled by on-board systems according to pre-programmed instructions are called drones. Those controlled and directed in real time by a "pilot", either on the ground or in another aircraft, using a television camera mounted on the vehicle for guidance, are called remotely piloted vehicles (RPVs). For the sake of simplicity, the term "remotely piloted vehicle" is used in this chapter to include drones as well.

operating lifetime as possible; they should be able to discriminate between signals originating from different sources; and they should be as cheap as possible. Designing sensors which have optimal characteristics according to these criteria is obviously a very complex procedure. Although some sensors, intended for short and/or temporary missions, could be designed to meet more restricted criteria—not to be more sophisticated or expensive than necessary—in most cases a choice will have to be made between these characteristics, according to the special circumstances of their use.

The trends in development of better sensors aim at reducing size and power requirements while maintaining operating efficiency, at increasing operating lifetimes, and at reducing unit costs. The lifetime of sensors can be increased considerably by arranging for them to be switched on only at certain times, for example, by remote control. However, it is perhaps worth pointing out at this stage that some of the above criteria can be met, and some of the problems solved, by thinking in terms of sensor *systems* rather than by designing specific factors into individual sensors. For example, a large sensor with a wide operating range and the capacity to transmit signals over long distances could be replaced by a system consisting of a large number of smaller and more easily camouflagable sensors, each with the ability to detect signals from a small area (but together covering the same area as the large sensor) and with the capacity to transmit their collected data over short distances, but to a relay device so that eventually the data can be received at a control station a long distance away. In fact, small sensors with small detecting ranges often have advantages over larger devices. For example, a large number of small sensors with short detecting ranges deployed in an area might give much more accurate information on the position of an enemy than just one sensor with a wider range covering the whole area. Discriminating ability can also be provided by employing systems of sensors. For example, a sensor responsive to seismic disturbances in the ground may be unable to differentiate between a group of marching men and a moving vehicle, but another sensor deployed at the same place, for example a chemical sensor activated by engine exhaust gases, may provide other, different information which allows a more positive identification of the source to be made. In such a case, the second sensor may be switched off, and hence not using power, until activated by a signal either from the central control station or from the primary sensor itself, and hence combining sensors can be a useful way of conserving power. Additional examples of sensor systems and combinations are included in the discussions of individual sensor types below.

### Acoustic sensors

An acoustic sensor works like an ordinary microphone: it detects sounds in its immediate vicinity and transmits information by radio to a remote receiver, which could be either a ground receiving station or relay or an overflying aircraft. These sensors can be hand-emplaced, air-dropped on a parachute to hang in foliage or air-dropped to bury themselves in the ground. Most of the acoustic sensors currently in use have detecting ranges approximately the same as that of a human ear, so that they can detect vehicles at a distance of about 300 metres and people at distances of some 30 metres. One sensor, however, named the ACOUBUOY phase II, is capable of detecting vehicles at distances of up to 1600 metres. The operating lifetime of most acoustic sensors is between 30 and 40 days, although they can provide useful information for much longer periods if they can be switched on only at certain times.

Because acoustic sensors may relay what they "hear" they do offer some possibility of discrimination between different sources of sound. The degree of discrimination, however, is limited by the fidelity of the signals received at the control station. New acoustic sensors currently under development, as well as having improved detection capabilities, longer operating ranges, less weight and smaller physical dimensions than previous models, will also offer the possibility of discrimination at the sensor itself. The Radio Corporation of America (RCA) has reportedly constructed a prototype acoustic sensor, about the same size as a packet of cigarettes, which should be able to differentiate between footsteps and other sounds, such that it will not report the presence of vehicles or low-flying aircraft, but only of men. The detection range of this device will probably be about 30 metres. [1]

*Seismic sensors*

Sensors capable of picking up seismic disturbances in the ground caused by moving people or vehicles are probably the most common types of sensor so far developed and deployed on the battlefield. They can be delivered by hand or air-dropped from aircraft or helicopters and they are usually buried in the ground with only an antenna visible. (The antenna can easily be camouflaged to resemble a bush, for example, in jungle regions.) The detection ranges of seismic sensors depend on the intensity of the seismic disturbance and the seismic transmission properties of the soil, but on average, moving people can be detected at a distance of about 30 metres and moving vehicles at distances of some 300 metres, ranges similar to those for acoustic sensors. The operating lifetimes of most of the seismic sensors currently available range from one to three months, depending on how many times, and for how long, they are switched on.

*Radio frequency sensors*

Monitoring radio transmissions in order to locate enemy headquarters, troop concentrations and so on, and to follow enemy movements or try to discover future intentions, is an activity which belongs more or less to conventional intelligence gathering in any combat situation, and will not be discussed here. In addition to these methods, however, radio frequency emissions can be monitored by sensors in two main ways. Ignition sparks from internal combustion engines emit energy in the radio frequency region of the electromagnetic spectrum, and this can be monitored by simple radio receivers. One sensor which probably uses this technique, the air-droppable or airborne Engine Detector (EDET), can detect trucks up to 250 metres away. The main shortcoming of this sensor is that it will only detect vehicles with electrical ignition systems, so that diesel-engined vehicles will go unnoticed. But recently, development has begun of another sensor system, the Commandable Audio Engine Detector (CAEDET), that will be able to provide data on the type of engine, the range of the vehicle and the direction of travel, and transmit this information to a receiver carried in an overflying aircraft. [2] It is not known what techniques will be used in this sensor, but they will probably include simple radio direction-finding systems.

As well as detecting "natural" radio emissions from enemy vehicles, it is also possible to arrange a sensor system such that the movement of troops or vehicles in an area produces other forms of radio frequencies. Very small, hand-emplaced, simple radio transmitters, called Noiseless Button Bomblets (NBB), have been developed which emit a radio frequency signal when touched. Disguised as animal droppings, these sensors can be spread along paths and trails without attracting special attention. They have an operating lifetime of about 2000 activations.

*Magnetic sensors*

Sensors able to detect metal objects have long been used for the detection of mines and so on, but they can of course be used to detect other metal objects, such as a vehicle or a rifle carried by a soldier. The detecting range of magnetic sensors is determined by the size and the magnetic properties of the metal object, so that it is rather difficult to distinguish between a small metal object close to the sensor and a large metal object some distance away. Common ranges for such sensors are said to be about three to four metres for armed personnel and up to some 20–25 metres for vehicles: it is even possible with some devices to count the number of armed personnel or vehicles passing the detector. [3a] One shortcoming with these sensors, however, is that they are activated by any nearby ferrous metal object, so that in addition to the lack of discriminating ability already mentioned, it would further be impossible to differentiate between a soldier carrying a rifle and a civilian carrying, say, a spade or other "peaceful" tool. On the other hand, magnetic sensors are not set off by animals, rain, moving trees, overflying aircraft and so on, so in this repect the "false alarm" rate is low.

*Chemical sensors*

Vehicle exhaust gases contain large quantities of characteristic chemical compounds—the combustion products of fuels. Sensors capable of reacting to the presence of such chemicals are therefore capable of detecting the presence of vehicles. Tests were carried out in the United States during 1972 involving more than a dozen different techniques for the detection of vehicles by such chemical means. [4]

Diesel exhaust and gasoline exhaust have different chemical compositions, and while some of the sensors tested reacted to chemicals found in both types of exhaust, some were capable of reacting specifically to the presence of sulphur-containing compounds found only in diesel exhaust, and others were affected only by the presence of carbon monoxide, hydrocarbons and hydrogen, chemicals which are characteristic of gasoline exhaust. Thus it is possible, by using both types of sensor together, to determine whether the vehicles are medium-weight or heavy vehicles (which normally have diesel engines) or light-weight vehicles (which are normally fitted with gasoline engines).

The detection ranges of chemical sensors depend very much on the environment. In urban or other areas where the air is polluted and contains considerable amounts of exhaust gases anyway, the detection range is, of course, rather short. In the countryside, on the other hand, the ambient air is generally much cleaner, and detection ranges are correspondingly longer. However, wooded terrain seems to hamper the diffusion of exhaust gases, and wind conditions also have a decisive influence on the ability of the sensors to operate efficiently: upwind detection has been proved impossible even a few metres away from a road, and so sensors must be deployed on both sides of a road or trail to ensure that at least some will be operational whatever the wind conditions. With these limitations in mind, typical detection ranges of up to 150 metres are possible, and some of the prototypes tested as mentioned above could detect vehicles 200–400 metres away across open country and 100 metres away through wooded terrain. Whatever technique was applied in the tests of these sensors, most of them responded only to vehicles, and were not "fooled" by dust.

Another type of chemical sensor has been developed to detect chemicals emanated from a human body. This sensor, code named XM-3, but with the alternative name of "People Sniffer", was tested in South East Asia, but did not prove entirely satisfactory. It could not, of course, distinguish friend from foe and occasionally it reacted even when no human being was within range (figures for the detection range of this sensor are not available). Also, it could be "fooled" rather easily, simply by hanging a bag of urine near it. However, development of an improved chemical personnel detector is proceeding, the main aim being to improve detection reliability. [5]

*Sensor combinations*

Generally speaking, it is necessary to deploy a range of sensor types in a particular area in order to be assured of detecting a large proportion of enemy targets: there is no single sensor that will detect every target. On the other hand, different types of sensors are often capable of detecting the same target, but in different ways, and the more information one is able to obtain about a particular target, the greater are the chances of making a positive identification. In some cases, even the lack of a response from a sensor can provide useful information. For example, if a seismic sensor indicates the presence of something moving in an area, and a chemical vehicle sensor also reacts, the conclusion must be that the "something" is a vehicle. If, in addition, a chemical vehicle sensor sensitive only to gasoline exhaust gases reacts, or alternatively, a chemical vehicle sensor sensitive only to diesel exhaust gases fails to react, there are strong indications that the vehicle is powered by a gasoline engine, and is therefore probably a light-weight vehicle.

In addition to these sensor combinations, others are specially designed in suitable combinations. One combination frequently used is that of a seismic sensor with an acoustic one. A seismic sensor may well "confuse" a heavy vehicle moving at some distance from it with a light vehicle much closer. If an acoustic sensor is also used to listen to the target, a more positive identification can be made. The usual arrangement with such combinations is to keep the seismic sensor monitoring the environment continuously, with the acoustic sensor normally switched off, thus conserving power. When the seismic sensor reacts, the acoustic sensor is either automatically activated by seismic signals, or switched on by remote control from a control station.

Another common sensor combination is that of a seismic sensor with a magnetic one. Often the magnetic sensor component of such a combination will not have a radio transmitter of its own, but will instead make use of the transmitter contained in its "parent" seismic device. If the seismic sensor detects something passing, but the magnetic sensor fails to respond, this might be an indication that the "something" is not a vehicle, an armed soldier or a civilian carrying metal tools.

*Radar and infrared sensors*

All of the sensors described above can be deployed remote from any radio receiver or human operator on, in or very near the ground on the battlefield itself. Some types are also produced in alternative configurations for deployment on aircraft flying over the battlefield, or for being dangled at the end of a cable from a helicopter. (The "People Sniffer" and some magnetic sensors are examples of the latter.) By contrast, radar devices and infrared sensors have relatively fewer remotely deployed

ground applications: they are more commonly carried on airborne platforms (either manned aircraft or remotely piloted vehicles) and they are
often man-attended. For these reasons, they perhaps do not fit in as well
as other sensors with the concept of a fully automated battlefield, but they
certainly do have applications in a partially automated system, either for the
detection of an enemy or for launching weapons against targets. They
will therefore be described briefly here, and will be referred to again in
later sections of this chapter.

Many devices sensitive to visible light can also be used for battlefield
surveillance. They include television cameras, laser devices and image in-
tensifiers able to amplify available light by up to 40000 times or more, thus
providing very efficient means of observation, even under starlight or
"night glow" conditions. Image intensification can be coupled with a
television camera, resulting in low light level television (LLLTV) systems. But because the number of such applications is so great, and
because, unlike the other sensors described above, they have not yet been
applied according to the concept of a fully automated intelligence-gathering system, they are not discussed here.

Information received by radars carried on manned aircraft, helicopters
or remotely piloted vehicles can be processed on board the aircraft and
relayed directly to ground control stations for evaluation, and can form
the basis for tactical decisions and subsequent action against ground targets. Radars can work in all weather conditions, which means that they
are also useful for night surveillance.

In recent years, many ground radar applications have been developed.
The United States has developed a family of short- and medium-range
battlefield surveillance radars, designed to detect personnel and vehicles
at ranges of between 150 metres, in the case of the small, portable sets
about the size of a cigar box and weighing less than 10 lbs, to some 20000
metres for much larger, more sophisticated devices. Although most of
these radars are crew served, some can be operated by remote control
from a special display unit. [6a, 7]

A special surveillance problem arose during the war in South East Asia
—that of radar detection of targets located or moving in the jungle. The
problem was solved by the development of foliage penetration radars, able
to "see" targets under the jungle canopy. Some versions of this radar are
airborne. [6b, 8]

One of the problems with radar, and indeed with all active devices that
themselves emit some kind of signal, is that their signals can be intercepted
and jammed. Radar transmissions, particularly if directed ahead of an aircraft, can give an enemy advance warning of the aircraft's approach, and
can even be used to locate the aircraft. (Ground patrols using radar devices
could be located in a similar way.) For this reason, among others, Side-
looking Airborne Radars (SLAR) have been developed for use in aircraft:

they scan to the sides and directly below the aircraft, and, in addition to decreasing the risk of interception of the radar signals, this technique offers better resolution and the opportunity for surveying areas without actually flying over them—an important advantage, particularly for surveying heavily defended regions. [9–10]

Infrared sensors can be either active devices, which locate targets by detecting an interruption or reflection of an infrared beam, or passive devices which simply detect differences between the infrared radiation coming from a particular person or object and the background radiation. As different objects radiate infrared energy in characteristic ways, the infrared radiation received by a sensor can be used to build up an image: this image can be either recorded on specially sensitized film or videotape, or converted to visible light for real-time observation. Passive infrared sensors can detect very small differences in temperature. Infrared radiation is absorbed less by fog, haze, rain or other sources of moisture than is visible light, and so, under certain circumstances, a range of some three to six times that possible with visible light is obtainable. [11a]

Like radars, infrared sensors for battlefield surveillance can have airborne or ground applications. Information from airborne infrared sensors can be relayed and displayed in real or near-real time at ground stations in a similar way to radar images. Among modern passive infrared applications, the so-called Forward Looking Infra-Red (FLIR) technology is being used and further developed for a wide variety of applications in air, naval and ground warfare. Of particular interest to the automated battlefield are FLIR devices for reconnaissance, target acquisition and fire control in RPVs and helicopter gunships. A new Army Advanced Attack Helicopter (AAH) will probably employ a rather advanced FLIR "visionics" system enabling real-time imagery of a scene at low altitude and target acquisition within ranges of two to five kilometres even at night, as well as controlling weapons firing at these targets. The device is developed by Hughes Aircraft and will include a laser rangefinder/designator and tracker. For RPVs, very small light-weight infrared devices have been supplied, weighing as little as about 5.5 kg. [11b]

Typical infrared ground applications have so far been active devices, such as infrared searchlights together with receiving equipment. But the present trend is towards the development of passive devices which cannot be monitored by an adversary. Typical passive infrared devices are infrared binoculars, night sights for weapons, and more sophisticated devices such as the Passive Infrared Intrusion Detector (PIRID) which has a line-of-sight detection range. Development of active devices is, however, still going on. The Directional Infrared Intrusion Detector (DIRID) uses an active infrared beam and can detect objects or persons which interfere with this beam. A small British-made sensor, the Infrared Intrusion System (IRIS), also uses such a beam. Designed for use in broken terrain or in jungle, it has a detection range of about 200 metres in average visibility conditions and about 50 metres in fog, snow or tropical rain. [12]

*Countermeasures against sensors*

Sensor activities can be hampered in a number of ways. A discovered sensor can, of course, easily be destroyed, but unless the majority of sensors in a particular area can be destroyed, there will still be a chance of detection. It would be much more useful, from an adversary's point of view, therefore, to capture the sensor and investigate means to develop more efficient countermeasures. For this reason, US remotely deployed sensors are as a rule designed for self-destruction if tampered with: they do not explode, but a few vital parts are destroyed mechanically. Nevertheless, the North Viet-Namese managed to develop effective countermeasures within a remarkably short time after these US sensors were deployed. A Pentagon representative reported in 1968 that it was "seldom more than a few months after we introduce something new before we capture a document that tells the enemy, in essence, how to counter the new device". [13]

One way of countering sensors is to bring in dummies to cause false alarms (or, in the official jargon, "non-targetable activations"). There is one report from experience in Viet-Nam that a number of water buffaloes carrying metal containers filled with gasoline were mistaken by the sensors for tanks, because the sloshing of the gasoline in the containers was mistaken for the sloshing of fuel inside tanks. [14] "People Sniffers" have been fooled by hanging bags of urine around them, as already mentioned. And there have been complaints from commanders that on occasion magnetic sensors did not work properly because there was too much metal scrap in the environment. Another technique is to overload the sensors: bulldozers working along the so-called Ho Chi Minh trail in South East Asia probably saturated the seismic, acoustic and magnetic sensors deployed there, and may thus have disguised the sounds of some 600 North Viet-Namese tanks which later appeared quite unexpectedly in South Viet-Nam, undetected by the sensors. [15]

## The intelligence-gathering system: data transmission

Information collected by the sensors deployed on the automated battlefield must be passed on to a central control station for analysis and processing, and for this purpose, most sensors incorporate a small radio transmitter. (Those sensors which do not have transmitters of their own forward their data through a transmitter contained in another sensor.) The sensor transmitter normally has a very short range, principally because the sensor must be small in size which limits its power supply. While some of the larger, more sophisticated sensors may have transmitter ranges of several kilometres, most of the small sensors have transmitters whose ranges are limited to the line of sight, that is, approximately 500–1 000 metres on the ground.

As a rule, therefore, signals from sensors deployed considerable distances from the control station have to be relayed. The radio frequency signals (with wavelengths of less than two metres) emitted by the sensor transmitters are blocked by hills and are attenuated after passing through vegetation, so that the relay stations on the ground usually have to be deployed on hills or ridges. Relays can, however, be airborne, a technique that has been used for a long time for collecting information from naval sensors deployed at sea. The first aircraft used in South East Asia for relay purposes was a specially modified configuration of a Lockheed Super Constellation, the EC-121R. It could relay information direct to ground control stations, but could also carry personnel capable of assessing the information from the sensors while airborne. [3b]

Since the EC-121R is rather vulnerable to enemy attack, another aircraft, the QU-22B Beech Debonair, was designed. Capable of flying at high altitudes, the QU-22B is a relatively small aircraft, carrying relay equipment but no assessment capabilities. It has been produced in both piloted and pilotless configurations, the unmanned version being especially useful in high-threat areas. After the introduction of this first unmanned aircraft, other, more sophisticated ones have been developed and put into operation. [3c]

Countermeasures against transmitters and relay stations are normally electronic techniques. Jamming the frequencies used by the sensors may render the information incomplete, distorted or incomprehensible. High transmission power could be used to obtain a signal that is stronger when received at the control station than the jamming signal, but this would probably require larger sensors with larger transmitters, which entails such other problems as those mentioned above. In any case, it is more difficult to detect and monitor low power sensor signals. In South East Asia there was probably no major capability to interfere with the US sensor signals, and so the effects of such jamming have not been tested under advanced battlefield conditions. This is a field, however, that will be of paramount importance in any war fought between industrialized countries. Such wars are likely to take place in areas where the radio frequency bands are very crowded, leaving little space for sensor signals, and where the combatants have considerable expertise and resources for electronic countermeasures.

**The decision-making phase**

Once the information from the battlefield sensors is received at a central control station, the next phase of the automated battlefield, the decision-making process, comes into operation: the information is collected, processed and analysed, and then used to decide what action to take against the targets detected on the battlefield. This phase can also be considered in two parts; the readout, processing and display of the information, and the decision-making itself.

## Readout, processing and display equipment

Sensor systems involving great numbers of sensors reporting information from the automated battlefield require special receivers, capable of monitoring many separate input channels simultaneously, if optimal use is to be made of the information. Each channel in such a receiver accommodates transmissions from a certain number of sensors, each of which identifies itself by means of its own special code. An example of such a receiver is the Portatale: an early model could monitor about 800 sensors and a later generation is capable of monitoring some 40 000.

With such large numbers of sensors, particularly during periods of great activity on the battlefield, it is impossible to operate such a receiver manually. The incoming information must therefore be recorded automatically, and for this purpose recorders are attached to the receivers, displaying graphically all the information received from the sensors. [3a]

Computers were introduced for data handling in the early stages of sensor system development. In an operation known as "Igloo White", a large Infiltration Surveillance Center (ISC) was organized by the United States at the Nakhon Phanom Air Base in Thailand to monitor the sensors deployed along the Ho Chi Minh trail in Laos. This large permanent installation was originally equipped with two IBM 360–65 computers[2] which produced readouts and displays showing the activation of various sensor emplacements. Immediately on arrival of new information, the computers produced activation patterns of the sensors on the battlefield by high-speed printout, and this information was used as a basis for air strikes against the areas of activity. [3d]

Memory devices with stored information, such as a road map, can be combined with incoming information from sensors planted in the area in a visual display, as in the "Igloo White" operation:

An assessment officer monitors sensor activations in his area of interest. When he recognizes a target signature from a . . . particular sensor string, he calls up on his cathode ray tube [CRT] a sketch of the roadnet which that string of sensors is monitoring: the computer automatically displays and updates on the CRT the movement of the target along that road. [3e]

This information was then used for direct orders, to carry out air strikes against the targets concerned.

In order to achieve mobility, development in this field has been focused on smaller, air-transportable equipment. A Deployable Automatic Relay

---

[2] One computer was later withdrawn.

Terminal (DART) with a limited emergency back-up capability for the ISC has been designed. Adding a limited computer facility to DART produces a Sensor Reporting Post (SRP) with functional capabilities similar to those of the larger permanent ISCs. [3f] The US Air Force has recently announced the development of a four-segment air-transportable system, the Tactical Information Processing and Interpretation System (TIPI), to provide collated, tactical information from many sources to a commander in the field. Two segments are devoted to the processing and computer-assisted interpretation of conventional air reconnaissance photographs; a third segment processes and evaluates remote sensor data; and a fourth stores, retrieves and displays intelligence data. The output information is said to be provided to a commander "in a useable timeframe". [16, 21c]

Countermeasures against the readout, processing and display systems of the automated battlefield would be, first, to attack the ground stations to destroy the equipment: it is to pre-empt this measure that mobile facilities have been designed. It might also be possible to feed the computers with false data, or to overburden them with activation reports, in much the same way as the sensors themselves can be saturated with signals. In fact, the amount of information received at the ISC in Thailand was more than could be handled at the time of the operation. [14] This shows that in systems involving large numbers of sensors, insignificant information must be sorted out at an early stage. Developments in this field will probably include new and better methods of computer processing so that only the most essential information is printed out or displayed. This might be problematic, however, in terms of programming the computer to ignore the insignificant information on the one hand, but not to ignore unexpected or surprise action on the part of the enemy on the other.

## Decison making

Data from sensors, automatically collected, transmitted, processed, analysed and displayed, forms the basis on which decisions concerning action against enemy targets are taken. Human operators, sitting in control stations remote from or flying over the battlefield, could of course perform this task, and this is the most common procedure at the present time. But modern technology introduces the potential for this phase of the automated battlefield sequence also to be fully automated. A computer may be programmed to react to certain information by issuing orders to other military units. When the computer identifies a target signature, it can transmit information on the location of the target, in terms of grid coordinates, either to a reconnaissance sortie for further investigation, or to a ground unit, a ship, an aircraft, a missile or a remotely piloted vehicle for immediate attack.

This phase of the automated battlefield is the one against which most criticism has been directed. It has been argued that deficiencies in sensor discriminating ability and imperfections in transmission equipment and computers are likely to lead the decision maker, whether a man or a computer, to make serious mistakes in determining counteractions, thereby using weapons indiscriminately. It has further been maintained that this would be particularly applicable to attacks on moving targets whose position is electronically *calculated:* critics claim that there might be a temptation to employ area weapons making a greater impact than might have been considered necessary if the targets had been continuously tracked by conventional reconnaissance means and their positions *known* in real time. It is important to note, however, that information from a sensor displayed on a cathode ray tube in real time, or near-real time, may provide a better basis for appropriate action than a delayed report from conventional reconnaissance which does not necessarily guarantee a better discrimination of the target signature. This is in no sense a denial of the fact that situations may have occurred in which automatically collected and displayed information has resulted in the launching of weapons in a way which could best be described as indiscriminate.

### Counteraction: weapon platforms, weapons and munitions

In theory, almost any weapon could be used against enemy targets detected and located on the automated battlefield by the sensors and associated systems described above. However, because an important motivation behind the development of automated battlefield systems is to be able to increase the distance between the attacker and the target, the delivery of weapons is complicated by two major factors: the great distances over which the weapons must be fired, and the decreasing probability of hitting the target. The weapons and systems described below have, therefore, been developed mainly with these problems in view.

*Weapon platforms*

In order to solve the first of the above-mentioned problems—the great distances over which weapons must be fired against targets on the automated battlefield—the major effort has been directed towards utilizing airborne weapon-delivery platforms. These can be either manned aircraft or unmanned remotely piloted vehicles.

F4 Phantom aircraft were commonly used for air attacks against targets identified by sensors in South East Asia. A computer on board the Phantom automatically guided the aircraft to the designated point, using target grid-coordinate data received from a ground control station, and automatically released the weapon load. Sometimes B-52 bombers were also used, in much the same way, because of their great weapon load capability.

Depending on anti-aircraft defences, low speed aircraft have also been used in attack roles. Transport aircraft such as the C-130, and helicopters such as the AH-1G Huey Cobra and the UH-1M Iroquois, have been converted to combine detection and destruction capabilities in single, self-contained night attack systems. These aircraft, often called gunships, are equipped with various sensors and other night-observation devices such as radar, low light level television cameras and forward-looking infrared devices, which enable them to navigate, detect and engage targets in darkness and low visibility conditions. They are armed with multi-barrel guns such as the Vulcan 20 mm aircraft gun—a weapon with six barrels, capable of high rates of fire (a maximum of about 6 600 rounds per minute) with a muzzle velocity of 1 036 metres per second. A further development is the "Pave Spectre" project, an advanced version of the AC-130 gunship, armed with 40 mm guns and equipped with an on-board computer which can automatically fly the aircraft and aim and shoot its cannon. [12, 17]

A remotely piloted vehicle, equipped with small television cameras, data transmission links and even missiles, can operate in hostile environments with little or no risk to personnel. It can be "piloted" by operators located in ground control stations or launch aircraft remote from the combat areas. But apart from relieving pilots from exposure to modern air defences, RPVs offer many other advantages. They can be considerably smaller, and in many cases simpler, than manned aircraft, because they do not need to carry such equipment as life support and ejection systems. They are considerably cheaper: it is assumed that a remotely piloted, multi-mission, low-altitude strike-reconnaissance vehicle will cost about $300 000 as compared with more than $15 million for a modern air-superiority fighter. And they can be designed to withstand turning rates and g-forces far greater than those which could be endured by a human. On the other hand, they can be as versatile as a manned aircraft. Tests have shown that an operator in a ground control station, controlling an RPV in real time with the aid of television presentations returned from the aircraft, can guide the vehicle as if he were present in the cockpit; can successfully deliver Maverick and Shrike missiles against targets identified by sensors carried in the vehicle, and can subsequently recover the vehicle. Of course there are still limitations to these systems, such as the restricted field of view of the television camera as compared with a human eye. But the field of remotely piloted vehicles has considerable potential for further development, and is likely to add new dimensions to automated warfare. [18–19]

*Location and navigation systems*

The effectiveness of action against targets detected on the automated battlefield depends very much on the accuracy and reliability of location and navigation systems. Not only must the position of the target be known accurately, but the aircraft and weapons must be capable of finding the target and hitting it, even under poor visibility conditions.

Aircraft and missiles operating near control stations could be guided by ground-based radar data, but if the battlefield targets are a long way from the control stations, this simple system will not be sufficient. In the Loran navigation system, radio beacons are deployed at known positions over the areas concerned, and aircraft can then monitor these beacons and determine their positions by triangulation methods. This system enables an aircraft to determine its position with a maximum accuracy of about one-half nautical mile in daytime. At night, however, changes in the radio frequency wave dispersion may degrade the available accuracy to more than five nautical miles. Furthermore, systems relying on radio frequency communications are always sensitive to jamming, but to be effective, such interference would require extensive and powerful installations. Although US forces in South East Asia faced virtually no jamming, and navigation systems relying on radio frequency signals could be used with little dif-ficulty, the situation would probably be very different in other regions, such as Europe, where radio beacons and radio links between remotely piloted vehicles and their control stations would be the weak links in the automated system.

The intended route of a vehicle or a missile can be pre-programmed with the aid of an on-board guidance system (inertial navigation). As all the in-formation required for the flight is contained inside the vehicle or missile, this system is almost completely insensitive to jamming. Its accuracy depends largely on the time of flight of the vehicle or missile, presently employed equipment offering a 50 per cent probability that position de-gradation will not be more than about one nautical mile per hour of flight time.

Neither of these systems alone seems capable of providing sufficient accuracy for effective strikes at distant targets. There is the possibility, however, of combining the systems in order to provide better accuracy. Data from both the radio beacon system and the intertial guidance system can be processed by an on-board computer which can then correct the navigation. Probable errors of the systems can be calculated and fed into the computer in advance. And the computer could even collect data from other sources in order to improve the accuracy of navigation even more. The aircraft's position could be calculated continuously by devices record-ing speed and course after take-off ("dead reckoning"). Where terrain features are known, appropriate information can be fed into the computer memory and, by means of sensors studying the ground during flight, the computer can collect information about the terrain below the vehicle or missile, compare it with the stored data, and automatically correct the flight direction. Once the computer has been able to identify the under-lying terrain, a very high degree of accuracy (some tens of metres) is ob-tainable. This system also has the advantage of being relatively insensitive to jamming, as it relies on the reception of signals emitted or reflected as narrow beams from below.

Finally, satellites can also be employed for position-fixing systems, providing, under certain circumstances, a very high degree of accuracy. Small man-portable terminals, weighing approximately 12 kg, are capable of determining their locations, in relation to calculated positions of satellites, with an accuracy of approximately 25–30 metres. More sophisticated equipment can even be used for monitoring the position of rapidly moving objects, such as supersonic aircraft, thus adding considerably to the accuracy of automated navigation. Orbiting satellites have the disadvantage of being available for such systems only intermittently, depending on the length of the orbit period, but satellites launched into a synchronous orbit (so that they remain stationary over a particular area) would be much more useful for this purpose.

There is clearly considerable variation in the degree of accuracy obtainable with these navigation systems, and this factor must be taken into account when choosing weapons and munitions for use against targets on the automated battlefield. If the positions of the targets, and of the weapon platforms, can be determined accurately, then highly accurate guided weapons can be used to great effect. If on the other hand, the positions of the targets are not accurately known, area weapons, capable of causing an impact over a rather wide area and for which highly accurate positioning is not required, are used. Examples of both types of weapons will be discussed in the following section.

### Weapons and munitions

*Guided weapons.* The development of guided weapons—surface-to-surface missiles, air-to-surface missiles and bombs—provides a most effective means for ensuring that a weapon is delivered to its target on the automated battlefield with a very high degree of accuracy.

Certain missiles can be equipped with on-board automatic homing devices and, when launched, these missiles will find their own way to the target without further assistance. Homing systems may be infrared-seeking devices which will guide the missile towards heat sources (in much the same way as the Soviet SA-7 and the US Redeye anti-aircraft missiles are attracted towards the hot exhausts of aircraft engines); radar-seeking devices, as contained in the US AGM-45 A Shrike missile which is used to attack ground radar stations; or inertial guidance systems, similar to those used for aircraft navigation as described above, which are carried in the US Lance Battlefield Support Missile. Different systems can be combined to give better reliability.

Guidance systems of other missiles or bombs must be "locked in" on a target by an observer, such as the pilot of an aircraft, and this technique offers even greater accuracy in hitting targets. Two major systems have been developed so far for this purpose. The US Paveway series is a family of laser-guided bombs. The target is illuminated with a laser beam from an aircraft, or even from the ground; a laser-seeking device in the bomb or missile then locks on to the laser beam reflected from the target, and a guidance system guides the projectile along this reflected beam to the target. In the second system, bombs, such as the US AGM-62A Walleye, or air-to-surface missiles, such as the US AGM-65A Maverick, are equipped with television cameras. An image of the target as seen by this television camera is displayed on a monitor screen in the aircraft and, using this image, the pilot is able to lock the missile's or bomb's electro-optical tracker on to the target. The accuracies of both of these systems are reportedly very high, with "circular error probabilities"[3] of no more than a few feet. Both systems also provide the delivering aircraft with stand-off capability. One restriction on effectiveness in both cases is that the targets must be visible. But the use of infrared technology for the tracking and guidance system will provide night operation capability and could also give superiority over other systems under certain daytime poor visibility conditions.

*Area weapons.* If a target's position is not known accurately, or the target is not visible to an aircraft or the aircraft's navigation system is not capable of determining its *precise* position, highly accurate guided weapons are of less use. The military requirement in these cases is for a weapon which can cause an impact over a rather wide area so that there will be at least some chance of hitting the target. In some cases, guided weapons can deliver such large warheads that they can be considered almost as area weapons. But another means of increasing the area of coverage of a warhead is to divide it into a large number of small "packages" (bomblets) and to spread these over the area before activating them. This technique was developed during World War II for attacks with incendiary bombs: large numbers of two-kilogramme thermite sticks were distributed over a wide area by a "mother bomb". One such bomb is the US M-36 indendiary bomb, containing 182 incendiary bomblets, which was used in South East Asia.

A very large number of cluster bombs, containing fragmentation or hollow charge warheads, incendiary agents, chemical agents and so on have been developed: the US inventory includes more than 80 types in the Cluster Bomb Unit (CBU) series. The CBU-24 bomb (often called the "Guava" bomb because the bomblets resemble a guava fruit in size and shape) is one of the most widely used antipersonnel and anti-truck munitions in South East Asia. The 600 bomblets contained in this cluster bomb are spread over an area approximately one kilometre long by 300 metres

---

[3] "Circular Error Probability" (CEP) is used to quote the radius of a circle, centered on the target aimed at, within which 50 per cent of the weapons or munitions aimed at the target will fall.

broad, and each bomblet detonates on impact ejecting about 300 steel pellets at high velocity. These pellets puncture tyres, fuel tanks and radiators on trucks and kill or wound the drivers and other persons in the area. Another version has also been developed, with time delay fuses designed to hinder rescue activities. Other weapons include rockets and artillery shells which contain thousands of small steel darts called flechettes.

The above are only a few examples of modern weapon developments which, either because of their high degree of accuracy or their ability to cover wide areas, are not only compatible with the concept of the automated battlefield, but indeed make such a concept more feasible.

## Impact monitoring

After weapons have been launched against targets detected and located on the automated battlefield, it is important to know how effective this action has been; if the targets have not been destroyed, then another "round" of the sequence, beginning again with the gathering of new intelligence, may be necessary. This final phase of the automated battlefield sequence—impact monitoring—could of course be carried out by manned aerial reconnaissance or ground patrols, but on the automated battlefield, where the object is to keep personnel remote from the action, it is more logical to use remote sensing devices and data transmission systems, that is, to use the same intelligence-gathering systems that provided the initial target identification and location.

One difficulty here is that the fact that sensors have reported the presence of a target before an attack, but report nothing after the attack, could be interpreted in two ways. Bearing in mind that the probability of any sensor or sensor system reporting the presence of a target is always less than 100 per cent, the fact that sensors are not activated after an attack could indicate that the action has been successful in destroying the target. But this inactivity could also be the result of the destruction of the sensors; after all, the targets at which missiles, bombs and so on have been aimed must have been within a few hundred metres (in most cases) of the sensors to have been detected at all. However, experience shows that in many cases sensors are able to survive weapon strikes. On one occasion, about 400 artillery rounds were fired directly at a small area in which a sensor was deployed, and the sensor continued to function normally. [3g] Buried sensors, of course, have the best chance of survival; they are unlikely to be hit by fragments, and consequently would probably only be destroyed or severely damaged by an almost direct hit. Moreover, sensors which are designed for deployment by free-fall air-drop or by being fired from artillery or mortars must be of fairly sturdy construction to survive their delivery, and so would have a good chance of surviving weapon strikes.

Impact monitoring, then, can be carried out using the same sensor systems that initially detect and locate the targets, although new ones can be deployed as well. Data collected by these sensors is transmitted back to control stations for assessment in the same way as the initial target detection data. Computers in the control stations can be programmed to compare this data with previous reports and also to initiate the appropriate action, for example, to give instructions to cease fire.

## III. *The automated battlefield and the war in South East Asia*

It was stated at the beginning of this chapter that the operation of a fully automated battlefield is not yet a practical military proposition, and the descriptions of the devices, equipment and systems involved in such an operation have borne this out by showing that, with present-day technology, human involvement is still necessary, to a greater or lesser degree, in certain areas. But some parts of the automated battlefield have already been used under warfare conditions, and so, before considering how development in military technology in the short- and medium-term future might affect the practical feasibility of deploying a fully automated battlefield, it will be interesting to examine this experience briefly.

During the period of maximum overt US engagement in the recent war in South East Asia, automated battlefield systems and techniques were employed both on small scales, involving a few sensors deployed in restricted areas and certain limited operations and command levels, and in major operations involving many sensors, lasting long periods and covering very large areas. Apart from the scale of the individual operations, automated battlefield techniques were used in a number of different ways, and in fact it is possible to discern three fundamental types of operation: a system employed for direct support of ground combat troops—the "ground tactical system"; a "conventional barrier system"; and an "air-supported anti-infiltration system".

The "ground tactical system" is perhaps the least easily definable of the three systems; it involves the use of sensors, including, in many cases rather short-range, wire-connected or man-attended ones, in a wide range of tactical situations. A frequently encountered example is the following:

Suppose we have a US infantry unit responsible for securing a given area of operation (AO). This unit emplaces sensors at known locations along trails leading into or near its AO. If the sensors detect an enemy column moving along a trail, this information is received by a readout equipment operator, and he can . . . determine the size of the force, direction in which it is moving, and the speed, and he passes this information on to his commander.

The commander applies his knowledge of the location of friendly troops and civilians, or other intelligence information, of the terrain and weather, of means available to attack, and of safety controls and rules of engagement. Only after weighing all these factors does the commander give his decision: attack by artillery fire, an ambush, or whatever means is appropriate. [3h]

Since this system is mainly used in direct connection with ground troop operations, it can be integrated in ordinary ground combat activities. Human discrimination and decision-making form an important part of the system (dependent, of course, on the actual conditions and application in the field) and so it tends more to complement conventional means of combat rather than replace them. In other words, this system can be considered as the least automated of the three.

The "conventional barrier system"—often popularly referred to as the McNamara Wall—was conceived in 1966 as a means for deterring infiltration across the demilitarized zone in Viet-Nam. The system was modelled on rather similar naval systems, but the date of its conception is generally taken to mark the start of the development of the automated battlefield devices, systems and tactics which evolved in subsequent years. The "barrier" was to consist of a combination of sensors to detect intrusions into the demilitarized zone, and physical obstacles to impede and canalize the adversary's movements. Action against intruding units was to be taken by mobile, quick-acting combat units operating from strong points and by fire strikes from fortified artillery positions. The system was, however, apparently never totally integrated as an automated system, mainly because continued dependence on troops for ground action entailed continued human participation in discrimination and decision making in the decisive phase of combat. [3i]

The "air-supported anti-infiltration system" (Igloo White), intended to prevent the flow of troops and supplies along the Ho Chi Minh trail into South Viet-Nam, was first fielded in 1967, but was discontinued in 1972. Various types of sensors were air-dropped along roads and trails to be monitored; some of the equipment used for processing the data collected by these sensors has been described above. [3j] Because all the components of this system, including decision-making, air navigation, weapon strikes and impact monitoring and evaluation, could theoretically be carried out automatically, it can be said to have corresponded fully to the concept of the automated battlefield. Even if not all these activities were always automated in practice, the system could still potentially have been fully automated. In fact, it was completely dependent on advanced technology, since the system was entirely air-supported and involved no ground forces.

When assessing the experience gained the automated battlefield systems in South East Asia, it is essential to bear in mind that most of the automated equipment used there was developed and procured very rapidly, and put into operational use without adequate time for testing and modification. Many items thus proved unworkable or not adaptable to the region.

With this in mind, it must be said that the automated battlefield applications in South East Asia met with only mixed success. The "McNamara Wall" was never fully operational in its original form, although it served to stimulate certain technological developments. The "Igloo White" programme did not appear to detect, let alone stop, a large number of tanks, trucks, men and supplies from entering South Viet-Nam from North Viet-Nam, Laos and Cambodia.

# IV. *Future developments in automated battlefield techniques*

In a speech given in 1969, General W. C. Westmoreland, then Chief of Staff, US Army, described his vision of the future of automated warfare:

On the battlefield of the future, enemy forces will be located, tracked and targeted almost instantaneously through the use of data links, computer assisted intelligence evaluation, and automated fire control. With first round kill probabilities approaching certainty, and with surveillance devices that can continually track the enemy, the need for large forces to fix the opposition physically will be less important . . .

Based on our total battlefield experience and our proven technological capability, I foresee a new battlefield array.

I see battlefields or combat areas that are under 24 hour real or near real time surveillance of all types.

I see battlefields on which we can destroy anything we locate through instant communications and the almost instantaneous application of highly lethal firepower . . .

Currently we have hundreds of surveillance, target acquisition, night observation and information processing systems either in being, in development or in engineering. These range from field computers to advanced airborne sensors and new night vision devices . . .

We are confident that from our early solutions to the problem of finding the enemy in Viet-Nam the evidence is present to visualize this battlefield of the future . . . a battlefield that will dictate organizations and techniques radically different from those we have now . . . With cooperative effort, no more than 10 years should separate us from the automated battlefield . . .

We will pioneer this new dimension in ground warfare and develop an integrated battlefield system. [20]

In some ways at least, the experience gained from the use of automated battlefield systems in South East Asia might be compatible with such a vision, even though many applications failed. But it must be remembered that all, or almost all, practical experience of such systems comes from this one specific war, this one specific region and a number of specific conditions. Therefore, before beginning any discussion of the future applications of such systems, it would be useful to examine the military validity of this experience for other situations.

Devices for use on the automated battlefield have been designed for the tropical conditions which prevail in South East Asia. Various technical adjustments would be necessary before these devices could be used in other areas, such as the Arctic, and these are now being investigated. Apart from modifications necessitated by different weather conditions— power sources, for example, might need to be protected from extreme cold—the question of camouflage might be rather important; sensor antennae which are disguised as jungle plants for use in South East Asia would have to be disguised as something quite different if they were to be deployed in Northern Europe or in a desert region. Generally, however, problems such as these would probably present little difficulty; most of the equipment used on the automated battlefield can be adapted for use in different environments.

Vastly more difficult problems are likely to arise if an automated war is fought between two industrialized states, rather than between an industrialized and a non-industrialized state. In spite of a comparatively low level of technological sophistication in South East Asia, some simple, but often very effective countermeasures against sensors were successfully developed. In a conflict between two industrialized states, countermeasures are likely to be even more significant. It is difficult to conceive of how a fully automated war between such states would be fought, or to visualize its implications. But it is certain that an industrialized opposing force would have better resources for locating sensors and destroying or fooling them. Special detecting techniques may be developed for this purpose: most sensors contain metal and so could perhaps be detected by magnetic means; sensors emitting energy themselves, such as active infrared devices, are more easily detectable than passive sensors; and monitoring sensor transmissions may also be a way to locate sensors. It is also certain that electronic countermeasures such as jamming sensor signals, relay transmitters, aircraft and remotely piloted vehicle navigation systems and missile guidance systems, which may render a whole automated system useless, will play a very significant role in any conflict between two industrialized states. The "electronic countermeasure environment" in South East Asia has been characterized as "beneficial" in that virtually no such countermeasures were employed against the US combat systems. Current development is therefore very much concerned with reducing sensitivity to jamming: this may involve rather sophisticated communications techniques and the use of high-altitude aircraft or satellites as relay stations.

While North Viet-Nam was never able seriously to challenge US air supremacy in South East Asia, there would probably be no overall air supremacy in a war between two industrialized states. In such a situation, it might be impossible to deliver sensors to predetermined locations, particularly so far as delivery deep within enemy-held territory is concerned. It may also be impossible to keep airborne relay stations operating for more than limited periods. These are really general problems of aerial warfare: one solution might be to deliver sensors by very small RPVs or missiles, and to use satellites for relay purposes.

Technology has, of course, a great potential for further development of automated battlefield equipment. Many of the devices used in South East Asia are already considered obsolete and are no longer operational. New generations of sensors and auxilliary equipment are under development and in production. One important area in sensor development aims at providing a capability to distinguish between friend and foe. Indeed, the development of an "Identification, Friend or Foe" system which should be "suitable for positive and automatic recognition and identification . . . [and] capable of reliably identifying targets detected by·sensory devices" is already in progress. [21a] It might be possible to equip friendly forces with a device which transmits a simple identification code, although it will probably not be possible to provide such equipment to every combatant, much less to a civilian population;[4] and in densely populated areas, the use of sensors will involve identification problems for a long time yet. In short, many more techniques than are currently employed will probably be explored with a view to finding improved automated battlefield devices and systems.

## Future applications of automated battlefield techniques

As well as becoming technically more sophisticated, automated battlefield systems may well find an increasing number of applications in tactical situations in the future. Sensor systems are likely to be used much more frequently as complements to ground intelligence systems, and in fact may well be used as substitutes for other intelligence-gathering means. The sensor systems will probably be used at all levels in the military struc-ture, the most complex ones being under the control of, for example, divi-sional headquarters, and the simplest, including the wire-connected and man-attended ones, being used wherever protection is needed for in-dividual platoons or patrols. This latter application is limited in the sense that it only covers the first phase of the automated battlefield sequence— the intelligence-gathering phase.

In offensive operations involving two industrialized states, the use of ground sensor systems will probably be limited; as already discussed, the deployment of ground sensors in enemy-held territory will be very dif-ficult, or even impossible, in such a situation. Instead, sensors will probab-

---

[4] Another difficulty will arise in the case of relief and medical personnel belonging to the opposing force. In the Draft additional protocols to the four Geneva Conventions of 1949, the International Committee of the Red Cross has made certain proposals regarding the identification of such personnel as "friends" rather than "foes".

ly be carried in remotely piloted vehicles, and such vehicles will probably be used extensively for direct and indirect support of attacking troops, relying on automatic navigation to reach targets and automatic release of bombs, missiles and so on for destroying them. Thus most of an automated battlefield system in offensive ground operations is likely to be airborne. Also, as offensive operations are dynamic, it is doubtful whether computers could be programmed to control the support automatically, and so human discrimination and decision making will probably retain an important role, not to be eliminated entirely from the system.

In defensive operations, it is possible to deploy sensors for protection in front of one's own positions, or for tracking an adversary. As most sensors will be located close to the defensive positions, it will be relatively easy to receive the signals transmitted, and relay aircraft will be able to operate within range of their own anti-aircraft units, thus reducing the risk of their being shot down by enemy aircraft. It is likely that remotely deployed as well as attended sensors will be used in such situations, and that all phases of the automated battlefield, as defined above, will be employed in an integrated programme with all other combat activities, thus giving them maximum effectiveness from a military point of view.

Within these two broad areas—offensive and defensive—other perhaps more specific applications of automated battlefield techniques can be envisaged. Delaying actions during withdrawal operations could involve the use of such sensor systems and, as the distance between one's own troops and the deployed sensors increases as withdrawal proceeds, it is likely that completely automated systems, involving remotely deployed sensors, will be used. Area interdiction techniques are likely to be used in defensive actions, for precluding the enemy's use of a particular terrain, as well as in offensive operations. In the latter area interdiction operations, area weapons such as those described above may be used to protect flanks. However, when operational plans foresee the prospect of recapturing such areas, weapons will have to be selected carefully, avoiding those with very long delay fuses. Another example is the use of automated battlefield systems for border surveillance, both in peace and wartime, and in fact some such applications already exist. Border surveillance systems could employ mainly intelligence-gathering techniques, as, for example, in the system deployed on the US-Mexican border, or could include an automatic weapon-launching capability as well. This latter type of system could be extremely dangerous, particularly in peacetime, as a warhead released automatically and eroneously by a computer might hit foreign territory or even foreign border troops, with very grave consequences.

## V. *Summary and conclusions*

Automated battlefield techniques used against technologically less sophisticated adversaries will certainly involve fewer military problems than if used against technologically advanced countries. While some of the difficulties that will arise in the latter case will be countered by technological improvements and developments, others, such as the problem of gaining air supremacy and the use of radio frequency waves in an overcrowded radio environment, may remain serious military obstacles for a long time. The increased use of sophisticated sensors is expensive. And countermeasures against sensors and other equipment must always be expected.

A fully automated battlefield, in the sense that human beings are replaced by machines in all phases of the combat, will probably only be feasible in certain restricted areas of the world. Selected techniques and functions, rather than a fully integrated automatic system, are likely to be employed as complements to other combat systems. Remotely deployed ground sensor systems will probably have wider applications in defensive than in offensive operations. Small, low-cost sensor systems are likely to be used extensively for the protection of small units, at the company, platoon or patrol level, in all kinds of combat.

Thus the fully automated battlefield as envisaged by General Westmoreland in his 1969 speech, with all-computerized control of vast areas and with the capability of unleashing instant and enormously destructive force without human involvement, should probably not be anticipated, at least on such a scale, in the foreseeable future. But this is not necessarily the correct interpretation of Westmoreland's speech. By contrast, he has also stressed the importance of and the continuing need for the soldier, the human being, as an integral part even of the automated battlefield system:

I certainly do not imply by this that I foresee "pushbutton" warfare just around the corner. Quite the contrary. We will always need people to man the equipment we produce. We will have to have combat forces to react to the information our sensors systems generate . . . Most important of all, we will need the tactical decisions that only human judgement can provide—just as we do today. [21b]

The main concern in the recent public debate has been focused on the possibility that indiscriminate use of weapons might follow from the introduction of automated battlefield systems. This statement by General Westmoreland, however, tends to support the idea that the automated systems will be divided up and integrated into existing combat systems, which could reduce somewhat the risk of indiscriminate use of weapons; in fact, when there is close cooperation between automated devices and human senses, automation may even enhance discriminative ability. It must also be borne in mind that—even aside from humanitarian and legal aspects—an indiscriminate use of weapons is seldom cost-effective, even from a military point of view.

However, this does not exclude the possibility—and in some cases even the probability—of completely automated systems being applied in certain areas under certain conditions. Even with improved sensor discriminating capability and very sophisticated computers, the confidence in the infallibility of these modern technological achievements is not so well founded that one could dare believe that weapons launched by these systems would not involve the risk of indiscriminate use. Given the long ranges and immense destructive power of many modern means of warfare, any mistake in target designation or weapon launching may have grave consequences. In such cases, when technology is used extensively as a substitute for human senses, all efforts should be made to avoid applications that are likely to promote such risks.

## References

1. *Ny Teknik*, No. 4, 1 February 1973.
2. *DMS Market, Intelligence Report, Igloo White* (Greenwich, DMS Inc., January 1972), p. 2.
3. *Hearings before the Electronic Battlefield Subcommittee of the Preparedness Investigating Subcommittee of the Committee on Armed Services, United States Senate*, Ninety-First Congress, Second Session, 18, 19 and 24 November 1970
    (a) –, p. 7.
    (b) –, pp. 121–22.
    (c) –, p. 122.
    (d) –, pp. 9–10.
    (e) –, p. 127.
    (f) –, p. 124–26.
    (g) –, p. 96.
    (h) –, p. 12.
    (i) –, pp. 8–9.
    (j) –, p. 109.
4. *Vehicle Detection and Classification Using Chemical Sensors* (IS Army Cold Regions Research and Engineering Laboratory, Hanover, New Hampshire, August 1972).
5. *Ordnance*, Vol. LVIII, No. 319, July–August 1973, p. 86.
6. *Department of Defense Appropriations for 1973, Hearings before a Subcommittee of the Committee on Appropriations, House of Representatives*, Ninety-Second Congress, Second Session, Part 4 (Washington, 1972).
    (a) –, p. 110.
    (b) –, pp. 1209–10.
7. *Ordnance*, Vol. LV, No. 305, March–April 1971, p. 439.
8. Brantman, F., "The Era of the Blue Machine, Laos 1969–," *The Washington Monthly*, July 1971.
9. *Interavia*, Vol. XXVII, No. 5, May 1972, p. 492.
10. *NATO's Fifteen Nations*, Vol. 18, No. 2, April–May 1973.

11. *Aviation Week & Space Technology,* Vol. 98, No. 19, 7 May 1973.
    (a) –, p. 43.
    (b) –, p. 45.
12. Pretty, R. T. and Archer, D.H.R., eds., *Jane's Weapon Systems 1972–73* (London, Sampson, Low, Marston & Co., Ltd., 1972).
13. Sullivan, L., "R & D for Vietnam", *Science and Technology,* October 1968, pp. 28–38.
14. *New Scientist,* Vol. 58, No. 844, 3 May 1973, p. 283.
15. *New York Times,* 23 October 1972.
16. *Interavia,* Vol. XXVII, No. 4, April 1972, p. 375.
17. *Armed Forces Journal,* Vol. 108, No. 12, 15 February 1971, pp. 18–22.
18. Greene, T. A., *Remotely Manned Systems—Origins and Current Capabilities* (Santa Monica, Cal., The Rand Corporation, February 1972).
19. *Aviation Week & Space Technology,* Vol. 98, No. 4, 22 January 1973, pp. 38–47.
20. Address by General W. C. Westmoreland, Chief of Staff, US Army, Annual Luncheon Association of the United States Army, Sheraton Park Hotel, Washington, D.C., 14 October 1969 (Congressional Record, US Senate, 16 October 1969).
21. *Department of Defense Appropriations for Fiscal Year 1972, Hearings before a Subcommittee of the Committee on Appropriations, United States Senate,* Ninety-Second Congress, First Session, Part 2 (Washington, 1971).
    (a) –, 1462.
    (b) –, p. 177.

# Part IV. Developments in arms control and disarmament

### Chapter 12. Disarmament negotiations in 1973

Strategic arms limitation / The prevention of nuclear war / Chemical disarmament / The cessation of underground nuclear-weapon testing / The Indian Ocean as a zone of peace / The reduction of military budgets / Prohibition of napalm and of other inhumane and indiscriminate weapons / The world disarmament conference / Basic principles of negotiations on the further limitation of strategic offensive arms. Agreement between the United States of America and the Union of Soviet Socialist Republics / Agreement between the United States of America and the Union of Soviet Socialist Republics on the prevention of nuclear war / List of states which have signed, ratified, acceded or succeeded to the Geneva Protocol of 17 June 1925, for the prohibition of the use in war of asphixiating, poisonous and other gases, and of bacteriological methods of warfare, as of 31 December 1973 / Documents relating to the question of a comprehensive test ban, presented for discussion at the 1973 session of the Conference of the Committee on Disarmament (CCD) / Treaties expressly prohibiting the use of specific conventional (non-nuclear) weapons / UN General Assembly resolutions on disarmament and related matters / Record of the nuclear-weapon powers' votes on the main resolutions concerning disarmament at the UN General Assembly in 1973

### Chapter 13. The status of the implementation of agreements related to disarmament

Bilateral US–Soviet agreements / Multilateral agreements / Bilateral arms control agreements between the USA and the USSR as of 31 December 1973 / Summary of the relevant provisions of the agreements / Multilateral agreements related to disarmament as of 31 December 1973 / Announced and presumed nuclear explosions in 1972 and 1973 / Protocols signed together with certain IAEA nuclear safeguards agreements / Treaty banning nuclear tests in the atmosphere, in outer space and under water / French nuclear explosions, as of 31 December 1973 / Chinese nuclear explosions, as of 31 December 1973 / Nuclear explosions 1945–1973 (announced and presumed)

### Chapter 14. Chronology of major events related to disarmament issues

# 12. Disarmament negotiations in 1973

*Square-bracketed references, thus [1], refer to the list of references on page 404.*

## I. *Strategic arms limitation*

Under Article VII of the Interim Agreement "on certain measures with respect to the limitation of strategic offensive arms", which was signed by the USA and the USSR on 26 May 1972, and which entered into force on 3 October 1972, the parties have undertaken to continue active negotiations for limitations on strategic offensive arms. [1a] This undertaking was reiterated in the US-Soviet agreement on seven "Basic Principles of Negotiations on the Further Limitation of Strategic Offensive Arms" of 21 June 1973. These principles are reviewed here and their significance is briefly evaluated. (For the text of the agreement, see appendix 12A.)

The *first principle* affirms the decision of both parties to negotiate an agreement of indefinite duration, replacing the interim one, that will be more comprehensive in limiting strategic offensive arms and will provide for their subsequent reduction.

The signing of the new agreement is envisaged in 1974.

Although reduction has been mentioned as a "subsequent" step rather than an immediate goal, it is the first time since the beginning of the Strategic Arms Limitation Talks (SALT) that the USA and the USSR have officially committed themselves to negotiate such a measure in addition to fixing numerical limits for strategic arms. Indeed, the 1972 SALT agreements resulted in establishment of levels of armaments higher than those which existed at the time they were concluded. However, the fifth basic principle, allowing modernization and replacement (see below), has restricted in advance the prospects for cuts in the most modern armaments; the initial steps would probably include elimination of some obsolete weapons.

The setting of a target date for the conclusion of an arms control agreement by the negotiating parties themselves is without precedent. It is remarkable that the parties considered 18 months sufficient time to reach a permanent agreement on "more complete" measures of strategic offensive arms limitation, while it took a much longer time—about 30 months—to get a provisional agreement.

The *second principle* establishes that the main guidelines for a permanent agreement will be a mutual recognition of the "equal security interests" of each side and a recognition that efforts to obtain unilateral advantage, directly or indirectly, would be inconsistent with the strengthening of US-

Soviet relations. These guidelines are drawn from the statement of Basic Principles of Relations between the USA and the USSR, signed on 29 May 1972.[1]

The requirement of "equal security", taken literally, is so self-evident as to appear superfluous. No sovereign state, especially a great power, would sign an arms control treaty which could harm its security as perceived by its leaders. As early as 1961, in a joint statement of agreed principles for disarmament negotiations subsequently approved by the United Nations, the USA and the USSR stressed that all measures of general and complete disarmament should be balanced so that at no stage could any state or group of states gain military advantage and so that "security is ensured equally for all". But in the context of SALT the same formula could be understood as an instruction to the negotiators to take into account each other's interests in a broad sense, including the interests of their respective allies, as well as the threats they may face outside their mutual confrontation, and not necessarily to deal with limits on individual weapons. As a matter of fact, with the differences in organization, equipment, technology, strategic thinking and geographical circumstances, it would be difficult to evolve formulae of strategic balances based on strict symmetry. If the above interpretation is correct, the principle of asymmetrical limitations, which was applied in the SALT I agreements, would seem to have been reaffirmed in the June 1973 agreement. The parties could, for example, establish general ceilings on all strategic weapons, allowing each side the freedom to determine which weapons it wished to emphasize within its forces, that is, which proportion of its forces would be made up of ICBMs, SLBMs and strategic bombers. Such an arrangement could be complemented, when necessary, by an agreement on the geographical disposition of the forces.

However, there is no evidence that either side envisages giving up the advantage it now enjoys. The USA has made it clear that it would not sign an agreement which would level off its technological superiority; neither would it accept equality as regards access to military bases close to the borders of the other side. But it would favour bringing down the total Soviet strategic missile payload to its own, lower level. [2] The USSR, on the other hand, does not seem to be prepared to renounce its numerical superiority as far as strategic nuclear delivery vehicles are concerned. On the contrary, it has proposed that this superiority, which was allowed under the Interim Agreement, should be consolidated in a permanent agreement, and that reductions should take place in the levels of strategic bomber forces in which the USA has an advantage.

---

[1] The relevant portion of the statement reads: "The prerequisites for maintaining and strengthening peaceful relations between the USA and the USSR are the recognition of the security interests of the parties based on the principle of equality and the renunciation of the use or threat of force."

No state would acquiesce in any unilateral advantages of its partner in an arms control treaty, and efforts to obtain such advantages would be of no avail if the requirement of equal security interests were observed. Therefore, the agreement recorded in the second basic principle to the effect that the USA and the USSR would desist from efforts to obtain unilateral advantages could not reasonably apply to the terms of the treaty itself. It must be understood as applying rather to activities preceding the conclusion of the treaty, or following it, in areas not covered by arms control.

Ever since SALT started, the two parties have been engaged in the tactics of acquiring "bargaining chips" in order to be in a better negotiating position. The attempts to secure at least some temporary gains have led to ever larger and costlier weapons programmes and the good faith of the negotiating parties has been repeatedly questioned. Were these tactics of *fait accompli* to be pursued, and were the deployment of new systems to be decided irrespective of the talks, the very sense of the second basic principle would be lost.

The *third principle* envisages the possibility of limits to be placed both on the numbers of strategic weapons and on their qualitative characteristics.

The Interim Agreement of 1972 dealt, almost exclusively, with quantitative restrictions on offensive weapons, the only qualitative restriction being a freeze on the size of ICBM launchers. In addition to the on-going rivalry in areas not controlled by the SALT I accords, constant technological improvements of weapons, with an emphasis on increasing the effectiveness of each missile, have been gradually undermining the significance of the agreed numerical ceilings. It is regrettable, therefore, that under the third basic principle, restrictions on the quality of arms are mentioned only as a possibility, not as a firm commitment (they "can" apply).

The most urgent, but also the most difficult measure in the field of qualitative limitations is the control of multiple independently-targetable re-entry vehicles (MIRVs). Since the signing of the SALT I agreements, the USSR has successfully flight-tested MIRVs (see chapter 6), thus narrowing the technological nuclear gap which in this respect has favoured the USA. This predictable development was described by some high US officials as jeopardizing the prospects for a US-Soviet understanding to control multiple warheads. In reality, it may improve the chances of an understanding by creating a mutual interest in limiting MIRV deployment; the USSR would probably never agree to freezing its technology and leaving to the USA the advantage of possessing MIRVs. If, however, a permanent agreement is to be reached quickly, the limit on the numbers of MIRVs would have to be different for each side because, according to US estimates, only by 1979 will the USSR have as many MIRV warheads deployed on its ICBMs as the USA has now, and also because Soviet MIRVs are likely to be of much larger yield.

An unhampered deployment of MIRVs provides a stimulus to the continuing competition between the two powers. The ever increasing accuracy of MIRVs could make them counterforce-capable and, thereby, affect the fixed ICBMs which form a basic component of the strategic deterrent systems of the USA and the USSR. Due mainly to the existence of submarine-based deterrence, which is considerably less vulnerable than land-based deterrence, neither side can hope to attain a first-strike capability, that is, the ability totally to destroy the other side's retaliatory forces. But, in view of the uncertainties which may arise because of unavoidable differences in yield and the degree of accuracy achieved by the two sides for their MIRVs, the latter could become a threat to the "equilibrium" of nuclear forces. The value of MIRV as a counterforce weapon would decrease if the missile sites were hardened even more than they are now, or if a computerized command were installed to launch missiles automatically "on warning", as soon as the enemy missiles crossed the horizon, or if a new generation of mobile ICBMs were developed and deployed by both sides to replace the fixed ones. The importance of MIRV would be further reduced if land-based missiles were removed from the armaments of the two powers, and the bulk of nuclear deterrence were transferred underwater—a prospect which is still far away.

The *fourth principle* states the requirement of adequate verification and records the agreement that this should be achieved by "national technical means". It confirms the approach to verification of compliance that was taken in the ABM Treaty and the Interim Agreement.

Reliance on "national technical means" is tantamount to reliance, chiefly, on satellite surveillance. Such verification is considered adequate to monitor the numbers and certain characteristics of the weapons deployed, but its applicability to qualitative factors is doubtful. Thus, for example, qualitative changes in missiles cannot be revealed by cameras orbiting in space; no method is known to have been developed to determine whether a missile has more than one re-entry vehicle, or whether multiple re-entry vehicles are independently-targetable or not. Limitations on flight tests of MIRVed missiles may be helpful in slowing down the development of highly accurate and reliable MIRVs and in thereby decreasing the threats to the deterrent forces. But even if the tests could be detected with complete confidence, it would be difficult to ensure that MIRV deployment had been halted or cut back.

In the absence of more effective methods of off-site control, and since on-site control has been excluded, the quality of missiles from the point of view of their MIRV capability could be checked, by necessity, through limitations on the number of missiles and their size. The fewer the missiles allowed, and the smaller their size, the lesser the number of MIRVs installed, because there is a limit to the number of warheads a missile of given dimensions can carry. This, of course, would not solve the problem of the quality of warheads; the accuracy of the re-entry vehicle has a bearing on its effectiveness. Total elimination of MIRVs would be impossible to verify with the use of satellites alone without elimination of the missiles themselves, but such a disarmament measure is not the goal the SALT negotiators are pursuing. In any event, by restricting themselves to national means, and by excluding more intrusive methods of verification, the parties have consciously narrowed down the scope of possible qualitative limitation measures.

The *fifth principle* permits modernization of weapons and their replacement under conditions to be agreed upon.

The insistence on the right to modernize offensive arms and to replace those becoming obsolete contradicts the third principle which carries a promise of limitations on the qualitative improvement of weapons. At best, it could be taken as the lack of determination to carry out *effective* qualitative limitations of the strategic systems.

It is stated that conditions for modernization and replacement of weapons would be spelled out in the agreements to be concluded. Some such conditions have been formulated in the ABM Treaty. But it should be remembered that specific restrictions on anti-ballistic missiles refer only to systems in the form they exist at the present time, not to the introduction of new means of anti-missile protection. It remains to be seen whether a different path will be followed with regard to offensive weapons, that is, whether new strategic offensive systems, which may be devised in the future, would be covered by the agreed restrictions in a more general way. This would require some monitoring of the development of strategic arms.

The rationale behind the fifth basic principle is that confidence in the capabilities of weapons should be maintained. In actual fact, this approach sanctions and even encourages a technological arms race. The cause of arms control would probably be better served if modernization and replacement were forbidden altogether. Once uncertainty rather than confidence became prevalent on both sides with regard to the performance of the strategic offensive arms, the threat of a nuclear first strike would be diminished.

The *sixth principle* provides for the possibility of concluding agreements on separate measures supplementing the Interim Agreement even before the negotiations on the permanent agreement are completed.

Under this principle, the strategic arms race in specific areas could be temporarily curbed to facilitate an agreement on permanent restrictions. By spring 1974 no such partial arrangement had been reached.

The *seventh principle* reaffirms that both sides will continue to take necessary measures for preventing accidental or unauthorized use of nuclear weapons under their control.

This principle reiterates the obligation of the USA and the USSR to abide by the agreement of 30 September 1971 on measures to reduce the risk of outbreak of nuclear war between the two powers. It is only loosely connected with the issues dealt with in the preceding principles. More significant is the omission of a reference to eventual nuclear disarmament to which the parties are committed under the Treaty on the Non-Proliferation of Nuclear Weapons; it may be an indication of the limits the nuclear powers have imposed on the process of restricting their strategic arms.

In sum, the US-Soviet document signed on 21 June 1973 is a declaration of intention to make "serious efforts" towards reaching a new SALT agreement. The only important element is the promise of progress before the end of 1974. Other provisions are vague. Some terms used are even more cryptic than those included in the 20 May 1971 joint US-Soviet statement which preceded the SALT I agreements. No mention has been made about the total abolition of anti-ballistic missile systems. The fundamental question is whether the two powers have really decided to stabilize the "strategic balance", and whether they have really renounced seeking "strategic superiority". In any event, unless some permanent treaty is concluded before May 1977, the five-year Interim Agreement on the limitation of strategic offensive arms will lapse, and even the treaty limiting ABMs may be jeopardized.

The strategic arms limitation talks continue to be conducted in secrecy. The parties consider these talks to be outside the purview of the United Nations and insist that the principle of confidentiality of bilateral transactions must be observed. Nevertheless, the twenty-eighth UN General Assembly invited the US and Soviet governments to keep it informed of the results of their negotiations. It also reaffirmed the responsibility of the United Nations with regard to all matters pertaining to disarmament. [3–4]

## II. *The prevention of nuclear war*

On 22 June 1973, the USA and the USSR signed an Agreement on the Prevention of Nuclear War. It was a follow-up of the 1971 accords on a direct US-Soviet communications link and on measures to reduce the risk of outbreak of nuclear war between the USA and the USSR.

The new agreement was described by the Soviet press and officials as one of the most important documents in contemporary international relations, as a step on the way to the creation of a system of real guarantees of international security. The US representatives characterized it as a landmark on the road towards a régime of peace, lifting the fears of nuclear war from mankind. The main features of the June 1973 agreement are examined here in the light of the above assertions. (For the full text of the agreement, see appendix 12B.)

**Assessment of the essential provisions**

Under Article I, the parties have pledged themselves to prevent the development of situations capable of causing a "dangerous exacerbation" of their relations and to avoid "military confrontations". They also agreed, in Article II, to refrain from the "threat or use of force" against each other.

Barely a few months after the signing of the agreement this commitment was subjected to a severe test in connection with the Middle East crisis in October 1973. The parties failed to share the information they had about the forthcoming military attack, and when the hostilities actually started they were in no hurry to cooperate with each other in ending them; both then encouraged the belligerents, through massive re-supplies of weapons, to secure maximum gains. Attempts were made to widen rather than limit the scope of the war by inviting other countries to join. The threats, actual or implied, used to intimidate each other, coupled with reports about alleged transfer of nuclear warheads, in addition to ground-to-ground missiles, to the crisis area, raised the tension between the USA and the USSR to the point at which a "very significant and potentially explosive crisis" developed. (This was the term used by the US President.)

It appears that irrespective of the *détente,* the big powers would make use of any opportunity to bring about a change in the balance of forces in their favour, the only problem being how far their involvement in crisis situations could go. The fact that a military confrontation in the Middle East between the USA and the USSR was avoided was not due to the recent obligation to refrain from the use of force. Rather, it was because of the overriding interest, already shown in the past by the two powers, in avoiding situations which might jeopardize the viability of each of them as a nation. This interest was evident, for example, during the 1962 Cuban crisis, when no formal bilateral non-use of force undertaking was in existence, and when what is now called *détente* was far from being a political reality.

The real significance of the agreement lies, therefore, in the fact that it goes beyond bilateral US-Soviet relations. It aims at excluding a nuclear war also "between either of the Parties and other countries" (Article I), and "anywhere in the world" (paragraph 4 of the preamble). The obligations assumed are even wider: the parties proceed from the premise that each will refrain from the threat or use of force "against the allies of the other Party and against other countries" (Article II).

The following points can be made in relation to the latter clause. Paragraph 5 of the preamble to the agreement refers to the provisions of the United Nations Charter "regarding the maintenance of peace, refraining from the threat or use of force, and the avoidance of war". The non-use of force provision is the most fundamental commitment of the UN members. Its reaffirmation in international accords concluded by states is, certainly, desirable, on condition that its essence remains intact. This, however, does not seem to be the case with the agreement under discussion.

Article 2(4) of the UN Charter established a principle that all members shall refrain in their international relations from the threat or use of force against the territorial integrity or political independence of "any state". Instead of using the blanket formula "any state", the US–Soviet agreement has categorized the states against whom force should not be used in the following way: (*a*) USA and USSR—in their mutual relations; (*b*) the allies of the other party; and (*c*) other countries (Article II). This enumeration may raise a question about the status of each party's own allies. If they were covered by the term "other countries", it would be difficult to understand why the "allies of the other Party" should be specifically mentioned. Unless each party's own allies are not covered by the non-use of force commitment, a general prohibition, as expressed in the UN Charter, should have sufficed.

It could be argued with reference to paragraph 5 of the preamble that the US–Soviet agreement is "in conformity with the agreements to which either Party has subscribed", and that the use of force against one's allies would obviously run counter to obligations already contracted. But so would the use of force against any other country, if the UN Charter were to be considered a binding international instrument.

The agreement also seems to be at variance with the UN Charter in another respect. Under the Charter, the undertaking to refrain from the threat or use of force in international relations is unconditional. Under the agreement, it is hedged with a proviso: it applies "in circumstances which may endanger international peace and security". No indication is given as to who will judge whether such circumstances have arisen or not. Evidently, the big powers themselves will decide whether the use of force can be condoned on the grounds that international peace and security will not be endangered. Thus, for example, the bombing of Cambodia in the summer of 1973 was not considered by the parties as inconsistent with the obligations assumed under the agreement. However, a military attack against China would be deemed, at least by the USA, as incompatible with the agreement. In other words, if either signatory wanted to go to war, it would be free to do so, provided the war remained sufficiently "small". Presumably, *détente* is meant to be practised on a selective basis.

The above provisions have been accepted by the USA and the USSR as guidelines "in the formulation of their foreign policies and in their actions in the field of international relations" (Article II). The two powers have undertaken to develop their relations with each other and with other countries in a way "consistent with the purposes of this Agreement" (Article III).

The agreement also provides for action to be taken if the risk of nuclear conflict appears. The parties have undertaken to enter immediately into urgent consultations with "each other" and to make "every effort" to avert this risk (Article IV). The other nuclear-weapon powers which are permanent members of the UN Security Council, or the Council as a whole which bears the main responsibility for international peace and security, would not be directly involved in handling such situations. The latter body will only be informed of the progress and outcome of the two-power consultations. It is not even obligatory to provide information to the Security Council, the UN Secretary-General and the governments of allied or other countries; each party "shall be free" to do so.

Although a nuclear war between the USA and the USSR would have "devastating consequences for mankind", as admitted in the preamble to the agreement (paragraph 3), the two parties seem to have excluded, in advance, possible contributions of other countries or international bodies to the removal of the nuclear menace. It is noteworthy that, according to the agreement, the two-power exclusive consultation procedure will also apply to relations of the USA and the USSR with other countries. Moreover, it will be applicable whenever relations between countries "not parties" to the agreement appear to involve the risk of nuclear war between the USA and the USSR or between either of them and other countries (Article IV).

These provisions may have been motivated by a desire to prevent possible degeneration of a local conflict into a major great-power confrontation. Nevertheless, they have given rise to suspicions, especially in Europe and in Japan, that the two powers accord absolute priority to their bilateral relations to the detriment of their engagements towards multilateral alliances, that they arrogate to themselves the role of referee in matters relating to the security of others, and that they try to impose their joint supremacy over the rest of the world. (Attempts to have a US–Soviet military presence established in the Middle East area have given credence to the latter allegation.)

Assurances were given in Article VI(c) that obligations undertaken by either party towards its allies or other countries "in treaties, agreements and other appropriate documents" will not be impaired. Statements have also been made by the representatives of the parties to the effect that the agreement is not directed against any country and that the alliance strategies are not affected, but these have not allayed the above-mentioned suspicions. Again, the events in the Middle East show that the allies of the big powers are not consulted when it comes to such momentous initiatives as the placing of military forces on worldwide alert, an action which is fraught with very serious consequences to world peace. All the allies are asked to do is to support *faits accomplis;* their particular interests notwithstanding. Refusal of support is considered an unfriendly act. While the two great powers are determined not to let themselves be drawn, against their will, into local conflicts, "other countries" continue to face the danger of suffering from great-power contests which are not their direct concern.

### Conclusion

The agreement of 22 June 1973 is politically significant in the sense that for the first time the two powers formally, and in a bilateral document, expressed the intention to minimize the probability of a nuclear war started by design; prior to that, their interest was limited to avoiding an accidental use of nuclear weapons. The principle of consultations was re-affirmed as a cornerstone of US–Soviet relations but the treatment accorded to other countries raised questions about the impact of the bilateral *détente* on multilateral international relations.

In practical terms, the importance of the agreement is questionable. Its most essential provisions, implying a special responsibility of the USA and the USSR for the preservation of world peace, were simply "forgotten" in the heat of the Middle East War. The new code of nuclear behaviour has not removed the danger of nuclear war between the two big powers or between either of them and another nuclear power, any further than has the 1972 UN resolution [5] on the renunciation of the use or threat of force in international relations and the "permanent" prohibition of the use of nuclear weapons.[2] Moreover, in the context of the agreement as a whole, Article VI(a) which reiterates the right of self-defence implies that the parties still consider themselves free to employ nuclear weapons against an adversary that uses only conventional weapons, that is, against a non-nuclear-weapon power as well. Neither the USA nor the USSR has committed itself to a non-first use of nuclear weapons under any circumstances. Consequently, nuclear war has not become less likely now than it was before.

## III. *Chemical disarmament*

In 1973, the international debate on the prohibition of chemical weapons, though inconclusive, succeeded in clarifying the main difficulties standing in the way of an agreement, as well as the approaches to their solution. It has become evident that the criteria used in formulating the biological disarmament convention, which was opened for signature on 10 April 1972, are only partly applicable to a ban on chemical weapons since the two areas pose different problems from the military and practical points of view. Chemical weapons are considered more reliable and predictable

---

[2] For the assessment of the resolution, see reference [1b].

in their effects than biological weapons; some of them have already been employed in war; they are in the inventory of armies; and the commercial use of chemicals which may be used in warfare is widespread.

## Scope of the prohibition

All the participants in the negotiations conducted at the Conference of the Committee on Disarmament (CCD) and in the discussions held at the United Nations General Assembly have formally reiterated their commitment to bring about comprehensive chemical disarmament. Some countries want to achieve this aim in a single international instrument, while others prefer a gradual approach—a series of partial agreements leading to the same goal.

A fully comprehensive convention would have to cover all chemical warfare agents, as well as weapons, that is, munitions filled with these agents, equipment or means of delivery designed to use them. The activities prohibited would include research, development, testing, production and acquisition by other means, retention, stockpiling and transfer to any recipient of the agents, weapons, equipment or means of delivery, as well as training in their use (including issuance of field manuals for the handling of chemical weapon systems), and assistance, encouragement or inducement in manufacturing or acquiring them. The activities prescribed would include the closure, elimination, or conversion to peaceful uses of facilities for the production of chemical warfare agents, weapons, and relevant equipment or means of delivery, as well as the destruction of stockpiles.

No proposal submitted in the course of the negotiations went that far. Even the draft convention put forward by the Socialist countries on 28 March 1972 [6] and generally considered as all-inclusive, did not cover the prohibition on the training of troops in the use of chemical weapons and only implicitly provided for the ban on research related to chemical warfare agents and for the abolition of chemical warfare productive capacity.

A partial approach could relate to some items and/or some activities enumerated above. Thus, for example, in a working paper presented on 21 August 1973, Japan proposed that, as a first step towards the ultimate goal of complete chemical disarmament, an agreement be concluded prohibiting only the development, production, transfer and acquisition of the so-called super-toxic agents; the existing stockpiles would not be affected in this initial stage. Chemical agents other than the super-toxic ones would remain temporarily outside the ban. [7] Were such a partial approach to be adopted, the non-producing countries would be prevented from embarking upon the manufacture of the most dangerous and militarily most important combat agents: proliferation of these agents would be rendered illegal. On the other hand, the producing countries which have already accumulated stocks of these agents, including munitions, would be allowed to retain them for an indefinite period—until provisions for their destruction could be agreed upon.

For those who have stockpiled super-toxic chemical weapons in quantities sufficient to meet their military requirements, the solution described above would amount to the banning of something which they have stopped or were about to stop doing, anyway, without a formal international commitment. The USA, for example, has not produced lethal chemical agents on any scale since 1968, and for some years has been phasing out parts of its chemical-weapon arsenal—principally mustard gas, which the US Army considers obsolete, and those nerve-gas munitions whose safe-storage lifetime has come to an end, or for which the delivery systems are now obsolete. A ban on the production of super-toxic warfare agents only could not inhibit developments in other areas not covered by the prohibition. Since the emphasis is now shifting to so-called binary munitions (see below), a production ban which did not include these munitions would have a limited value.[3] Moreover, the partial convention, as proposed by Japan, would not prohibit the possession and further development of special equipment and means of delivery; the chemical warfare capability of the "have" states would be fully retained and could even increase.

Most countries do not have the technical capability to manufacture super-toxic warfare agents in meaningful quantities and may not be in a position to acquire it in the foreseeable future. To them, any limitation, even partial, imposed on the chemical warfare potential of the "haves" could be a gain. On the other hand, those which have such capability and, as a matter of policy, have abstained from producing the agents in question, may consider a permanent renunciation of the option they now possess as clearly discriminatory, if a few other powers were given the right to retain their stockpiles.

To avoid discrimination between countries at different levels of military preparedness, so as to achieve a balanced agreement, it would be more judicious to start, precisely, with the destruction of stockpiles. This was the position taken by a number of countries, including Brazil which also thought that an undertaking not to develop and produce chemical weapons should be nullified after a fixed period of time, unless there is evidence that stocks had been effectively destroyed. [9–10] In any event, elimination of super-toxic agents would not remove the danger of chemical warfare. Under certain circumstances, in the absence of adequate protection which is the case for most countries, less toxic agents, such as those used in World War I, could also create a great danger to the combatants and the population.

---

[3] It has been reported that the US Army plans to spend at least $200 million to produce binary nerve-gas munitions, and about as much to detoxify the nerve gases that the binaries will replace; see reference [8].

## Definition of the agents

Another controversial question is the definition of chemical warfare agents. They are grouped into two main categories: single-purpose agents which have no use other than for warfare, and dual-purpose agents which are commonly used for civilian purposes but which can also be used in war.

In a general way, the agents to be banned under a convention could be defined by a general purpose criterion as those of types and in quantities that have no justification for protective or peaceful purposes. This would leave outside the prohibition certain, presumably small, amounts of single-purpose warfare agents which may be needed for medical research and the development of defences against a chemical attack, as well as dual-purpose agents, in quantities which can be shown to be needed for normal industrial or other peaceful activities. A similar approach could be taken with regard to munitions and means of delivery: only those which are specifically designed to use chemical agents for hostile purposes or in armed conflict would be included in the ban.

Definitions based on purpose or intended use are useful, but may be found insufficient for an internationally binding legal instrument. In the absence of other criteria, the implementation of an agreement could be very difficult in practice; it might give rise to divergent interpretations as to what should be controlled, accounted for or destroyed.

Thus, a comprehensive convention would require a clear demarcation line separating single-purpose agents which would be completely prohibited (with the exceptions mentioned above) from dual-purpose agents which would be subject only to restrictions. In a partial convention, covering a certain category of agents, the prohibited agents would have to be unambiguously distinguishable from the agents allowed, irrespective of the uses the latter may be put to. Such qualifications, supplementing a general purpose criterion, could serve as technical guidelines; considering constant advances in chemical technology, they would have to be revised and updated, whenever necessary, according to an agreed procedure. To this end, levels of toxicity, or general structural formulae, or specific structural formulae, could be used either separately or in combination with each other.[4] A list of agents might be helpful as an illustration of what is prohibited; it could not be exhaustive. A definition based only on physiological effects, such as the one contained in the 1925 Geneva Protocol prohibiting the use in war of "asphyxiating, poisonous or other gases", has been found insufficient for disarmament purposes. [11] In a convention banning the production and stockpiling of chemical weapons, the prohibited substances would have to be qualified as warfare agents before, not after, they had produced the described effects.

---

[4] For a discussion of the technical definitions, their advantages and drawbacks, see reference [1c].

Much attention has been devoted to definitions based on toxicity. Canada suggested that two thresholds of toxicity might be set—one to include the super-toxic agents, the production of which could be entirely prohibited, and another, lower threshold, to encompass less toxic agents, the production of some of which, namely those having a dual purpose, might be permitted for legitimate civil purposes, but the use of which in military munitions and means of delivery could be prohibited. The scope of a treaty with regard to development, production and stockpiling would depend on the adequacy of the verification system adopted. [12–13]

However, a lethal toxicity criterion would not cover the incapacitating agents; nor would it cover binary agent components. The latter, which by themselves may be relatively harmless and easy to handle and store, generate nerve gas when they are mixed together, the mixing process taking place when the munition is on the way to the target. The components of binary weapons would, therefore, have to be identified and treated in accordance with the general purpose criterion: those which may have peaceful industrial uses could be considered dual-purpose agents and their production would be permitted but restricted, while those capable of being used only in binary munitions would be prohibited. An explicit ban against the filling of munitions with binary weapon components could provide some additional guarantees against circumvention of the provisions regarding the agents.

**Verification**

As distinct from the arms control treaties concluded hitherto, verification of an agreement on chemical disarmament would imply the monitoring of different activities connected with large quantities of different substances. Consequently, various control methods would be required.

Sweden presented a concept of "amplified verification", according to which the overall effectiveness of a verification system would be enhanced once several independent methods were combined, even if each of them, separately, had limited prospects of success. [14]

It is agreed that a verification system should include both national and international measures which would complement each other.

As far as national measures are concerned, the Socialist states members of the CCD (Bulgaria, Czechoslovakia, Hungary, Mongolia, Poland, Romania and the USSR) proposed that control committees should be set up, possibly composed of representatives of governmental and public organizations, as determined by individual parties, who would be assisted by specialists in chemistry and economics. Their duty would be to supervise, by way of random verifications on their own territory, the destruction of stockpiles of chemical weapons and the closure or conversion to peaceful production of those enterprises which before the conclusion of the convention had been engaged in the manufacture of chemical means of warfare, as well as compliance with the prohibition on the production of the means of delivery of chemical weapons. The committee staff engaged in control activities could use detection apparatus, carry out analyses of waste gases, waste water and soil, visit the enterprises and install their sealed sensing devices. The committees should be able to examine reports on research work carried out by research institutions in the chemical industry; patenting of chemical warfare agents, weapons, equipment and means of delivery would be prohibited. Reports of the national committees on their activities would be submitted to national governments and, possibly, published for general information. [10] It is noteworthy that Finland has already started a project for the creation on a national basis of a "chemical weapons control capacity for possible future international use".[5] [18]

Whatever the organizational structure of the national committees, it is doubtful whether self-imposed control over the fulfilment of obligations undertaken by states internationally could meet all the criteria of impartiality needed to provide reasonable assurance to other parties. As a rule, chemical agents and weapons are manufactured at the initiative and under the control of governments and in some countries they may be produced by government-owned enterprises. The observance of the prohibition on the production and stockpiling of chemical weapons would depend, primarily, on the behaviour of governments: if the governments decided not to buy these items, the industries would lose the market and would, consequently, stop producing them. Thus, the governments and not individual enterprises would be responsible for violations under international law. Government-appointed controllers would be unlikely to denounce those who designated them, even if they had unimpeded access to all relevant facilities and a real possibility of disclosing the breaches committed, which may not be the case in all countries. It is conceivable that a privately-owned industry might manufacture chemical weapons for non-parties to the convention or for groups of individuals or organizations abroad, without the knowledge of the national government. But, in such cases, the exportation of the prohibited products would require the approval of the national authorities and, again, national controllers would be either unable or unwilling to reveal the infractions.

Enforcement of nationally adopted laws and regulations is an internal matter for each country. Nevertheless, national agencies performing this task could become constituents of a treaty verification machinery, if they applied uniform methods of accounting, control and reporting and if they were linked to independent surveillance on an international level. States

---

[5] For a discussion of the organization of national agencies and the methodology of control of non-production of CW agents, see reference [17].

could also use their own technical means, such as remote sensors to detect open air tests of CW agents, and other methods to verify the observance of the prohibition by others. But in this respect they would not be in an equal position, considering the differences in technological development, capabilities of intelligence gathering and so on.

In the view of the Socialist countries, the international element of verification should consist of voluntary exchanges of information among countries in the form of discussions on data which may be obtained as a result of scientific research on the development of new chemical products for peaceful uses. Conclusions of these discussions (which might take place at international meetings of experts convened whenever the need arose) would be submitted, along with possible recommendations, to periodic conferences reviewing the implementation of the convention. The experts could consider assistance to be provided to states, at their request, in carrying out national measures of verification; they could also meet to solve problems relating to complaints of violation. There would be no institutionalized international machinery and no centralized analysis of statistics on relevant raw materials and semi-finished products. Each party would be free to use information from open publications in order to compare the amount of chemicals manufactured and consumed in other countries, and to draw its own conclusions as to whether a state was living up to its commitments under the agreement. [15–16, 19] With regard to the destruction of stocks, declarations by governments would have to be accepted as "appropriate and adequate indications" that obligations were being observed. [20]

The USA was critical of the Socialist countries' approach to verification, but did not make specific proposals of its own.

Argentina, Brazil, Burma, Egypt, Ethiopia, Mexico, Morocco, Nigeria, Sweden and Yugoslavia considered that it would be necessary to have an international control organ, designated by the parties, which would carry out continuous surveillance by collecting, analysing and circulating relevant data provided by the national bodies on a regular basis. They assumed that at the time of entering into force of the prohibition, states party to the treaty would make declarations as regards their national activities related to chemical weapons and agents. Measures of international verification would encompass the development, production and stockpiling, as well as the destruction of stocks, and the results of verification would be available to all parties. [21]

The Netherlands suggested that a standing organ for the "operational support" of a CW convention (with a potential of enlarging its field of action to include other disarmament measures) should be constructed in the same way as many other international organizations. A plenary conference of the parties to the convention would meet at certain intervals, while a board, elected by the conference, would function continuously and provide practical guidance to the work of the organ on the basis of a programme established by the conference. A secretariat, headed by an administrator, would consist of a permanent staff and such panels of experts as may be required for the performance of *ad hoc* specialized activities. [22–23] Japan thought that an international verification organization might include a verification committee composed of parties to the chemical convention who were members of the CCD. [13] Sweden felt that a special UN body should be set up, possibly in the form of a disarmament council, to deal with the implementation of disarmament measures in general and was of the opinion that an exchange of information and data regarding chemical agents could start even before a treaty was concluded. [24]

As in previous arms control agreements, such as the BW Convention or the Sea-Bed Treaty, problems which may arise in relation to the application of the provisions of a chemical weapon convention, including suspicions of breaches, could be clarified through consultation among the parties. The need for international consultations has been generally recognized. However, in case of unresolved controversies, a third-party inquiry may prove unavoidable. An inquiry procedure could start with requests for explanation; it may or may not include on-site inspection.

It seems that on-site inspection would be particularly useful when a party suspected of violation was willing to prove its innocence by inviting international inspectors. A party guilty of violation would most certainly resort to all possible excuses to avoid foreign control on its territory, even if such control were mandatory under the treaty. Therefore, also in cases when the international verification organization finds that a party seems to be acting contrary to the obligations under the treaty and has not provided a satisfactory explanation, or when a request for on-site inspection is filed by any other party, the inspection could take place only with the consent of the suspected state. Indeed, the concept of "inspection by cooperation" rather than "by obligation", so as to place the onus of proof on the part accused rather than on the accuser, is receiving ever wider support. [13]

The Soviet Union and other Socialist states hold the view that on-site inspections of any kind would create difficulties of a political and technical nature; they could be used as a "pretext for unwarranted violation of the sovereignty of states" and for gathering information unrelated to the purposes of an agreement prohibiting chemical weapons. These countries also consider on-site inspections to be impractical in view of the close link between the production of chemical substances for military and for peaceful purposes; visits of foreign experts to chemical enterprises would "violate the protection of industrial property". [25–26]

It must be recognized that inspection *in loco* is an intrusive type of verification. Nevertheless, it probably can be implemented in such a way as to avoid disclosure of scientific, industrial and commercial secrets. As a matter of fact, it has already been accepted in certain arms control agreements, for example in the Non-Proliferation Treaty in connection with IAEA safeguards. Most states do not consider it an infringement upon their national sovereignty.

There are different opinions as to the practicability of direct inspection of production plants but the method would certainly be applicable in dealing with the destruction of stockpiles. Verification of the destruction of stocks could not reveal matters of vital national importance; it would be carried out primarily on the basis of declarations from the parties concerned and would have to take place at depots specified by these parties. Whatever the adopted procedure, physical presence of controllers at the site of destruction would be advisable. Considering the nature of the weapons to be banned, and given the present degree of trust or lack of trust between nations, governmental statements reaffirming compliance with the treaty, though useful as a reassurance, may not suffice.

It has been suggested that, as a last resort, after an investigation had been carried out by an international control organ, a complaint concerning an alleged breach of the provisions of the convention could be submitted to the UN Security Council for political judgement. [21] Several countries stressed the need for a clear distinction between factual investigation of a complaint and the decision to be taken by the Security Council in the light of the facts reported. [27–29] Others, like Japan, [13] thought that a special clause allowing for complaints to the Security Council was superfluous, as the UN Charter already provides for such eventualities. In any event, it is unlikely that the Security Council, under the prevailing political conditions and considering the record of failures to enforce its own resolutions, would be able to take effective action against a defaulting state. A withdrawal from the treaty will probably remain the only ultimate sanction a party could apply in case of treaty violation. Conclusive proof of violation may be difficult to obtain. Some countries have, therefore, argued that patent lack of goodwill to cooperate on the part of the suspected offender, namely refusal to provide adequate clarification or to allow on-site inspection, should also be considered as sufficient reason to withdraw from the treaty.

**Other provisions**

The negotiators agree that any future CW convention, partial or comprehensive, should, together with the BW convention, reinforce the 1925 Geneva Protocol prohibiting the use of chemical and biological weapons, and should not detract from any obligations assumed under the Protocol. They also agree that the convention should prohibit transfer to other countries of relevant weapons and substances, as well as assistance in carrying out the banned activities; that it should not hamper research, development, production, possession, transfer and application of chemical materials for peaceful purposes, or hinder the economic and technological development of states; and that exchange of chemical substances, equipment, material and scientific and technological information for the use of agents for peaceful purposes should be facilitated.

As regards the last provision, it is easy to imagine that the adoption of an imprecise formulation regarding the scope of the prohibition of chemical substances could impede commercial exchanges between the countries. But it should not be taken for granted that a clause calling for a more extensive international cooperation in the chemical field will necessarily produce the expected effects. A similar commitment under the Non-Proliferation Treaty, for example, has not resulted in developments which would not have taken place without the treaty. Competition between industries of different countries is bound to impose limits on cooperation.

Some nonaligned countries have insisted that the convention confirm the principle that a substantial portion of the savings derived from measures in the field of disarmament should be devoted to promoting economic and social development, particularly in the developing countries. [10, 21] The USA questioned the applicability of this principle to CW disarmament. It argued that destruction of stocks, which would require elaborate environmental and safety precautions and disposal operations, was likely to result in substantial costs rather than savings. And in the case of the prohibition of production, it could be difficult to identify savings attributable to the agreement. [16] Poland stated that it was too early to raise the question of the distribution of financial resources released by individual disarmament measures and that this could only further complicate the negotiation of a CW convention. [30]

Security guarantees, going beyond those envisaged in existing arms control agreements, have also been requested in connection with a future CW convention. [21] These have not been spelled out. A formal undertaking not to use chemical weapons under *any circumstances,* combined with a provision for collective action in defence of the country attacked or exposed to danger as a result of violations by another country could, perhaps, meet the concern of smaller states.

**Format of the agreement**

If it is decided that a partial CW agreement should be signed, whatever the initial scope of the prohibition, the question will arise as to what kind of guarantee the parties should be given that a comprehensive convention will be subsequently negotiated and eventually concluded.

In the Partial Test Ban Treaty, the commitment to seek ''to achieve the discontinuance of all test explosions of nuclear weapons'' has been included in the preamble. Other partial agreements in the field of disarmament—the Non-Proliferation Treaty, the Sea-Bed Treaty or the BW Convention—contain a special article under which the parties have undertaken to continue negotiations with the aim of reaching more comprehensive measures. All these undertakings have, so far, proved ineffectual. In the case of the Sea-Bed Treaty, which entered into force more than two years ago, further measures for the prevention of an arms race in the environment in question have not even been considered by the parties. Provisional measures tend to remain provisional.

It is certainly impossible to set a concrete date for the conclusion of a comprehensive agreement, but the above-mentioned failures to secure meaningful negotiations have made it necessary to look for an improved format for a partial treaty. Japan suggested [7] that two documents should be signed simultaneously: a comprehensive treaty setting the ultimate goal to be achieved and a supplementary document, inseparable from the treaty, which would determine the scope of the initial prohibitions. The latter could either specify what is prohibited in the first stage or list "temporary" exceptions from the total ban. The text of the treaty itself would include a provision by which the parties undertake to negotiate on measures to bring about, at an early date, a comprehensive ban. Further steps could result either in expansion of the prohibitions or in elimination of exceptions, gradually or at one stroke. The method of striking off exceptions would seem more practical, although it is unusual for a disarmament agreement to record what is allowed rather than what is prohibited.

The Japanese suggestion has been received with considerable interest by a number of countries, including the USA and the USSR. Its attraction lies in the fact that the commitment to a comprehensive agreement would be politically stronger than in the previous arms control treaties.

### Assessment of the approaches to chemical disarmament

The basic controversy in the chemical disarmament negotiations concerns the scope of the agreement. Some countries (mainly the USA) argue that the prohibitions should be strictly related to the possibility of verifying that the commitments undertaken by states are fully respected. Since—in their view—there are, as yet, no such possibilities with regard to a comprehensive CW convention, a partial or gradual approach would be more in order. Chemical substances to be dealt with in the first place would be single-purpose warfare agents, preferably the most toxic ones, which are produced in comparatively limited quantities. Other agents, particularly those which are widely used in peaceful industries, but which may also have military applications, would be temporarily put aside as their control would present great difficulties.

Besides restricting the classes of agents to be covered by the prohibition, the proponents of a partial agreement suggest limiting the activities to be banned to development, manufacture and inter-state transfer. Stockpiles of agents as well as munitions would remain unaffected by a first-stage convention, because—it is contended—there are uncertainties over their size and composition and it would not be possible to provide adequate assurance that all the stocks had been actually and concurrently eliminated. The opposition to the destruction of stockpiles is justified by the need to maintain a CW deterrent capability. [31]

As regards the range of agents to be covered in a CW convention, there can be no doubt that the prohibition of production of the super-toxics is particularly important. These are the most threatening chemicals, since they have the characteristics of weapons of mass destruction; some verification measures could be devised to check compliance with non-production obligations. To monitor the production of the remaining warfare agents, in particular dual-purpose agents, may be more complicated and, to be sure, more cumbersome, but difficulties of control can hardly justify the omission of a large group of chemicals. Their lethal potential is much lower than that of the super-toxic chemicals and only on rare occasions could they be of importance in combat. Consequently, the incurred risk of evasion would also be smaller and the verification measures would not need to be as severe as in the case of super-toxics. The principle that the scope of the prohibitions should depend entirely on verification possibilities has not always been observed in arms control negotiations; as a matter of fact, it was disregarded in the BW Convention. It may be valid in certain cases, but only with a proviso that not all the activities banned under a treaty necessarily require the same degree of stringency in verification provisions; the military significance of what is to be controlled ought to be of primary importance.

One of the main reasons why a CW production ban should be all-inclusive is the appearance of binary nerve gas weapons, the ingredients of which, taken separately, cannot be classified as super-toxic. Some of them are chemical compounds obtainable through commercial channels, and their manufacture cannot be prohibited. The "production" of the lethal agent takes place only when the components chemically react with each other, that is, when the weapon is actually used. Binary-weapon production should, therefore, be prohibited as a whole, including munitions specially constructed for the purpose, even though verification of compliance will pose a problem (binary technology could be used for peaceful purposes as well).

The argument regarding stockpiles may appear more plausible. There is no practical way to discover hidden weapons; storage is not a readily identifiable activity. Some countries may feel that there is an advantage to be gained by concealing at least a part of their stockpiles. But it is questionable whether the cheating party would really get an advantage, or, rather, whether the cheated party or parties would actually suffer a significant disadvantage.

To escape detection, the proscribed weapons would probably have to be stored in remote places on the territory of the defaulting state, away from the regions of possible confrontation, which are usually under close intelligence surveillance by the opposing sides. Not being destined for long-distance or intercontinental use, they would have to be shipped to the areas of combat before being employed. But, as shown by recent experience in the USA, transfer of toxic munitions or bulk chemical warfare agents is not an easy operation; it is a complex procedure which presents certain dangers. The public has become highly sensitive towards chemical weapon transportation and considers it a threat to its safety. In view of the increasing worldwide concern about the protection of the environment, this sensitivity will probably persist. It is, therefore, less likely now than it was in the past that a shipment of significant quantities of chemical weapons over long distances could take place in absolute secrecy. The element of surprise, which is of paramount importance in chemical warfare, would be lost if a future victim discovered enemy preparations for an attack and could minimize its effects by taking certain precautionary measures. Marginal military gains that might still be obtained from such an attack would be definitely outweighed by the international political consequences of a violation of the long-standing ban on the first use of chemical weapons. For similar reasons, precisely because chemical weapons are essentially first-strike weapons, the deterrence value of retained stocks, constituting a second-strike capability, is not of great value or credibility: before striking the offender would obviously take all the necessary precautions in order to reduce the effectiveness of a retaliation.[6]

Indeed, adequate anti-chemical warfare defences could contribute to the weakening of the incentive to use chemical weapons. Such defences may include protective clothing, respirators and alarms, as well as medical countermeasures, in the form of therapeutic drugs and antidotes or even prophylactic treatment. It is, of course, assumed that under a CW convention activities aimed at obtaining protection against a chemical attack would be allowed. Besides, other weapons may be an effective counter to the possible use of chemical weapons; there is no overriding military requirement that every enemy action or weapon be deterred by a response in kind. In other words, the risk that some state will somewhere conceal chemical agents or weapons is not so great as described by those who refer to security interests in opposing a treaty obligation for the elimination of all stockpiles. It should also be borne in mind that unless replenished at regular intervals, which would not be possible under a production ban, chemical weapon stockpiles may be subject to losses resulting

---

[6] For a detailed discussion of the value of a deterrent CW capability, see reference [32].

from deterioration. The size of hidden arsenals could, therefore, gradually diminish.

Whatever the validity of the arguments put forward by those who favour the retention of chemical weapon stockpiles under a partial chemical convention, and however complex and expensive it may be to detoxify chemical agents, there can be no justification for keeping the stockpiles completely intact. Such a convention would be only remotely related to disarmament, unless at least a partial destruction took place. A cut-down could be expressed either in absolute terms or in percentages of existing stocks. (The first method might be found more acceptable to the possessors of the chemical weapons, as it would not involve revealing the entire stocks.) The greater the amounts destroyed, the more significant would be the disarmament measure and its political and psychological impact.

## Conclusions

A fully comprehensive agreement prohibiting all activites related to chemical warfare agents and weapons, and providing for their total destruction, would be the best solution from the point of view of disarmament. If there is a choice between a partial convention and no convention at all, a partial solution will be desirable if it is meaningful. To be meaningful, a partial agreement would have to prescribe the destruction of a significant part of existing stockpiles, especially of super-toxic agents and munitions, and to proscribe the development and production of all chemical warfare agents, and of weapons, equipment or means of delivery designed to use them, as well as inter-state transfer of the prohibited items. In addition, areas of possible military confrontation should be made entirely free from chemical weapon stockpiles; such disengagement would further reduce the likelihood of chemical warfare.

As long as the stockpiles remain, be it in reduced proportions, the possibility of chemical weapons being resorted to in international conflicts will not disappear. Even after the elimination of military stockpiles, some countries, especially those with highly developed industries, would always be in a position to divert to military purposes such readily available industrial chemicals as phosgene and chlorine, which could be sprayed from relatively simple dispersal devices. Countries which have already acquired the knowledge of binary-weapon technology would continue to possess a chemical warfare potential that is much more formidable. These dangers cannot be removed by any new international instrument. Hence the need for reaffirmation and strengthening of the 1925 Geneva Protocol prohibiting the use of chemical weapons. The strengthening could be achieved by universal adherence to the Protocol;[7] general recognition of

[7] For the list of parties to the 1925 Geneva Protocol, see appendix 12C.

the comprehensiveness of the prohibition under the Protocol; withdrawal of reservations limiting its applicability;[8] and, finally, by establishing an international machinery to investigate allegations of breaches.

The twenty-eighth UN General Assembly requested the CCD to continue negotiations, as a matter of high priority, on the problem of chemical methods of warfare, with a view to reaching early agreement on effective measures for the prohibition of the development, production and stock-piling of all chemical weapons, and for their elimination from the arsenals of all states. It also invited states that have not yet done so to accede to the 1925 Geneva Protocol and/or to ratify it, and called for the strict ob-servance by all states of the principles and objectives contained in the Protocol. [33]

The resolution embodying the above points was adopted unanimously, but China and France did not participate in the vote. China expressed the view that the USA and the USSR were using the problem of CW to cover their actual intention of continuing the arms race. France favours a com-prehensive prohibition of chemical weapons, but only on condition that there would be effective international control; it furthermore believes that the CCD is not an appropriate body to deal with this question. [34]

## IV. *The cessation of underground nuclear-weapon testing*

The discussions regarding a comprehensive test-ban (CTB) continued throughout 1973 at the political and technical expert levels. Working papers pertaining to verification were submitted to the CCD and examined there (see appendix 12D).

### The usefulness of tests

A basic question which underlies the debate on the cessation of under-ground nuclear-weapon tests concerns the military usefulness of such tests for the USA and the USSR, considering the high degree of sophistication of their nuclear arsenals. Some experts contend that the possibility of achieving further progress in nuclear explosive technology, through test-ing, is very limited. They point out that, at the present stage, non-nuclear rather than nuclear developments determine the advances in the military technology relating to strategic weapons of the two big powers, the char-acteristics of the weapon systems themselves—accuracy, warhead carry-ing capacity and so on—being of primary importance. A CTB, therefore, though politically desirable to reinforce the ban on the proliferation of

---

[8] By 31 December 1973, only Ireland withdrew its reservations made at the time of acces-sion to the Geneva Protocol.

nuclear weapons, would, in their view, not result in an appreciable slow-down of the nuclear arms race between the USA and the USSR.

The official position of the USA, however, is that testing could bring about "significant" improvements in nuclear weapon design: the yield of weapons could be increased while their weights and dimensions could be diminished to make them suitable for certain delivery systems; they could be made less radioactive and more safe in handling; their reliability could be improved; and the cost of their production could be reduced. The developments in the field of nuclear devices could be translated into improvements in the weapon delivery systems employing these devices and even small refinements could become important in the context of a full weapon system. In the opinion of US officials, all these innovations would be impossible if testing were to stop altogether. The USA has, however, declared its readiness to give up whatever advantage might result from continued testing provided that reasonable confidence can be obtained that other parties have given up the same advantage. [35]

Indeed, as in previous years, the debate centred on the problem of verification.

**Verification**

The general, uncontested opinion is that seismic monitoring is the most useful control method for a comprehensive test ban, that a very high verification capability is already available for strong and intermediate explosions and that international cooperation and coordination can reduce the uncertainty relating to very weak explosions. The importance of multilateral cooperation and coordination in the field of seismology has been stressed particularly by Japan, [36] Sweden, [28, 37] Canada [20] and Italy. [38–39] Sufficiently rapid exchange of relevant seismic data is considered important to improve the identification of nuclear explosions and to make these data available to all states; the setting up of a body specifically designed for this purpose has also been suggested.

Identification capabilities could be rendered better if more modern seismic stations were built, but it is understood that there exists an ultimate threshold of explosion yield below which explosions cannot be detected even by teleseismic means. Moreover, under some conditions it is not possible, by seismic means alone, to identify certain weak events which have been detected. Some experts have estimated that at present the detection/identification threshold for underground nuclear explosions in hard rock in the Northern hemisphere lies in the yield-range of two to three kilotons. [40] One should also bear in mind that, however weak the test, a would-be violator could never be entirely sure what seismic signal it would cause.

A teleseismic network may not be able to counter completely certain

385

evasion techniques, such as "medium de-coupling", involving the emplacement of the nuclear device in a loosely compacted material (for example, dry alluvium); "cavity de-coupling", involving the emplacement of the nuclear device in a large cavity in hard rock or salt medium; "earthquake simulation", employing a series of appropriately spaced and timed nuclear explosions to generate seismic signals which resemble those of earthquakes; or "earthquake masking", by deliberately detonating nuclear devices after earthquakes have occurred. The described techniques are, admittedly, complicated and costly. Some have probably never been proved in practice and may be purely imaginary. An evader would have to restrict himself to explosions of a yield low enough to ensure a safety margin, and he could not, in advance, have sufficient assurance of non-detection and non-identification.

Some countries assume that, to be of value, whole series of tests are needed, making discovery practically unavoidable. They doubt whether a "successful" violator of a CTB would stand to gain much, as compared with the risk incurred, by an isolated, clandestine nuclear test. The official view of the USA, however, is that even a single low-yield test could be of significant military value, and that tests at small yield could be related to devices of large yields. The USA claims that a series of tests, involving many explosions, would not be essential for weapon system development; if necessary, a series could be conducted over an extended period of time.

Among other, non-seismic, methods of verifying an underground test ban,[9] detection by satellites was for the first time discussed at some length in an international forum.

To be a primary control system, satellite observation would require total coverage at frequent intervals of all potential sites for violation. Satellite photography could detect activities associated with the preparation of tests, such as transportation of equipment to the site or drilling, and possible effects of tests, such as subsidence craters or dust clouds. In practice, in view of the costs involved, probably only known or suspected test sites would be covered. The opinion widely shared is that satellites would be particularly useful in photographing the site of a dubious event whose location has been established by seismic means. They would thus play a complementary role by magnifying the risks of detection of possible violations. The application of the suggested technique will be subject to limitations as long as satellite reconnaissance remains a monopoly of a few powers, but these are the powers most concerned.

Some attention was devoted to the perennial question of on-site inspection. The inspection is viewed by the USA as an obligatory follow-up in regard to events detected and located, but not conclusively identified, in

---

[9] For a review of non-seismic methods of detecting underground nuclear tests, see reference [41].

order to deter clandestine testing. [42] An examination of the site of a suspected nuclear test could reveal radioactive leakages if the violator has not succeeded in fully containing the explosion underground. Also certain relatively small changes on the surface could be observed by inspectors after a test, the assumption being that these effects would remain for a substantial period of time. Since the early 1960s, no indication has been provided by the USA as to the desired frequency of obligatory inspections, the way in which the sites would be selected and the modalities of inspection operations, including the technical methods used at the site.

Other countries consider that obligatory on-site inspections would not change in any significant way the number of events which can be identified through seismological means, and would not change the possibilities for evading a test ban. [16, 40] They believe that deterrence needed against cheating can be obtained without such inspections. Sweden has suggested that, as a last resort, once the potentialities of a consultation procedure to clarify dubious events have been exhausted, inspection "by invitation" could be applied, that is, inspection agreed upon by the parties involved in the dispute concerning compliance.

The USSR continues to be opposed to any kind of on-site inspection. It requires that reliance should be placed exclusively on national means of detection and identification, which it considers a sufficient guarantee of the observance of the obligation to stop underground tests. [42–45]

## Conclusions

No arms control treaty can completely rule out the possibility of evasion; all it can do is to minimize its probability. According to the overwhelming opinion, the existing verification capabilities make the probability of discovery of clandestine tests very high, except for some very weak explosions. These capabilities would be further increased by a formal undertaking not to interfere with the national technical means of verification, as has been done in the 1972 US–Soviet ABM Treaty. A similar clause in a comprehensive test ban treaty, combined with a consultation procedure between the parties, which is also envisaged in the ABM Treaty, should provide increased confidence in the monitoring capability. Whatever the methods of verification employed, the risk that some weak explosions will remain undetected must be taken, if an underground test-ban treaty is to be concluded. In this field, as in the whole area of arms control, insistence on 100 per cent assurance would be tantamount to a rejection of any agreement.

Ever since the test ban debate began, verification has posed problems to the negotiators, but has probably never constituted the main obstacle to an agreement: considerations of a political and military nature have been of greater importance. Testing programmes have been motivated

387

chiefly by the desire to develop new weapons or to improve the existing ones. At the present stage, it may well be the development of new tactical weapons that adds to the difficulties of reaching a comprehensive test ban.

Recently, there has been a growing concern among non-nuclear-weapon states about highly accurate tactical nuclear weapons of subkiloton yields, which could blur the distinction between conventional and nuclear weaponry (see chapter 5). Possible pernicious repercussions of this tendency for the Non-Proliferation Treaty and its continued validity have been described in the CCD, [46] and some countries, for example Ethiopia, have suggested a moratorium on the further development of tactical nuclear weapons. [47] If all the nuclear-weapon powers decided to acquire the so-called nuclear mini-weapons, the prospects of a CTB could also be pushed further away, as more tests might be needed. A complicating factor is that the testing of very small-yield devices underground could not be detected or identified from outside the territory of the testing state. It is also regrettable that the question of underground peaceful explosions has not been discussed in sufficient detail. In the present world energy situation, explosions which could be used to release new sources of energy may pose additional problems for reaching a comprehensive test-ban treaty. (According to preliminary data, 14 of the 35 nuclear explosions conducted by the USSR in 1972 and 1973 may have been part of a programme for peaceful uses of nuclear energy.)

The twenty-eighth UN General Assembly condemned "with the utmost vigour" all nuclear-weapon tests; reiterated its conviction that, whatever may be the differences on the question of verification, there is no valid reason for delaying the conclusion of a comprehensive test ban; and urged the governments of nuclear-weapon states to bring all nuclear-weapon tests to a halt without delay, either through a permanent agreement or through unilateral or agreed moratoria. [48] China and France voted against the UN resolution, while the USA, the USSR and the UK abstained. The USA regretted the failure of the resolution to recognize the importance of verification, while the USSR opposed partial solutions, such as moratoria, agreements banning tests above a certain level of magnitude and, in particular, unilateral commitments.

# V. *The Indian Ocean as a zone of peace*[10]

The *Ad Hoc* Committee which was set up in 1972 to study the implications of the Indian Ocean peace zone proposal [49] held 11 meetings in 1973. The report produced by the committee [50] provided information

[10] A discussion of the proposal to declare the Indian Ocean a zone of peace can also be found in the *SIPRI Yearbooks 1972* and *1973*. [1, 41]

about the questions discussed but contained no recommendation as to what measures should be taken to halt the great powers' accelerating military build-up in the Indian Ocean, and to eliminate from it all bases, military installations, logistical supply facilities, nuclear weapons and weapons of mass destruction and any manifestation of great power military presence in this ocean conceived in the context of great power rivalry—an objective stated in the UN declaration of 1971. [51]

The twenty-eighth UN General Assembly did not debate the issue in much detail. Its action was restricted to the adoption of a resolution by which the *Ad Hoc* Committee was requested to carry out its mandate and the Secretary-General was asked to prepare a "factual statement of the great Powers' military presence in all its aspects, in the Indian Ocean, with special reference to their naval deployments, conceived in the context of great Power rivalry". [52] The purpose of the "statement" is to provide the *Ad Hoc* Committee with authoritative information which would help it to assess the implications of foreign military presence in the area. However, it is not the lack of knowledge about the situation in the Indian Ocean that has prevented progress in the work of the committee. Even if the area were now free of the great powers' military presence, there would be an advantage in immunizing it against their future intrusion.

At the present stage the difficulty lies in the fact that there is no common understanding of the basic principles underlying the concept of the Indian Ocean as a zone of peace.

Taken literally, the declaration on the Indian Ocean of 1971, if implemented, would result in the military absence of the great powers in the territories of states belonging to the region, and in strict limitations on their military movements in the ocean.

Whether the great powers are present or absent in the territories of states in the region depends exclusively on the coastal and hinterland nations: any sovereign state can refuse to allow foreign bases or other military facilities on its national territory. But the proposal is so formulated as to allow exceptions. It would prohibit only such great powers' military presence as is "conceived in the context of great power rivalry" and it has been stressed that "there is no question of any attempt at limiting the sovereignty of any country in the maintenance of such establishments as it considers necessary for its own security". [53–54]

A question, therefore, may arise whether military presence of the great powers not conceived in the context of rivalry between them, and not considered as limiting the sovereignty of the host country, would be condoned and, if so, who would decide what is allowed and what is banned: the host country, all the countries in the region or the great power concerned? It is very doubtful whether an objective criterion could be agreed upon to pass a judgement of this nature. No great power would ever admit that it is using foreign territory to gain strategic advantages over its rival;

the usual justification given is the protection of the interests of the host country. Certainly the country allowing foreign installations on its territory would consider them necessary for its own security. This ambiguous position on the question of foreign military bases is also apparent in the fact that the only concrete proposal refers to a freeze on the numbers of bases or to a prohibition on the enlargement of the existing ones but not to their complete elimination.

The restrictions applying to the great powers' activities in the ocean are accompanied by similar qualifications. It has been pointed out in the discussions in the *Ad Hoc* Committee [55] that not only the passage of warships, which in any event cannot be forbidden, but even their presence in the Indian Ocean would not be found objectionable if they did not pose a threat to the sovereignty and territorial integrity of the littoral and hinterland states and were not prejudicial to the peace or security of these states. This could imply allowance for the stationing of the great powers' fleets and for the overflight of the area by their military aircraft on the conditions spelled out above. Again, it is not clear who would decide whether the conditions were met: each state individually, all the countries in the region or the great powers themselves. Moreover, the qualification attached to the presence of warships might not be compatible with the requirement that military presence conceived in the context of great power rivalry should be banned. Thus, for example, the presence of nuclear missile-carrying submarines could be justified only on strategic grounds, as a factor in the arms competition between nuclear-weapon powers, but it may not threaten the sovereignty and territorial integrity of the littoral and hinterland states. A ban hedged with so many reservations would seem to be of doubtful value. It could be interpreted as changing nothing in the present situation: the great powers could retain and increase their military presence in the Indian Ocean, and even those now absent in the zone could enter it at any time, claiming that they do so not in the context of great power rivalry and that they do not threaten the sovereignty of the states in the zone. They might even be supported in these assertions by some of the countries belonging to the region.

The *Ad Hoc* Committee's report has listed the following 36 states as littoral and hinterland states of the Indian Ocean:

| | | |
|---|---|---|
| Afghanistan | Ethiopia | Madagascar |
| Australia | India | Malawi |
| Bahrain | Indonesia | Malaysia |
| Bhutan | Iran | Maldives |
| Botswana | Iraq | Mauritius |
| Burma | Kenya | Nepal |
| Democratic Yemen | Kuwait | Oman |
| Egypt | Lesotho | Pakistan |

| Qatar | Sri Lanka | Uganda |
|---|---|---|
| Saudi Arabia | Sudan | United Republic of Tanzania |
| Singapore | Swaziland | Yemen |
| Somalia | Thailand | Zambia |

The list is meant to include coastal states directly bordering the Indian Ocean or any of its natural extensions, as well as hinterland states whose main access to the sea is the Indian Ocean. This criterion, which seems to have the merit of comprehensiveness, has not been consistently applied: states that have part of their seaboard in the Indian Ocean but whose concerns or interests are—in the opinion of the drafters of the list—related primarily to the Atlantic seaboard, are not treated as littoral states. The list is, therefore, not only incomplete, but contains incongruities. Thus a number of land-locked states would qualify as Indian Ocean nations, while South Africa, with most of its approximately 2 000-mile sea frontage on the Indian Ocean, would not. The Portuguese colony of Mozambique has been disregarded as well, and not all countries with interests both in the Mediterranean Sea and the Indian Ocean have been taken into account.

It is true that under the present political conditions it is difficult to envisage negotiations, and even more difficult to expect an agreement with certain states in the region, but it would be short-sighted to ignore the existence of these states. South Africa, for example, because of its policy of apartheid, creates conditions of conflict rather than peace. But it is one of the biggest and richest countries in the region, it is well armed and is generally considered a potential nuclear-weapon country. The behaviour of South Africa is, therefore, bound to have a bearing on the situation in the whole area; its accession to the treaty on the non-proliferation of nuclear weapons would be an important event.

There is also the problem of overseas territories of European states. Some countries in the region contend that the status of these territories, which they regard as colonies, is incompatible with the idea of the zone of peace and they seem to make the implementation of the idea contingent on decolonization. However, if the goal is to reduce the levels of military presence, there is no reason why it should not be achieved before decolonization: the administering powers could assume obligations also with regard to their overseas territories. This was the case, for instance, with Protocol I to the Treaty of Tlatelolco prohibiting nuclear weapons in Latin America, under which states have undertaken to apply the statute of denuclearization in territories for which, *de jure* or *de facto*, they are internationally responsible and which lie within the limits of the geographical zone established by the treaty. Introduction of extraneous political considerations, unrelated to the basic concept of the Indian Ocean as a zone of peace, would hamper rather than promote the implementation of the concept itself.

One of the arms control objectives of the declaration on the Indian Ocean is to remove or prevent the deployment of nuclear weapons or other weapons of mass destruction in the area. This is a demand for unilateral obligations on the part of nuclear-weapon powers. However justified the demand may be it would carry greater weight if all the countries in the region were to commit themselves to a non-nuclear-weapon policy by acceding to the Non-Proliferation Treaty. This would be especially important in the case of so-called nuclear-threshold states. Nevertheless, some countries have placed less emphasis on the accession to the Non-Proliferation Treaty than on the accession to the Sea-Bed Treaty, even though the latter may be considered as redundant for states which have formally renounced the possession of nuclear weapons.

A complete prohibition of nuclear weapons in the littoral and hinterland states of the Indian Ocean would entitle these states to ask for guarantees that nuclear weapons would never be used against them.

It is understood that the geographical limits of the zone would have to be defined in terms of latitude and longitude, but there exists some confusion as concerns the territorial limits. The view of at least certain members of the *Ad Hoc* Committee is that possible restrictions on military activities in the Indian Ocean should apply solely beyond the limits of national jurisdiction. This would mean that the waters within the jurisdiction of the coastal states would be exempt from the ban on the military presence of the great powers. Frequent references to the Sea-Bed Treaty as a possible model for the determination of the territorial limits of the peace zone suggest that this may be the case. Under the latter treaty, which prohibits the emplacement of nuclear weapons and other weapons of mass destruction on the sea-bed and the ocean floor and in the subsoil thereof, beyond a 12-mile limit, nuclear-weapon powers retain the possibility of installing weapons of mass destruction on the sea-bed beneath the territorial waters of other states, within the 12-mile sea-bed zone, with the consent and authorization of these states.[11] If the same provision were used in an agreement concerning the Indian Ocean, the very idea of the peace zone would be in jeopardy. It is not clear why there should be any exception at all. The restrictions are meant to be imposed, in the first place, on the great powers. It would seem, therefore, natural that they should apply to the entire ocean, significantly including territorial waters.

The following conclusions could be drawn from the above review. The idea of the Indian Ocean as a zone of peace, accepted in general terms almost three years ago by the United Nations, remains ill-defined. The distinction made by the promoters of the idea between measures related to disarmament and the "strengthening of international peace and security" is misleading. If the arms race in the Indian Ocean were arrested, the cause of peace and security in the area would certainly be enhanced,

[11] For the discussion of the relevant provision of the Sea-Bed Treaty, see reference [56].

while without concrete disarmament or arms control undertakings any proclamation of peace would be no more than an expression of good intentions: an armed peace usually rests on shaky foundations.

Some countries in the region assume that peace in the Indian Ocean would be ensured once the great powers "disappeared" from the area. They insist that commitments should be taken unilaterally by these powers and they do not envisage any specific obligations of their own. The fallacy of this approach is obvious: foreign presence—although an important source of friction and conflict—is not solely responsible for the absence of peace. More often than not it is justified precisely by unstable situations in the regions concerned and by the need to assist those who ask for protection, whatever the real motives of the powers providing the assistance. Consequently, the "disappearance" of the great powers would not automatically bring about tranquillity in the area. It should complement rather than subsitute for the obligations to be contracted by the countries of the region themselves. As has been pointed out by one of the members of the *Ad Hoc* Committee, states of the region cannot in all earnestness advocate the concept of a peace zone without themselves first practising what they preach to the outside world, beginning with the renunciation of the threat or use of force against each other.

The countries to be involved in the realization of the proposal are: (*a*) the littoral and hinterland states, (*b*) the great powers, and (*c*) the major maritime users of the Indian Ocean. None of these categories has been properly defined. The list of littoral and hinterland states, established by the *Ad Hoc* Committee, contains notable omissions; it is not clear whether the term "great powers" refers only to the USA and the USSR or to all the permanent members of the Security Council; neither is it known what criterion will be used to decide whether a country is or is not a "major user" of the ocean and, in particular, whether such a determination will be based on the absolute volume of the maritime traffic or on the relative importance of this traffic to the country concerned.

Similar uncertainties exist with regard to the limits of the area to be included in the peace zone. There is a tendency to exclude from it not only the territories of some coastal or hinterland states, but even certain portions of the Indian Ocean itself.

Precise definitions may not be indispensable for setting up a peace zone. It is unlikely that all the countries directly concerned would simultaneously agree to contract corresponding obligations. The zone may, therefore, initially embrace only those states which have accepted the concept; others could join later. Also the geographical scope of the zone may not, from the very start, include the whole area of the Indian Ocean. But it would seem important to identify the countries whose participation in the future agreement is absolutely essential, as well as to delineate the areas that must be covered in order to render the agreement meaningful.

There appears to be hesitation among the Indian Ocean states even as regards the extent of the possible disengagement obligations of the great powers. The qualifications which accompany the demands for their withdrawal, such as "military presence conceived in the context of great power rivalry" or constituting a threat to the "sovereignty, territorial integrity and independence" of littoral and hinterland states, tend to create a distinction between "good", or tolerable, presence and "bad", or intolerable, presence, based on subjective judgements of individual states. It is unlikely that concrete progress towards an Indian Ocean peace zone could be made before the above inconsistencies are smoothed away. The matter is becoming ever more urgent in the light of reports that US and Soviet naval activity in the Indian Ocean is expanding, while the military build-up of the coastal states continues unabated due to massive supplies of weapons by the great powers.

## VI. *The reduction of military budgets*

On 25 September 1973, in a letter addressed to the UN Secretary-General, the USSR proposed that the permanent members of the UN Security Council "should reduce their military budgets by 10 per cent from the 1973 level during the next financial year". Ten per cent of the funds released, or 1 per cent of the current military budgets of these states, was to be used for assistance to developing countries. Other states especially those with a major economic and military potential were invited to take similar steps. A special international committee was to be established, on a temporary basis, to distribute the funds and it was suggested that priority should be given to states afflicted by natural disasters. [57–58]

Subsequently, the USSR explained that the envisaged assistance to developing countries would be in addition to existing aid programmes. It also specified that the projected special committee would have to comprise representatives of China, France, the UK, the USA and the USSR, as well as those from Africa, Asia, Latin America, and Eastern and Western Europe. [59–60]

The following conditions for the implementation of the suggested measure were put forward by the Soviet Union: (a) all the five great powers, China, France, the UK, the USA and the USSR, without exception, should reduce their military budgets by the same percentage, and they should do so simultaneously; (b) only officially published figures could be used as a basis for the reduction of budgets; (c) the reduction must not be offset by increased military spending by other members of the military alliances; and (d) no control of compliance with the reduction commitments undertaken by states was to be carried out. [61] The great powers' reaction to the proposal was either reserved or outright negative.

The USA considered it impractical and inequitable, because there was no common standard for measuring the military budgets of the states concerned: those countries whose military budget covered only a part of their defence expenditures would have the advantage of effecting a relatively smaller reduction in their military strength than others, and also their development assistance contribution would be relatively smaller. Even if such a standard could be agreed upon—ran the argument—there was no assurance that all the states concerned would be willing to submit their military budgets to international scrutiny, which would be necessary to ensure that the standard was applied. Furthermore, in the absence of verification, there could be no assurance that the budgetary cuts were in fact carried out, or, if they were, that actual military expenditures had been decreased or that the funds had not been subsequently restored. Besides, the USA was of the opinion that there was no direct relationship between the size of a country's defence budget and the funds it may make available for development purposes abroad. Therefore, it did not believe it useful to link defence budgetary levels to a capacity to provide development assistance; it was up to each state to decide what financial mechanism to use to allocate funds for foreign aid. [62]

Similar arguments were formulated by the UK which stressed particularly the point that there was no valid basis for the comparison of military budgets. In its view, it was not budgetary cuts that were needed, but rather agreed disarmament measures resulting in reductions in military expenditure and hence in additional funds becoming available for development and other purposes. [62–63]

Like many other nations, France thought that it was important to determine how military budgets were drawn up, because states may, for various reasons, account only for part of their military expenditures in their military budgets. It considered that commonly agreed definitions were essential and that, to start with, figures should be provided regarding the actual ratio that existed between military expenditures and development aid. Its suggestion was that the problem involved in the Soviet proposal would be practically resolved if the USA and the USSR were to subscribe to the targets laid down in the Development Decade.[12] [64]

China understood the Soviet proposal as directed primarily against its interests. It accused the USSR of including in its military budget only one-third or one-fourth of its actual military expenditures and stated that a

---

[12] The target for development assistance to the developing countries by the economically advanced countries, to be reached by 1975, has been set, under the United Nations International Development Strategy, as 0.7 per cent of the gross national product of the latter countries. [65]

reduction of military budgets of all the five permanent members of the Security Council by the same proportion was unacceptable. [62, 64]

Most of the developing countries found the Soviet-proposed measure interesting and commendable. Some of them qualified their endorsement with remarks concerning the size of the budget reduction and the amount of development aid, which they considered too modest, or disapproved of the suggested mode of the implementation of the proposal. Brazil was of the opinion that no less than 5 per cent of the military budgets of the most highly armed states should be channelled to developing countries, and that the proposed measure should be realized on a staggered basis so that countries could adhere to it at different stages. [66] Liberia suggested setting up a fund in the United Nations to which each of the permanent members of the Security Council would be requested to contribute a 5 per cent deduction from its military budgets until disarmament was achieved, and to ask the UN Secretary-General to distribute the funds on an equitable basis to the developing nations. [67] Sri Lanka believed that it would be more sensible to apply the proposed reduction to the combined military expenditure of each military alliance—NATO and the WTO powers—[67] and Kuwait and India expressed a wish that a portion of the development assistance funds should be in convertible currency. [67–68] Nepal, however, thought that the first step should be a freeze on the level of spending for military purposes and that attempts could be subsequently made to effect reductions from that level. [59] A few countries considered that it was unnecessary to establish a separate committee for the purpose of distributing the funds released following the adoption of the Soviet proposal, as there were already in existence international bodies competent to perform this task. Others criticized the distribution of seats in the proposed committee. Still others, while appreciating the Soviet idea in principle, expressed doubts about its practicability.

The Soviet proposal was accepted by 83 votes (including those of the WTO countries) against two (Albania and China), with 38 abstentions (including those of the NATO countries). [69] At the same time, at the initiative of Mexico, the General Assembly requested the Secretary-General to prepare, with the assistance of experts, a report on the reduction of the military budgets of the permanent members of the Security Council, which should also cover other states with a major economic and military potential, and on the utilization of a part of the funds thus saved to provide international assistance to developing countries. [70] The voting record was better than on the previous resolution: 93 in favour, two against (Albania and China) and 26 abstentions; the USSR supported this recommendation, and the three Western powers—France, the UK and the USA—though abstaining, welcomed the suggested expert study.

A freeze on, or a reduction of, military budgets has been on the disarmament agenda since the early 1950s, with the USSR as the main proponent.

At one time, the Western powers also seemed interested in such a measure. Thus, the Anglo-French memorandum of 11 June 1954 suggested that "Over-all military expenditure, both atomic and non-atomic, shall be limited to amounts spent in the year ending 31 December 1953"; [71] in a memorandum of 21 July 1955, the French government proposed that "a reduction in the amount of military expenditure borne by the states be agreed by them, and that the financial resources thus made available be, either in whole or in part, allocated to international expenditure on equipment and mutual aid"; [72] and on 18 March 1957, the US representative to the Disarmament Subcommittee expressed the view that a target could be set that "each state in its first step should bring its military expenditure down by 10 per cent". [73] In recent years, the Western powers lost interest in an internationally agreed reduction of military budgets, while the USSR continued to press for it. The Soviet move at the twenty-eighth General Assembly can be understood as corroborating the link between disarmament and development.[13] It is noteworthy in the sense that the distribution of the funds to the developing countries was not to be left to the discretion of each of the great powers, but was to be decided internationally. Nevertheless, the proposal suffers from the same shortcoming as all the previous Soviet proposals on the subject of budgetary reductions: it seems to ignore that the meaning and the contents of military budgets are different in different countries.[14]

Even if accepted at its face value, the proposal might prove unworkable. It does not take into account the fact that the financial year in the USSR does not coincide, for example, with that of the USA, and it is not clear whether the cuts should be effected from the projected or from the actual levels of budgetary expenditure. It is not known how the requirement of simultaneous reduction is to be met, considering the existing differences in the constitutional processes of countries with different political and economic systems. Neither has it been explained whether the assistance to developing countries would be expressed in the price levels prevailing at the time the budgetary cuts were made, or in current prices prevailing at the time the funds were transferred, and whether these funds would be provided in national currencies or converted into a common currency; in the latter case there would be problems with the choice of currency, and particularly with the rate of exchange.

For all these reasons, and also because China has not published any budget figures since 1960, it is difficult to say what the proposed reduc-

---

[13] The report of the group of experts on the economic and social consequences of disarmament, published in 1972, has concluded that "disarmament and development can be linked to each other because the enormous amount of resources wasted in the arms race might be utilized to facilitate development and progress". It also stated that "efforts to promote development should be neither postponed nor allowed to lag merely because progress in disarmament is slow". [74]
[14] See *SIPRI Research Report No. 10,* August 1973. [75]

tion of military budgets would amount to and how much it would yield for the developing countries. According to Soviet estimates, the implementation of the proposal would "free more than a thousand million dollars to help the developing countries". [64] This means that the 10 per cent cuts in the military budgets of the five permanent members of the Security Council would add up to more than $10 billion; the exact amount was not indicated. The USSR has put its own military budget in 1973 at approximately $24 billion, which is probably a considerable overestimation. (See appendix 8C.) Czechoslovakia and Poland have calculated that under the Soviet proposal the military spending of the five great powers would be reduced by $15 billion and, consequently, $1.5 billion would be released for development assistance. The estimates given by Bulgaria were $13 billion and $1.3 billion dollars, respectively. It is likely that other countries would produce still other sets of figures, and that the discrepancies could be in the range of billions of dollars. There is no provision in the Soviet proposal as to how these, as well as other seemingly technical problems, should be dealt with. The mandate of the special committee is limited to the distribution of the contributions declared; it does not include the task of checking the accuracy of the declarations, or of determining the global amount to be distributed. For the great powers the question of assessment is essential. For the developing countries, it is of lesser importance; whatever the figures and whatever the political motivations of the donors, they would stand to benefit from a transfer of resources in addition to what they receive at present through the existing channels; as recipients they cannot lose. However, from the point of view of disarmament, the merits of the proposal are doubtful. The provision of development assistance would not be a sufficient proof that military expenditures had been reduced. Besides, a 10 per cent reduction is too low to produce noticeable effects on the military potential of the nuclear-weapon powers, especially since it is meant as a one-time operation without a follow-up.[15] In any event, in view of the opposition of the remaining permanent members of the Security Council, the Soviet proposal, which presupposes unanimity of the great powers, is unlikely to become even a basis for a serious discussion. The special committee charged with the distribution of funds was still-born; there will be no funds to distribute. The USSR could hardly have expected a different outcome, and those who supported its initiative could have had no illusion that it would materialize. The proposal gave rise to harsh polemics between the great powers, especially between

---

[15] A much more substantial reduction was envisaged in the Soviet proposal of 11 June 1954, containing "Basic provisions of a draft international convention for the prohibition of atomic, hydrogen, and other weapons of mass destruction, for a substantial reduction in armaments and armed forces, and for the establishment of international control over the observance of the convention", namely, an obligation of states party to the convention "to reduce their military expenditure within one year by not less than one-third of the 1953–54 level of exexpenditure". [76]

the USSR and China—polemics, which had nothing to do either with disarmament or with development.

On the other hand, the study which the experts appointed by the UN Secretary-General are to prepare can be useful, if it provides a generally acceptable definition of a military budget, if it elaborates a basis for possible cuts in the military expenditure and, also, if it suggests means for carrying them out and for verifying compliance. But even if it succeeds in achieving this very complicated task, it is improbable that under the existing political circumstances the Soviet proposal would be found less objectionable.

A flat rate of percentage reduction of the military expenditure of all the five great powers, placing them on an equal footing, has only an appearance of fairness. In actual fact, because of considerable differences in the volume of expenditure, in the quantity and quality of armaments and, consequently, in the levels of military preparedness, identical percentage cuts would affect the military establishments concerned in different degrees; they would certainly favour the greatest spenders—the USA and the USSR. These two countries are responsible for about two-thirds of the total world military outlays. It would be appropriate for them to be the first to reduce military expenditures, without making it conditional on similar moves by others. A mere halt in the strategic arms race between the USA and the USSR would release considerable resources for peaceful purposes, without endangering the security of either power. They could even substantially reduce their arsenals without giving up the position of superiority with regard to other nuclear-weapon powers. To avoid disputes over comparability of military expenditure, or verification, which are unlikely to end in an agreement, the USA and the USSR could apply the method of mutual example: a cut in the expenditures by one power would be reciprocated by a cut which the other power considered equivalent. Since there is no agreed starting point from which percentage deductions should be calculated, cuts in absolute terms would be, perhaps, preferable. There would be no need to state which parts of the military budget and, for that matter, which components of the military potential were affected. The problem of balance which is considered highly relevant in the limitation or reduction of specific categories of armaments may prove to be less controversial in the case of military expenditures. In the absence of formal treaty obligations, the voluntary reduction process could stop without formal denunciation, if one of the powers found that there was no reciprocation at all, or that it was inadequate. The bigger the reductions, the more difficult and improbable the concealment; significant cuts in military spending are bound to produce observable shifts in the economy of a country.

The reduction by 300 million roubles in the Soviet military budget for 1974, announced last December, [77] though small, could have been taken as an invitation to a process of mutual example, but it has found no response on the part of the USA. The latter country is planning to increase its military spending considerably in the next fiscal year, though much of the increase stems from rising prices and manpower costs.

A reduction of overall military expenditure, by itself, is not the most effective method of bringing about disarmament, but as a collateral measure it could promote disarmament by building up confidence among nations. In addition, certain arms control or disarmament agreements could be usefully accompanied by a freeze on, or corresponding cuts in, military appropriations, depending on the nature of the agreement. This would make it more difficult for the parties to compensate armament restrictions in one area by an expansion in another. On the other hand, agreed substantial cuts in armaments would inevitably have to be followed by cuts in expenditure, whether or not the latter were specifically provided for in the disarmament treaty.

## VII. *Prohibition of napalm and of other inhumane and indiscriminate weapons*

The UN Secretary-General's report on *Napalm and other incendiary weapons and all aspects of their possible use,* [78] issued in October 1972, was circulated to UN member states for comments. The report stated the necessity to work out measures for the prohibition of the use, production, development and stockpiling of napalm and other incendiaries.[16] Over 20 countries sent in communications. [79] Most of them favoured early action to impose restraints on or an outright prohibition of the use of the weapons in question, especially against civil populations, and suggested that attention should be focused, at least in the first stage of the debate, on this aspect rather than on a possible ban on production, development and stockpiling. The reason for taking this approach was that it might be difficult to set up adequate control to ensure total abolition of incendiary weapons. The Netherlands, for example, thought that an agreement to dispense with these weapons could never be satisfactorily verified, and since napalm and other incendiaries can be produced with relative ease, the agreement could be nullified almost instantaneously. In the view of the Netherlands, which was shared by Norway, [47] effective disarmament in this field was unattainable. Furthermore, it was generally felt that the prohibition of use should be broadened to include other conventional weapons which tend to cause excessive suffering and particularly severe injuries or which may, either by their nature or because of the way in which they are commonly used, affect civilians and combatants indiscriminately.

---

[16] For a summary of the report, see reference [1d].

Some of the weapons belonging to this category were described in a report which was prepared in the summer of 1973 by a group of military, medical and legal experts convened by the International Committee of the Red Cross (ICRC). [80] Besides incendiaries, the report discussed high-velocity ammunition for small arms, fragmentation weapons, antipersonnel mines and other delayed action weapons, as well as some new or contemplated weapons, such as laser devices. A more detailed list has appeared in the recommendations submitted by a Swedish working group. [81] The group formulated guidelines for the establishment of international rules concerning the following weapons which cause needless suffering or super-fluous injury, and/or are capable of producing indiscriminate effects: small calibre weapons with an impact velocity of the projectile exceeding 800 m/sec; fragmentation warheads; flechette warheads with an impact velocity exceeding 900 m/sec; land mines; ambush weapons; long delayed action weapons; weapons for area bombardment; weapons based solely on blast effects; and incendiary weapons.

The 22nd International Conference of the Red Cross, held in Tehran in November 1973, adopted a resolution on the "Prohibition or restriction of use of certain weapons". Recalling that the right of parties to a con-flict to adopt means of injuring the enemy is not unlimited, the Red Cross Conference urged that the Diplomatic Conference on the reaffirmation and development of international humanitarian law applicable in armed con-flicts, to be convened in February 1974 at Geneva, should begin considera-tion, at its first session, of the question of the prohibition or restriction of use of conventional weapons which may cause unnecessary suffering or have indiscriminate effects. It invited the ICRC to call a conference of government experts to study the question in depth and to transmit a re-port to all governments participating in the Diplomatic Conference. [82] Also the twenty-eighth UN General Assembly asked the Diplomatic Con-ference to consider "the question of the use of napalm and other in-cendiary weapons, as well as other specific conventional weapons which may be deemed to cause unnecessary suffering or to have indiscriminate effects, and to seek agreement on rules prohibiting or restricting the use of such weapons". [83] The UN resolution was adopted by a vote of 103 to none, with 18 abstentions. Of the great powers, only China voted in favour of the resolution; France, the United Kingdom, the USA and the USSR abstained. Those abstaining argued that the introduction of a major controversial subject into the agenda of the Diplomatic Conference might jeopardize the successful conclusion of its scheduled work on two draft protocols to the 1949 Geneva Conventions, relating to the protection of victims of international armed conflicts and the protection of victims of non-international conflicts. They thought that the matter would be best dealt with in a separate body, such as the CCD.

Another UN General Assembly resolution, dealing with "respect for human rights in armed conflicts'', urged the participants in the Diplomatic Conference to reach agreement on additional rules which might help to alleviate the suffering brought by armed conflicts and to protect non-combatants and civilian objects. It called upon all parties to armed conflicts to acknowledge and to comply with their obligations under the humanitarian instruments and to observe the international humanitarian rules, in particular the Hague Conventions of 1899 and 1907, the Geneva Protocol of 1925 and the Geneva Conventions of 1949. It urged that instruction concerning such rules be provided to armed forces and information concerning these rules be given to civilians, with a view to securing their strict observance. It also requested the UN Secretary-General to encourage the study and teaching of principles of international humanitarian rules applicable in armed conflicts. [84]

The question of particularly cruel and inhumane weapons can be dealt with both under humanitarian law and in the context of disarmament. In the first case, the aim is to prohibit or impose restraints on the use of the weapons in question; in the second case, the aim is to prohibit the development, production and stockpiling, that is, the very possession of these arms. The two approaches complement each other.

There exist rules of international law condemning, in a general way, the use of weapons that cause unnecessary suffering or which could lead to indiscriminate destruction and there is no need to revise or reformulate them. But, as it appears from the survey prepared by the UN Secretariat in 1973, [85] there are only a few treaties expressly prohibiting the use of specific weapons (see appendix 12E). Some of them are already obsolete; others, such as the Geneva Protocol of 1925, prohibiting the use of chemical and bacteriological methods of warfare, should be strengthened through a uniform, universally accepted interpretation of its provisions. A reaffirmation of the general as well as the specific rules in a new international instrument would be useful, but would have little practical value, unless supplemented by new bans. These bans, in turn, would be effective, if they were made all-inclusive and absolute, covering the use of inhumane weapons under any circumstances. Restrictions applying to the mode of employment, or to certain targets or to certain conditions only, regulating the use rather than prohibiting it altogether, could give rise to practical difficulties and controversies and prove unenforceable, even if an international mechanism were set up to ensure compliance. Thus, for example, it would be insufficient to prohibit the use of selected types of incendiaries, because new types of incendiary weapons could be developed and deployed, reducing or even nullifying the effectiveness of a selective ban. Moreover, a distinction between combatants and civilian populations would have little meaning in the case of weapons which by their very nature are indiscriminate in their effects. This applies, in the first place, to weapons of mass destruction. It would be logical, therefore, to focus the attention primarily on these weapons. Nevertheless, in the whole discussion on indiscriminate means of warfare, the most important category of weapons of mass destruction, namely nuclear weapons, which are mainly directed against population centres, has hardly been mentioned. Apparently, under the overruling pressure of the nuclear deterrence doctrine, most countries have opted for minimum solutions by concentrating on certain conventional weapons which have acquired notoriety in recent conflicts. (At the twenty-fifth UN General Assembly, Portugal was again accused of using napalm in the territories under its administration [86] and Israel of employing incendiaries and other cruel types of weapons in the Middle East War. [87]) The objective is, thus, rather limited. It is, nonetheless, worth pursuing in so far as progress in the development of humanitarian international law is concerned.

A prohibition of use of a given weapon does not necessarily lead to a cessation of its production. As is known, the existence of the Geneva Protocol banning the use of chemical and bacteriological weapons has not, by itself, prevented states from developing and deploying ever new types of warfare agents, especially chemical ones. However, a ban on use could facilitate negotiations on the physical elimination of weapons from the arsenals of states. While the conference on humanitarian law applicable in armed conflicts seems to be the proper forum to settle the question of the prohibition of the use of inhumane weapons, the disposal of these weapons could be discussed in a disarmament body.

# VIII. *The world disarmament conference*

No progress was made in 1973 in preparing a world disarmament conference which most countries consider desirable to promote and facilitate the adoption of effective measures of disarmament. As expected, [1c] the special committee whose members were appointed by the President of the UN General Assembly failed to perform the modest task of examining the views and suggestions expressed by governments on the convening of the conference. As a matter of fact, the committee was never properly constituted and did not produce a formal report. Only a few informal meetings and consultations took place, devoted almost exlusively to the composition of the committee. [88–89] The main problem was the participation of the nuclear-weapon powers, and it proved politically impossible to reconcile the presence of one of them, namely the USSR, which was specifically appointed by the UN General Assembly President as a member of the committee, with the absence of the remaining great powers—China, France, the UK and the USA—which had their seats "reserved", but refused to attend. As a result, the mandate of the General Assembly remained unfulfilled. Nevertheless, the twenty-eighth General Assembly decided to pursue the matter and established an *Ad Hoc* Committee consisting exclusively of non-nuclear-weapon member states: Algeria, Argentina, Austria, Belgium, Brazil, Bulgaria, Burundi, Canada, Chile, Colombia, Czechoslovakia, Egypt, Ethiopia, Hungary, India, Indonesia, Iran, Italy, Japan, Lebanon, Liberia, Mexico, Mongolia, Morocco, Netherlands, Nigeria, Pakistan, Peru, Philippines, Poland, Romania, Spain, Sri Lanka, Sweden, Tunisia, Turkey, Venezuela, Yugoslavia, Zaïre and Zambia.

The nuclear-weapon powers were not designated as members; they were invited to cooperate or maintain contact with the *Ad Hoc* Committee, "it being understood that they will enjoy the same rights as the designated members of the Committee". The latter provision is somewhat ambiguous as regards the status of the great powers, but there seems to be a tacit agreement that at least at the initial stage the work of the committee will be carried out without their direct involvement. The committee has not been entrusted with actual preparations for a world disarmament conference; like its unsuccessful predecessor, it has only to examine the views and suggestions on the convening of the conference and related problems, "including conditions for the realization of such a conference", and to submit a report on the basis of consensus. [90] The main purpose of this decision was to keep the whole idea alive.

## References

1. *World Armaments and Disarmament, SIPRI Yearbook 1973* (Stockholm, Almqvist & Wiksell, 1973, Stockholm International Peace Research Institute).
   (a) —, chapter 1.
   (b) —, p. 396.
   (c) —, chapter 12.
   (d) —, chapter 5.
2. *US Congressional Record-Senate*, S 21757, 4 December 1973.
3. UN document A/RES/3184A (XXVIII).
4. UN document A/RES/3184C (XXVII).
5. UN document A/RES/2936 (XXVII).
6. Disarmament Conference document CCD/361.
7. Disarmament Conference document CCD/413.
8. *New York Times*, 10 December 1973.
9. Disarmament Conference document CCD/PV.597.
10. Disarmament Conference document CCD/PV.625.
11. Disarmament Conference document CCD/PV.594.
12. Disarmament Conference document CCD/414.
13. Disarmament Conference document CCD/PV.623.
14. Disarmament Conference document CCD/395.
15. Disarmament Conference document CCD/403.
16. Disarmament Conference document CCD/PV.608.

17. *Chemical Disarmament: Some Problems of Verification,* SIPRI Monograph (Stockholm, Almqvist & Wiksell, 1973, Stockholm International Peace Research Institute).
18. Disarmament Conference document CCD/412.
19. Disarmament Conference document CCD/PV, 616.
20. Disarmament Conference document CCD/PV.591.
21. Disarmament Conference document CCD/400.
22. Disarmament Conference document CCD/410.
23. UN document A/C.1/PV.1948.
24. Disarmament Conference document CCD/PV.610.
25. Disarmament Conference document CCD/PV.593.
26. Disarmament Conference document CCD/PV.612.
27. Disarmament Conference document CCD/PV.587.
28. Disarmament Conference document CCD/PV.590.
29. Disarmament Conference document CCD/PV.617.
30. Disarmament Conference document CCD/PV.611.
31. Disarmament Conference document CCD/PV.624.
32. *The Problem of Chemical and Biological Warfare, Volume II: CB Weapons Today* (Stockholm, Almqvist & Wiksell, 1973, Stockholm International Peace Research Institute).
33. UN document A/RES/3077 (XXVIII).
34. UN document A/C.1/PV.1970.
35. Disarmament Conference document CCD/PV.625.
36. Disarmament Conference document CCD/PV.588.
37. Disarmament Conference document CCD/PV.614.
38. Disarmament Conference document CCD/PV.621.
39. Disarmament Conference document CCD/409.
40. Disarmament Conference document CCD/416.
41. *World Armaments and Disarmament, SIPRI Yearbook 1972* (Stockholm, Almqvist & Wiksell, 1972, Stockholm International Peace Research Institute) chapter 12.
42. Disarmament Conference document CCD/PV.604.
43. Disarmament Conference document CCD/PV.585.
44. Disarmament Conference document CCD/PV.596.
45. UN document A/C.1/PV.1938.
46. Disarmament Conference document CCD/PV.620.
47. UN document A/C.1/PV.1953.
48. UN document A/RES/3078A (XXVIII).
49. UN document A/RES/2992 (XXVII).
50. UN document A/9029.
51. UN document A/RES/2832 (XXVI).
52. UN document A/RES/3080 (XXVIII).
53. UN document A/C.1/PV.1955.
54. UN document A/C.1/PV.1969.
55. UN document A/AC.159/L.2 and Corr. 1.
56. *SIPRI Yearbook of World Armaments and Disarmament 1969/70* (Stockholm, Almqvist & Wiksell, 1970, Stockholm International Peace Research Institute) pp. 163–68.
57. UN document A/9191.
58. UN document A/L.701.
59. UN document A/PV.2178.
60. UN document A/L.701/Rev.1.

61. UN document A/PV.2154.
62. UN document A/PV.2194.
63. UN document A/PV.2180.
64. UN document A/PV.2175.
65. UN document A/RES/2626 (XXV).
66. UN document A/PV.2171.
67. UN document A/PV.2179.
68. UN document A/PV.2173.
69. UN document A/RES/3093A (XXVIII).
70. UN document A/RES/3093B (XXVIII).
71. UN document DC/SC.1/10.
72. Conference document CF/DOC/13 in the Geneva Conference of Heads of Government, 18–23 July 1955.
73. UN document DC/SC.1/PV.87.
74. Disarmament and Development, United Nations publication. Sales No. E.73.IX.1.
75. *The Meaning and Measurement of Military Expenditure,* SIPRI Research Report No. 10 (Stockholm, Almqvist & Wiksell, 1973, Stockholm International Peace Research Institute).
76. UN document DC/SC.1/9.
77. *Pravda,* 15 December 1973.
78. United Nations publication. Sales No. E.73.I.3.
79. UN document A/9207 and Corr.1.
80. *Weapons That May Cause Unnecessary Suffering or Have Indiscriminate Effects,* Report on the work of experts (Geneva, 1973, International Committee of the Red Cross).
81. *Conventional Weapons, Their Deployment and Effects From a Humanitarian Aspect,* A Swedish Working Group Study (Stockholm, 1973).
82. UN document A/9123/Add.2.
83. UN document A/RES/3076 (XXVIII).
84. UN document A/RES/3102 (XXVIII).
85. UN document A/9215.
86. UN document A/RES/3113 (XXVIII).
87. UN document A/C.6/SR.1454.
88. UN document A/9228.
89. UN document A/C.1/PV.1934.
90. UN document A/RES/3183 (XXVIII).

# Appendix 12A

*Basic principles of negotiations on the further limitation of strategic offensive arms Agreement between the United States of America and the Union of Soviet Socialist Republics*

The President of the United States of America, Richard Nixon, and the General Secretary of the Central Committee of the CPSU, L. I. Brezhnev,

Having thoroughly considered the question of the further limitation of the strategic arms, and the progress already achieved in the current negotiations,

Reaffirming their conviction that the earliest adoption of further limitations of strategic arms would be a major contribution in reducing the danger of an outbreak of nuclear war and in strengthening international peace and security,

Have agreed as follows:

*First.* The two Sides will continue active negotiations in order to work out a permanent agreement on more complete measures on the limitation of strategic offensive arms, as well as their subsequent reduction, proceeding from the Basic Principles of Relations between the United States of America and the Union of Soviet Socialist Republics signed in Moscow on May 29, 1972, and from the Interim Agreement between the United States of America and the Union of Soviet Socialist Republics of May 26, 1972 on Certain Measures with Respect to the Limitation of Strategic Offensive Arms.

Over the course of the next year the two Sides will make serious efforts to work out the provisions of the permanent agreement on more complete measures on the limitation of strategic offensive arms with the objective of signing it in 1974.

*Second.* New agreements on the limitation of strategic offensive armaments will be based on the principles of the American-Soviet documents adopted in Moscow in May 1972 and the agreements reached in Washington in June 1973; and in particular, both Sides will be guided by the recognition of each other's equal security interests and by the recognition that efforts to obtain unilateral advantage, directly or indirectly, would be inconsistent with the strengthening of peaceful relations between the United States of America and the Union of Soviet Socialist Republics.

*Third.* The limitations placed on strategic offensive weapons can apply both to their quantitative aspects as well as to their qualitative improvement.

*Fourth.* Limitations on strategic offensive arms must be subject to adequate verification by national technical means.

*Fifth.* The modernization and replacement of strategic offensive arms would be permitted under conditions which will be formulated in the agreements to be concluded.

*Sixth.* Pending the completion of a permanent agreement on more complete measures of strategic offensive arms limitation, both Sides are prepared to reach agreements on separate measures to supplement the existing Interim Agreement of May 26, 1972.

*Seventh.* Each Side will continue to take necessary organizational and technical measures for preventing accidental or unauthorized use of nuclear weapons under its control in accordance with the Agreement of September 30, 1971 between the United States of America and the Union of Soviet Socialist Republics.

Washington, June 21, 1973

# Appendix 12B

*Agreement between the United States of America and the Union of Soviet Socialist Republics on the prevention of nuclear war*

The United States of America and the Union of Soviet Socialist Republics, hereinafter referred to as the Parties,

Guided by the objectives of strengthening world peace and international security,

Conscious that nuclear war would have devastating consequences for mankind,

Proceeding from the desire to bring about conditions in which the danger of an outbreak of nuclear war anywhere in the world would be reduced and ultimately eliminated,

Proceeding from their obligations under the Charter of the United Nations regarding the maintenance of peace, refraining from the threat or use of force, and the avoidance of war, and in conformity with the agreements to which either Party has subscribed,

Proceeding from the Basic Principles of Relations between the United States of America and the Union of Soviet Socialist Republics signed in Moscow on May 29, 1972,

Reaffirming that the development of relations between the United States of America and the Union of Soviet Socialist Republics is not directed against other countries and their interests,

Have agreed as follows:

ARTICLE I

The United States and the Soviet Union agree that an objective of their policies is to remove the danger of nuclear war and of the use of nuclear weapons.

Accordingly, the Parties agree that they will act in such a manner as to prevent the development of situations capable of causing a dangerous exacerbation of their relations, as to avoid military confrontations, and as to exclude the outbreak of nuclear war between them and between either of the Parties and other countries.

ARTICLE II

The Parties agree, in accordance with Article I and to realize the objective stated in that Article, to proceed from the premise that each Party will refrain from the threat or use of force against the other Party, against the allies of the other Party and against other countries, in circumstances which may endanger international peace and security. The Parties agree that they will be guided by these considerations in the formulation of their foreign policies and in their actions in the field of international relations.

ARTICLE III

The Parties undertake to develop their relations with each other and with other countries in a way consistent with the purposes of this Agreement.

ARTICLE IV

If at any time relations between the Parties or between either Party and other countries appear to involve the risk of a nuclear conflict, or if relations between countries not parties to this Agreement appear to involve the risk of nuclear war between the United States of America and the Union of Soviet Socialist Republics or between either Party and other countries, the United States and the Soviet Union, acting in accordance with the provisions of this Agreement, shall immediately enter into urgent consultations with each other and make every effort to avert this risk.

ARTICLE V

Each Party shall be free to inform the Security Council of the United Nations, the Secretary General of the United Nations and the Governments of allied or other countries of the progress and outcome of consultations initiated in accordance with Article IV of this Agreement.

ARTICLE VI

Nothing in this Agreement shall effect or impair:

(a) the inherent right of individual or collective self-defense as envisaged by Article 51 of the Charter of the United Nations,

(b) the provisions of the Charter of the United Nations, including those relating to the maintenance or restoration of international peace and security, and

(c) the obligations undertaken by either Party towards its allies or other countries in treaties, agreements, and other appropriate documents.

ARTICLE VII

This Agreement shall be of unlimited duration.

ARTICLE VIII

This Agreement shall enter into force upon signature.

DONE at Washington on June 22, 1973, in two copies, each in the English and Russian languages, both texts being equally authentic.

# Appendix 12C

*List of states which have signed, ratified, acceded or suceeded to the Geneva Protocol of 17 June 1925, for the prohibition of the use in war of asphyxiating, poisonous and other gases, and of bacteriological methods of warfare, as of 31 December 1973*

**Note**

Some states, former non-self-governing territories, acceded to the Geneva Protocol without referring to the obligations previously undertaken on their behalf by the colonial power. In these cases, the date of the notification by the government of France, the depositary government, is indicated as the date of entry into force of the accession for the countries concerned, in accordance with paragraph 2 of the operative part of the Protocol.

Other states, former non-self-governing territories, officially informed the government of France that they consider themselves bound by the Geneva Protocol by virtue of its ratification by the power formerly responsible for their administration. In such cases of continuity of obligations under the Geneva Protocol, the date of receipt of the country's notification by the French government is indicated. In the absence of a statement to the contrary the succession is regarded as applying also to reservations attached to the ratification of the Protocol.

States which, upon attaining independence, made general statements of continuity to the treaties concluded by the power formerly responsible for their administration, but have not notified the government of France that their statements specifically applied to the Geneva Protocol, are not listed here.

To determine the actual number of parties to the Geneva Protocol, account should also be taken of the facts that Estonia, Latvia and Lithuania, which signed and ratified the Protocol, no longer have independent status; both the Federal Republic of Germany and the German Democratic Republic are bound by ratification on behalf of Germany; both the People's Republic of China and Taiwan are bound by accession on behalf of China.

(The text of the Geneva Protocol can be found in appendix 12E.)

## I. List of signatories and ratifications

| *Signatory* | *Deposit of ratification* | |
|---|---|---|
| Austria | 9 May | 1928 |
| Belgium | 4 Dec | 1928[1] |

| | | |
|---|---|---|
| Brazil | 28 Aug | 1970 |
| British Empire | 9 Apr | 1930[2] |
| Bulgaria | 7 Mar | 1934[3] |
| Canada | 6 May | 1930[4] |
| Chile | 2 Jul | 1935[5] |
| Czechoslovakia | 16 Aug | 1938[6] |
| Denmark | 5 May | 1930 |
| Egypt | 6 Dec | 1928 |
| El Salvador | | |
| Estonia | 28 Aug | 1931[7] |
| Ethiopia | 20 Sep | 1935[8] |
| Finland | 26 Jun | 1929 |
| France | 10 May | 1926[9] |
| Germany | 25 Apr | 1929[10] |
| Greece | 30 May | 1931 |
| India | 9 Apr | 1930[11] |
| Italy | 3 Apr | 1928 |
| Japan | 21 May | 1970 |
| Latvia | 3 Jun | 1931 |
| Lithuania | 15 Jun | 1933 |
| Luxembourg | 1 Sep | 1936 |
| Netherlands | 31 Oct | 1930[12] |
| Nicaragua | | |
| Norway | 27 Jul | 1932 |
| Poland | 4 Feb | 1929 |
| Portugal | 1 Jul | 1930[13] |
| Romania | 23 Aug | 1929[14] |
| Serbs, Croats and Slovenes, | | |
| Kingdom of the (Yugoslavia) | 12 Apr | 1929[15] |
| Siam (Thailand) | 6 Jun | 1931 |
| Spain | 22 Aug | 1929[16] |
| Sweden | 25 Apr | 1930 |
| Switzerland | 12 Jul | 1932 |
| Turkey | 5 Oct | 1929 |
| USA | | |
| Uruguay | | |
| Venezuela | 8 Feb | 1928 |

## II. List of accessions and successions

| Country | Notification | |
|---|---|---|
| Argentina | 12 May | 1969 |
| Australia | 24 May | 1930[17] |

| | | |
|---|---|---|
| Central African Republic | 31 Jul | 1970 |
| Ceylon (Sri Lanka) | 20 Jan | 1954 |
| China | 24 Aug | 1929[18] |
| Cuba | 24 Jun | 1966 |
| Cyprus | 29 Nov | 1966[19] |
| Dominican Republic | 8 Dec | 1970 |
| Ecuador | 16 Sep | 1970 |
| Fiji | 21 Mar | 1973[20] |
| Gambia | 5 Nov | 1966[21] |
| Ghana | 3 May | 1967 |
| Holy See | 18 Oct | 1966 |
| Hungary | 11 Oct | 1952 |
| Iceland | 2 Nov | 1967 |
| Indonesia | 21 Jan | 1971[22] |
| Iraq | 8 Sep | 1931[23] |
| Irish Free State (Ireland) | 29 Aug | 1930[24] |
| Israel | 20 Feb | 1969[25] |
| Ivory Coast | 27 Jul | 1970 |
| Jamaica | 28 Jul | 1970[26] |
| Kenya | 6 Jul | 1970 |
| Kuwait | 15 Dec | 1971[27] |
| Lebanon | 17 Apr | 1969 |
| Lesotho | 10 Mar | 1972[28] |
| Liberia | 17 Jun | 1927 |
| Libyan Arab Republic | 29 Dec | 1971[29] |
| Malagasy Republic | 2 Aug | 1967 |
| Malaysia | 10 Dec | 1970 |
| Malawi | 14 Sep | 1970 |
| Maldives | 27 Dec | 1966[30] |
| Malta | 9 Oct | 1970[31] |
| Mauritius | 23 Dec | 1970[32] |
| Mexico | 28 May | 1932 |
| Monaco | 6 Jan | 1967 |
| Mongolia | 6 Dec | 1968[33] |
| Morocco | 13 Oct | 1970 |
| Nepal | 9 May | 1969 |
| New Zealand | 24 May | 1930[34] |
| Niger | 5 Apr | 1967[35] |
| Nigeria | 15 Oct | 1968[36] |
| Pakistan | 15 Apr | 1960[37] |
| Panama | 4 Dec | 1970 |
| Paraguay | 22 Oct | 1933[38] |
| Persia (Iran) | 5 Nov | 1929 |
| Philippines | 8 Jun | 1973 |

| | | |
|---|---|---|
| Rwanda | 11 May | 1964[39] |
| Saudi Arabia | 27 Jan | 1971 |
| Sierra Leone | 20 Mar | 1967 |
| South Africa | 24 May | 1930[40] |
| Syrian Arab Republic | 17 Dec | 1968[41] |
| Togo | 5 Apr | 1971 |
| Tonga | 28 Jul | 1971 |
| Trinidad and Tobago | 24 Nov | 1970[42] |
| Tunisia | 12 Jul | 1967 |
| Uganda | 24 May | 1965 |
| United Republic of Tanzania | 22 Apr | 1963 |
| Upper Volta | 3 Mar | 1971 |
| USSR | 15 Apr | 1928[43] |
| Yemen | 17 Mar | 1971 |

[1] (1) The said Protocol is only binding on the Belgian government as regards States which have signed or ratified it or which may accede to it. (2) The said Protocol shall *ipso facto* cease to be binding on the Belgian government in regard to any enemy State whose armed forces or whose allies fail to respect the prohibitions laid down in the Protocol.

[2] The British Plenipotentiary declared when signing: "my signature does not bind India or any British Dominion which is a separate Member of the League of Nations and does not separately sign or adhere to the Protocol".

(1) The said Protocol is only binding on His Britannic Majesty as regards those Powers and States which have both signed and ratified the Protocol or have finally acceded thereto. (2) The said Protocol shall cease to be binding on His Britannic Majesty towards any Power at enmity with Him whose armed forces, or the armed forces of whose allies, fail to respect the prohibitions laid down in the Protocol.

[3] The said Protocol is only binding on the Bulgarian government as regards States which have signed or ratified it or which may accede to it. The said Protocol shall *ipso facto* cease to be binding on the Bulgarian government in regard to any enemy State whose armed forces or whose allies fail to respect the prohibitions laid down in the Protocol.

[4] (1) The Said Protocol is only binding on His Britannic Majesty as regards those States which have both signed and ratified it, or have finally acceded thereto. (2) The said Protocol shall cease to be binding on His Britannic Majesty towards any State at enmity with Him whose armed forces, or whose allies *de jure* or in fact fail to respect the prohibitions laid down in the Protocol.

[5] (1) The said Protocol is only binding on the Chilean government as regards States which have signed and ratified it or which may definitely accede to it. (2) The said Protocol shall *ipso facto* cease to be binding on the Chilean government in regard to any enemy State whose armed forces, or whose allies, fail to respect the prohibitions which are the object of this Protocol.

[6] The Czechoslovak Republic shall *ipso facto* cease to be bound by this Protocol towards any State whose armed forces, or the armed forces of whose allies, fail to respect the prohibitions laid down in the Protocol.

[7] (1) The said Protocol is only binding on the Estonian government as regards States which have signed or ratified it or which may accede to it. (2) The said Protocol shall *ipso facto* cease to be binding on the Estonian government in regard to any enemy State whose armed forces or whose allies fail to respect the prohibitions laid down in the Protocol.

[8] The document deposited by Ethiopia, a signer of the Protocol, is registered as an accession. The date given is therefore the date of notification by the French government.

[9] (1) The said Protocol is only binding on the government of the French Republic as regards States which have signed or ratified it or which may accede to it. (2) The said Protocol shall *ipso facto* cease to be binding on the government of the French Republic in regard to any enemy State whose armed forces or whose allies fail to respect the prohibitions laid down in the Protocol.

[10] On 2 March 1959, the embassy of Czechoslovakia transmitted to the French Ministry for Foreign Affairs a document stating the applicability of the Protocol to the German Democratic Republic.

[11] (1) The said Protocol is only binding on His Britannic Majesty as regards those States which have both signed and ratified it, or have finally acceded thereto. (2) The said Protocol shall cease to be binding on His Britannic Majesty towards any Power at enmity with Him whose armed forces, or the armed forces of whose allies, fail to respect the prohibitions laid down in the Protocol.

[12] Including Netherlands Indies, Surinam and Curaçao.

As regards the use in war of asphyxiating, poisonous or other gases, and of all analogous liquids, materials or devices, this Protocol shall *ipso facto* cease to be binding on the Royal Netherlands government with regard to any enemy State whose armed forces or whose allies fail to respect the prohibitions laid down in the Protocol.

[13] (1) The said Protocol is only binding on the government of the Portuguese Republic as regards States which have signed and ratified it or which may accede to it. (2) The said Protocol shall *ipso facto* cease to be binding on the government of the Portuguese Republic in regard to any enemy State whose armed forces or whose allies fail to respect the prohibitions which are the object of this Protocol.

[14] (1) The said Protocol only binds the Romanian government in relation to States which have signed and ratified or which have definitely acceded to the Protocol. (2) The said Protocol shall cease to be binding on the Romanian government in regard to all enemy States whose armed forces or whose allies *de jure* or in fact do not respect the restrictions which are the object of this Protocol.

[15] The said Protocol shall cease to be binding on the government of the Serbs, Croats and Slovenes in regard to any enemy State whose armed forces or whose allies fail to respect the prohibitions which are the object of this Protocol.

[16] Declares as binding *ipso facto,* without special agreement with respect to any other Member or State accepting and observing the same obligation, that is to say, on condition of reciprocity, the Protocol for the Prohibition of the Use in War of Asphyxiating, Poisonous and other Gases and of Bacteriological Methods of Warfare, signed at Geneva on 17 June, 1925.

[17] Subject to the reservations that His Majesty is bound by the said Protocol only towards those Powers and States which have both signed and ratified the Protocol or have acceded thereto, and that His Majesty shall cease to be bound by the Protocol towards any Power at enmity with Him whose armed forces, or the armed forces of whose allies, do not respect the Protocol.

[18] On 13 July 1952, the People's Republic of China issued a statement recognizing as binding upon it the accession to the Protocol in the name of China. The People's Republic of China considers itself bound by the Protocol on condition of reciprocity on the part of all the other contracting and acceding powers.

[19] In a note of 21 November 1966, Cyprus declared that it was bound by the Protocol which had been made applicable to it by the British Empire.

[20] In a declaration of succession of 26 January 1973 addressed to the depositary government, the government of Fiji confirmed that the provisions of the Protocol were applicable to it by virtue of the ratification by the United Kingdom. The Protocol is only binding on Fiji as regards states which have both signed and ratified it and which will have finally acceded thereto. The Protocol shall cease to be binding on Fiji in regard to any enemy state whose armed forces or the armed forces of whose allies fail to respect the prohibitions which are the object of the Protocol.

[21] In a declaration of 11 October 1966, Gambia confirmed its participation in the Protocol which had been made applicable to it by the British Empire.

[22] In an official declaration of 13 January 1971 addressed to the French government, the government of Indonesia reaffirmed its acceptance of the Geneva Protocol which had been ratified on its behalf by the Netherlands on 31 October 1930, and stated that it remained signatory to that Protocol.

[23] On condition that the Iraq government shall be bound by the provisions of the Protocol only towards those States which have both signed and ratified it or have acceded thereto, and that it shall not be bound by the Protocol towards any State at enmity with Iraq whose armed forces, or the forces of whose allies, do not respect the provisions of the Protocol.

[24] The government of the Irish Free State does not intend to assume, by this accession, any obligation except towards the States having signed and ratified this Protocol or which shall have finally acceded thereto, and should the armed forces or the allies of an enemy State fail to respect the said Protocol, the government of the Irish Free State would cease to be bound by the said Protocol in regard to such State. In a note of 7 February 1972, received by the depositary government on 10 February 1972, the government of Ireland declared that it had decided to withdraw the above reservations made at the time of accession to the Protocol.

[25] The said Protocol is only binding on the State of Israel as regards States which have signed and ratified or acceded to it. The said Protocol shall cease *ipso facto* to be binding on the State of Israel as regards any enemy State whose armed forces, or the armed forces of whose allies,

or the regular or irregular forces, or groups or individuals operating from its territory, fail to respect the prohibitions which are the object of this Protocol.

[26] On this date Jamaica declared to the depositary government that it considered itself bound by the provisions of the Protocol on the basis of the ratification by the British Empire in 1930.

[27] The accession of the State of Kuwait to this Protocol does not in any way imply recognition of Israel or the establishment of relations with the latter on the basis of the present Protocol. In case of breach of the prohibition mentioned in this Protocol by any of the Parties, the State of Kuwait will not be bound, with regard to the Party committing the breach, to apply the provisions of this Protocol. In a note of 25 January 1972, addressed to the depositary government, Israel objected to the above reservations.

[28] By a note of 10 February 1972 addressed to the depositary government, Lesotho confirmed that the provisions of the Protocol were applicable to it by virtue of the ratification by the British Empire on 9 April 1930.

[29] The accession to the Protocol does not imply recognition or the establishment of any relations with Israel. The present Protocol is binding on the Libyan Arab Republic only as regards States which are effectively bound by it and will cease to be binding on the Libyan Arab Republic as regards States whose armed forces, or the armed forces of whose allies, il to respect the prohibitions which are the object of this Protocol. In a note of 25 January 1972 addressed to the depositary government, Israel objected to the above reservations.

[30] In a declaration of 19 December 1966, Maldives confirmed its adherence to the Protocol.

[31] By a notification of 25 September 1970, the government of Malta informed the French government that it considered itself bound by the Geneva Protocol as from 21 September 1964, the provisions of the Protocol having been extended to Malta by the government of the United Kingdom, prior to the former's accession to independence.

[32] By a notification of 27 November 1970, the government of Mauritius informed the French government that it considered itself bound by the Geneva Protocol as from 12 March 1968, the date of its accession to independence.

[33] In the case of violation of this prohibition by any State in relation to the People's Republic of Mongolia or its allies, the government of the People's Republic of Mongolia shall not consider itself bound by the obligations of the Protocol towards that State.

[34] Same reservations as Australia. (See footnote 17.)

[35] In a letter of 18 March 1967, Niger declared that it was bound by the adherence of France to the Protocol.

[36] The Protocol is only binding on Nigeria as regards States which are effectively bound by it and shall cease to be binding on Nigeria as regards States whose forces or whose allies' armed forces fail to respect the prohibitions which are the object of the Protocol.

[37] By a note of 13 April 1960, Pakistan informed the depositary government that it was a party to the Protocol by virtue of Paragraph 4 of the Annex to the Indian Independence Act of 1947.

[38] This is the date of receipt of the instrument of accession. The date of the notification by the French government "for the purpose of regularization" is 13 January 1969.

[39] In a declaration of 21 March 1964, Rwanda recognized that it was bound by the Protocol which had been made applicable to it by Belgium.

[40] Same reservations as Australia. (See footnote 17.)

[41] The accession by the Syrian Arab Republic to this Protocol and the ratification of the Protocol by its government does not in any case imply recognition of Israel or lead to the establishment of relations with the latter concerning the provisions laid down in this Protocol.

[42] By a note of 9 October 1970, the government of Trinidad and Tobago notified the French government that it considered itself bound by the Protocol, the provisions of which had been made applicable to Trinidad and Tobago by the British Empire prior to the former's accession to independence.

[43] (1) The said Protocol only binds the government of the Union of Soviet Socialist Republics in relation to the States which have signed and ratified or which have definitely acceded to the Protocol. (2) The said Protocol shall cease to be binding on the government of the Union of Soviet Socialist Republics in regard to any enemy State whose armed forces or whose allies de jure or in fact do not respect the prohibitions which are the object of this Protocol.

On 2 March 1970, the Byelorussian Soviet Socialist Republic stated that "it recognizes itself to be a Party" to the Geneva Protocol of 1925 (United Nations doc. A/8052, Annex III).

# Appendix 12D

*Documents relating to the question of a comprehensive test ban, presented for discussion at the 1973 session of the Conference of the Committee on Disarmament (CCD)*

1. CCD/397; Sweden: Working Paper with points to be considered by experts on the verification of a ban on underground nuclear explosions.
2. CCD/399; Japan: Working Paper on problems in determining the body wave magnitudes.
3. CCD/401; United Kingdom: Working Paper on a review of the United Kingdom seismological research and development programme.
4. CCD/402; United Kingdom: Working Paper on the estimation of depth of seismic events.
5. CCD/404; United States: A programme of research related to problems in seismic verification.
6. CCD/405; Sweden: Working Paper reviewing recent Swedish scientific work on the verification of a ban on underground nuclear explosions.
7. CCD/406; Canada: The verification of a comprehensive test ban by seismological means.
8. CCD/407; United States: Comments on CCD/399 (Japan), concerning magnitude determinations.
9. CCD/408; Japan: Working Paper on comparison between earthquakes and underground explosions observed at Mutsushiro Seismological Observatory.
10. CCD/409; Italy: Some observations on detection and identification of underground nuclear explosions—prospects of international co-operation.
11. CCD/411; Norway: Working Paper on seismic research at the Norwegian Seismic Array (NORSAR).
12. CCD/416; Netherlands: Some observations on the verification of a ban on underground nuclear test explosions.

# Appendix 12E

*Treaties expressly prohibiting the use of specific conventional (non-nuclear) weapons*

## I. *Poison and poisoned weapons; chemical and bacteriological weapons*

1. At the 1899 Hague International Peace Conference the following Declaration (IV, 2) was signed on 29 July 1899: "The contracting Powers agree to abstain from the use of projectiles the sole object of which is the diffusion of asphyxiating or deleterious gases."

2. The regulations annexed to the 1899 Hague Convention (II) and to the 1907 Hague Convention (IV) state in article 23 (a) that besides the prohibitions provided by special conventions it is especially prohibited or forbidden . . . "to employ poison or poisoned arms".

3. On 7 February 1923, the Convention on the Limitation of Armaments of Central American States was signed at Washington. Article 5 of that Convention states that:

The Contracting Parties consider that the use in warfare of asphyxiating gases, poisons, or similar substances as well as analogous liquids, materials or devices, is contrary to humanitarian principles and to international law, and obligate themselves by the present Convention not to use said substances in time of war.

4. The Protocol for the prohibition of the use in war of asphyxiating, poisonous or other gases, and of bacteriological methods of warfare was signed at Geneva on 17 June 1925:

The undersigned Plenipotentiaries, in the name of their respective Governments:
Whereas the use in war of asphyxiating, poisonous or other gases, and of all analogous liquids, materials or devices, has been justly condemned by the general opinion of the civilised world; and
Whereas the prohibition of such use has been declared in Treaties to which the majority of Powers of the world are Parties; and
To the end that this prohibition shall be universally accepted as a part of International Law, binding alike the conscience and the practice of nations;
Declare:
That the High Contracting Parties, so far as they are not already Parties to Treaties prohibiting such use, accept this prohibition, agree to extend this prohibition to the use of bacteriological methods of warfare and agree to be bound as between themselves according to the terms of this declaration.
The High Contracting Parties will exert every effort to induce other States to accede to the present Protocol. Such accession will be notified to the Government of the French Republic, and by the latter to all signatory and acceding Powers,

and will take effect on the date of the notification by the Government of the French Republic.

The present Protocol, of which the French and English texts are both authentic, shall be ratified as soon as possible. It shall bear to-day's date.

The ratifications of the present Protocol shall be addressed to the Government of the French Republic, which will at once notify the deposit of such ratification to each of the signatory and acceding Powers.

The instruments of ratification of and accession to the present Protocol will remain deposited in the archives of the Government of the French Republic.

The present Protocol will come into force for each signatory Power as from the date of deposit of its ratification, and, from that moment, each Power will be bound as regards other Powers which have already deposited their ratifications.

## II. *Projectiles of various kinds;*[1] *incendiary weapons*

1. The St. Petersburg Declaration of 29 November 1868 includes the following:

The contracting parties engage, mutually, to renounce, in case of war among themselves, the employment, by their military or naval forces, of any projectile of less weight than four hundred grammes which is explosive, or is charged with fulminating or inflammable substances.

2. The Hague Declaration (IV, 3) concerning expanding bullets ("Dum-Dum" bullets) was signed on 29 July 1899:

The contracting Parties agree to abstain from the use of bullets which expand or flatten easily in the human body, such as bullets with a hard envelope which does not entirely cover the core or is pierced with incisions.

---

[1] The 1899 Hague Declaration (IV,2) concerning projectiles, the sole object of which is the diffusion of asphyxiating or deleterious gases, is included in section I.

# Appendix 12F

*UN General Assembly resolutions on disarmament and related matters*

## I. *Member states of the United Nations as of 18 September 1973*

Total membership: 135.

| Member | Date of admission | |
|---|---|---|
| Afghanistan | 19 Nov | 1946 |
| Albania | 14 Dec | 1955 |
| Algeria | 8 Oct | 1962 |
| Argentina | 24 Oct | 1945 |
| Australia | 1 Nov | 1945 |
| Austria | 14 Dec | 1955 |
| Bahamas | 18 Sep | 1973 |
| Bahrain | 21 Sep | 1971 |
| Barbados | 9 Dec | 1966 |
| Belgium | 27 Dec | 1945 |
| Bhutan | 21 Sep | 1971 |
| Bolivia | 14 Nov | 1945 |
| Botswana | 17 Oct | 1966 |
| Brazil | 24 Oct | 1945 |
| Bulgaria | 14 Dec | 1955 |
| Burma | 19 Apr | 1948 |
| Burundi | 18 Sep | 1962 |
| Byelorussian Soviet Socialist Republic | 24 Oct | 1945 |
| Cameroon | 20 Sep | 1960 |
| Canada | 9 Nov | 1945 |
| Central African Republic | 20 Sep | 1960 |
| Chad | 20 Sep | 1960 |
| Chile | 24 Oct | 1945 |
| China | 24 Oct | 1945 |
| Colombia | 5 Nov | 1945 |
| Congo | 20 Sep | 1960 |
| Costa Rica | 2 Nov | 1945 |

| | | |
|---|---|---|
| Cuba | 24 Oct | 1945 |
| Cyprus | 20 Sep | 1960 |
| Czecholovakia | 24 Oct | 1945 |
| Dahomey | 20 Sep | 1960 |
| Democratic Yemen[a] | 14 Dec | 1967 |
| Denmark | 24 Oct | 1945 |
| Dominican Republic | 24 Oct | 1945 |
| Ecuador | 21 Dec | 1945 |
| Egypt[b] | 24 Oct | 1945 |
| El Salvador | 24 Oct | 1945 |
| Equatorial Guinea | 12 Nov | 1968 |
| Ethiopia | 13 Nov | 1945 |
| Fiji | 13 Oct | 1970 |
| Finland | 14 Dec | 1955 |
| France | 24 Oct | 1945 |
| Gabon | 20 Sep | 1960 |
| Gambia | 21 Sep | 1965 |
| German Democratic Republic | 18 Sep | 1973 |
| Germany, Federal Republic of | 18 Sep | 1973 |
| Ghana | 8 Mar | 1957 |
| Greece | 25 Oct | 1945 |
| Guatemala | 21 Nov | 1945 |
| Guinea | 12 Dec | 1958 |
| Guyana | 20 Sep | 1966 |
| Haiti | 24 Oct | 1945 |
| Honduras | 17 Dec | 1945 |
| Hungary | 14 Dec | 1955 |
| Iceland | 19 Dec | 1946 |
| India | 30 Oct | 1945 |
| Indonesia[c] | 28 Sep | 1950 |
| Iran | 24 Oct | 1945 |
| Iraq | 21 Dec | 1945 |
| Ireland | 14 Dec | 1955 |
| Israel | 11 May | 1949 |
| Italy | 14 Dec | 1955 |
| Ivory Coast | 20 Sep | 1960 |
| Jamaica | 18 Sep | 1962 |
| Japan | 18 Dec | 1956 |
| Jordan | 14 Dec | 1955 |
| Kenya | 16 Dec | 1963 |
| Khmer Republic | 14 Dec | 1955 |
| Kuwait | 14 May | 1963 |
| Laos | 14 Dec | 1955 |
| Lebanon | 24 Oct | 1945 |

| | | |
|---|---|---|
| Lesotho | 17 Oct | 1966 |
| Liberia | 2 Nov | 1945 |
| Libyan Arab Republic | 14 Dec | 1955 |
| Luxembourg | 24 Oct | 1945 |
| Madagascar | 20 Sep | 1960 |
| Malawi | 1 Dec | 1964 |
| Malaysia[d] | 17 Sep | 1957 |
| Maldives | 21 Sep | 1965 |
| Mali | 28 Sep | 1960 |
| Malta | 1 Dec | 1964 |
| Mauritania | 27 Oct | 1961 |
| Mauritius | 24 Apr | 1968 |
| Mexico | 7 Nov | 1945 |
| Mongolia | 27 Oct | 1961 |
| Morocco | 12 Nov | 1956 |
| Nepal | 14 Dec | 1955 |
| Netherlands | 10 Dec | 1945 |
| New Zealand | 24 Oct | 1945 |
| Nicaragua | 24 Oct | 1945 |
| Niger | 20 Sep | 1960 |
| Nigeria | 7 Oct | 1960 |
| Norway | 27 Nov | 1945 |
| Oman | 7 Oct | 1971 |
| Pakistan | 30 Sep | 1947 |
| Panama | 13 Nov | 1945 |
| Paraguay | 24 Oct | 1945 |
| Peru | 31 Oct | 1945 |
| Philippines | 24 Oct | 1945 |
| Poland | 24 Oct | 1945 |
| Portugal | 14 Dec | 1955 |
| Qatar | 21 Sep | 1971 |
| Romania | 14 Dec | 1955 |
| Rwanda | 18 Sep | 1962 |
| Saudi Arabia | 24 Oct | 1945 |
| Senegal | 28 Sep | 1960 |
| Sierra Leone | 27 Sep | 1961 |
| Singapore | 21 Sep | 1965 |
| Somalia | 20 Sep | 1960 |
| South Africa | 7 Nov | 1945 |
| Spain | 14 Dec | 1955 |
| Sri Lanka[e] | 14 Dec | 1955 |
| Sudan | 12 Nov | 1956 |
| Swaziland | 24 Sep | 1968 |
| Sweden | 19 Nov | 1946 |

| | | |
|---|---|---|
| Syrian Arab Republic[b] | 24 Oct | 1945 |
| (resumed | 13 Oct | 1961) |
| Thailand | 16 Dec | 1946 |
| Togo | 20 Sep | 1960 |
| Trinidad and Tobago | 18 Sep | 1962 |
| Tunisia | 12 Nov | 1956 |
| Turkey | 24 Oct | 1945 |
| Uganda | 25 Oct | 1962 |
| Ukrainian Soviet Socialist Republic | 24 Oct | 1945 |
| Union of Soviet Socialist Republics | 24 Oct | 1945 |
| United Arab Emirates | 9 Dec | 1971 |
| United Kingdom | 24 Oct | 1945 |
| United Republic of Tanzania[f] | 14 Dec | 1961 |
| United States of America | 24 Oct | 1945 |
| Upper Volta | 20 Sep | 1960 |
| Uruguay | 18 Dec | 1945 |
| Venezuela | 15 Nov | 1945 |
| Yemen | 30 Sep | 1947 |
| Yugoslavia | 24 Oct | 1945 |
| Zaïre | 20 Sep | 1960 |
| Zambia | 1 Dec | 1964 |

[a] Formerly listed as People's Democratic Republic of Yemen.

[b] Egypt and Syria were original members of the United Nations from 24 October 1945. Following a plebiscite on 21 February 1958, the United Arab Republic was established by a union of Egypt and Syria and continued as a single member. On 13 October 1961, Syria, having resumed its status as an independent state, resumed its separate membership in the United Nations. On 2 September 1971, the United Arab Republic changed its name to Arab Republic of Egypt.

[c] By letter of 20 January 1965, Indonesia announced its decision to withdraw from the United Nations "at this stage and under the present circumstances". By telegram of 19 September 1966, it announced its decision "to resume full co-operation with the United Nations and to resume participation in its activities". On 28 September 1966, the General Assembly took note of this decision and the president invited representatives of Indonesia to take seats in the Assembly.

[d] The Federation of Malaya joined the United Nations on 17 September 1957. On 16 September 1963, its name changed to Malaysia, following the admission to the new federation of Singapore, Sabah (North Borneo) and Sarawak. Singapore became an independent State on 9 Augusti 1965 and a member of the United Nations on 21 September 1965.

[e] Formerly Ceylon.

[f] Tanganyika was a member of the United Nations from 14 December 1961 and Zanzibar was a member from 16 December 1963. Following the ratification on 26 April 1964, of Articles of Union between Tanganyika and Zanzibar, the United Republic of Tanganyika and Zanzibar continued as a single member, changing its name to United Republic of Tanzania on 1 November 1964.

## II. *List of UN resolutions adopted in 1973*

The list includes resolutions exclusively concerning disarmament, as well as those dealing with economic, colonial, legal and general political questions, but referring to disarmament matters. In the latter case, the negative votes or abstentions do not necessarily reflect the positions of states on the disarmament paragraphs of the relevant resolutions.

Only the essential parts of each resolution are given here. The text has been abridged, but the wording is close to that of the resolution.

The resolutions are grouped according to subjects, irrespective of the agenda items under which they were discussed.

In the case of non-recorded votes, the voting results may be incomplete.

| Resolution no. and date of adoption | Subject and contents of resolution | Voting results |
|---|---|---|
| | **Strategic nuclear weapons** | |
| 3184 A (XXVIII) 18 December 1973 | Appeals to the governments of the USSR and the USA to bear constantly in mind in the current phase of the Strategic Arms Limitation Talks the necessity and urgency of reaching agreement on important qualitative limitations and substantial reductions of their strategic nuclear-weapon systems and again invites the two governments to keep the General Assembly informed of the results of their negotiations. | *In favour* 94 *Against* 1: Albania *Abstentions* 19: Belgium, Bulgaria, Byelorussian SSR, Cuba, Czechoslovakia, France, German Democratic Republic, Greece, Hungary, Italy, Mongolia, Poland, Romania, South Africa, Turkey, Ukrainian SSR, USSR, United Kingdom, United States *Absent or not participating in the vote*: Bahamas, Bolivia, Botswana, Chad, China, Colombia, Costa Rica, Democratic Yemen,[a] Gambia, Guyana, Haiti, Honduras, Iraq, Khmer Republic, Maldives, Mauritius, Panama, Sudan,[a] Trinidad and Tobago, Upper Volta, Yemen |
| 3184 B (XXVIII) 18 December 1973 | **Non-proliferation of nuclear weapons** Bearing in mind that the Treaty on the Non-Proliferation of Nuclear Weapons will have been in force for five years on 5 March 1975 and expecting that the review conference called for in the Treaty will take place soon after that date, notes that, following appropriate consultation, a preparatory committee has been formed of parties serving on the Board of Governors of the International Atomic Energy Agency (IAEA) or represented at the Conference of the Committee on Disarmament (CCD); and requests the Secretary-General to provide assistance requested for the conference and its preparation. | *In favour* 100 *Against* 2: Albania. China *Abstentions* 11: Algeria, Argentina, Brazil, Cuba, Democratic Yemen, France, India, Saudi Arabia, Spain, United Republic of Tanzania, Zambia *Absent or not participating in the vote*: Bahamas, Bolivia, Botswana, Chad, Colombia, Costa Rica, Equatorial Guinea, Gambia, Guyana, Haiti, Iraq, Israel, Khmer Republic, Madagascar, Malawi, Maldives, Mauritius, Panama, Sudan,[a] Trinidad and Tobago, Upper Volta, Yemen |

**3078 A (XXVIII)**
6 December 1973

### Nuclear weapon tests

Condemns with the utmost vigour all nuclear weapon tests; reiterates its conviction that, whatever may be the differences on the question of verification, there is no valid reason for delaying the conclusion of a comprehensive test ban of the nature contemplated as long as 10 years ago in the preamble to the Treaty Banning Nuclear Weapon Tests in the Atmosphere, in Outer Space and under Water; once more urges the governments of nuclear-weapon states to bring all nuclear weapon tests to a halt without delay, either through a permanent agreement or through unilateral or agreed moratoria.

*In favour* 89
*Against* 5: Albania, China, France, Gabon, Portugal
*Abstentions* 33: Afghanistan, Algeria, Belgium, Bulgaria, Burundi, Byelorussian SSR, Central African Republic, Cuba, Czechoslovakia, Democratic Yemen, German Democratic Republic, Germany (Federal Republic of), Greece, Haiti, Hungary, Iraq, Italy, Japan, Luxembourg, Malawi, Mongolia, Netherlands, Poland, Romania, Rwanda, Saudi Arabia, South Africa, Syrian Arab Republic, Turkey, Ukrainian SSR, USSR, United Kingdom, United States
*Absent or not participating in the vote:* Ecuador, El Salvador, Equatorial Guinea, Gambia, Guyana, Maldives, Mauritius, Paraguay

**3078 B (XXVIII)**
6 December 1973

Emphasizes its deep concern at the continuance of nuclear weapon tests, both in the atmosphere and underground, and at the lack of progress towards a comprehensive test ban agreement; again calls upon all nuclear-weapon states to seek, as a matter of urgency, the end of all nuclear weapon tests in all environments; insists that the nuclear-weapon states which have been carrying out nuclear weapon tests in the atmosphere discontinue such tests forthwith; urges states which have not yet adhered to the Treaty Banning Nuclear Weapon Tests in the Atmosphere, in Outer Space and under Water (Partial Test Ban Treaty) to do so without further delay; vigorously urges the states members of the Conference of the Committee on Disarmament (CCD), especially those which are nuclear-weapon states and parties to the Partial Test Ban Treaty, immediately to start negotiations for elaborating a treaty designed to achieve the objective of a comprehensive test ban; requests the CCD to continue, as a matter of highest priority, its deliberations on this treaty.

*In favour* 65
*Against* 7: Albania, China, France, Gabon, Portugal, Saudi Arabia, Senegal
*Abstentions* 57: Afghanistan, Algeria, Bahrain, Belgium, Bulgaria, Burundi, Byelorussian SSR, Central African Republic, Chad, Congo, Cuba, Czechoslovakia, Democratic Yemen, Egypt, Gambia, German Democratic Republic, Germany (Federal Republic of), Greece, Haiti, Hungary, Iraq, Italy, Ivory Coast, Jordan, Kuwait, Lebanon, Luxembourg, Madagascar, Malawi, Mali, Mauritania, Mongolia, Morocco, Netherlands, Niger, Oman, Pakistan, Poland, Qatar, Romania, Rwanda, Somalia, South Africa, Spain, Syrian Arab Republic, Togo, Tunisia, Turkey, Uganda, Ukrainian SSR, USSR, United Arab Emirates, United Kingdom, United States, Upper Volta, Yemen, Zaire
*Absent or not participating in the vote:* Dahomey, El Salvador, Equatorial Guinea, Lesotho, Maldives, Mauritius

| Resolution no. and date of adoption | Subject and contents of resolution | Voting results |
|---|---|---|
| 3063 (XXVIII) 9 November 1973 | **Atomic radiation** Requests the UN Scientific Committee on the Effects of Atomic Radiation to meet as soon as possible in order to make a study of the most recent documents and to update the conclusions contained in its latest report. | *In favour* 86 *Against* 0 *Abstentions* 13: Bulgaria, Byelorussian SSR, Central African Republic, Czechoslovakia, German Democratic Republic, Hungary, Mongolia, Pakistan,[a] Poland, Romania, Ukrainian SSR, USSR, United States *Absent or not participating in the vote*: Albania, Bahamas, Bhutan, Burundi, Chile, China, Colombia, Costa Rica, Dominican Republic, Egypt, El Salvador, Ethiopia, Gabon, Gambia, Ghana, Guatemala, Guinea, Iran, Iraq,[a] Jordan, Kenya, Lebanon, Lesotho,[a] Liberia, Malaysia, Maldives, Mauritius, Niger, Nigeria, Paraguay, Saudi Arabia, Senegal, Sierra Leone, Sudan, Uganda, Zaire |
| 3154 A (XXVIII) 14 December 1973 | Noting the report submitted by the UN Scientific Committee on the Effects of Atomic Radiation, and noting with concern that there has been additional radioactive fall-out resulting in additions to the total doses of ionizing radiation since the Committee prepared its last report, deplores environmental pollution by ionizing radiation from the testing of nuclear weapons. | *In favour* 86 *Against* 0 *Abstentions* 28: Belgium, Central African Republic, Chad, Democratic Yemen, Denmark, Equatorial Guinea, France, Gabon, Germany (Federal Republic of), Ghana,[a] Greece, Ireland, Italy, Luxembourg, Morocco, Netherlands, Nicaragua, Pakistan, Portugal, Qatar, Romania, Saudi Arabia, Senegal, South Africa, Spain, Tunisia, United Kingdom, United States *Absent or not participating in the vote*: Albania, Bahamas, Bahrain, Botswana, China, Dominican Republic, Egypt, El Salvador, Gambia, Iraq, Jamaica, Kuwait, Lebanon, Maldives, Mauritius, Niger, Nigeria,[a] Sierra Leona, Swaziland, Syrian Arab Republic, Trinidad and Tobago[a] |
| 3154 B (XXVIII) 14 December 1973 | Requests the UN Scientific Committee on the Effects of Atomic Radiation to continue, at its twenty-third session to be held in October 1974, to review and assess the levels, effects and risks of radiation from all sources and to report to the General Assembly at its twenty-ninth session. | *In favour* 117[b] *Against* 0 *Abstentions* 5: Qatar, Saudi Arabia, Uganda, United Republic of Tanzania, Zambia *Absent or not participating in the vote*: Albania, Bahamas, Botswana, China, Dominican Republic, El Salvador, Gambia, Lebanon, Liberia,[c] Maldives, Mauritius, Sierra Leone, Trinidad and Tobago[d] |

**3154 C (XXVIII)**
**14 December 1973**

Decides to increase the membership of the UN Scientific Committee on the Effects of Atomic Radiation to a maximum of 20 members, while reaffirming the need for members of the Committee to be represented by scientists; urges the Scientific Committee to request from member states, as frequently as may be necessary, the detailed information which it needs to assist it in its work; and authorizes the Scientific Committee, in response to a request by the government of a country which is situated in an area of nuclear arms testing or which considers that it is exposed to atomic radiation by reason of such testing, to appoint a group of experts from among its members for the purpose of visiting that country, at the latter's expense, and of consulting with its scientific authorities and informing the Committee of the consultations.

*In favour* 91
*Against* 0
*Abstentions* 33: Belgium, Bulgaria, Byelorussian SSR, Central African Republic, Chad, Czechoslovakia, Dahomey, Denmark, Fiji, Finland, France, Gabon, German Democratic Republic, Guinea, Hungary, Iceland, India, Italy, Japan, Luxembourg, Mongolia, Netherlands, Norway, Poland, Portugal, Qatar, Saudi Arabia, South Africa, Sweden, Ukrainian SSR, USSR, United Kingdom, United States
*Absent or not participating in the vote*: Albania, Bahamas, China, Dominican Republic, Gambia, Jordan, Lebanon, Maldives, Mauritius, Sierra Leone, Trinidad and Tobago[a]

**3079 (XXVIII)**
**6 December 1973**

### Latin American nuclear-free zone

Notes with satisfaction that Additional Protocol II of the Treaty for the Prohibition of Nuclear Weapons in Latin America (Treaty of Tlatelolco), which entered into force for the United Kingdom and the United States of America in 1969 and 1971, respectively, has been signed in 1973 by France and by the People's Republic of China and that the governments of both countries have already decided to take the necessary measures for its ratification; urges the Union of Soviet Socialist Republics to sign and ratify Additional Protocol II of the Treaty of Tlatelolco in conformity with the repeated appeals of the General Assembly.

*In favour* 116
*Against* 0
*Abstentions* 12: Bulgaria, Byelorussian SSR, Cuba, Czechoslovakia, German Democratic Republic, Guyana, Hungary, Malawi, Mongolia, Poland, Ukrainian SSR, USSR
*Absent or not participating in the vote*: Bahamas, Belgium,[a] Gambia, Ireland,[a] Maldives, Mauritius, Syrian Arab Republic

**3056 (XXVIII)**
**29 October 1973**

### Peaceful uses of nuclear energy

Observes that there has been a further increase in the technical cooperation activities of the International Atomic Energy Agency (IAEA) and in the number of large-scale projects that the IAEA is executing for the United Nations Development Programme; notes the work carried out by the IAEA in surveying present and future nuclear energy requirements in developing countries and its aim of carrying out such surveys as an ongoing activity; commends the IAEA for the progress it has made in meeting its safeguards responsibilities and in negotiating agreements for the application of safeguards with non-nuclear-weapon states, in particular the agreements arrived at with the European Atomic Energy Community and the non-nuclear-weapon states of that organization.

Adopted without vote.

427

| Resolution no. and date of adoption | Subject and contents of resolution | Voting results |
|---|---|---|
| | **Indian Ocean as a zone of peace** | |
| 3080 (XXVIII) 6 December 1973 | Requests the Secretary-General to prepare a factual statement of the great powers' military presence in all its aspects, in the Indian Ocean, with special reference to their naval deployments, conceived in the context of great power rivalry; recommends that the statement should be based on available material and prepared with the assistance of qualified experts and competent bodies selected by the Secretary-General. | *In favour* 95<br>*Against* 0<br>*Abstentions* 35: Austria, Belgium, Bulgaria, Byelorussian SSR, Canada, Central African Republic, Cuba, Czechoslovakia, Denmark, El Salvador, Finland, France, German Democratic Republic, Germany (Federal Republic of), Greece, Guatemala, Guinea, Hungary, Ireland, Israel, Italy, Luxembourg, Malawi, Mongolia, Netherlands, Norway, Oman, Poland, Portugal, South Africa, Turkey, Ukrainian SSR, USSR, United Kingdom, United States<br>*Absent or not participating in the vote:* Gambia, Libyan Arab Republic, Maldives, Mauritius, Syrian Arab Republic |
| | **Chemical and biological weapons** | |
| 3077 (XXVIII) 6 December 1973 | Requests the Conference of the Committee on Disarmament (CCD) to continue negotiations, with a view to reaching early agreement, on effective measures for the prohibition of the development, production and stockpiling of all chemical weapons and for their elimination from the arsenal of all states; invites all states that have not yet done so to accede to the Protocol for the Prohibition of the Use in War of Asphyxiating, Poisonous or Other Gases, and of Bacteriological Methods of Warfare of 17 June 1925 and/or to ratify this Protocol, and again calls for the strict observance by all states of the principles and objectives contained therein. | *In favour* 118<br>*Against* 0<br>*Abstentions* 0<br>*Absent or not participating in the vote:* Albania, Bahamas, Chile, China, Ecuador, Equatorial Guinea, France, Gambia, Guyana, Iceland, Lebanon, Malawi, Maldives, Mauritius, Nicaragua, Nigeria, Swaziland |
| | **Napalm and other incendiary weapons** | |
| 3076 (XXVIII) 6 December 1973 | Invites the Diplomatic Conference on the Reaffirmation and Development of International Humanitarian Law Applicable in Armed Conflicts to consider the question of the use of napalm and other incendiary weapons, as well as other specific conventional weapons which may be deemed to cause unnecessary suffering or to have indiscriminate effects, and to seek agreement on rules prohibiting or restricting the use of such weapons. | *In favour* 103<br>*Against* 0<br>*Abstentions* 18: Belgium, Bulgaria, Byelorussian SSR, Central African Republic, Czechoslovakia, France, German Democratic Republic, Greece, Hungary, Israel, Italy, Mongolia, Poland, Saudi Arabia, Ukrainian SSR, USSR, United Kingdom, United States<br>*Absent or not participating in the vote:* Bahamas, Chile, Ecuador, Equatorial Guinea, Gambia, Guyana, Iceland, Kenya,[a] Lebanon, Malawi, Maldives, Mauritius, Nigeria, Swaziland |

3113 (XXVIII)
12 December 1973

Condemns the intensified armed repression by Portugal of the peoples of the territories under its domination, including the massacre of villagers, the mass destruction of villages and property and the use of napalm and chemical substances.

*In favour* 105
*Against* 8: Bolivia, Brazil, France, Portugal, South Africa, Spain, United Kingdom, United States
*Abstentions* 16: Austria, Belgium, Colombia, Costa Rica, El Salvador, Germany (Federal Republic of), Guatemala, Honduras, Israel, Italy, Japan, Luxembourg, Malawi, Nicaragua, Paraguay, Uruguay
*Absent or not participating in the vote:* Dominican Republic, Gabon, Gambia, Maldives, Mauritius, Upper Volta

**Outer space**

3182 (XXVIII)
18 December 1973

Invites states which have not yet become parties to the Treaty on Principles Governing the Activities of States in the Exploration and Use of Outer Space, including the Moon and Other Celestial Bodies, the Agreement on the Rescue of Astronauts, the Return of Astronauts and the Return of Objects Launched into Outer Space, and the Convention on International Liability for Damage Caused by Space Objects, to give early consideration to ratifying or acceding to those international agreements, so that they may have the broadest possible effect.

Recommends that the Legal Sub-Committee of the Committee on the Peaceful Uses of Outer Space should make efforts to complete the draft treaty relating to the Moon and the draft convention on registration of objects launched into outer space, consider the question of elaborating principles governing the use, by states, of artificial Earth satellites for direct television broadcasting with a view to concluding an international agreement or agreements, respond to the request for its views on the legal implications of the Earth resources survey by remote sensing satellites, and consider matters relating to the definition and/or delimitation of outer space and outer space activities.

Welcomes the various efforts envisaged by the Scientific and Technical Sub-Committee of the Committee on the Peaceful Uses of Outer Space and the Working Group on Remote Sensing of the Earth by Satellites with a view to bringing the benefit of this new technology to all countries, especially developing countries.

*In favour* 77
*Against* 0
*Abstentions* 10: Bulgaria, Byelorussian SSR, Czechoslovakia, German Democratic Republic, Hungary, Mongolia, Poland, Saudi Arabia, Ukrainian SSR, USSR

| Resolution no. and date of adoption | Subject and contents of resolution | Voting results |
|---|---|---|
| 3075 (XXVIII) 6 December 1973 | **Reduction of military budgets** Calls upon all states to make renewed efforts aimed at adopting effective measures for the cessation of the arms race, especially in the nuclear field, including the reduction of military budgets, particularly of the strongly armed countries, with a view to achieving progress towards general disarmament. | Adopted without objection. |
| 3093 A (XXVIII) 7 December 1973 | Recommends that all states permanent members of the Security Council should reduce their military budgets by 10 per cent from the 1973 level during the next financial year; appeals to the aforementioned states to allot 10 per cent of the funds released as a result of the reduction in military budgets for the provision of assistance to developing countries so as to permit the execution in those countries of the most urgent economic and social projects; expresses the desire that other states, particularly those with a major economic and military potential, should also take steps to reduce their military budgets and allot part of the funds thus released for the provision of assistance to developing countries; and establishes a Special Committee to distribute the funds released as a result of the reduction of military spending to developing countries as an addition to the assistance that is already provided to them through the existing channels. | *In favour*   83 *Against*   2: Albania, China *Abstentions*   38: Australia, Austria, Bahamas, Belgium, Brazil, Canada, Congo, Denmark, France, Germany (Federal Republic of), Greece, Guinea, Guyana, Iceland, Ireland, Israel, Italy, Ivory Coast, Jamaica, Japan, Luxembourg, Malawi, Mauritania, Netherlands, New Zealand, Norway, Pakistan, Portugal, South Africa, Sweden, Thailand, Trinidad and Tobago, Turkey, United Kingdom, United Republic of Tanzania, United States, Zambia *Absent or not participating in the vote:* Bolivia, Burundi, Equatorial Guinea, Gambia, Maldives, Mauritius,[a] Morocco, Paraguay, Sierra Leone, Somalia, Upper Volta, Zaire[a] |
| 3093 B (XXVIII) 7 December 1973 | Requests the Secretary-General to prepare, with the assistance of qualified consultant experts appointed by him, a report on the reduction of the military budgets of the permanent members of the Security Council, which should also cover other states with a major economic and military potential, and on the utilization of a part of the funds thus saved to provide international assistance to developing countries. | *In favour*   93 *Against*   2: Albania, China *Abstentions*   26: Bahamas, Barbados, Belgium, Brazil, Canada, Congo, Denmark, France, Germany (Federal Republic of), Greece, Guinea, Ireland, Israel, Italy, Ivory Coast, Japan, Liberia, Luxembourg, Mauritania, Netherlands, Portugal, South Africa, Spain, Togo, United Kingdom, United States *Absent or not participating in the vote:* Bolivia, Burundi, Cameroon, Equatorial Guinea, Gambia, Maldives, Mauritius, Morocco, Nepal, Paraguay, Rwanda, Sierra Leone, Somalia, Upper Volta |

3176 (XVIII)
17 December 1973

In reviewing the progress in the implementation of the International Development Strategy for the Second UN Development Decade, states:

Taking into account the link that should exist between the process of *détente* and the creation of better conditions for international cooperation in all fields, all countries should actively promote the achievement of general and complete disarmament through effective measures. The resources that may be released as a result of effective measures of actual disarmament should be used for the promotion of economic and social development of all nations. The release of resources resulting from those measures should increase the capacity of developed countries to provide support to developing countries in their efforts towards accelerating their economic and social progress.

Adopted without vote.

### General and complete disarmament

3184 C (XXVIII)
18 December 1973

Reaffirms the responsibility of the United Nations with regard to all matters pertaining to disarmament, in particular the ultimate goal of general and complete disarmament under effective international control; invites the states, parties to disarmament negotiations, to ensure that the disarmament measures adopted in one region should not result in increasing armaments in other regions, thus upsetting their stability; and invites the governments of all states to keep the General Assembly suitably informed of their disarmament negotiations so as to allow the proper performance of its functions.

*In favour*      93
*Against*          0
*Abstentions*    20: Belgium, Bulgaria, Byelorussian SSR, Canada, Cuba, Czechoslovakia, France, German Democratic Republic, Germany (Federal Republic of), Greece, Hungary, Italy, Mongolia, Poland, Portugal, South Africa, Ukrainian SSR, USSR, United Kingdom, United States
*Absent or not participating in the vote:* Albania, Bahamas, Bolivia, Botswana, Chad, China, Colombia, Costa Rica, Equatorial Guinea, Gambia, Guyana, Haiti, Iraq, Khmer Republic, Maldives, Mauritius, Panama, Rwanda, Sudan,[a] Trinidad and Tobago, Upper Volta, Yemen

### World disarmament conference

3183 (XXVIII)
18 December 1973

Decides to establish an *Ad Hoc* Committee to examine all the views and suggestions expressed by governments on the convening of a world disarmament conference and related problems, including conditions for the realization of such a conference, and to submit, on the basis of consensus, a report to the General Assembly at its twenty-ninth session; the *Ad Hoc* Committee shall consist of the following 40 non-nuclear-weapon member states appointed by the President of the General Assembly: Algeria, Argentina, Austria, Belgium, Brazil, Bulgaria, Burundi, Canada, Chile, Colombia, Czechoslovakia, Egypt, Ethiopia, Hungary, India, Indonesia, Iran, Italy, Japan, Leba-

Adopted unanimously.

| Resolution no. and date of adoption | Subject and contents of resolution | Voting results |
| --- | --- | --- |
| | non, Liberia, Mexico, Mongolia, Morocco, Netherlands, Nigeria, Pakistan, Peru, Philippines, Poland, Romania, Spain, Sri Lanka, Sweden, Tunisia, Turkey, Venezuela, Yugoslavia, Zaire and Zambia.<br><br>Invites the states possessing nuclear weapons to cooperate or maintain contact with the *Ad Hoc* Committee, it being understood that they will enjoy the same rights as the designated members of the Committee. | |
| | **Human rights in armed conflicts** | |
| 3102 (XXVIII) 12 December 1973 | Welcoming the convocation of the Diplomatic Conference on the Reaffirmation and Development of International Humanitarian Law Applicable in Armed Conflicts, urges all participants in the conference to do their utmost to reach agreement on additional rules which may help to alleviate the suffering brought by armed conflicts and to protect non-combatants and civilian objects in such conflicts; calls upon all parties to armed conflicts to acknowledge and to comply with their obligations under the humanitarian instruments and to observe the international humanitarian rules which are applicable, in particular the Hague Conventions of 1899 and 1907, the Geneva Protocol of 1925 and the Geneva Conventions of 1949; urges that instruction concerning such rules be provided to armed forces and information concerning the same rules be given to civilians everywhere, with a view to securing their strict observance; and requests the Secretary-General to encourage the study and teaching of principles of international humanitarian rules applicable in armed conflicts. | *In favour* 107<br>*Against* 0<br>*Abstentions* 6: Costa Rica, Israel, Paraguay,[a] Portugal, Spain, United States<br>*Absent or not participating in the vote*: Albania, Bolivia, Chile, Colombia, Dominican Republic, Ethiopia, Fiji, Gambia, Haiti, Jordan, Maldives, Malta, Mauritius, Morocco, Nepal, Nicaragua, Saudi Arabia, Somalia, Swaziland,[a] Thailand, Upper Volta, Venezuela |
| 3105 (XXVIII) 12 December 1973 | **Definition of aggression**<br>Decides that the Special Committee on the Question of Defining Aggression shall resume its work early in 1974, with a view to completing its task and to submitting a draft definition of aggression to the General Assembly at the twenty-ninth session. | *In favour* 119<br>*Against* 0<br>*Abstentions* 0 |

3185 (XXVIII)
18 December 1973

**Strengthening of international security**

Expresses the hope that the favourable trends currently emerging in bilateral, regional and multilateral relations, including the establishment of zones of peace and cooperation in various parts of the world, will be maintained and that efforts along these lines will be pursued and intensified so as to promote the strengthening of international security, in accordance with the purposes and principles of the Charter of the United Nations; reaffirms the recommendation that all States should contribute to the efforts to assure peace and security for all nations and to establish, in accordance with the Charter, an effective system of universal collective security without military alliances; appeals to all militarily significant States to exert efforts in order to extend the political *détente* so far achieved to military *détente*, to stop the arms race as well as to take practical steps to reduce armaments, with a view to making available additional resources for economic and social development, particularly to the developing countries.

*In favour*     97
*Against*       2: Portugal, South Africa
*Abstentions*  18

3073 (XXVIII)
30 November 1973

**Strengthening of the role of the United Nations**

Reaffirms that it is imperative that the United Nations should become a more effective instrument in safeguarding and strengthening the independence and sovereign equality of all states, as well as the inalienable right of every people to decide its own fate without any outside interference, and that it should take firm action, in accordance with the Charter of the United Nations, to oppose foreign domination and to prevent and suppress acts of aggression or any other acts which, in violating the Charter, may jeopardize international peace and security; reiterates its appeal to all member states to take full advantage of the framework and means provided by the United Nations in order to prevent the perpetuation of situations of tension, crisis and conflict, avert the creation of such new situations which endanger international peace and security, and settle international problems exclusively by peaceful means.

Adopted without vote.

| Resolution no. and date of adoption | Subject and contents of resolution | Voting results |
|---|---|---|
| 3091 (XXVIII) 7 December 1973 | **Peace-keeping operations**<br>Notes the progress made by the Special Committee on Peace-keeping Operations in the fulfilment of its mandate and the work of its Working Group, and requests them to intensify their efforts to complete by the twenty-ninth session of the General Assembly the task of achieving agreed guidelines for carrying out peace-keeping operations in conformity with the Charter of the United Nations. | Adopted unanimously. |
| 3065 (XXVIII) 9 November 1973 | **Peace research**<br>Having considered with interest and appreciation the first informative report on scientific works produced by national and international, governmental and non-governmental, public and private institutions with regard to peace research, which was submitted by the Secretary-General to the General Assembly, and considering that fundamental research on the foundations of and conditions for peace, and on the origins, motivations and spreading of conflicts, can contribute considerably to the peace mission of the United Nations, requests the Secretary-General to submit to the Assembly, at its thirtieth session, a second informative report containing, in addition to the titles of the studies carried out, a brief summary of their contents. | *In favour* 74<br>*Against* 10: Bulgaria, Byelorussian SSR, Cuba, Czechoslovakia, German Democratic Republic, Hungary, Mongolia, Poland, Ukrainian SSR, USSR<br>*Abstentions* 3: Democratic Yemen, Qatar, Somalia |

[a] Later advised the Secretariat it had intended to vote in favour.
[b] Ghana and Nigeria, which voted in favour, later advised the Secretariat they had intended to abstain.
[c] Later advised the Secretariat it had intended to abstain.

434

# Appendix 12G

*Record of the nuclear-weapon powers' votes on the main resolutions concerning disarmament at the UN General Assembly in 1973*

| Subject | Resolution No. | China | France | USSR | UK | USA |
|---|---|---|---|---|---|---|
| Strategic nuclear weapons | 3184 A | Not voting | Abstaining | Abstaining | Abstaining | Abstaining |
| Non-proliferation of nuclear weapons | 3184B | No | Abstaining | Yes | Yes | Yes |
| Nuclear weapon tests | 3078 A | No | No | Abstaining | Abstaining | Abstaining |
|  | 3078B | No | No | Abstaining | Abstaining | Abstaining |
| Atomic radiation | 3154 A | Not voting | Abstaining | Yes | Abstaining | Abstaining |
|  | 3154B | Not voting | Yes | Yes | Yes | Yes |
|  | 3154 C | Not voting | Abstaining | Abstaining | Abstaining | Abstaining |
| Latin American nuclear-free zone | 3079 | Yes | Yes | Abstaining | Yes | Yes |
| Indian Ocean as a zone of peace | 3080 | Yes | Abstaining | Abstaining | Abstaining | Abstaining |
| Chemical and biological weapons | 3077 | Not voting | Not voting | Yes | Yes | Yes |
| Napalm and other incendiary weapons | 3076 | Yes | Abstaining | Abstaining | Abstaining | Abstaining |
| Reduction of military budgets | 3093 A | No | Abstaining | Yes | Abstaining | Abstaining |
|  | 3093B | No | Abstaining | Yes | Abstaining | Abstaining |
| World disarmament conference | 3183 | Yes | Yes | Yes | Yes | Yes |
| Human rights in armed conflicts | 3102 | Yes | Yes | Yes | Yes | Abstaining |

# 13. The status of the implementation of agreements related to disarmament

*Square-bracketed references, thus [1], refer to the list of references on page 446.*

## I. *Bilateral US-Soviet agreements*

### Strategic arms limitation

The ABM Treaty, which entered into force in October 1972, restricted the deployment of anti-ballistic missile systems to two areas in the United States and the Soviet Union—one for the defence of the national capital, and the other for the defence of an intercontinental ballistic missile (ICBM) site. When the treaty was signed in May 1972, the USSR had 64 ABM launchers deployed around Moscow and no ABM protection of ICBM sites. Under the treaty, the USSR is permitted to expand the capital defence system to 100 launchers and 100 interceptor missiles and to construct a new site with the same number of launchers and missiles to protect some of its ICBMs. The USA, which in May 1972 had no ABMs deployed, is permitted to complete the construction of one ABM complex for the protection of ICBMs, and to build an ABM system around Washington, also with 100 launchers and 100 interceptor missiles. While the USA has been proceeding with the construction of its ABM system at Grand Forks, North Dakota, there is no evidence that the USSR has been expanding its ABM system around Moscow, and there is no indication that either country is planning to take advantage of the option under the treaty to build another ABM site. Nevertheless, work on the qualitative improvement of the existing systems has not stopped; it has been reported that new, advanced anti-ballistic missile defence technology is being developed in both the USA and the USSR. The official justification for this activity is that the treaty can be abrogated if one of the parties decides that some extraordinary events "have jeopardized its supreme interests" and that each party should guard against a technological "surprise" by the other.

As a matter of fact, the treaty permits, within certain limits, the modernization and replacement of ABM systems and their components, including testing. The competition in this field is, therefore, unlikely to cease as long as the parties do not give up missile defence altogether. It may even be expected to escalate. Recently the USA disclosed the development of a manoeuvrable re-entry vehicle (MARV), a new type of missile warhead that can be manoeuvred during the final part of its trajectory so as to avoid enemy defences and strike its target with high accuracy (see chapter 6). Such a "contingency" development of strategic weapons would be more difficult to justify if the parties were firmly resolved to put up with the existing ABM systems, which offer only negligible resistance to the penetration of offensive missiles, and if they trusted each other that no further attempts would be made at securing the invulnerability of their strategic nuclear weapons.

The Interim Agreement on "certain measures with respect to the limitation of strategic offensive arms", which entered into force simultaneously with the ABM Treaty, has not slowed down the development and deployment of new weapons, of which MIRVs and MARVs are among the most important. Ever more accurate guidance systems combined with ever more numerous nuclear warheads have helped to resuscitate the elusive goal of reaching a first-strike capability. In January 1974, the US Secretary of Defense announced a change in US strategy in precisely that direction: some US missiles would be aimed at Soviet military targets instead of almost solely at cities and industrial areas. The official reason given for this important move was that the USSR, with its more numerous and more powerful missiles equipped with MIRVs (which have already been successfully tested), might gain the capability to attack the US missile bases and destroy them, and that the USA needed to have alternatives other than a strike against the cities of the other side. The shift from a countervalue strategy to a counterforce strategy, albeit not complete, is based on the assumption that a strategic nuclear war can actually be waged (and possibly contained), not simply deterred. And since missile silos are contemplated as the main object of a counterforce strike, the "novel" approach is bound to spur a new round of the strategic arms race.[1] None of these developments contradicts the letter or the spirit of the SALT I agreements which were drafted so as to permit a new dimension in the nuclear rivalry between the USA and the USSR, rather than to put a stop to it. Consequently, there have been no complaints by either side of noncompliance with the substantive clauses of the agreements. Also the formal provisions have been observed: the Standing Consultative Commission for the promotion of the implementation of the ABM Treaty and the Interim Agreement was constituted and held meetings; and the follow-on negotiations (SALT II) on "more complete measures limiting strategic offensive arms" have continued (see chapter 12).

### The prevention of accidental nuclear war

In accordance with the "Hot Line" Modernization Agreement of 1971, US and Soviet experts have worked out technical details for transferring

---

[1] For a more detailed discussion of the new counterforce strategy and its implications, see chapter 5.

the Washington-Moscow direct communications link entirely to a network of satellites. [1] The new system is meant to improve the emergency communications and to put the line beyond the reach of human interference. It will thus provide technical means for the implementation of the US-Soviet agreement on measures to reduce the risk of an accidental outbreak of nuclear war between the two countries. It has also been reported that the USA was equipping its nuclear weapons stationed abroad with advanced electronic controls to guard against unauthorized use. [2]

Further progress was made toward the prevention of incidents on the high seas. On 22 May 1973, the USA and the USSR signed a protocol to the agreement of 1972 on measures to improve the safety of navigation of the ships of the two powers' armed forces on, and flight of their military aircraft over, the high seas. The protocol provides that ships and aircraft of the parties "shall not make simulated attacks by aiming guns, missile launchers, torpedo tubes and other weapons at non-military ships of the other party, nor launch nor drop any objects near non-military ships of the other party in such a manner as to be hazardous to these ships or to constitute a hazard to navigation".

## II. *Multilateral agreements*

### The BW Convention

By 31 December 1973, the convention on the prohibition of the development, production and stockpiling of bacteriological (biological) and toxin weapons and on their destruction, which was opened for signature on 10 April 1972, was still not in force, although it had been signed by 112 states and ratified by 31.

The important ratifications missing were those of the depositary governments—the UK, the USA and the USSR. In the United Kingdom, the House of Commons passed a biological weapons bill, which provides that it shall be an indictable offence, punishable with imprisonment for life, for a person to do any of the things prohibited by the BW Convention. [3] The only difficulty seemed to be with the US ratification, because of the divergent views in the US Congress. However, the USA stated that, pursuant to its unilateral decisions taken in 1969, the destruction of all stocks of biological and toxin agents and of all associated munitions had been completed, except for small quantities for laboratory defensive research purposes, and facilities where biological warfare activities were conducted had been converted to medical research centres. [4] The 28th UN General Assembly expressed the hope for the widest possible adherence to the convention. [5]

Negotiations on measures of chemical disarmament, provided for in the BW Convention, continued in 1973, but no progress was made (for a review of the debate, see chapter 12). As far as the 1925 Geneva Protocol (prohibiting the use in war of chemical and biological weapons) is concerned, there were only two accessions—by Fiji and the Philippines. The USA was still not a party even though the American Chemical Society, which had for many years been one of the strongest opponents of the protocol, reversed its position and expressed support for its ratification without any qualification regarding tear gas or herbicides. [6]

The example of Ireland, which withdrew its reservations limiting the applicability of the protocol only to nations party to it, and only to first use, was not followed by other countries. On the contrary, one of the new accessions was accompanied by the same reservations. The United Kingdom expressed the view that the practical result of some of the reservations had been to strengthen the operation of the protocol. It linked the question of their withdrawal with the degree of success in the negotiations on the prohibition of the production and possession of chemical weapons and suggested that a future CW convention contain an explicit reaffirmation of the prohibition on the use of CW. [7]

### The Sea-Bed Treaty

In 1973 six states—Australia, India, Lesotho, Nicaragua, South Africa and Yugoslavia—joined the treaty on the prohibition of the emplacement of nuclear weapons and other weapons of mass destruction on the sea-bed and the ocean floor and in the subsoil therof, bringing the total number of parties to 52.

India stated that its accession to the treaty is based on the position that, as a coastal state, it has full and exclusive sovereign rights over the continental shelf adjoining its territory and beyond its territorial waters and the subsoil thereof. It is the view of India that other countries cannot use its continental shelf for military purposes. There cannot, therefore, be any restriction on, or limitation of, the sovereign right of India as a coastal state to verify, inspect, remove or destroy any weapon, device, structure, installation or facility which might be emplanted or emplaced on or beneath its continental shelf by any other country, or to take such other steps as may be considered necessary to safeguard its security.

In response to the Indian statement, the US government expressed the view that under existing international law the rights of coastal states over their continental shelves are exclusive only for purposes of exploration and exploitation of natural resources, and are otherwise limited by the 1958 Convention on the Continental Shelf and other principles of international law. [8]

In the 1958 convention, the term "continental shelf" is used as referring to the sea-bed and subsoil of the submarine areas adjacent to the coast but outside the area of the territorial sea, to a depth of 200 metres or, beyond that limit, to where the depth of the superjacent waters admits the exploitation of the natural resources of the said areas; and to the sea-bed and subsoil of similar submarine areas adjacent to the coasts of islands.

## The Non-Proliferation Treaty

Article VIII (3) of the Treaty on the Non-Proliferation of Nuclear Weapons (NPT) provides that five years after the entry into force of the treaty, a conference of parties shall be held in Geneva, "in order to review the operation of this Treaty with a view to reassuring that the purposes of the Preamble and the provisions of the Treaty are being realized". In March 1975 the treaty will have been in force for five years and because the review conference is expected to take place soon after that date, a preparatory committee was set up during the 28th UN General Assembly. [9] The Committee is composed of those parties to the NPT which serve on the Board of Governors of the International Atomic Energy Agency (IAEA) or which are represented at the Conference of the Committee on Disarmament (CCD). As of December 1973, there were 24 countries in these two categories: Australia, Bulgaria, Canada, Costa Rica, Czechoslovakia, Denmark, Ethiopia, Ghana, Hungary, Ireland, Lebanon, Mexico, Mongolia, Morocco, Nigeria, Peru, the Philippines, Poland, Romania, Sweden, the UK, the USA, the USSR and Yugoslavia.

It is understood that all parties to the NPT, whether members of the preparatory committee or not, may express their views on the conference preparations.

The conference is expected to concentrate on two questions: the implementation of the non-proliferation obligations undertaken by the non-nuclear-weapon states, including control; and the implementation of the nuclear-weapon powers' commitments to pursue negotiations on effective measures "relating to cessation of the nuclear arms race at an early date and to nuclear disarmament".

Although no new nuclear-weapon power has emerged since the NPT entered into force, the basic purpose of the treaty has not yet been fulfilled. A number of militarily important countries, usually referred to as near-nuclear countries, had not ratified or even signed the NPT by 31 December 1973.[2] At that time, 79 non-nuclear-weapon states were parties

---

[2] The government of the Federal Republic of Germany considers itself bound by the NPT provisions as of the date of signature, irrespective of the pending ratification. [10] In February 1974, the Bundestag, the lower house of the FRG parliament, approved the NPT. South Africa, another near-nuclear country (and one of the world's major producers of uranium), which has not signed the NPT and which has often been accused by African states of clandestinely developing a nuclear weapon, stated that its atomic programme was devoted exclusively to peaceful purposes. It proposed to negotiate, at the appropriate time, an agreement with the IAEA for the application of safeguards to enriched uranium, so as to ensure that the product was used solely for peaceful purposes. [11]

to the treaty. In the field of control, the situation was worse. Only 29 countries had concluded safeguards agreements with the IAEA, as required by the NPT, that is, 36 per cent of those under obligation to do so (the nuclear-weapon powers have no such obligation); 15 additional states had signed the agreements, but were not yet bound by them, as entry into force was subject to notification that the statutory and constitutional requirements had been met; and four more agreements had been approved by the IAEA Board of Governors but had not been signed by 31 December 1973. Some safeguards agreements were signed together with protocols (see appendix 13 D).

As regards nuclear disarmament, the nuclear-weapon powers will most certainly be under heavy pressure to undertake more specific pledges. Demands may even be put forward to reformulate the relevant provision of the treaty (Article VI).

Other proposals may include guarantees of non-use of nuclear weapons against non-nuclear-weapon countries, obligatory IAEA control of peaceful nuclear activities of nuclear-weapon powers, a ban on the proliferation of nuclear weapons and nuclear-weapon technology among the nuclear-weapon states and restrictions on the right to withdraw from the NPT.[3]

### The Treaty of Tlatelolco

The number of parties to the treaty for the prohibition of nuclear weapons in Latin America did not increase in 1973, but two more nuclear-weapon powers, in addition to the UK and the USA, signed Additional Protocol II which provides for an undertaking to respect the statute of military denuclearization of the area.

France signed the protocol on 18 July 1973 and stated that it interprets the undertaking contained in Article 3 to mean that it presents no obstacle to the full exercise of the right of self-defence under Article 51 of the UN Charter; it takes note of the interpretation of the treaty given by the preparatory commission for the denuclearization of Latin America and reproduced in its final act, according to which the treaty does not apply to transit, the granting or denying of which lies within the exclusive competence of each state party in accordance with the pertinent principles and rules of international law; and it considers that the application of the legislation referred to in Article 3 of the treaty relates to a legislation which is consistent with international law. In the view of France, the provisions of Articles 1 and 2 of the protocol apply to the text of the treaty as it stood at the time the protocol was signed. Consequently, no amendment to the treaty that might come into force under the provisions of Article 29 thereof

[3] A detailed discussion of these and other questions can be found in *Nuclear Proliferation Problems*. [12]

would be binding on the government of France without its express consent. If this declaration of interpretation is contested in part or in whole by one or more contracting parties to the treaty or to Additional Protocol II, these instruments would be null and void as far as relations between France and the contesting state or states are concerned.

China signed Additional Protocol II on 21 August 1973 and made a declaration in which it repeated its undertaking of 14 November 1972 never to use or threaten to use nuclear weapons against non-nuclear Latin American countries and the Latin American nuclear-weapon-free zone; not to test, manufacture, produce, stockpile, install or deploy nuclear weapons in these countries or in this zone; and not to send "means of transportation and delivery carrying nuclear weapons to cross the territory, territorial sea or air space of Latin American countries". It pointed out that the signing of the protocol by the Chinese government did not imply any change whatsoever in China's stand on the disarmament and nuclear-weapon issue and, in particular, did not affect the Chinese government's opposition to the treaty on the non-proliferation of nuclear weapons and the partial nuclear test ban treaty. The Chinese government holds that, in order that Latin America may truly become a nuclear-weapon-free zone, "all nuclear countries, and particularly the super-powers," must undertake not to use or threaten to use nuclear weapons against Latin American countries and the Latin American nuclear-weapon-free zone, and they must be asked to undertake to observe and implement the following: (*a*) the dismantling of all foreign military bases in Latin America and refraining from establishing any new foreign military bases there; and (*b*) the prohibition of the passage of any means of transportation and delivery carrying nuclear weapons through Latin American territory, territorial sea or air space.

The 28th UN General Assembly noted "with satisfaction" the signing of Additional Protocol II of the Treaty of Tlatelolco by China and France as well as the fact that the governments of both countries had decided to take the necessary measures for its ratification. It also urged the USSR, the only remaining nuclear power which has not signed the protocol, to sign and ratify it in conformity with the repeated appeals of the General Assembly. [13]

The USSR maintained its objections to certain clauses of the treaty. It reiterated that it would respect the denuclearized status of the Latin American countries only if transit of nuclear weapons over the territories of these countries as well as conduct of peaceful nuclear explosions, contrary to the NPT, were prohibited, and if the principle of the freedom of the high seas were observed.[4] [14] Mexico suggested that the Soviet

---

[4] For a discussion of the relevant provisions of the Treaty of Tlatelolco, see the *SIPRI Yearbook 1972*. [15]

government follow the procedure adopted by the governments of the other nuclear-weapon powers, that is, to sign the protocol and make a declaration of its own interpretation of the points in respect of which it feels special concern.

**The Outer Space Treaty**

In 1973 the UN Committee on the peaceful uses of outer space continued discussions on principles governing the use by states of artificial Earth satellites for direct television broadcasting, with a view to concluding an international agreement or agreements on the subject. It made progress towards the completion of the draft treaty relating to the Moon and the draft convention on registration of objects launched into outer space. Attention was also given to the promotion of international cooperation in the field of remote sensing of the Earth by satellites. Two nations joined the treaty on principles governing the activities of states in the exploration and use of outer space, including the Moon and other celestial bodies, bringing the total number of parties to 71. The 28th UN General Assembly invited states which have not yet become party to the treaty to ratify or accede to it. [16]

**The Partial Test Ban Treaty**

On 5 August 1973, 10 years had elapsed since the signing of the treaty banning nuclear weapon tests in the atmosphere, in outer space and under water (see appendix 13 E). By 1 January 1974 it had been adhered to by as many as 106 states.

The record of compliance with the treaty is generally considered as good; there has been no complaint of a significant breach by any party. In a few incidents when radioactive substances released from underground explosions crossed the state boundaries of the USA and the USSR, the parties preferred to treat the occurrences as "technical" violations. [17]

However, it is questionable whether the pledge given in the Partial Test Ban Treaty and reiterated in the Non-Proliferation Treaty, by the UK, the USA and the USSR, to negotiate the discontinuance of all test explosions of nuclear weapons is being fulfilled. During the past decade there have been no real negotiations on the subject of underground tests. In the discussion of verification, which is ostensibly the most important stumbling block to achieving a comprehensive agreement, the positions of the main parties have remained unchanged since 1963 (see chapter 12). Other provisions of the agreement have not even been meaningfully discussed.

A few militarily important countries, such as Argentina and Pakistan, and especially China and France, are still missing from the list of parties.

China and France have been testing nuclear weapons in the atmosphere (see appendices 13 F and 13 G). The French explosions carried out in the Pacific region were found most objectionable, mainly because of the danger of radioactive contamination. On 9 May 1973, the matter was brought before the International Court of Justice (ICJ): proceedings against France were instituted by Australia and also by New Zealand both on its own behalf and on behalf of the external territories for which it is responsible. The Court was asked to declare that the carrying out of atmospheric nuclear-weapon tests in the south Pacific Ocean was not consistent with applicable rules of international law, and to order that France should not carry out any further such tests. The complaining states also asked the Court to lay down interim measures of protection by ordering France to desist from carrying out these tests pending a judgement in the case.

France denied that it was violating any existing rule of international law. It took the position that the ICJ was not competent in the case because nuclear testing was an activity connected with national defence, and the French government's declaration of 1966 on the acceptance of the compulsory jurisdiction of the Court excluded disputes concerning such activities. Nevertheless, on 22 June 1973, the ICJ indicated, by eight votes to six (in two separate but analogous orders) that, pending its final decision, the governments of Australia, New Zealand and France should each ensure that "no action of any kind is taken which might aggravate or extend the dispute submitted to the Court or prejudice the rights of the other party in respect of the carrying out of whatever decision the Court may render in the case; and in particular, that the French government should avoid nuclear tests causing the deposit of radioactive fall-out" on the territory of Australia, New Zealand, the Cook Islands, Niue or the Tokelau Islands.

The ICJ stated that its orders in no way prejudged the question of the jurisdiction of the Court to deal with the merits of the case, or any questions relating to the admissibility of the applications, or relating to the merits themselves.[5]

France did not consider itself bound by the order of the Court. A few weeks later, on 21 July, it started a new series of atmospheric tests. The series, consisting of five explosions of low yield, ended on 28 August 1973, and some radioactive fall-out was detected in Australia and New Zealand. Subsequently, France notified the UN Secretariat that it had terminated its recognition of the compulsory jurisdiction of the ICJ.

At the initiative of France, the UN General Assembly requested the UN Scientific Committee on the Effects of Atomic Radiation to meet in order

[5] For a review of the legal arguments put forward by the parties to the dispute and a discussion of the arms control implications of the possible outcome of the litigation, see *French Nuclear Tests in the Atmosphere*. [18]

to study some recent documents transmitted to it and to update the conclusions contained in the Committee's report of 1972.

The Scientific Committee held a special session on 26 and 27 November
1973 and gave attention to radioactive contamination of the environment
by all nuclear tests, including those carried out between the end of 1970
and the time of its session.

The Committee noted that

the estimates of the total doses to the world population to be received by the year
2000 from such long-lived radio-nuclides as strontium-90 and caesium-137 that had
been given by the Committee in its latest report did not appear to require revision
on the basis of the data available as at 1 January 1973. This is because the
estimated increases in the doses are smaller than the uncertainties in the estimates
of the total doses. The amounts of strontium-90 and caesium-137 released in the
environment by nuclear tests carried out in 1971 and 1972 added slightly to the
totals reported in the latest report of the Committee. While the additions of radioactivity were greater in the southern hemisphere, the total amounts produced by all
tests carried out up to the end of 1972 remain much higher in the northern hemisphere. The resulting additions to the total doses are small in the southern hemisphere and even smaller in the northern hemisphere.

The Committee further noted that

in 1972 and 1973 the short-lived radio-nuclide iodine-131 was detected for a few
weeks at a number of sites in both hemispheres. In 1973 the levels, and the
corresponding thyroid doses, were generally of the same magnitude as in 1972. In
both years and in both hemispheres, the levels and thyroid doses were equal to or
lower than those observed in the southern hemisphere in 1970 and 1971. [19]

While the data on levels of radioactivity collected in 1972 were available,
those relating to 1973 were more limited, so that the assessment of the
1973 levels could only be considered as preliminary.

The UN General Assembly adopted three resolutions, in which it de-
plored environmental pollution by ionizing radiation from the testing of
nuclear weapons; requested the Scientific Committee to continue to review
and assess the levels, effects and risks of radiation from all sources; and
authorized the Committee to respond to a request from the government of
a country which is situated in an area of nuclear arms testing or which
considers that it is exposed to atomic radiation because of such testing,
by appointing a group of experts from among its members for the purpose
of visiting that country, at the latter's expense, and of consulting with its
scientific authorities and informing the Committee of the consultations.
[20–22]

The reaction of world opinion to Chinese nuclear tests in the atmosphere
was considerably weaker probably because, unlike France, China is not
testing overseas and the number of its tests is relatively small: in 1973 it
conducted only one test. Nevertheless, Japan [23] and Mongolia [24]
complained about increased radioactivity which resulted from the Chinese
test of June 1973.

The USA and the USSR have continued intensive testing underground. Last year, according to preliminary data, the USA carried out nine nuclear explosions, and the USSR 14 (see appendix 13 C). Both powers together are responsible for 865 nuclear explosions (announced and presumed) conducted from 1945 to 1973, that is, for some 90 per cent of the total of 956, and it is noteworthy that approximately 50 per cent of the explosions were carried out (underground) after the signing of the Partial Test Ban Treaty (see appendix 13 H).

## The Antarctic Treaty

A proposal has been put forward by a group of scientists [25] that the Antarctic be used for the disposal of radioactive wastes accumulating from the production of nuclear energy. It is believed that if the wastes were fused into a solid glass matrix, they could be safely transported to the interior of the ice cap and removed from all contact with the biosphere. If placed on the surface of the ice, they would melt their own emplacement shafts which would rapidly reseal by freezing. The average temperature in the Antarctic has remained below freezing for more than a million years, so that the large thickness of polar ice may be expected to provide a reliable seal for a very long time.

The Antarctic Treaty prohibits the disposal there of radioactive waste material (Article V). But it also provides that in the event of the conclusion of international agreements concerning the disposal of radioactive wastes, to which all the contracting parties whose representatives are entitled to participate in the consultative meetings are parties, the rules established under such agreements shall apply in the Antarctic. The proposal has not yet come up for official consideration. If it proves workable, the establishment of an international régime in the Antarctic may become an inescapable necessity. Many countries will have radioactive waste disposal problems, including those which are not parties to the treaty.

## References

1. *New York Times,* 8 December 1973.
2. *International Herald Tribune,* 18 December 1973.
3. Parliamentary Debates (Hansard) House of Commons Official Report, 17 December 1973, Volume 866, No. 35, column 1028.
4. Disarmament Conference document CCD/PV.585.
5. UN document A/RES/3077 (XXVIII).
6. The American Chemical Society, News Service, 8 October 1973.
7. Disarmament Conference document CCD/PV.625.
8. Note of the US Acting Secretary of State to the Ambassador of India, of 4 October 1973.
9. UN document A/RES/3184B (XXVIII).
10. UN document A/C.1/PV.1944.

11. UN document A/PV.2141.

12. *Nuclear Proliferation* Problems (Stockholm, Almqvist & Wiksell, 1974, Stockholm International Peace Research Institute).

13. UN document A/RES/3079 (XXVIII).

14. UN document A/C.1/PV.1956.

15. *World Armaments and Disarmament, SIPRI Yearbook 1972* (Stockholm, Almqvist & Wiksell, 1972, Stockholm International Peace Research Institute) chapter 19.

16. UN document A/RES/3182 (XXVIII).

17. *Ten Years of the Partial Test Ban Treaty, 1963–1973,* SIPRI Research Report No. 11, August 1973 (Stockholm, Almqvist & Wiksell, 1973, Stockholm International Peace Research Institute).

18. *French Nuclear Tests in the Atmosphere: The Question of Legality* (Stockholm, Almqvist & Wiksell, 1974, Stockholm International Peace Research Institute).

19. UN document A/9349.

20. UN document A/RES/3154A (XXVIII).

21. UN document A/RES/3154B (XXVIII).

22. UN document A/RES/3154C (XXVIII).

23. *Japan Times,* 30 June 1973.

24. UN document A/PV.2194.

25. Zeller, E. J., Saunders, D. F. and Angino, E. E., "Putting Radioactive Wastes on Ice", *Bulletin of the Atomic Scientists,* January 1973.

# Appendix 13A

*Bilateral arms control agreements between the*
*USA and the USSR as of 31 December 1973*

*Summary of the relevant provisions of the agreements*

### Memorandum of understanding regarding the establishment of a direct communications link ("Hot Line" Agreement)

Establishes a direct communications link between the governments of the USA and the USSR for use in time of emergency. An annex attached to the memorandum provides for two circuits, namely a duplex wire telegraph circuit and a duplex radio telegraph circuit, as well as two terminal points with telegraph-teleprinter equipment between which communications are to be exchanged.

Signed at Geneva on 20 June 1963.
Entered into force on 20 June 1963.

### Agreement on measures to improve the USA–USSR direct communications link ("Hot Line" Modernization Agreement)

Establishes, for the purpose of increasing the reliability of the direct communications link set up pursuant to the Memorandum of understanding of 20 June 1963, two additional circuits between the USA and the USSR each using a satellite communications system (the US circuit being arranged through Intelsat and the Soviet circuit through the Molniya II system), and a system of terminals (more than one) in the territory of each party. Matters relating to the implementation of these improvements are set forth in an annex to the agreement.

Signed at Washington on 30 September 1971.
Entered into force on 30 September 1971.

### Agreement on measures to reduce the risk of outbreak of nuclear war between the USA and the USSR (Nuclear Accidents Agreement)

Provides for immediate notification in the event of an accidental, unauthorized incident involving a possible detonation of a nuclear weapon (the party whose nuclear weapon is involved should take necessary measures to render harmless or destroy such weapon), immediate notification in the event of detection by missile warning systems of unidentified objects, or in the event of signs of interference with these systems or with related

448

communications facilities, as well as advance notification of planned missile launches extending beyond the national territory in the direction of the other party.

Signed at Washington on 30 September 1971.

Entered into force on 30 September 1971.

### Agreement on the prevention of incidents on and over the high seas

Provides for measures to assure the safety of navigation of the ships of the armed forces of the USA and the USSR on the high seas and flight of their military aircraft over the high seas, advance notification of actions on the high seas which represent a danger to navigation or to aircraft in flight, as well as exchange of information concerning instances of collision or other incidents at sea between ships and aircraft of the parties.

Signed at Moscow on 25 May 1972.

Entered into force on 25 May 1972.

### Treaty on the limitation of anti-ballistic missile systems (SALT ABM Treaty)

Prohibits the deployment of ABM systems for the defence of the whole territory of the USA and the USSR or of an individual region, except as expressly permitted. Permitted ABM deployments are limited to two areas in each country—one for the defence of the national capital, and the other for the defence of some intercontinental ballistic missiles (ICBMs). No more than 100 ABM launchers and 100 ABM interceptor missiles may be deployed in each ABM deployment area. ABM radars should not exceed specified numbers and are subject to qualitative restrictions.

Signed at Moscow on 26 May 1972.

Entered into force on 3 October 1972.

### Interim agreement on certain measures with respect to the limitation of strategic offensive arms (SALT Interim Agreement)

Provides for a freeze for up to five years of the aggregate number of fixed land-based intercontinental ballistic missile (ICBM) launchers and ballistic missile launchers on modern submarines. The parties are free to choose the mix, except that conversion of land-based launchers for light ICBMs, or for ICBMs of older types, into land-based launchers for modern "heavy" ICBMs is prohibited.

A protocol which is an integral part of the Interim Agreement specifies that the USA may have not more than 710 ballistic missile launchers on submarines and 44 modern ballistic missile submarines, while the USSR may have not more than 950 ballistic missile launchers on submarines and 62 modern ballistic missile submarines. Up to those levels, additional SLBMs—in the USA over 656 ballistic missile launchers on nuclear-powered submarines and in the USSR over 740 ballistic missile launchers on nuclear-powered submarines, operational and under construction—may become operational as replacements for equal numbers of ballistic missile launchers of types deployed prior to 1964, or of ballistic missile launchers on older submarines.

Signed at Moscow on 26 May 1972.

Entered into force on 3 October 1972.

## Protocol to the Agreement on the prevention of incidents on and over the high seas, signed on 25 May 1972

Provides that ships and aircraft of the parties shall not make simulated attacks by aiming guns, missile launchers, torpedo tubes and other weapons at non-military ships of the other party, nor launch nor drop any objects near non-military ships of the other party in such a manner as to be hazardous to these ships or to constitute a hazard to navigation.

Signed at Washington on 22 May 1973.

Entered into force on 22 May 1973.

## Agreement on the prevention of nuclear war

Provides that the parties will act in such a manner as to exclude the outbreak of nuclear war between them and between either of the parties and other countries. Each party will refrain from the threat or use of force against the other party, against the allies of the other party and against other countries in circumstances which may endanger international peace and security. If at any time relations between the parties or between either party and other countries appear to involve the risk of a nuclear conflict, or if relations between countries not parties to this agreement appear to involve the risk of nuclear war between the USSR and the USA or between either party and other countries, the Soviet Union and the United States, acting in accordance with the provisions of this agreement, shall immediately enter into urgent consultations with each other and make every effort to avert this risk.

Signed at Washington on 22 June 1973.

Entered into force on 22 June 1973.

# Appendix 13B

*Multilateral agreements related to disarmament as of*
*31 December 1973*

## I. *Summary of the relevant provisions of the agreements*

### Antarctic Treaty

Declares the Antarctic an area to be used exclusively for peaceful purposes. Prohibits any measure of a military nature in the Antarctic, such as the establishment of military bases and fortifications, the carrying out of military manoeuvres, as well as the testing of any type of weapons.

Signed at Washington on 1 December 1959.
Entered into force on 23 June 1961.
The depositary government: USA.

### Treaty banning nuclear weapon tests in the atmosphere, in outer space and under water (Partial Test Ban Treaty)

Prohibits the carrying out of any nuclear weapon test explosion, or any other nuclear explosion: (*a*) in the atmosphere, beyond its limits, including outer space, or under water, including territorial waters or high seas, or (*b*) in any other environment if such explosion causes radioactive debris to be present outside the territorial limits of the state under whose jurisdiction or control the explosion is conducted.

Signed at Moscow on 5 August 1963.
Entered into force on 10 October 1963.
The depositary governments: UK, USA, USSR.

### Treaty on principles governing the activities of states in the exploration and use of outer space, including the moon and other celestial bodies (Outer Space Treaty)

Prohibits the placing in orbit around the Earth of any objects carrying nuclear weapons or any other kinds of weapons of mass destruction, the installation of such weapons on celestial bodies, or stationing them in outer space in any other manner. The establishment of military bases, installations and fortifications, the testing of any type of weapons and the conduct of military manoeuvres on celestial bodies are also forbidden.

Signed at London, Moscow and Washington on 27 January 1967.

Entered into force on 10 October 1967.

The depositary governments: UK, USA, USSR.

## Treaty for the prohibition of nuclear weapons in Latin America (Treaty of Tlatelolco)

Prohibits the testing, use, manufacture, production or acquisition by any means, as well as the receipt, storage, installation, deployment and any form of possession of any nuclear weapons by Latin American countries.

The parties should conclude agreements with the International Atomic Energy Agency (IAEA) for the application of safeguards to their nuclear activities.

Under *Additional Protocol I,* annexed to the treaty, the extra-continental or continental states which, *de jure* or *de facto,* are internationally responsible for territories lying within the limits of the geographical zone established by the treaty (France, the Netherlands, the UK and the USA), undertake to apply the statute of military denuclearization, as defined in the treaty, to such territories.

Under *Additional Protocol II,* annexed to the treaty, the nuclear-weapon states undertake to respect the statute of military denuclearization of Latin America as defined in the treaty, not to contribute to acts involving a violation of the treaty, and not to use or threaten to use nuclear weapons against the parties to the treaty.

Signed at Mexico City on 14 February 1967.

The treaty enters into force for each state that has ratified it when the requirements specified in the treaty have been met, that is, that all states in the region deposit the instruments of ratification, that Additional Protocols I and II be signed and ratified by those states to which they apply (see above), and that agreements on safeguards be concluded with the IAEA. The signatory states have the right to waive, wholly or in part, those requirements.

The Additional Protocols enter into force for the states that have ratified them on the date of the deposit of their instruments of ratification.

The depositary government: Mexico.

## Treaty on the non-proliferation of nuclear weapons (Non-Proliferation Treaty—NPT)

Prohibits the transfer by nuclear-weapon states to any recipient whatsoever of nuclear weapons or other nuclear explosive devices or of control over them. Prohibits the receipt by non-nuclear-weapon states from any transferor whatsoever, as well as the manufacture or other acquisition by those states, of nuclear weapons or other nuclear explosive devices.

Non-nuclear-weapon states undertake to conclude safeguards agreements with the International Atomic Energy Agency (IAEA) with a view to preventing diversion of nuclear energy from peaceful uses to nuclear weapons or other nuclear explosive devices.

Signed at London, Moscow and Washington on 1 July 1968.

Entered into force on 5 March 1970.

The depositary governments: UK, USA, USSR.


## Treaty on the prohibition of the emplacement of nuclear weapons and other weapons of mass destruction on the sea-bed and the ocean floor and in the subsoil thereof (Sea-Bed Treaty)

Prohibits emplanting or emplacement on the sea-bed and the ocean floor and in the subsoil thereof beyond the outer limit of a sea-bed zone (coterminous with the 12-mile outer limit of the zone referred to in the 1958 Geneva Convention on the Territorial Sea and the Contiguous Zone) of any nuclear weapons or any other types of weapons of mass destruction as well as structures, launching installations or any other facilities specifically designed for storing, testing or using such weapons.

Signed at London, Moscow and Washington on 11 February 1971.

Entered into force on 18 May 1972.

The depositary governments: UK, USA, USSR.


## Convention on the prohibition of the development, production and stockpiling of bacteriological (biological) and toxin weapons and on their destruction (BW Convention)

Prohibits the development, production, stockpiling, acquisition by other means or retention of microbial or other biological agents, or toxins, whatever their origin or method of production, of types and in quantities that have no justification for prophylactic, protective or other peaceful purposes, as well as weapons, equipment or means of delivery designed to use such agents or toxins for hostile purposes or in armed conflict. The destruction of the agents, toxins, weapons, equipment and means of delivery in the possession of the parties, or their diversion to peaceful purposes, should be effected not later than nine months after the entry into force of the convention.

Signed at London, Moscow and Washington on 10 April 1972.

The depositary governments: UK, USA, USSR.

## II. *List of states which have signed, ratified, acceded or succeeded to multilateral agreements related to disarmament, as of 31 December 1973*

**Total number of parties**

| | |
|---|---|
| Antarctic Treaty | 17 |
| Partial Test Ban Treaty | 106 |
| Outer Space Treaty | 71 |
| Treaty of Tlatelolco | 18 |
| Non-Proliferation Treaty | 82 |
| Sea-Bed Treaty | 52 |
| BW Convention | 31 ratifications, but the convention was still not in force |

**Note**

1. Abbreviations used in the list:

S: signature

R: deposit of instruments of ratification, accession or succession. Place of signature and/or deposit of the instrument of ratification, accession or succession:

L: London

M: Moscow

W: Washington

P.I: Additional Protocol I to the Treaty of Tlatelolco

P.II: Additional Protocol II to the Treaty of Tlatelolco

S.A.: Safeguards agreement concluded with the International Atomic Energy Agency (IAEA) under the Non-Proliferation Treaty or the Treaty of Tlatelolco.

2. The footnotes at the end of the table are grouped separately for each agreement.

| | Antarctic Treaty | Partial Test Ban Treaty | Outer Space Treaty |
|---|---|---|---|
| Afghanistan | | S: 8 Aug. 1963 LW<br>9 Aug. 1963 M<br>R: 12 Mar. 1964 L<br>13 Mar. 1964 W<br>23 Mar. 1964 M | S: 27 Jan. 1967 W<br>30 Jan. 1967 M |
| Algeria | | S: 14 Aug. 1963 LW<br>19 Aug. 1963 M | |
| Argentina | S: 1 Dec. 1959<br>R: 23 Jun. 1961 | S: 8 Aug. 1963 W<br>9 Aug. 1963 LM | S: 27 Jan. 1967 W<br>18 Apr. 1967 M<br>R: 26 Mar. 1969 MW |
| Australia | S: 1 Dec. 1959<br>R: 23 Jun. 1961 | S: 8 Aug. 1963 LMW<br>R: 12 Nov. 1963 LMW | S: 27 Jan. 1967 W<br>R: 10 Oct. 1967 LMW |
| Austria | | S: 11 Sep. 1963 MW<br>12 Sep. 1963 L<br>R: 17 Jul. 1964 LMW | S: 20 Feb. 1967 LMW<br>R: 26 Feb. 1968 LMW |
| Barbados | | | R: 12 Sep. 1968 W |
| Belgium | S: 1 Dec. 1959<br>R: 26 Jul. 1960 | S: 8 Aug. 1963 LMW<br>R: 1 Mar. 1966 LMW | S: 27 Jan. 1967 LM<br>2 Feb. 1967 W<br>R: 30 Mar. 1973 W<br>31 Mar. 1973 LM |
| Bolivia | | S: 8 Aug. 1963 W<br>21 Aug. 1963 L<br>20 Sep. 1963 M<br>R: 4 Aug. 1965 MW<br>25 Jan. 1966 L | S: 27 Jan. 1967 W |

| Treaty of Tlatelolco | Non-Proliferation Treaty | Sea-Bed Treaty | BW Convention |
|---|---|---|---|
| | S: 1 Jul. 1968 LMW<br>R: 4 Feb. 1970 W<br>5 Feb. 1970 M<br>5 Mar. 1970 L | S: 11 Feb. 1971 LMW<br>R: 22 Apr. 1971 M<br>23 Apr. 1971 L<br>21 May 1971 W | S: 10 Apr. 1972 LMW |
| S:[1] 27 Sep. 1967 | | S:[1] 3 Sep. 1971 LMW | S: 1 Aug. 1972 M<br>3 Aug. 1972 L<br>7 Aug. 1972 W |
| | S:[1] 27 Feb. 1970 LMW<br>R: 23 Jan. 1973 LMW | S: 11 Feb. 1971 LMW<br>R: 23 Jan. 1973 LMW | S: 10 Apr. 1972 LMW |
| | S: 1 Jul. 1968 LMW<br>R: 27 Jun. 1969 LMW<br>S.A.:[2] 23 Jul. 1972 | S: 11 Feb. 1971 LMW<br>R: 10 Aug. 1972 LMW | S: 10 Apr. 1972 LMW<br>R:[7] 10 Aug. 1973 LMW |
| S: 18 Oct. 1968<br>R:[2] 25 Apr. 1969 | S: 1 Jul. 1968 W | | S: 16 Feb. 1973 W<br>R: 16 Feb. 1973 W |
| | S: 20 Aug. 1968 LMW<br>S.A.:[28, 29] 5 Apr. 1973 | S: 11 Feb. 1971 LMW<br>R: 20 Nov. 1972 LMW | S: 10 Apr. 1972 LMW |
| S: 14 Feb. 1967<br>R:[2] 18 Feb. 1969 | S: 1 Jul. 1968 W<br>R: 26 May 1970 W<br>S.A.:[18, 22, 27] | S: 11 Feb. 1971 LMW | S: 10 Apr. 1972 W |

|  | Antarctic Treaty | Partial Test Ban Treaty | Outer Space Treaty |
|---|---|---|---|
| Botswana |  | R:[1]  5 Jan. 1968  M<br>14 Feb. 1968  L<br>4 Mar. 1968  W | S:   27 Jan. 1967  W |
| Brazil |  | S:   8 Aug. 1963  LW<br>9 Aug. 1963  M<br>R:  15 Dec. 1964  M<br>15 Jan. 1965  W<br>4 Mar. 1965  L | S:   30 Jan. 1967  M<br>2 Feb. 1967  LW<br>R:[1]  5 Mar. 1969  LMW |
| Bulgaria |  | S:   8 Aug. 1963  LMW<br>R:  13 Nov. 1963  W<br>21 Nov. 1963  M<br>2 Dec. 1963  L | S:   27 Jan. 1967  LMW<br>R:  28 Mar. 1967  M<br>11 Apr. 1967  W<br>19 Apr. 1967  L |
| Burma |  | S:  14 Aug. 1963  LMW<br>R:  15 Nov. 1963  LMW | S:  22 May 1967  LMW<br>R:  18 Mar. 1970  LMW |
| Burundi |  | S:   4 Oct. 1963  W | S:   27 Jan. 1967  W |
| Byelorussian Soviet Socialist Republic |  | S:   8 Oct. 1963  M<br>R:[2] 16 Dec. 1963  M | S:[2] 10 Feb. 1967  M<br>R:  31 Oct. 1967  M |
| Cameroon |  | S:[3] 27 Aug. 1963  W<br>6 Sep. 1963  L | S:   27 Jan. 1967  W |
| Canada |  | S:   8 Aug. 1963  LMW<br>R:  28 Jan. 1964  LMW | S:   27 Jan. 1967  LMW<br>R:  10 Oct. 1967  LMW |

| Treaty of Tlatelolco | Non-Proliferation Treaty | Sea-Bed Treaty | BW Convention |
|---|---|---|---|
| | S:  1 Jul. 1968  W<br>R:  28 Apr. 1969  L | S:  11 Feb. 1971  W<br>R:  10 Nov. 1972  W | S:  10 Apr. 1972  W |
| S:[3]  9 May 1967<br>R:[4]  29 Jan. 1968 | | S:[2]  3 Sep. 1971  LMW | S:  10 Apr. 1972  LMW<br>R:  27 Feb. 1973  LMW |
| | S:  1 Jul. 1968  LMW<br>R:  5 Sep. 1969  W<br>   18 Sep. 1969  M<br>   3 Nov. 1969  L<br>S.A.: 29 Feb. 1972 | S:  11 Feb. 1971  LMW<br>R:  16 Apr. 1971  M<br>   7 May 1971  W<br>   26 May 1971  L | S:  10 Apr. 1972  LMW<br>R:  2 Aug. 1972  L<br>   13 Sep. 1972  W<br>   19 Sep. 1972  M |
| | | S:  11 Feb. 1971  LMW | S:  10 Apr. 1972  LMW |
| | R:  19 Mar. 1971  M | S:  11 Feb. 1971  MW | S:  10 Apr. 1972  MW |
| | | S:  3 Mar. 1971  M<br>R:  14 Sep. 1971  M | S:  10 Apr. 1972  M |
| | S:  17 Jul. 1968  W<br>   18 Jul. 1968  M<br>R:  8 Jan. 1969  W | S:  11 Nov. 1971  M | |
| | S:  23 Jul. 1968  LW<br>   29 Jul. 1968  M<br>R:  8 Jan. 1969  LMW<br>S.A.: 21 Feb. 1972 | S:  11 Feb. 1971  LMW<br>R:[8] 17 May 1972  LMW | S:  10 Apr. 1972  LMW<br>R:  18 Sep. 1972  LMW |

|  | Antarctic Treaty | Partial Test Ban Treaty | Outer Space Treaty |
|---|---|---|---|
| Central African Republic |  | R:  22 Dec. 1964  W<br>    24 Aug. 1965  L<br>    25 Sep. 1965  M | S:  27 Jan. 1967  W |
| Chad |  | S:  26 Aug. 1963  W<br>R:   1 Mar. 1965  W |  |
| Chile | S:   1 Dec. 1959<br>R:  23 Jun. 1961 | S:   8 Aug. 1963  W<br>    9 Aug. 1963  LM<br>R:   6 Oct. 1965  L | S:  27 Jan. 1967  W<br>    3 Feb. 1967  L<br>    20 Feb. 1967  M |
| China |  |  |  |
| Colombia |  | S:  16 Aug. 1963  MW<br>    20 Aug. 1963  L | S:  27 Jan. 1967  W |
| Costa Rica |  | S:   9 Aug. 1963  L<br>    13 Aug. 1963  W<br>    23 Aug. 1963  M<br>R:  10 Jul. 1967  W |  |
| Cuba |  |  |  |
| Cyprus |  | S:   8 Aug. 1963  LMW<br>R:  15 Apr. 1965  L<br>    21 Apr. 1965  M<br>    7 May 1965  W | S:  27 Jan. 1967  W<br>    15 Feb. 1967  M<br>    16 Feb. 1967  L<br>R:   5 Jul. 1972   LW<br>    20 Sep. 1972  M |

| Treaty of Tlatelolco | Non-Proliferation Treaty | Sea-Bed Treaty | BW Convention |
|---|---|---|---|
| | R: 25 Oct. 1970 W | S: 11 Feb. 1971 W | S: 10 Apr. 1972 W |
| | S: 1 Jul. 1968 M<br>R: 10 Mar. 1971 W<br>11 Mar. 1971 M<br>23 Mar. 1971 L | | |
| S: 14 Feb. 1967 | | | S: 10 Apr. 1972 LMW |
| P.II:[13]<br>S: 21 Aug. 1973 | | | |
| S: 14 Feb. 1967<br>R:[2] 4 Aug. 1972 | S: 1 Jul. 1968 W | S: 11 Feb. 1971 W | S: 10 Apr. 1972 W |
| S: 14 Feb. 1967<br>R:[2] 25 Aug. 1969 | S: 1 Jul. 1968 W<br>R: 3 Mar. 1970 W<br>S.A.:[17,18,22] 12 Jul. 1973 | S: 11 Feb. 1971 W | S: 10 Apr. 1972 W<br>R: 17 Dec. 1973 W |
| | | | S: 12 Apr. 1972 M |
| | S: 1 Jul. 1968 LMW<br>R: 10 Feb. 1970 M<br>16 Feb. 1970 W<br>5 Mar. 1970 L<br>S.A.:[18] 26 Jan. 1973 | S: 11 Feb. 1971 LMW<br>R: 17 Nov. 1971 LM<br>30 Dec. 1971 W | S: 10 Apr. 1972 LW<br>14 Apr. 1972 M<br>R: 6 Nov. 1973 L<br>13 Nov. 1973 W<br>21 Nov. 1973 M |

461

|  | Antarctic Treaty | Partial Test Ban Treaty | Outer Space Treaty |
|---|---|---|---|
| Czechoslovakia | R: 14 Jun. 1962 | S: 8 Aug. 1963 LMW<br>R: 14 Oct. 1963 LM<br>17 Oct. 1963 W | S: 27 Jan. 1967 LMW<br>R: 11 May 1967 L<br>18 May 1967 M<br>22 May 1967 W |
| Dahomey |  | S:[3] 27 Aug. 1963 W<br>3 Sep. 1963 L<br>9 Oct. 1963 M<br>R: 15 Dec. 1964 W<br>23 Dec. 1964 M<br>22 Apr. 1965 L |  |
| Democratic Yemen |  |  |  |
| Denmark | R: 20 May 1965 | S: 9 Aug. 1963 LMW<br>R: 15 Jan. 1964 LMW | S: 27 Jan. 1967 LMW<br>R: 10 Oct. 1967 LMW |
| Dominican Republic |  | S: 16 Sep. 1963 W<br>17 Sep. 1963 L<br>19 Sep. 1963 M<br>R: 3 Jun. 1964 M<br>18 Jun. 1964 L<br>22 Jul. 1964 W | S: 27 Jan. 1967 W<br>R: 21 Nov. 1968 W |
| Ecuador |  | S: 27 Sep. 1963 W<br>1 Oct. 1963 LM<br>R: 6 May 1964 W<br>8 May 1964 L<br>13 Nov. 1964 M | S: 27 Jan. 1967 W<br>16 May 1967 L<br>7 Jun. 1967 M<br>R: 7 Mar. 1969 W |
| Egypt |  | S:[4] 8 Aug. 1963 LMW<br>R: 10 Jan. 1964 LMW | S: 27 Jan. 1967 MW<br>R: 10 Oct. 1967 W<br>23 Jan. 1968 M |
| El Salvador |  | S: 21 Aug. 1963 W<br>22 Aug. 1963 L<br>23 Aug. 1963 M<br>R: 3 Dec. 1964 W<br>7 Dec. 1964 L<br>9 Feb. 1965 M | S: 27 Jan. 1967 W<br>R: 15 Jan. 1969 W |

| Treaty of Tlatelolco | Non-Proliferation Treaty | Sea-Bed Treaty | BW Convention |
|---|---|---|---|
| | S: 1 Jul. 1968 LMW<br>R: 22 Jul. 1969 LMW<br>S.A.: 3 Mar. 1972 | S: 11 Feb. 1971 LMW<br>R: 11 Jan. 1972 LMW | S: 10 Apr. 1972 LMW<br>R: 30 Apr. 1973 LMW |
| | S: 1 Jul. 1968 W<br>R: 31 Oct. 1972 W | S: 18 Mar. 1971 W | S: 10 Apr. 1972 W |
| | S: 14 Nov. 1968 M | S: 23 Feb. 1971 M | S: 26 Apr. 1972 M |
| | S: 1 Jul. 1968 LMW<br>R: 3 Jan. 1969 LMW<br>S.A.:[19,20] 1 Mar. 1972 | S: 11 Feb. 1971 LMW<br>R: 15 Jun. 1971 LMW | S: 10 Apr. 1972 LMW<br>R: 1 Mar. 1973 LMW |
| S: 28 Jul. 1967<br>R:[2] 14 Jun. 1968 | S: 1 Jul. 1968 W<br>R: 24 Jul. 1971 W<br>S.A.:[18] 11 Oct. 1973 | S: 11 Feb. 1971 W<br>R: 11 Feb. 1972 W | S: 10 Apr. 1972 W<br>R: 23 Feb. 1973 W |
| S: 14 Feb. 1967<br>R:[2] 11 Feb. 1969 | S: 9 Jul. 1968 W<br>R: 7 Mar. 1969 W | | S: 14 Jun. 1972 W |
| | S: 1 Jul. 1968 LM | | S: 10 Apr. 1972 LM |
| S: 14 Feb. 1967<br>R:[2] 22 Apr. 1968 | S: 1 Jul. 1968 W<br>R: 11 Jul. 1972 W | | S: 10 Apr. 1972 W |

|  | Antarctic Treaty | Partial Test Ban Treaty | Outer Space Treaty |
|---|---|---|---|
| Equatorial Guinea |  |  |  |
| Ethiopia |  | S:   9 Aug. 1963 LW<br>    19 Sep. 1963  M | S:   27 Jan. 1967  LW<br>    10 Feb. 1967  M |
| Fiji |  | R:[1] 14 Jul. 1972 M<br>    18 Jul. 1972  W<br>    14 Aug. 1972 L | R:[7] 18 Jul. 1972  W<br>    14 Aug. 1972 L<br>    29 Aug. 1972 M |
| Finland |  | S:   8 Aug. 1963 LMW<br>R:   9 Jan. 1964  LMW | S:   27 Jan. 1967  LMW<br>R:   12 Jul. 1967  LMW |
| France | S:   1 Dec. 1959<br>R:   16 Sep. 1960 |  | S:   25 Sep. 1967 LMW<br>R:    5 Aug. 1970 LMW |
| Gabon |  | S:   10 Sep. 1963  W<br>R:   20 Feb. 1964  W<br>     4 Mar. 1964 L<br>     9 Mar. 1964 M |  |
| Gambia |  | R:[1] 27 Apr. 1965  MW<br>     6 May 1965  L | S:    2 Jun. 1967  L |
| German Democratic Republic |  | S:   8 Aug. 1963 M<br>R:[5] 30 Dec. 1963 M | S:   27 Jan. 1967  M<br>R:[3]   2 Feb. 1967  M |

| Treaty of Tlatelolco | Non-Proliferation Treaty | Sea-Bed Treaty | BW Convention |
|---|---|---|---|
| | | S: 4 Jun. 1971 W | |
| | S: 5 Sep. 1968 LMW<br>R: 5 Feb. 1970 M<br>5 Mar. 1970 LW | S: 11 Feb. 1971 LMW | S: 10 Apr. 1972 LMW |
| | R:[13] 18 Jul. 1972 W<br>14 Aug. 1972 L<br>29 Aug. 1972 M<br>S.A.:[18] 22 Mar. 1973 | | S: 22 Feb. 1973 L<br>R: 4 Sep. 1973 W<br>1 Oct. 1973 L |
| | S: 1 Jul. 1968 LMW<br>R: 5 Feb. 1969 LMW<br>S.A.:[3] 9 Feb. 1972 | S: 11 Feb. 1971 LMW<br>R: 8 Jun. 1971 LMW | S:[10] 10 Apr. 1972 LMW |
| P.II:[14]<br>S: 18 Jul. 1973 | | | |
| | | | S: 10 Apr. 1972 L |
| | S: 4 Sep. 1968 L<br>20 Sep. 1968 W<br>24 Sep. 1968 M | S: 18 May 1971 L<br>21 May 1971 M<br>29 Oct. 1971 W | S: 2 Jun. 1972 M<br>8 Aug. 1972 L<br>9 Nov. 1972 W |
| | S: 1 Jul. 1968 M<br>R:[4] 31 Oct. 1969 M<br>S.A.: 7 Mar. 1972 | S:[3] 11 Feb. 1971 M<br>R: 27 Jul. 1971 M | S: 10 Apr. 1972 M<br>R: 28 Nov. 1972 M |

| | Antarctic Treaty | Partial Test Ban Treaty | Outer Space Treaty |
|---|---|---|---|
| Germany, Federal Republic of | | S:  19 Aug. 1963 LMW<br>R:⁶  1 Dec. 1964 LW | S:  27 Jan. 1967  LMW<br>R:⁴ 10 Feb. 1971 LW |
| Ghana | | S:   8 Aug. 1963 M<br>    9 Aug. 1963 W<br>    4 Sep. 1963 L<br>R: 27 Nov. 1963 L<br>    9 Jan. 1964 W<br>   31 May 1965 M | S:  27 Jan. 1967 W<br>   15 Feb. 1967 M<br>    3 Mar. 1967 L |
| Greece | | S:   8 Aug. 1963 W<br>    9 Aug. 1963 LM<br>R:  18 Dec. 1963 LMW | S:  27 Jan. 1967 W<br>R:  19 Jan. 1971 L |
| Guatemala | | S:  23 Sep. 1963  W<br>R:³  6 Jan. 1964  W | |
| Guinea | | | |
| Guyana | | | S:   3 Feb. 1967 W |
| Haiti | | S:   9 Oct. 1963 W | S:  27 Jan. 1967 W |
| Holy See | | | S:   5 Apr. 1967 L |

| Treaty of Tlatelolco | Non-Proliferation Treaty | Sea-Bed Treaty | BW Convention |
|---|---|---|---|
| | S:[5] 28 Nov. 1969 LMW<br>S.A.:[28, 29] 5 Apr. 1973 | S:[4] 8 Jun. 1971 LMW | S: 10 Apr. 1972 LMW |
| | S: 1 Jul. 1968 MW<br>24 Jul. 1968 L<br>R: 4 May 1970 L<br>5 May 1970 W<br>11 May 1970 M<br>S.A.:[17, 18] 23 Aug. 1973 | S: 11 Feb. 1971 LMW<br>R: 9 Aug. 1972 W | S: 10 Apr. 1972 MW |
| | S: 1 Jul. 1968 MW<br>R: 11 Mar. 1970 W<br>S.A.:[21] 1 Mar. 1972 | S: 11 Feb. 1971 M<br>12 Feb. 1971 W | S: 10 Apr. 1972 L<br>12 Apr. 1972 W<br>14 Apr. 1972 M |
| S: 14 Feb. 1967<br>R:[2] 6 Feb. 1970 | S: 26 Jul. 1968 W<br>R: 22 Sep. 1970 W | S: 11 Feb. 1971 W | S: 9 May 1972 W<br>R: 19 Sep. 1973 W |
| | | S: 11 Feb. 1971 MW | |
| | | | S: 3 Jan. 1973 W |
| S: 14 Feb. 1967<br>R:[2] 23 May 1969 | S: 1 Jul. 1968 W<br>R: 2 Jun. 1970 W<br>S.A.:[18, 22, 27] | | S: 10 Apr. 1972 W |
| | R:[6] 25 Feb. 1971 LMW<br>S.A.:[18] 1 Aug. 1972 | | |

|  | Antarctic Treaty | Partial Test Ban Treaty | Outer Space Treaty |
|---|---|---|---|
| Honduras | | S: 8 Aug. 1963 W<br>15 Aug. 1963 L<br>16 Aug. 1963 M<br>R: 2 Oct. 1964 W<br>2 Dec. 1964 L | S: 27 Jan. 1967 W |
| Hungary | | S: 8 Aug. 1963 LMW<br>R: 21 Oct. 1963 L<br>22 Oct. 1963 W<br>23 Oct. 1963 M | S: 27 Jan. 1967 LMW<br>R: 26 Jun. 1967 LMW |
| Iceland | | S: 12 Aug. 1963 LMW<br>R: 29 Apr. 1964 LMW | S: 27 Jan. 1967 LMW<br>R: 5 Feb. 1968 LMW |
| India | | S: 8 Aug. 1963 LMW<br>R: 10 Oct. 1963 L<br>14 Oct. 1963 M<br>18 Oct. 1963 W | S: 3 Mar. 1967 LMW |
| Indonesia | | S: 23 Aug. 1963 LMW<br>R: 20 Jan. 1964 M<br>27 Jan. 1964 W<br>8 May 1964 L | S: 27 Jan. 1967 W<br>30 Jan. 1967 M<br>14 Feb. 1967 L |
| Iran | | S: 8 Aug. 1963 LMW<br>R: 5 May 1964 LMW | S: 27 Jan. 1967 L |
| Iraq | | S: 13 Aug. 1963 LMW<br>R: 30 Nov. 1964 L<br>1 Dec. 1964 W<br>3 Dec. 1964 M | S: 27 Feb. 1967 LW<br>9 Mar. 1967 M<br>R: 4 Dec. 1968 M<br>23 Sep. 1969 L |
| Ireland | | S: 8 Aug. 1963 LW<br>9 Aug. 1963 M<br>R: 18 Dec. 1963 LW<br>20 Dec. 1963 M | S: 27 Jan. 1967 LW<br>R: 17 Jul. 1968 W<br>19 Jul. 1968 L |

| Treaty of Tlatelolco | Non-Proliferation Treaty | Sea-Bed Treaty | BW Convention |
|---|---|---|---|
| S:  14 Feb. 1967<br>R:[2]  23 Sep. 1968 | S:  1 Jul. 1968  W<br>R:  16 May 1973  W | S:  11 Feb. 1971  W | S:  10 Apr. 1972  W |
| | S:  1 Jul. 1968  LMW<br>R:  27 May 1969 LMW<br>S.A.: 30 Mar. 1972 | S:  11 Feb. 1971  LMW<br>R:  13 Aug. 1971  LMW | S:  10 Apr. 1972 LMW<br>R:  27 Dec. 1972 LMW |
| | S:  1 Jul. 1968  LMW<br>R:  18 Jul. 1969  LMW<br>S.A.:[17,18] 12 Jul. 1972 | S:  11 Feb. 1971  LMW<br>R:  30 May 1972  LMW | S:  10 Apr. 1972 LMW<br>R:  15 Feb. 1973  LMW |
| | | R:[10] 20 Jul.  1973  LMW | S:[8]  15 Jan.  1973  LMW |
| | S:[7]  2 Mar. 1970  LMW | | S:  20 Jun. 1972  MW<br>21 Jun. 1972  L |
| | S:  1 Jul. 1968   LMW<br>R:  2 Feb. 1970  W<br>10 Feb. 1970  M<br>5 Mar. 1970  L<br>S.A.:[17,26] 19 Jun. 1973 | S:  11 Feb. 1971  LMW<br>R:  26 Aug. 1971  LW<br>6 Sep. 1972  M | S:  10 Apr. 1972  MW<br>16 Nov. 1972  L<br>R:  22 Aug. 1973  LW<br>27 Aug. 1973  M |
| | S:  1 Jul. 1968  M<br>R:  29 Oct. 1969 M<br>S.A.: 29 Feb. 1972 | S:  22 Feb. 1971  M<br>R:[6] 13 Sep. 1972  M | S:  11 May 1972  M |
| | S:  1 Jul. 1968  MW<br>4 Jul. 1968  L<br>R:  1 Jul. 1968  W<br>2 Jul. 1968  M<br>4 Jul. 1968  L<br>S.A.:[18,19] 29 Feb. 1972 | S:  11 Feb. 1971  LW<br>R:  19 Aug. 1971  LW | S:[1]  10 Apr. 1972  LW<br>R:  27 Oct. 1972  LW |

| | Antarctic Treaty | Partial Test Ban Treaty | Outer Space Treaty |
|---|---|---|---|
| Israel | | S: 8 Aug. 1963 LMW<br>R: 15 Jan. 1964 LW<br>28 Jan. 1964 M | S: 27 Jan. 1967 LMW |
| Italy | | S: 8 Aug. 1963 LMW<br>R: 10 Dec. 1964 LMW | S: 27 Jan. 1967 LMW<br>R: 4 May 1972 LW |
| Ivory Coast | | S: 5 Sep. 1963 W<br>R: 5 Feb. 1965 W | |
| Jamaica | | S: 13 Aug. 1963 LMW | S: 29 Jun. 1967 LMW<br>R: 6 Aug. 1970 W<br>10 Aug. 1970 L<br>21 Aug. 1970 M |
| Japan | S: 1 Dec. 1959<br>R: 4 Aug. 1960 | S: 14 Aug. 1963 LMW<br>R: 15 Jun. 1964 LMW | S: 27 Jan. 1967 LMW<br>R: 10 Oct. 1967 LMW |
| Jordan | | S: 12 Aug. 1963 LW<br>19 Aug. 1963 M<br>R: 29 May 1964 L<br>7 Jul. 1964 M<br>10 Jul. 1964 W | S: 2 Feb. 1967 W |
| Kenya | | R: 10 Jun. 1965 L<br>11 Jun. 1965 W<br>30 Jun. 1965 M | |
| Khmer Republic | | | |

| Treaty of Tlatelolco | Non-Proliferation Treaty | Sea-Bed Treaty | BW Convention |
|---|---|---|---|
| | S:[8] 28 Jan. 1969 LMW<br>S.A.:[28, 29] 5 Apr. 1973 | S:[5] 11 Feb. 1971 LMW | S: 10 Apr. 1972 LMW |
| | S: 1 Jul. 1968 W<br>R: 6 Mar. 1973 W | R: 14 Jan. 1972 W | S: 23 May 1972 W |
| S: 26 Oct. 1967<br>R:[2] 26 Jun. 1969 | S: 14 Apr. 1969 LMW<br>R: 5 Mar. 1970 LMW | S: 11 Oct. 1971 LW<br>14 Oct. 1971 M | |
| | S:[9] 3 Feb. 1970 LMW | S: 11 Feb. 1971 LMW<br>R: 21 Jun. 1971 LMW | S: 10 Apr. 1972 LMW |
| | S: 10 Jul. 1968 W<br>R: 11 Feb. 1970 W | S: 11 Feb. 1971 LMW<br>R: 17 Aug. 1971 W<br>30 Aug. 1971 M<br>1 Nov. 1971 L | S: 10 Apr. 1972 W<br>17 Apr. 1972 L<br>24 Apr. 1972 M |
| | S: 1 Jul. 1968 W<br>R: 11 Jun. 1970 M | | |
| | R: 2 Jun. 1972 W | S: 11 Feb. 1971 W | S: 10 Apr. 1972 W |

|  | Antarctic Treaty | Partial Test Ban Treaty | Outer Space Treaty |
|---|---|---|---|
| Korea, South |  | S: 30 Aug. 1963 LW<br>R:[3] 24 Jul. 1964 LW | S: 27 Jan. 1967 W<br>R:[8] 13 Oct. 1967 W |
| Kuwait |  | S:[7] 20 Aug. 1963 LMW<br>R: 20 May 1965 W<br>21 May 1965 L<br>17 Jun. 1965 M | R:[9] 7 Jun. 1972 W<br>20 Jun. 1972 L<br>4 Jul. 1972 M |
| Laos |  | S: 12 Aug. 1963 LMW<br>R: 10 Feb. 1965 L<br>12 Feb. 1965 W<br>7 Apr. 1965 M | S: 27 Jan. 1967 W<br>30 Jan. 1967 L<br>2 Feb. 1967 M<br>R: 27 Nov. 1972 M<br>29 Nov. 1972 W<br>15 Jan. 1973 L |
| Lebanon |  | S: 12 Aug. 1963 W<br>13 Aug. 1963 LM<br>R: 14 May 1965 W<br>20 May 1965 L<br>4 Jun. 1965 M | S: 23 Feb. 1967 LMW<br>R: 31 Mar. 1969 LM<br>30 Jun. 1969 W |
| Lesotho |  |  | S: 27 Jan. 1967 W |
| Liberia |  | S: 8 Aug. 1963 W<br>16 Aug. 1963 L<br>27 Aug. 1963 M<br>R: 19 May 1964 W<br>22 May 1964 L<br>16 Jun. 1964 M |  |
| Libyan Arab Republic |  | S: 9 Aug. 1963 L<br>16 Aug. 1963 MW<br>R: 15 Jul. 1968 L | R: 3 Jul. 1968 W |
| Luxembourg |  | S: 13 Aug. 1963 L<br>3 Sep. 1963 W<br>13 Sep. 1963 M<br>R: 10 Feb. 1965 LMW | S: 27 Jan. 1967 MW<br>31 Jan. 1967 L |

| Treaty of Tlatelolco | Non-Proliferation Treaty | Sea-Bed Treaty | BW Convention |
|---|---|---|---|
| | S:[10]  1 Jul. 1968  W | S:[6]  11 Feb. 1971  LW | S:[2]  10 Apr. 1972  LW |
| | S:  15 Aug. 1968  MW<br>22 Aug. 1968  L | | S:  14 Apr. 1972  MW<br>27 Apr. 1972  L<br>R:[3] 18 Jul.  1972  W<br>26 Jul.  1972  L<br>1 Aug. 1972  M |
| | S:  1 Jul. 1968  LMW<br>R:  5 Mar. 1970  LW<br>20 Feb. 1970  M | S:  11 Feb. 1971  LW<br>15 Feb. 1971  M<br>R:  19 Oct. 1971  L<br>22 Oct. 1971  M<br>3 Nov. 1971  W | S:  10 Apr. 1972  LMW<br>R:  20 Mar. 1973  M<br>22 Mar. 1973  W<br>25 Apr. 1973  L |
| | S:  1 Jul. 1968  LMW<br>R:  15 Jul. 1970  LM<br>20 Nov. 1970  W<br>S.A.:[18] 5 Mar. 1973 | S:  11 Feb. 1971  LMW | S:  10 Apr. 1972  LW<br>21 Apr. 1972  M |
| | S:  9 Jul. 1968  W<br>R:  20 May 1970  W<br>S.A.:[18] 12 Jun. 1973 | S:  8 Sep. 1971  W<br>R:  3 Apr. 1973  W | S:  10 Apr. 1972  W |
| | S:  1 Jul. 1968  W<br>R:  5 Mar. 1970  W | S:  11 Feb. 1971  W | S:  10 Apr. 1972  W<br>14 Apr. 1972  L |
| | S:  18 Jul. 1968  L<br>19 Jul. 1968  W<br>23 Jul. 1968  M | | |
| | S:  14 Aug. 1968  LMW<br><br>S.A.:[28, 29] 5 Apr. 1973 | S:  11 Feb. 1971  LMW | S:  10 Apr. 1972  LM<br>12 Apr. 1972  W |

|  | Antarctic Treaty | Partial Test Ban Treaty | Outer Space Treaty |
|---|---|---|---|
| Madagascar |  | S:  23 Sep. 1963  W<br>R:  15 Mar. 1965  W | R:[5] 22 Aug. 1968  W |
| Malawi |  | R:[1] 26 Nov. 1964  MW<br>7 Jan. 1965  L |  |
| Malaysia |  | S:  8 Aug. 1963  W<br>12 Aug. 1963  L<br>21 Aug. 1963  M<br>R:  15 Jul. 1964  M<br>16 Jul. 1964  LW | S:  20 Feb. 1967  W<br>21 Feb. 1967  L<br>3 May 1967  M |
| Maldives |  |  |  |
| Mali |  | S:  23 Aug. 1963  LMW | R:  11 Jun. 1968  M |
| Malta |  | R:[1] 25 Nov. 1964  MW<br>1 Dec. 1964  L |  |
| Mauritania |  | S:  13 Sep. 1963  W<br>17 Sep. 1963  L<br>8 Oct. 1963  M<br>R:  6 Apr. 1964  W<br>15 Apr. 1964  L<br>28 Apr. 1964  M |  |
| Mauritius |  | R:[1] 30 Apr. 1969  MW<br>12 May 1969  L | R:[7] 7 Apr. 1969  W<br>21 Apr. 1969  L<br>13 May 1969  M |

| Treaty of Tlatelolco | Non-Proliferation Treaty | Sea-Bed Treaty | BW Convention |
|---|---|---|---|
| | S:   22 Aug. 1968 W<br>R:    8 Oct. 1970  W<br>S.A.:[18] 14 Jun. 1973 | S:   14 Sep. 1971  W | S:   13 Oct. 1972  L |
| | | | S:   10 Apr. 1972  W |
| | S:    1 Jul. 1968   LMW<br>R:    5 Mar. 1970 LMW<br>S.A.:[18] 29 Feb. 1972 | S:   20 May 1971  LMW<br>R:   21 Jun. 1972  LMW | S:   10 Apr. 1972  LMW |
| | S:   11 Sep. 1968  W<br>R:    7 Apr. 1970  W | | |
| | S:   14 Jul. 1969   W<br>      15 Jul. 1969   M<br>R:   10 Feb. 1970  M<br>       5 Mar. 1970  W | S:   11 Feb. 1971  W<br>      15 Feb. 1971  M | S:   10 Apr. 1972  W |
| | S:   17 Apr. 1969  W<br>R:    6 Feb. 1970  W | S:   11 Feb. 1971  LW<br>R:    4 May 1971  W | S:   11 Sep. 1972  L |
| | S:    1 Jul. 1968   W<br>R:    8 Apr. 1969  W<br>      14 Apr. 1969  L<br>      25 Apr. 1969  M<br>S.A.:[18] 31 Jan. 1973 | S:   11 Feb. 1971  W<br>R:   23 Apr. 1971  W<br>       3 May 1971  L<br>      18 May 1971  M | S:   10 Apr. 1972  W<br>R:    7 Aug. 1972  W<br>      11 Jan.  1973  L<br>      15 Jan.  1973  M |

|  | Antarctic Treaty | Partial Test Ban Treaty | Outer Space Treaty |
|---|---|---|---|
| Mexico |  | S: 8 Aug. 1963 LMW<br>R: 27 Dec. 1963 LMW | S: 27 Jan. 1967 LMW<br>R: 31 Jan. 1968 LMW |
| Mongolia |  | S: 8 Aug. 1963 LM<br>R: 1 Nov. 1963 M<br>7 Nov. 1963 L | S: 27 Jan. 1967 M<br>R: 10 Oct. 1967 M |
| Morocco |  | S: 27 Aug. 1963 MW<br>30 Aug. 1963 L<br>R: 1 Feb. 1966 L<br>18 Feb. 1966 M<br>21 Feb. 1966 W | R: 21 Dec. 1967 LM<br>22 Dec. 1967 W |
| Nepal |  | S: 26 Aug. 1963 LM<br>30 Aug. 1963 W<br>R: 7 Oct. 1964 LMW | S: 3 Feb. 1967 MW<br>6 Feb. 1967 L<br>R: 10 Oct. 1967 L<br>16 Oct. 1967 M<br>22 Nov. 1967 W |
| Netherlands | R:[1] 30 Mar. 1967 | S: 9 Aug. 1963 LMW<br>R:[8] 14 Sep. 1964 LMW | S: 10 Feb. 1967 LMW<br>R:[10] 10 Oct. 1969 LMW |
| New Zealand | S: 1 Dec. 1959<br>R: 1 Nov. 1960 | S: 8 Aug. 1963 LMW<br>R: 10 Oct. 1963 LW<br>16 Oct. 1963 M | S: 27 Jan. 1967 LMW<br>R: 31 May 1968 LMW |
| Nicaragua |  | S: 13 Aug. 1963 LW<br>16 Aug. 1963 M<br>R: 26 Jan. 1965 L<br>26 Feb. 1965 MW | S: 27 Jan. 1967 W<br>13 Feb. 1967 L |
| Niger |  | S: 24 Sep. 1963 LW<br>R: 3 Jul. 1964 M<br>6 Jul. 1964 L<br>9 Jul. 1964 W | S: 1 Feb. 1967 W<br>R: 17 Apr. 1967 L<br>3 May 1967 W |

| Treaty of Tlatelolco | Non-Proliferation Treaty | Sea-Bed Treaty | BW Convention |
|---|---|---|---|
| S:[5] 14 Feb. 1967<br>R:[2] 20 Sep. 1967<br>S.A.: 6 Sep. 1968 | S:[11] 26 Jul. 1968 LMW<br>R: 21 Jan. 1969 LMW<br>S.A.:[22] 14 Sep. 1973 | | S:[4] 10 Apr. 1972 LMW |
| | S: 1 Jul. 1968 M<br>R: 14 May 1969 M<br>S.A.:[18] 5 Sep. 1972 | S: 11 Feb. 1971 LM<br>R: 8 Oct. 1971 M<br>15 Nov. 1971 L | S: 10 Apr. 1972 LMW<br>R: 5 Sep. 1972 W<br>14 Sep. 1972 L<br>20 Oct. 1972 M |
| | S: 1 Jul. 1968 LMW<br>R: 27 Nov. 1970 M<br>30 Nov. 1970 L<br>16 Dec. 1970 W<br>S.A.:[17,18] 30 Jan. 1973 | S: 11 Feb. 1971 MW<br>18 Feb. 1971 L<br>R: 26 Jul. 1971 L<br>5 Aug. 1971 W<br>18 Jan. 1972 M | S: 2 May 1972 L<br>3 May 1972 W<br>5 Jun. 1972 M |
| | S: 1 Jul. 1968 LMW<br>R: 5 Jan. 1970 W<br>9 Jan. 1970 M<br>3 Feb. 1970 L<br>S.A.:[18] 22 Jun. 1972 | S: 11 Feb. 1971 MW<br>24 Feb. 1971 L<br>R: 6 Jul. 1971 L<br>29 Jul. 1971 M<br>9 Aug. 1971 W | S: 10 Apr. 1972 LMW |
| P.I.:[6]<br>S: 15 Mar. 1968<br>R: 26 Jul. 1971 | S: 20 Aug. 1968 LMW<br>S.A.:[28,29,25] 5 Apr. 1973 | S: 11 Feb. 1971 LMW | S: 10 Apr. 1972 LMW |
| | S: 1 Jul. 1968 LMW<br>R: 10 Sep. 1969 LMW<br>S.A.:[18] 29 Feb. 1972 | S: 11 Feb. 1971 LMW<br>R: 24 Feb. 1972 LMW | S: 10 Apr. 1972 LMW<br>R: 13 Dec. 1972 W<br>18 Dec. 1972 L<br>10 Jan. 1973 M |
| S: 15 Feb. 1967<br>R:[2,7] 24 Oct. 1968 | S: 1 Jul. 1968 LW<br>R: 6 Mar. 1973 W<br>S.A.:[18,22,27] | S: 11 Feb. 1971 W<br>R: 7 Feb. 1973 W | S: 10 Apr. 1972 LW |
| | | S: 11 Feb. 1971 W<br>R: 9 Aug. 1971 W | S: 21 Apr. 1972 W<br>R: 23 Jun. 1972 W |

|  | Antarctic Treaty | Partial Test Ban Treaty | Outer Space Treaty |
|---|---|---|---|
| Nigeria |  | S: 30 Aug. 1963 M<br>2 Sep. 1963 L<br>4 Sep. 1963 W<br>R: 17 Feb. 1967 L<br>25 Feb. 1967 M<br>28 Feb. 1967 W | R: 14 Nov. 1967 L |
| Norway | S: 1 Dec. 1959<br>R: 24 Aug. 1960 | S: 9 Aug. 1963 LMW<br>R: 21 Nov. 1963 LMW | S: 3 Feb. 1967 LMW<br>R: 1 Jul. 1969 LMW |
| Pakistan |  | S: 14 Aug. 1963 LMW | S: 12 Sep. 1967 LMW<br>R: 8 Apr. 1968 LMW |
| Panama |  | S: 20 Sep. 1963 W<br>R: 24 Feb. 1966 W | S: 27 Jan. 1967 W |
| Paraguay |  | S: 15 Aug. 1963 LW<br>21 Aug. 1963 M |  |
| Peru |  | S: 23 Aug. 1963 LMW<br>R: 20 Jul. 1964 W<br>4 Aug. 1964 L<br>21 Aug. 1964 M | S: 30 Jun. 1967 W |
| Philippines |  | S: 8 Aug. 1963 LW<br>14 Aug. 1963 M<br>R:[3] 10 Nov. 1965 L<br>15 Nov. 1965 W<br>8 Feb. 1966 M | S: 27 Jan. 1967 LW<br>29 Apr. 1967 M |
| Poland | R: 8 Jun. 1961 | S: 8 Aug. 1963 LMW<br>R: 14 Oct. 1963 LMW | S: 27 Jan. 1967 LMW<br>R: 30 Jan. 1968 LMW |

| Treaty of Tlatelolco | Non-Proliferation Treaty | Sea-Bed Treaty | BW Convention |
|---|---|---|---|
| | S: 1 Jul. 1968 LMW<br>R: 27 Sep. 1968 L<br>   7 Oct. 1968 W<br>   14 Oct. 1968 M | | S: 3 Jul. 1972 M<br>   10 Jul. 1972 L<br>   6 Dec. 1972 W<br>R: 3 Jul. 1973 W<br>   9 Jul. 1973 L<br>   20 Jul. 1973 M |
| | S: 1 Jul. 1968 LMW<br>R: 5 Feb. 1969 LMW<br>S.A.:[19] 1 Mar. 1972 | S: 11 Feb. 1971 LMW<br>R: 28 Jun. 1971 LM<br>   29 Jun. 1971 W | S: 10 Apr. 1972 LMW<br>R: 1 Aug. 1973 LW<br>   23 Aug. 1973 M |
| | | | S: 10 Apr. 1972 LMW |
| S: 14 Feb. 1967<br>R:[2] 11 Jun. 1971 | S: 1 Jul. 1968 W | S: 11 Feb. 1971 W | S: 2 May 1972 W |
| S: 26 Apr. 1967<br>R:[2] 19 Mar. 1969 | S: 1 Jul. 1968 W<br>R: 4 Feb. 1970 W<br>   5 Mar. 1970 L | S: 23 Feb. 1971 W | |
| S: 14 Feb. 1967<br>R:[2] 4 Mar. 1969 | S: 1 Jul. 1968 W<br>R: 3 Mar. 1970 W | | S: 10 Apr. 1972 LMW |
| | S: 1 Jul. 1968 W<br>   18 Jul. 1968 M<br>R: 5 Oct. 1972 W<br>   16 Oct. 1972 L<br>   20 Oct. 1972 M<br>S.A.:[17, 24] 21 Feb. 1973 | | S: 10 Apr. 1972 LW<br>   21 Jun. 1972 M<br>R: 21 May 1973 W |
| | S: 1 Jul. 1968 LMW<br>R: 12 Jun. 1969 LMW<br>S.A.: 11 Oct. 1972 | S: 11 Feb. 1971 LMW<br>R: 15 Nov. 1971 LMW | S: 10 Apr. 1972 LMW<br>R: 25 Jan. 1973 LMW |

479

|  | Antarctic Treaty | Partial Test Ban Treaty | Outer Space Treaty |
|---|---|---|---|
| Portugal | | S:   9 Oct. 1963  LW | |
| Qatar | | | |
| Romania | R:[2] 15 Sep. 1971 | S:   8 Aug. 1963  LMW<br>R:  12 Dec. 1963  LMW | S:  27 Jan. 1967  LMW<br>R:   9 Apr. 1968  LMW |
| Rwanda | | S:  19 Sep. 1963  W<br>R:  22 Okt. 1963  L<br>     16 Dec. 1963  M<br>     27 Dec. 1963  W | S:  27 Jan. 1967  W |
| San Marino | | S:  17 Sep. 1963  W<br>     20 Sep. 1963  L<br>     24 Sep. 1963  M<br>R:   3 Jul. 1964  L<br>      9 Jul. 1964  W<br>     27 Nov. 1964  M | S:  21 Apr. 1967  W<br>     24 Apr. 1967  L<br>      6 Jun. 1967  M<br>R:  29 Oct. 1968  W<br>     21 Nov. 1968  M<br>      3 Feb. 1969  L |
| Saudi Arabia | | | |
| Senegal | | S:  20 Sep. 1963  W<br>     23 Sep. 1963  L<br>      9 Oct. 1963  M<br>R:   6 May 1964  L<br>     12 May 1964  M<br>      2 Jun. 1964  W | |
| Sierra Leone | | S:   4 Sep. 1963  L<br>      9 Sep. 1963  M<br>     11 Sep. 1963  W<br>R:  21 Feb. 1964  L<br>      4 Mar. 1964  W<br>     29 Apr. 1964  M | S:  27 Jan. 1967  LM<br>     16 May 1967  W<br>R:  13 Jul. 1967  M<br>     14 Jul. 1967  W<br>     25 Oct. 1967  L |

| Treaty of Tlatelolco | Non-Proliferation Treaty | Sea-Bed Treaty | BW Convention |
|---|---|---|---|
| | | | S:  29 Jun. 1972  W |
| | | | S:  14 Nov. 1972  L |
| | S:  1 Jul. 1968  LMW<br>R:  4 Feb. 1970  LMW<br>S.A.:  27 Oct. 1972 | S:  11 Feb. 1971  LMW<br>R:[9]  10 Jul. 1972  LMW | S:  10 Apr. 1972  LMW |
| | | S:  11 Feb. 1971  W | S:  10 Apr. 1972  MW |
| | S:[10]  1 Jul. 1968  W<br>29 Jul. 1968  L<br>21 Nov. 1968  M<br>R:  10 Aug. 1970  L<br>20 Aug. 1970  M<br>31 Aug. 1970  W | | S:  12 Sep. 1972  W<br>30 Jan. 1973  M<br>21 Mar. 1973  L |
| | | S:  7 Jan. 1972  W<br>R:  23 Jun. 1972  W | S:  12 Apr. 1972  W<br>R:  24 May 1972  W |
| | S:  1 Jul. 1968  MW<br>26 Jul. 1968  L<br>R:  17 Dec. 1970  M<br>22 Dec. 1970  W<br>15 Jan. 1971  L | S:  17 Mar. 1971  W | S:  10 Apr. 1972  W |
| | | S:  11 Feb. 1971  L<br>12 Feb. 1971  M<br>24 Feb. 1971  W | S:  7 Nov. 1972  W<br>24 Nov. 1972  L |

| | Antarctic Treaty | Partial Test Ban Treaty | Outer Space Treaty |
|---|---|---|---|
| Singapore | | R:[1] 12 Jul. 1968  MW<br>23 Jul. 1968  L | |
| Somalia | | S:  19 Aug. 1963 MW | S:   2 Feb. 1967  W |
| South Africa | S:    1 Dec. 1959<br>R:  21 Jun. 1960 | R:  10 Oct. 1963  LW<br>22 Nov. 1963  M | S:   1 Mar. 1967 W<br>R:  30 Sep. 1968  W<br>8 Oct. 1968  L |
| Spain | | S:  13 Aug. 1963  W<br>14 Aug. 1963  L<br>R:  17 Dec. 1964  LW | R:  27 Nov. 1968 L<br>7 Dec. 1968  W |
| Sri Lanka | | S:  22 Aug. 1963  LW<br>23 Aug. 1963  M<br>R:   5 Feb. 1964  W<br>12 Feb. 1964  M<br>13 Feb. 1964  L | S:  10 Mar. 1967 L |
| Sudan | | S:   9 Aug. 1963 LMW<br>R:   4 Mar. 1966 LW<br>28 Mar. 1966  M | |
| Swaziland | | R:  29 May 1969  LW<br>3 Jun. 1969  M | |
| Sweden | | S:  12 Aug. 1963 LMW<br>R:   9 Dec. 1963 LMW | S:  27 Jan. 1967  LMW<br>R:  11 Oct. 1967  LMW |

| Treaty of Tlatelolco | Non-Proliferation Treaty | Sea-Bed Treaty | BW Convention |
|---|---|---|---|
| | S:   5 Feb. 1970 LMW | S:   5 May 1971 LMW | S:   19 Jun. 1972 LMW |
| | S:   1 Jul. 1968 LMW<br>R:   5 Mar. 1970 L<br>     12 Nov. 1970 W | | S:   3 Jul. 1972 M |
| | | S:   11 Feb. 1971 W<br>R:   14 Nov. 1973 W<br>     26 Nov. 1973 L | S:   10 Apr. 1972 W |
| | | | S:   10 Apr. 1972 LW |
| | S:   1 Jul. 1968 LMW | | S:   10 Apr. 1972 LMW |
| | S:   24 Dec. 1968 M<br>R:   31 Oct. 1973 W<br>     22 Nov. 1973 M<br>     10 Dec. 1973 L | S:   11 Feb. 1971 L<br>     12 Feb. 1971 M | |
| | S:   24 Jun. 1969 L<br>R:   11 Dec. 1969 L<br>     16 Dec. 1969 W<br>     12 Jan. 1970 M<br>S.A.:[18,27] | S:   11 Feb. 1971 W<br>R:   9 Aug. 1971 W | |
| | S:   19 Aug. 1968 LMW<br>R:   9 Jan. 1970 LMW | S:   11 Feb. 1971 LMW<br>R:   28 Apr. 1972 LMW | |

|  | Antarctic Treaty | Partial Test Ban Treaty | Outer Space Treaty |
|---|---|---|---|
| Switzerland |  | S:  26 Aug. 1963  LMW<br>R:  16 Jan. 1964  LMW | S:  27 Jan. 1967  LW<br>     30 Jan. 1967  M<br>R:  18 Dec. 1969  LMW |
| Syrian Arab Republic |  | S:  13 Aug. 1963  LMW<br>R:   1 Jun. 1964  LMW | R:[11]  14 Nov. 1968  M |
| Taiwan |  | S:  23 Aug. 1963  W<br>R:  18 May 1964  W | S:  27 Jan. 1967  W<br>R:  24 Jul. 1970  W |
| Thailand |  | S:   8 Aug. 1963  LMW<br>R:  15 Nov. 1963  L<br>     21 Nov. 1963  M<br>     29 Nov. 1963  W | S:  27 Jan. 1967  LMW<br>R:   5 Sep. 1968  L<br>      9 Sep. 1968  M<br>     10 Sep. 1968  W |
| Togo |  | S:  18 Sep. 1963  W<br>R:   7 Dec. 1964  W | S:  27 Jan. 1967  W |
| Tonga |  | R:[1] 22 Jun. 1971  M<br>      7 Jul. 1971  W | R:[7] 22 Jun. 1971  L<br>      7 Jul. 1971  W<br>     24 Aug. 1971  M |
| Trinidad & Tobago |  | S:  12 Aug. 1963  LW<br>     13 Aug. 1963  M<br>R:  14 Jul. 1964  W<br>     16 Jul. 1964  L<br>      6 Aug. 1964  M | S:  24 Jul. 1967  L<br>     17 Aug. 1967  M<br>     28 Sep. 1967  W |
| Tunisia |  | S:   8 Aug. 1963  W<br>     12 Aug. 1963  L<br>     13 Aug. 1963  M<br>R:  26 May 1965  LM<br>      3 Jun. 1965  W | S:  27 Jan. 1967  LW<br>     15 Feb. 1967  M<br>R:  28 Mar. 1968  L<br>      4 Apr. 1968  M<br>     17 Apr. 1968  W |

| Treaty of Tlatelolco | Non-Proliferation Treaty | Sea-Bed Treaty | BW Convention |
|---|---|---|---|
|  | S:[12] 27 Nov. 1969 LMW | S: 11 Feb. 1971 LMW | S:[5] 10 Apr. 1972 LMW |
|  | S: 1 Jul. 1968 M <br> R:[10] 24 Sep. 1969 M |  | S: 14 Apr. 1972 M |
|  | S: 1 Jul. 1968 W <br> R: 27 Jan. 1970 W | S: 11 Feb. 1971 W <br> R: 22 Feb. 1972 W | S: 10 Apr. 1972 W <br> R:[9] 9 Feb. 1973 W |
|  | R: 7 Dec. 1972 L |  | S: 17 Jan. 1973 W |
|  | S: 1 Jul. 1968 W <br> R: 26 Feb. 1970 W | S: 2 Apr. 1971 W <br> R: 28 Jun. 1971 W | S: 10 Apr. 1972 W |
|  | R:[13] 7 Jul. 1971 LW <br> 24 Aug. 1971 M |  |  |
| S: 27 Jun. 1967 <br> R:[12] 3 Dec. 1970 | S: 20 Aug. 1968 W <br> 22 Aug. 1968 L |  |  |
|  | S: 1 Jul. 1968 LMW <br> R: 26 Feb. 1970 LMW | S: 11 Feb. 1971 LMW <br> R: 22 Oct. 1971 M <br> 28 Oct. 1971 L <br> 29 Oct. 1971 W | S: 10 Apr. 1972 LMW <br> R: 18 May 1973 W <br> 30 May 1973 M <br> 6 Jun. 1973 L |

| | Antarctic Treaty | | Partial Test Ban Treaty | | Outer Space Treaty | |
|---|---|---|---|---|---|---|
| Turkey | | | S: 9 Aug. 1963 LMW | R: 8 Jul. 1965 LMW | S: 27 Jan. 1967 LMW | R: 27 Mar. 1968 LMW |
| Uganda | | | S: 29 Aug. 1963 LW | R: 24 Mar. 1964 L<br>2 Apr. 1964 W | R: 24 Apr. 1968 W | |
| Ukrainian Soviet Socialist Republic | | | S: 8 Oct. 1963 M | R:[2] 30 Dec. 1963 M | S:[2] 10 Feb. 1967 M | R: 31 Oct. 1967 M |
| Union of Soviet Socialist Republics | S: 1 Dec. 1959 | R: 2 Nov. 1960 | S: 5 Aug. 1963 M | R: 10 Oct. 1963 LMW | S: 27 Jan. 1967 LMW | R: 10 Oct. 1967 LMW |
| United Arab Emirates | | | | | | |
| United Kingdom of Great Britain and Northern Ireland | S: 1 Dec. 1959 | R: 31 May 1960 | S: 5 Aug. 1963 M | R:[9] 10 Oct. 1963 LMW | S: 27 Jan. 1967 LMW | R:[6] 10 Oct. 1967 LMW |
| United Republic of Tanzania | | | S: 16 Sep. 1963 L<br>18 Sep. 1963 W<br>20 Sep. 1963 M | R: 6 Feb. 1964 L | | |
| United States of America | S: 1 Dec. 1959 | R: 18 Aug. 1960 | S: 5 Aug. 1963 M | R: 10 Oct. 1963 LMW | S: 27 Jan. 1967 LMW | R: 10 Oct. 1967 LMW |

| Treaty of Tlatelolco | Non-Proliferation Treaty | Sea-Bed Treaty | BW Convention |
|---|---|---|---|
| | S: 28 Jan. 1969 LMW | S: 25 Feb. 1971 LMW<br>R: 19 Oct. 1972 W<br>25 Oct. 1972 L<br>30 Oct. 1972 M | S: 10 Apr. 1972 LMW |
| | | S: 3 Mar. 1971 M<br>R: 3 Sep. 1971 M | S: 10 Apr. 1972 M |
| | S: 1 Jul. 1968 LMW<br>R: 5 Mar. 1970 LMW | S: 11 Feb. 1971 LMW<br>R: 18 May 1972 LMW | S: 10 Apr. 1972 LMW |
| | | | S: 28 Sep. 1972 L |
| P.I:[8]<br>S: 20 Dec. 1967<br>R: 11 Dec. 1969<br>P.II:[8]<br>S: 20 Dec. 1967<br>R: 11 Dec. 1969 | S: 1 Jul. 1968 LMW<br>R:[14] 27 Nov. 1968 LW<br>29 Nov. 1968 M | S:[7] 11 Feb. 1971 LMW<br>R: 18 May 1972 LMW | S:[6] 10 Apr. 1972 LMW |
| | | S: 11 Feb. 1971 W | S: 16 Aug. 1972 L |
| P.II:[9]<br>S: 1 Apr. 1968<br>R: 12 May 1971 | S: 1 Jul. 1968 LMW<br>R: 5 Mar. 1970 LMW | S: 11 Feb. 1971 LMW<br>R: 18 May 1972 LMW | S: 10 Apr. 1972 LMW |

|  | Antarctic Treaty | Partial Test Ban Treaty | Outer Space Treaty |
|---|---|---|---|
| Upper Volta | | S:  30 Aug. 1963  W | S:  3 Mar. 1967  W<br>R:  18 Jun. 1968  W |
| Uruguay | | S:  12 Aug. 1963  W<br>27 Sep. 1963  LM<br>R:  25 Feb. 1969  L | S:  27 Jan. 1967  W<br>30 Jan. 1967  M<br>R:  31 Aug. 1970  W |
| Venezuela | | S:  16 Aug. 1963  MW<br>20 Aug. 1963  L<br>R:  22 Feb. 1965  M<br>3 Mar. 1965  L<br>29 Mar. 1965  W | S:  27 Jan. 1967  W<br>R:  3 Mar. 1970  W |
| Viet-Nam, South | | S:  1 Oct. 1963  W | S:  27 Jan. 1967  W |
| Western Samoa | | S:  5 Sep. 1963  L<br>6 Sep. 1963  MW<br>R:  15 Jan. 1965  W<br>19 Jan. 1965  L<br>8 Feb. 1965  M | |
| Yemen | | S:  13 Aug. 1963  M<br>6 Sep. 1963  W | |
| Yugoslavia | | S:  8 Aug. 1963  LMW<br>R:  15 Jan. 1964  L<br>31 Jan. 1964  M<br>3 Apr. 1964  W | S:  27 Jan. 1967  LMW |
| Zaïre | | S:  9 Aug. 1963  LW<br>12 Aug. 1963  M<br>R:  28 Oct. 1965  W | S:  27 Jan. 1967  W<br>29 Apr. 1967  M<br>4 May 1967  L |

| Treaty of Tlateloco | Non-Proliferation Treaty | Sea-Bed Treaty | BW Convention |
|---|---|---|---|
| | S:   25 Nov. 1968  W<br>      11 Aug. 1969  M<br>R:    3 Mar. 1970  W | | |
| S:   14 Feb. 1967<br>R:[2] 20 Aug. 1968<br>S.A.:[10] 24 Sep. 1971 | S:   1 July 1968  W<br>R:  31 Aug. 1970  W<br>S.A.:[15,17] 24 Sep. 1971 | S:  11 Feb. 1971  W | |
| S:   14 Feb. 1967<br>R:[2,11] 23 Mar. 1970 | S:   1 Jul. 1968  W | | S:  10 Apr. 1972  W |
| | S:   1 Jul. 1968  W<br>R:  10 Sep. 1971  W<br>S.A.:[17,23] 3 Oct. 1972 | S:  11 Feb. 1971  W | S:  10 Apr. 1972  W |
| | | | |
| | S:   23 Sep. 1968  M | S:  23 Feb. 1971  M | S:  10 Apr. 1972  W<br>     17 Apr. 1972  M<br>     10 May 1972  L |
| | S:  10 Jul. 1968  LMW<br>R:[16]  4 Mar. 1970  W<br>     5 Mar. 1970  LM<br>S.A.: 28 Dec. 1973 | S:   2 Mar. 1971  LMW<br>R:  25 Oct. 1973  LMW | S:  10 Apr. 1972  LMW<br>R:  25 Oct. 1973  LMW |
| | S:  22 Jul. 1968  W<br>     26 Jul. 1968  M<br>     17 Sep. 1968  L<br>R:   4 Aug. 1970  W<br>S.A.: 9 Nov. 1972 | | S:  10 Apr. 1972  LMW |

| | Antarctic Treaty | Partial Test Ban Treaty | Outer Space Treaty |
|---|---|---|---|
| Zambia | | R:[1] 11 Jan. 1965  MW<br>8 Feb. 1965  L | R:  20 Aug. 1973  W<br>21 Aug. 1973  M<br>28 Aug. 1973  L |

*The Antarctic Treaty*

[1] The Netherlands stated that the accession is also valid for Surinam and the Netherlands Antilles.

[2] Romania stated that the provisions of the first paragraph of Article XIII of the Antarctic Treaty are not in accordance with the principle according to which multilateral treaties whose object and purposes concern the international community, as a whole, should be opened for universal participation.

*The Partial Test Ban Treaty*

[1] Notification of succession.

[2] The United States considers that the Byelorussian SSR and the Ukrainian SSR are already covered by the signature and deposit of ratification by the USSR.

[3] With a statement that this does not imply the recognition of any territory or régime not recognized by this state.

[4] Egypt stated that its ratification of the Treaty does not mean or imply any recognition of Israel or any treaty relations with Israel.

[5] The United States did not accept the notification of signature and deposit of ratification by the German Democratic Republic.

[6] The Federal Republic of Germany stated that the Treaty applies also to Land Berlin.

[7] Kuwait stated that its signature and ratification of the Treaty does not in any way imply its recognition of Israel, nor does it oblige it to apply the provisions of the Treaty in respect of the said country.

[8] The Netherlands stated that the ratification is also valid for Surinam and the Netherlands Antilles.

[9] The UK stated its view that if a régime is not recognized as the government of a state, neither signature nor the deposit of any instrument by it nor notification of any of those acts will bring about the recognition of that régime by any other state.

*The Outer Space Treaty*

[1] The Brazilian government interprets Article 10 of the Treaty as a specific recognition that the granting of tracking facilities by the parties to the Treaty shall be subject to agreement between the states concerned.

[2] The United States considers that the Byelorussian SSR and the Ukrainian SSR are already covered by the signature and deposit of ratification by the USSR.

[3] The USA stated that this did not imply recognition of the German Democratic Republic.

[4] The Federal Republic of Germany stated that the Treaty applies also to Land Berlin.

[5] Madagascar acceded to the Treaty with the understanding that under Article 10 of the Treaty the state shall retain its freedom of decision with respect to the possible installation of foreign observation bases in its territory and shall continue to possess the right to fix, in each case, the conditions for such installation.

[6] The United Kingdom's ratification is in respect of the United Kingdom of Great Britain and Northern Ireland, the Associated States (Antigua, Dominica, Grenada, Saint Christopher-Nevis-Anguilla and Saint Lucia) and Territories under the territorial sovereignty of the United Kingdom, as well as the State of Brunei, the Kingdom of Swaziland, the Kingdom of Tonga and the British Solomon Islands Protectorate. On depositing its instrument of ratification, the United Kingdom declared that the Treaty will not be applicable in regard to Southern Rhodesia unless and until the United Kingdom informs the other depositary governments that it is in a position to ensure that the obligations imposed by the Treaty in respect of that territory can be fully implemented.

[7] Notification of succession.

[8] With a statement that this does not imply the recognition of any territory or régime not recognized by this state.

490

| Treaty of<br>Tlatelolco | Non-Proliferation<br>Treaty | Sea-Bed<br>Treaty | BW<br>Convention |
|---|---|---|---|
| | | R: 9 Oct. 1972 L<br>1 Nov. 1972 W<br>2 Nov. 1972 M | |

[9] Kuwait acceded to the Treaty with the understanding that this does not in any way imply its recognition of Israel and does not oblige it to apply the provisions of the Treaty in respect of the said country.

[10] The Netherlands stated that the ratification is also valid for Surinam and the Netherlands Antilles.

[11] The Syrian Arab Republic acceded to the Treaty with the understanding that this should not mean in any way the recognition of Israel, nor should it lead to any relationship with Israel that could arise from the Treaty.

### The Treaty of Tlatelolco

[1] Argentina stated that it understands Article 18 as recognizing the right of the parties to carry out, by their own means or in association with third parties, explosions of nuclear devices for peaceful purposes, including explosions which involve devices similar to those used in nuclear weapons.

[2] The Treaty is in force for this country due to a declaration, annexed to the instrument of ratification (in the case of Colombia the declaration was made subsequent to the deposit of ratification—on 6 September 1972) in accordance with § 2 of Article 28, which waived the requirements specified in § 1 of that article, namely, that all states in the region deposit the instruments of ratification; that Additional Protocol I and Additional Protocol II be signed and ratified by those states to which they apply; and that agreements on safeguards be concluded with the IAEA.

[2] On signing the Treaty, Brazil stated that, according to its interpretation, Article 18 of the Treaty gives the signatories the right to carry out, by their own means or in association with third parties, nuclear explosions for peaceful purposes, including explosions which involve devices similar to those used in nuclear weapons.

[4] Brazil stated that it did not waive the requirements laid down in Article 28 of the Treaty. (The Treaty is therefore not yet in force for Brazil.) In ratifying the Treaty, Brazil reiterated its interpretation of Article 18, which it made upon signing.

[5] In signing the Treaty, Mexico said that if technological progress makes it possible to differentiate between nuclear weapons and nuclear devices for peaceful purposes it will be necessary to amend the relevant provisions of the Treaty, according to the procedure established therein.

[6] The Netherlands stated that the Protocol shall not be interpreted as prejudicing the position of the Netherlands as regards its recognition or non-recognition of the rights of or claims to sovereignty of the parties to the Treaty, or of the grounds on which such claims are made. With respect to nuclear explosions for peaceful purposes on the territory of Surinam and the Netherlands Antilles no other rules apply than those operative for the parties to the Treaty.

[7] Nicaragua stated that it reserved the right to use nuclear energy for peaceful purposes such as the removal of earth for the construction of canals, irrigation works, power plants, and so on, as well as to allow the transit of atomic material through its territory.

[8] When signing and ratifying Additional Protocol I and Additional Protocol II, the United Kingdom made the following declarations of understanding:

In connection with Article 3, defining the term "territory" as including the territorial sea, air space and any other space over which the state exercises sovereignty in accordance with "its own legislation", the UK does not regard its signing or ratification of the Additional Protocols as implying recognition of any legislation which does not, in its view, comply with the relevant rules of international law.

The Treaty does not permit the parties to carry out explosions of nuclear devices for peaceful purposes unless and until advances in technology have made possible the development of devices for such explosions which are not capable of being used for weapons purposes.

Its signing and ratification could not be regarded as affecting in any way the legal status of any territory for the international relations of which the UK is responsible lying within the limits of the geographical zone established by the Treaty.

Should a party to the Treaty carry out any act of aggression with the support of a nuclear-weapon state, the UK would be free to re-consider the extent to which it could be regarded as committed by the provisions of Additional Protocol II.

In addition, the UK declared that its undertaking under Article 3 of Additional Protocol II not to use or threaten to use nuclear weapons against the parties to the Treaty extends also to territories in respect of which the undertaking under Article 1 of Additional Protocol I becomes effective.

[9] The United States signed and ratified Additional Protocol II with the following understandings and declarations:

In connection with Article 3 defining the term "territory" as including the territorial sea, air space and any other space over which the state exercises sovereignty in accordance with "its own legislation", the US ratification of the Protocol could not be regarded as implying recognition of any legislation which did not, in its view, comply with the relevant rules of international law.

Each of the parties retains exclusive power and legal competence, unaffected by the terms of the Treaty, to grant or deny non-parties transit and transport privileges.

As regards the undertaking not to use or threaten to use nuclear weapons against the parties, the United States would consider that an armed attack by a party, in which it was assisted by a nuclear-weapon state, would be incompatible with the party's obligations under Article 1 of the Treaty.

The definition contained in Article 5 of the Treaty is understood as encompassing all nuclear explosive devices; Articles 1 and 5 of the Treaty restrict accordingly the activities of the parties under paragraph 1 of Article 18.

Paragraph 4 of Article 18 permits, and US adherence to Protocol II will not prevent, collaboration by the USA with the parties to the Treaty for the purpose of carrying out explosions of nuclear devices for peaceful purposes in a manner consistent with a policy of not contributing to the proliferation of nuclear-weapon capabilities.

The United States will act with respect to such territories of Protocol I adherents, as are within the geographical area defined in Paragraph 2 of Article 4 of the Treaty, in the same manner as Protocol II requires it to act with respect to the territories of the parties.

[10] The Safeguards Agreement was concluded in accordance with Article III of the NPT. An additional protocol provides that the safeguards under the NPT shall also apply to Uruguay's obligations under Article 13 of the Treaty of Tlatelolco.

[11] Venezuela stated that in view of the existing controversy between Venezuela on the one hand and the United Kingdom and Guyana on the other, § 2 of Article 25 of the Treaty should apply to Guyana. This paragraph provides that no political entity should be admitted, part or all of whose territory is the subject of a dispute or claim between an extra-continental country and one or more Latin American states, so long as the dispute has not been settled by peaceful means.

[12] The Treaty is not yet in force for Trinidad and Tobago; the requirements laid down in Article 28 of the Treaty have not been waived.

[13] On signing Protocol II, China stated, *inter alia:* "China will never use or threaten to use nuclear weapons against non-nuclear Latin American countries and the Latin American nuclear-weapon-free zone; nor will China test, manufacture, produce, stockpile, install or deploy nuclear weapons in these countries or in this zone, or send her means of transportation and delivery carrying nuclear weapons to cross the territory, territorial sea or air space of Latin American countries. It is necessary to point out that the signing of Additional Protocol II to the Treaty for the Prohibition of Nuclear Weapons in Latin America by the Chinese Government does not imply any change whatsoever in China's principled stand on the disarmament and nuclear weapons issue and, in particular, does not affect the Chinese Government's consistent stand against the treaty on non-proliferation of nuclear weapons and the partial nuclear test ban treaty . . ."

"The Chinese Government holds that, in order that Latin America may truly become a nuclear-weapon-free zone, all nuclear countries, and particularly the super-powers, which possess huge numbers of nuclear weapons, must first of all undertake earnestly not to use or threaten to use nuclear weapons against the Latin American countries and the Latin American nuclear-weapon-free zone, and they must be asked to undertake to observe and implement the following: (1) dismantling of all foreign military bases in Latin America and refraining from establishing any new foreign military bases there; (2) prohibition of the passage of any means of transportation and delivery carrying nuclear weapons through Latin American territory, territorial sea or air space."

[14] On signing Protocol II, France stated that it interprets the undertaking contained in article 3 of the Protocol to mean that it presents no obstacle to the full exercise of the right of self-defence enshrined in Article 51 of the United Nations Charter; it takes note of the interpretation of the Treaty given by the Preparatory Commission and reproduced in the Final Act, according to which the Treaty does not apply to transit, the granting or denying of which lies within the exclusive competence of each state party in accordance with the pertinent principles and rules of international law; it considers that the application of the legislation referred to in article 3 of the Treaty relates to a legislation which is consistent with international law. The provisions of articles 1 and 2 of the Protocol apply to the text of the Treaty of Tlatelolco as it stands at the time when the Protocol is signed by France. Consequently, no amendment to the Treaty that might come into force under the provisions of article 29 thereof would be binding on the government of France with-

out the latter's express consent. If this declaration of interpretation is contested in part or in whole by one or more contracting parties to the Treaty or to Protocol II, these instruments would be null and void as far as relations between the French Republic and the contesting state or states are concerned.

## The Non-Proliferation Treaty

[1] On signing the Treaty, Australia stated, *inter alia,* that it wanted to be assured that there was sufficient degree of support for the Treaty, regarded it as essential that the Treaty should not affect security commitments under existing treaties of mutual security, and considered that the safeguards agreement to be concluded by Australia with the IAEA in accordance with Treaty Art. III must in no way subject Australia to treatment less favourable than is accorded to other states which, individually or collectively, conclude safeguards agreements with that agency.

[2] Together with a protocol on finance and a protocol suspending the trilateral safeguards agreement between Austria, the USA and the IAEA.

[3] Together with a protocol on finance.

[4] The United States notified its non-acceptance of notification of signature and ratification by the German Democratic Republic.

[5] On signing the Treaty, the Federal Republic of Germany stated, *inter alia,* that it understood that its security shall continue to be ensured by NATO and that the Treaty shall not hamper European unification. It did not intend to ratify the Treaty before an agreement in accordance with Art. III of the Treaty had been concluded between Euratom and the IAEA, and reaffirmed its view that, until the conclusion of the agreement between the IAEA and Euratom, the supply contracts concluded between Euratom and the parties to the Treaty shall remain in force.

[6] On acceding to the Treaty, the Holy See stated, *inter alia,* that the Treaty will attain in full the objectives of security and peace and justify the limitations to which the states party to the Treaty submit, only if it is fully executed in every clause and with all its implications. This concerns not only the obligations to be applied immediately but also those which envisage a process of ulterior commitments. Among the latter, the Holy See considers it suitable to point out the following:
(a) The adoption of appropriate measures to ensure, on a basis of equality, that all non-nuclear weapon states party to the Treaty will have available to them the benefits deriving from peaceful applications of nuclear technology.
(b) The pursuit of negotiations in good faith on effective measures relating to cessation of the nuclear arms race at an early date and to nuclear disarmament, and on a treaty on general and complete disarmament under strict and effective international control.

[7] On signing the Treaty, Indonesia stated, *inter alia,* that the government of Indonesia attaches great importance to the declarations of the United States of America, the United Kingdom and the Soviet Union, affirming their intention to provide immediate assistance to any non-nuclear-weapon state party to the Treaty that is a victim of an act of aggression in which nuclear weapons are used.

Of utmost importance, however, is not the action *after* a nuclear attack has been committed but the guarantees to prevent such an attack. The Indonesian government trusts that the nuclear-weapon states will study further this question of effective measures to ensure the security of the non-nuclear-weapon states. Its decision to sign the Treaty is not to be taken in any way as a decision to ratify the Treaty. Its ratification will be considered after matters of national security, which are of deep concern to the government and people of Indonesia, have been clarified to their satisfaction.

[8] On signing the Treaty, Italy stated, *inter alia,* that in its belief nothing in the Treaty was an obstacle to the unification of the countries of Western Europe; noted full compatibility of the Treaty with the existing security agreements; noted further that when technological progress would allow the development of peaceful explosive devices different from nuclear weapons, the prohibition relating to their manufacture and use shall no longer apply; and that pending the conclusion of the agreement between IAEA and Euratom, the understandings reached on the matter of supplies between Euratom and the signatories to the Treaty would remain in force.

[9] On signing the Treaty, Japan stated, *inter alia,* that pending the ratification of the Treaty it would pay particular attention to developments in disarmament negotiations and progress in the implementation of the UN Security Council resolution on the security of non-nuclear-weapon states, and that the safeguards agreement to be concluded by Japan with the IAEA in accordance with Art. III of the Treaty must not be such as would subject it to disadvantageous treatment as compared with the safeguards agreements which other parties conclude with the agency.

[10] A statement was made containing a disclaimer regarding the recognition of states party to the Treaty.

[11] On signing the Treaty, Mexico stated, *inter alia,* that none of the provisions of the Treaty shall be interpreted as affecting in any way, whatsoever, the rights and obligations of Mexico as a state party to the Treaty for the Prohibition of Nuclear Weapons in Latin America (Treaty of Tlatelolco).

It is the understanding of Mexico that at the present time any nuclear explosive device is capable of being used as a nuclear weapon and that there is no indication that in the near future it will be possible to manufacture nuclear explosive devices that are not potentially nuclear weapons. However, if technological advances modify this situation, it will be necessary to amend the relevant provisions of the Treaty in accordance with the procedure established therein.

[12] On signing the Treaty, Switzerland stated that the Treaty would not be submitted to Parliament for approval until such time as a sufficient measure of universal support has been obtained by the Treaty.

[13] Notification of succession.

[14] The Treaty was ratified in respect of the United Kingdom of Great Britain and Northern Ireland, the Associated States (Antigua, Dominica, Grenada, Saint Christopher-Nevis-Anguilla and Saint Lucia) and Territories under the territorial sovereignty of the United Kingdom, as well as the State of Brunei, the Kingdom of Tonga and the British Solomon Islands Protectorate. The United Kingdom recalled its view that if a régime is not recognized as the government of a state, neither signature nor the deposit of any instrument by it, nor notification of any of those acts will bring about recognition of that régime by any other state. The provisions of the Treaty shall not apply in regard to Southern Rhodesia unless and until the government of the United Kingdom informs the other depositary governments that it is in a position to ensure that the obligations imposed by the Treaty in respect of that territory can be fully implemented. Cameroon stated that it was unable to accept the reservation concerning Southern Rhodesia. Also Mongolia stated that the obligations assumed by the United Kingdom under the Non-Proliferation Treaty should apply equally to Southern Rhodesia. In a note addressed to the UK Embassy in Moscow, the Soviet government expressed the view that the United Kingdom carries the entire responsibility for Southern Rhodesia until the people of that territory acquire genuine independence, and that this fully applies to the Non-Proliferation Treaty.

[15] Together with a Protocol on finance and a Protocol relating to Article 13 of the Treaty of Tlatelolco.

[16] In connection with the ratification of the Treaty, Yugoslavia stated, *inter alia,* that it considered a ban on the development, manufacture and use of nuclear weapons and destruction of all stockpiles of these weapons to be indispensable for the maintenance of a stable peace and international security; it held the view that the chief responsibility for the progress in this direction rested with the nuclear-weapon powers, and expected these powers to undertake not to use nuclear weapons against the countries which have renounced them as well as against non-nuclear-weapon states in general, and to refrain from the threat to use them. It also emphasized the significance it attached to the universality of the efforts relating to the realization of the NPT.

[17] Entry into force is subject to notification that the statutory and constitutional requirements for entry into force have been met.

[18] Together with a Protocol for states having minimal quantities of nuclear material.

[19] Together with a Protocol for states that have signed a Treaty of accession to Euratom.

[20] Together with a Protocol suspending the trilateral safeguards agreement between the IAEA, Denmark and the UK; and a Protocol suspending the trilateral safeguards agreement between the IAEA, Denmark and the USA.

[21] Together with a Protocol suspending the trilateral safeguards agreement between the IAEA, Greece and the USA.

[22] Covers the NPT and the Treaty of Tlatelolco.

[23] Together with a Protocol suspending the trilateral safeguards agreement betwen the IAEA, Viet-Nam and the USA.

[24] Together with a Protocol suspending the trilateral safeguards agreement between the IAEA, the Philippines and the USA.

[25] Agreement was signed by the Netherlands for Netherlands Antilles and Surinam, covering the NPT and the Treaty of Tlatelolco, together with a Protocol for states having minimal quantities of nuclear material and a Protocol for the application of the Euratom NPT Agreement in the event of a declaration by the Netherlands that the Euratom Treaty becomes applicable. Entry into force is subject to notification that the statutory and constitutional requirements for entry into force have been met.

[26] Together with a Protocol suspending the trilateral safeguards agreement between the IAEA, Iran and the USA.

[27] Agreements approved by the IAEA Board of Governors but not signed by 31 December 1973.

[28] Together with a Protocol on cooperation in the application of safeguards between Euratom and the IAEA.

[29] Entry into force is subject to notification that the requirements of Euratom and all states concerned (Belgium, Denmark, Federal Republic of Germany, Ireland, Italy, Luxembourg and Netherlands) for entry into force have been met.

### The Sea-Bed Treaty

[1] On signing the Treaty, Argentina made an interpretative declaration. It stated that it interprets the references to the freedoms of the high seas as in no way implying a pronouncement or judgment on the different positions relating to questions connected with international maritime law. It understands that the reference to the rights of exploration and exploitation by coastal states over their continental shelves was included solely because those could be the rights most frequently affected by verification procedures. Argentina precludes any possibility of strengthening, through this Treaty, certain positions concerning continental shelves to the detriment of others based on different criteria.

[2] On signing the Treaty, Brazil stated that nothing in the Treaty shall be interpreted as prejudicing in any way the sovereign rights of Brazil in the area of the sea, the sea-bed and the subsoil thereof adjacent to its coasts. It is the understanding of the Brazilian government that the word "observation", as it appears in paragraph 1 of Article III of the Treaty, refers only to observation that is incidental to the normal course of navigation in accordance with international law.

[3] The United States has not accepted the notification of signature by the German Democratic Republic.

[4] On signing the Treaty, the Federal Republic of Germany stated that its signature does not imply recognition of the German Democratic Republic under international law.

[5] On signing the Treaty, Italy stated, *inter alia,* that in the case of agreements on further measures in the field of disarmament to prevent an arms race on the sea-bed and ocean floor and in their subsoil, the question of the delimitation of the area within which these measures would find application shall have to be examined and solved in each instance in accordance with the nature of the measures to be adopted.

[6] A statement was made containing a disclaimer regarding the recognition of states party to the Treaty.

[7] The instrument of ratification states that the Treaty is ratified in respect of the United Kingdom of Great Britain and Northern Ireland, the Associated States (Antigua, Dominica, Grenada, St. Christopher-Nevis-Anguilla, St. Lucia and St. Vincent) and Territories under the territorial sovereignty of the United Kingdom, as well as the State of Brunei and the British Solomon Islands Protectorate. The United Kingdom recalled its view that if a régime is not recognized as the government of a state, neither signature nor the deposit of any instrument by it, nor notification of any of those acts, will bring about recognition of that régime by any other state.

[8] In depositing the instrument of ratification Canada declared: Article I, paragraph 1, cannot be interpreted as indicating that any state has a right to implant or emplace any weapons not prohibited under Article I, paragraph 1, on the seabed and ocean floor, and in the subsoil thereof, beyond the limits of national jurisdiction, or as constituting any limitation on the principle that this area of the seabed and ocean floor and the subsoil thereof shall be reserved for exclusively peaceful purposes. Articles I, II and III cannot be interpreted as indicating that any state but the coastal state has any right to implant or emplace any weapon not prohibited under Article I, paragraph 1, on the continental shelf, or the subsoil thereof, appertaining to that coastal state, beyond the outer limit of the seabed zone referred to in Article I and defined in Article II. Article III cannot be interpreted as indicating any restrictions or limitation upon the rights of the coastal state, consistent with its exclusive sovereign rights with respect to the continental shelf, to verify, inspect or effect the removal of any weapon, structure, installation, facility or device implanted or emplaced on the continental shelf, or the subsoil thereof, appertaining to that coastal state, beyond the outer limit of the seabed zone referred to in Article I and defined in Article II.

[9] Romania stated that it considered null and void the ratification of the Treaty by the Taiwan authorities.

[10] On the occasion of its accession to the Treaty, the Government of India stated that as a coastal state, India has, and always has had, full and exclusive sovereign rights over the continental shelf adjoining its territory and beyond its territorial waters and the subsoil thereof. It is the considered view of India that other countries cannot use its continental shelf for military purposes. There cannot, therefore, be any restriction on, or limitation of, the sovereign right of India as a coastal state to verify, inspect, remove or destroy any weapon, device, structure, installation or facility, which might be implanted or emplaced on or beneath its continental shelf by any other country, or to take such other steps as may be considered necessary to safeguard its security. The accession by the Government of India to the Sea-Bed Treaty is based on this position. In response to the Indian statement, the US Government expressed the view that under existing international law, the rights of coastal states over their continental shelves are exclusive only for purposes of exploration and exploitation of natural resources, and are otherwise limited by the 1958 Convention on the Continental Shelf and other principles of international law.

### The BW Convention

[1] Ireland considers that the Convention could be undermined if reservations made by the parties to the 1925 Geneva Protocol were allowed to stand, as the prohibition of possession is incompatible

with the right to retaliate, and that there should be an absolute and universal prohibition of the use of the weapons in question. Ireland notified the depositary government for the Geneva Protocol of the withdrawal of its reservations to the Protocol, made at the time of accession in 1930. The withdrawal applies to chemical as well as to bacteriological (biological) and toxin agents of warfare.

[2] The Republic of Korea stated that the signing of the Convention does not in any way mean or imply the recognition of any territory or régime which has not been recognized by the Republic of Korea as a state or government.

[3] In the understanding of Kuwait, its ratification of the Convention does not in any way imply its recognition of Israel, nor does it oblige it to apply the provisions of the Convention in respect of the said country.

[4] Mexico considers that the Convention is only a first step towards an agreement prohibiting also the development, production and stockpiling of all chemical weapons, and notes the fact that the Convention contains an express commitment to continue negotiations in good faith with the aim of arriving at such an agreement.

[5] Switzerland stated that the Convention would not be submitted to the parliamentary procedure of approval preceding ratification, until such time as the convention has obtained a measure of universal support, considered necessary by the Swiss government. Switzerland reserves the right to decide for itself which means fall under the category of weapon, equipment or means of delivery designed to use biological agents or toxins, to which the Convention is applicable. With regard to Article VII of the Convention, Switzerland has made a general reservation, namely, that its cooperation within the framework of the Convention cannot go beyond its obligations resulting from its status of permanent neutrality.

[6] The United Kingdom recalled its view that if a régime is not recognized as the government of a state, neither signature nor the deposit of any instrument by it, nor notification of any of those acts will bring about recognition of that régime by any other state.

[7] Considering the obligations resulting from its status as a permanently neutral state, the Republic of Austria declares a reservation to the effect that its cooperation within the framework of this Convention cannot exceed the limits determined by the status of permanent neutrality and membership with the United Nations.

This reservation refers in particular to Article VII of this Convention as well as to any similar provision replacing or supplementing this article.

[8] In a statement made on the occasion of the signature of the Convention, India reiterated its understanding that the objective of the Convention is to eliminate biological and toxin weapons, thereby excluding completely the possibility of their use, and that the exemption in regard to biological agents or toxins, which would be permitted for prophylactic, protective or other peaceful purposes would not, in any way, create a loophole in regard to the production or retention of biological and toxin weapons. Also, any assistance which might be furnished under the terms of the Convention, would be of medical or humanitarian nature and in conformity with the Charter of the United Nations.

[9] The USSR stated that it considered the deposit of the instrument of ratification by Taiwan as an illegal act, because the government of the Chinese People's Republic is the sole representative of China.

[10] Finland deposited the instrument of ratification in February 1974.

# Appendix 13C

*Announced and presumed nuclear explosions in 1972 and 1973*

*Note:*

1. The following sources have been used in compiling the lists:

(*a*) Research Institute of the Swedish National Defence,

(*b*) US Atomic Energy Commission (AEC),

(*c*) US Geological Survey,

(*d*) Press reports.

2. The geographical coordinates for the US tests are given in degrees, minutes and seconds, while those for the Soviet and Chinese tests are given in degrees (using decimal notation).

3. The events marked with an asterisk (*) may be part of a programme for peaceful uses of nuclear explosions.

4. $m_b$, $M_s$ indicate the size of the event; the data have been provided by the Hagfors Observatory of the Research Institute of the Swedish National Defence.

5. The yields of explosions are AEC announcements.

6. In the case of very weak events, it is impossible to distinguish, through seismological methods only, between chemical and nuclear explosions.

## I. Revised list of nuclear explosions in 1972[a]

| Date GMT | Latitude deg | Longitude deg | Region | $m_b$ | $M_s$ | Yield kt |
|---|---|---|---|---|---|---|
| **USSR** | | | | | | |
| 10 Feb | 49.986 N | 78.886 E | E Kazakh | 6.2 | | 20–200 |
| 10 Mar | 49.755 N | 78.180 E | E Kazakh | 5.8 | | 20–200 |
| 28 Mar | 49.730 N | 78.186 E | E Kazakh | 5.5 | | 20–200 |
| 7 Jun | 49.761 N | 78.175 E | E Kazakh | 5.7 | | 20–200 |
| 6 Jul | 49.724 N | 77.979 E | E Kazakh | 4.7 | | |
| 9 Jul | 49.9 N | 35.2 E | N of Black Sea* | 5.0 | 2.8 | |
| 14 Jul | 55.8 N | 47.4 E | N of Caspian Sea* | 3.5 | | |
| 16 Aug | 49.759 N | 78.146 E | E Kazakh | 5.5 | 3.5 | 20–200 |
| 20 Aug | 49.462 N | 48.179 E | W Kazakh* | 6.0 | 3.6 | 20–200 |
| 26 Aug | 49.994 N | 77.781 E | E Kazakh | 5.7 | | 20–200 |
| 28 Aug | 73.336 N | 55.085 E | Novaya Zemlya | | 4.7 | 1 000 |
| 2 Sep | 49.957 N | 77.726 E | E Kazakh | 5.2 | | |
| 4 Sep | 67.689 N | 33.445 E | W Russia* | | 3.1 | |
| 21 Sep | 52.127 N | 51.994 E | W Russia* | 5.1 | | 20–200 |
| 3 Oct | 46.848 N | 45.010 E | NW of Caspian Sea* | 6.1 | 3.0 | 200–1 000 |
| 2 Nov | 49.913 N | 78.837 E | E Kazakh | | 3.9 | 200–1 000 |
| 24 Nov | 52.779 N | 51.067 E | W Russia* | 5.1 | | |
| 24 Nov | 51.843 N | 64.152 E | W Kazakh* | 5.2 | | 20–200 |
| 10 Dec | 49.847 N | 78.099 E | E Kazakh | 5.9 | | 20–200 |
| 10 Dec | 50.114 N | 78.808 E | E Kazakh | 6.7 | 4.3 | 200–1 000 |
| 28 Dec | 51.7 N | 77.2 E | E Kazakh | 4.5 | | |
| **USA** | | | | | | |
| 19 Apr | 37.07.19 N | 116.05.02 W | Nevada Test Site | | | <20 |
| 17 May | 37.07.14 N | 116.05.16 W | Nevada Test Site | | | <20 |
| 19 May | 37.03.53 N | 116.00.06 W | Nevada Test Site | 4.9 | | <20 |
| 20 Jul | 37.12.52 N | 116.11.00 W | Nevada Test Site | 4.8 | | <20 |
| 21 Sep | 37.04.55 N | 116.02.12 W | Nevada Test Site | 5.7 | 4.1 | 20–200 |
| 26 Sep | 37.07.17 N | 116.05.09 W | Nevada Test Site | | | <20 |
| 21 Dec | 37.08.24 N | 116.05.00 W | Nevada Test Site | 5.1 | | 20–200 |
| **France** | | | | | | |
| 25 Jun | | | Mururoa | | | |
| 30 Jun | | | Mururoa | | | |
| 29 Jul | | | Mururoa | | | |
| **China** | | | | | | |
| 7 Jan | | | Lop Nor | | | <20 |
| 18 Mar | | | Lop Nor | | 4.3 | 20–200 |

[a] A preliminary list of nuclear explosions in 1972 was published in the *SIPRI Yearbook 1973*, pp. 475–76.

## II. Preliminary list of nuclear explosions in 1973

| Date GMT | Latitude deg | Longitude deg | Region | $m_b$ | $M_s$ | Yield kt |
|---|---|---|---|---|---|---|
| **USSR** | | | | | | |
| 16 Feb | 49.835 N | 78.232 E | E Kazakh | 5.6 | | 20–200 |
| 19 Apr | 50.006 N | 77.725 E | E Kazakh | 5.6 | | 20–200 |
| 10 Jul | 49.780 N | 78.058 E | E Kazakh | | | 20–200 |
| 23 Jul | 49.986 N | 78.853 E | E Kazakh | 7.1 | | |
| 15 Aug | 42.711 N | 67.410 E | Central Kazakh* | 5.6 | | 20–200 |
| 28 Aug | 50.550 N | 68.395 E | Central Kazakh* | 5.5 | | 20–200 |
| 12 Sep | 73.3 N | 55.2 E | Novaya Zemlya | 5.8 | | 3 000–6 000 |
| 19 Sep | 45.635 N | 67.850 E | Central Kazakh* | | | 20–200 |
| 27 Sep | 70.756 N | 53.872 E | Novaya Zemlya | 5.9 | | 20–200 |
| 30 Sep | 51.608 N | 54.582 E | W Russia* | 5.7 | | 20–200 |
| 26 Oct | 49.765 N | 78.196 E | E Kazakh | 5.5 | | 20–200 |
| 26 Oct | 53.656 N | 55.375 E | S Ural* | | | < |
| 27 Oct | 70.779 N | 54.177 E | Novaya Zemlya | 5.9 | | ~3 000–6 000 |
| 14 Dec | | | E Kazakh* | 6.6 | | |
| **USA** | | | | | | |
| 8 Mar | 37.06.12 N | 116.01.36 W | Nevada Test Site | 5.7 | | 20–200 |
| 25 Apr | 37.00.17 N | 116.01.42 W | Nevada Test Site | 4.7 | | 20–200 |
| 26 Apr | 37.07.23 N | 116.03.30 W | Nevada Test Site | 5.8 | | 20–200 |
| 17 May | 39.47.34 N | 108.21.59 W | Colorado* | 5.4 | | 3×30 |
| 5 Jun | 37.11.06 N | 116.12.54 W | Nevada Test Site | | | <20 |
| 6 Jun | 37.14.42 N | 116.20.45 W | Nevada Test Site | 6.5 | | 200–1 000 |
| 21 Jun | 37.08.4 N | 115.99.3 W | Nevada Test Site | 5.8 | | |
| 28 Jun | 37.08.54 N | 116.05.09 W | Nevada Test Site | 5.3 | | 20–200 |
| 12 Oct | 37.12.01 N | 116.12.11 W | Nevada Test Site | 4.8 | | <20 |
| **France** | | | | | | |
| 21 Jul | | | Mururoa | | | ~5 |
| 28 Jul | | | Mururoa | | | low |
| 19 Aug | | | Mururoa | | | 5–10 |
| 25 Aug | | | Mururoa | | | |
| 28 Aug | | | Mururoa | | | |
| **China** | | | | | | |
| 27 Jun | 40.559 N | 89.532 E | Lop Nor | 4.6 | | 2 000–3 000 |

# Appendix 13D

*Protocols signed together with certain IAEA nuclear safeguards agreements*

## Protocol on finance

This protocol provides that the finance clause of the safeguards agreement shall become definitive on condition that the 1971 IAEA General Conference endorses the arrangements for the financing of safeguards which the IAEA Board of Governors approved on 20 April 1971. As the General Conference supported these arrangements, no further protocol of this type has become necessary.

## Protocol suspending trilateral safeguards agreements

This protocol provides that the safeguards transfer agreement shall be suspended upon the application of safeguards under the NPT safeguards agreement.

## Protocol relating to article 13 of the Treaty of Tlatelolco

At the request of the state concerned (Uruguay), the safeguards agreement covers only obligations under Article III.1 of the NPT but it is provided in this protocol that the safeguards shall also cover the obligations arising from Article 13 of the Treaty of Tlatelolco.

## Protocol for states having minimal quantities of nuclear material

This protocol applies to states which at the time of the conclusion of the NPT safeguards agreement have only very small quantities of nuclear material or no nuclear material to be safeguarded; it provides that the implementation of safeguards under the agreement will be held in abeyance until such time as the state has nuclear material in quantities exceeding certain specified limits.

## Protocol for states that have signed a treaty of accession to Euratom

The NPT safeguards agreement signed by the IAEA, the European Atomic Energy Community (Euratom) and the non-nuclear-weapon states members of Euratom will (upon its entry into force) replace the NPT safeguards agreements concluded by those states which had signed a treaty of accession to the Euratom Treaty but were not yet members of the Community when the Euratom safeguards agreement was negotiated.

**Protocol on cooperation in the application of safeguards**

This protocol specifies the conditions and means for cooperation in the application of safeguards between Euratom and the IAEA.

# Appendix 13E

*Treaty banning nuclear weapon tests in the atmosphere, in outer space and under water*

The Governments of the United States of America, the United Kingdom of Great Britain and Northern Ireland, and the Union of Soviet Socialist Republics, hereinafter referred to as the "Original Parties",

Proclaiming as their principal aim the speediest possible achievement of an agreement on general and complete disarmament under strict international control in accordance with the objectives of the United Nations which would put an end to the armaments race and eliminate the incentive to the production and testing of all kinds of weapons, including nuclear weapons,

Seeking to achieve the discontinuance of all test explosions of nuclear weapons for all time, determined to continue negotiations to this end, and desiring to put an end to the contamination of man's environment by radioactive substances,

Have agreed as follows:

ARTICLE I

1. Each of the Parties to this Treaty undertakes to prohibit, to prevent, and not to carry out any nuclear weapon test explosion, or any other nuclear explosion, at any place under its jurisdiction or control:

(a) in the atmosphere; beyond its limits, including outer space; or under water, including territorial waters or high seas; or

(b) in any other environment if such explosion causes radioactive debris to be present outside the territorial limits of the State under whose jurisdiction or control such explosion is conducted. It is understood in this connection that the provisions of this subparagraph are without prejudice to the conclusion of a treaty resulting in the permanent banning of all nuclear test explosions, including all such explosions underground, the conclusion of which, as the Parties have stated in the Preamble to this Treaty, they seek to achieve.

2. Each of the Parties to this Treaty undertakes furthermore to refrain from causing, encouraging, or in any way participating in, the carrying out of any nuclear weapon test explosion, or any other nuclear explosion, anywhere which would take place in any of the environments described, or have the effect referred to, in paragraph 1 of this Article.

ARTICLE II

1. Any Party may propose amendments to this Treaty. The text of any proposed amendment shall be submitted to the Depositary Governments which shall circulate it to all Parties to this Treaty. Thereafter, if requested to do so by one-third or more of the Parties, the Depositary Governments shall convene a conference, to which they shall invite all the Parties, to consider such amendment.

2. Any amendment to this Treaty must be approved by a majority of the votes of all the Parties to this Treaty, including the votes of all of the Original Parties. The amendment shall enter into force for all Parties upon the deposit of instruments of ratification by a majority of all the Parties, including the instruments of ratification of all of the Original Parties.

ARTICLE III

1. This Treaty shall be open to all States for signature. Any State which does not sign this Treaty before its entry into force in accordance with paragraph 3 of this Article may accede to it at any time.

2. This Treaty shall be subject to ratification by signatory States. Instruments of ratification and instruments of accession shall be deposited with the Governments of the Original Parties—the United States of America, the United Kingdom of Great Britain and Northern Ireland, and the Union of Soviet Socialist Republics—which are hereby designated the Depositary Governments.

3. This Treaty shall enter into force after its ratification by all the Original Parties and the deposit of their instruments of ratification.

4. For States whose instruments of ratification or accession are deposited subsequent to the entry into force of this Treaty, it shall enter into force on the date of the deposit of their instruments of ratification or accession.

5. The Depositary Governments shall promptly inform all signatory and acceding States of the date of each signature, the date of deposit of each instrument of ratification of and accession to this Treaty, the date of its entry into force, and the date of receipt of any requests for conferences or other notices.

6. This Treaty shall be registered by the Depositary Governments pursuant to Article 102 of the Charter of the United Nations.

ARTICLE IV

This Treaty shall be of unlimited duration.

Each Party shall in exercising its national sovereignty have the right to withdraw from the Treaty if it decides that extraordinary events, related to the subject matter of this Treaty, have jeopardized the supreme interests of its country. It shall give notice of such withdrawal to all other Parties to the Treaty three months in advance.

ARTICLE V

This Treaty, of which the English and Russian texts are equally authentic, shall be deposited in the archives of the Depositary Governments. Duly certified copies of this Treaty shall be transmitted by the Depositary Governments to the Governments of the signatory and acceding States.

IN WITNESS WHEREOF the undersigned, duly authorized, have signed this Treaty.

DONE in triplicate at the city of Moscow the fifth day of August, one thousand nine hundred and sixty-three.

# Appendix 13F

*French nuclear explosions, as of 31 December 1973*

| Date GMT | Region | Environment and mode of explosion | Yield |
|---|---|---|---|
| 13 Feb 1960 | Sahara | Atmosphere: from tower | 60–70 kt |
| 1 Apr 1960 | Sahara | Atmosphere: ground surface | <20 kt |
| 27 Dec 1960 | Sahara | Atmosphere: from tower | <20 kt |
| 25 Apr 1961 | Sahara | Atmosphere: from tower | <20 kt |
| 7 Nov 1961 | Sahara | Underground | <20 kt |
| 1 May 1962 | Sahara | Underground | >20 kt |
| 18 Mar 1963 | Sahara | Underground | <20 kt |
| 30 Mar 1963 | Sahara | Underground | <20 kt |
| 20 Oct 1963 | Sahara | Underground | >20 kt |
| 14 Feb 1964 | Sahara | Underground | <20 kt |
| 15 Jun 1964 | Sahara | Underground | <20 kt |
| 28 Nov 1964 | Sahara | Underground | <20 kt |
| 27 Feb 1965 | Sahara | Underground | >20 kt |
| 30 May 1965 | Sahara | Underground | <20 kt |
| 1 Oct 1965 | Sahara | Underground | <20 kt |
| 1 Dec 1965 | Sahara | Underground | <20 kt |
| 16 Feb 1966 | Sahara | Underground | <20 kt |
| 2 Jul 1966 | Pacific Tests Centre | Atmosphere: from tower | 25–30 kt |
| 19 Jul 1966 | Pacific Tests Centre | Atmosphere: dropped from airplane | 70–80 kt |
| 11 Sep 1966 | Pacific Tests Centre | Atmosphere: from balloon | 120 kt |
| 24 Sep 1966 | Pacific Tests Centre | Atmosphere | 150 kt |
| 4 Oct 1966 | Pacific Tests Centre | Atmosphere | 200–300 kt |
| 5 Jun 1967 | Pacific Tests Centre | Atmosphere: from balloon | <20 kt |
| 27 Jun 1967 | Pacific Tests Centre | Atmosphere: from balloon | <20 kt |
| 2 Jul 1967 | Pacific Tests Centre | Atmosphere: from balloon | <20 kt |
| 7 Jul 1968 | Pacific Tests Centre | Atmosphere | <20 kt |
| 15 Jul 1968 | Pacific Tests Centre | Atmosphere: from balloon | 0.5 mt |
| 3 Aug 1968 | Pacific Tests Centre | Atmosphere: from balloon | <1 000 kt |
| 24 Aug 1968 | Pacific Tests Centre | Atmosphere: from balloon | 2.5 mt (First French thermonuclear explosion) |
| 8 Sep 1968 | Pacific Tests Centre | Atmosphere: from balloon | 1 mt |
| 15 May 1970 | Pacific Tests Centre | Atmosphere: from balloon | <20 kt |
| 22 May 1970 | Pacific Tests Centre | Atmosphere: from balloon | <20 kt |
| 30 May 1970 | Pacific Tests Centre | Atmosphere: from balloon | 100–1 000 kt |
| 24 Jun 1970 | Pacific Tests Centre | Atmosphere: from balloon | <20 kt |
| 3 Jul 1970 | Pacific Tests Centre | Atmosphere: from balloon | ~1 mt |
| 27 Jul 1970 | Pacific Tests Centre | Atmosphere: from balloon | <20 kt |
| 2 Aug 1970 | Pacific Tests Centre | Atmosphere: from balloon | <20 kt |
| 6 Aug 1970 | Pacific Tests Centre | Atmosphere: from balloon | <20 kt |
| 5 Jun 1971 | Pacific Tests Centre | Atmosphere: from balloon | Low |
| 12 Jun 1971 | Pacific Tests Centre | Atmosphere: from balloon | 400–500 kt |
| 4 Jul 1971 | Pacific Tests Centre | Atmosphere: from balloon | Low |
| 8 Aug 1971 | Pacific Tests Centre | Atmosphere: from balloon | Low |
| 14 Aug 1971 | Pacific Tests Centre | Atmosphere: from balloon | ca. 1 mt |
| 25 Jun 1972 | Pacific Tests Centre | Atmosphere | <20 kt |
| 30 Jun 1972 | Pacific Tests Centre | Atmosphere | <20 kt |
| 29 Jul 1972 | Pacific Tests Centre | Atmosphere | <20 kt |

| Date GMT | Region | Environment and mode of explosion | Yield |
|---|---|---|---|
| 21 Jul 1973 | Pacific Tests Centre | Atmosphere: from balloon | ~5 kt |
| 28 Jul 1973 | Pacific Tests Centre | Atmosphere: from balloon | Low |
| 19 Aug 1973 | Pacific Tests Centre | Atmosphere | 5–10 kt |
| 25 Aug 1973 | Pacific Tests Centre | Atmosphere | — |
| 28 Aug 1973 | Pacific Tests Centre | Atmosphere | — |

*Sources:*
1. Research Institute of the Swedish National Defence.
2. US National Oceanic and Atmospheric Administration.
3. Press reports.

# Appendix 13G

*Chinese nuclear explosions, as of 31 December 1973*

| Date GMT | Region | Environment and mode of explosion | Yield |
|---|---|---|---|
| 16 Oct 1964 | Lop Nor | Atmosphere: from tower | ~20 kt |
| 14 May 1965 | Lop Nor | Atmosphere: dropped from airplane | >20 kt |
| 9 May 1966 | Lop Nor | Atmosphere: dropped from airplane | 200–500 kt |
| 27 Oct 1966 | Lop Nor | Atmosphere: missile (400 miles range) | <20 kt |
| 28 Dec 1966 | Lop Nor | Atmosphere: from tower | 300 kt |
| 17 Jun 1967 | Lop Nor | Atmosphere: dropped from airplane | 3 mt (First Chinese thermonuclear weapon test) |
| 24 Dec 1967 | Lop Nor | Atmosphere: dropped from airplane | 15–25 kt |
| 27 Dec 1968 | Lop Nor | Atmosphere: dropped from airplane | 3 mt |
| 22 Sep 1969 | Lop Nor | Underground | ~25 kt |
| 29 Sep 1969 | Lop Nor | Atmosphere: dropped from airplane | 3 mt |
| 14 Oct 1970 | Lop Nor | Atmosphere: dropped from airplane | 3 mt |
| 18 Nov 1971 | Lop Nor | Atmosphere: from tower | ~20 kt |
| 7 Jan 1972 | Lop Nor | Atmosphere | <20 kt |
| 18 Mar 1972 | Lop Nor | Atmosphere | 20–200 kt |
| 27 Jun 1973 | Lop Nor | Atmosphere | 2–3 mt |

*Sources:*
1. US Atomic Energy Commission (AEC).
2. US National Oceanic and Atmospheric Administration.
3. Press reports.

# Appendix 13H

*Nuclear explosions 1945–73 (announced and presumed)*

a atmospheric
u underground and underwater (the latter are put in brackets)

| Year | USA a | USA u | USSR a | USSR u | United Kingdom a | United Kingdom u | France a | France u | China a | China u | Total |
|---|---|---|---|---|---|---|---|---|---|---|---|
| **I. 1945–5 August 1963 (the signing of the Partial Test Ban Treaty)** | | | | | | | | | | | |
| 1945 | 3 | 0 | | | | | | | | | 3 |
| 1946 | 1 | 1 (1) | | | | | | | | | 2 |
| 1947 | 0 | 0 | | | | | | | | | 0 |
| 1948 | 3 | 0 | | | | | | | | | 3 |
| 1949 | 0 | 0 | 1 | 0 | | | | | | | 1 |
| 1950 | 0 | 0 | 0 | 0 | | | | | | | 0 |
| 1951 | 15 | 1 | 2 | 0 | | | | | | | 18 |
| 1952 | 10 | 0 | 0 | 0 | 1 | 0 | | | | | 11 |
| 1953 | 11 | 0 | 2 | 0 | 2 | 0 | | | | | 15 |
| 1954 | 6 | 0 | 2 | 0 | 0 | 0 | | | | | 8 |
| 1955 | 13 | 2 (1) | 4 | 0 | 0 | 0 | | | | | 19 |
| 1956 | 14 | 0 | 7 | 0 | 6 | 0 | | | | | 27 |
| 1957 | 26 | 2 | 13 | 0 | 7 | 0 | | | | | 48 |
| 1958 | 53 | 13 (2) | 26 | 0 | 5 | 0 | | | | | 97 |
| | 155 | 19 (4) | 57 +33[a] | 0 | 21 | 0 | | | | | 252 33[a] |
| 1945–1958 | 155 | 19 (4) | 90 | 0 | 21 | 0 | | | | | 285 |
| 1959 | 0 | 0 | 0 | 0 | 0 | 0 | | | | | 0 |
| 1960 | 0 | 0 | 0 | 0 | 0 | 0 | 3 | 0 | | | 3 |
| 1961 | 0 | 9 | 30 | 2 (1) | 0 | 0 | 1 | 1 | | | 43 |
| 1962 | 38 | 50 (1) | 41 | 1 | 0 | 2 | 0 | 1 | | | 133 |
| 1963–5 Aug 1963 | 0 | 11 | 0 | 0 | 0 | 0 | 0 | 2 | | | 13 |
| 1959–5 Aug 1963 | 38 | 70 (1) | 71 | 3 (1) | 0 | 2 | 4 | 4 | | | 192 |
| 1945–1958 | 155 | 19 (4) | 90 | 0 | 21 | 0 | 0 | 0 | | | 285 |
| *1945–5 Aug 1963* | *193* | *89 (5)* | *161* | *3 (1)* | *21* | *2* | *4* | *4* | | | *477* |
| **II. 5 August 1963 – 31 December 1973** | | | | | | | | | | | |
| 5 Aug 1963 – Dec 1963 | 0 | 14 | 0 | 0 | 0 | 0 | 0 | 1 | | | 15 |
| 1964 | 0 | 28 | 0 | 6 | 0 | 1 | 0 | 3 | 1 | 0 | 39 |
| 1965 | 0 | 28 | 0 | 9 | 0 | 1 | 0 | 4 | 1 | 0 | 43 |
| 1966 | 0 | 40 | 0 | 14 | 0 | 0 | 5 | 1 | 3 | 0 | 63 |
| 1967 | 0 | 28 | 0 | 14 | 0 | 0 | 3 | 0 | 2 | 0 | 47 |
| 1968 | 0 | 37[b] | 0 | 12 | 0 | 0 | 5 | 0 | 1 | 0 | 55 |
| 1969 | 0 | 28 | 0 | 15 | 0 | 0 | 0 | 0 | 1 | 1 | 45 |
| 1970 | 0 | 30 | 0 | 13 | 0 | 0 | 8 | 0 | 1 | 0 | 52 |
| 1971 | 0 | 11 | 0 | 18 | 0 | 0 | 5 | 0 | 1 | 0 | 35 |
| 1972 | 0 | 7 | 0 | 21 | 0 | 0 | 3 | 0 | 2 | 0 | 33 |
| 1973 | 0 | 9 | 0 | 14 | 0 | 0 | 5 | 0 | 1 | 0 | 29[d] |
| *5 Aug 1963–1973* | *0* | *260 +23[c]* | *0* | *136* | *0* | *2* | *34* | *9* | *14* | *1* | *456[d] 23[c]* |

| Year | USA | | USSR | | United Kingdom | | France | | China | | Total |
|------|-----|-----|------|-----|------|-----|------|-----|------|-----|-------|
| | a | u | a | u | a | u | a | u | a | u | |
| **III. 1945–31 December 1973** | | | | | | | | | | | |
| *1945–5 Aug 1963* | *193* | *89 (5)* | *161* | *3 (1)* | *21* | *2* | *4* | *4* | *0* | *0* | *477* |
| *5 Aug 1963–1973* | *0* | *260* | *0* | *136* | *0* | *2* | *34* | *9* | *14* | *1* | *456[d]* |
| | | *+23[c]* | | | | | | | | | *23[c]* |
| **1945–1973** | **193** | **372 (5)** | **161** | **139 (1)** | **21** | **4** | **38** | **13** | **14** | **1** | **956[d]** |

[a] Up to 1958. The dates of these explosions are unknown.
[b] Including five devices used simultaneously in the same test (Buggy) counted here as five.
[c] Explosions conducted between 15 September 1961 and 20 August 1963. Their dates are not specified in the lists available; at least one of them must have been conducted after 5 August 1963.
[d] The data for 1973 are preliminary.

# 14. Chronology of major events related to disarmament issues

*12 January*   The French-Soviet communiqué, issued at the conclusion of the French President's visit to the USSR, reiterates both countries' support for a world disarmament conference and states that the implementation of general and complete disarmament under effective international control requires, first of all, an examination of the question of nuclear disarmament.

*27 January*   The agreement on ending the war and restoring peace in Viet-Nam is signed in Paris. It provides for a ceasefire from 28 January; the withdrawal of all US forces from South Viet-Nam and the release of all US prisoners of war within 60 days; the formation of a four-party joint military commission to enforce these provisions; the establishment of an international commission of control and supervision (ICCS); the setting up, by agreement between the South Viet-Namese parties, of a national council of national reconciliation and concord to organize general elections; and the holding of an international conference on Viet-Nam within 30 days of the signing of the agreement. Four protocols, which deal with the ceasefire, the ICCS, the return of prisoners and the removal of mines from North Viet-Namese waters, accompany the agreement.

*31 January*   Preparatory consultations relating to force reductions in Central Europe open in Vienna.

*21 February*   The agreement on restoring peace and achieving national concord in Laos is signed in Vientiane by the Vientiane government and the Lao Patriotic Forces (Pathet Lao). It provides for a ceasefire beginning on 22 February; the ending of all bombing and other military activities by foreign forces; the withdrawal of all foreign forces within 60 days after the establishment of a provisional government; the release of prisoners of war; the establishment, within 30 days after the signing of the agreement, of a provisional government composed of equal numbers of representatives of the Vientiane government and the Pathet Lao, and of a similarly composed national political consultative council to organize general elections; as well as the formation of a joint commission for the implementation of the agreement.

*23 February* In a joint communiqué issued at the conclusion of the visit of the prime minister of Australia to Indonesia, Australia expresses support for the initiatives of the Association of South East Asian Nations (ASEAN) for a zone of peace, freedom and neutrality in the region.

*2 March* The foreign ministers of Canada, China, the USA, France, the Provisional Revolutionary Government of the Republic of South Viet-Nam, Hungary, Indonesia, Poland, the Democratic Republic of Viet-Nam, the United Kingdom, the Republic of Viet-Nam and the USSR sign, in the presence of the UN Secretary-General, a declaration in which they express their approval of, and support for, the Paris agreement of 27 January 1973 on ending the war and restoring peace in Viet-Nam, and the four protocols to the agreement of the same date.

*12 March* US-Soviet strategic arms limitation talks (SALT) resume in Geneva.

*5 April* The agreement for the application of nuclear safeguards under the Non-Proliferation Treaty is signed by the European Atomic Energy Community (Euratom), its seven non-nuclear-weapon member states—Belgium, the Federal Republic of Germany, Denmark, Ireland, Italy, Luxembourg and the Netherlands—and the International Atomic Energy Agency (IAEA).

*6 April* The North Korean Assembly declares that the Democratic People's Republic of Korea will be prepared to reduce its army strength to 200 000 men or less if US forces withdraw from South Korea.

*9 May* Australia and New Zealand institute proceedings against France in the International Court of Justice in connection with the French nuclear tests in the Pacific region. They contend that the conduct of these tests is not consistent with international law.

*21 May* In a joint Soviet-West German statement the two countries share the view that the implementation of the Non-Proliferation Treaty constitutes a step towards disarmament and contributes to a lessening of the danger of nuclear war and to the strengthening of international security.

*22 May* The USA and the USSR sign a protocol to the 1972 agreement on measures to improve the safety of navigation of the ships of the two powers' armed forces on, and flight of their military aircraft over, the high seas. The protocol is aimed at preventing incidents between warships or military aircraft and nonmilitary ships.

*6 June* In a joint communiqué the prime ministers of Australia and India agree that the creation of a zone of peace in the Indian Ocean would be a positive step towards the reduction of tensions and rivalries in this region and also agree to cooperate bilaterally, and with all states concerned, towards this end.

*7 June*   Ministers participating in the NATO defence planning committee's meeting discuss the practical implications of negotiations on force reductions in Europe and stress that the maintenance of undiminished security at lower levels of forces remains the objective of NATO. They reiterate their conviction that unilateral action on the part of countries of the alliance to reduce or withdraw forces would erode the conditions of stability essential to the negotiation of a satisfactory agreement.

*8 June*   The participants in the Helsinki consultations on the question of the Conference on Security and Cooperation in Europe adopt final recommendations concerning the organization, agenda, participation, date, place, rules of procedure and financial arrangements for that conference.

*8 June*   It is reported that France will not continue its contribution to the South East Asia Treaty Organization (SEATO) budget after 30 June 1974.

*11 June*   In the final communiqué of the meeting of the council of ministers of the Central Treaty Organization (CENTO) at Tehran, a hope is expressed that current negotiations for the purpose of reducing armaments and fostering conditions for peace and stability in Europe will not fail to take into consideration the interests of the CENTO region.

*12 June*   The prime minister of New Zealand states that his country will steadily reduce the level of its participation in SEATO.

*21 June*   The treaty on the basis of relations between the German Democratic Republic and the Federal Republic of Germany,which was signed on 21 December 1972, enters into force.

*21 June*   The USA and the USSR sign an agreement on basic principles of negotiations on the further limitation of strategic offensive arms.

*22 June*   The USA and the USSR sign an agreement on the prevention of nuclear war.

*22 June*   The International Court of Justice orders that, pending the Court's final decision in the case submitted to it on 9 May 1973 (see above), the French government should avoid nuclear tests causing the deposit of radioactive fall-out on the territory of Australia, New Zealand, the Cook Islands, Niue or the Tokelau Islands.

*23 June*   The president of North Korea reiterates his proposal to South Korea to cease arms reinforcement, bring about the withdrawal of all foreign troops, reduce armed forces and armaments, stop the introduction of weapons from foreign countries and conclude a peace agreement.

*24 June*   Ministers of the five member states of the Association of South East Asian Nations (ASEAN)—Indonesia, Malaysia, the Philippines, Singapore and Thailand—meet at Baguio (Philippines) and agree on joint procedures for the neutralization of the South East Asian region.

*24 June*   In a joint Soviet-US communiqué the two sides agree to continue their efforts to conclude an international agreement with respect to chemical weapons and to make every effort to facilitate the work of the CCD, and state that they will actively participate in negotiations aimed at working out new measures to curb and end the arms race. They reaffirm that the ultimate objective is general and complete disarmament, including nuclear disarmament, under strict international control, and that a world disarmament conference could at an appropriate time play a role in this process.

*28 June*   Preparatory consultations relating to Central Europe end with a decision to hold negotiations on mutual reduction of forces and armaments and associated measures in Central Europe, and an agreement on the participation in and procedures for these negotiations.

*3–7 July*   The first stage of the Conference on Security and Cooperation in Europe is held on the foreign-minister level in Helsinki. The ministers adopt the 8 June 1973 recommendations of the Helsinki consultations and decide that the second stage of the conference will pursue the study of the questions on the agenda and prepare drafts of declarations, recommendations, resolutions or any other final documents on the basis of the proposals submitted during the first stage as well as those to be submitted.

*5 July*   The European (EEC) parliament adopts a resolution disapproving of atomic tests regardless of where they take place in the world and regardless of which state is responsible. It urges the realization of overall and supervised nuclear disarmament.

*10 July*   Australia announces that it has withdrawn from the scheduled SEATO joint naval exercise.

*18 July*   France signs Additional Protocol II of the treaty for the prohibition of nuclear weapons in Latin America (the Treaty of Tlatelolco), which provides for an undertaking to respect the statute of military denuclearization of the area.

*5 August*   On the occasion of the 10th anniversary of the signing of the treaty banning nuclear-weapon tests in the atmosphere, in outer space and under water, the heads of government of the Commonwealth, meeting in Ottawa, appeal to all powers, and in particular the nuclear powers, to take up as an urgent task the negotiation of a new agreement to bring about the total cessation of nuclear-weapon tests in all environments.

*15 August*   The US bombing of Cambodia ends following a ban by the US Congress on further appropriations for this purpose.

*17 August*   The US Secretary of Defense announces that the USSR successfully tested multiple independently-targetable re-entry vehicles (MIRVs).

*21 August*   China signs Additional Protocol II of the treaty for the prohibition of nuclear weapons in Latin America (the Treaty of Tlatelolco), which provides for an undertaking to respect the statute of military denuclearization of the area.

*24 August*   A joint Thai-US communiqué states that the USA will take immediate steps for an initial withdrawal of 3 550 US military personnel from Thailand and a reduction of over 100 aircraft, and that representatives of the two governments will continue to hold discussions with a view to agreeing on plans for further gradual reductions of the level of US forces in Thailand, including strategic, tactical and support aircraft, while taking into consideration the security requirements in South East Asia.

*9 September*   The fourth conference of heads of state and government of non-aligned countries, held in Algiers, declares itself in favour of general and complete disarmament and especially of a total ban on the use and manufacture of nuclear weapons and the total destruction of existing stocks, as well as the cessation of nuclear tests in all environments and in all regions of the world. In this connection, it demands the suspension of French nuclear tests in the South Pacific. The conference also declares itself in favour of the banning of all chemical and bacteriological weapons; demands that an international conference on disarmament, with the participation of all states, be convened as soon as possible; and emphasizes the enormous benefit which could ensue from the peaceful uses of nuclear technology and the release of resources as a result of disarmament.

*18 September*   The UN General Assembly decides to admit the German Democratic Republic and the Federal Republic of Germany as members of the United Nations.

*18 September*   The second stage of the Conference on Security and Co-operation in Europe opens in Geneva.

*23 September*   At a press conference held in the USA, the prime minister of Pakistan says that it is worth considering reducing armed forces on the Indian subcontinent.

*25 September*   In a letter addressed to the UN Secretary-General, the USSR proposes that the permanent members of the UN Security Council should reduce their military budgets by 10 per cent and that 10 per cent of the funds released should be used for assistance to developing countries.

514

*28 September*   At the 18th SEATO council meeting in New York, member countries agree to reduce SEATO's military activities and to place greater emphasis on supporting the internal security and development programmes of the two regional members—the Philippines and Thailand.

*6 October*   A war between the Arab states and Israel breaks out with an Egyptian offensive across the Suez Canal and a Syrian offensive on the Golan Heights.

*7 October*   The American Chemical Society, one of the strongest opponents of the 1925 Geneva Protocol prohibiting the use in war of chemical and biological weapons, reverses its position and expresses support for the ratification of the Protocol without any qualification regarding tear gas or herbicides.

*17 October*   The Arab oil ministers meet in Kuwait and decide to reduce oil production forthwith by not less than 5 per cent of the September 1973 level of output in each Arab oil-exporting country, with a similar reduction to be applied each successive month, computed on the basis of the previous month's production, until such time as total evacuation of Israeli forces from all Arab territory occupied during the June 1967 War is completed, and the legitimate rights of the Palestinian people are restored.

*22 October*   The UN Security Council adopts a resolution calling for a ceasefire in the Middle East.

*30 October*   Negotiations open in Vienna on the mutual reduction of forces and armaments and associated measures in Central Europe.

*31 October*   The World Congress of Peace Forces, held in Moscow, adopts a communiqué stating that the treaties and agreements on disarmament which have already been signed should be strictly fulfilled and should be subscribed to by countries that have not yet signed or ratified them; that all the five nuclear powers should sign a pact on the non-use of force, containing a commitment to a permanent ban on nuclear weapons; reduce their military spending; employ part of the funds released to assist the peoples of the developing countries; ensure the termination of nuclear tests in all environments; and take practical steps to end the nuclear-missile race and to achieve disarmament. It also points out that the proposals for the creation of nuclear-free zones, the dismantling of foreign military bases and the banning of the installation of nuclear weapons on foreign territory should be implemented; that a world disarmament conference should be held as soon as possible; and that the success of the talks on reducing armaments and armed forces in Europe should be ensured.

*4 November*   The Arab oil ministers decide that the reduction in oil production in each Arab country which is party to the decision of 17 October 1973 (see above) shall be 25 per cent of the September production including quantities deducted as a result of the embargo on oil supplies to the US and Dutch markets. A further reduction amounting to 5 per cent of the November output will follow in December, provided that such reduction shall not affect the share that any friendly state was importing from any Arab exporting country during the first nine months of 1973.

*7 November* In the final communiqué of the NATO nuclear planning group's meeting, the defence ministers of eight NATO countries state that they have reviewed the progress that has been made in implementing the political guidelines pertaining to the possible use of atomic demolition munitions (ADMs) that were approved by the defence planning committee in 1970.

*8 November* It is reported that at the Vienna negotiations on mutual reduction of forces in Central Europe, the Warsaw Treaty countries have proposed a three-stage reduction of all armed forces in the area.

*8–15 November* The 22nd International Conference of the Red Cross meets in Tehran. It adopts a resolution urging the diplomatic conference on the reaffirmation and development of international humanitarian law applicable in armed conflicts to begin consideration at its 1974 session of the question of the prohibition or restriction of the use of conventional weapons which may cause unnecessary suffering or have indiscriminate effects.

*22 November* Addressing the Assembly of the Western European Union, the West German defence minister states that the inclusion of Western Europe in the nuclear strategic protection by the United States will remain indispensable for the USA as long as North America has a vital interest in a stable European peace arrangement; and that East-West negotiations on relevant matters of security policy, be it in the nuclear or in the conventional field, contribute to diminishing the security risks while the rivalry between East and West continues. He also states that on no account could a political union of Western Europe replace the presence of the USA in Europe or the deterrent function of the US nuclear strategic capabilities, and that cooperative efforts should be made for the harmonization of operational doctrines, joint development, procurement, supply and maintenance of equipment, common training systems and an assignment of military roles that have to be accomplished for the overall purposes of the alliance.

*22 November* It is reported that at the Vienna negotiations on the mutual reduction of forces in Central Europe, the NATO countries have proposed cuts in US and Soviet armed forces stationed in the area, to be followed by the setting of a common ceiling for all NATO and Warsaw Treaty forces in the region.

*6 December*   The UN General Assembly adopts resolutions condemning all nuclear-weapon tests; insisting that the nuclear-weapon states which have been carrying out nuclear tests in the atmosphere discontinue such tests forthwith; urging immediate negotiations for elaborating a comprehensive test ban treaty; urging the USSR to sign and ratify Additional Protocol II of the Treaty of Tlatelolco; requesting the Secretary-General to prepare a factual statement of the great powers' military presence in the Indian Ocean; requesting the CCD to continue negotiations with a view to reaching agreement on effective measures for the prohibition of the development, production and stockpiling of all chemical weapons and for their elimination from the arsenals of all states; and inviting the diplomatic conference on the reaffirmation and development of international humanitarian law applicable in armed conflicts to consider the question of the use of napalm and other incendiary weapons, as well as other specific conventional weapons causing unnecessary suffering or having indiscriminate effects and to seek agreement on the prohibition or restriction of the use of such weapons.

*7 December*   At a meeting of the NATO defence planning committee the participating ministers reaffirm that the fundamental purpose of NATO forces is to deter aggression and to preserve all members of the alliance from an attack or a threat of attack from outside. They stress that the fulfillment of this purpose depends on maintaining a capability of conventional, as well as nuclear, forces balanced with the Warsaw Treaty Organization. They agree to give new impetus to the programmes to provide protection for aircraft and airfields, to improve the anti-armour capability of NATO forces, and to raise the levels of war reserve stocks.

*7 December*   The UN General Assembly adopts resolutions recommending that all the permanent members of the Security Council reduce their military budgets by 10 per cent from the 1973 level during the next financial year and allot 10 per cent of the released funds for the provision of assistance to developing countries, and establishes a special committee to distribute the funds. The Assembly also requests the Secretary-General to prepare a report on the reduction of the military budgets and on the utilization of a part of the funds thus saved to provide international assistance to developing countries.

*10–11 December*   At the North Atlantic Council meeting, the participating ministers express appreciation for the continuing efforts undertaken by the USA in SALT II towards a permanent agreement limiting strategic offensive arms.

*11 December*   Czechoslovakia and the Federal Republic of Germany sign a treaty on the normalization of relations between the two countries.

*14 December*   In a declaration of policy issued by the European Economic Community, the members of the community which are also members of the Atlantic alliance consider that in the present circumstances there is no alternative to the security provided by the nuclear weapons of the USA and by the presence of North American forces in Europe; and they agree that in the light of the relative military vulnerability of Europe, the Europeans should, if they wish to preserve their independence, hold to their commitments and make constant efforts to ensure that they have adequate means of defence at their disposal.

*14 December*   The UN General Assembly adopts resolutions deploring environmental pollution by radiation from the testing of nuclear weapons; requesting the UN Committee on the Effects of Atomic Radiation to review and assess the levels, effects and risks of radiation from all sources; and authorizing the committee to appoint a group of experts from among its members for the purpose of visiting a country which is situated in an area of nuclear arms testing or which considers that it is exposed to atomic radiation as a result of testing.

*18 December*   The UN General Assembly adopts resolutions appealing to the USA and the USSR to bear in mind the necessity and urgency of reaching agreement on important qualitative limitations and substantial reductions of their strategic nuclear weapon systems; noting the establishment of a preparatory committee for the 1975 NPT review conference; and setting up an *ad hoc* committee to examine the views and suggestions expressed by governments on the convening of a world disarmament conference and related problems.

*21 December*   A peace conference on the Middle East opens in Geneva.

# Errata

*World Armaments and Disarmament, SIPRI Yearbook 1973*

*Page 76, Table 3A.1.* For SAMOS 2 (1961α) the lifetime should read 13 years instead of 15 years.

*Page 83, Table 3A.1.* For USAF[h] (1972-52A) the lifetime should read 68 instead of 49; for USAF (1972-68A) the lifetime should read 29 instead of 30; for USAF[h] (1972-79A) the lifetime should read 90 instead of 60; for USAF[f] (1972-103A) the lifetime should read 33 instead of 30.

*Page 85, Table 3A.2.* For USAF (1968-86A) the lifetime should read 2.5 instead of 3.

*Page 86, Table 3A.2.* For USAF (1969–65A) the lifetime should read 3.4 instead of 6.

*Page 86, Table 3A.3.* For MIDAS 2 (1960 ξ 1) the lifetime should read 15 instead of 20.

*Page 87, Table 3A.3.* For Vela 7 (1967-40A) the orbital inclination should read 33.06 instead of 30.06 and the period should read 6671.8 instead of 667.8; for Vela 8 (1967-40B) the orbital inclination should read 33.06 instead of 30.06.

*Page 88, Table 3A.3.* For BMEWS 3 (1970-46A) the lifetime should read 5 instead of 3.

*Page 97, Table 3B.1.* For Cosmos 491[c] (1972-38A) the launch date should read 25 May instead of 15 May; for Cosmos 502[c] (1972-55A) the lifetime should read 11.7 instead of 14.

*Page 99, Table 3B.2.* For Cosmos 200 (1968-06A) the lifetime should read 1 863 days instead of 10 years.

*Page 100, Table 3B.2.* For Cosmos 440 (1971-79A) the lifetime should read 401.18 days instead of 1 year.


# Addendum

*World Armaments and Disarmament, SIPRI Yearbook 1974*

*Appendix 8C.* In the tables showing military expenditure as a percentage of gross domestic product (GDP), the military expenditure and GDP figures used for the calculation were in local currency, current price figures.

# INDEX

arms trade 264, 280; nuclear-weapon tests 289, 292–93, 444–45, 498–99, 507–509; disarmament agreements 427, 435, 442–43, 460–61, 514

Colombia 157, 228–29, 255–57, 285, 460–61

Command and control 59. *See also* Strategic nuclear weapons: Command data-buffer system

Comprehensive Test Ban Treaty (CTBT) 2, 384, 386, 388, 417, 425

Conference of the Committee on Disarmament (CCD) 2, 371, 374, 384, 401, 417, 424–25, 428, 440, 513, 517

Congo (Brazzaville) 220–25

Conventional weapons 30, 43, 48–54, 69, 143–44, 153, 403, 418–19, 428–29, 435; anti-aircraft missiles (incl. Soviet "SA-2 Guideline", "SA-3 Goa", "SA-6 Gainful", "SA-7 Grail") 6–7, 11, 18, 21, 89, 118, 144, 238–43, 256, 260–61, 264, 267–77, 282–84; anti-tank missiles (incl. Soviet "Sagger" "Snapper", US Maverick, TOW) 6–8, 18, 144, 150–51, 153, 238–43, 256, 260–63, 266–69, 271, 280, 347; other missiles and munitions (incl. anti-personnel weapons) 2, 10–11, 15, 17–21;

fighter aircraft 5, 12, 33, 50–54, 59, 84, 137–38, 144–51, 153, 231–36, 252–55, 260–62, 264–67, 269–78, 280–81, 283–85;

tanks 5, 11, 49, 52–54, 138, 145, 150, 153, 249–51, 258, 260, 262–63, 267–69, 271, 274, 285–86, 342;

strategy and tactics 1, 5–8, 17, 21, 31–32, 43, 66, 68, 72–94. *See also* Nuclear-weapon doctrine

*See also* Antisubmarine warfare, Automated battlefield, Biological disarmament, Chemical disarmament, Incendiary weapons

Costa Rica 226–27, 440, 460–61

Cruise missiles. *See* under Strategic nuclear weapons

Cuba 92, 226–27, 281, 413, 460–61

Cyprus 52, 153, 212–14, 413, 460–61

Czechoslovakia 25–26, 28–30, 42, 45, 48, 53–54, 374, 412, 440, 462–63, 517; military expenditure 142, 156, 208–11, 398; indigenous weapon development 235, 250; arms trade 263, 269; receipt of arms and aid 263

**D**

Dahomey 220–25, 462–63

Democratic Yemen 271, 462–63

Denmark 25–28, 38, 45, 48, 52, 206–209, 239, 244, 260–62, 412, 440, 462–63, 511

Disarmament chronology 510–18

Dominican Republic 226–27, 413, 462–63

Dubai 267

Dulles, John F. 74, 76

**E**

Ecuador 157, 228–29, 285, 413, 462–63

Egypt 5–6, 92, 142, 148–53, 212–15, 267, 277, 376, 412, 462–63. *See also* Middle East War

Einstein, Albert 1

Eisenhower, Dwight D. 74, 93

El Salvador 226–27, 282, 412, 462–63

Equatorial Guinea 464–65

Estonia 412

Ethiopia 220–25, 278, 376, 388, 412, 440, 464–65

Euratom (European Atomic Energy Committee) 427, 493, 500–501, 511

Europe 21, 355, 391, 512–14; military expenditure 127, 131, 133, 206–209, 212–13, 394; indigenous weapon development 236, 242, 247, 251; licensed weapon production 253, 256–58; receipt of arms and aid 264; mutual force reductions (MFR) 1–2, 24–55, 155–56, 510, 512–13, 515–16. *See also* North Atlantic Treaty Organization, Warsaw Treaty Organization

European Economic Community (EEC) 513, 518

**F**

Far East 127, 206–207, 216–17, 237, 243, 247, 251, 254, 256, 272. *See also* individual countries

Fiji 413, 439, 464–65

Finland 132, 210–13, 236, 253, 264, 266, 375, 412, 464–65

France 25–27, 35, 48–52, 64, 77, 79–80, 92, 384, 388, 401, 403, 412, 510–11; military expenditure 130, 141–43, 153, 155, 206–209, 394–95, 397; indigenous weapon development 143–44, 231–32, 238–39, 244, 249; arms trade 146, 148–49, 260–64, 266–67, 270–72, 274, 276–81, 283–86; receipt of arms and aid 261; nuclear-weapon tests 2, 289, 292–94, 444–45, 498–99, 505–506, 508–509, 511, 513–14; disarmament agreements 427, 452, 464–65; and the Viet-Nam War 19

**G**

Gabon 220–25, 464–65

Gambia 413, 464–65

General and complete disarmament (GCD) 431

Geneva Protocol of 1925, 2, 373, 378, 383–84, 402–403, 411–16, 418, 428, 432, 439

Germany, Democratic Republic of 1, 25, 28–30, 37, 42, 45, 48, 53–54, 464–65, 514; military expenditure 142, 156, 208–11; indigenous weapon development 246; receipt of arms and aid 263

521